日英対訳

世界の歴史

増補改訂版

A HISTORY OF THE WORLD :
FROM THE ANCIENT PAST TO THE PRESENT

山久瀬洋二 =著
ジェームス・M・バーダマン =訳

IBCパブリッシング

装　　幀 = 岩目地英樹（コムデザイン）

校　　閲 = 神余 秀樹

翻訳協力 = Ed Jacob

編集協力 = 株式会社 iTEP Japan

本書は2021年に小社から刊行された『日英対訳 世界の歴史』を加筆・修正したものです。

まえがき

　今回、本書を改訂し出版するにあたって、前回に執筆して以来、いかに世界が変化したかを痛感させられています。

　新型コロナウイルスが世界で猛威を振るい、それに伴って世界経済に甚大な打撃を与えたのみならず、人々のライフスタイルが大きく変化しました。また、ロシアのウクライナ侵攻は、「新冷戦」とも呼ばれる新たな大国同士の対立を刺激し、世界では民主主義を信奉する国家と中国に代表される権威主義国家との確執も深刻になっています。

　一方、社会全般でもこうした世界の動きと呼応するように、教育や経済格差、さらには持てる国と持たざる国との間の格差が広がり、中東でもイスラエルに右派政権ができると、パレスチナとの紛争が頻発するようになりました。

　今、世界の人々は未来に対して不安を抱いています。あの2つの世界大戦への道と似た歩みを始めているのではと警告する人も増えてきました。しかも、当時と比較すれば、現在はネット社会で、そしてAIが進化を続けている時代です。そうした技術革新の中で、武器も一段と進化し、人と人とは瞬時に世界規模で交流できるようになりました。人々は情報源をインターネットに頼り、自らが欲する情報へとどんどん傾斜し、そのことが他の立場や政治的なスタンスを持つ人との間に埋めがたい疎外を増幅・深刻化させています。

　こうした難しい時代にあって、私たちが今まで歩んできた道を振り返ることがどれだけ大切かを痛感しています。世界史へのアプローチは、人によって異なるにせよ、それを英語という共通の言語で共有することは価値のあることといえましょう。世界史をバイリンガルで読むことで、国を超えた理解を深めるツールが生み出されることを祈念しているところです。特に、欧米の知人に向けて私たちの生きるアジアの歴史をぜひ語っていただければ、よりお互いのことを知り合う機会になるはずです。そうした意味で、本書は数千年の人類の歴史を、東西の交流という視点を横軸に置いて制作してみました。ローマ帝国のことを扱うときには同じ時代に中国にあった前漢、後漢について平行した目線で語っています。

　そうすれば、お互いが同じ人類の歴史を共有しながら、それでいて各々の文化や宗教、社会の特性をいかに育てていったかが、見えてくるはずです。

今、私たちがしなければならないことは、この世界史の延長ともいえる未来について、考えることでしょう。そして考えながら、どのような困難があろうとその課題を克服するノウハウを培わなければならないのです。未来学は歴史学と同じ線とベクトルの上にあるもので、地球で最も進化した動物といわれる私たち人類の地球に対する責任を理解し、少しでも良い未来へと私たちを導くツールであるべきなのです。

　この数年で起こったありとあらゆる事件は、未来の人々から見れば、ちょうど私たちが20世紀を見ているように映るはずです。そんな未来の人々が人権に守られ、心身ともに豊かな人生を送ることができるのか。それが、本書を読み終え、未来へのベクトルを見つめるときに皆さんに考えていただきたいことなのです。

2023年7月10日

山久瀬　洋二

A Word from the Translator

The world is a complicated place. What happened in Europe in the seventeenth century affects life in the Americas today. What happens in the Middle East today affects East Asia almost instantaneously. We are interconnected politically, economically, and culturally. Because of that, gaining an understanding of history and present-day affairs is essential.

World history as it appears in textbooks in Japan and most other countries tends to ignore the dynamics of events. Textbooks carefully divide events into small independent pieces composed of dates, people, and actions that form clear-cut patterns. One by one, they seem very clear and straightforward. Put these pieces together and, if we are lucky, we may see that they form a mosaic, a broader picture, but still one that is flat and two-dimensional.

The present volume brings world history into three dimensions, crossing time zones, eras, and regions and bringing multiple events into perspective. As a narrative history, it tells a series of stories of what occurred and also why it occurred, and allows us to consider how it affected the history of the world at that time and perhaps how it affects us today. While the significant dates, places, people, and events are included, they are woven into stories that we can enjoy reading. These stories both provide the details and leave us wondering what might have happened if things had been different.

While translating this volume, I hoped that young people would encounter this volume early in their lives. Surely it would change their view of world history as a subject, for the better. History is not simply something to be memorized for examinations without thinking deeply. World history is filled with stories that tell us where we came from and how people developed completely different cultures. We can learn from history what we share and what we don't share in the twenty-first century.

The value of the author's presentation is that it stimulates us to learn more, to look for the big picture, and to consider how each chapter affected what happened afterward and whether it has an impact on our world.

The side-by-side Japanese-English format allows the reader to grasp history in context and grasp it in two languages at the same time. The translations are not word-for-word but paragraph-for-paragraph, so please read with that in mind. I hope that you enjoy reading both sides as you consider the history of the human race in a new way.

James M. Vardaman

Table of Contents

Part One:
Before Talking about History 1
001-006

Part Two:
Human Progress Begins (The Ancient World) 21
007-033

Part Three:
The Stabilization of Life and the Age of Stagnation
(The Medieval World) 103
034-071

Part Four:
The Expansion of the Human World
(The Early-Modern World) 225
072-108

Part Five:
Freedom and Revolution, Chaos and Colonization
(The Modern World) 339
109-139

Part Six:
The Age of War, Freedom and Globalization
(The Contemporary World) 439
140-193

目次

第一部
歴史の話をする前に 1
001–006

第二部
人類の歩みが始まる（古代の世界）................................21
007–033

第三部
暮らしの安定と停滞の時代（中世の世界）........................103
034–071

第四部
人間の世界が広がっていく時代（近世の世界）................225
072–108

第五部
自由と革命、混乱と植民地化の時代（近代の世界）.......339
109–139

第六部
戦争と自由・グローバルの時代（現代の世界）................439
140–193

時代・地域別項目一覧

本書の内容を関連する時代と地域ごとにまとめています（全世界・地域に共通する項目は除く、数字は項目ナンバー）。

時代 / 地域		アメリカ	西ヨーロッパ	中央ヨーロッパ	東ヨーロッパ
B.C.	3,000				
	2,000				
	1,000	83			11
	6世紀				
	5世紀				16
	4世紀				17
	3世紀				
	2世紀				
	1世紀			22, 23	
A.D.	1世紀			24, 25, 26	
	2世紀			25, 26	
	3世紀			25, 26	
	4世紀		27	25, 26	
	5世紀		27, 34	25, 34	34
	6世紀		37		
	7世紀				
	8世紀		37, 43, 44, 71	43, 44, 71	43, 44, 71
	9世紀		43, 44, 71	43, 44, 71	43, 44, 71
	10世紀		43, 44, 45, 47, 71	43, 44, 45, 47, 71	43, 44, 45, 47, 71, 101
	11世紀		43, 44, 45, 48, 71	43, 44, 45, 51, 54, 71	43, 44, 45, 51, 54, 71, 101
	12世紀		65, 71	54, 56, 71	54, 56, 71, 101
	13世紀	83	57, 65, 71	54, 56, 62, 71, 78	54, 56, 62, 71, 101
	14世紀		57, 65, 66, 69, 71, 74	66, 69, 71, 74, 78	66, 69, 70, 71, 74, 101
	15世紀		66, 71, 74, 92	66, 71, 74, 78, 92	66, 70, 71, 74, 92, 101, 104
	16世紀	83, 84	72, 73, 75, 76, 77, 85, 86, 89, 92, 120	72, 73, 75, 76, 77, 78, 85, 92	70, 75, 76, 77, 85, 91, 92, 101, 104
	17世紀	87, 100	87, 88, 89, 97, 98, 99, 100, 102, 103, 120	78, 96	70, 91, 101, 104, 106
	18世紀	100, 107, 108, 109, 110, 111	98, 99, 100, 102, 103, 108, 111, 112, 113, 114, 116, 120	114	101, 104, 106, 114
	19世紀	123, 124, 125, 130, 139, 144	115, 116, 117, 118, 120, 122, 128, 131, 132, 137, 144	115, 131	115, 119, 127, 131, 138, 139
	20世紀	139, 141, 144, 150, 155, 158, 159, 163, 166, 172, 177, 178, 179	144, 148, 149, 150, 152, 155, 158, 159, 162, 163, 164, 165, 172, 173, 179, 181, 185	147, 148, 149, 150, 152, 155, 158, 159, 160, 162, 163, 164, 165, 172, 173, 179, 181, 185	139, 140, 141, 147, 148, 151, 155, 158, 159, 162, 163, 164, 165, 172, 173, 179, 181, 184, 185
	21世紀以降	189			

本書を読みながら、いま自分が歴史のどこを辿っているのか、文脈を理解する手助けとしてご活用ください。

アフリカ	中東（西アジア）	中央アジア	インド（南アジア）	東南アジア	中国	朝鮮	日本
	7						
9			9				
8	8, 11				11		
	13						
	16						
			18		20		
	19	19	19				
					21		
	25		29, 30				
	25		29, 30				
	25		29, 30		28		
	25		29, 30		28		
	25		29, 30		28		
			29		28, 32		
	35, 36, 39		29, 50		32, 39, 50		33, 50
	36, 38, 39, 41		50	63	39, 40, 41, 50		50
	41, 42		50	63	41, 42, 50		50
		49, 53	50	63	49, 50		50
55	54, 55	53	50	63	50, 58, 59		50, 54
	54	53	50	63	50, 58, 59		50, 54
	54, 62	67		63	58, 59, 60, 61, 62, 68	68	54, 68
	70	67		63	68, 95	68	68, 95
	70			63	82, 95		81, 95
	70, 79, 91, 93, 94		93	63	95, 120	120	81, 90, 95, 120
	70, 91, 93, 94		93	63	95, 105, 120	106, 120	90, 95, 106, 120
107					120, 121	106, 120	106, 120, 121
135	122, 127		132, 133, 154	126	119, 120, 121, 122, 126, 129, 133, 134, 139	120, 134	120, 121, 122, 126, 129, 133, 134, 138, 144
186	147, 175, 176, 182, 187		154	177	139, 140, 141, 142, 149, 152, 161, 162, 163, 164, 166, 180, 185	140, 141, 171, 181	140, 141, 144, 149, 150, 161, 162, 163, 164, 166, 181
	189						

第一部

歴史の話をする前に

....

Part One:
Before Talking about History

....

　銀河系の隅にある太陽という恒星の惑星の一つに、人類へと進化をした動物のグループがありました。

　道具を使うことを覚え、火を操り、そしてついに農作物の生産を始め、社会を構成するようになりました。知識の進化が肉体の進化に付加されたとき、ヒトと呼ばれる動物は、自らを他の動物とは切り離し、地球上を支配するようになったのです。

　ヒトは農耕社会の中でさらに鉄を手に入れ、家畜を養い、やがて社会は支配する者と支配される者とに分離します。階級が社会に生まれたとき、ヒトは現代の競争社会に至る長い歴史という旅路を歩み始めたのです。

　ヒトは、自らをヒトとして意識した瞬間から、道具と社会という二つの大きな車輪を、現在に向けて推し進め始めます。時には、その車輪同士が衝突を起こし、またははじき合いながら、民族というさらに大きな集団が形成され、国家を創造するようになったのです。

001 Language and science become two tools for talking about history

"In the beginning was the Word" is the famous quote that begins the New Testament's Book of John. That people were able to establish civilizations is due entirely to their ability to handle languages. Language promoted communication between people, transmitted information, and became a catalyst for the accumulation of all manner of wisdom and experience.

The word "history" includes the notion of transmitting and accumulating language and records. For words to be recorded, written letters or characters are necessary. The great majority of civilizations have set down records and wisdom from each period in writing, communicating them to future generations. With this accumulated knowledge as capital, new knowledge is created, and the continuation leads to the development of culture and civilization.

In order to discuss the history of humankind, it is necessary to observe the enormous accumulations of records of the past. At the same time, unless we obtain hints from records of the past for the establishment of new civilizations, the whole meaning of discussing history becomes diluted.

However, "language" also caused humankind various forms of confusion. As conveyed by the expression "manipulate language," in some cases history has been intentionally distorted by records, and the basis upon which our common knowledge has been founded has sometimes been embellished. No matter how we look at it, we cannot forget that there is always a possibility that "language" and history set down in "writing" may diverge from reality due to circumstances and intentions at that time.

Furthermore, language can give birth to misunderstanding. Given that people manipulate language, their motivations for writing reflect their character, the culture to which they belong, and their environment at the time, and the fact that this is not accurately conveyed to other people has given birth to countless tragedies, stagnation, and conflicts. When we look at history in which these elements are interwoven, they become factors that we must take into account.

Therefore, when we discuss history, together with analyzing the record "based on language" we should make free use of the various sciences in our efforts to clarify what is real. Analysis of language and writing together with scientific proof are two inseparable tools that we need to employ in clarifying history itself.

言葉と科学は人類の歴史を語る二つのツールとなる

　「はじめに言葉ありき」とは、新約聖書『ヨハネによる福音書』の有名な言葉です。人が文明を築けたのは「言葉」を操れたからに他なりません。言葉が人と人とのコミュニケーションを促進し、情報を伝達し、様々な知恵や経験を蓄積してゆく触媒となりました。

　歴史を意味する「History」という言葉は、言葉や記録を伝承し、集積することという意味を含みます。言葉が記録されるには文字が必要です。大多数の文明は文字によって時代ごとの記録や知恵が記され、後世に伝わります。また、集められた知識を原資にして、新たな知識が創造され、その継続が文化、そして文明の発展へと繋がります。

　このように、人類の歴史を語るために、我々は過去の記録という膨大な堆積物を紐とかなければならないのです。同時に、過去の記録から新たな文明を築くヒントを得なければ、歴史を語る意味は希薄になります。

　しかし、「言葉」は人類に様々な混乱ももたらしました。「言葉を操る」という表現がありますが、記録によって歴史が意図的にゆがめられたり、我々の常識そのものの土台が粉飾されたりということもありました。あくまでも「言葉」、そして「文字」によって綴られた歴史は、その時々の人の都合や意図によって事実から乖離し、傾斜していった可能性があることを我々は忘れてはなりません。

　また、言葉は誤解も生み出します。人が言葉を操る以上、その人の性格、所属している文化、そのときの環境などによって様々な意図が生まれ、それが他の人に正確に伝達されないことが、無数の悲劇や停滞、紛争を生み出しました。このことも歴史に綴られている記録を見るときに、我々が意識してゆかなければならない要素となります。

　そこで、歴史を語るとき、我々は「言葉ありき」という記録の分析とともに、多種多様な科学を駆使して事実が何であったか解明しなければなりません。言葉、そして文字への解析と、科学的立証の両輪が、歴史そのものを解明してゆく道具となるのです。

時代
総合

地域
共通

分類
文化【言語】

キーワード
言葉の力・歴史は言葉が作る

History is an incomplete creature. No perfect source is passed down to posterity. Furthermore, humans are forgetful creatures. When it comes to world history, the distortion is enormous. History is being continually composed, and on each occasion, misunderstandings come into existence, and at the same time, new attempts are made to elucidate it.

The endeavors of relating history and conveying it to successive generations is a strenuous effort that depends on how much light human beings can shed on an imperfect process.

002 Darwin shed light on the theme of where humans came from

The French painter Paul Gauguin, who was born in Paris in 1848 and died in the Marquesas Islands in the South Pacific, painted during his sojourn in Tahiti a work titled *Where do we come from? Who are we? Where are we going?*

Disenchanted with civilized community and living in French Polynesia, Gauguin became known as a representative Post-Impressionist painter. He was also a rebellious artist who resisted the Christian values and colonial policies that were deeply rooted in Europe, which surpassed the rest of the world at the time. Turning to the ingenuous culture of the Southern Pacific, Gauguin must have shared something with Lafcadio Hearn, who at roughly the same time arrived in Japan, became fascinated with the customs and myths of Izumo, and became a naturalized Japanese citizen, taking the name Koizumi Yakumo.

The title of Gauguin's masterpiece expresses clearly that we are creatures who are born, mature, and die. At the same time, it connotes that humanity itself comes into existence, evolves, and is ultimately destroyed. Just as an individual has no recollection of his or her own birth, humankind has no clear recollection of how it has evolved.

On the Origin of Species by Means of Natural Selection, published in 1859 by the British naturalist Charles Darwin, who was a bit older than Gauguin and Koizumi Yakumo, shed some light on the world of the distant past. In this work, Darwin put forth his theory of evolution, presenting the thesis that all living things have evolved over a long period of time until the present.

人類は不完全な生き物です。完璧な資料が後世に伝わっているわけではありません。さらに人類は忘却する生き物です。世界の歴史となれば、その歪みは甚大なはずです。歴史は常に綴られ、その都度誤解も生まれ、同時に解明への試みも進化してゆくのです。

　世界の歴史を語り、それを後世に伝える作業は、こうした人類の不完全な歩みにどこまで光をあててゆけるのかという、壮大な作業でもあるのです。

ヒトはどこからきたのかというテーマにダーウィンは光をあてた

　1848年にパリに生まれ、1903年に南太平洋のマルキーズ諸島で死去したフランスの画家ポール・ゴーギャンが、タヒチに滞在していた頃に描いた作品に、『我々はどこから来たのか　我々は何者か　我々はどこへ行くのか』という絵画があります。

　文明社会を嫌い、フランス領南太平洋の島で生活していたゴーギャンは、ポスト印象派を代表する画家といわれています。彼は、当時世界を凌駕したヨーロッパに深く根ざしていたキリスト的な価値観や、植民地政策に抗う反骨の芸術家でもありました。南太平洋の素朴な文化に身を寄せた彼の発想は、同じ頃に日本を訪れ、出雲の風俗や神話に魅せられ、日本に帰化したラフカディオ・ハーンこと、小泉八雲にも通じるものがあったはずです。

　ゴーギャンのこの代表作の表題は、我々が生まれ、育ち、死んでゆく生き物であることを明示します。同時に、人類そのものも、発生し、進化し、いずれは滅亡するのではという暗示も含みます。ヒトは個々の誕生の記憶を持たないように、人類がどのように進化してきたのかという記憶が定かではないのです。

　ゴーギャンや小泉八雲より少し先輩のイギリスの自然科学者チャールズ・ダーウィンが1859年に発表した『種の起源』という著作が、そんな記憶の彼方の世界へ光をあてました。ダーウィンは同書で進化論を説き、全ての生

時代
総合

地域
共通

分類
人類【進化】

キーワード
霊長類から進化した人類
・二足歩行・道具の使用
・言語の使用

ポール・ゴーギャン『我々はどこから来たのか 我々は何者か 我々はどこへ行くのか』
Paul Gauguin —Where do we come from? Who are we? Where are we going?

Subsequently, progress in genetic research has corroborated this theory, and we now know that humans share the same ancestry as other primates, including gorillas and orangutans. At present, we know that we are connected via direct ancestry with an ape-man referred to as *Australopithecus* that was active some five million years ago. We also believe now that several types of primitive humans appeared, evolved, and went extinct. Fossil remains discovered in east Africa support those assumptions.

In order for these to develop into human species, the brain had to become stable and then develop further. One necessary condition for this was becoming bipedal. For further development, the brain had to develop enough to enable the use of tools. Typical of the first tools employed was a chipped stone tool made by striking a stone. It is thought that ape-man and primitive man made use of such tools in groups to protect themselves and to hunt.

By becoming bipedal, using tools, and then by eventually manipulating words, these creatures developed from primates, through the process of evolution, to become ape-man, primitive man, archaic humans, and finally *Homo sapiens*. Through recent developments in archaeology and the sciences, we are beginning to achieve at least a hazy answer to Gauguin's query "Where do we come from?"

003 *Homo sapiens* departed from the African continent and spread throughout the world

The brain capacity of ape-men such as *Australopithecus*, which are considered to be distant ancestors of *Homo sapiens*, appears to be some 500 cc, less than one-third that of present-day human beings. Approximately 2.5 million years ago, that capacity developed. Our ancestor *Homo habilis*, somewhere between ape-man and primitive man, appeared. Subsequently, this ancestor began to contrive new ways of using tools. Early man, who had developed from ape-man, smashed rock, processed the pieces, and created hand axes and held them as tools.

When one looks at the fossils of Java Man, held to have been active some 1.3 million years ago, and Peking Man, which was discovered in Zhoukoudian on the outskirts of Beijing and is thought to date back to 500,000 years ago, one

き物は長い年月を通して進化し、現在に至っているという学説を発表したのです。

その後、遺伝子学などの進歩により進化論が裏付けられ、人類の祖先はゴリラやオランウータンなどと同じ霊長類であることがわかってきます。今では、我々に繋がる直接の祖先は、500万年ほど前から地球上で活動していた猿人、アウストラロピテクスをはじめ、様々な原人が進化と絶滅を繰り返してきながら現在に至ったものではないかといわれており、その化石は東アフリカ各地で発見されているのです。

人類へ進化するためには頭脳が安定して発達しなければなりません。それには二足歩行が欠かせない要素となります。そして発達した頭脳によって、道具を使うことができるようになることが、さらなる進化への条件となりました。最初に使った道具の代表が、石を砕いて使用した打製石器でした。猿人や原人は、こうした道具を使い、集団で身を守り、狩猟をしていたものと思われます。

二本足で歩き、道具を使い、やがて言葉を操るようになることが、霊長類から、猿人、そして原人、旧人という過程を経て、人類へと繋がる進化を押し進めます。近年の考古学や科学の発達で、ゴーギャンの命題の中で「我々がどこから来たのか」という部分が、おぼろげながら見えてきたのです。

人類はアフリカ大陸から世界各地へと旅立った

人類の遠い祖先とされるアウストラロピテクスなど猿人の脳の容積は、現代人の3分の1弱の500ccしかなかったようです。そして、約250万年前には、それがさらに進化します。ホモ・ハビリスという猿人と原人の中間に位置する我々の祖先が出現したのです。その後、道具の使用方法にも工夫が加わります。猿人から進化した原人は、石を打ち砕き、加工し、ハンドアックス、つまり手斧として、それを握って使用したのです。

130万年前頃に活動していたとされるジャワ原人や、北京郊外の周口店付近で発見され、50万年以前に遡る北京原人などの化石を見ると、既に彼らは猿人より倍の脳の容積を持っていたことがわかっています。

時代
BC10,000以前
先史

地域
共通

分類
人類【進化】

キーワード
道具の加工・埋葬の習慣・新人の登場・集団での生活・世界に拡散

recognizes that both already possessed double the brain capacity of ape-man. This is the primitive man called *Homo erectus*. It is conjectured that these beings were already leading a hunting-gathering lifestyle and employing fire.

Following them came Neanderthals, which have been unearthed in Europe and elsewhere, who buried their dead and developed various methods of hunting and gathering and used stone tools in various ways. Referred to as archaic humans, these peoples branched out between Europe and Central Asia between approximately 600,000 and 35,000 years ago. In due course, a new, more developed ancestor of human species appeared. This included Cro-Magnon Man in Europe and the Peking Man in Zhoukoudian in China. The cave paintings at Altamira in Spain and Lascaux in France are believed to have been left by the Cro-Magnon people.

While Neanderthals are known as archaic humans, Cro-Magnons are known as *Homo Sapiens*. It is these people who are our direct ancestors. At present, the Neanderthal people are not considered the direct progenitors of the human species. It is speculated that these archaic humans and *Homo sapiens* mingled together as they dispersed, eventually joining together to form modern man.

In the latter part of the period known as the Pleistocene, some 200,000 years ago, rugged glaciers repeatedly spread across the earth.

These peoples, in order to survive the ice age, acquired knowledge, formed

それがホモ・エレクトゥスといわれる原人たちです。彼らは既に狩猟採集生活をしながら、火も使用していたのではないかといわれています。

　その後、ヨーロッパなどで発掘されたネアンデルタール人などは、死者の埋葬なども行い、狩猟や採集の方法も、様々な石器を使用するなど、多様になってゆきます。彼らのことを旧人といい、約60万年前から3万5千年前までの間に、ヨーロッパから中央アジアにかけて進出をしていました。やがてより進化した新しい人類の祖先が現れます。ヨーロッパのクロマニョン人や中国の周口店上洞人などがそれにあたります。スペインのアルタミラや、フランスのラスコーには、クロマニョン人が描いたとされる壁画が残っています。

　ネアンデルタール人を旧人と呼ぶのに対して、クロマニョン人たちは新人と呼ばれています。彼らこそ、我々の直接の祖先です。今ではネアンデルタール人は人類の直系の祖先ではなく、彼ら旧人と新人は共に混ざったり拡散したりしながら、現代人へと繋がっていったのではとも推測されています。

　約20万年前の更新世（あるいは洪積世）と呼ばれる時代の後期から、厳しい氷河が何度も地球を見舞います。

　彼らは氷河期を生き抜く中で知恵をつけ、集団でチームを構成して、気候に適応します。石器を使った原始的な武器で、グループでマンモ

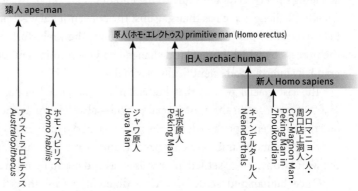

実年代 Absolute age	500万年前〜 5M years ago	250万年前〜 2.5M years ago	150万年前〜 1.5M years ago	60万年前〜 600,000 years ago	20万年前〜 200,000 years ago	1万年前〜 10,000 years ago
考古年代 Timeline of prehistoric technology			旧石器時代（打製石器） Old Stone Age (chipped stone tool)			新石器時代（磨製石器） New Stone Age (polished stone tool)

猿人 ape-man

原人（ホモ・エレクトゥス）primitive man (Homo erectus)

旧人 archaic human

新人 Homo sapiens

アウストラロピテクス
Australopithecus

ホモ・ハビリス
Homo habilis

ジャワ原人
Java Man

北京原人
Peking Man

ネアンデルタール人
Neanderthals

クロマニョン人・
周口店上洞人
Cro-Magnon Man・
Peking Man in
Zhoukoudian

人類の進化
Human Evolution

bands, and adapted to the climate. Try to imagine a scene in which these people using stone tools as primitive weapons capture and make a prize of a mammoth. It is these archaic humans and new people that we call modern human beings, *Homo sapiens*.

Later, over long spans of time, human species spread widely. Departing from Africa, they completed a migration into Europe, Asia, and North and South America by 13,000 years ago. During the ice age, Japan and the Asian continent were connected by land. The ancestors of human species, it is thought, reached the Japanese archipelago as early as 100,000 or even 120,000 years ago.

004 The formation of the livelihood sphere brought forth a revolution in human consciousness

The period in which Darwin, Gauguin, and Koizumi Yakumo lived was one in which humankind harnessed steam to provide power and in which industry advanced considerably.

Together with developments in science, a major change occurred in how people thought, and there was an increase in the number of people who entertained doubts regarding long-held religious views and ways of looking at the world. Representative of this revolution was Darwin's theory of evolution, which said that humans were not created by God but had evolved from primates. Struggling against the power and feeling of alienation that was created in this constantly changing society, Gauguin came to the end of his life on an isolated island in the Pacific. Challenges such as theirs against the conventional wisdom that had been believed in the past stimulated curiosity about the prehistoric world. Further, the process by which humankind changed and evolved into modern people was gradually inferred and scientifically clarified.

The last glacial period that humankind experienced ended approximately 10,000 years ago. In the post-glacial period—also known as the alluvial epoch and the Holocene epoch—due to the influence of the temperate climate, hunting activities expanded and were energized. Humankind, after spreading throughout the world from Africa, settled in various areas and began living there.

Once humankind settled in these different places, they took up diverse

ス象を捕獲していた光景を想像してみてください。そんな旧人や新人を、我々は現生人類（ホモ・サピエンス）と呼んでいます。

その後人類は長い年月をかけて世界に拡散しました。アフリカから旅立ってヨーロッパ、アジア、そして南北アメリカへと人々が移動を終えたのは1万3千年ほど前のことだったようです。氷河期は、日本も大陸と陸続きでした。人類の祖先が日本列島にも到着したのは、10万年から12万年以上前のことではないかといわれています。

生活圏の形成が人としての意識に変革を生み出した

ダーウィンやゴーギャン、そして小泉八雲の生きた時代は、人類が蒸気などの力を利用して動力を生み出し、産業が急激に発展した時代でした。

科学の発展と共に人々の発想にも革命がおこり、旧来の宗教観や世界観に疑念を持つ人も増えてきます。人類は神が創ったものではなく、霊長類から進化したものだというダーウィンの進化論はそれを象徴したものでした。そして、ゴーギャンは変化する社会の中に生まれた権力や疎外感に抗いながら、太平洋の孤島で生涯を閉じました。彼らのような過去に信じられていた常識への挑戦が、太古の世界への好奇心を刺激します。そして、人類が現代人へと変化し、進化する過程が少しずつ類推され、学術的にも解明されてゆくのです。

時代
BC4,000以前
先史

地域
共通

分類
文化【社会】

キーワード
氷河期の終了・定住生活の開始・火の使用・宗教の発生

我々人類が迎えた最後の氷河期は約1万年前に終わります。そして、後氷期（沖積世とか完新世とも呼ばれます）になると、温暖な気候の影響で、狩猟活動にも広がりが生まれ、太古の人類の活動がにわかに活発になります。人類は、アフリカから世界中に拡散した後、それぞれの地域に定着して、生活を始めたのです。

人類が各地で定着してゆくと、それぞれの場所で生活圏が生まれま

livelihoods. In order to protect those ways of life, they attempted to create social structures. Naturally enough, there would have been commercial activity, such as trade with groups in different environments, and conflicts over those areas from time to time. In order to maintain this social behavior and ensure the group's continued existence, one would assume that the idea of "organization" came about. Sometime later, as generation after generation maintained a certain location for their livelihood, the people living there would probably have developed a sense of attachment to that land. That would develop into a sense of pride regarding the land itself and their culture, which would become the energy for solidarity as a tribe or a nation. This starting point of the psychology of modern people in terms of ethnic awareness and national awareness began to be cultivated at the end of the glacial epoch, as the climate became more livable, when people began to put down roots.

During the period when primitive man and modern *Homo sapiens* were intermingling, humankind was making use of fire. Fire could be used not simply for warmth, but in changing eating habits, and that in turn led to development of the jaw and other bone structures. That tied in with the development of the ability to communicate via spoken language. When *Homo sapiens* spread throughout the world, it is believed that they already possessed the type of cranium people today have, and as a result, those people had the ability to use words.

Language strengthens human bonds and the capacity for strengthening organizations. A "village" is born, and to promote its prosperity, religious ceremonies are carried out. Stone tools and bone or horn implements are put together and used for more detailed working processes to create precise tools. Through this, our ancestors were able to bring about a new dawn in the social activities of humankind.

す。そして生活圏を守るために、社会の仕組みを作ろうとします。当然生活圏の違う集団同士の交易などの商業活動、時には生活圏を巡った戦争もあったはずです。こうした社会的行為を維持し、集団で生き残るためにも、生活圏の中に「組織」という発想が生まれてきたのではないでしょうか。やがて、世代から世代へと維持された生活圏は、そこに住む人にその土地への愛着と執着を生み出します。それが土地や文化へのプライドとなり、部族や国家の結束のエネルギーともなりました。そんな民族意識や国家意識という現代人の心理の原点が、氷河期が終わり、過ごしやすい気候になり、人々が大地に根ざして生活を始めたときに育成され始めたのです。

　原人と新人とが交錯していた時代、人類は既に火を使用していました。火を使用すれば単に暖がとれるのみならず、食生活が進化し、そのことは顎などの骨格の進化にも影響を与えます。それは言語の発話能力の発達にも繋がります。新人が世界中に拡散した時代には、既に人々は今のような頭蓋骨に覆われ、それによって言葉を操れる能力を有するようになっていたのではと思われます。

　言葉は人の紐帯を強め、組織力を高めます。「村」が生まれ、その繁栄のための宗教的儀式が行われるようになったはずです。石器も、石を骨角器と呼ばれる骨などを加工した部品と組み合わせて使用され始め、より細かい作業工程による精密な道具が制作されます。こうして、我々の祖先は、人類の社会活動の黎明期を迎えたのです。

005 The development of agriculture led to the growth of ancient civilizations

The ice age came to an end. With the warming of the planet, firm ground for activity expanded. One day on this solid ground, people gathering plants discovered that sprouts came out of seeds and that they could cultivate those plants. Elsewhere, other people noticed that they could domesticate animals and breed them.

Once the ice age ended and sea levels rose, separating Japan from the continent, the inhabitants of the Japanese archipelago learned to mix clay with sand, bake it, and produce earthenware. These people took pleasure in creating interesting designs by wrapping rope around these clay vessels. This is the start of the straw-rope patterned Jomon pottery. Earthenware was produced not only in Japan but almost everywhere else on the planet. At about the same time, ever more precise stone tools came into use. People polished stones, giving them an even sharper edge. They shattered obsidian, a volcanic glass, and ground it to produce arrowheads for use in hunting. The Old Stone Age, in which chipped stone tools were used, gave way to a new age in which polished stone tools came into existence. This was the advent of the New Stone Age. This great revolution began some 9,000 years ago, and by degrees, people began to combine agriculture with hunting and commenced raising domesticated animals, settling and living in one place on a regular basis.

Recent archaeological research suggests that during the Jomon period, inhabitants of Japan practiced a primitive form of agriculture. It may have been simply a matter of spreading seeds, letting them sprout in the rain, and then gathering the grain that developed.

However, progress in agricultural activity in different parts of the world was already undergoing various changes. Villages were growing into towns, and people were even constructing cities in some places. They managed rivers and acquired the technology necessary for constructing aqueducts and irrigating land. Agricultural activities employing the control of water were a highly significant revolution in production. With agrarian culture taking hold and people benefiting from the expanded harvests, a variety of other activities commenced. Inhabitants developed regulations and ceremonies for festivals and living communally, which in turn made it necessary to have tools for sharing information. Such needs led to the creation of writing. The first form is called hieroglyphics, which pictorially

農耕の発達が古代文明の発生に繋がった

　氷河期が終わります。そして地球が温暖化し、活動できる大地も拡大します。ある日、そんな大地で植物を採集していた人々が、種から芽がでて、それが育ってゆくことを発見します。また、ある所では、動物をなつかせて飼育できることに気付きます。

　氷河期が終わり、水面が上昇し、大陸と分断された日本では、人々は粘土に砂を混ぜて焼くことで、土器を生産することを覚えます。そしてそんな土器に縄目などの面白い文様を施し創作を楽しみました。縄文土器の誕生です。土器は日本に限らず世界各地で生産されました。同時により精度の高い石器が使用され始めます。石を磨いて切れ味をよくしたり、黒曜石などを砕いて研磨して鏃を造ったりして、狩猟に使用したのです。人々は打製石器を使う旧石器時代から、磨製石器を使う時代へと進化します。新石器時代の到来です。こうした大変革は、約9000年前から始まり、次第に人々は農耕と狩猟、そして動物の飼育を両立させながら、定住して生活をするようになるのです。

時代
BC4,000以前
先史

地域
共通

分類
文化【技術】

キーワード
磨製石器の製作・土器の製作・農耕の開始・文字の発明

　日本では、最近の考古学者の研究もあって、縄文時代に原始的な農耕が行われていたのではないかといわれています。当時はまだ種をまいて雨によって発芽成長した穀物を採集する程度のものだったかもしれません。

　しかし、世界の中には農耕活動の進化によって既に様々な変化がおきていました。村が町へと成長し、さらに都市を築いていった人々もいたのです。彼らは川を管理し、水路を造り灌漑をする技術を取得します。水を管理して農耕活動をすることは、人類にとっての大きな生産革命となったのです。農耕文化が定着すれば、収穫を享受するために人々は様々な活動を始めます。祭礼や集団生活のための規則や儀式、そこでの情報を共有するためのツールが必要となるのです。そうしたニーズが文字を生み出します。それは象形文字と呼ばれる、自然界の生き物や現象を絵文字化したものでした。やがて文字は様々な形式を持つようになり、進化します。例えば中国人の祖先は、そんな象形文

symbolize living things and phenomena in the natural world. In due course, these symbols took different forms and continued to develop. For example, the ancestors of the Chinese people created Chinese characters based on these hieroglyphics.

The Jomon people, unfortunately, did not possess a written form of language. Despite the fact that they were able to produce sophisticated earthenware, manufacture bows and arrows with sharp arrowheads, and carry on trade with these products, the people were unable to establish either a power structure or a state.

The first people to possess writing and begin to form a state lived in Mesopotamia, today's Iraq. The Sumerians, who lived in the fertile lands between the Tigris and the Euphrates Rivers, developed a society that employed cuneiform characters. Today we call this area which extends from northern Iraq through the Mediterranean to Egypt the Fertile Crescent.

006 Religion led to the division of labor and developed the notion of an occupation

Before explaining the Sumerians in greater detail, let us consider a bit more carefully the process by which religion causes the evolution of a social system while it cultivates civilization.

In the beginning, humans hunted in close-knit groups, sharing what they caught. Once individuals with physical strength were able to obtain game by using weapons, such as stone implements, everyone from children to old people probably joined together in dismembering the catch. At that point, people must have been simply terrified by such things as volcanic activity and weather disasters.

In due time, humans who had attained high levels of technique in hunting and agriculture and had grown accustomed to settled habitation, because they maintained a stable livelihood, must have felt the need to bring natural changes and calamities under some degree of control. They became conscious of the power of deities in the overwhelming strength possessed by nature, and sought to in some way negotiate with those deities.

The act of negotiation transformed into religion. Not only did people pray to the gods for an abundant harvest but spiritual mediums, priests, and prophets conveying divine messages also began to appear. These figures devised ceremonies

字から漢字を作り出しました。

　縄文人は残念ながら文字を持ちませんでした。ですから先進的な土器を作成し、鏃から弓矢を造り、それをもって交易もしていましたが、それ以上の強い権力構造や国家を造ることはできませんでした。

　文字を最初に持って国家を造り始めたのが、メソポタミア、今のイラク周辺の人々です。チグリス川とユーフラテス川に挟まれた肥沃な大地で生活していたシュメール人が、楔形文字をもって社会を発展させたのです。この二つの大河に挟まれ、文明が交錯したイラク北部から地中海沿岸を経てエジプトに至る地域を、我々は「肥沃な三日月地帯」と呼んでいます。

楔形文字
Cuneiform

宗教は分業を生み出し、職業という概念を育んだ

　シュメール人についてさらに詳しく解説する前に、人類が宗教を持ち、宗教が文明を育みながら社会制度を進化させてゆくプロセスについて、もう少し詳しく考えてみます。
　原始、人類は身近な集団で狩猟をし、獲物を分かち合って生活をしていました。腕力のある者が石器などの武器で獲物を手にいれると、子供から老人まで、総出でそれを解体していたのでしょう。その時点では、人々は火山活動や天候異変などの自然の脅威に対して、単純に恐怖心をもって怯えていたはずです。
　やがて、より高度な狩猟や農耕技術を身につけ、定住することを覚えた人類は、安定した生活を維持するために、自然の変化や異変を克服する必要に迫られます。人々は圧倒的な力を持つ自然の側に神の力を意識し、その力と交渉しようとするのです。

　この交渉の行為が宗教へと変化します。豊作を求め神に祈る者のみならず、神のお告げを語る巫女や神官、預言者が現れます。彼らは宗教行為を実行するための儀式を編み出します。宗教行為に関わる人々

時代
BC4,000以前
先史

地域
共通

分類
社会【宗教】

キーワード
社会制度の進化 ● 宗教の組織化 ● 階級の成立 ● 分業の発生

in order to perform religious practices. Those who were involved in these religious activities were not necessarily the people who wielded the most authority. However, when ceremonies and systems came into being, it is easy to imagine how it would become necessary to have someone to carry them out and take leadership over them. Written language may well have been devised as a means of preserving these systems of religion to pass them on to succeeding generations.

To exercise leadership over groups and carry out religious activities, social classes may have come into existence among the people. There would have been high and low status not only within one's own society, but also between conquerors and the conquered. To protect their own group from someone who might attempt to attack it, a sophisticated leadership and maintenance of status were required.

In the social system based on this status, people learned how to sustain society based on the division of labor, comprised of those who were producers, those who ruled, those who prayed, and those who fought.

Through the wisdom of the specialization of labor, the social structure became even more complex. Even among those who offered prayers, the division of labor progressed further, leading to people like shamans who conversed directly with the gods, people who recorded divine oracles, and others whose duty it was to serve at a shrine or sanctuary.

This division of labor provided humans with the concept of an occupation. The more society developed, the more diverse human occupations became, and people came to subsist on the accumulation of what was produced by these various occupations.

Some occupations became hereditary. In modern society, as humankind has cast aside class or caste systems and acquired the concept of equality, more people have been released from the constraints of heredity and have secured the freedom to select their own occupations. As a result, occupations have become open to everybody and have been further subdivided, providing specialization. This evolution through the division of labor is apparent almost everywhere in the world, a process common to all humankind.

が必ずしも権力の頂点に立っていたわけではありません。しかし、儀式や制度が生まれれば、それを管理し、集団を統率する人々が必要になったことは十分に想像できます。文字もこうした宗教制度を世代を超えて維持するために、発明されたのかもしれません。

　集団を統率し、宗教行為を行うために、人々の間に階級が生まれます。身分の上下は自らの社会のみならず、征服者と被征服者との間にもありました。むしろ、人々が自らの集団への征服を試みる者から守るためにも、より洗練された統率と身分による管理が求められていたはずです。
　この身分に基づいた社会制度の中で、生産をする者、国を統治する者、祈る者、戦う者など、人々は仕事を分担して社会を維持することを覚えたのです。
　分業の知恵によって、社会構造はさらに複雑になってゆきました。同じ祈る者の中にも、シャーマンのように神と直接語る者もいれば、お告げを記録する者、神殿を守る者など、制度の中で分業がさらに進んでいったのです。

　分業は職業という概念を人類に与えます。社会が発展すればするほど、人類は多様な職業を持ち、それぞれの職業によって生産されるものを集積して生活を営むようになったのです。

　職業は世襲されたこともありました。人類が身分制度を捨て、平等の概念を獲得した近代社会では、世襲という束縛から人々は解放され、職業の選択の自由が保障されます。その結果職業は万人に解放され、ますます細分化し、専門性を備えていったのです。この分業による進化は、世界のあらゆるところで見受けられる、人類共通の過程なのです。

第二部

人類の歩みが始まる
（古代の世界）

....

Part Two:
Human Progress Begins
(The Ancient World)

....

　ヒトは国家を作り、その巨大な集団同士がさらに競争しながら、文明を育ててゆきました。四大文明と呼ばれる古代文明を通して、人は物事を記録するための文字も発展させました。ヒトの活動が文字に記録されたとき、ヒトは歴史という時代に入りました。

　そして、階層の分化と共に、人々を統合する要としての宗教も進化を続けました。古代文明は、現在の我々の日常生活につながる、様々な風俗習慣を生み出したのです。文字、神、そして社会秩序など、我々が今も受け継ぐ、ヒトがヒトとしての特徴を誇示するすべての理由が、この時代に育まれたのです。

　国家は時に破壊され、再生され、膨張し、縮小し、そして消滅もしました。こうした幾多の過程を通して、ヒトは世界の要所要所に巨大な帝国を築き、周辺民族をも支配しました。ローマや漢といった古代の超大国は、その周辺にも文明を伝播させ、今も残る遺跡の数々によって現代人をも魅了しているのです。

007 Ethnic groups mingled together searching for abundance nurtured in fertile lands

In prehistoric times, in the process of humankind's spread to all parts of the world, as human beings adapted to different environments, from time to time they mingled with people who had different roots. Out of that mixing together were born various races and diverse spoken languages.

It is said that in the present day there are close to 7,000 languages spoken around the world. They are classified into a number of subgroupings, but it has not yet been clearly proven which of the languages has as its progenitor the Sumerians, who were active in the early period of the Mesopotamian civilization.

The invention of writing as a means of transmitting these languages was a watershed development for humankind. The Sumerian's syllabic script, known as cuneiform, appears to be human beings' earliest type of writing. With the invention of characters, technology could be transmitted and social systems could be made more complete.

At this point we enter the period which seeks to answer the second question posited by the aforementioned title of Paul Gauguin's painting, *Where do we come from? Who are we? Where are we going?* When we attempt to discuss who we are, we are entering the historical period.

According to legend, among the Sumerians who settled in Mesopotamia and built a city-state, there was a wandering king who shared Gauguin's anxiety about fate. It is the story of King Gilgamesh, in the *Gilgamesh Epic*, which describes his realization after fighting with the gods and losing his close friend to death that he too is mortal and tells of his search for an elixir that will provide him with eternal youth and immortality.

By 3500 B.C. the Sumerians already possessed the technology for casting metals including bronzeware, and their village had developed into a city-state. The remains of the city known as Ur or Uruk still exist. It is believed that a king named Gilgamesh actually resided in Uruk around 2600 B.C., but the details are not clear. The tale has many elements common to legends around the world. They describe a sage or king who wanders the world, feuding with the gods, searching for a potion that will provide him with eternal youth and make him immortal, and suffering in a flood. Interestingly enough, this myth of the Sumerians has counterparts later in history, including the Old Testament of the Bible.

肥沃な大地に育まれた豊かさを求めて
民族が交錯した

先史時代に人類が世界各地に拡散する過程の中で、人類は異なる環境に適応しながら、時には異なるルーツの人々とも交流します。その混合の中から様々な人種が生まれ、多様な言語が喋られるようになりました。

現在では世界に7000近くの言語があるといわれています。それらはいくつかの系列に分類はされていますが、メソポタミア文明の初期に活動したシュメール人がどの言語系の祖先なのか、まだはっきりと証明されてはいないのです。

そしてこの言語を伝承するために文字が発明されたことは、人類にとって画期的なことでした。シュメール人が所有した楔形文字は、人類にとって最も初期の文字だったことになります。文字の発明によって、技術も伝承され、社会制度もより整ってゆくのです。

先に紹介したポール・ゴーギャンの『我々はどこから来たのか　我々は何者か　我々はどこへ行くのか』という絵画の中で、「我々は何者か」という命題に応える時代、すなわち歴史時代へとこれから入ってゆきます。

ところで、メソポタミア地方に定住し都市国家を築いたシュメール人の中に、ゴーギャンと同じ「人の定め」について悩み、放浪した王の伝説が遺されています。神々と戦いながら、親友を失ったことから自らも死すべき人間だということを悟り、不老不死の薬を求めて旅をするギルガメシュ王の物語『ギルガメシュ叙事詩』がそれにあたります。

シュメール人は、紀元前3500年頃には既に青銅器などの金属をも鋳造する技術をもち、村落は、都市国家へと成長していました。ウルやウルクといった都市が今でも遺跡として残っているのです。ギルガメシュは紀元前2600年頃にウルクに実在した王であるといわれていますが、詳しいことはわかりません。賢者や王が世界を放浪したり、神々との確執を切り抜けたり、不老不死の薬を求めたり、洪水に見舞われたりという話は、世界の多くの神話に共通したものでした。シュメール人のこの神話は、その後の旧約聖書などでの物語にも通じる興味深いものなのです。

時代
BC3,000年代
先史/古代

地域
メソポタミア(イラク)

分類
文化【民族】

キーワード
歴史はシュメールに始まる・文字の使用・最古の文学・都市の成立・戦争の開始

In affluent civilizations supported by agricultural technology, such as that of the Sumerians, when peoples' livelihoods improve, people of other ethnic origins, seeking the riches that have been cultivated there, come to pillage and plunder that wealth. In such scrambles for riches, Mesopotamia witnessed the birth and destruction of any number of dynasties. Following the Sumerians came the Semitic-speaking Akkadians. They in turn were overthrown by another Semitic-speaking people known as the Amorites, who gained control of Mesopotamia and founded the First Babylonian dynasty.

Under these people, the productive Fertile Crescent became even more affluent. This occurred in roughly the 18th century B.C.

008 The confusion and chaos of war and exchanges supported the four great civilizations

The four great civilizations that are representative of the ancient world are those of Mesopotamia, Egypt, the Indus, and the Yellow River. We tend to mistakenly think that these regions were dominated by powerful and stable dynasties protected by power structures that supported the civilization. However, many civilizations were established in unstable and dynamic chaos through strife for supremacy and conflict among ethnic groups.

For a civilization to flourish, synergy is necessary, and it is attained by diverse ethnic groups carrying out cultural exchanges, enhancing their respective qualities through that interaction. Ironically these exchanges were carried out not only through trade but also through violent invasions and warfare. When one area became prosperous, another ethnic group, seeking its riches and hoping to enjoy them, invaded that area and on occasion totally destroyed the state that existed there. Through repetition of such activities, civilizations spread and their qualities were enhanced.

Think back to Japan after World War II. Faced with defeat, Japan accepted an inflow of culture from America, against which Japan had fought during the war. However, as a result of this, both Japan and America accepted the influence of the other culture, so that one finds sushi in America, and one can easily enjoy hamburgers in Japan. In ancient times, something similar was always happening in the regions where the four great civilizations flourished.

農耕技術に支えられたシュメール人のような豊かな文明の中で、人々の暮らしが向上すると、そこで育まれた富を求めて他の民族がその略奪のためにやってきます。メソポタミアはこうした富を巡る争奪戦の中で、様々な王朝が生まれ滅びていったのです。シュメール人にとって代わったのは、アッカド人と呼ばれるセム語系の人々でした。そしてさらに同じセム語系のアムル人が彼らを滅ぼしてメソポタミア全域を支配したバビロン第一王朝を開きます。

　彼らのもと、肥沃な三日月地帯はさらに豊かになってゆくのです。紀元前18世紀頃のことでした。

戦争と交流による混乱と混沌が
四大文明を支えてきた

　古代世界を代表する四大文明は、メソポタミア、エジプト、インダス、そして黄河文明です。我々は、これらの地域には権力構造に守られた強力で安定した王朝が君臨し、文明を支えていたと誤解しがちです。しかし、文明の多くは民族同士の覇権争いと抗争を通した不安定でダイナミックな混沌の中で築かれたのです。

　文明が栄えるには、多民族同士が文化交流を行い、その質を高め合うという相乗効果が必要です。皮肉なことに、その交流は交易だけではなく侵略や戦争といった暴力によっても促進されたのです。一つの場所が豊かになれば、その富を求め、富を享受しようと別の部族がそこに侵入し、時にはそこにあった国家を崩壊させることもあります。そうした行為を重ねることで、文明はより深く浸透し、その質も向上しました。

　第二次世界大戦の後の日本を思い出してください。敗戦を迎えた日本には、戦争中敵として戦ったアメリカの文化が洪水のように流入しました。しかし、そのことによって、日本とアメリカ双方がお互いの文化の影響を受け合い、今やアメリカに行っても寿司があり、日本でもハンバーガーを簡単に楽しめます。古代、四大文明が栄えた地域にも、同様なことが常におこっていたのです。

時代
BC1,500以前
先史/古代

地域
メソポタミア(イラク)・
エジプト

分類
文化【戦争】

キーワード
文明の交流・侵略と戦争
・暦の誕生・最古の法律
・鉄器の使用

One notices particularly throughout Mesopotamia, where from ancient times agricultural techniques progressed, this sort of subjugation and subjection repeated again and again, and in that process people intermingled, cultures mixed together, and the result was progress toward an even greater civilization. The conquering ethnic group that zealously benefited from the culture that the Sumerians had assembled in the Fertile Crescent were Semite-speaking people.

In the state called the First Babylonian dynasty which they established, they used the sexagesimal system and a lunisolar calendar. This calendar corrected the errors that resulted from the use of the lunar calendar by using the rules of the solar calendar.

The First Babylonian dynasty is also famous for the Code of Hammurabi, which was compiled by the king of that name. It is the world's oldest legal code and is known for its principle of retaliation: "An eye for an eye, a tooth for a tooth." The invaders who came in the First Babylonian dynasty were a typical ethnic group that had suddenly risen in what is today's eastern Turkey, a group known as the Hittites. These people already possessed iron weapons and with those powerful weapons they were able to overwhelm the Bronze Age civilization of Mesopotamia.

Meanwhile, through contact and mutual stimulation with the Mesopotamian civilization, Egyptian civilization also developed.

At present, this entire area takes the form of a broad cultural area holding Islamic beliefs, but from earliest times, there were close political and cultural ties connecting the region from North Africa to the Middle East.

009 Rivers were the original sources of civilization

Two sources of the Nile River, Lake Victoria in the central part of the African continent and another source on the Ethiopian Plateau, become one great river at present-day Khartoum, the capital city of Sudan, and then flow north toward the desert and the Mediterranean Sea. Throughout history large rivers like the Nile have repeatedly flooded their banks, tormenting people along the rivers. In contrast, people who were able to control floods were able to enjoy the benefits of abundant fertile soil which the great raging rivers carried and deposited. Providing both trials and bounties to people, these rivers became instructors providing guideposts along the path toward civilization.

In order to bring the wrath of the Nile River under control, the ancient

中でも特に古くから農耕技術の進化がみられたメソポタミア一円も、このような征服と服属を繰り返しながら、人が混ざり文化が混ざり、さらに大きな文明へと進化していったのです。肥沃な三日月地帯で太古に活躍したシュメール人の築いた文化を貪欲に享受した征服民族はセム語系の人々でした。

　彼らが築いたバビロン第一王朝と呼ばれる国家では、60進法が使われ、太陰太陽暦が使用されたといいます。これは太陰暦ででてくるカレンダーの誤差を太陽暦の法則で修正する暦法のことです。
　バビロン第一王朝は、ハムラビ王の作ったハムラビ法典でも有名です。これは世界最古の法典で、「目には目を、歯には歯を」という復讐法の原則で知られた法典です。そんなバビロン第一王朝を侵略したのが、現在のトルコ東部に勃興したヒッタイト人に代表される民族でした。彼らは既に鉄器を使っており、その強力な武器で青銅器文明に依存していたメソポタミア地域を席巻したのです。

　一方、メソポタミア文明と接し、刺激を受け合いながら成長したのが、エジプト文明でした。
　現在、この地域一帯はイスラム教を信奉する広大な文化圏を形成していますが、その当時から、北アフリカと中東とは政治的にも文化的にも密接な繋がりを持っていたのです。

川は文明の源たる教師だった

【時代】
BC2,000以前
先史/古代

【地域】
エジプト・インド

【分類】
文化【社会】

【キーワード】
絶大な王権・霊魂の不滅の思想・都市の発達(インド)・アーリア人の侵入(インド)

　アフリカ大陸の中心部にあるヴィクトリア湖と、エチオピア高原を二つの源流とするナイル川は、現在のスーダンの首都ハルツームで一本の大河となって砂漠を北に、地中海に向かって流れてゆきます。ナイル川などの大河は、氾濫を繰り返していました。氾濫は人々に試練を与えますが、逆にそれを克服した人々は、荒れる大河が運ぶ豊かな土壌の恵みを享受できたのです。川は人々に試練と恵みを与え、文明への道標となった教師だったのです。

　古代エジプト人は、ナイル川の怒りを抑えるために、季節を把握し

Egyptians worked out a solar calendar to grasp the seasons and a complex system of measurement technology, enabling them to build a strong social structure that made it possible to implement enormous construction projects. This organized control with the king at the top used its efficient administrative hierarchy to build the famous group of pyramids. A unified country was established in Egypt in about 3000 B.C. The king was called a pharaoh, and under the pharaohs, from the Old Kingdom through the Middle Kingdom to the New Kingdom, some 30 dynasties were formed and handed down to the next one. The pyramids were intended to serve as residences of the pharaohs in the afterlife. The Giza pyramids constructed by King Khufu during the Old Kingdom period are particularly well known. It is believed that they were constructed not solely by ruthlessly driven slaves but also by hired workers and engineers, all working in close teamwork. The dynasties of the Old Kingdom also suffered invasions by the Hyksos people from what is today's Syria, but they always retained their own religious views. Ancient Egyptians continued to believe in the immortality of the soul, the necessity of mummifying the dead, and producing, in hieroglyphs, *The Book of the Dead*, to guide the dead to the netherworld.

The story of the four great civilizations is also the story of the rivers that flowed through them and the story of the ethnic groups that mingled within them. This is true not only of Egypt and is best represented by the Tigris River and the Euphrates River, which were the sources of the Mesopotamian civilization.

Further, if we look at the basin of the Indus River, which flows through present-day Pakistan, we notice that there were a number of city-states like those in Mesopotamian civilization.

These became the Indus civilization, one that flourished in city-states such as Harappa and Moenjo-daro around 2600 B.C., and then vanished into the desert. Some hold that this was caused by climate change, while others believe it was due to invasions by other ethnic groups, but the actual cause remains unclear. After the whole area of present-day India and Pakistan flourished through the Indus civilization, it was exposed to a great migration of Indo-European-speaking peoples from Central Asia. The Aryans came from Afghanistan over the Khyber Pass in the mountainous region of the Punjab. And this became the base of the ethnic mosaic of contemporary India.

ようと太陽暦を編み出し、複雑な測量技術を、そして大工事を進める
ことを可能にする強力な社会組織を作り出します。それは王を頂点と
した支配組織で、その絶大な権力のもと、有名なピラミッド群も造ら
れます。エジプトに統一国家が造られたのは紀元前3000年頃のことで
した。王はファラオと呼ばれ、王の元、古王国から中王国を経て新王
国まで、30の王朝が生まれては引き継がれてゆきました。ピラミッド
は王の来世の居宅でした。古王国の頃に造られたクフ王が建設したギ
ザのピラミッドなどは特に有名です。それは、単に奴隷のみを酷使し
て造ったのではなく、普通に雇用された労働者と技術者との連携プレー
により建設されたのではないかといわれてい
ます。古代エジプトの王朝は、例えば現在の
シリアあたりに展開していたヒクソス人など
の侵入を受けたりもしますが、常に自らの宗
教観を維持してきました。古代エジプト人は
霊魂の不滅を信じ、死者をミイラにし冥界へ
案内するために『死者の書』を象形文字（ヒ
エログリフ）で記しました。

象形文字（ヒエログリフ）
Hieroglyphs

　四大文明は、そこを流れた川の物語でもあ
り、そこで交錯した民族の盛衰史でもありま
す。エジプトのみならず、メソポタミア文明の源となったチグリス川
やユーフラテス川などがその代表です。
　さらに現在のパキスタンを流れるインダス川流域に目をやれば、そ
こにはメソポタミア文明と同様にいくつかの都市国家が存在していま
した。
　インダス文明です。その文明を代表するハラッパやモヘンジョダロ
など、紀元前2600年頃から繁栄していた都市文明は、その後砂漠の中
に消滅してしまいました。その理由は気候変動とも民族の侵入ともい
われますが、いまだ定かではないのです。現在のインドやパキスタン
一帯は、インダス文明が繁栄した後に、中央アジアからインドヨーロッ
パ語族の大移動にさらされます。アーリア人がアフガニスタンからカ
イバル峠のある山岳地を越え、パンジャブ地方からさらにインドへと
進出したのです。そして現在のインドの人種模様のベースを作っていっ
たのです。

四大文明
Four great civlizations

	エジプト文明 Egyptian civilization	メソポタミア文明 Mesopotamian civilization	インダス文明 Indus civilization	黄河文明 Yellow River civilization
誕生 Started from	紀元前3000年頃 3000 B.C.	紀元前3500年頃 3500 B.C.	紀元前2600年頃 2600 B.C.	紀元前5000年頃 5000 B.C.
流域 Prospered basin of	ナイル川 Nile River	チグリス川 Tigris River ユーフラテス川 Euphrates River	インダス川 Indus River	黄河 Yellow River
特徴 Features	・象形文字 （ヒエログリフ） hieroglyphs ・太陽暦 solar calendar ・ピラミッドの建設 construction of pyramids	・楔形文字 cuneiform ・60進法 sexagesimal system ・太陰太陽暦 lunisolar calendar ・ウル/ウルク Ur/Uruk	・都市文明の繁栄 city-states civilization ・ハラッパ/モヘンジョダロ Harappa/Moenjo-daro	・農耕文明 agrarian civilization ・文字の使用 use of written characters

010 The discord between those who ruled over civilizations and the surrounding ethnic groups colored ancient history

When we observe the vicissitudes of civilizations, it is always necessary to pay attention to the surrounding areas. There were always people outside of these civilizations who were waiting for an opportunity to gain for themselves the benefits enjoyed by those civilizations.

In the case of Mesopotamia, to the west there was another civilization in Egypt. Northeast of this delicate equilibrium were present-day Turkey, Ukraine, Central Asia, and Iran, where ethnic groups already used iron and copper weapons and rode horseback. Representative of these people were the Scythians, who roamed southern Russia. What these people had their eyes on were the Fertile Crescent and the rich, temperate Indus world. Looking far to the east, along the banks of the Yellow River, the ancient Chinese civilization was emerging. From their locations in Central Asia and neighboring regions, such affluent regions were approximately equidistant.

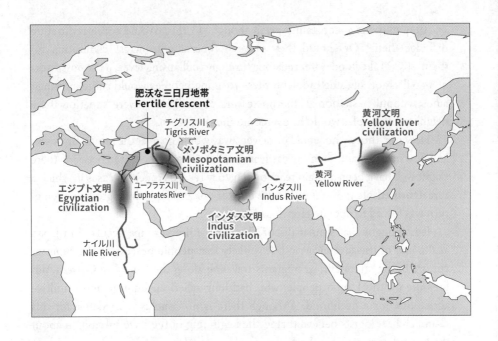

肥沃な三日月地帯
Fertile Crescent

チグリス川
Tigris River

メソポタミア文明
Mesopotamian civilization

黄河文明
Yellow River civilization

黄河
Yellow River

エジプト文明
Egyptian civilization

ユーフラテス川
Euphrates River

インダス川
Indus River

インダス文明
Indus civilization

ナイル川
Nile River

文明を司る人々と、その周辺の民族との確執が古代史を彩った

　文明の変遷を見るときに、その地域の周辺に常に注目する必要があります。そこには、文明の外にいながら、虎視眈々と文明の恩恵にあずかる機会をうかがう人々がいました。

　メソポタミア文明の場合、西にはエジプトというもう一つの文明がありました。この微妙な均衡の北東側、今のトルコからウクライナ、そして中央アジア、イランなどでは、既に鉄器や青銅器を使い、騎馬を操る部族があちこちで活動していました。ロシア南部で活動し、スキタイ文明をつくり上げた人々などはその代表でした。彼らの目に映ったのが、肥沃な三日月地帯やインダスの温暖で豊かな世界でした。ずっと東を展望すれば、黄河の流れに沿って、古代中国の文明も萌芽していたのです。中央アジアとその周辺に展開していた彼らの位置からは、こうした豊かな地域はおおよそ似た距離の彼方にありました。

時代
BC1,500以前
先史/古代

地域
共通

分類
文化【侵略】

キーワード
鉄器を使う騎馬民族・文明の波及・移住と略奪・中国と日本の古代文化

They must have constantly given thought to this. Would some civilization dislodge them? Or should they make it their aim to wrest civilization for themselves? Like flood waters gushing through a collapsing levee, if the possessors of a civilization became indolent, these roaming peoples would surge into their lands without hesitation. If the possessors of civilization were superior, these neighboring peoples would be overcome and driven out.

However, those who would be driven away would go over the mountain passes and flow into the lands of more easily invaded civilized regions. On occasion there might well have been a chain reaction. History records repeated cases in which a threatened ethnic group invaded the territory of another ethnic group, which in turn was forced to migrate elsewhere.

It is thought that similar discord between ethnic groups occurred in Japan at the end of the Jomon period. It is likely that people possessing the superior culture of the continent, or migrants traveling along the Kuroshio Current, put pressure on the Jomon people, who had long relied on hunting and primitive agriculture for a livelihood. Although there is no conclusive evidence for this claim, archaeologists believe that at the beginning of the Yayoi period, in about the second century B.C., the Jomon people were driven north and other people settled the lands that had become available. Subsequently, the Jomon people and the new settlers contended with one another and managed to coexist, and out of this mixing of people came present-day Japanese.

China has a great number of large rivers, and from ancient times agriculture and cattle-breeding were practiced in the basins of the Yellow River and the Yangzi River. It is said that already by 5000 B.C., particularly in the basin of the Yangzi, rice was being cultivated and inhabitants were producing detailed colored earthenware. A culture called Yangshao had formed.

It is also thought that although there was no rice culture in the Yellow River basin, from an even earlier date, various grains were cultivated and city-states began to expand.

The long history of successive dynasties is faithfully recorded in written records. Setting aside the issue of just how historically accurate these records are, the fact that from ancient times some variety of written characters was utilized in recording their names is truly remarkable, when compared with any other civilization.

彼らは常に考えます。文明が我々を駆逐するか。それとも我々が文明を奪い、そこの主になってゆくか。堤防が決壊すれば洪水がおきるように、文明の所有者が怠惰になれば、彼らはすかさずそこになだれ込みます。そして、文明の所有者が優秀であれば、彼らは手なずけられるか、逆に駆逐され追い払われます。

　しかし、追い払われた人々は草原を駈け、峠を越えてより侵入しやすい文明地域へと流れてゆきます。時には、それが玉突き現象を起こすこともあったはずです。圧迫された部族が、他の部族の領域に流入し、そこにいた元々の部族が移動を余儀なくされるといったようなことが歴史上繰り返されたのです。
　日本でもそんな民族同士の確執が縄文時代の末期にあったのではないかといわれています。大陸の優秀な文化を持った人々や、黒潮にのって海を渡ってきたハングリーな移住者が、長年狩猟生活や原始的な耕作に依存していた縄文人を圧迫したこともあったはずです。まだ確証はないにせよ、紀元前2世紀頃の弥生時代のはじめは、縄文人が北に追われ、新たな人々が移住してきた時代ではなかったかと考古学者は考えます。その後、縄文人と新たな移住者とが争いながらも共存し、今の日本人が形成されたのではないかといわれています。

　中国にはいくつもの大河がありますが、黄河と揚子江（長江）はその流域で古くから農耕や牧畜が行われていました。特に長江の流域では紀元前5000年頃には既に稲が栽培されていたといわれ、人々は彩陶と呼ばれる精密な土器を作っていました。仰韶文化（ヤンシャオ文化）と呼ばれる文化圏が形成されていたのです。
　黄河流域では稲作はありませんでしたが、それより以前から雑穀が栽培され、都市国家が次第に膨張を始めていたのではないかといわれています。
　中国の長い王朝史は漢字で克明に記録されています。それがどこまで史実に正確かはさておき、古代から一貫して同種の文字が歴史を記録するために使用されていたことは、他の文明と比較しても際立った特徴であるといえましょう。

When dynasties began to appear in China, the civilizations of the Middle East expanded toward the Mediterranean

According to history books, the Xia, China's first dynasty, was established in Henan sometime around 2000 B.C.

It is unclear whether the Xia dynasty is mythological or not, and at present archaeologists debate the scale of the state. However, ancient ruins have been uncovered that support its existence, and it is a fact that some sort of country did exist there.

As is often the case, the people in China in those days put forth their greatest efforts in flood control works. Yu, held to be the progenitor of Xia, is believed to have become king because of his successful Yellow River riparian improvement. The Yin toppled the Xia dynasty in approximately 1500 B.C., and it is well-known that the capital city Yin Xu, which was built midway through their dynasty, was excavated in the 20th century. The king of Yin, as a god-like figure who unified the feudal lords, is said to have conducted various ceremonies. Some tortoise shells with inscriptions that may have been used in such ceremonies have been unearthed at the Yin Xu site.

There were various city-states and tribal states scattered around China in that era. The Yin flourished in an area along the middle of the Yellow River and are believed to have been the leading power in a group of such states. It was the Zhou, originally subordinate to the Yin, who overthrew the Yin. That is believed to have occurred in the 11th century B.C. The Zhou established their royal palace along the Wei River, a tributary of the Yellow River, at present-day Xi'an. From that base, they established a feudal system in which they reigned over the leaders of various countries north of the river while guaranteeing the territories of their subordinates. Through this feudal organization between the Zhou and the local lords, civilization on the Yellow River was disseminated throughout every part of China.

China came to dominate the eastern portion of Eurasia, while Mesopotamia and Egypt dominated the western portion. In the middle, the Indus civilization advanced through various unique systems of administration. With each of these civilizations as a nucleus, people of differing ethnic groups intermingled in the vast territories, while the four great civilizations themselves expanded. For example, Egyptian and

中国に王朝が生まれた頃、中東の文明は、地中海へと拡大した

史書によれば、中国最初の王朝は「夏」という王朝で、紀元前2000年前後に現在の河南省に建国されたといわれています。

夏王朝が伝説上のものなのかどうかは、そしてどれほどの規模の国家であったかは、目下考古学上の論争となっています。しかし、その存在を裏付けるような遺跡も発見されており、当時なんらかの国家があったことは事実のようです。

ご多分に漏れず、当時の中国の人々が最も力を入れたのが治水事業でした。夏の始祖とされる禹は、黄河の治水事業の成功によって、王になったとされています。そんな夏王朝を紀元前1500年頃に倒したという殷は、王朝中期に造成された首都であった殷墟が20世紀になって発掘されたことで有名です。殷の王は、諸侯を統治する神的な存在として、様々な儀式を司っていたといわれています。その時に使用した亀の甲（亀甲）などに掘られた甲骨文字が、殷墟などから発見されています。

当時、中国にはあちこちに都市国家や部族国家があり、殷は黄河中流域を中心に繁栄し、そうした国家群の盟主的な存在だったのではと考えられています。殷を滅ぼしたのは、元々殷に従属していた周でした。紀元前11世紀のことといわれています。周は黄河の支流である渭水沿い、現在の西安に王城をおきます。そして河北の国々の指導者を諸侯として、彼らの領地を保全しながら、その上に君臨するという封建制度を樹立します。この周と諸侯による封建体制を通し、黄河文明は中国各地へと伝播されてゆくことになったのです。

こうして、ユーラシア大陸の東には中国、西にはメソポタミア、そしてエジプト。中間にはインダス文明がそれぞれ独自の統治機構によって文明を開花させました。それらの文明を大きな核とするならば、核に挟まれた広大な面を様々な民族が行き交い、四大文明はそうした地域へも拡散します。例えば、エジプト文明、メソポタミア文明は地中

時代
BC1,500以前
先史/古代

地域
中国・中東・ヨーロッパ

分類
文化【国家】

キーワード
国家の発生・大規模土木工事・政治の発生・文明の拡散

Mesopotamian civilization expanded northward toward the Mediterranean and penetrated Europe. The palace of Knossos, on the island of Crete in the Aegean Sea, conveys the fact that it was a relay point in the northward advance of that civilization. The Cretan civilization dates from approximately 2000 B.C.

At that time, the European world remained dormant deep in the inland forests. Out of those forests came people who migrated to the shores of the Mediterranean in search of benefits from the civilization that had not spread further north. These people were the Greeks, who built cities and carried on trade in the coastal areas of what is now Greece and Turkey. The Mycenaean civilization, which blossomed around 1600 B.C., is known for its dynastic states dotting the sea coasts, including Troy, which is known for the legend of the Trojan Horse. It is this Troy which Homer tells about in the *Iliad*, his epic poem from the 8th century B.C. Troy's existence was proven in the 19th century by the archaeologist Heinrich Schliemann.

シュリーマンらによるミケーネの調査
Investigation of Mycenae by
Schliemann and others

012 The Caucasoid and the Mongoloid, said to be the roots of modern humankind

Since the 19th century, together with the success of the Industrial Revolution, European culture has swept across the globe. It cannot be denied that Darwin and Gauguin, mentioned at the beginning of this volume, and Schliemann, who excavated Troy, lived during the most thriving period of European society.

On the one hand, the success of the Industrial Revolution gave birth to a negative legacy, that of so-called "white supremacy," relentless racial prejudice, and racial discrimination. Out of this way of thinking came efforts to use anthropology

海を北上し、ヨーロッパに浸透します。エーゲ海に浮かぶクレタ島に残るクノッソス宮殿は、地中海に浮かぶ島々が、そんな文明が北上する中継地点となっていたことを物語っています。この文明をクレタ文明と呼んでいます。紀元前2000年頃のことでした。

　当時、ヨーロッパ世界はまだ深い森の中に眠っていました。その森のなかから、地中海から香る文明を享受しようと、ある民族が沿岸部に移住します。ギリシア人です。彼らは、現在のギリシアからトルコなどの海岸部に都市を築き交易を行います。紀元前1600年頃に開花したミケーネ文明は、あの木馬の伝説で知られるトロイアなどの王朝国家群が点在していたことで知られています。紀元前8世紀頃の詩人ホメロスによる叙事詩『イーリアス』に語られるトロイア。その存在を証明したのが19世紀の考古学者ハインリッヒ・シュリーマンだったのです。

ハインリッヒ・シュリーマン
Heinrich Schliemann (1822–1890)

コーカソイドとモンゴロイドは現代人のルーツといわれた

　19世紀以降、産業革命の成功と共に、ヨーロッパ文明が世界を席巻しました。冒頭で触れたダーウィンやゴーギャン、そしてトロイアを発見したシュリーマンは、西欧社会が最も繁栄していた時代を生きた人に他なりません。

　一方で、産業革命の成功は、いわゆる「白人優越論」をも生み出し、執拗な人種偏見、人種差別という負の遺産も生み出しました。中には「白人優越論」を人類学的にも裏付け証明しようとする動きまであった

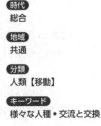

時代
総合

地域
共通

分類
人類【移動】

キーワード
様々な人種・交流と交換

to provide evidence to support the theory that white people were superior. The classic example of this was Nazi Germany's contention regarding the superiority of Aryan northern Europeans. Following World War II, out of soul-searching regarding such prejudice, cautious research approaches have been carried out employing abundant application of genetics to elucidate the races of humankind and their roots. What has drawn special attention as a result of this research has been the study of two races: the Caucasoid, which flowed north from the Middle Eastern regions, and the Mongoloid, which spread eastward to become the Chinese, the Japanese, and the varied peoples of Southeast Asia.

The Caucasoid are called Caucasians in English. The name refers to the Caucasus region wedged between the Black Sea and the Caspian Sea, thought to be the place from which they originated. They came out of Africa through present-day Iran into the Caucasus and into Central Asia. They spread from eastern Turkey in the west to the Western Regions of China, through present-day Iran and Uzbekistan, spreading throughout the entirety of southwest India. This broad dispersal of Caucasian peoples settled there and came to be called Aryans. One group of these people advanced in the direction of the Ganges; another moved southward through the Middle East toward the Mediterranean and subsequently throughout Europe.

Later, the famous Silk Road became a trade route through Central Asia linking China, the Middle East, and Europe. This route was the stage for the activities of diverse groups of Caucasians and Mongoloids. Along the Mediterranean Sea, we see that the civilization that evolved in Egypt and Mesopotamia was carried by these people as they moved into the European world.

This current gave birth to Greek civilization. It was then inherited by the Roman Empire and transmitted to every part of Europe. At the turn of the epoch from B.C. to A.D. waves of Roman civilization flowed over Gaul, present-day France, and the surrounding regions, extending its influence as far as England. The Aryan people absorbed Indus civilization and moved farther south, building city-states in the vicinity of the Ganges, and then in the 6th century B.C., giving birth to the countries of Kosala and Magadha. These successive waves went as far as Southeast Asia. There Chinese culture developed by the Mongoloid people merged with Indus culture transmitted by the Aryans.

That culture first began to reach Japan, farthest to the east, in 400 B.C., the beginning of the Yayoi period.

のです。その典型的な事例が、ナチスドイツのアーリア系北ヨーロッパ人種への優越論でした。戦後、そうした偏見への反省から、世界の人種とそのルーツの解明には遺伝子学などを駆使した慎重なアプローチが繰り返されました。そんな研究の中で特に注目されたのが、中東地域から北上したコーカソイドと、東進し中国人や日本人となり、さらに東南アジアなどへと拡散したモンゴロイドという二つの人種系列への研究でした。

　コーカソイドは英語ではCaucasianといいます。これはコーカサスという黒海とカスピ海とに挟まれた地域を源流とする白色系人種をさす言葉です。彼らはアフリカから現在のイランを経由してコーカサスへ、そして中央アジアへと拡散してゆきました。西はトルコの東部から東は中国の西域まで、現在のイランやウズベキスタンなどを経て、南西インド一円を占める広大な地域にコーカソイドの流れを組む人々がアーリア人として定住したのです。その一部はガンディース川方面へと進出します。また、別の人々は南下して中東から地中海へ、その後ヨーロッパ各地へと移動します。

　後年、中央アジアは中国と中東、ヨーロッパとの交易ルートとして有名なシルクロードの舞台となります。それは、この地域で活動するコーカソイド系、モンゴロイド系の様々な部族の活動とも無縁ではありません。一方、地中海を見れば、エジプトやメソポタミアで発生した文明が、これらの人々に担われて、さらにヨーロッパ世界へと浸透していったことがわかります。
　その流れがギリシア文明を生み出し、それを引き継いだローマ帝国によって文明はヨーロッパ全域に広がります。ローマ文明の波がガリアと呼ばれた現在のフランスとその周辺を経て、イギリスにまで影響を与えたのは、紀元前後のことでした。そして、インダス文明を消化し、更に南下したアーリア人がインドのガンディース川周辺に都市国家を築いた後、コーサラやマガダという国家の誕生をみたのが、前6世紀頃のことでした。その波は東南アジアまで及び、そこで、モンゴロイドのもたらした中国の文化と、アーリア系の人々が伝えてきたインドの文化とが融合したのでした。
　東の端の島国日本にそうした文明が届き始めたのが、紀元前400年頃でした。弥生時代の始まりです。

013

The Babylonian Captivity became the emotional support for the founding of the nation of Israel

Let us direct our attention once again to subsequent events in Mesopotamia.

Among the people who were active in the region between the Middle East and Egypt were the Hebrews, also known as the Jews.

These people held a single deity named Yahweh to be a transcendent, almighty power. According to the Old Testament of the Bible, which tells the story of the Hebrew people, they migrated for a while to Egypt, where they were eventually put to work as slaves. The Hebrews suffered under the oppressive, tyrannical rule of the New Kingdom of Egypt. The story of the Book of Exodus tells how the Hebrews escaped from Egypt, led by the prophet Moses, an event that legend says occurred in the 13th century B.C. Discord between the polytheistic Egyptians and monotheistic Hebrews may have given birth to this mythology.

The nomadic Hebrew people established a kingdom in Palestine around the 11th century B.C. During the reign of King Solomon, this Hebrew kingdom flourished. This occurred in approximately 1000 B.C., the same period in which the Zhou dynasty was established in China.

The Hebrew kingdom broke into two parts following the reign of King Solomon. One region, the Kingdom of Israel, was destroyed by Assyria, which was expanding its territory from the north. The name Israel is another name for Jacob, grandson of Abraham in the Old Testament. Assyria, in the northern part of present-day Iraq, established its capital at Nineveh and rapidly expanded so that by the 7th century B.C. it controlled all of Mesopotamia.

However, shortly thereafter a struggle for power broke out in Assyria and in the end, the country collapsed. A kingdom known as New Babylonia evolved and conquered the Kingdom of Judah, the other kingdom that the Hebrews had built. The inhabitants of Judah were then detained in Babylon for fifty years beginning in 586 B.C. This event, called the Babylonian Captivity, had a great long-term impact on the religious views of the Jewish people.

At the beginning of the 20th century, Zionism seeking the establishment of an Israeli nation, in a place they considered sacred, considered the Babylonian Captivity to be a highly symbolic event.

バビロンの捕囚は現代のイスラエル建国の
精神的支柱になった

　さて、再びメソポタミア文明のその後に目を向けてみます。

　中東からエジプトにかけて、古代から活動していた人々の中に、ヘブライ人（ユダヤ人）がいました。

　彼らは全てを超越する偉大なパワーであるヤハウェ神を唯一の神として崇める人々です。ヘブライ人の来歴を示す書として知られる旧約聖書によれば、彼らは一時エジプトに移動し、そこで奴隷として使役されていたといわれています。その後エジプト新王国の圧政に苦しんでいたヘブライ人が、預言者であるモーゼに率いられてエジプトを脱出した「出エジプト」の物語は、紀元前13世紀あたりに起きたことを元に描かれた神話であるとされています。元々多神教の王国であったエジプトと、一神教であるユダヤ教を信奉するヘブライ人との確執が、こうした神話を生み出したのかもしれません。

　遊牧の民であったヘブライ人は、紀元前11世紀頃に今のパレスチナにヘブライ王国を建国しました。ソロモン王の時代にヘブライ王国は繁栄します。それは紀元前1000年頃のこと、中国では周の時代になります。

　ユダヤ人のおこしたヘブライ王国は、ソロモン王の統治の後に分裂しますが、その一つであったイスラエル王国を滅ぼしたのが、北から版図を拡げてきたアッシリアだったのです。イスラエルとは、旧約聖書にあるアブラハムの孫、ヤコブの別名です。アッシリアは今のイラク北部にあったニネベに首都をおいた国家で、その後急速に拡大し、紀元前7世紀にはメソポタミア一帯を支配したのです。

　しかし、アッシリアは間もなく権力闘争がおきたのか、内部崩壊の末に滅亡します。その時にできた新バビロニアという王国が、ヘブライ人の造ったもう一つの国ユダ王国を席巻し、そこにいた人々を前586年から50年にわたってバビロニアに拘束したのです。バビロンの捕囚というこの事件は、その後のユダヤ人の宗教観に大きな影響を与えました。

　20世紀におきたシオニズムというイスラエル建国の動きの原点に、自らの聖地での建国を求める動きがあり、バビロンの捕囚は、その象徴的事件として、その後人々の間で語られてきたのです。

時代
BC6世紀以前
古代

地域
パレスチナ・ペルシア
（イラン）

分類
宗教【国家】

キーワード
ユダヤ人の世界・ユダヤ教の発生・ペルシア帝国の成立

After the conquest of Judah, a new power arose in the Middle East. The Persians came onto the scene. Under the rule of the emperor Darius I, the Achaemenid dynasty, which had been expanding its territory since 550 B.C., unified the area between present-day Iran and Mesopotamia. During that period, there were also major activities in the Mediterranean region. The civilizations that had matured in Egypt and Mesopotamia began to develop further on a small peninsula in southeast Europe, the Peloponnesian Peninsula in present-day Greece. By 800 B.C. a group of city-states called poleis began to gain strength.

014 "God" gives humankind the eternal task of achieving peaceful coexistence

The people of ancient times gave birth to all sorts of myths, including those found in the Old Testament, Japan's *Kojiki* (Record of Ancient Matters), and Greek mythology. Fear of natural phenomena gave birth to religion, and people began to believe in and worship deities. Especially in the activities of cultivating land and hunting, prayer became a necessary act in supporting their livelihood by means of partaking of the blessings of nature. In those days, many of the deities took after human beings. They had the same kinds of emotions, and many ancient religions were polytheistic, revering multiple deities.

The Japanese language has the expression "all the gods of heaven and earth," which refers to "the myriads of gods and deities." This way of thinking is close to animistic notions that everything in nature has a spirit. The sun must have been an especially impressive figure, and in Japan, Amaterasu, the Sun Goddess, became especially revered. In ancient times it was also believed that there were people such as shrine maidens and spiritualistic mediums who could communicate with various powers that floated around in the realm of the gods and transmit their will to people on earth. In some countries, the king served in that intermediary role.

With such intermediaries as central figures, religious ceremonies and observances were cultivated to ask for the blessings of an abundant harvest or rainfall, dancing and music were brought into being as expressions of devotion, and various customary practices evolved around human life and death. It is believed that religions such as Confucianism, which greatly influenced Chinese culture, originated as forms of etiquette and ceremonial rituals.

その後中東に新たな勢力が現れます。ペルシア人の登場です。ダレイオス1世という帝王の元、紀元前550年以来版図を拡大したアケメネス朝ペルシアという国家が、現在のイランからメソポタミア一帯を統一します。この時期、地中海世界でも大きな動きがありました。エジプトやメソポタミアで円熟した文明が、ヨーロッパ南東の小さな半島で、さらに進化しようとしていたのです。現在のギリシアがあるペロポネソス半島でのことでした。そこには紀元前800年頃までにポリスと呼ばれる都市国家群が台頭していたのです。

「神」は平和共存という人類永遠の課題を与える

旧約聖書や日本の古事記、あるいはギリシア神話などのように、古代の人々は様々な神話を生み出しました。自然現象への畏れが宗教を生み出し、人々は「神」の存在を思い敬います。特に農耕や狩猟活動において、祈りは自然の恵みを得て生活を維持してゆくために必要な行為だったのです。当時、多くの神は人間を模したものでした。ですから神々には我々と同様の喜怒哀楽がありました。そして、古代の宗教の多くは、複数の神を敬う多神教だったのです。

日本には八百万の神という言葉があります。それは、森羅万象全てに霊魂があるというアニミズム的な発想に近い考え方です。特に太陽は大きな存在であったはずです。日本では天照大神が太陽神として崇められました。古代には、神々の世界に漂う力と、人とを繋ぐ霊能力のある巫女のような人もいましたが、国によっては王がそうした媒介者の役割を担いました。

そうした媒介者を中心に、豊作や降雨を願う宗教上の儀式や儀礼が育まれ、舞踊や音楽を生み出し、人間の生と死に関する様々なしきたりの創造にも繋がりました。中国文化に大きな影響を与えた儒教なども、元々はそうした儀式を司る様式やしきたりから進化したものだといわれています。

時代
総合

地域
共通

分類
宗教【対立】

キーワード
宗教の成り立ち・多神教と一神教・宗教をめぐる対立

In contrast with polytheistic religions, monotheism takes the position that there is one and only one deity. The most well known of this type is Judaism, which is the religious root of the other traditions that developed in that region: Christianity and Islam.

It is a matter of course that in many religions the deities are heavenly beings who present moral precepts and demand absolute obedience to those precepts. If these become societal norms, then breaking precepts established by the deity cultivates within humankind a consciousness of sinfulness. Throughout history, countries and authority figures have intervened as agents of absolute deities and adapted religious authority to political goals.

Humankind has experienced repeated religious upheavals. In the present day, for example, Pakistan, which follows the Muslim faith, and India, where many people are followers of the polytheistic Hindu faith, are bitterly opposed to one another, not only in religious terms but also in political terms.

Human history is no less than an accumulation of activities carried out in order to find a way for believers of different faiths to live together in peace. Whether it is the coexistence of polytheistic and monotheistic faiths or the prolonged conflicts between Christianity and Islam that persist to this day, monotheistic religions have fiercely sought to eliminate one another throughout history. As the world knows, the result of the confrontation has been the spilling of much blood through gruesome warfare and persecution.

As religions grew in size and became more strongly rooted in society, they became more organized and systematized. To maintain that system, religion has sometimes allied itself with secular authority. The combination, together with confrontation between religious and secular authority, has caused numerous wars. Only recently, out of a degree of soul-searching regarding such tragedies, have countries established legal systems that guarantee freedom of religion and the coexistence of diverse religions and cultures. Even with this, however, human beings lacking broad-mindedness and acceptance of other faiths still wage war against one another.

一方、多神教に対して、神は唯一であるという立場をとるのが一神教です。その代表がすでに紹介したユダヤ教です。ユダヤ教は、その後そこから発展するキリスト教や、イスラム教などのルーツともなる宗教です。

　当然のことですが多くの宗教では、神は絶対の戒律を要求する天上の存在として個人に様々な道徳律を提示します。それが、社会規範にもなれば、神の定めた戒律を破ることへの罪の意識をも人々の間に育みます。長い歴史の中では、国家や時の権力者が、その絶対神の代理人として介在し、宗教的権威を政治利用したこともありました。

　そして人類は、宗教をめぐって何度も騒乱を経験しています。例えば現在でもイスラム教を信奉するパキスタンと、多神教のヒンドゥー教徒の多いインドとは、宗教的のみならず政治的にも鋭く対立しています。

　人類の歴史は、宗教の異なる者といかに共存するかというテーマを模索する行為の集積に他なりませんでした。多神教と一神教のみならず、現在も続くキリスト教とイスラム教との長年の対立のように、一神教同士も歴史を通して激しく相手を排除してきました。その結果、長い歴史の中で凄惨な戦争や迫害で多くの血が流されてきたことはご存知の通りです。

　宗教はその規模が大きくなり、社会に強く根ざしてゆく過程で、組織化され、制度化されてゆきます。その制度を維持するために、宗教が世俗の権力と提携したこともありました。宗教的権威と世俗の権威との融合や対立が、人類の歴史を通して多くの戦争の原因となりました。そんな悲劇への反省から、国家が信教の自由や、多様な宗教や文化との共存を保障する法制度を整備するようになったのは、ごく最近のことなのです。しかし、それでもなお人類は、他の宗教を受け入れる寛容さを持てずに、世界各地で紛争を起こしているのです。

015 The milestone in the formation of unified states was a common process throughout ancient history

The period of 1,200 years between the First Babylonian dynasty and the Achaemenid dynasty was approximately the same length of time that passed between the Heian periods in Japan and the present day. Ancient history deals not only with long periods of time but with large numbers of facts that remain unclear.

When one looks closely, throughout this period, human beings have gained enormous advantages. Tools and weapons have progressed from copper implements to those made of iron; hence productivity in agriculture and other fields have improved—together with greater destructive power in warfare. Countries have also evolved from primitive states to advanced states with complex administrative functions and intricate organizational structures. During the Achaemenid dynasty in Persia, in order to maintain the control functions of the monarch, a secret police force was organized in order to serve as the eyes and ears of the sovereign, and a system of local governments was worked out to carry out directives from the central authorities efficiently in remote areas. Through these means, the country was able to smoothly expand and maintain its territories.

In China, the feudal system under the leadership of the Zhou began to fall apart, and from 770 B.C. regional states began to struggle for power, in what is known as the Spring and Autumn and Warring States periods. From that period onward, while showing respect to the Zhou as the leading power, these states competed among themselves. From 403 B.C. onward they fought with one another in a series of merciless wars in an attempt to form an even stronger state. Close to 550 years of civil war continued until 221 B.C., when the country was unified.

Viewed from a different perspective, China's Spring and Autumn and Warring States periods can be interpreted as the time when small states becoming independent gave way to a large unified country that maintained sophisticated control functions and organizations. This bears a resemblance to the process through which Mesopotamian city-states were created by the Sumerians, ultimately unified under Assyria, and then evolved into the Achaemenid dynasty.

In the process of the formation of a unified state, through fierce and repeated conflicts and also natural interchange between the regions, conspicuous progress was made in culture and civilization. In the case of the Fertile Crescent, the

統一国家組成へのマイルストーンは
古代史に共通したプロセスだった

　バビロン第一王朝からアケメネス朝ペルシアに至る1200年という年月は、平安時代初期から現代に至る時間と同じ長期間にわたるものです。古代史は、解明されていない事実が多い分だけ、長い年月をまとめて扱います。

　よく見ると、この年月を通し、人類は多くのものを手に入れています。青銅器から鉄器へと道具や武器が進化し、農耕などでの生産力も戦争による破壊力も強靭になります。国家も原始的な国家からより統治機能を充実させ、複雑な組織運営を可能にした国家が出現します。アケメネス朝ペルシアでは帝王の統治機能を維持するための「王の目」「王の耳」といった秘密警察まで組織され、遠隔地を効率的に統治するために中央の指令で動く地方行政の制度も整えました。こうしたことで、国家はその版図を拡大し、維持しやすくなったのです。

時代
BC3世紀以前
古代

地域
共通

分類
国家【政治】

キーワード
生産の増大・国家の発生・中国の戦国時代・ギリシアの都市国家・統一国家への道

　中国では、周を盟主とした封建制度がほころび、紀元前770年以降、地方の国家がそれぞれ覇権を争い戦う春秋戦国時代に突入します。周を盟主として敬いながら覇権を争っていた春秋時代から、紀元前403年以降の国家同士がより強大な国家形成を目指し「仁義なき戦い」を繰り広げた戦国時代へと、紀元前221年に中国が統一されるまでの550年近くに及ぶ動乱の時代が訪れます。

　中国の春秋戦国時代は、別の見方をするならば、小国が分立していた太古から、より洗練された統治機能と制度を維持できる統一国家へと、中国全体が移行していった時代といえます。それは、ちょうどメソポタミアでシュメール人による都市国家が興り、最終的にアッシリアを経てアケメネス朝ペルシアが統一王朝を築き上げた過程と類似しています。

　統一国家形成への過程では、地域同士が激しく競いながらも交流を重ね、文化や文明も著しく進化してゆきました。肥沃な三日月地帯の場合、そこで円熟した様々な文化現象がギリシアに伝播し、さらにギ

various mature cultural phenomena spread to Greece, fostering the Greek city-states. For example, from approximately the 12th century B.C., the Phoenicians, who became quite active in trade in the Mediterranean, established their own city-states throughout the region. Carthage, which was located on the outskirts of what is now Tunis, the capital of Tunisia, maintained hegemony over the central Mediterranean as a city-state supported by a powerful naval force.

It was the Roman Empire that unified this group of city-states within the larger framework of the Mediterranean world. The process began with the Cretan civilization and the Mycenaean civilization, which sprang from the early Greek city-states, continuing through Greek civilization to the Roman Empire. This was the exact same process that occurred in China, starting with the Spring and Autumn and Warring States periods, through the Qin and the Han unifications. The common element in each of these two processes was the existence of a written language. The spread of Chinese character culture and the diffusion of the European-related languages, Greek, and Latin, formed the foundation for the unification of monarchial governments.

016   The Persian Wars were glorified by Herodotus

The city-states of the Mycenaean civilization on the Mediterranean coast of Greece and Turkey that flourished at Troy and other places later declined. Although there is no conclusive evidence to prove it, the 400-year period beginning in 1200 B.C. is held to have been a dark age in which the whole of Greece was in a state of turmoil, resulting from invasions and plundering by various ethnic groups.

Following this, in about the 8th century B.C., Greek-related people speaking different dialects called Ionians, Aeolians, and Dorians began to form city-states (poleis) in the region. Among these city-states was Athens, established by the Ionians. It chief rival was Sparta, founded by the Dorians. The Aeolians advanced into the coastal areas of present-day Turkey. Contemporary Greeks already possessed iron implements and traded widely throughout the Mediterranean. It is even thought that cities such as present-day Marseilles, France, and Naples, Italy, may have begun as Greek city-states.

リシアなどの都市国家を育ててゆきます。例えば、紀元前12世紀頃から地中海での交易を通して活発に活動していたフェニキア人なども、各地に都市国家を形成しました。現在のチュニジアの首都チュニス近郊にあったカルタゴなどは、強力な海軍力に支えられた都市国家として、地中海中部での覇権を維持していたのです。

そんな国家群を、地中海世界という大きな枠組みで統一したのが古代ローマ帝国でした。クレタ文明や、ギリシアの初期の都市国家が育んだミケーネ文明に始まり、ギリシア文明を経てローマ帝国に至る過程は、まさに中国での春秋戦国時代を経て秦、そして漢という統一王朝が組成される過程と同じなのです。そしてその両方の過程に共通しているのが文字の存在です。漢字文化とギリシア語やラテン語といったヨーロッパ系の言語の拡散が、こうした統一王朝の組成の基礎を造っていったのです。

ペルシア戦争はヘロドトスによって美化された

ギリシアやトルコの地中海沿岸の都市国家は、トロイアなどが栄えたミケーネ文明のあと衰退を続けます。暗黒の時代と呼ばれる紀元前1200年からの400年間、ギリシア一帯は様々な民族が入り乱れた混乱状態にあったのではといわれていますが、定かな記録が残されていません。

その後、紀元前8世紀頃に、イオニア人、アイオリス人、そしてドーリア人と呼ばれる異なった方言を話すギリシア系の人々で構成される都市国家（ポリス）が、この地域に形成されます。その内、イオニア人が造った都市国家として知られるのがアテナイです。そのライバルでもあったスパルタはドーリア人の造ったポリスです。アイオリス人は現在のトルコ沿岸に進出していました。当時ギリシア人は既に鉄器を使用し、広く地中海で交易を行っていました。現在のフランスのマルセイユや、イタリアのナポリなども、その起源はギリシアのポリスであったといわれています。

時代
BC5世紀以前
古代

地域
ギリシア・ペルシア（イラン）

分類
戦争【政治】

キーワード
ギリシア人の成り立ち・都市国家の成立・ペルシア戦争とアテナイの覇権

Recall for a moment the history of Japan. Long ago, Japan was divided into various domains, each speaking its own dialect, and fighting with one another from time to time. Abroad, however, they were all considered to be Japanese. The Greeks were like that. The various poleis constantly competed for dominance, yet they possessed a strong self-awareness of being Greeks. They held Ancient Olympic Games once every four years. They shared the same gods in their legends. There was interchange between their people and on occasion they joined together in alliances.

The ties that united them were particularly strengthened by the invasion of the Achaemenid dynasty. Persia invaded Greece on three occasions during the fifty-year period commencing in 499 B.C. The opposing Greek city-states united in a military alliance known as the Delian League in order to repel the invaders. The Greek alliance achieved victory at the Battle of Marathon in 490 B.C. and the Battle of Salamis ten years later, giving Athens leadership of the confederated states.

What exactly was the Persian War? It was recorded by the historian Herodotus from the side of the victors. In modern times, as European civilization swept across the world, ancient Greece became idealized as its point of origin. Consequently, the Persian War came to be colored with the image of Greece resolutely confronting the powerful, autocratic Persian Empire. In actual fact, the fighting could be understood more accurately as a conflict over trade routes and commercial rights on the Mediterranean. Furthermore, not every city-state joined in the Greek alliance and some Greeks sided with the Persians. Persia was at that time a civilized country and the confederation of the various Greek poleis was in a joint struggle for domination over the Mediterranean Sea.

In later times, the Christian society of Europe came into strained relationships and even confrontations with the Ottoman Empire and then with the Middle East—the so-called Orient—and Turkey as well, areas in which Islam had gained religious ascendance. This is all the more reason why the victory by the European world in the Persian War was glorified as a symbolic event in ancient history.

日本の歴史を思い出してください。昔、日本も色々な国に分かれ、異なった方言を話し、時には国同士で戦うこともありましたが、海外には日本人として対応していました。ギリシア人も同様でした。ポリス同士は覇権を争い頻繁に戦争をします。しかし、ギリシア人としての自覚は強く、4年に一度の古代オリンピックや、ギリシア神話の世界にみられる共通の神々の存在によって、人々は交流し、時には同盟関係をも結んでいました。

　彼らの絆を特に強めたのがアケメネス朝ペルシアの侵入でした。ペルシアは紀元前499年から50年間にわたり3度遠征してきました。対するギリシアは、ポリス間でデロス同盟という軍事同盟を結び、これを撃退したのです。この戦争は、紀元前490年のマラトンの戦いや、その10年後のサラミスの海戦など、ギリシア側の勝利を通して、その盟主であるアテナイが台頭する原因にもなりました。

　ではペルシア戦争は、実際はどのような戦争だったのでしょう。ペルシア戦争は、勝者であるギリシア側の歴史家ヘロドトスによって描かれます。近代、ヨーロッパ文明が世界を席巻すると、その源流とされる古代ギリシアが美化されます。従って、強大な専制君主の帝国ペルシアに果敢に挑んだ自由なギリシアというイメージがペルシア戦争にはついてまわりますが、実際は地中海の商圏や交易権などの利害を巡った争いであったと思われます。さらに、ギリシアのポリス全てが一つにまとまっていたわけではなく、ペルシア側についた人々もいたようです。ペルシアは当時の文明国で、ギリシアのポリス集団は、それに対して自らの地中海での覇権を守ろうとして共闘したのでしょう。

　後年、キリスト教社会であるヨーロッパは、オスマン帝国など、いわゆるオリエントと呼ばれる中東やトルコに拡大したイスラム教勢力との対立と緊張関係に見舞われます。それだけに、ペルシア戦争はヨーロッパ世界が勝利した古代史の象徴的な事件として美化されてきたのです。

017 Greek culture established the Hellenistic world

Greek culture calls to mind the democratic form of government in Athens. However, Athens was originally a monarchy, supported by an aristocracy. The city-state was defended by soldiers called hoplites, armed with iron weapons. These troops were composed of plebians, or common people, and as a result, these common people who were actually protecting Athens sought reforms of the privileges held by the aristocrats. Hence, when Pericles became leader following the Persian War, the government of Athens was transformed into a direct democratic system governed by a gathering of young men. In those days, there was a system of Ostracism, under which an overly powerful citizen could be banished by popular vote by writing their names on a shell or potsherd in an election vote. Nevertheless, it is inaccurate to say that human rights in Athens were fully safeguarded. Democratic government in Athens was also founded upon a system of slavery, and women did not have the right to vote.

The Athenians built the Parthenon temple on the Acropolis knoll in the center of the city and below that, in a public square called the Agora, citizens gathered to carry out the business of the city government.

Sparta, which is commonly invoked as a contrast with Athens as a polis, maintained a monarchial system. It is also known as a state possessing a powerful military force. It was Sparta that defeated Athens in the Peloponnesian War for supremacy in 404 B.C. after the end of the Persian War. Following that victory, however, Sparta continued fighting with other city-states, to the point that eventually Greece as a whole fell into decline. It is said that the politics of Athens also fell under the sway of demagogues, and that led to complications with other city-states. At that point, professional political "consultants" began to appear in Athens. These teachers came to be called Sophists. Before long, as Greece fell into disorder, Macedonia in the north attempted to absorb Greece as a whole. One of the Greek city-states, Macedonia, under Philippos II, ousted Athens and Thebes, became the leader of a confederacy of powers called the League of Corinth and gained influence over every part of Greece except Sparta in 337 B.C.

This action, which was nothing less than the organization of a confederation of city-states into a single, strong unified state appeared threatening to neighboring

ギリシア文化はヘレニズム世界を築いていった

　ギリシア文明といえば、誰もがアテナイでの民主政治を思い起こします。しかし、アテナイも元々は貴族に支えられた王国でした。アテナイの防衛にあたっていたのは、重装歩兵と呼ばれる鉄器で武装した人々でした。重装歩兵は平民によって構成されていました。その結果、貴族の特権に対して、実際に国を守っていた平民が改革を求めてゆきます。最終的にペルシア戦争の勝利の後に指導者となったペリクレスの時代に、アテナイでは成年男子が集まって国家の運営を決める直接民主政治へと移行したのです。当時、独裁者になるおそれのある者を陶片に書いて投票し、追放する陶片追放の制度もありました。とはいえ、アテナイで人権がしっかり保護されていたかというとそうではありません。アテナイの民主政治は奴隷制度の上に成り立ち、女性に参政権はなかったのです。

　アテナイでは、中心にあるアクロポリスの丘にパルテノン神殿を建設し、その下のアゴラと呼ばれる広場に人々が集まり、集会などをひらき都市国家を運営していたのです。

　一方アテナイと対照的なポリスとして引き合いに出されるスパルタは、王政を維持していました。そして強力な軍事国家として知られていました。ペルシア戦争のあと、ペロポネソス戦争と呼ばれるアテナイとの覇権を巡る戦いに紀元前404年に勝利したのはスパルタです。しかしその後、スパルタと他のポリスとの対立などからポリス同士の戦争が続き、次第にギリシア全体が衰退していったのです。アテナイもデマゴークと呼ばれる煽動家によって政治が壟断され、その事が周辺のポリスとの関係をさらに複雑にしたともいわれています。そんなアテナイにおいて、職業的な政治コンサルタントも現れます。ソフィストと呼ばれる人たちでした。やがて混乱するギリシアに対し、北から台頭したマケドニアが、ギリシア全体を飲み込もうとします。ギリシアの都市国家の一つであったマケドニアは、フィリッポス2世の時にアテナイとテーバイを駆逐し、紀元前337年にはコリントス同盟の盟主として、スパルタ以外のギリシア全域を勢力下においたのです。

　この動きは、一つの地域が都市国家群から強大な統一国家に再編されてゆく過程に他なりませんが、隣国ペルシアから見ればこれは脅威

時代
BC5, 4世紀 古代

地域
ギリシア

分類
政治【統一】

キーワード
アテナイの民主政治・アテナイの発展と衰退・マケドニアによる統一・アレクサンドロスの東征

パルテノン神殿
The Parthenon in Athens

Persia. That threat became a reality in the form of a military expedition to the east by Philippo II's son, Alexander the Great. In 333 B.C. Alexander defeated Persian forces under Darius III at the Battle of Issos. Three years later Persia was conquered. As a result of taking over the extensive territories of Persia, Greek culture came into contact with the civilization of South Asia centered in India.

Due to the fact that Alexander the Great also incorporated Egypt in his empire, the Fertile Crescent, Greece, and Central Asia became merged into a single global cultural area. That culture became known as Hellenism.

With Hellenism as its main source, global interchange expanded through India and China into the Korean Peninsula. By the 7th century, it reached Japan, lending color to the Asuka period, during which Horyuji was constructed, and the 8th-century Nara period.

018   India also developed from city-states

Alexander the Great was certainly a genius when it came to military strategy. Like a small animal that knows the weak points of an enormous dinosaur, going for the weak points in the Persian army, which was composed of large numbers of non-uniformed tribal fighters and mercenary troops, he overthrew the enemy's organization from within. In a short period of time, Alexander the Great, having conquered Egypt and Persia, further expanded his domain until it came into contact with the Indian world.

Let us turn to ancient India. As a result of the great migration of Aryan peoples in 1500 B.C., these incoming people mixed with the original inhabitants, city-states came into existence, and a caste system unique to India came into being.

The system of four castes held at the top the Brahmans, who carried out complex festival rituals. The second caste was the Kshatriya, the military caste. Third was the Vaishya, comprised of merchants and farmers. The lowest caste was the servile Shudra. This four-caste system became a permanent, widespread characteristic of Indian society, and although it has now been abolished, it still remains influential.

です。この脅威が現実のものとなったのが、フィリッポス2世の息子、アレクサンドロス大王の東征だったのです。大王は前333年にイッソスの戦いでダレイオス3世の率いるペルシア軍を破り、3年後に最終的にペルシアを滅ぼします。ペルシアの広大な版図を手中にしたアレクサンドロス大王ですが、これによって、ギリシア文明がインドを中心とした南アジアの文明と接点を持つようになったのです。

アレクサンドロス大王は、エジプトをも自らの帝国に組み込んでいたために、「肥沃な三日月地帯」とギリシア、そして中央アジアというグローバルな文化圏が融合したことになります。それがヘレニズム文化です。

このヘレニズム文化を源流とした世界の交流が、その後インドから中国、そして朝鮮半島を経て、7世紀に日本にも伝わり、法隆寺などが建立された飛鳥時代、さらには8世紀の奈良時代を彩るのです。

インドも都市国家から発展した

アレクサンドロス大王は軍事戦略の天才だったのでしょう。図体の大きい恐竜の短所をよく知っていた小動物のように、非征服民族の兵士や、傭兵の多いペルシアの弱点をつき、敵の組織を内部からも崩壊させてゆきました。短期間に、エジプトとペルシアを手中に収めたアレクサンドロス大王は、さらにインド世界との接点まで版図を広げます。

ここで古代インドに目を向けてみます。紀元前1500年頃にアーリア民族の大移動によって、先住民と混合した都市国家が生まれると、そこにインド独特の身分制度ができあがります。

それが複雑な祭礼を司る神官バラモンを頂点とし、軍人であるクシャトリア、交易や農耕をするヴァイシャ、そして隷属民であるシュードラという4つの身分に分けて人々を統治するカースト制度です。カースト制度はその後インド社会に深く浸透し、制度が廃止された現在も社会に影響を与えています。

時代
BC2世紀以前
古代

地域
インド

分類
文化【宗教】

キーワード
カーストの成立・小規模国家群の成立・仏教の発生・統一王朝の形成・バラモン教の成立

Within these city-states, in about the 6th century B.C., in eastern India, there came into existence a confederation of states including Magadha. The story of this period is the same as that of the myths of the Yamato period in Japan. The story tells of an imperial prince in Kosala, one of the states in what is present-day southern Nepal. The prince's name is Gautama Siddhartha, or Buddha. Gautama Siddhartha overcame suffering, aging, illness, and death, and traveled around preaching how one could achieve enlightenment, also called nirvana, cultivating the teachings that we refer to as Buddhism.

In this way, at the time when city-states were flourishing in Greece, new city-states were springing up in the chaos of the migration of ethnic groups in southern Asia, and both religious systems and social systems were becoming established.

Appearing in India from the west was Alexander the Great. But he suddenly died in 323 B.C. at the young age of 33 years.

After the army of Alexander withdrew, a hero was born in India. In the late 4th century B.C., Chandragupta founded the Maurya Empire, the first dynasty in India.

Under Ashoka, the third ruler of the Maurya Empire, the empire reached its peak. He is known as an ardent guardian of Buddhism and under his influence Buddhism spread throughout India. In addition to Buddhism, at about the same time, another religion known as Jainism appeared preaching the importance of freeing oneself from the cycles of life. These various religious movements spread throughout Asia and are one reason why even today there is a great diversity in the beliefs of the region.

The mythologies which have been passed down from ancient India have been collected in the Vedas and inherited by Brahmanism. The latter is the religious source of Hinduism, which is considered to be the established religion of India.

こうした都市国家の中から、紀元前6世紀頃にはインド東部に興ったマガダ国などの国家群が成立します。当時の物語はちょうど日本にとっての大和時代初期のように神話の中で語られます。そんな国家の一つで、現在のネパール南部にあったとされるコーサラ国の皇子だったと伝えられているのが、ゴータマ・シッダールタ、すなわちブッダです。ブッダは紀元前6世紀頃に、生きる苦しみや老病死への畏れを克服し、涅槃の境地に至ろうと人々に説いてまわり、仏教を開きました。

　このように、ギリシアで都市国家が繁栄した頃、南アジアでも民族の移動による混乱の中から新たな都市国家が生まれ、宗教や社会制度が整えられていったのです。
　そんなインドに西方から現れたのが、アレクサンドロス大王だったのです。大王は不幸にして33歳の若さで紀元前323年に急逝します。
　大王の軍隊が撤退したあと、インドでは一人の英雄が現れます。紀元前4世紀終盤に登場しインド世界初の統一王朝を造ったマウリヤ王朝のチャンドラグプタ大帝です。
　マウリヤ王朝は3代目のアショーカ王の頃に最盛期を迎えます。王は仏教を熱心に保護した人物としても知られており、その影響もあって、仏教はインド世界に広がっていったのです。仏教の他に、輪廻からの脱却を説くジャイナ教などが生まれたのも当時のことです。これら様々な宗教活動は、インドからアジア各地に広がり、今なおそれらの地域の多様性の一因となっているのです。

　一方、古代インドに受け継がれてきた神話の世界は、ヴェーダという聖典群にまとめられ、バラモン教として人々に受け継がれてゆきます。バラモン教は現代インドの国教ともいわれているヒンドゥー教の源流となる宗教です。

019 From Bactria, Greek civilization streamed into India

As one civilization advances and then retreats, it leaves behind certain elements that are blended into the recipient civilization, transforming it into a new civilization. Within that repeated metamorphosis, a cosmopolitan civilization is created. Waves of Greek civilization flowed eastward from Iran into India and westward to Rome, the supreme political power in the Mediterranean world. All the more so because Rome was so close to Greece, regardless of the fact that Rome subjugated the Mediterranean regions, Greek civilization so deeply influenced Rome that it might well be claimed that in cultural terms Rome was conquered by Greece.

To the east, it was Bactria in Central Asia that was influenced by the expanding civilization of Greece.

Hellenism was not perfected in the lifetime of Alexander the Great. Following his death, bitter conflicts commenced over who was to succeed to his territories. As a result, the Seleucid Empire flourished in a broad area between present-day northern Mesopotamia and Pakistan. This occurred in 312 B.C. The founder, Seleucus, was one of Alexander's generals. Seven years later Ptolemy, another of Alexander's generals, established the Ptolemaic dynasty in Egypt.

Thus, a state with the Greeks at its head was founded in the region of the great king's expeditions, which created the Hellenistic cultural sphere.

The Seleucid Empire was unable to maintain its broad domain, and in the eastern regions separatist and independence movements appeared. As a result, in the middle of the third century B.C. the region between present-day Afghanistan through northeastern Iran was established as the Bactrian Kingdom. As it carried on Greek civilization, it was even referred to as the Greco-Bactrian Kingdom. This was during the period when the Maurya Empire flourished under Ashoka. Bactria applied pressured on the Maurya Empire from the north. Following the death of Ashoka, the Maurya Empire began to weaken and its territories were gradually stripped away.

Thereafter, however, the Bactria Kingdom also fell into decline and fragmented, and in about 130 B.C. it was destroyed. It is thought that the Yuezhi people were in some way connected with Bactria's collapse. These people created within the Bactria region a state called Greater Yuezhi.

バクトリアからギリシア文明がインドへと
流れ込んだ

　一つの文明が押し寄せ、それが去ったあと、元々あった大地の香り
にその文明の香りが混ざり、新たな文明へと変貌します。その変貌の
繰り返しの中で、次第にコスモポリタンな文明が創造されます。ギリ
シア文明の波は、東はイランからインドに、西はやがて地中海世界の
覇者となるローマへと拡大します。ローマはギリシアに近いだけに、
ローマ人は地中海世界を征服したものの、文化によってはギリシアに
征服され続けたといわれているほど、ギリシア文明がローマに与えた
影響は甚大でした。

　一方、東へ拡大したギリシア文明の影響を考えるときに注目される
のが、バクトリアという中央アジアに興った国家なのです。

　ヘレニズム文化はアレクサンドロス大王一代で完成したわけではあ
りません。大王の死後その版図の継承を巡って熾烈な争いが始まりま
す。その結果、現在のメソポタミア北部からパキスタンに至る広大な
地域にセレウコス帝国が興ります。紀元前312年のことです。創始者
のセレウコス一世は、アレクサンドロス大王の側近の一人でした。そ
の7年後には、もう一人の側近であるプトレマイオスによって、プト
レマイオス朝という国家がエジプトにできあがります。

　こうして、ギリシア人を上に抱く国家が大王の遠征した地域に建国
し、それがヘレニズム文化圏を造り出したのです。

　セレウコス朝は広い版図を維持できず、東方地域で分離独立運動が
おこります。その結果、紀元前3世紀中盤に現在のアフガニスタンか
らイラン北東部に至る地域に出来上がったのがバクトリア王国だった
のです。この国家はグレコ・バクトリア王国ともいわれるように、ギ
リシア文明を継承していました。マウリヤ王朝がアショーカ王の元で
全盛期を迎えていた頃のことです。バクトリア王国はそんなマウリヤ
王朝を北から圧迫します。そしてアショーカ王の死後衰退を始めたマ
ウリヤ王国の領土を蝕みます。

　しかし、バクトリア王国もその後分裂し、紀元前130年頃には滅亡
します。バクトリアの滅亡劇に関わったのではないかといわれるのが
月氏と呼ばれる人々でした。彼らはバクトリア王国のあった地域に大
月氏という国家を造ります。

時代
BC3, 2世紀
古代

地域
中東・インド・中央アジア

分類
交流【国家】

キーワード
ギリシア文化の波及・ヘ
レニズム文化の成立・シ
ルクロードによる交流・
多文化融合の中央アジア

As can be understood from the fact that the name of this country is written in Chinese characters, a Chinese cultural area had already been established in East Asia.

The history of Central Asia is the history of nomadic peoples, the details of which are mostly cloaked in mystery. Two languages elucidate this matter. One is the alphabetic letters of the Greeks from the west; the other is the characters which the Chinese from the east used in documents. Hellenistic culture and Chinese culture came together and overlapped in this region, and the Buddhist culture that evolved in India merged here and spread to China. The Silk Road which became the central focus of interchange between the two civilizations first flourished just as Bactria was expanding its territories. The Khyber Pass, which is on the border between Pakistan and Afghanistan, is known as the pass that serves as the point of contact in relations between the East and the West.

020 China attracted the world with its China-centered view of the world

The Greeks were people who originally migrated from inland European areas and spread along the coastline of the Mediterranean Sea. Later they migrated with Alexander the Great into Central Asia.

In complete contrast were the Han Chinese. The Han Chinese remained permanently in the Chinese homeland, exposed to threats from surrounding ethnic groups as they built their own civilization. Needless to say, from the perspective of the neighboring peoples, the Han Chinese who possessed the characteristics of a civilization were themselves a threat to their neighbors. The two sides intimidated each other and, as occurred in later centuries, neighboring people, including the Mongols, seized China and built powerful states there.

When neighboring peoples invaded China, they tended to maintain Chinese systems and culture by adapting themselves to the Chinese ways of thinking and governing. When the Han Chinese were strong, they expelled the invaders, bestowed the products of culture on those who pledged fealty, and encouraged outsiders to adopt Chinese culture. As the expression Middle Kingdom suggests, the Chinese always thought of themselves as being at the center of the world. Unlike the Greeks, who of their own accord spread outward and around the world, the Chinese wanted the world to come to them. China remained as it was, where

この名前が漢字名であることからも理解できるように、既に東アジアには中国文化圏ができあがっていました。

　中央アジアの歴史は、遊牧民の歴史で、その詳細の多くが謎に包まれています。それを解き明かす二つの言語。それが西からきたギリシア人の文字と、東から拡大してきた中国人の漢字による文献です。ヘレニズム文化と中国文化がこの地域を接点に重なり合い、インドに興った仏教文化もこの地域で融合して中国へと伝播されてゆくことになります。「絹の道」として注目を集めたシルクロードでの文明の交流が活発になり始めたのが、バクトリアが版図を拡大した頃のことだったのです。パキスタンとアフガニスタンの国境にあるカイバル峠は、こうした東西交渉の接点となる峠として知られています。

中国は中華思想をもって世界を招いた

　ギリシア人は元々内陸から移動し、海伝いに地中海沿岸に拡散し、その後アレクサンドロス大王と共に中央アジアにまで至った移動する民でした。

　彼らと対照的だったのが漢民族でした。漢民族は常に中国にあって周辺民族の脅威にさらされながら文明を築きました。もちろん周辺民族から見れば、文明を持っていた漢民族のほうが脅威で、双方は威嚇し合い、時には後年のモンゴル人のように、周辺民族が中国を奪取し強大な国家を造ったこともありました。

時代
BC3世紀以前
古代

地域
中国

分類
文化【学問】

キーワード
中華と周辺民族・小国の分裂・多様な学問の開花・漢字文化の浸透・統一国家の出現

　周辺民族は、中国に侵入したとき、中国の制度や文化を利用し、自らを中国化することで存続を図ります。漢民族が強いときは、周辺民族を駆逐しながらも、恭順する民族には中国の文物を与え、中国文化を学ぶことを奨励しました。中華という言葉の通り、中国は常に世界の中心でした。ギリシア人のように、進んで世界に拡散したのではなく、世界が中国に集まることを欲していたのです。中国は、漢民族が膨張したときも、周辺民族が膨張し漢民族を脅かしたときも、中華として存在したのです。そして、この膨張と縮小の繰り返しこそが、中国の

it was, regardless of whether the Han were expanding or the neighboring peoples were intruding on their homeland. This repeated expansion and contraction is what makes up Chinese history.

During the Spring and Autumn and Warring States periods that followed the Zhou, the small countries competed for supremacy. During this period, each country invited various tacticians and thinkers to instruct them in how they might gain and sustain their strength. This assortment of people are referred to as Teachers of the Hundred Schools of Thought. Later Confucius, founder of Confucianism, which had a major impact on morals and political ideology in the region, was active in spreading his ideas around 500 B.C. in the small country of Lu in north-central China. He traveled with his disciples from country to country throughout that area teaching the principles of order, hierarchy, and how a sovereign should govern. Elsewhere Laozi, founder of Daoism, and Zhuangzi preached belief in divine providence, being in harmony with nature, and the sanctification of nature apart from existing systems. Confucianism and Daoism thereafter spread among the people of China and the neighboring peoples, eventually becoming the underpinnings of the East Asian cultural sphere.

Among the Teachers of the Hundred Schools of Thought were people of various specialties, from advisers who explained the know-how of negotiating with other countries to that of how to fight and defeat others, such as Sun Tzu, who set forth military tactics and Mozi, who advocated defense and peaceful tactics.

What spread Chinese political institutions and culture to every corner of the Chinese world was the weapons of war and the written characters we call Chinese characters. Already by the Zhou period, these characters were put to various uses, such as in government and ceremonies. Diverse ethnic groups built towns and cities, as well as states, across China's vast landmass. During the Zhou period, systematized Chinese characters cultivated these assorted people into a single communicating group.

During the Warring States period, under the strengthened state of Qin, Qin Shi Huang accomplished the first true unification of China. This occurred in 221 B.C. The state of Qin took command of the country through a system of prefectures and districts, suppressed the ideology of Confucianism, and aimed at state administration through a rigorous legal system. Qin Shi Huang's suppression of Confucianism consisted of burning books and burying scholars alive. Following the death of Qin Shi Huang, as a result of internal strife for power, the Qin state collapsed. The next government to reunify China in 206 B.C. was the Han dynasty.

歴史そのものだったのです。

周の後に続く春秋戦国時代には、小国が覇権を争って戦っていました。この時代は、それぞれの国が国力を維持するために、様々な戦術家や思想家を招聘します。こうした人々を諸子百家と呼んでいます。その後の東アジア社会の道徳や政治理念に大きな影響を与える儒教の創始者孔子も、紀元前500年頃に中国中北部にあった魯という小国で活動しました。孔子は、社会のあり方、君主の心得について弟子の集団と共に国々を説いてまわったのです。また、自然や宇宙の摂理への洞察から、既存の制度などから離れた自然体を説き、道教の元祖とされた老子や荘子も当時の人です。儒教と道教は、その後の中国とその周辺国家の人々に浸透し、東アジア文化圏の価値観の支柱となってゆきました。

湯島聖堂の孔子像。世界で最大の孔子像である。
Confucius Statue at the Yushima Seido (This is the world's largest statue of Confucius.)

諸子百家の中には、他国との交渉や戦争のノウハウを語るアドバイザーもいれば、兵法を解く孫氏、守城と和平を説く墨子など、多彩な人々がいたのです。

中国の政治制度や文化を中国世界の隅々に浸透させたのは、戦争と、漢字という文字の武器でした。漢字は周の時代に既に政治や儀式など、様々な用途で使用されていました。中国という広大な大地では、多様な民族が各地で都市を築き、国家をつくりました。周の時代に体系化された漢字が、そうした人々を一つのコミュニケーション集団へと育てていったのです。

中国は、戦国時代に強国となった秦の始皇帝により、初めて本格的に統一されます。紀元前221年のことでした。秦は、国を郡県制度によって統率し、儒教などの思想を弾圧し、厳格な法による国家運営を目指します。始皇帝による儒教の弾圧は焚書坑儒と呼ばれ、儒教に関係した書籍も焼却されました。秦は、始皇帝の死後、帝国内部の権力抗争の末に、あえなく滅亡します。その中国を紀元前206年に受け継ぎ、再統一したのが漢王朝だったのです。

021 When the Han unified China, the world was still immense

The word Zhongyuan refers to the vast interior plain that extends along the Yellow River from its middle reaches to its lower reaches. In this area were established the capital cities of the successive dynasties: Luoyang and Chang'an. Zhongyuan is considered to be the place where Chinese culture originated and developed, and protecting that area was thought to be identical with protecting Chinese culture. Qin Shi Huang of the Qin state initiated the construction of the Great Wall of China, an enormous project, specifically in order to protect Zhongyuan from migrants flowing in from the north. The construction of the Great Wall continued until the Ming dynasty.

The Han, who unified China after the Qin, temporarily lost power to the Xin between A.D. 8 and A.D. 23, dividing the Han regime into two parts—the Earlier Han and the Later Han—but unified the country for more than 400 years.

The heyday of the Han was the period of Wu Di, in the second half of the 2nd century B.C. During that period, Confucianism, under the Confucianist Dong Zhongshu, became the scholarly underpinning of the government, and its ideas ordered the social system. From that point onward, Confucian values became the basis of the political system and permeated society as a whole.

Wu Di drove the threatening Xiongnu from the north out of Zhongyuan, expanded into territories to the west, and interacted with groups including the Yuezhi. At that time, to the west of the Yuezhi, who succeeded Bactria, was the Parthian Empire, which was independent of the Seleucid Empire. The Chinese name for Parthia reflected its image as a "refuge" and a "safe haven," and the Chinese engaged in exchanges with the Parthians. In this way, Hellenistic culture spread eastward.

The Han advanced into the Korean Peninsula, and from intermediate destinations such as the Lelang Commandery, they promoted relations with Japan. This was during the Yayoi period in Japan, where small states were forming under powerful regional families. It was not only these Yayoi period mini-states but also countries and city-states on all sides of China who were sending envoys to the Han and absorbing Chinese culture. They brought tribute to the Han, and in return received official endorsement from the Han to administer their respective regions. This exchange was mutually beneficial. China, by its beneficence toward

漢が中国を統一した当時、世界はまだ広大だった

中原という言葉。それは中国の大河、黄河の中流から下流に至る内陸の平原を指す言葉です。そこには、洛陽や長安といった歴代王朝の首都がありました。中原は中国文化が生まれ育まれた場所とされ、人々は中原を守ることが、中国文化を守ることだと考えていました。秦の始皇帝が始めた大事業、万里の長城の建築は、まさに北方の移民から中原を守るためのものでした。万里の長城の建築事業は始皇帝の後も明代に至るまで続けられます。

秦の後に中国を統一した漢は、西暦8年から23年まで新という王朝に政権を奪われていた時代があることから、それ以前の漢を前漢、それ以降を後漢とし、約400年以上に渡って中国を統治しました。

漢の全盛期は、前2世紀後半の武帝の時代です。その時代、董仲舒という儒者によって、儒教は国の学問の支柱になり、その考え方で社会制度が整えられました。儒教はその後歴代の政権によって、政治制度の根本をなす価値観として、社会に浸透してゆくのです。

武帝は北から中原を脅かす匈奴を駆逐し、領土を西へと広げ、月氏などとも交流します。当時、バクトリアの後を継いだ月氏の西には、バクトリアと同じようにセレウコス朝から自立したパルティア帝国がありました。パルティアは中国語で安息国と呼ばれたように、漢は西域世界と交流をしていたのです。ヘレニズム文化はこうして東へと伝播されます。

漢は朝鮮半島にも進出し、楽浪郡などの出先を通して、日本との交流も進めました。当時の日本は弥生時代にあたり、豪族による小国家が生まれていました。こと弥生時代の小国家に限らず、中国周辺の国や都市国家は、漢に使者を送り中国文化を吸収します。中国に朝貢し、中国の皇帝からその地域を治めるお墨付きを貰ったのです。これはお互いの利益に合致していました。中国は朝貢する国を懐柔することで脅威を減らし、周辺の国家は中国に進んで朝貢することで、その文明を学び、中国から安全を保証されたのです。朝貢は命がけの旅でした。

時代
紀元前後
古代

地域
中国

分類
統一【国家】

キーワード
漢の成立と超大国化・儒教の浸透・グローバルな文化交流・周辺諸国と朝貢貿易を開始

the tributary states, reduced any potential threat they might pose; the surrounding states through their offerings of tribute were able to learn from Chinese civilization, and their security was guaranteed. To carry tribute to China was to put one's life at risk. The world was vast and the greater part was uncivilized. There were no roads and the few maps that did exist were primitive at best.

It is dangerous, therefore, to analyze the world situation of that day from the perspective of contemporary sensibilities. China was able to grasp conditions in the outside world from information gathered from tributary envoys and merchants who traded overseas. Because Wu Di opposed Xiongnu, he sent Zhang Qian to probe the western districts, but Zhang Qian's journey lasted a dozen or so years, including a period during which he was detained by the Xiongnu. As a result of the accumulation of knowledge during that long period of time, exchanges between the three civilized worlds of the Hellenist lands, India, and China were deepened.

The period of the rise and decline of the Han overlapped with that of Rome. As the Han were advancing westward gathering information from the Parthian Empire, the Roman Empire was beginning to advance eastward. Gaius Julius Caesar, who we know as Julius Caesar, was just preparing to invade Parthia.

022 Rome reigned over the Mediterranean for a period of 800 years

"Rome was not built in a day" goes the saying, and true enough, it took 800 years for Rome to unify and develop a great empire around the Mediterranean. That is comparable to the length of time that has passed between the Kamakura period and the present day.

The masters of Rome were people of Latin descent. They were one branch of speakers of Indo-European languages, who migrated from the periphery of the Caucasus Mountains and scattered across Europe. One subgroup of these Latin-related migrants moved southward down the Italian Peninsula, and in about the 8th century B.C. they created a city-state along the Tiber River: the city of Rome.

The history of Rome, just as with Greece, began with a city-state. The process of its development resembled that of Athens. Originally a monarchy, Rome in the 6th century B.C. evolved into a republican form of government under its aristocracy. Thereafter, repeated conflicts arose between the common people,

当時世界はまだ広大で、大地の大部分は未開でした。道路もなければ、地図ですら極めて原始的なものでした。

　従って当時の世界情勢を現在の感覚で分析することは危険です。中国は朝貢してくる人々や、海外と交流する商人などから情報を収集し、外の世界の事情を把握します。武帝は匈奴と対抗するために、張騫という人物を西域に送り探索を進めますが、その旅は匈奴に拘束された時期も含め、十数年に及ぶものでした。こうした十年単位での情報の蓄積によって、ヘレニズム、インド、そして中国の3つの世界が交流を深めてゆくことになるのです。

　漢の盛衰はローマの盛衰の時期と重なります。漢が西域に進出して、パルティア帝国の情報をキャッチしていた頃、ローマ帝国も東方への進出を始めます。ジュリアス・シーザーの名前で知られるガイウス・ユリウス・カエサルも、パルティアへの侵攻を計画していたのです。

ローマは800年の年月をかけて
地中海に君臨した

　「ローマは一日にしてならず」という言葉があるように、ローマが地中海世界を統合した大帝国に成長するには800年以上の年月がかかっています。それは鎌倉時代から現在までに匹敵する時間です。

　ローマの主はラテン系の人々です。彼らはコーカサス山脈周辺から移動し、ヨーロッパ各地へと拡散したインドヨーロッパ語族の一派です。そんな一派の一つでイタリア半島を南下してきたラテン系の人々によって、紀元前8世紀頃にティベル川のほとりに都市国家が生まれます。それがローマの興りです。

　ローマの歴史は、ギリシアと同様、都市国家から始まったのです。その成長の過程は、アテナイと似通っています。元々王政をしいていたローマは、紀元前6世紀頃に貴族による共和政国家となります。その後、重装歩兵としてローマの成長を担った平民と、その上に立つ貴族

時代
BC1世紀以前
古代

地域
ローマ

分類
国家【戦争】

キーワード
ローマの成り立ち・カルタゴとの対立・ポエニ戦争と西地中海の覇権・ギリシアを制圧

who bore the burden of the development of Rome serving in the heavily armed infantry units, and the aristocracy who ruled them. As a result, the city-state came to be administered by a democratic system composed of the Senate, controlled by the aristocrats and the plebeian assembly, composed of plebian commoners. Under this government, Rome expanded its territories to include the entirety of the Italian Peninsula.

In order for Rome to advance into the Mediterranean world, however, it had to subjugate a powerful rival: Carthage, a city-state founded by the Phoenicians.

The Phoenicians first became active in the region in about the 15th century B.C. They subsequently used Canaan script, which evolved into Greek letters, and established city-states throughout the Mediterranean. Rome and Carthage clashed three times between 264 and 146 B.C. We refer to these conflicts as the Punic Wars. As an aside, the term Punic comes from the Latin word "Punicus" from the Greek word "Phoinix" meaning Phoenician.

A famous episode from the Punic Wars involves the military expedition of Hannibal, a resourceful general from Carthage. As a result of this incident, Hannibal became famous together with Napoleon as one of the greatest generals in all of European history. Hannibal led his troops from North Africa across the sea to the Iberian Peninsula and then over the Alps to suddenly appear at the heart of the Roman Empire. The strategy he used to defeat the Roman army at the Battle of Cannae, leaving Rome in a critical state, is still taught in military academies today. However, the Roman general Scipio the Elder made use of Hannibal's extended campaign, which left the army bottled up in Italy, to send Roman troops to Carthage. When Hannibal hurriedly returned to Carthage, Scipio annihilated Hannibal's army in 202 B.C.

Ultimately the Punic Wars concluded with Rome destroying Carthage entirely.

At the same time, Rome suppressed Macedonia and then Greece, and by the 2nd century B.C., Rome had achieved hegemony throughout the Mediterranean. Thereafter, Rome faced a century-long series of conflicts, including domestic struggles for power and the rebellion led by the gladiator Spartacus. As a result, the people began to hope for a stable, stronger leadership, which ultimately led to an imperial regime. Through the establishment by imperial Rome of a unified Mediterranean world in the 1st century B.C., the region rejoiced at the achievement of an unprecedented period of peace and stability.

との間の長い権力闘争が繰り返されました。その結果、貴族が運営する元老院と、平民による平民会による民主制によって国家が運営され、ローマはイタリア半島全域に版図を拡大したのです。

　しかし、ローマが地中海世界に進出するためには、克服しなければならない強大なライバルがありました。フェニキア人の都市国家カルタゴです。

　地中海世界で元々フェニキア人が活動を始めたのは、紀元前15世紀頃ではないかといわれています。彼らは後にギリシア文字へと進化するフェニキア文字を使い、地中海各地に都市国家を築いていました。紀元前264年から146年にかけて、3回にわたりローマとカルタゴは衝突します。ポエニ戦争です。ちなみに、ポエニとはラテン語でフェニキア人を意味する単語です。

　ポエニ戦争での有名なエピソードに、カルタゴの知将ハンニバルの遠征があります。ハンニバルは後年のナポレオンと共に、ヨーロッパ史に残る将軍といわれています。彼は北アフリカからスペインに渡り、アルプスを越えてローマの喉元に忽然と現れます。そして、今でも士官学校などでの戦術論で取り上げられるカンネーの戦いでローマ軍を打ち破り、ローマは瀕死の状態となったのです。しかし、ハンニバルが長引く遠征で、イタリアに釘付けになっている状況を利用したローマの将軍スキピオは、カルタゴ本国に兵を送り、慌てて舞い戻ったハンニバル軍を撃滅します。紀元前202年のことでした。

アルプス山脈を越えるハンニバル軍
Hannibal's crossing of the Alps

　ポエニ戦争は最終的にローマがカルタゴを滅ぼす形で終結します。
　同時にローマはマケドニア、そしてギリシアを制圧し、紀元前2世紀には地中海での覇権を獲得するのです。その後のローマは、権力闘争や、スパルタクスという剣奴がおこした反乱など、約一世紀にわたって混乱が続きます。その結果、安定したより強い指導力を人々が欲したことが、帝政への移行の背景となるのです。紀元前1世紀に地中海世界を統一した帝政ローマによって、その地域は今までにない平和で安定した時代を謳歌するのでした。

023 Unifying the Mediterranean was not all Rome accomplished

At about the time that Rome gained ascendancy in the Mediterranean, in Egypt, the Ptolemaic dynasty, which had carried on Hellenistic culture from the period of Alexander the Great, remained in power. Its capital was Alexandria. In the library there, the country preserved and maintained collections of books from all around the world. Volumes were gathered from abroad by means of the trading ships that entered the port at Alexandria, and it is believed that transcriptions of books on papyrus, a form of paper invented in Egypt, numbered over 700,000 volumes. This was the largest library collection in the world at that time.

However, the technology for preserving books was still in its early stages, and this enormous collection was damaged not only by warfare and fire but also by insect damage. And in the end, the library building itself ceased to exist. Some say that if this library had continued to exist, not only would it have unraveled mysteries of ancient history but it would also have speeded up the progress of human civilization by some 500 years.

At the time of the last monarch of the Ptolemaic dynasty, the famous Cleopatra VII, Rome destroyed and annexed the monarchy symbolic of Hellenistic culture. The tale of the love affair between Cleopatra and the Roman general Mark Antony and the war with Caesar Augustus were later dramatized by William Shakespeare and, in the recent past, made into a motion picture.

Caesar consigned the Ptolemaic dynasty to oblivion in 30 B.C., and Rome thereby unified the Mediterranean region. Before attacking Egypt, however, in about 58 B.C., Caesar led an expedition through Gaul, present-day France and its periphery, to England, placing the region under Roman jurisdiction. After participating along with Pompey and Crassus in the Roman triumvirate which administered the political world, Caesar became an autocrat, ultimately earned political enemies, and was assassinated. This tale, like that involving Cleopatra, became the subject of theatrical dramas in later generations.

In any event, through this political turmoil, Caesar's adopted son Octavian eventually took the title Augustus, and in 27 B.C., he attained imperial status and Rome became an empire.

ローマは地中海を統一しただけではなかった

ローマが地中海で覇権を握ろうとしていた頃、エジプトにはアレクサンドロス大王以来のヘレニズム文化を継承したプトレマイオス王朝が残っていました。首都はアレクサンドリア。ここの図書館では世界中からの蔵書を国家が保護して管理していました。アレクサンドリアに入港する船などを通して海外から収集され、エジプトで発明された紙、パピルスに写本された書籍は70万巻を超えていたといわれています。それは世界最大規模の図書館でした。

書籍の保存技術が未熟であったこともあり、この図書館はその後の戦争や火災、そして虫害などで蝕まれ、最終的には建物自体も消滅します。人によれば、この図書館が現存していれば、古代史の謎の解明のみならず、人類の文明そのものが500年は早く進んでいたのではといわれています。

プトレマイオス朝最後の女王として有名なクレオパトラ7世の頃、ローマはそんなヘレニズム文化の象徴であった王国を滅亡させ、併合します。クレオパトラとローマの将軍マルクス・アントニウスとの恋、そしてアウグストゥスとの戦争の物語は、その後シェイクスピアなどによって戯曲化され、近年になっても映画などでも取り上げられる伝説となりました。

カエサルが、このプトレマイオス朝を紀元前30年に葬ったことで、ローマは地中海を統一したのです。ところで、カエサルは、エジプトを攻める前、紀元前58年頃には現在のフランスとその周辺にあたるガリアから、イギリスへと遠征をして、そこをローマの傘下に加えます。彼はポンペイウスやクラッススといった重鎮との三頭政治をもってローマの政界で活躍した後、独裁者となりますが、最終的に政敵を生み、暗殺されます。この物語も、クレオパトラの物語と同様に後世、戯曲などの題材にされました。

いずれにせよ、こうした政争を経てカエサルの養子であったオクタヴィアヌスがアウグストゥスという称号をもらい、ローマの最高指導者として紀元前27年に帝位に就き、ローマは帝政へと移行したのでした。

時代
BC1世紀以前
古代

地域
ローマ

分類
政治【統一】

キーワード
学問の中心アレクサンドリア・エジプト征服と地中海の統一・共和国から帝国へ

In a sense, the account of Caesar may have been somewhat glorified by Augustus after he ascended the imperial throne and by those who succeeded him. Yet there is no denying that Caesar was the one who assembled a great empire that governed a realm extending from Spain in the west to the Middle East.

While patterning itself after Greek civilization, Rome took upon itself the role of successor to Hellenist civilization. At the same time, Rome constructed cities modeled on itself throughout the provinces under its control. Through this activity, various forms and technologies that would one day serves as sources for European civilization were disseminated across the entire Mediterranean world. It is an irony of history that the library in Alexandria, which compiled resources that served as the origin of that civilization, was destroyed in part by the fires of war initiated by Roman expeditions.

ガイウス・ユリウス・カエサル
Gaius Julius Caesar (100 B.C.?–44 B.C.)

024 The Roman world was standardized under the Pax Romana

When the Greek city-states were flourishing, scientific awareness was also coming to the fore. By observing phenomena objectively and seeking to grasp the physical forces that govern them, the members of the Ionian school in ancient Greece were actively engaged in science and mathematics. The 6th century B.C. philosopher and mathematician Pythagoras, whose name was given to the Pythagorean Theorem, is considered to be the starting figure in the study of geometry.

In the 5th century B.C., Socrates and Plato were actively involved in philosophy. Plato's disciple Aristotle is praised as the founder of logic for his systematization of the methodology of thought. As an aside, Aristotle is also known as the tutor of Alexander the Great. Another significant mathematician of the period is Euclid, who is known for giving birth to what became known as Euclidean geometry.

Such knowledge was passed down from the ancient Grecian city-states and

ある意味で、カエサルの物語は、帝位についたアウグストゥスやその後継者によって美化された側面があるかもしれません。しかし、カエサルが西はスペインから東は中東に至る広範な地域を支配する大帝国を築いた人物であることには間違いありません。

　ローマはギリシア文明を模倣しながらも、ヘレニズム文明の後継者としての役割を担います。同時にローマは支配地域全体にローマを模倣した都市を築きました。こうした活動を通して、ヨーロッパ文明の原点となる様々な様式や技術が、地中海世界全体に伝播されてゆくことになったのです。そんな文明の源の資料を集積していたアレクサンドリアの図書館が、ローマの遠征などの戦火の中で消滅していったことも、また歴史の皮肉といえましょう。

アウグストゥス
Augustus (63 B.C.–A.D. 14)

パクス・ロマーナの元で、ローマ世界は規格化された

　ギリシアの都市国家が繁栄した時代は、科学という意識が芽生えた時代でもありました。ものごとを客観的に観察し、そこから法則を導きだそうと、古代ギリシアではイオニア学派と呼ばれる人々が科学や数学の分野で活躍したのです。ピタゴラスが幾何学の原点ともいえるピタゴラスの定理を発見したのは、紀元前6世紀のことでした。

　一方で、哲学の分野ではソクラテスやプラトンが紀元前5世紀に活躍します。プラトンの弟子であるアリストテレスは、哲学的な思考方法を体系付けたことで、論理学の始祖と賞賛されました。ちなみにアリストテレスは、アレクサンドロス大王の家庭教師であったことでも知られています。ユークリッド幾何学を生み出したエウクレイデスも、同時代の人でした。

　古代ギリシアの都市国家から、中東や地中諸国に受け継がれたこ

時代
BC1〜AD2世紀
古代

地域
ローマ

分類
政治【学問】

キーワード
ギリシアの多様な学問・技術の向上・計画都市とローマの繁栄・法の整備・周辺民族への対応

disseminated throughout the states of the Middle East and the Mediterranean were later passed on to the Romans. Rome inherited cultural activities themselves from Greece and then in turn played a role in spreading that culture throughout the Roman world. Particularly in Rome's case, due to the necessity for managing the empire, the technology that came out of this knowledge was put to practical use in fields such as public works and architecture. Throughout the urban areas, in Greek-style architecture, aqueducts, and road development, every aspect of city planning was standardized.

In the Roman Empire, once Augustus established the imperial government, there was a period of political instability. However, in the first century A.D., the domains of the empire spread to include all territories from western Europe to the Mediterranean and eastward as far as Turkey. At that point, the empire entered a period of stability. This period of peace based on Rome is called the Pax Romana. During this period, Rome was governed by five leaders called the Five Good Emperors, known for their contributions to Roman prosperity. In A.D. 98, when Trajan, one of the five, took the throne, the empire reached its greatest expanse. Rome gave citizenship to the inhabitants of all the lands it included, sustaining an expansive empire administered by Roman laws. The completion of this system became the secret of the longevity of the empire.

While Rome flourished, the Han dynasty in China prospered, and the culture of written Chinese characters spread widely across East Asia. Similarly, Greek letters evolved in Rome, and the alphabets of present-day European languages came into wide use. The Latin language which they used became the progenitor of European languages. The foundation of these written languages that had such a great impact on present-day Asia and Europe were formed at approximately the same time.

Once the Han dynasty and the Roman Empire became cultural nexuses, they had to deal with one common issue: how to deal with frontier districts far away from the center of the empire. In Rome's case, this meant the northeast European region called Germania, as well as the periphery of eastern Europe and Turkey. The defense of these borderlands placed an increasingly heavy economic burden on the Roman Empire. One can see in virtually any empire that at the height of its prosperity there are initial indications of its eventual decline.

うした知識は、ローマ時代にも継承されます。ローマは文化活動そのものをギリシアから継承し、それをローマ世界全体に広める役割を担いました。特にローマの場合、帝国の経営の必要性から、そうした知識から生み出された技術を土木工事や建築などの分野で実用化します。都市はどこもギリシア風の建物と、水道や街道の整備などによる、都市計画によって規格化されたのです。

　ローマ帝国は、アウグストゥスによって帝政に移行した後、しばらく政治的には不安定な時代もありました。しかし、紀元1世紀頃になると、帝国の版図も西ヨーロッパから地中海全域、そしてトルコに至る広大なものとなり、帝国は安定期を迎えます。このローマによる平和を「パクス・ロマーナ」と呼んでいます。この時代を治めた5人の皇帝は五賢帝と呼ばれ、ローマの繁栄を担った皇帝として知られています。五賢帝の一人で98年に即位したトラヤヌス帝の頃、帝国の版図は最大となりました。ローマは征服した地域の人々にも市民権を与えて広大な帝国を維持し、ローマ法と呼ばれる法によって国を運営します。こうした制度を整えたことが、ローマ帝国の長寿の秘訣となったのです。

　ローマが栄えた頃、中国では漢王朝が繁栄し、漢字文化圏が広く東アジアに広がります。同様にローマでもギリシア文字から進化し、現代ヨーロッパのアルファベットとなったローマ字が普及し、彼らの言語であるラテン語がヨーロッパ言語の始祖となりました。アジアとヨーロッパとで、それぞれ現代に直接影響を与えている文字文化の土台が、同じ時代に築かれたことになります。

　そして、漢王朝もローマ帝国も、共に文化の中心となった以上、双方に共通した課題にも取り組まなければなりませんでした。それが辺境対策です。ローマの場合は、ゲルマニアと呼ばれた北東ヨーロッパ、そして東ヨーロッパやトルコ周辺がそれにあたります。版図が拡大したローマにとって、辺境の防衛は、ローマ世界に次第に経済的負担となってのしかかってゆきます。どのような帝国も、その最盛期に、既に衰亡の兆しが見え始めているのです。

五賢帝
The Five Good Emperors

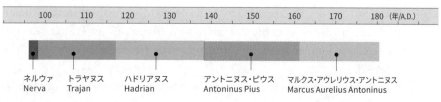

025 Rome's decline becomes the foundation of Europe

At the time when Rome aimed for domination of the Mediterranean Sea, the heart of the Eurasian continent was extremely unstable. In the 2nd century B.C., Wu Di of the Earlier Han attacked the Xiongnu, pushing them westward. The Xiongnu over time migrated across the vast steppes into northern Central Asia. This was following the death of Alexander the Great, when various tribes and states became entangled in claiming land after his death.

Following this, the Sassanid Empire, which overthrew Parthia in 224, expanded its influence in the area between the Roman and Indian worlds. Under the influence of such conditions, in the territories to the north of the Caspian Sea, the Huns, nomadic peoples with the same roots as the Xiongnu, moved westward, encroaching on Europe. Under this pressure, it was the inhabitants of Germania who began migrating. Between the Han dynasty and the Roman Empire, these various ethnic groups collided in chain reactions over a period of more than four centuries. Sometimes these people became migrants; sometimes they were hired as mercenaries by the Romans on the frontiers. And on occasion they entered Roman territories as refugees or as invaders.

As the Sassanid Empire expanded, it began to exert pressure on Rome's eastern frontier. At that time, in order to maintain its territories, Rome was carrying out a partitioned administration, but in 324 Constantine the Great, who reconsolidated the government, moved his capital city to Byzantium in order to counter the threat of the Sassanians.

The threats, however, came not only from east. In 375 people from Germania, who until then came into frequent contact with Romans, began to move into Roman lands in earnest. There was a Great migration of these Germanic peoples. In addition, the Huns expanded from the Ukrainian region around the Black Sea. In 395, upon the death of Theodosius, the Roman Empire split into the Western and Eastern Empires, never to be unified again.

In the 5th century, the Huns led by Attila began to aggressively invade Roman territories. Immediately after the fear fueled by Attila passed, the Western Roman Empire collapsed under attack by German mercenaries from its own army. The year was 476.

When an edifice becomes larger and technology cannot keep pace with its

ローマは衰亡して、ヨーロッパの石礎になった

　ローマが地中海の覇権を目指していた頃、ユーラシア大陸の中心部は極めて不安定な状態にありました。紀元前2世紀の前漢の武帝による匈奴の攻撃で、彼らが西へと押しやられます。匈奴は広大な草原地帯を年月をかけて移動し、中央アジアの北部に進出します。それはアレクサンドロス大王の死後、その遺領を巡り、様々な民族や国家が交錯していた頃のことでした。

　その後、西暦224年になると、パルティアを倒したサ サン朝が、ローマ世界とインド世界との間で勢力を拡大します。そうした情勢に影響され、カスピ海北部一帯に展開していた遊牧民で匈奴と同じルーツを持つといわれるフン族が西へと動き、ヨーロッパへと侵入してきたのです。これに押されるように動き出したのが、ゲルマニアに住んでいた人々でした。まさに、漢帝国とローマ帝国の間で、様々な民族が400年以上の歳月をかけて、玉突き現象をおこしていたのです。彼らは、あるときは移民として、またあるときはローマの傭兵として辺境で雇われます。さらに時には難民として、同時に侵入者としてローマ帝国領に入ってきたのです。

　一方サ サン朝ペルシアが拡大すると、ローマの東部を圧迫し始めます。当時ローマでは、広大な領土を維持するために、分割統治が行われていましたが、324年にローマを再びまとめあげたコンスタンティヌス1世は、サ サン朝からの脅威に対抗するために、帝国の首都をビザンティウムへと移します。

　しかし、脅威は東からだけではありませんでした。それまでも頻繁にローマと接触していたゲルマニアの人々が、375年に本格的にローマ領内へ移動を始めたのです。ゲルマン人の大移動です。また、フン族もウクライナ地方から黒海沿岸へと展開します。395年、テオドシウス帝が亡くなると、ローマ帝国は西と東とに分割され、以後統一されることはありませんでした。

　5世紀になると、フン族はアッティラという王の元で積極的にローマへ侵入を始めます。そして、アッティラの脅威が去った直後、西ローマ帝国はゲルマン人の傭兵によって滅ぼされてしまうのです。476年のことでした。

　技術が追いつかないままに建物が肥大化すると、その重みのために

growth, due to the increased weight of the structure, its pillars and its foundation begin to crack. The Roman Empire also collapsed due to the fact that it could not withstand the weight of its own prosperity. If Rome's economy tilted in favor of maintaining the frontier, this in turn affected the budget and equipment for maintaining the frontier. Additionally, in terms of civic life, economic turmoil created a gap between the rich and the poor, and a so-called society of inequality undermined the city. Following the era of the Five Good Emperors, Rome declined over a period of 200 years, and less than 100 years after that, the Western Roman Empire collapsed.

When that happened, people from the north and east seeking wealth surged in, as if a levee had suddenly collapsed. These people were the ones who later formed states in various regions, mainly in Europe. And just as the Romans had learned from the Greeks, these people used the authority of Rome to govern their own domains. Hence the Roman world made a major contribution as the center of the spiritual culture of Europe thereafter. That contribution was Christianity.

026 Christianity used Rome to become the master of Europe

It may be that the current of religious reform within Judaism brought Christianity into being. In Judaism, it is said that people who believe in it are a chosen people who will be saved by God. When Moses brought the Hebrews out of their captivity in Egypt, where, as is recorded in the Old Testament, they had been treated as slaves, God led and protected only those who believed in him and followed His commandments. However, this did not mean that Judaism was to be a religion of the Jews as a race. Rather, it meant that it was open to everyone who believed in Judaism. Therefore, the definition of Jew also refers to anyone who believes in Judaism.

Criticizing Judaism for its formalism and adherence to the legalism of the Pharisees, who were a mainstream sect of Judaism, Jesus was prosecuted by people like the Pharisees. Jesus was brought before the court of Pilate, the Roman governor-general, was sentenced to crucifixion, and was executed in approximately A.D. 30.

柱や土台そのものが軋みだします。ローマも、自らの繁栄の重みに耐えられなくなり、衰亡していったのでした。辺境の維持のために、ローマの経済が傾けば、それは逆に辺境の維持のための予算や装備にも影響を与えます。そして、市民生活でいうならば、経済的混乱は貧富の差を生み、いわゆる格差社会が都市を蝕みます。五賢帝時代の後、ローマは200年かけて衰退し、その後さらに100年足らずで西ローマ帝国の滅亡に至ったのです。

　当時、堤防が決壊したかのように、北や東から富を求めて人々がなだれ込んできました。彼らは、後のヨーロッパ世界の主として、各地に国家を造ります。そしてローマがギリシアに習ったように、彼らはローマの権威を利用して自らの領地を統治したのです。そんなローマ世界がその後のヨーロッパの精神文化の軸となってゆくために大きく貢献したもの。それがキリスト教だったのです。

キリスト教は、ローマを利用して
ヨーロッパの主になった

　もしかすると、ユダヤ教の中でおきた宗教改革の流れが、キリスト教を生み出したのかもしれません。ユダヤ教には、ユダヤ教を信ずる人こそは神から救済されるという選民意識があるといわれています。モーゼがエジプトから奴隷として酷使されていたヘブライ人を伴って脱出したとき、神は自らを信じ、戒律を守る人のみを導いていったと旧約聖書には記されています。しかし、このことは、ユダヤ教は人種としてのユダヤ人のための宗教ではなく、ユダヤ教を信ずる全ての人を受け入れる宗教であるということにもなります。従って、ユダヤ人という定義も、ユダヤ教を信仰する全ての人を指すものとされているのです。

　このユダヤ教が形骸化し、ファリサイ人と呼ばれるユダヤ教の主流派のみの戒律に縛られた宗教になっていると批判したことで、そうした人々に訴えられたのがイエスでした。イエスは、ローマの総督ピラトによる裁判で、十字架の刑に処せられます。処刑されたのは、紀元30年頃でした。

時代
1～4世紀
古代

地域
ローマ

分類
宗教【政治】

キーワード
ユダヤ教の戒律化とイエスの出現・キリスト教の発生・ローマとキリスト教

When it comes to determining just what kind of person Jesus was, there remain a considerable number of elements that are unclear. As believers in Christianity spread, they became the object of persecution by the Roman Empire, some being executed in public spectacles. Innumerable examples of martyrdom are recorded as purifying believers' faith in Christ.

Why were Christians persecuted from the outset? Christianity is a world religion. Therefore, because it accepted followers beyond members of a specific race of people and spread so rapidly, one theory holds, it incurred the wrath of the authorities. However, the same is true of other religions including Islam, so that argument is hardly persuasive. Rather, because Christianity did not acknowledge the authority of the Emperor and because it treated polytheistic beliefs as heresy, that may have been the motive for persecution by the Roman authorities. Christianity was officially legalized in A.D. 313 by Emperor Constantine, who granted freedom of religion.

Not only are there many aspects of Christianity during the Roman period that remain unknown but subsequent events have been dramatized or adapted. Having said that, it is a fact that during the Roman era, a Christian religious order was founded, its doctrines were compiled in the Bible, and there was continuous debate regarding orthodoxy. Following that, the religious order became systematized to the degree that Christianity became the established religion of Rome, and the Roman Catholic Church was founded. In this process, Yahweh, who had been worshiped as the only God within Judaism, was considered to be one with Jesus, and various groups such as the Arians, who asserted that Christ was a human being, and the Nestorians, who recognized both divinity and humanity within Christ, were expelled as heretics.

In passing, one should note that the teachings of Christianity at that time were such that if someone alive today were to try to follow them, he or she would be so strictly bound by rigid precepts and conventions that it would be impossible to live in normal society. The common understanding of Christianity today shows how it was later authorized, adapted, and reformed.

では実際のイエスとはどんな人物なのかといえば、まだまだ解明されていないことが多すぎます。キリスト教の信者は、その後ローマ各地に拡散する中で、ローマ帝国による迫害の対象となり、中には見せ物として処刑されたこともありました。そんな数えきれない殉教例が、キリストへの信仰を純化するために記録されていきました。

　何故、キリスト教は、当初迫害されたのでしょうか。キリスト教は世界宗教です。従って特定の人種以外の人々も受け入れたことで急速に拡大し、それが権力者の逆鱗に触れたのだという説があります。しかし、それはイスラム教をはじめ他の宗教にもあったことで、充分な説得力はありません。むしろ、キリスト教が皇帝の権威を認めないこと、多神教を邪宗としたことなどが、ローマでの迫害の動機であったのかもしれません。コンスタンティヌス帝によって信教の自由が認められたことで、キリスト教が事実上公認されたのは313年のことでした。

　ローマ時代のキリスト教の状況については、未知の事柄が多いだけではなく、後世の脚色もありました。とはいえ、ローマ時代にキリスト教に教団ができ、教義として聖書が編纂され、何が正当かという議論も繰り返されたことは事実です。その後、キリスト教がローマの国教となるまで、こうした教団としての制度が整えられ、いわゆるローマカトリックが成立してくるのです。ユダヤ教の中で唯一の神として崇められてきたヤハウェが、イエスと一体であるとされ、キリストは人であると主張するアリウス派や、キリストの中に神性と人格の二つを認めるネストリウス派などが異端として追放されたのも、この過程でのことでした。

　ちなみに当時のキリスト教の教えそのものも、もし現代人がその教え通りに生活したら、社会生活を送れないほど、厳格な戒律やしきたりに縛られたものでした。今の常識で見るキリスト教は、あきらかに後年、権威付けされ、脚色され、変革されていったものなのです。

027 At the dawn of the Middle Ages, science and religion split

It is interesting to take a quick peek at American society. Many of those who are globally active in employing leading-edge technology and working in facilities capable of launching space vehicles attend church with their families on the weekends, offer prayers, and lead their lives according to Christian morals. Even among those who are not devout believers in Christianity one can detect in their social standards and sense of values the influences of Christian morality that their parents and siblings believe in.

Science and religion, which at first glance would appear to be conceptually contradictory, have in American society maintained an incredible balance as they created the cultural climate of the country. America is a society of immigrants, many of whom are of Protestant lineage and believe in being diligent. As a people who had to overcome severe conditions, they placed value on their success and courage. For that reason, the unusual balance of science and religion was never seen as being inconsistent, but was taken for granted.

In the long history of humankind, however, that idiosyncratic balance was broken everywhere. The wrecking of this balance between science and religion began at the end of the Roman Empire. Under the leadership of Emperor Theodosius, who made Christianity the state religion of the Roman Empire in 395, a wide variety of religions disappeared. Within Christianity, taking the doctrine that God, the Holy Spirit, and Christ were united as one and holding that as orthodoxy, this teaching reigned throughout western Europe. The deification of Christ as an individual was actively promoted in religious conferences, such as the Council of Nicaea in 325 and the Council of Ephesus in 431. From then onward, any way of thinking or acting that went against such ideas of Divine Providence were taken to be heresy and were harshly persecuted. Scientific rationality, which had been explored up to that point, became the object of that type of persecution.

A Greek scientist named Hypatia was active in Alexandria during the period when Christianity became the orthodox religion of the empire. She was known for her accomplishments in the fields of astronomy and mathematics, and was well-versed in the philosophy of the period of Socrates and Plato. There are some who believe she had even developed a heliocentric theory based on her scientific observations of the heavens. Following the Council of Ephesus, in Alexandria

中世の夜明けの頃、科学と宗教が絶縁した

　アメリカの社会を垣間見ると面白いことが見えてきます。最先端の技術をもってグローバルに活躍したり、宇宙船を打ち上げる施設で働いたりしている人の多くが、週末には家族と教会に行って祈りを捧げ、キリスト教のモラルに従った生活をおくっています。特にキリスト教への信仰を強く持たない人ですら、その生活規範や価値観には、彼らの親や兄弟が信じてきたキリスト教の道徳観の影響がみられます。

　科学と宗教。一見矛盾した二つの概念が、アメリカの社会で不思議な均衡を保ちながら国の風土をつくっているのです。アメリカは移民社会で、多くが勤勉をよしとするプロテスタント系の人々です。過酷な条件を克服しなければならない移民であった彼らは、自らが成功し、強く生きることを価値観の中心においていました。そのためにも、科学と宗教との不思議な均衡は、アメリカ人の中では特に矛盾として指摘されることなく、ごく自然に受け入れられてきたのです。

　しかし、人類の長い歴史の過程を見ると、この不思議な均衡は、至るところで破られていました。ローマ帝国末期は、この科学と宗教の均衡が壊され始めた時代でした。テオドシウス帝が395年にキリスト教をローマ帝国の国教として以来、その統率のもと、多様な宗教が消滅しました。キリスト教の中でも、神と精霊とキリストの三つの存在を一体であると説くカトリックが正当であるとして、西ヨーロッパ全体に君臨することになります。キリスト個人の神格化も、325年のニケーア公会議や、431年のエフェソス公会議などの宗教会議を通して積極的に進められました。以来、こうした摂理に反する考え方や行為は異端として、過酷な迫害に直面します。それまで探求されてきた科学的な合理性も、そうした迫害の対象となったのです。

　ヒュパティアという女性が、アレクサンドリアでキリスト教が国教となった時代に活躍していました。彼女は聡明な科学者で、天体観測と数学、そしてソクラテスやプラトン以来のギリシア哲学にも通じていました。彼女は天体を科学的に観測することにより、地動説にたどり着いていたのではと指摘する人もいるほどでした。エフェソス公会議の後、アレクサンドリアでは、ギリシア以来受け継がれていた科学

時代
4, 5世紀
古代

地域
ローマ

分類
宗教【学問】

キーワード
キリスト教の発展・公会議による教義の統一・学問(科学)との軋轢

ヒュパティア
Hypatia (350~370?-415)

those who pursued the sciences and philosophy inherited from the Greeks, those who believed in multiple religions and followers of Christian orthodoxy fell into frequent conflict with one another. And unfortunately, various resources of intellectual heritage that had been collected at Alexandria were destroyed.

Among the events that occurred was the kidnapping and brutal murder of Hypatia by Christian believers. This occurred in 415. In the Middle Ages, the leader of a group of monks, the Ecumenical Patriarch of Alexandria, Saint Cyril of Alexandria, who declared Nestorianism to be heretical, was declared a saint by the Pope for his contributions to the founding of the Roman Catholic Church. It would take a thousand years before the balance between religion and science could once again be restored.

028 At the time of the downfall of the Roman Empire, in Asia too, Chinese society was invaded by different ethnic groups

From the 4th century through the 5th century, as the Roman Empire treaded its downward path, in Japan the Yamato Court was solidifying the foundations of its authority and actively adopting civilization from China. In China, the Later Han had lost hold and collapsed in 220. Following this, its territories were divided into three states—Wei, Wu, and Shu—which competed among themselves for dominance. The story of the conflicts between these three kingdoms is familiar to many people even today through the Record of the Three Kingdoms and the Romance of the Three Kingdoms. The Jin dynasty reunified China, but that dynasty did not last long.

The unified dynasty of the Han Chinese disappeared for a period of time thereafter. This period is referred to as the Sixteen Kingdoms of the Five Barbarians era. The northern half of the land was conquered by northern tribes. And beginning with the Jin, in South China a number of dynasties sprang up and then disappeared.

Just as the Roman Empire was divided by the Germanic peoples, the same process occurred in East Asia. In the same manner that a tsunami occurred in the epicenter of Central Asia and flowed outward in both directions across the Eurasian Continent, from the 4th through the 5th century, different ethnic groups blended together as they reached the two cultural poles. At the same time, after the floods of Chinese and Roman culture ebbed, they once again poured back into

や哲学を探求する者や、多様な宗教を信じる者と、正当とされたキリスト教徒の間で騒乱が重なります。そして、アレクサンドリアに蓄積されていた様々な知的遺産も破壊されつつありました。

そうした中、キリスト教信徒によって、ヒュパティアは拉致され、惨殺されたのです。415年のことでした。中世になり、その修道士の一団を指導していたアレクサンドリアの総主教キュリロスは、ネストリウス派などを異端とし、ローマカトリックの創建に貢献したとして、法王により聖人に列せられます。宗教と科学の均衡がその後復活するには、1000年以上の年月を経なければならないのです。

ローマの衰亡の時期、アジアでも中華社会に異民族が侵攻した

ローマが衰亡への道を歩んでいた4世紀から5世紀にかけて、日本では大和朝廷が政権基盤を整え、中国からも積極的に文明を取り入れていました。そんな中国では、後漢が求心力を失い220年に滅亡したあと、国が魏、呉、蜀の三つにわかれ、覇権を争います。三国間の争乱の物語は、三国志、あるいは三国志演義として、今でも多くの人に親しまれています。中国を再度統一したのが晋王朝ですが、王朝は長くは続きませんでした。

漢民族による統一王朝は、その後しばらくなくなります。4世紀は、五胡十六国と呼ばれる時代です。この時代、中国の北半分は北方民族によって席巻されてしまうのです。そして、晋の末裔に始まって、華南にはいくつもの王朝が生まれては消えてゆきます。

ローマがゲルマン人などによって分断されてゆく過程と同じ状況が、東アジアでもおきるのです。ちょうど、中央アジアを震源地として発生した津波が、ユーラシア大陸の両側に伝わるかのように、4世紀から5世紀にかけて、異民族が交錯しながら二つの文化の極に到達します。同時にローマ、そして中国の文化が津波のあとの引き潮のように、中央アジアへも再度流れ込みます。この波に乗って、極東に伝播したの

時代
3〜6世紀
中国中古代

地域
中国

分類
交流【国家】

キーワード
三国志の時代・仏教の伝来・異民族の侵入・陸と海のシルクロードによる東西交流

Central Asia. With that, Buddhism was disseminated to the Far East. In addition, in China Zoroastrianism, which was venerated by the Sassanid Empire and is known for the worship of fire, and Nestorian Christianity, which was considered heresy in Rome, became active and spread.

One of the Xiongnu's rival groups, the Xianbei, spread across all of northern Asia. When the Later Han were powerful, these people paid tribute to the Han and deferred to China. However, the Xianbei extended their domains northward across the territory of the Later Han, and after the Xiongnu declined, the Xianbei conquered large areas. Eventually, within the Xianbei, the Tuoba clan gained power and established a dynasty known as the Northern Wei. Ultimately, they crossed over the Great Wall and invaded northern China, unifying all of the northern region of China in 439.

Meanwhile in southern China four independent dynasties followed after the Jin. Because various dynasties rose and fell in both the northern and southern parts of China, the period up to 589 is known as the period of the Northern and Southern Dynasties. What is important to note is that during these movements the northern peoples absorbed Chinese culture and the dynastic system, intermingled with the Chinese and assimilated. This was a global movement similar to the assimilation phenomenon that occurred between the Romans and the Germanic peoples during the Roman era.

During this period, Buddhism was transmitted to China in earnest. Among the Northern Wei, Buddhism was at one point suppressed, but on the whole, the successive monarchs earnestly protected the religion. When one observes the cave temples created in those times at places like Yungang and Longmen, one realizes just how widely East-West relations were cultivated in Central Asia after the Hellenist period.

Two regions became the stage for such East-West relations: the region stretching from northern India through Afghanistan, which was called Gandhara, and the region that stretches from south India into Southeast Asia. These are the land and sea components of the Silk Road.

Buddhism and various other religions and cultures that sprang up around Asia passed along those two routes. Over a period of several hundred years, they became rooted throughout the Far East.

が仏教です。また、中国にはその後、ササン朝で崇拝され、火を拝むことで知られるゾロアスター教や、ローマで異端とされたキリスト教ネストリウス派も伝播し、宗教活動を行っています。

　匈奴のライバルの一つで、北アジア一帯に展開していた民族に鮮卑族があります。彼らは後漢の力が強かった頃には朝貢し、中国に恭順していた時期もありました。しかし、鮮卑族は後漢の北部に拡大し、最終的には匈奴が衰退した後の広大な領土を征服します。やがて鮮卑族の中から拓跋氏が台頭し、北魏という王朝を樹立します。そしてついに彼らは万里の長城を越え、華北に侵入。西暦439年に華北全体を統一したのでした。

　一方で、華南では晋の系列から自立した4つの王朝が続きます。華北と華南にそれぞれ王朝が興亡したことから、589年までのこの時期は、南北朝時代と呼ばれているのです。大切なことは、こうした動きの中で、北方民族が中華の文化や王朝制度を吸収し、在来の中国人と混ざりながら同化していったことです。これはローマ時代にゲルマン人などとローマ人との間におこった同化現象にも似た世界的な動きでした。

　この時代、仏教が本格的に中国に伝来します。北魏では、一時仏教が弾圧されたこともありましたが、歴代の王は概ねそれを手厚く保護します。雲岡や龍門などにみられる当時の石窟寺院を見ると、そこにはヘレニズム時代以降、中央アジアに培われた東西交渉の証が見てとれます。

　そんな、東西交渉の舞台となったのは、ガンダーラと呼ばれる北部インドからアフガニスタンにかけての地域と、南インドから東南アジアにかけての二つの地域でした。陸と海のシルクロードです。

　仏教など、アジア各地でおこった様々な宗教や文化は、この二つのルートを通り、数百年という年月をかけて極東地域に流れ込み、定着していったのでした。

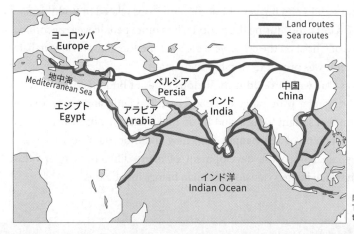

陸と海のシルクロード
The land and sea routes of
the Silk Road

029 Images transformed a human into a deity

From the period of Bactria through that of Greater Yuezhi, the people from Greece who settled in Central Asia greatly influenced the culture of the lands they eventually inhabited.

Iranian nomads in the first century A.D. defeated Greek rulers and created the Kushan Empire in northern India. Coins that the monarchy used in commerce with the Later Han in about A.D. 90 have Greek letters engraved on them. At the time, Roman territories extended from the Mediterranean into the Middle East, and there was a flourishing trade with a region called Gandhara.

In the mid-2nd century during the reign of Kanishka, the Kushan Empire extended its sway as far as the Ganges in eastern India, ruling over the territories that had once been the domain of the Maurya Empire.

Surely they were at least vaguely conscious of both memories of Hellenistic elements and Chinese society far to the east. We know that in the 3rd century there were interactions between the Kushans and the Wei.

Buddhism, which arose in India, was patronized by Kanishka and propagated widely.

The founder of Buddhism was perhaps not so much a religious figure as he was an intellectual or a philosopher. At the very least, Buddhism itself was more a way of thinking or a philosophy than a religion. Buddha as a philosopher began his teachings with an explanation of suffering in human life.

As his teachings were passed down, however, a movement began that turned him into an object of veneration. This overlapped the process in which followers began to worship statues and images of Buddha and icons related to Buddhism.

Within Christianity, too, during the period when more people were becoming believers, images of Christ on the cross were created, and there was furious debate regarding whether it was proper to worship such images.

The same was true within Buddhism. Various types of Buddhist images were being created, bringing a wide range of believers to the faith, and there was an attempt at reform that sought to turn Buddhism into a faith that had the capacity to save a large segment of the people. The new tradition became Mahayana Buddhism. One can find in the development of many different religions this process through which images transform human beings into deities.

偶像が人を神へと変身させた

　中央アジアは、バクトリア王国の時代から大月氏の時代を通し、ギリシアから入植した人々が、土地の文化に大きな影響を与えていました。

　イラン系の遊牧民が、紀元1世紀頃に、そんなギリシア系の支配者を倒し、インド北部にクシャーナ朝を興します。西暦90年頃に後漢とも交流していた王朝のコインを見ると、そこにギリシア文字が刻まれています。当時、ローマは地中海から中東地域にまで領土を拡大し、ガンダーラと呼ばれたこの地域とも盛んに交易をしていました。

　2世紀中盤に王となったカニシカの頃に、クシャーナ朝はガンディース川に沿ってインド東部まで勢力を拡大し、マウリヤ王朝の旧領を凌ぐ版図を統治します。

　彼らの意識の中には、ヘレニズムの記憶と、遠く東にある中華社会の双方がぼんやりと投影されていたはずです。3世紀には、中国の魏とクシャーナ朝とが交流していたこともわかっているのです。

　そんなインドにおこった仏教は、カニシカ王に保護されて、より広範な人々に信奉されるようになったのです。

　宗教の創始者は宗教家ではなく、思想家や哲学者だったのかもしれません。少なくとも、仏教ではそうでした。ブッダは人が生きる苦しみから解脱することを説いた哲学者でした。

　しかし、その教えを引き継ぐ中で、ブッダを信仰の対象として崇める動きが起こります。それはブッダや仏教に関する様々な偶像を拝むようになるプロセスと重なります。

　キリスト教も、より多くの人に信仰されるようになった時代になって、十字架にかかるキリスト像などが造られ、偶像を崇拝するかどうかをめぐって、激しい議論が展開されました。

　仏教も同様だったのです。仏教に関連した様々な偶像が積極的に造られ、より広範な人々を信仰に引きつけ、多くの人を仏教という器で救済しようという改革が試みられました。そうした新しい仏教を大乗仏教と呼んでいます。このように、偶像が人を神へと変身させてゆく過程が、様々な宗教の成長過程に見受けられるのです。

時代
1〜7世紀
古代

地域
インド

分類
宗教【文化】

キーワード
仏教の発展・国家の仏教保護・仏教の波及

One can see quite easily in the Buddhist images created at that time the influence of Greek culture. In the course of time, using the image of Buddha conveyed through the statues, Buddhism spread rapidly eastward. It spread through China and the Korean Peninsula and reached Japan in the first half of the 6th century.

The Kushan Empire was ousted as the Sassanid Empire gained power and expanded, and eventually the Kushan fell under the latter's control. During the more than two centuries in which the Kushan controlled northern India, civilization in the region began to undergo a transformation from one based on Hellenistic elements to one based on particularly Indian elements.

030 The winds bore culture

The activities of humankind are closely related with the planet's weather conditions. From early summer through early autumn, winds from the southwest blow from the Indian Ocean toward the Arabian Sea; from late autumn through spring northeasterly winds blow in the opposite direction. These winds are caused by changes in the atmospheric pressure over the mainland and over the ocean. These seasonal winds are called monsoons, a word derived from Arabic. In ancient times, people made use of these changing winds to engage in cultural exchange.

The dry winds from the continent in winter and the humid winds from the sea in summer are known as the dry monsoon and wet monsoon, respectively.

In early-modern times, Europeans traveled along the west coast of Africa all the way around the Cape of Good Hope to reach the India. But long before the Europeans discovered that route, people in the Middle East had perfect command of the monsoon winds, using them to sail back and forth across the Arabian Sea and the Indian Ocean.

When the Kushan Empire controlled northern India, the Satavahana Kingdom ruled the south. This was during the period when the Roman Empire was flourishing.

A merchant in one of the major cities, such as Alexandria along the Mediterranean Sea, might sail by way of the Red Sea to the Arabian Sea, catching the dry monsoon winds to reach the eastern coast of India. The jewels that could be procured in India and Ceylon would bring large profits in Rome. Coins from the Roman Empire have been found in excavated ruins from the Satavahana Kingdom.

当時の仏像には明らかにギリシア文化の影響が見受けられます。やがて、仏像の持つブッダへの明快なイメージによって、仏教は急速に東へと伝播します。中国に、朝鮮半島に、そして日本に仏教が伝来したのは、6世紀前半頃だったといわれています。

クシャーナ朝は、ササン朝が勢力を拡大する中で駆逐され、最終的にはその支配下におかれます。クシャーナ朝が北インドを支配した200年強の間、ヘレニズムから、よりインド独特の文化圏へと文明が変貌を始めたといわれています。

風が文化を運んでいった

人の行動は地球の気象とも深く関わります。初夏から初秋にかけて南西の風が、逆に晩秋から春にかけて北東の風がインド洋からアラビア海におこります。それは、大陸と海との気圧の変化によっておきる風です。元々アラビア語を語源とするモンスーンというこの季節風。人々は古来、この風を捉えて航海をして、文物の交流をしていました。

時代
1〜5世紀
古代

地域
インド

分類
交流【経済】

キーワード
海上での交易・季節風に
乗った貿易・ヒンドゥー
教の発展

冬は大陸からの乾燥した風、そして夏は海の湿気を吸い上げて吹く湿気の多い風がおこることから、それぞれの季節風をドライモンスーン、そしてウエットモンスーンと呼んでいます。

近世にヨーロッパの人々がはるばる喜望峰をまわってインドへの道を発見する遥か以前から、中東の人々は、モンスーンを捉えて航海をする技術を駆使して、アラビア海からインド洋にかけて航海をしていたのです。

クシャーナ朝が北インドを制圧していた頃、その南にはサータヴァーハナという王朝がありました。それはちょうどローマ帝国の最盛期でもありました。

例えばアレクサンドリアなどの地中海に面した主要都市の商人は、紅海からドライモンスーンにのってアラビア海を経てインドの東海岸まで航海します。インドやセイロンで採れる宝石などがローマで珍重されていたのです。サータヴァーハナ王朝の遺跡からはローマ帝国のコインが発掘されているのです。

Voyages making use of these monsoon winds passed along the sea-route version of the Silk Roads, traveling east and west by ship.

The land and sea Silk Roads were first used long ago.

As early as *The History of the Later Han*, one finds references to the Roman Empire in Chinese records. A delegation from the Roman Empire is recorded in this particular historical account in the Later Han Empire in 166. Whether this entourage was an official one or not is unclear. It is also possible that India had become a transfer point. A merchant from the Middle East might arrive in India with goods from the West to sell. Another merchant from India or Southeast Asia might then transfer those goods to China.

Following the collapse of Kushan and the extinction of the Satavahana Kingdom, the Gupta Empire arose in the 3rd century in eastern India. Chandragupta I became king in 320 and unified the Indian world, with the exception of south India. These people continued the trade using the monsoon winds.

At that time, Hinduism adopted ancient Brahman ceremonies and religious precepts and began taking on unique aspects of indigenous Indian beliefs, and these spread throughout the Indian world. The Gupta adopted Hinduism as the orthodox state religion, and in Indian society today it is the mainstream belief.

Incidentally, Hindu is the origin of the word India.

031 History is further told by the encounter between writing and paper

There were two famous historians in ancient Greece.

Herodotus wrote an account of the history of Greece through the world of the Middle East in his *Historia*, focusing on the 5th century B.C. Persian Wars. Thucydides, a contemporary of Herodotus, wrote about the Peloponnesian War in his *History of the Peloponnesian War*. While Herodotus viewed the war with Persia from the Greek point of view, Thucydides took a more even-handed approach, objectively portraying the surrounding conditions. Although history at that time was not a science, that does not change the fact that it was a resource that transmitted through the written word what was observed.

Chinese society from ancient times recorded various historical tales on

この風に乗った航海が海のシルクロードと呼ばれ、海を利用した東西交易のルートとなるのです。

　陸のシルクロード、そして海のシルクロードを通って東西交流が始まったのはかなり古い時代からでした。

　後漢の史書である『後漢書』には既にローマ帝国についての記述がみられます。後漢の頃西暦166年にローマ帝国の使節が訪ねてきたというのですが、それが公式な使節であったかどうかは、定かでありません。インドが中継地点となっていたのかもしれません。インドまで到達した中東の商人がもたらした西の文物が、今度はインドや東南アジアの商人によって中国に届けられたのではないかといわれています。

　クシャーナ朝が滅び、サータヴァーハナ朝も消滅した後、東インドに3世紀に興ったグプタ朝は、チャンドラグプタ1世が王となった320年に、南インドを除くインド世界を統一します。彼らはこのモンスーンを使った交易を引き継ぎます。

　その当時、古代のバラモン教の儀式や戒律に、インド独特の土着信仰が加味されたヒンドゥー教がインド世界に拡散します。グプタ朝ではヒンドゥー教は国教となり、現代のインド社会の源流となるのです。

　ちなみに、ヒンドゥーとは、インドという単語の語源でもあるのです。

ヘロドトス
Herodotus

トゥキディデス
Thucydides (?–395 B.C.)

文字と紙の出会いで歴史は さらに語られる

　古代ギリシアには二人の有名な歴史家がいました。

　一人は、紀元前5世紀のペルシア戦争を軸に、ギリシアから中東世界の歴史を記述し『ヒストリア』という著述を残したヘロドトス。そしてもう一人は、ヘロドトスとほぼ同時代に生き、ペロポネソス戦争の時代を『ギリシア史』としてまとめたトゥキディデスです。ヘロドトスがよりギリシアの見解からペルシアとの戦いを見ていたのに対して、トゥキディデスはより、客観的に周囲の状況を描いた公正さが評価されています。しかし、当時の歴史が科学ではなく、言葉と文字によってのみ伝承され、見聞したことがその記述のリソースであったことには変わりはありません。

　中国社会は、古来竹簡に様々な歴史物語が記述されていました。春

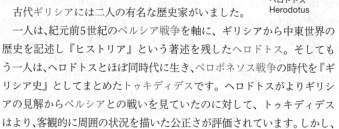

時代
総合

地域
共通

分類
文化【言語】

キーワード
歴史の記述・紙と文字

bamboo writing strips. From the Spring and Autumn and Warring States periods come writings that range from the consolidation of teachings of Confucianism known as the Nine Chinese Classics to Sun Tzu's *The Art of War*. The writings of these and other prominent thinkers who shared the limelight as the Hundred Schools of Thought have been handed down to the present.

Sima Qian, who lived in the first century A.D., is known for compiling the ancient history of China. In the period of Wu Di in the Earlier Han, Sima Qian compiled an immense record of historical episodes from ancient China through the Earlier Han. This work is known as the *Historical Records*. Sima Qian was well-traveled and was employed as a senior official under Wu Di. However, for having defended a friend, he was made a eunuch, and ended up devoting the rest of his life to compiling this history.

In 105 Cai Lun invented paper. It is well known that papyrus was used in Egypt as a form of paper, but papyrus was coarse and took up a lot of space. With the invention of paper, it became possible for the various dynasties of China to record detailed histories of the previous dynasty and preserve these records. Further, the writings of a large number of thinkers were passed on to later generations.

In the historical records of China one finds information regarding the neighboring states and the ethnic groups who came to China to pay tribute as well as accounts of people who were sent forth on expeditions and investigations under orders from the rulers. Although Japan's ancient history is blurry at best, the fact that we are able to grasp any information about Japan at that time is thanks to accounts in the *Record of Encounters with the Eastern Barbarians in the History of the Later Han* and the *Record of Japan in The History of Wei*.

It is hard to know just how accurate historical records at that time actually were. For historians such as Sima Qian to carefully gather information by traveling, actually gathering material, and putting together hearsay must have required considerable effort. Within a civilization that possessed a written culture, where even the writing itself is not elucidated, there are many ways in which the state of affairs of that history remain hard to grasp. Maya civilization, which was created in Central America by descendants of human immigrants who reached the American continent in the glacial period, formed a monarchy that excelled in mathematics and astronomy, but there are many elements of their written language which remain unclear, and the details of their history remains partially undecipherable. By contrast, China invented paper, and based on Chinese characters and paper, they have left a treasure trove of historical works.

秋戦国時代になると、四書五経と呼ばれる儒教の教えをまとめた著作物や、『孫子』などの戦略書に至るまで、当時諸子百家として脚光を浴びた思想家の記述が残されています。

　そんな古代中国の歴史をまとめたことで知られているのが、紀元1世紀を生きた司馬遷でした。司馬遷は前漢の武帝の時代に、古代中国から前漢に至る膨大な歴史上のエピソードをまとめました。『史記』と呼ばれる歴史書です。司馬遷は、旅行家でもあり、武帝に高官としても用いられていました。しかし、友人をかばったことから宦官にされ、残りの人生のほとんどを、この『史記』の編纂に費やしたのです。

　西暦105年に、蔡倫という人物が紙を発明します。エジプトで、パピルスが紙のように使用されていたことは有名ですが、それは粗くかさばるものでした。本格的な紙の発明で、中国でのそれぞれの王朝が、その前の王朝の詳細な歴史を記述し、保存することができるようになりました。また、多くの思想家の著述も後世に伝えられました。
　中国の歴史書には、王朝に朝貢してきた周辺の国家や民族、さらには国の命令で探検や探索に出た人々の記録も収録されています。日本の古代史がおぼろげながら我々に見えてくるのは、当時の日本の状況が、『後漢書東夷伝』や『魏志倭人伝』などに記されていたからです。

　当時の歴史書がどこまで信頼できるか、それはなんともいえません。司馬遷のような歴史家が旅をして実際に収集した情報と、伝聞によって綴られた話の中から、丁寧に事実をあぶり出してゆくには、相当の作業が必要です。文字文化を持った文明の中には、まだその文字自体が解明されず、その歴史の実態がつかめないものも沢山あります。氷河期にアメリカ大陸に移住した人類の子孫が中米でおこしたマヤ文明は、数学や天文学に秀でた王国を形成していたとされていますが、解明されていない文字も多く、歴史の詳細は不明です。逆に、紙を発明した中国は、漢字と紙とによって史書の宝庫となってゆくのです。

032 In the Sui era, canals shortened distances in the Chinese world

In order for Chinese civilization, including the paper invented by Cai Lun, to spread westward, a powerful dynasty needed to be established in China and its influence had to reach Central Asia. The sudden rise of the Chinese Empire that began with the Sui and continued with the Tang met that requirement.

The Chinese expression about traveling in the south by boat and in the north on horseback is used to refer to restless wandering or constant traveling. In the south of China there are a large number of rivers, and a large number of canals linking these rivers so that people can interact by way of navigation. In the north, however, because the land is dry, winters are harsh, and deserts are numerous, people are forced to travel about on horseback.

Emperor Yang of the Sui dynasty, was the one who opened the great canal that linked northern and southern China. Emperor Wen, Emperor Yang's father, reorganized northern China after it broke apart following the decline of the Northern Wei. At the same time, he ousted the monarchies in southern China, unifying all of China in 589. Perhaps Emperor Yang felt that the construction of this major canal would be essential for unifying China and managing it militarily. Through its construction, distribution logistics throughout China improved significantly.

To be sure, the saying about travel by water in the south and on horseback in the north applied not only to methods of distribution from ancient times but also accurately describes the geographical features themselves. It was in the south that rice cultivation took hold early on, and it is thought that rice culture was transmitted to Japan from that region.

In the north, there was a continuous mingling of northern tribal people and Han Chinese. During the time of Emperor Wen, a group known as the Tujue, who excelled in the production of iron, expanded their influence, placing large areas of Central and North Asia under their control while also watching for opportunities in north China.

Numerous horse-riding peoples, including the Xiongnu, Xianbei, and Tujue, moved south, crossing over the Great Wall. Sometimes they cooperated in the administration of China; other times they invaded China, became assimilated, and established kingships there. Emperor Yang of the Sui had such roots in these northern ethnic groups.

Among these northern groups were the horse-riding people of Tungus derivation. They migrated south into the Korean Peninsula and established the

隋の時代に運河が中国世界の距離を縮めた

　蔡倫の発明した紙をはじめ、中国文明が西へと伝播するには、中国に強大な王朝が生まれ、その影響が中央アジアに及ばなければなりません。隋から唐に至る中華帝国の勃興がその要望に応えてゆきます。

　南船北馬という言葉があります。中国の南部は河川が多く、そこを縫う運河なども発達し、人は船で航行し交流します。しかし、北部は土地が乾燥し、冬は厳しく砂漠も多いため、人は馬で移動していました。

【時代】
6, 7世紀
中国中古代

【地域】
中国

【分類】
統一【経済】

【キーワード】
隋による中国の再統一・大運河による南北の交通・周辺民族との攻防・唐の成立

　この華北と華南とを結ぶ大運河を開通させたのが、隋の皇帝であった煬帝でした。煬帝の父に当たる楊堅が、北魏以降分裂再編を繰り返していた華北をまとめあげ、同時に華南の王朝も駆逐して中国世界を統一したのが589年のことでした。煬帝にとっては、中国を統一し、軍事的にも管理するために、この大運河の工事が必要だったのかもしれません。これによって中国の物流状況は大幅に改善されました。

　確かに、南船北馬という言葉の通り、華北と華南では古来より物流手段のみならず、風土そのものが異なっていました。稲作文化が早くから根付いたのは華南で、そこから日本へも稲作が伝わったのではないかといわれています。

　華北を見ると、そこでは常に北方民族と漢民族とが交錯していました。楊堅の時代、鉄の製造に長けた突厥という民族が膨張し、中央アジアから北アジアにかけて広大な大地を傘下におさめながら、華北を狙っていたのです。
　匈奴に始まり、鮮卑、そして突厥など、幾多の騎馬民族が、万里の長城を越えて南下し、時には中華の政権に協力したり、逆に侵略と共に中国社会と同化しながら、そこに王朝を造ったのでした。隋の煬帝も、そのルーツには北方民族の血が混じっていました。

　そうした北方民族の一つにツングース系の騎馬民族がありました。彼らは、その後朝鮮半島に南下し、高句麗を建国します。彼らは、匈

country of Koguryo. They, along with groups like the Xiongnu, the Xianbei, and the Göktürks, would have been a threat in the eyes of the Chinese dynasties.

Koguryo developed into a strong country occupying land from the northeast of present-day China to the middle of the Korean Peninsula, and the Sui could not simply let them be.

Emperor Yang deployed a large army to deal with Koguryo, but the attempt failed. Exhausted by the economic burden of constructing the canal and by the defeat of his military expedition, Emperor Yang turned into a tyrant of unprecedented brutality. He was assassinated in 618 and, all too quickly, the Sui were overthrown.

Just as the short-lived Qin dynasty concluded the Warring States period and the subsequent Han dynasty unified China for over 400 years through the earlier and later Han dynasties, the Tang dynasty, which unified China after the Sui dynasty, maintained a powerful centralized rule over China for 289 years, much like the Roman Empire, establishing itself as a great superpower.

Under the Tang rulers, various neighboring states were able to enjoy the benefits of Chinese civilization, and the entire East Asian cultural world thrived as a result. The Korean Peninsula and Japan were no exceptions. In the middle of the 7th century, the Yamato Court in Japan strengthened its administrative foundations and completed a version of the legal system that it had learned from China.

033 **From the diplomatic policy of the Yamato administration, one can see the international situation at that time**

How did China appear to statesmen in ancient Japan?

When we consider ancient history, there is one thing that we should always be cautious about. As we understand when we look at contemporary history, the world can change significantly in a 20-year period. However, there is a tendency when looking at ancient history to summarize past events in terms of centuries, rather than decades. If we do this, it is easy to fall into the habit of thinking in stereotypes and generalizations.

The history of the Korean Peninsula, which had close relations with Japan's ancient history, is a perfect example of this unfortunate tendency.

Between the Chinese dynasties of Qin, Han, and Tang, over a period of 800

奴や鮮卑、そして突厥などと共に、中国の王朝から見れば脅威であったはずです。

　高句麗は現在の中国東北地方から朝鮮半島中部までを領有する強大な国家に成長し、隋にとっても、放置できない存在となりました。

　煬帝は大軍を送って高句麗に対応しますが、失敗します。運河建設などの経済的負担と、遠征の失敗による疲弊により、煬帝は歴代希有の暴君とされ、618年に暗殺され、隋はあっけなく滅んでしまったのです。

　ちょうど、戦国時代をまとめあげた秦が短命に終わり、それを受け継いだ漢が、前漢と後漢を通して400年以上中国を統一したように、隋の後に中国を統一した唐は、ローマと同様の超大国として、289年間にわたって中国に強大な統一政権を維持しました。

　唐のもと、周辺諸国も中国文明の恩恵にあずかり、東アジア文化圏全体が繁栄したのです。朝鮮半島、そして日本も例外ではありませんでした。7世紀中盤に、日本でも大和朝廷がその政権基盤を強化し、中国に習った法律制度を整えていったのでした。

大和の外交政策から、当時の国際情勢が見えてくる

　古代日本の為政者には、中国はどのように映ったのでしょうか。
　我々は古代史を語るときにも、気をつけなければならないことがあります。現代史を見れば理解できるように、世の中は20年も経てば大きく変化します。しかし、古代史は、百年単位の出来事をまとめて語る傾向があり、ともすれば、そこに当時の状況に対するステレオタイプが生まれがちなのです。

　日本の古代史と密接な関わりを持つ、朝鮮半島の歴史はその典型です。
　中国の秦や漢の時代から唐に至るまで、朝鮮半島は800年以上にか

時代
7世紀以前
古代

地域
日本

分類
国家【交流】

キーワード
日本のあけぼの・大陸との交流・百済の滅亡と日本の動揺・遣隋使と遣唐使

years and more, the Korean Peninsula changed rapidly. Those changes occurred in periods of basically a decade or so. The Korean Peninsula was constantly menaced by China in the west and various groups in the north. And from the perspective of the Korean Peninsula, it was necessary to keep in mind the influence of another people to the south: the Wa, in other words, the people of ancient Japan.

The people called Japanese are said to have descended from various peoples from the continent and the south who came across the sea. In order to maintain its power base, the Yamato Court actively adopted culture from the mainland. Particularly important in that function were those who came from Baekje in the southern part of the Korean Peninsula. It is believed that the descendants of the Baekje and Koguryo were Tungus people. They were exposed to the threat of Koguryo, which was expanding its influence from the north, and sought to strengthen their relations not only with Silla, the neighboring country to the east but also with the emerging Yamato court. Of course, the Yamato court must have considered how to support Baekje in order to absorb continental culture.

However, from the late 4th century until the 5th century, conditions changed completely. The strength of Silla as a country expanded significantly. In particular, the Sui military expedition against Koguryo provided a perfect opportunity for Silla to counter threats from the north. The newly strengthened Silla became a new menace to Baekje. Silla strengthened diplomatic relations with the Tang, who had unified China, and pitted itself against Baekje and Koguryo.

The Yamato Court attempted to support Baekje, but ultimately Silla destroyed Baekje, and in 663 the reinforcements sent by the Yamato Court were absolutely devastated by the Tang navy. Five years later, Koguryo was also wiped out by the Tang.

The Yamato Court had sent envoys to the Sui dynasty and did the same to the Tang dynasty, continuing to absorb Chinese civilization. At the same time, political affairs on the Korean Peninsula remained edgy, and on occasion there were fierce confrontations with China.

Scrutinizing the Japanese state of affairs from the perspective of Tang China, we can see it as one model of how the neighboring peoples dealt with the powerful country the Tang developed.

In order to strengthen their own countries and absorb Chinese civilization, they used cooperation with neighboring countries, as well as confrontation with them, as strategies. This may well have been the strategy adopted by the neighboring peoples to ensure their survival when Chinese dynasties were expanding. The Yamato Court was in no way an exception to this pattern.

けてめまぐるしく変化します。それはまさに数十年単位の変化でした。朝鮮半島には、常に西にあった中国と、北方民族の脅威がありました。そして、朝鮮半島から見るならば南方の民族である「倭」、すなわち古代日本の影響も考慮しなければなりません。

　日本人という民族は、大陸や南方などから海を渡ってきた人々が、その祖先であるといわれています。大和朝廷は政権基盤を維持するために、積極的に大陸の文化を取り入れました。特に朝鮮半島南西部にあった百済から渡来した人々が、その役割を担っていたのです。百済の子孫も高句麗と同じツングース系の民族ではないかといわれています。彼らは、北方から勢力を拡大してきた高句麗の脅威に晒され、東の隣国の新羅のみならず、積極的に黎明期の大和朝廷との関係を強化したかったのです。もちろん大和朝廷も、大陸の文化を吸収するために、いかに百済を支援しようかと考えたはずです。

　しかし、4世紀の終わり頃から5世紀にかけて情勢が一変します。新羅の国力が著しく伸長してきたのです。特に隋の高句麗遠征は、新羅にとっては北方の脅威に対抗する絶好の機会であったはずです。強国となった新羅は、百済にとっての新たな脅威となりました。新羅は、中国を統一した唐と外交関係を強化し、百済と高句麗に対抗しようとしたのです。
　大和朝廷は百済を支援しようとしますが、最終的に新羅が百済を滅ぼし、大和朝廷の援軍も663年に唐の水軍によって壊滅させられます。その5年後には、高句麗も唐によって滅ぼされてしまうのです。

　大和朝廷は、隋には遣隋使を送っていました。その後唐にも遣唐使を送り、中国文明を吸収します。同時に、朝鮮半島の政治情勢には常に神経を尖がらせ、時には中国とも政治的に激しく対立します。

　この日本の状況を、中国を中心にした視点で眺めると、唐という強大な国家に対して、周囲の民族がどう対応をしたのかという一つのモデルが見えてきます。
　国力を充実させるために、中国の文明を吸収しながらも、常に隣国との連携や対立を利用して中国との外交を考える。これが、中華王朝が膨張したときの周辺民族のサバイバル術だったのかもしれません。大和朝廷も決して例外ではなかったのです。

第三部

暮らしの安定と停滞の時代（中世の世界）

Part Three:
The Stabilization of Life and the Age of Stagnation (The Medieval World)

　この時代、世界の多くの地域では、ヒトは古代に生まれた宗教の下に統率されていました。一方で、古代文明が築き上げた伝統と権威は、富を求めて様々な地域から移動してきた民族によって受け継がれ、地球上の版図が目まぐるしく塗り替えられてゆきました。

　そこに、三大宗教の最後のプレイヤーであるイスラム教世界が急速な拡大を続け、現代にまで続くキリスト教社会との確執が始まりました。中国は、北方民族の度重なる南下にさらされます。その過程で、次第に中国文明も各地に広がってゆきました。西欧世界、中近東、そして南アジアと東アジア。これらの文化圏がだんだんと固定され、その接点を通した交流も活発になったのです。

　中世という一見宗教と戒律に縛られていたかのように見える世界の中で、何万年も前に地球の隅々に拡散したヒトたちは、お互いの存在を知るようになり、拡散から交流へと舵をきり始めたのでした。それは、決して平和な活動だけではなく、時には血によって贖われ、剣によって切り裂き合う交流でもあったのです。

034 The Roman Empire was encroached upon, while its culture and authority spread

Throughout the 5th and 6th centuries, at the time the Yamato dynasty was establishing its ruling system in Japan and northern peoples were sweeping through the northern part of China, there was a turbulent situation with numerous competing states. Simultaneously, Europe and the Mediterranean world were also experiencing a transitional phase, preparing for the unfolding of the next era of history.

The process of the decline of the Roman Empire was, in turn, a process of the penetration of Roman civilization by the invading Germanic peoples and other ethnic groups from the north. It would not be an exaggeration to say that as Roman power declined, the incoming Germanic people who settled in that fading empire actually protected it. The means by which different ethnic groups protected their own footing by using Roman authority resembled the actions of the peoples around China who used Chinese authority on their own behalf.

The Germanic people were not one single group. The various ethnic groups repeatedly cooperated with and then confronted each other, each learning from Roman civilization how to construct their own respective states.

The German Odoacer, a mercenary in the Roman army, led a revolt that destroyed the Western Roman Empire in 476. From that point onward, the Eastern Roman Empire, which succeeded to Roman traditions, granted authority to such peoples while resorting to a subtle use of influence throughout the European world.

In due course, Theodoric the Amal, with the support of the Eastern Roman Empire, led the Goths against and defeated Odoacer, turning Italy into the Kingdom of the Ostrogoths. Although it was merely for appearance's sake, the establishment of this kingdom was recognized by the Eastern Roman Empire.

The same thing had occurred previously. As a result of the decline of the Western Roman Empire, when it became impossible to govern what is now southern France, the same Goths took possession of that territory, ostensibly as a delegation of authority. When the Western Roman Empire collapsed completely, these peoples migrated into the Iberian Peninsula and established the Visigothic Kingdom.

Another Germanic people, the Vandals—after they were pressured by the

ローマは侵食され、文化と権威を
浸透させた

　日本では大和朝廷が支配体制を整えていた頃、そして、中国では北方民族が華北一帯を席巻し、いくつもの国家が乱立していた5世紀から6世紀にかけて、ヨーロッパや地中海世界も次の歴史のうねりに向けた過渡期にありました。

　ローマ帝国の衰亡の過程は、逆にローマの文明が北方から侵入したゲルマン人などの民族に浸透する過程だったのです。衰亡期のローマの権威は、そこに移住していたゲルマン系の人々によって守られていたといっても過言ではありませんでした。ローマの権威を使って自らの基盤を維持する異民族のやり方は、中華の権威を活用する中国周辺の民族の動きとも似たものがありました。

　ゲルマン人は一つのかたまりではありません。種族ごとに協調と対立とを繰り返しながら、それぞれがローマにならって国家を築いてゆきました。

　ローマの傭兵だったゲルマン人のオドアケルが、西ローマ帝国を滅ぼしたのが476年。その後ローマの伝統を引き継いだ東ローマ帝国は、そうした民族に権威を与えながら、ヨーロッパ世界に微妙な影響力を行使していたのです。

　やがて、東ローマに支援された、ゴート族のテオドリックがオドアケルを破り、イタリアに東ゴート王国をひらきます。建前とはいえ、それはローマ帝国が承認した国家の建設という形式をとりました。

　以前にも、同様のことがありました。西ローマ帝国の衰退によって統治ができなくなった現在の南フランスを、同じゴート族が西ローマ帝国から権限を委譲される名目で占有していたのです。やがて、西ローマ帝国が滅亡すると、彼らはイベリア半島に移住し、そこで西ゴート王国を建国します。

　一方、ゲルマン民族の一つヴァンダル族は、5世紀初頭にフン族に押

時代
5世紀
欧州中世

地域
ヨーロッパ

分類
民族【侵略】

キーワード
ゲルマン民族の大移動・西ローマ帝国の崩壊・ゲルマン国家の成立・東ローマ帝国の存続

Huns at the start of the 5th century into Spain—under the command of Gunderic and his successor Gaiseric, migrated to northern Africa. Establishing his base of operations at Carthage, capital of the ancient Phoenicians, Gaiseric founded the Vandal Kingdom. The Vandal peoples, one tribal group at a time, carried out a long march from northeastern Europe into north Africa.

In this manner, the Mediterranean world that had been governed by the Roman Empire changed into states taken over by Germanic peoples and northern ethnic groups. In the growth process, they made use of the authority of the collapsed Western Roman Empire, while at the same time applying powerful military pressure on the Roman Empire and expanding their own rights and interests.

Following the complete disappearance of the Western Roman Empire, the Eastern Roman Empire became in real terms the Roman Empire. In the first half of the 6th century, under the leadership of Justinian I, it was able to momentarily restore the better part of its power around the Mediterranean Sea and was able to destroy the Vandal and Ostrogoth kingdoms. Further, while maintaining a balance with the neighboring Sassanid Empire, it was able to control the entirety of what is now Turkey.

All of this military activity, however, required enormous sums of money. After that, the Eastern Roman Empire was exposed to invasion by foreign enemies, and although it repeatedly expanded and contracted, it was never able to unite the Mediterranean world again.

035 Islam spread as a religion of Abraham

Justinian I was an emperor who sought to regain the power and influence of the Roman Empire. He is known not only for his foreign military expeditions, but also for his compilation of the Roman legal system, known as the *Corpus Iuris Civilis*, which formed the basis of the state's organization. The Eastern Roman Empire filled the role of successor to Greco-Roman culture.

Let us for a moment think about religions. In Shinto, Japan's ancient religion, Amaterasu Omikami, the Sun Goddess, is held to be the god among gods. Amaterasu is enshrined and worshipped at Ise Shrine. In Greece, the god among the gods was Zeus. In Hinduism, there are three gods who together are considered

されるようにスペインに流れ込んだ後、グンデリックとその遺志をついだガイセリックに率いられ、北アフリカに移動します。そして昔フェニキア人が首都にしたカルタゴを本拠地にして、ヴァンダル王国をつくります。ヴァンダル族は、一つの民族集団ごと北東ヨーロッパから北アフリカへの大行軍を成し遂げたのです。

このように、ローマ帝国が統治していた地中海世界は、そのままゲルマン人や北方民族の国家へと変わっていったのです。彼らは、成長の過程で、衰弱した西ローマ帝国の権威を利用し、同時にローマ帝国にも強い軍事的な圧力をかけながら自らの権益を拡大したのでした。

西ローマ帝国なきあとは、東ローマ帝国が実質上のローマ帝国でした。6世紀前半には、ユスティニアヌス1世の強い指導力の元で、地中海の大半を一時的に回復し、ヴァンダルや東ゴートといった王国も滅ぼしました。また、隣国ササン朝ペルシアとの均衡も保ちながら、現在のトルコ一帯を支配します。

しかし、こうした軍事活動には膨大な経費がかかります。その後も東ローマ帝国は外敵の侵入にさらされながら、膨張と縮小を繰り返しはしたものの、二度と地中海世界をまとめ上げることはできなかったのです。

イスラム教は「アブラハムの宗教」として拡大した

ユスティニアヌス1世は、ローマ帝国の威光を取り戻そうとした皇帝でした。彼は外征のみならず、『ローマ法大全』とよばれるローマ時代の法体系を集大成し、国家制度の基本に据えたことでも知られています。東ローマ帝国は、ギリシアローマ文化の継承者としての役割を担っていったのでした。

ここで宗教について考えます。日本古来の宗教である神道では、天照大神が数多くの神の中の神とされています。その天照大神が祀られ、敬われているのが伊勢神宮です。ギリシアでは神々の神はゼウスでした。ヒンドゥー教では、ブラフマー、ヴィシュヌ、シヴァという3体

時代
7世紀
イスラム初期

地域
アラビア

分類
宗教【社会】

キーワード
多神教、自然崇拝と一神教・イスラム教の成立・イスラム教とキリスト教

the greatest of the many gods: Brahma, Vishnu, and Shiva. In many polytheistic religions around the world there are certain deities that are seen as particularly worthy of worship and have become objects of veneration and faith. In Shinto the mirror is symbolic of the presence of the deity and things in the natural world such as rocks and trees are seen as possessing divine nature. In the same way, many other religions project upon natural phenomena the manifestations of deities.

The Arabian Peninsula is no exception. A similar form of polytheistic religion is found there, too. The god among gods is Allah. The various gods were worshipped at a shrine in Mecca. Among those who follow the faith of Islam today, the most important shrine is the Kaaba, formerly the shrine where all the various gods were enshrined. It was the Prophet Muhammad who declared that Allah was the one and only absolute deity, and that believers could worship no other deities or worship any kind of idol. The Islamic faith which he founded later created a major rivalry not only with the Eastern Roman Empire but also with the entire European world.

Muhammad claimed that the prophet Abraham, then Moses, and finally Jesus all insisted upon the worship of only one absolute deity, and Muhammad himself was the final prophet that would appear with the same message. Muhammad claimed that God had entrusted all the teachings for humankind in the Quran and that followers should keep faith with those words entrusted to Muhammad. Muhammad was persecuted and forced out of Mecca in 622. This flight from Mecca is called the Hijra, and it is, in Islamic history, considered the founding date of the faith.

世界のおもな宗教
Major Religions of the World

	ユダヤ教 Judaism	キリスト教 Christianity	イスラム教 Islam	仏教 Buddhism	ヒンドゥー教 Hinduism
神 God	ヤハウェ (一神教) Yahweh (monotheism)	父なる神ー子なるイエスー聖霊（三位一体） God the Father - Jesus the Son of God - the Holy Spirit (Trinity)	アラー (一神教) Allah (monotheism)	なし None	ブラフマー，ヴィシュヌ，シヴァ (多神教) Brahma, Vishnu, Shiva (polytheism)
開祖 Founder	モーゼ Moses	イエス Jesus	ムハンマド Muhammad	ゴータマ・シッダールタ（ブッダ） Gautama Siddhartha (Buddha)	特定できない unspecified
聖典 Scriptures	『旧約聖書』 Old Testament	『旧約聖書』 Old Testament 『新約聖書』 New Testament	『コーラン』 Quran	多数の仏典 Many Buddhist scriptures	ヴェーダなど 多数 The Vedas and many more

の神が最高神であると信じられています。このように、世界中の多神教の多くには、神々の神と呼ばれ崇拝される最高神がいて、信仰の対象となっているのです。そして、神道では神の存在を象徴する鏡があり、石や木など自然界の造物にも神性を見るように、多くの宗教は、神の化身を自然現象に投影します。

　アラビア半島も例外ではありませんでした。そこにも同様の多神教があり、その神々の神がアラーであったといわれています。メッカには、そうした神々を祀る神殿がありました。それが、現在イスラム教を信奉する人々にとって、最も大切な神殿とされるカーバの昔の様子だったのです。そのアラーを絶対唯一の神とし、他の神を拝んではならず、偶像も崇拝してはならないと主張したのが、ムハンマドという預言者でした。彼がおこしたイスラム教は、その後東ローマ帝国のみならず、ヨーロッパ世界との大きな対立項を作ってゆきます。

　ムハンマドは、唯一絶対の神を拝むように主張した過去の預言者アブラハムや、モーゼ、そしてキリストの後、自らが最後に現れた預言者で、彼に神が託した言葉であるコーランをもってその教えを守るように人々に訴えたのです。622年に彼は迫害されメッカを追われます。この逃避行をヒジュラとよび、それがイスラム暦の元年となりました。

Muhammad left Mecca to take refuge in Medina, and there he created the Ummah, the community of Muslims. With the Ummah as its center, the Muslims retook Mecca in 630. Muhammad destroyed the Kaaba shrine where all the various gods were venerated, and it was transformed into a holy site where Allah, the one and only absolute deity was worshipped. The Kaaba is believed to be the place where the Black Stone, which has been passed down since the time of Adam and Eve and is considered significant in the Old Testament as the descendant of Abraham's son Ishmael, is housed.

From this one realizes that originally Islam, Judaism, and Christianity all spring from the same source. That is why the three religions are referred to as Abrahamic religions. It is ironic that these three "siblings" have from their very foundations to the present day violently opposed one another and fought among themselves. The new world religion called Islam was born in the Middle Ages, a period in which, under its influence, people repeated a cycle of opposition and unification among themselves time and time again.

036 Islam was flexible when it came to other religions

Once Mecca became a holy site, in the mosques, or Islamic places of worship, a niche in the wall called a mihrab was constructed. This niche indicated the point nearest to the Kaaba in Mecca, toward which the congregations faced when they prayed. In accord with the Quran worshippers were to face that direction when they prayed five times a day.

Islam, with the solidarity of belief in a single deity, rapidly gained influence across the Arabian Peninsula, and in 651, it destroyed the Sassanid dynasty, which had weakened due to conflict with the Eastern Roman Empire. It advanced further, even into territories of the Eastern Roman Empire, continuing its conquests, even forcing Egypt under its wing.

Where converts grew in number, it was necessary to obtain a place to settle. In one sense, a new religion penetrates not so much people with vested interests but, first of all, people of the lower social strata. The religious piety of those people becomes a surge under a capable leader and can evolve into a powerful military capability. One example of this phenomenon in Japan, for example, occurred

メッカからメディナに避難したムハンマドがそこにイスラム教徒、ムスリムの共同体ウンマを作ります。このウンマを中心に、ムスリムが最終的にメッカを奪還したのが630年です。ムハンマドは、カーバ神殿に安置されていた様々な神を破壊し、アラーを崇める一神教の聖地にします。カーバは、旧約聖書で人類の祖先とされるアブラハムの息子であるイシュマエルの命令で、アダムとイブの時代から伝わる黒石を収めているとされる場所なのです。

　このことからもおわかりのように、元はといえば、イスラム教もユダヤ教も、そしてキリスト教も、源流を共有する宗教なのです。この三つの宗教を「アブラハムの宗教」と呼んでいるのはそうした理由によるものです。その兄弟が、その後厳しく対立し、争い、今に至るのは皮肉なことです。中世はイスラム教という新しい世界宗教が生まれ、その影響の中で人々が対立と融合を繰り返した時代でもあったのです。

イスラム教徒は、他の宗教に対して柔軟だった

　メッカが聖地となって以来、イスラム教寺院であるモスクには、ミフラーブという窪んだ場所が設けられます。その場所はメッカのカーバの方向を指し、礼拝者はコーランの教えに従って、メッカに向かって日に5回祈りを捧げます。

　イスラム教は、一神教による団結力で、みるみるアラビア半島から勢力を拡大し、651年には東ローマ帝国との摩擦などで衰弱していたササン朝ペルシアを滅ぼします。また東ローマの領土にも侵入し、エジプトを傘下におさめ、征服活動を続けます。

　入信者が多くなれば、その人たちの入植地が必要になります。ある意味で、新しい宗教は、既得権益のある人々ではなく、階層の低い人々の間にまず浸透します。そうした人々の信仰心が、有能な指導者によってうねりとなったとき、それは強力な戦力へと変化します。日本にも室町時代から戦国時代にかけて各地で活動を行い、独立した領国まで

時代
7, 8世紀
イスラム初期

地域
中東

分類
国家【政治】

キーワード
イスラム帝国の成立・シーア派とスンナ派・他宗教政策・イスラム帝国の発展

during the Muromachi and Sengoku periods when the Ikko Sect was active in various regions, even holding one fief entirely under its control.

Following the death of Muhammad, a leader referred to as a caliph was selected from among his relatives and close aides. However, internal struggles for power were endless. Among the competitors, Mu'awiya, one of those who had gained influence in Syria, assumed the position of caliph following the assassination of Ali, the 4th caliph, in 661. This marked the beginning of the Umayyad Caliphate.

The four caliphs until that point are called the Rightly Guided Caliphs. Those who insisted that Islam should be spread on the authority of these orthodox leaders gave rise to the greatest faction of Islam today: the Sunni. In contrast, those followers of Islam who believe that Ali was the legitimate successor formed the Shia branch. Although these two groups are the main leaders of Islam, Islamic society today is composed of even more branches.

Under the Umayyad Caliphate, which was predominantly Sunni, the Islamic forces continued to expand and spread along the southern coast of the Mediterranean. This military action was called jihad, or "holy war." This term is still used as a justification for warfare by Islamic fundamentalists, but at that time, believers in Islam refrained entirely from persecuting believers of other religions. As long as the non-believers paid land taxes and poll taxes, they were free to continue their lives as they had been doing. This was an important policy not only for the peaceful coexistence of different religious communities but also as a source of funding for the expansion of Islam.

This policy succeeded and the Umayyad Caliphate, in the early 8th century, succeeded in attaining control over a large country stretching from northern India in the east to the Iberian Peninsula, after destroying the Visigothic Kingdom there. However, during the process of achieving this expansion, confrontations arose between the new converts and original followers of Islam. As a result, the Abbasid descendants of a relative of Muhammad led a rebellion in 750, and established Baghdad as the capital of the Abbasid Caliphate.

The Abbasid Caliphate on the whole treated all believers of Islam, including converts, as equals in a more universal community of believers, and maintained quite flexible policies in dealing with followers of other religions. By means of a policy that is the exact opposite of the fundamentalist Islamic jihad that we think of today, the empire extended through territories under its control.

持った一向宗の事例があります。

　ムハマンドの死後、縁者や側近の中から指導者であるカリフが選出
されました。しかし、内部では権力抗争が絶えません。そうした中、
シリアで勢力を拡大していた有力者の一人ムアーウィヤが、4代目のカ
リフであったアリーが暗殺された後にカリフの座につきます。661年
のことです。ウマイヤ朝の誕生です。

　それ以前の4代のカリフを正統カリフといいます。この正統カリフ全
ての権威の元でイスラム教を広げるべきだと主張する人々が、現在イ
スラム教の最大派閥となるスンナ派のおこりとなります。逆に、アリー
を正統として、イスラム教を信奉する集団がシーア派となり、この2派
を中心としながら、さらにいくつかの派閥を含めてイスラム社会が構
成されるようになるのです。

　イスラム教勢力は、スンナ派を主流とするウマイヤ朝の元で拡大を
続け、地中海世界の南岸に拡大します。こうした戦闘行為を聖戦、ジハー
ドと呼びます。それは今でもイスラム原理主義者が戦いの大義名分と
して使用している言葉ですが、その当時のイスラム教徒は決して他の
宗教を強く迫害しておらず、地租や人頭税を払えば、人々が以前通り
生活をすることを許されていました。イスラム教を拡大する資金源と
しても、それは重要な政策だったのです。

　そんな政策が成功し、ウマイヤ朝は、8世紀の初めには東はインド北
部から、西は西ゴート王国を滅ぼしてイベリア半島に至る強大な国家
へと成長したのです。しかし、その成長の過程で、新しい改宗者と元々
のイスラム教徒との間に対立がおこります。その結果、ムハンマドの
縁戚にあたるアッバース家が750年に革命を起こし、バグダードを首
都にアッバース朝を開きます。

　アッバース朝は、改宗者も含め、支配下のイスラム教徒に対して、
おしなべて平等に対処し、異教徒に対しても極めて柔軟な政策をとっ
たのです。今、我々が思い描くイスラム原理主義者のジハードとは全
く逆の政策によって、帝国はその支配地域を拡大していったのでした。

The Kingdom of the Franks built Medieval Europe with the authority of the Catholic Church

If suppression can intensify religious activity, it also strengthens religions' organization.

When Christianity was persecuted by the Roman Empire, believers gathered in clandestine meeting places called catacombs to offer prayers and expand the network of their organization. In later years, a religious reform within Christianity led to a new religion, referred to as Protestantism. When believers in the newly formed Protestant forms of Christianity were persecuted by the older forms of Catholicism, there was great bloodshed across Europe. Proponents of some new sects escaped to the New World, and in due course large numbers of Protestant denominations put down roots on American soil.

Followers of Islam at the time of Muhammad banded together during their battles with prominent figures who believed in polytheistic religions, and eventually they extended their influence from the Arabian Peninsula to the northern coast of Africa. A hundred years was more than enough time for people to strengthen the position of this new religion in society.

So, what was happening in the European world at that time?

It was the Germanic peoples who employed the authority of the Western Roman Empire to establish states throughout Europe, but in the 6th century due to aggression by the Eastern Roman Empire, a large portion of the Mediterranean world once again placed itself under the wing of the Roman Empire. Yet that lasted only a short period of time. Thereafter, northern Africa was incorporated into the Umayyad Caliphate, which succeeded the Islamic Empire.

North of the Alps, one group of Germanic peoples called the Franks gained ascendancy. Immediately following the destruction of the Western Roman Empire in 481, Clovis I consolidated the Frankish people and established the Merovingian dynasty of Frankish kingdoms.

The territory of these kingdoms was called Gaul. When these kingdoms began to expand, the Roman Empire had already weakened, but in order to extend and administer territories centering in Gaul, these kingdoms needed to work together with Roman migrants and actively adopt Roman culture.

The Roman Empire held Christianity as the state religion, and through a series of religious conferences, a religious system was developed based on Roman

フランク王国はカトリックの権威で中世ヨーロッパ世界を築いていった

　宗教活動は、弾圧によって先鋭化もすれば、組織として強化もされます。

　キリスト教がローマ帝国で弾圧されたとき、人々はカタコンベと呼ばれる密会所で祈りを捧げ、組織としてのネットワークを拡大しました。後年キリスト教の中で、宗教改革を経て新教がおこり、プロテスタントと呼ばれた新教徒が旧教派から弾圧されたとき、ヨーロッパで多くの血が流れました。彼らの一部は新天地アメリカに逃れ、やがてアメリカの多数派の宗教へと成長します。

　イスラム教徒もムハンマドの時代は、多神教を信奉する有力者との戦いを通して団結し、最終的にはアラビア半島から北アフリカ沿岸へと、拡大しました。100年という歳月は、人々が新しい宗教によって社会での地位を強化するには余りある時間なのです。

　では、その時、ヨーロッパ世界はどうなっていたのでしょうか。

　西ローマ帝国の権威を利用しながら、ヨーロッパ各地で国家を建設したゲルマン人でしたが、6世紀には東ローマ帝国の攻勢によって地中海世界の多くは再びローマの傘下に復帰します。しかし、それもつかの間のことでした。その後北アフリカはイスラム帝国を受け継いだウマイヤ朝へと編入されたのです。

　一方、アルプスの北側は、フランク族というゲルマン人の一派が力を蓄えていました。特に西ローマ帝国滅亡直後の481年には、クローヴィス1世がフランク族をまとめてメロヴィング朝フランク王国を開いたのです。

　フランク王国の領土は、ガリアとよばれていました。フランク王国が拡大した当時、すでにローマ帝国は衰弱していましたが、ガリアを中心とした広大な領土を運営するには、ローマ人入植者と連携し、同時にローマの文化を積極的に導入する必要がありました。

　ローマ帝国はキリスト教を国教とし、いくつかの宗教会議を経てローマカトリックを正統とした教会制度を作りました。その過程で異端と

時代
6〜8世紀
欧州中世

地域
西ヨーロッパ

分類
国家【宗教】

キーワード
東ローマ帝国の発展と衰退・フランク族の改宗・フランク王国の発展・キリスト教の強化

Catholic beliefs as orthodoxy. In this process, offshoots such as Arianism, which were considered heretical, continued to propagate in dependencies and remote territories of the Roman Empire, gathering followers even among the Germanic peoples. A large number of clans, such as the Vandals, who opposed the Roman Empire, were influenced by Arianism.

However, Clovis I, in the process of strengthening his power base, converted to Catholicism and strengthened ties with the Catholic Church.

After his death, his territory fragmented. It was the powerful court minister Pepin III who brought them back together in 751. From that point on, the Frankish kingdoms were referred to as the Carolingian dynasty. For Pepin III to unify the state and solidify the power base, he donated the northern Italian territory of Ravenna to the Vatican as the Papal States, seeking to deepen ties with the Catholics. This event symbolized the tying of the Vatican's need for military protection with the secular king's need for religious authority.

There was, however, another reason for the commencement of the Carolingian monarchy. That was the war with the Umayyad Caliphate which invaded the Iberian Peninsula from northern Africa.

038 World history changed dramatically with the Battle of Tours-Poitiers and the Battle of Talas

European history was significantly affected by the Battle of Tours-Poitiers in France in October 732.

The Umayyad Caliphate, which destroyed the Visigothic Kingdom in the Iberian Peninsula in 711, then invaded the peninsula and continued on into France, that is, the center of the European world. The one who confronted the surging Islamic forces was Charles Martel, father of Pepin III, who founded the Carolingian dynasty in France. As a result of attaining victory in this battle, Martel was able to lay the foundations of the Kingdom of the Franks, to which his son would succeed.

トゥール・ポワティエ間の戦いでのカール・マルテル
Charles Martel in the Battle of Tours-Poitiers

It is said that if the Muslims had been victorious at the Battle of Tours-Poitiers

されたアリウス派などは、ローマの属領や遠隔地で布教を続け、ゲルマン人にも信者をつくり、ヴァンダル族のようにアリウス派の影響を受けローマと対立した部族も多くありました。

　しかしクローヴィス1世は、権力基盤を強化してゆく過程で、自らがカトリックに改宗し、カトリックとの結びつきを強化したのです。
　その後、クローヴィス1世の遺領は分裂します。751年になってそれをまとめたのが、有力な宮廷宰相であったピピン3世でした。以後のフランク王国をカロリング朝といいます。ピピン3世は国家を統一し、権力基盤を固めるために、北イタリアのラヴェンナ地方を教皇領として寄進し、ローマカトリックとの紐帯をさらに深めます。これは、軍事的庇護を必要としたローマ教皇庁と宗教的権威を必要とした世俗の王との連携を象徴する出来事でした。
　ところで、カロリング家が王朝を開くきっかけがもう一つありました。それは北アフリカからイベリア半島へと侵攻してきたウマイヤ朝との戦争だったのです。

トゥール・ポワティエ間の戦いとタラス河畔の戦いが世界史を大きく変えた

　732年10月に、トゥール・ポワティエ間の戦いという、ヨーロッパ史を左右する戦争がフランスでありました。
　711年にイベリア半島の西ゴート王国を滅ぼしたウマイヤ朝は、その後イベリア半島から、フランスへ、つまりヨーロッパ世界の中枢へと侵攻しました。雪崩れ込んできたイスラム勢力と対峙したのが、カロリング朝フランク王国を開いたピピン3世の父親にあたる、カール・マルテルでした。この戦いの勝利で、カール・マルテルはフランク王国の中で強い基盤を作り、息子がそれを継承したのです。

時代
8世紀
欧州中世

地域
中東

分類
戦争【交流】

キーワード
イスラム帝国の東西拡大の限界・ヨーロッパの成立・文化技術の伝播

　もしトゥール・ポワティエ間の戦いで、イスラム教徒がカール・マ

and had put Martel to the sword, Europe would thereafter have held the Quran—not the Bible—as its sacred scripture. Conversely, due to the fact that the Kingdom of the Franks won, 760 years later Christianity would drive the followers of Islam out of Spain and would unify western Europe under a Christianized culture.

This battle, therefore, is the beginning of the consciousness of "Europe" as an entity.

Meanwhile, Islamic forces continued to expand toward the east. Nineteen years after the Battle of Tours-Poitiers, the Umayyad Caliphate underwent a revolutionary upheaval and became the Abassid Caliphate. This occurred in 750. The military forces of the Abassid clashed with those of the Tang, which had extended Chinese influence into Central Asia as far west as the Talas River in current-day Kazakhstan.

This battle resulted in a defeat for the Chinese side. As a result, there was an increase in the number of Muslims from Central Asia to western regions of China, and people who studied the Quran began to spread into China. This can be seen as one of the underlying factors behind the separatist movement of the Uyghur ethnic group in present-day China.

After the Battle of Talas, the Tang Dynasty's expansion into Central Asia was halted. Simultaneously, this war marked the beginning of cultural exchange between Islamic and Chinese civilizations. It is profoundly interesting to compare the Battle of Tours-Poitiers with the later Crusades in terms of the strife that resulted between Islamic society and Christian society. Actually, the struggle between Muslims and Christians was the origin of the spread of civilization of the Islamic world into Europe.

A representative example of this exchange between civilizations was the spread of paper. Chinese who were taken prisoner at the Battle of Talas transferred the paper manufacturing process to the Islamic side, and they in turn passed it on to the Europeans. Six hundred years had elapsed since Cai Lun invented paper-making in 105, during the Later Han period.

The empire that began with the period of the Rightly Guided Caliphs, the Umayyad, and the Abbasid came to be referred to as an Islamic empire. People who believed in Allah as the one and only deity spread from North Africa to Central Asia, and from there, making use of the monsoon trade routes reached Southeast Asia. The extensive territory of the Islamic empire thus played a role as a catalyst in East-West exchange.

ルテルを打ち果たしていたら、ヨーロッパではその後聖書ではなく、コーランを学ぶようになっただろうといわれています。逆に、この戦いでフランク王国が勝利したことで、それから760年の後にキリスト教がイスラム教徒をスペインから完全に駆逐して、西ヨーロッパ世界をキリスト教文化でまとめあげることになるのです。

この戦争は、「ヨーロッパ」という意識を生み出す原点になったわけです。

一方、イスラム勢力は、東方へも拡大を続けます。トゥール・ポワティエ間の戦いから19年後のこと、すでにウマイヤ朝は、革命によってアッバース朝に変わっていました。750年のことです。そのアッバース朝の軍隊が、現在の中央アジアにあるカザフスタンに流れるタラス川の河畔で当時西域にまで勢力を拡大してきた唐の軍隊と衝突したのです。

この戦いは中国側の敗北に終わります。そのことから、中央アジアから中国の西部にイスラム教徒が増加し、コーランを学ぶ人々が中国へと拡散していったのです。それは、現在のウイグル族による中国からの分離運動の遠因であるともいえましょう。

タラス河畔の戦いの後、唐の中央アジアへの侵攻に歯止めがかかります。同時に、この戦争でイスラム文化と中国文化の二つの文明の交流が始まるのです。それは、トゥール・ポワティエ間の戦いと、その後の十字軍の遠征により、イスラム社会とキリスト教社会に生まれる対立と確執の歴史と比較しても興味深い事実です。実際、イスラム教徒とキリスト教徒の抗争は、逆にイスラム世界の文明がヨーロッパに伝播される原因となったのです。

そんな文明の交流の代表例が、紙の西への伝播でした。タラス河畔の戦いに敗れた中国人捕虜が、紙の製法をイスラム側に伝え、やがて、それがヨーロッパにも伝播したのです。後漢初期、105年に蔡倫が紙を発明して600年以上が経過した後の出来事でした。

正統カリフの時代に始まり、ウマイヤ朝、アッバース朝と続く帝国は、別名イスラム帝国とも呼ばれています。アラーを唯一神として信ずる人々は、その後北アフリカから中央アジアに、そしてモンスーンの交易ルートに乗って東南アジア方面にも広がります。イスラム帝国の広大な領土は、東西交流の触媒の役割も果たしたのでした。

039 Both the Abbasid Caliphate and the Tang dynasty contributed to the globalization of civilizations

The Abbasid Caliphate and the Tang dynasty, which unified China after the Sui, were global states. Although these two countries held contrasting world views, they both played major roles in interchange between Eastern and Western civilization.

As previously explained, while the Islamic and Christian worlds opposed one another, as religions they shared a common background as Abrahamic monotheistic faiths. The Chinese world, however, had no monotheistic belief that could serve as a centripetal force. In China, that role was played by the emperor, who was believed to govern the country under the mandate of heaven.

Confucianism, which preached the ideal that the country should be governed by reverence for the emperor, had roots in ancient ceremonial prayers and formalities. However, as it developed over time, Confucianism became more focused on pursuing the proper social order in the present world. On the other hand, in China, alongside Confucianism, there is Taoism, which takes a contrasting approach by perceiving the flow of nature, the universe, and human consciousness through concepts such as yin and yang. None of these was a religion. Within the Chinese tradition, there are also beliefs in the pursuit of extraordinary abilities, such as immortality, by those who seek to transcend the human realm. This too was entirely unrelated to a religion that respected a deity and possessed religious precepts.

Confucianism, which began during the Warring States period, was at the time used as a tool by people in positions of power to govern the country. In approximately the same period, the philosophy of Laozi and Zhuangzi expounded the art of living, merging with ancient Daoism, adding the influence of Buddhism, and giving birth to a uniquely Chinese worldview. This occurred during the period of the Northern and Southern Dynasties.

When one considers the disparity between Middle Eastern and European religious views and those of the Chinese worldview, which does not have a strong focal point of monotheism, one can understand how China absorbed the world's civilizations with very little resistance. With the exception of several emperors who persecuted Buddhists, when Tang China was flourishing, the country was flooded with Buddhism, Islam, Zoroastrianism from Persia, and even Nestorianism, an offshoot of Christianity which European religious councils had

アッバース朝と唐は共に文明の
グローバル化に貢献した

アッバース朝と共に、隋の滅亡のあとに中国を統一した唐も、グローバルな国家でした。この二つの国家は、対照的な世界観を持ちながらも、共に東西文明の交流に大きな役割を果たします。

既に解説したように、イスラム教とキリスト教の世界はお互いに対立しながらも、宗教としては、「アブラハムの宗教」といわれるように共通した背景を持つ一神教でした。しかし、中国世界には、求心力を持つ一神教は存在していません。中国でその役割を果たしたのは、天から命を受けて国家を運営しているとされる皇帝だったのです。

皇帝を仰いで国家を運営するための理想を説いた儒教は、そのルーツは古代の祈りの儀式や儀礼を伝えるものでした。しかし、時と共に体系化された儒教は、あくまでも現世での社会のあるべき姿を追求しています。一方、中国には儒教と対照的な位置にあって、自然や宇宙の流れ、人の意識などを陰と陽などの発想で捉える道教がありますが、これも宗教ではありません。中国に昔から伝わる、人界を離れて不老不死など超人的な能力を求めようとする神仙思想なども、道教の一部ですが、そこで敬われる人格は、社会と隔絶した隠者のような者への崇拝で、戒律をもって神を敬う宗教とは無縁のものでした。

戦国時代に始まる儒教は、国家運営のツールとして時の権力者に取り入れられてゆきます。そして同じ頃に老子や荘子によって広められたとされる老荘思想は、処世術を説きながら、古来の道教と融合し、そこに仏教の影響も加わり、中国独特の世界観を育みます。それは南北朝時代のことでした。

中東や西欧の宗教観と、一神教という強い軸のない中国の世界観の相違を考えれば、いかに中国に世界の文明が抵抗なく吸収されてゆくかが理解できます。一部の皇帝による仏教への迫害など例外はあるものの、中国で唐が繁栄すると、仏教のみならず、イスラム教も、ペルシアなどで信仰されたゾロアスター教、ヨーロッパの宗教会議で異端とされたキリスト教の一派であるネストリウス派までもが唐へと流入します。ゾロアスター教は中国では祆教、ネストリウス派キリスト教

時代
7, 8世紀
中国中世

地域
中東・中国

分類
交流【文化】

キーワード
唐の成立・東アジア文化圏・東西交流

declared to be heretical. Zoroastrian and Nestorian beliefs each came to be known under Chinese names, and in the Tang city of Chang'an there were facilities where believers of each could assemble. The Chinese world, in which there was no monotheistic conformity, provided a breeding ground for every conceivable ideology and religion.

Under Taizong (Li Shimin), the second emperor, Tang China extended its territories into Western Regions, and individuals such as Xuanzang, who traveled to India in search of Buddhist scriptures, promoted East-West exchanges.

When Xuanzong became emperor in 712, Tang China reached the peak of its prosperity. Chang'an became a major city where people from around the world gathered. Emissaries from Japan visited the city with considerable frequency. With the arrival of peaceful relations stretching across the broad territory from Islamic North Africa across Eurasia to Tang China, East-West interchange accelerated.

Under the Abbasid Caliphate, as mentioned earlier, while Islamic influence spread through wider domains, there was no censure of other religious beliefs. There was no religious persecution or oppression, and yet there was a connected flourishing of these two empires in Asia.

040 Tang China, like all world superstates, bore the destiny of all multi-ethnic countries

In both the past and the present, a country that has become a superstate bears a common fate.

In order to maintain extensive territories, these states have to include different ethnic groups. The various activities of other ethnic groups enable a country to absorb culture from around the world and this becomes the foundation of that country's prosperity. At the same time, however, the country always faces the issue of dissension and conflict between these ethnic groups. Present-day superstates like the United States, China, and Russia, each with its own unique policies, are consistently addressing the task of how to harmonize and integrate diverse races and ethnicities in order to sustain their vitality.

In the ancient world, the Roman Empire repeatedly used trial and error to deal with the Germanic and other neighboring peoples. At that time the Romans hired people of different ethnic groups as mercenary soldiers or granted them

は景教と呼ばれ、唐の都長安にはそうした人々が集う施設もあったのです。一神教の規制のない中国世界には、ありとあらゆる思想や宗教を受け入れる土壌があったのです。

　唐は、2代目の皇帝太宗（李世民）の時に、版図を西域へと広げ、仏典を求めインドまで旅をした玄奘三蔵のような人々が、東西交流を促進させました。

　そして、712年に皇帝になった玄宗の時代に、唐は繁栄の頂点を迎えました。長安は世界中の人々が集まる大都会となり、日本からも遣唐使が頻繁に訪れます。イスラム帝国と唐によって、ユーラシア大陸から北アフリカまでの広大な土地に平和が訪れたことが、東西交流を促進させたのです。

　アッバース朝も、勢力を拡大すると共に領土にイスラム教を広めますが、他の宗教を弾劾しなかったことは既に記した通りです。宗教的迫害を行わなかったことが、アジアにおけるこの二つの帝国の繁栄に繋がったのです。

唐も、世界の全ての超大国同様、多民族国家の宿命を背負っていた

　今も昔も、超大国となった国家は、一つの宿命を背負います。

　それは、広大な版図を維持するために、国家の中に多民族を包含しなければならないという宿命です。他民族が多彩に活動することは、世界中の文化を吸収でき、国が豊かになる基盤となります。しかし、同時に民族同士の抗争や、対立という課題に常に直面させられます。現在の超大国アメリカ、中国、そしてロシアも、それぞれの政策は異なっても、常に多様な人種や民族をいかに融和させ、国家の活力を維持してゆくかという課題に取り組んでいるのです。

　古代ではローマ帝国が、ゲルマン人などの周辺民族とそうした試行錯誤を繰り返しました。彼らは、時には異民族を傭兵にしたり、市民権を与えたりして、国力の維持をはかりました。それは成功します。

時代
8世紀
中国中世

地域
中国

分類
国家【政治】

キーワード
超大国の宿命・異民族の登用・多民族国家の成立・初期の政策の綻び・安禄山の乱

citizenship as a means of maintaining the power of the state. This succeeded. Ironically, however, it was a Germanic mercenary named Odocaer who ultimately overthrew the Western Roman Empire.

Tang China, the superpower of the East, also actively took in people of different ethnic groups. Abe no Nakamaro, who was sent to the Tang court as an envoy from Japan, spent the rest of his life as a high-level official in the Chinese government. It was not only Japanese but also people from regions to the west of China who were employed by the Chinese. After the Sassanid dynasty of Persia was destroyed in 651, a large number of migrants streamed into Tang China. A large number of Sogdians, an Iran-related people who were active in Central Asia, were also numerous in the Tang capital city of Chang'an. As a result of these various ethnic groups gathering in China, the Tang enjoyed unprecedented prosperity.

The first half of the 8th century is referred to as the second and most prosperous of four sub-periods of the Tang dynasty. During this period the famous Li Bo, said to be from one of the western minority ethnic groups, became a leading figure.

It was in that period that the Tang inherited from the Sui the system of centralized government called the ritsuryo codes, which were fixed laws and statutes for governing, with a system of local administration. Under this supervision, grain was taxed, labor was levied, a tax system for gathering silk was created, and a draft system for military service was instituted in order to maintain military strength.

However, in the 8th century, the number of manors owned by nobles increased and the system for taxes in produce or labor gave way. On top of that, the military system to protect the provinces changed from a system sustained by levies on the peasantry to a system of military conscription, with military units led by military commanders who also administered the people's livelihood and local finances.

An Lushan, one of these commanders, together with a subordinate named Shi Siming started an insurrection in 755 that brought the Tang to the verge of collapse. The rebellion continued after the two leaders died, lasting until 763. This was about the time when the Tang Emperor Xuanzong bestowed favors on the famous Yang Guifei, and when her family played a leading role in the country's power structure. It was also the same time as Abe no Nakamaro's activities in Tang China.

An Lushan's lineage went back to the Sogdians and the Tujue.

As with Odocaer in the Western Roman Empire, in the cosmopolitan superstate of Tang China, a life-or-death crisis was brought about by a different ethnic group that the country had of its own accord recruited. Both prosperity and chaos resulted from the inclusion of various ethnic groups. From the ancient past

しかし、皮肉なことに、最終的に西ローマ帝国を滅ぼしたのはゲルマン人の軍人オドアケルでした。

そして、東の超大国であった唐も、異民族を積極的に登用します。日本から遣唐使として派遣された阿倍仲麻呂は、唐の高級官僚として一生を終えました。日本人のみならず、西域からの人々も同様でした。イスラム帝国に651年に滅ぼされたササン朝ペルシアからも、多くの人々が唐に流入します。中央アジアでは、元々ソグド人というイラン系の人々が活動していましたが、そうしたイラン系の人々が唐の首都長安に多数生活していたといわれています。多様な民族によって唐はかつてない繁栄を享受したのです。

唐が最も栄えた8世紀前半を盛唐といいますが、この時期を代表する詩人李白も実は西域の少数民族の出身だったという説もあるのです。

唐は当初、律令制度という中央集権的な政治制度を隋から引き継ぎ、地方行政は州県制度をもって統率しました。そうした管理のもとに、穀物を収める租、労役を課す庸、絹などを収める調という税制度も整え、府兵制度という徴兵制度によって軍事力を維持しました。

しかし、8世紀には貴族の荘園も増え、租庸調の税制そのものが崩れてゆきます。そして地方の防衛は府兵制度から募兵制度へと変化し、節度使と呼ばれる長官がその指揮にあたったのです。
そんな節度使の一人であった安禄山が、部下の史思明と755年の反乱を起こし、唐は滅亡寸前にまで追い込まれます。乱は二人の死後763年まで続きました。玄宗皇帝が有名な楊貴妃を寵愛し、楊貴妃の一族が国の権限を牛耳っていた頃のことでした。それは阿倍仲麻呂が唐で活躍していた頃の出来事でもありました。
安禄山は、ソグド人と突厥の血が流れる人物でした。
西ローマのオドアケル同様、コスモポリタンな超大国であった唐も、自らが採用した異民族によって、存亡の危機に見舞われたのです。多民族を包含することによる繁

李白
Li Bo (701–762)

阿倍仲麻呂
Abe no Nakamaro (698–770)

to the present day, this contradiction has continued to be an issue that superstates inevitably confront.

041 Turkish people commence activities in the center of Asia

The height of the flourishing of the Tang dynasty was during the reign of Emperor Xuanzong.

Various well-cultured figures were active, but among them two were equally admired as prominent: Li Bo and Du Fu. Du Fu is known for his poem which translates roughly as "The country collapses, but the mountains and rivers remain," which laments the devastation caused by the An Lushan Rebellion. It is believed that Li Bo lost his official post during that period and was swept away into some outlying region. Judging from the life circumstances of these two poets, one can understand just how sharp a blow the An Lushan Rebellion was to the Tang government.

When the rebellion spread to Chang'an, Emperor Xuanzong was routed and forced to flee to present-day Sichuan. Along the way, Yang Guifei and her clan were executed at the demand of the army. This tragedy was taken as the subject matter in a long epic poem by the poet Bai Juyi.

In efforts to suppress the An Lushan Rebellion, the Tang depended on the military power of the northern Uyghurs.

Elsewhere, at the time of the rebellion, the monarchy of Tufan, founded in Tibet in 633, matured to the point that it at one time threatened Chang'an. The movements of these various neighboring peoples drove the Tang down the road to ruin.

After the An Lushan Rebellion, the local Tang military administrators themselves took power in their own hands and came to be called fanzhen, a kind of military governor. Eventually they took control of local administration, making it harder for the central government to exert itself.

When one looks to the west, the Abbasid Caliphate, which reached its high point at the same time as the Tang dynasty, began in the latter half of the 9th century to lose its own vigor. As a result, in the vacuum left behind when the two great empires declined, nomadic peoples in Central Asia and North Asia became increasingly active.

Taking the lead among these nomadic peoples were the Turkish people. These

栄と混乱。この矛盾は、古代から現在まで、超大国が常に直面してきた課題であるといえましょう。

アジアの中心から、トルコ系の人々が活動を始める

玄宗皇帝の時代こそが唐が最も栄えた盛唐期でした。

当時、様々な文化人が活躍しましたが、中でも既に紹介した李白と常に並び称される詩人が杜甫でした。杜甫に「国破れて山河あり」という有名な詩がありますが、これは安禄山の乱の頃の荒廃を嘆いた詩だといわれています。一方の李白は、この動乱の時期に失脚し、辺境に流されそうになったといわれています。この二人の詩人の人生の顛末からも、いかに安禄山の乱が唐に大きな打撃を与えたかがうかがえます。

安禄山の乱が長安に及ぶと、玄宗皇帝は長安を逃れ、現在の四川省へと敗走します。途中、楊貴妃とその一族も兵士の要求で処刑されます。その悲劇は9世紀の詩人白居易の長恨歌に綴られています。

唐は安禄山の乱を平定するにあたり、北方民族のウイグル族の武力に頼ります。

また、安禄山の乱の頃、チベットで633年に建国した吐蕃という王国が、一時長安を脅かすまでに成長します。唐の衰亡に乗じるように周辺民族の活動が活発になったのです。

安禄山の乱の後、節度使が地方で権力を握り、藩鎮と呼ばれるようになりました。やがて藩鎮は地方行政を牛耳り、中央の制御もききにくくなったのです。

目を西に向けるなら、唐と同じ時期に栄華を極めたアッバース朝も、9世紀後半には次第に勢いがなくなります。その結果、これらの世界帝国の凋落によって生まれた空間で、中央アジアや北アジアの遊牧民が活発に活動するようになったのです。

遊牧民の主役は、トルコ系の人々でした。しかし、彼らは今のトル

時代
8,9世紀
中国中世

地域
中東・中国

分類
国家【民族】

キーワード
東西巨大帝国の動揺・周辺民族の侵入・他民族のイスラム改宗

people, however, did not live in present-day Turkey. The Tujue, who swept through Central Asia during the Northern and Southern dynasties, the Sui, and the Tang periods, and the Uyghur, who cooperated with the Tang army during the rebellion led by An Lushan, were both Turkic peoples. Even today, the term "Turkestan" is used to refer to the unified region of Central Asia, reflecting this historical background.

Also in this region lived Iranian people including the Sogdians. When Islamic forces poured in from the west with the rise of the Abbasid, many of the people mentioned above converted to Islam.

As a result, in present-day Xianjiang Uyghur Autonomous Region—which is the eastern part of Turkestan—there remain large numbers of Muslims. Media today report on how a portion of the inhabitants of that region are dissatisfied with the Chinese government's policies regarding minority ethnic peoples and have launched a movement to separate from China and gain independence. Many of these people are descendants of converts to Islam during the Tang period.

In the 9th century when both the Tang and the Abbasid were politically weakening, these people found themselves in the eye of a hurricane powered by a new migration of ethnic groups.

042 The decline and fall of the Tang dynasty and the Abbasid Caliphate brought forth chaos in Asia

In 875, a large-scale insurrection known as the Huang Chao Rebellion dealt a devastating blow to the Tang dynasty. The military leader Zhu Quanzhong, who was credited with bringing the rebellion under control, on the contrary ended up calling the shots, and in 907 the Tang dynasty collapsed. The monarchy that Zhu Quanzhong brought about is known as the Later Liang. Including the Later Liang, a total of five short-lived monarchies governed North China, while ten regimes divided and ruled over South China. This chaotic period is therefore known as the Five Dynasties and Ten Kingdoms period.

The loss of a centripetal force in China had a major influence on Japan as well. The sending of missions to Tang dynasty China was discontinued, and the relationship between China and Japan became distant. As a result, the culture which until then had been brought from the Tang evolved and matured with uniquely Japanese features.

コで生活していたわけではありません。中国の南北朝、隋、そして唐にわたって中央アジアを席巻していた突厥、そして安禄山の謀反の折に唐軍と連携したウイグル族は、ともにトルコ系の人々でした。今でも、中央アジア一体がトルキスタンと呼ばれている背景はそこにあります。

そこにはソグド人などイラン系の人々も生活していました。アッバース朝の隆盛によってイスラム教の勢力が西から流入してくると、彼らの多くがイスラム教に改宗します。

その結果、トルキスタンの東部にあたる、現在の中国の新疆ウイグル自治区は今でもイスラム教徒が多く、一部の人々が中国政府の少数民族政策に対して不満を抱き、中国からの分離独立運動を展開していることがニュースなどで取り上げられます。彼らの多くは、唐の時代にイスラム教に改宗した人々の子孫なのです。

そんな彼らが、9世紀になって、唐とアッバース朝の双方の勢いが減速したとき、新たな民族移動の台風の目となっていったのでした。

唐とアッバース朝の衰亡がアジアに混沌を生み出した

唐は875年に起きた黄巣の乱という大規模な内乱で壊滅的な打撃を受けてしまいます。そして、その乱の制圧に功のあった朱全忠という軍人が逆に唐の政権を牛耳ることになり、907年に唐を滅亡させたのでした。朱全忠が興した王朝を後梁といいます。その後梁を含め、53年の間に5つの王朝が短命な政権を華北にたて、華南では10の政権が中国を分断していたことから、この混乱した時代を五代十国といいます。

時代
9世紀
イスラム初期

地域
中東・中国

分類
国家【独立】

キーワード
東西巨大帝国の滅亡・地域政権の勃興・日本の国風文化・イスラム中世の始まり

中国に求心力がなくなったことは、日本にも大きな影響を与えます。遣唐使は廃止され、中国と日本は疎遠になります。その結果、それまで唐からもたらされた文化が、日本の風土の中で独自に熟成され進化します。

The indigenous culture of the Heian period is known through literary works by women writers including *The Tale of Genji*, and in these works one is able to catch glimpses of accomplishments of Chinese culture. From this, we can grasp the notion that Chinese culture, in the form of knowledge, changed inside the Japanese environment into a distinctively indigenous culture.

Turning to the west of China, the desert regions studded with oases in Central Asia during the period when the Tang and the Abbasid were powerful prospered as important transfer points in East-West interchange. At the time, the journey between the Mediterranean world and Tang China was a life-risking venture requiring several years to complete. In many cases, by way of the oasis towns, travelers coming from the west encountered and mingled with travelers coming in the opposite direction, and by means of multiple encounters, one after another, cultures were transmitted in both directions.

As mentioned earlier, in the 9th century, the Abbasid Caliphate, too, due to internal discord and the feudal lords establishing their own independence, was unable to maintain its expansive territories and began to decline. Various peoples began to fill the vacuum that resulted from its downfall. Islam was already spreading among the nomadic peoples. Just as the Germanic peoples made use of the authority of the Roman Empire, these nomadic people obtained the divine protection of Islam by making a show of reverence for the Abbasid caliphs, while governing their own states.

After the Umayyad Caliphate was overthrown in what is now Spain in the Iberian Peninsula, in 756 descendants of the Umayyad family established the Andalusian Umayyad dynasty. The capital city of Cordoba later became the western base of Islamic culture. Cordoba and Baghdad, capital city of the Abbasid Caliphate, prospered together. The monarch of the Andalusian Umayyad took the title of caliph.

In the 10th century, commencing in Tunisia, in North Africa, and expanding power into Egypt as its center, another leader expanded territory and took the title of caliph in creating the Fatimid Caliphate.

The Fatimid Caliphate was a Shia Islamic country which embraced a strong sense of rivalry vis-à-vis the Abbasid, who succeeded to the title of caliph within Sunni Islam.

While Islamic strength was divided among a number of different countries, the constantly moving nomadic peoples also continued to spread. In this course of events, the Turkic people in Central Asia embraced Islam and later migrated

平安時代の国風文化は、『源氏物語』などの女流文学で知られていますが、作品の中には、中国文化の素養をあちこちに垣間見ることができるのです。中国文化が知識として日本の風土で独自な国風文化へと変化していったことが、このことからもわかるのです。

　西へ目を向ければ、中央アジアの砂漠地帯に点在するオアシスは、唐とアッバース朝が強大であった時代には、東西交流の重要な中継地点として繁栄しました。当時地中海世界から唐までの旅は、数年を要した命がけの旅でした。多くの場合、オアシスの都市などを介して西から来た旅人は、東からの旅人と出会い交流しながら、何人もの人の手を経て、文化が伝達されていったのです。

　前述のように、9世紀になるとアッバース朝も内紛と諸侯の自立などによって、広大な領土を維持できず衰退します。その隙間を様々な民族が埋めてゆくのです。元々イスラム教は、遊牧民の間に広がりました。ゲルマンの人々が、ローマの権威を利用したように、こうした遊牧民は、イスラム教の守護神としてのアッバース朝のカリフをたてながら、自らの国を運営してゆくのです。

　一方、現在スペインがあるイベリア半島では、アッバース家がウマイヤ朝を滅ぼした後、756年にウマイヤ家の子孫が後ウマイヤ朝を建国します。首都のコルドバはその後西方のイスラム文化の拠点となり、アッバース朝の首都バグダードと共に繁栄しました。後ウマイヤ朝の王もカリフを名乗ります。

　そして、10世紀に北アフリカのチュニジアでおこり、エジプトを中心に勢力を拡大したファーティマ朝の王も同じくカリフを名乗ります。

　ファーティマ朝はシーア派の国家で、スンナ派のカリフを引き継ぐアッバース朝に強い対抗意識を持っていたのです。

　イスラム勢力は、こうしていくつもの国家に分かれながらも、移動を常とした遊牧民によって更に拡大を続けます。その流れの中で、中央アジアに展開したトルコ系の人々がイスラム化し、その後西へ移動

westward, establishing the Seljuk Empire in the 11th century. This occurred in the year 1038.

043 Both the Eastern and Western European civilizations, as well as Islamic civilization, have become the origins of the present-day Western civilization

In the process of the rise and decline of the Islamic Empire and the Tang dynasty in China, when Asia was undergoing bewildering changes, in Western Europe under Charlemagne, the Carolingian dynasty of the Frankish Kingdom was approaching its zenith.

As mentioned earlier, Pepin III, who established the Carolingian dynasty, donated the domain of Ravenna to the Roman Catholic Pope. Originally, that was a domain belonging to the Kingdom of the Lombards, a group of Germanic peoples. The Kingdom of the Franks ultimately destroyed the Kingdom of the Lombards in 774, and with an alliance with the pope, controlled the Western European world. Then in the year 800 Charlemagne was recognized as the successor to the Roman Empire by the Pope and was crowned in a coronation ceremony.

Later, the Kingdom of the Franks fragmented over issues regarding succession. Through the Treaty of Verdun in 843 and the Treaty of Mersen in 876, the kingdom was divided into three parts. These three became the prototypes of France, Germany, and Italy.

At the same time, this meant that the European world would become divided into two cultural parts: Western Europe, centered on the Kingdom of the Franks, and the Roman Catholic Church and Eastern Europe, centered on the Eastern Roman Empire.

Thereafter, Europe would have two Christian powers. One would be the Roman Catholics in alliance with the Germanic secular government of the Kingdom of the Franks and others. The second would be the Eastern Roman Empire in alliance with the Orthodox Church. Over a period of several centuries following the breakup of the Roman Empire in 395, these two churches changed subtly in both doctrine and methods of proselytizing.

The Roman Catholics in particular felt the need to proselytize among the

して11世紀にセルジューク朝トルコを建国します。1038年のことでした。

東西ヨーロッパとイスラム文明が現在の
西欧文明の原点となった

イスラム帝国や唐の盛衰の過程で、アジアがめまぐるしく変化していた頃、西ヨーロッパでは、カロリング朝フランク王国がカール大帝（シャルルマーニュ）の元、全盛期を迎えていました。

時代
8〜11世紀
欧州中世

地域
ヨーロッパ

分類
政治【文化】

キーワード
教皇領の寄進・カールの戴冠・フランク王国の分裂・東西教会の分裂・学問はイスラムで発展

カロリング朝を興したピピン3世が、751年にラヴェンナ地方をローマ教皇に寄進したことはすでに解説しました。もともとそこはゲルマン人の一派が造ったランゴバルド王国の領地だったのです。フランク王国は774年に最終的にランゴバルド王国を滅ぼし、ローマ教皇と提携しながら、西ヨーロッパ世界を統治していったのです。そして、800年にカール大帝はローマ教皇からローマ帝国の後継者とされ、戴冠式を行ったのです。

その後、フランク王国は相続問題などで分裂し、843年のヴェルダン条約、876年のメルセン条約を経て、3つに分割されます。これが、現在のフランス、ドイツ、そしてイタリアの原型となるのです。

同時に、この動きは、ヨーロッパ世界がフランク王国とローマカトリックを中心とした西ヨーロッパ世界と、東ローマ帝国を軸とした東ヨーロッパ世界という二つの文化圏に分かれてゆくことを意味しています。

ヨーロッパには、二つのキリスト教の権威が存在することになります。フランク王国などのゲルマン系の世俗政権と連携したローマカトリックと、東ローマ帝国と連携した正教会がそれにあたります。この二つの教会は、395年にローマ帝国が分裂して以来数百年の年月を経てゆく中で、宗旨も布教政策も微妙に変化してゆきました。

特にローマカトリックでは、ゲルマン人への布教の必要性

アルブレヒト・デューラー『カール大帝』
Albrecht Dürer
—Emperor Charlemagne

Germanic peoples and encouraged idol worship to achieve that goal. The Orthodox Church, in contrast, denied that policy. Out of this confrontation in 1054 evolved the circumstances in which the institutions mutually excommunicated the other. The result was a complete split into separate churches with separate activities: the Roman Catholic Church and the Orthodox Church.

At the time, in point of fact, since the days of the ancient Greeks, science and philosophy had been protected in the Islamic regions by caliphs of the Abbasid Caliphate, such as Harun al-Rashid and Al-Ma'mun. In a library called Bayt al-Hikma—"the hall of wisdom"—constructed in 830 in Baghdad, the writings of Plato and Aristotle were translated and that in turn contributed to the systematization of Islamic theology.

In addition, with the addition of the mathematics developed in India and the paper-making technology that was transmitted from China, the knowledge and technology that form the basis of present-day medicine, science, and chemistry were cultivated. The domains which the Islamic Empire possessed were originally the territories conquered by Alexander the Great's military expedition. Hellenist civilization was deeply rooted there and those were the areas that succeeded Greek civilization.

Current Western civilization is the result of the fusion, maturation, and blossoming of the moral values and religious beliefs established separately by the Western European world and the Eastern Roman world in Christianity, along with the scientific and technological knowledge nurtured in the Islamic world.

044 Europe in the Middle Ages was based on feudalism

In Japan, the term Middle Ages calls to mind the Kamakura period and the Muromachi period.

But prior to that, just as the Nara period was giving way to the Heian period, Europe was already in the middle of its own Middle Ages.

What was Europe like in the Middle Ages?

Prior to the breakup of the Roman Empire, within the empire the gap between the haves and the have-nots grew larger. Invaders from outside, including the Germanic peoples, in the process of changing European society, became have-

もあり、偶像崇拝を奨励していましたが、正教会はそれを否定します。こうした対立から、1054年には、お互いにお互いを破門するという事態にまで至り、二つの教会はそれぞれ分裂したまま、片方はローマカトリック、片方は正教会として、別々に活動をしてゆくようになるのです。

その当時、実はギリシア以来の科学や哲学は、ハールン・アッラシードやマアムーンといったアッバース朝のカリフの指導のもと、イスラム圏で保護されていました。バグダードに830年に創建された「知恵の館」と呼ばれる図書館では、プラトンやアリストテレスの著書が翻訳され、それがイスラム教の神学の体系化にも貢献しました。

さらに、インドなどで進化した数学、中国から伝わった製紙技術なども加わり、現在の医学や科学、化学の基礎となった知識や技術が育まれました。イスラム帝国が領有した地域は、元々アレクサンドロス大王が遠征した地域で、ヘレニズム文明が深く根付き、ギリシア文明が継承された地域だったのです。

現在の西欧文明は、この西ヨーロッパ世界と東ローマ世界でそれぞれが打ち立てたキリスト教の道徳と宗教観に、イスラムで育てられた科学技術が後年融合し、熟成され、開花したものなのです。

中世ヨーロッパは封建制度を基盤にした

日本で中世というと、鎌倉時代から室町時代を想像します。

しかし、それ以前、ちょうど奈良時代から平安時代へと移っていく頃、ヨーロッパでは既に中世のまっただ中でした。

中世のヨーロッパとはどんなところだったのでしょう。

ローマ帝国が分裂する前、帝国の中は持てる者と持たざる者との格差が開いていました。ゲルマン人など、外部からの侵入者がヨーロッパ社会を変えてゆく中で、持たざる者は、持てる者に保護され、農耕

時代
8~11世紀
欧州中世

地域
ヨーロッパ

分類
社会【制度】

キーワード
領主による農民支配・封建秩序の成立・キリスト教の浸透・神聖ローマ帝国の成立

nots seeking protection under the haves. The former engaged in agriculture and paid taxes to the latter.

In due course, the haves became feudal lords who controlled the agriculturalists both physically and legally. The have-nots were turned into serfs. They lost freedom of movement and were tied to the land of their lord. The lands they labored on came to be called manors.

In Japan, from approximately the Nara period, such private estates that were controlled not by the imperial court but by prominent nobles were called *shoen*. In the Heian period, the Fujiwara clan, using income from their estates as a base, maintained significant influence in the court's government.

In Europe, such prominent figures, in order to protect their lands, pledged allegiance to monarchs or even to powerful feudal lords. They followed a system of mutual obligation wherein the local lord in essence donated his land to the more powerful lord and then that land was given back to him as fief. This system came to be known as feudalism. This relationship of master and servant also included military service as a knight. This aspect bears some similarity to the relationship of obligation and duty between master and vassal during the Edo period. The only thing is, within the estate of a powerful feudal lord, the monarch could exercise no administrative or legal authority. This relationship of superior and subordinate was maintained as a contractual relationship. In this sense, rather than the Edo period relationship between *daimyo* and vassal, in which the vassal pledged absolute obedience for the benevolences received, the European form may have been closer to the lord-vassal relationship of the Sengoku period between powerful warriors or powerful regional families and a daimyo.

During that time, outside the cultivated lands, there were deep forests. It was a world inhabited by spirits that the Germanic people had imagined in their hearts since ancient times, with the darkness and dappled sunlight filtering through the trees, and the distant howling of wolves. The darkness of the night was not just pitch black; it was quiet, and when there was no moonlight, countless stars adorned the sky. People were sensitive even to the slightest movements of the gentle breeze.

It was the Roman Catholic Church that ruled over the entirely of this European world. With the pope at the top of the hierarchy and bishops and priests below, the church's prominent figures accepted donations of land from monarchs and feudal lords. From the period of Charlemagne and the Kingdom of the Franks, within a fief, it became an established custom for the church to gather from the inhabitants

に従事し、持てる者に税を支払います。

　やがて、彼らは持てる者を領主とし、領主はその領地で耕作をする者を物理的にも法的にも支配するのです。持たざる者は農奴となり、移動の自由を奪われ、領主の所有する土地に縛られます。こうした土地を荘園といいます。

　日本では、奈良時代頃から、朝廷の支配の外にあって、有力貴族が所有する土地が荘園と呼ばれるようになりました。平安時代には荘園からの収入を土台に藤原氏が朝廷の政治にも大きな影響を及ぼすことになりました。

　ヨーロッパでは、有力者は自らの土地を守り保護してもらうために、王やさらに有力な諸侯に忠誠を誓っていました。彼らは自らの土地を寄進し、改めてその土地を与えられる恩貸地制度に従っていました。この制度が封建制度です。彼らは主従関係の中で騎士として従軍することもありました。このあたりは、江戸時代の主従関係にある恩と義理の関係と似たところがあります。ただ、有力な領主の荘園には、王といえども行政や司法権を行使できず、あくまでも彼らは契約関係によって上下関係を維持していたのです。その点においては、恩に対して絶対服従を誓っていた江戸時代の大名と家臣の構造というよりは、戦国時代の有力武士や地方の豪族と大名との主従関係に近いものがあるのかもしれません。

　当時、耕作地の外は深い森でした。森を支配する闇や木漏れ日、狼の遠吠えなど、そこはゲルマン人が昔から心に描いてきた精霊の宿る世界でした。夜の闇はただ暗いだけではなく、静かで、月明かりのないときは、無数の星が空を彩っていました。人々は、ささやかな風の動きにも敏感でした。

　そんなヨーロッパ世界全体に君臨していたのが、ローマカトリック教会でした。教皇を頂点に、司教や司祭など、教会の有力者は王や諸侯から土地の寄進を受けていました。フランク王国のカール大帝の時代から、領土内の住民が、十分の一税という特別な税を教会に納める制度が定着し、有力な聖職者は徴税のみならず司法権すら行使して、

a tithe, a special ten-percent tax. Not only did prominent clergymen collect this tax but they also exercised judicial powers, and this combination strengthened the foundation of the church.

In the 10th century, the lineage of the Kingdom of the Franks died out and one of the leading feudal lords was chosen to be the monarch. One of these monarchs, Otto I, gained power, and the Pope recognized him as successor to the Roman Empire. Thus was founded the Holy Roman Empire.

045 The Magyars and the Normans brought forth a new era in Europe

After surviving a long struggle for power, Otto I was crowned by the Pope as heir to the throne of the Roman Empire in 962.

Ten years earlier, Otto I had driven back the Magyars at the Battle of Lechfeld.

Hungary, the name of the eastern European country is, in the Hungarian language, Magyarorszag, which means the country of the Magyar people. The Magyars were originally nomadic peoples from the southern Ural Mountains in Russia. When Turkic-speaking people migrated westward from Central Asia, the Magyars were pressured to migrate to the area north of the Black Sea.

ブダペストを流れるドナウ川
The Danube River running through Budapest

The long Danube River flows toward the Black Sea past the cities of Budapest and Vienna, where the House of Habsburg was located. The Magyars later migrated along this river in Hungary.

From the perspective of Western Europe, this was a period of incessant discord.

Although they are referred to as Germanic peoples, they were not one single ethnic group. Like the indigenous people of the American continents, they were a diverse collection of ethnic groups, who were active over a broad area.

People of Germanic roots collaborated with the civilization of the Roman Empire to create the European society of the Middle Ages. Into this medieval European world came the Magyars and Normans, who were also called Vikings.

In viewing the history of this ethnic migration, one ought not forget the details

教会の基盤を盤石にしていました。

　10世紀になるとフランク王国は血統が絶え、諸侯の有力者が王を選んでいました。そんな王の一人、オットー1世が台頭し、ローマ教皇からローマ帝国の後継者とされます。彼がひらいたのが、神聖ローマ帝国だったのです。

マジャール人とノルマン人はヨーロッパに新時代をもたらした

　長い政争を乗り越えて、オットー1世がローマ教皇からローマ帝国の後継者として戴冠したのは962年のことでした。

　その10年前、オットー1世は、西ヨーロッパに侵入してきたマジャール人をレヒフェルトの戦いで撃退しています。

　東ヨーロッパの国家ハンガリー。この国名をハンガリー語にすればマジャロスザク、つまりマジャール人の国ということになります。マジャール人は、もともとロシアのウラル山脈南部にいた遊牧民であるといわれています。トルコ系の人々が、中央アジアから西へと移動してくると、彼らはそれに圧迫されて黒海北部へと移動します。

　ドナウ川は、近世に東ヨーロッパに君臨したハプスブルク家の本拠地となるウィーンやブダペストといった都市を経て黒海に流れ込む大河です。マジャール人は、その後この大河に沿ってハンガリーへと移動したのです。

　それは、西ヨーロッパから見れば周辺民族との摩擦の絶えない時代でした。

　ゲルマン人といっても、一つの単純な民族ではありません。ちょうどアメリカ大陸の先住民のように、様々な部族が広範な地域で活動していたのです。

　ゲルマン人をルーツにする人々と、ローマ帝国が培った文明とのコラボが中世ヨーロッパ社会を作ってゆきます。そんな中世ヨーロッパ世界に侵入してきたのがマジャール人と、別名バイキングと呼ばれたノルマン人でした。

　こうした民族移動の歴史を見てゆくためには、中国、ローマ帝国、

時代
10, 11世紀
欧州中世

地域
ヨーロッパ

分類
侵略【民族】

キーワード
マジャール人の侵入・ノルマン人の活動・周辺民族のキリスト教化・地球の温暖化

of the discord between the superpower Islamic Empire and the neighboring people. At the same time, natural phenomena including climate change also had a major influence on the movements of people.

From the time when Otto I was active, temperatures began to rise globally. In Europe in particular, this tendency continued until about the end of the 14th century, and records show that land suitable for agriculture increased and wine was produced even as far north as England. This warming rid the oceans of ice. And as the temperature of the oceans' surface rose, navigation deeper into the interior became possible. The Normans, who lived in the various lands of present-day northern Europe, supported by this change in the climate, began using large, highly mobile boats to make raids throughout Europe and began to settle in various lands.

As one can grasp from the fact that Greenland today is a Danish territory, one party of Normans navigated through the North Atlantic, reaching as far as Newfoundland and establishing permanent settlements there. That was roughly during the 11th century.

The activities of the Normans were not limited to the coasts of North Europe. They also extended throughout Europe from the Mediterranean Sea to the Black Sea. At that time, Spain and many other lands facing the Mediterranean were under the umbrella of the Islamic empire. The Normans not only invaded western Europe, but by converting to Christianity, they played a role in protecting the Roman Catholic Church from threats from Muslims.

046 Through the migration of ethnic groups, the three great religions became world religions

The general who led the Magyar people and swept across Europe, confronting Otto I, was named Árpád. He founded the Kingdom of Hungary, but eventually the people converted to Roman Catholicism, and it grew into a powerful East European country.

The Germanic peoples, the Magyars, and the Normans who moved to the west, with support from the Roman Catholic Church, each went on to strengthen their respective bases for their authority.

Not only these but other peoples as well, who from ancient times through the Middle Ages invaded civilized regions, were not content to passively enjoy

あるいはイスラム帝国といった超大国と周辺民族との軋轢の経緯を忘れてはなりません。同時に、気候変動などの自然現象も人々の移動に大きな影響を与えていました。

オットー1世が活躍していた頃から、地球規模で気温の上昇が始まります。特にヨーロッパでは14世紀頃までその傾向が続き、耕作可能な土地が増え、イギリスでもワインが製造されていたという記録が残っています。温暖化は海から氷を取り除きます。そして水面が上がれば、より奥地まで航海が可能になります。現在の北欧各地に居住していたノルマン人は、こうした気候変動にも後押しされ、機動力のある大型ボートを使って、ヨーロッパ各地を侵略し、定住を始めたのです。

現在もグリーンランドがデンマーク領となっていることからもおわかりのように、ノルマン人の一派は北大西洋を航行し、グリーンランドからカナダの一部となっているニューファンドランド島まで到達し、定住したのです。11世紀頃のことでした。

ノルマン人の活動は、北ヨーロッパの沿岸だけではなく、地中海から黒海に至るヨーロッパ全域に及んでいました。当時、スペインや地中海に面した多くの地域は、イスラム帝国の影響下にありました。ノルマン人は、単に西ヨーロッパを侵略するのではなく、彼らがキリスト教に帰依することによって、イスラム教徒の脅威からローマカトリックを守る役割も担ったのです。

三大宗教は民族移動によって世界宗教と
なってゆく

マジャール人を率いてヨーロッパを席巻し、オットー1世と対決したのはアールパードという将軍でした。彼を始祖としてハンガリー王国が成立しますが、彼らはやがてローマカトリックに改宗し、東ヨーロッパの強国へと成長します。

ゲルマン人、マジャール人、そして西へ移動したノルマン人も、ローマカトリックを支柱において、それぞれ自らの権力基盤を強化してゆきました。

彼らのみならず、古代から中世にかけて、文明のある地域に侵入した人々や、その周辺に生きた人々は、ただ受動的に文明の恩恵を享受

| 時代 |
| 10, 11世紀 |
| 欧州中世 |

| 地域 |
| 共通 |

| 分類 |
| 宗教【交流】 |

| キーワード |
| 三大宗教(キリスト教、イスラム教、仏教)の波及と定着・ロシアの地の開発 |

the benefits of civilization. By importing the thinking, philosophy, and religions that had been cultivated in civilized countries, they used these elements to obtain authority and to work out government functions. One example of this was how the Imperial Court in Japan during the Yamato and Nara periods made great efforts to introduce Buddhism and make use of that religion to administer the country. The Uyghurs and Turkic peoples, when they spread westward, converted to Islam. The only reason why Christianity, Islam, and Buddhism evolved into world religions is because people over broad regions took up religious faiths.

At the eastern extremity of the Eurasian landmass, the Korean Peninsula and, by extension across the sea, the land that became Japan became the ultimate destinations of Buddhism, which poured forth from China. The ultimate destination in the west was Western Europe, into which both Islam and Christianity flowed. Ultimately, Christianity drove Islam out onto the southern coast of the Mediterranean. At the same time, a vast Islamic sphere evolved in the interior of the Eurasian landmass.

At that point, more actors appeared on the stage.

These were people who spread from the Baltic Sea through Russia to the Eastern Roman Empire. This region was inhabited by Eastern Slavs, part of a larger Slavic population. Ryurik, a member of one of the Norman people called Swedish Vikings, or Rus, appeared. He built a city-state in Novgorod in present-day northwestern Russia. This was in the 9th century. Later, Ryurik's descendants moved to Kiev, where they established the Kievan Rus, a grand duchy. The ruler of this state selected as its religion the Eastern Roman Empire's Orthodox Church.

As a consequence of this, from the Baltic Sea, through Novgorod and Kiev to the Eastern Roman Empire's capital city of Constantinople, East European trade flourished. This created the foundation for present-day Russia and Ukraine. From that time to the present, the Russian world has adhered to the Orthodox Church, and the various monarchies that have evolved in Russia have reigned as that religion's guardians. This closely resembles the relationship between the Kingdom of the Franks and Roman Catholicism.

In the 10th century, the Bulgarian Empire, which was created by the Bulgars, a Turkic people who inhabited lands west of the Grand Duchy of Kiev, flourished and confronted the Grand Duchy of Kiev. Gradually the original form of today's East Europe was taking form.

しただけではありません。文明国家に育まれた思想や哲学、宗教を移入することで、自らに権威をつけ、統治機能を整えたのです。例えば、大和や奈良時代に朝廷が仏教を取り入れ、国家の運営に役立てようと腐心したこともその例です。そして、ウイグル族やトルコ系の人々は、西へと展開したときに、イスラム教に帰依したのです。キリスト教、イスラム教、そして仏教が世界宗教へと成長していったのは、こうした広範な人々が宗教に帰依してきたからに他なりません。

　朝鮮半島とそこから海を渡った日本がユーラシア大陸の東端であれば、仏教は中国から日本という終着駅に流れ込んだことになります。西の終着駅であった西ヨーロッパにはイスラム教とキリスト教がともに流れ込み、最終的にはキリスト教がイスラム教を地中海の南岸に追いやります。同時にユーラシア大陸の内陸部には広大なイスラム圏が生まれていたのです。

　そこにもう一つのプレイヤーが登場します。
　それはバルト海からロシアを経て東ローマ帝国に至る地域に展開した人々です。この地域はスラブ人のうち東スラブ族の住む土地でした。そこにノルマン人の一派といわれるスウェーデンバイキング、別名ルーシ族のリューリクという人物が登場します。彼は、現在のロシア北西部にあるノヴゴロドに都市国家を建国します。9世紀のことでした。その後リューリクの子孫はキエフに移動し、キエフ大公国が建国されます。その支配者が選んだ宗教が、東ローマ帝国の正教会だったのです。
　これによって、バルト海から、ノヴゴロド、キエフを経由して東ローマ帝国の首都コンスタンティノープルに至る東ヨーロッパの交易ルートが栄えます。現在のロシア、ウクライナの基礎ができあがったのです。当時から現在に至るまで、正教会はロシア世界で信奉され、ロシアに展開した代々の王朝は、その保護者として君臨します。それはちょうどフランク王国とローマカトリックとの関係に似ていました。

　10世紀には、キエフ大公国の西側にトルコ系のブルガール人が建国したブルガリア帝国が栄え、キエフ大公国と対峙します。現在の東ヨーロッパの原型が形成されつつあったのです。

047 The Normans brought the Celts under their control

The earth's climatic change undoubtedly had various impacts on Japan. And at the chaotic time when the Frankish Kingdom, the Grand Duchy of Kiev, and Tang China were collapsing, the Heian period was beginning in Japan. During that time, lords of manors in Japan became powerful landowners, and the samurai class was formed. According to records, Japanese society was thrown into confusion in the late Heian period due to a large number of natural calamities, including famines and damage done by insect pests. Europe suffered under the same kinds of climatic phenomena.

The Normans, who were known as Vikings, were pushed out to the seas by such a temperate climate and expanded their activities, reaching as far as the Mediterranean. However, the Islamic Empire held control over the seas in that region. People threatened by the empire engaged the Normans as mercenaries. In due course, the Normans established the Kingdom of Sicily in 1130, which spanned the island of Sicily and the southern end of the Italian Peninsula, driving a wedge into the activities of the Islamic Empire.

Present-day Britain was another region greatly affected by the Normans. Originally the Normans were people based in the Scandinavian Peninsula, and from a broad point of view, they were one portion of the Germanic peoples. Despite being descendants of the Germanic migrations, they reshaped the map of Europe 700 years later.

Let us turn the hands of the clock back to the remote past, when the speakers of Indo-European languages were spreading across the Eurasian landmass. Among them were Celtic-speaking people. Within the great migration of the Indo-European-speaking peoples in the epicenter of Central Asia, the main wings of the migration into Europe were composed of these Celtic speakers. Deploying war machines and carrying iron weaponry, in about 1000 B.C., they migrated farther west out of Central Europe toward what is now France, Britain, and Spain, settling and creating their own unique cultural sphere.

Britain is now officially called the United Kingdom of Great Britain and Northern Ireland, and it includes England in the south, Wales in the west, and Scotland in the north, as well as Northern Ireland across the Irish Sea. Ireland is an independent nation, where a pronounced Celtic cultural influence remains. The

ノルマン人はケルト人を支配下においた

　地球の気象変動は、日本にも様々な影響を与えたに違いありません。フランク王国、キエフ大公国、そして中国で唐が滅び世情が混沌としていた頃、日本は平安時代でした。当時、日本では地方の荘園領主が土豪化し、武士階級が形成されています。記録によると、平安後期には飢饉や害虫など、天変地異が多く、そのことによって世が乱れたといわれています。ヨーロッパをも見舞った温暖化現象と無縁ではなかったはずです。

　バイキングと呼ばれたノルマン人が、そんな温暖な気候に押し出されるように、海に展開し、地中海まで進出した場所は、イスラム帝国が制海権を握っていました。その脅威にさらされていた人々が、ノルマン人を傭兵として雇ったのです。やがて、ノルマン人はイスラム帝国の活動に楔を打つように、1130年にシチリア島と南イタリアにまたがったシチリア王国を建国します。

　さらにノルマン人の影響を大きく受けたのが現在のイギリスでした。ノルマン人は元々スカンジナビア半島を拠点としていた人々ですが、大局的にいえばゲルマン人の一派です。そんな彼らがゲルマン人の大移動から700年後にヨーロッパの地図を塗り替えていったのです。

　時計の針を太古に戻してみましょう。あのインドヨーロッパ語族がユーラシア大陸に拡散した頃のことです。彼らの一派にケルト語族と呼ばれる人々がいました。中央アジアが震源地となったインドヨーロッパ語族の大移動の中で、ヨーロッパへの移動の主翼を担ったのがこのケルト語族に属する人々でした。戦車を使い、鉄器をもって、紀元前1000年頃にはヨーロッパ中部からさらに西へと、現在のフランスやイギリス、スペイン方面に定住し、独自の文化圏を造っていました。

　現在イギリスはグレート・ブリテン及び北部アイルランド連合王国という正式名称を持っていますが、イギリス西部のウェールズ、北部のスコットランド、そして北アイルランド、加えて現在独立国となっているアイルランドにはケルト文化が色濃く残っています。ケルト人

<table>
<tr><td>時代</td></tr>
<tr><td>11世紀以前
欧州中世</td></tr>
<tr><td>地域</td></tr>
<tr><td>ヨーロッパ</td></tr>
<tr><td>分類</td></tr>
<tr><td>民族【移動】</td></tr>
<tr><td>キーワード</td></tr>
<tr><td>ケルト人の社会・ゲルマン民族の定着・ノルマン人の定着と国家</td></tr>
</table>

Celts also settled in Gaul, present-day France. Two thousand years ago a heroic figure from Rome appeared in Gaul and placed the Celts under the umbrella of the Roman Empire. His name was Gaius Julius Caesar. From that point onward, these ethnic groups under Roman control repeatedly merged, separated, and then merged again, transforming into today's French, Spanish, and other peoples.

A region in western France is now called Brittany, a name which recalls its relationship with Britain. The country of the Celtic people spanned France and Britain. When the Germanic peoples made a major migration, one group, the Anglo-Saxons, gained control of Britain and broke away from Roman control. The Celts, too, came under control of these new rulers, and in that way the foundation of present-day Great Britain was laid. The people who conquered this Anglo-Saxon country in the 11th century were the Normans.

048 Great Britain was transformed by the Norman Conquest

"England" is referred to as *Igirisu* in Japanese, and it specifically refers to the central region of the present-day United Kingdom. Scotland in the north, Wales in the west, and Ireland across the Irish Sea are not part of England.

What is this all about? When the Romans abandoned Britain in 407, the Anglo-Saxons, one group of the Germanic peoples, crossed from the north coast of Germany and settled in Britain. Scotland later became an independent monarchy. When the Normans invaded in the 10th century, the heart of the territory they controlled was England, but in the surrounding territories the culture of the Celts, the original European masters, remained pronounced. This process resembled the manner in which the Jomon people in Japan were affected by the more sophisticated Yayoi people. In Britain, the equivalent of the Jomon people were the Celtic people.

For a time in Britain, it was the Danes, people from Denmark, who created a monarchy, but in basic terms it was the Anglo-Saxon monarchy that continued through the 11th century. Within that monarchy, while Normans were migrating and settling, Anglo-Saxons preserved royal authority while maintaining a subtly strained relationship with the other ethnic groups.

は、ガリアと呼ばれた現在のフランスにも定住していました。2000年前、一人の英雄がローマから現れ、彼らをローマの傘下におきました。ジュリアス・シーザーです。以後、彼らはローマの支配下で民族同士の融合や分離にさらされながら、現在のフランス人、スペイン人などへと変化していったのです。

フランス西部にブルターニュ地方と呼ばれる地域がありますが、その名の通り、ブルターニュはブリテンと同じ意味で、ケルト人の国家はフランスとイギリスにまたがっていました。ゲルマン人が大移動をすると、その一派であるアングロ・サクソン人がイギリスを支配し、ローマの支配から離脱します。そして、ケルト人もこの新しい支配者を受け入れます。このようにして、現在のイギリスの土台が築かれました。そんなアングロ・サクソン人の国家を11世紀に席巻したのが、ノルマン人だったのです。

イギリスはノルマンコンクエストによって変貌した

「イギリス」はイングランドと呼ばれていますが、イングランドとは現在のイギリスの中心部一帯のことを指しています。北のスコットランド、西のウェールズからアイルランドはイングランドではありません。

それはどういうことでしょうか。407年にイギリスをローマが放棄したとき、ゲルマン人の一派であるアングロ・サクソン人が現在のドイツ北岸より海を渡り、イギリスに入植します。スコットランドはその後王国として自立しています。10世紀にノルマン人が進攻してきたときも、支配の中心はイングランドで、周辺には元々ヨーロッパの支配者だったケルト人の文化が色濃く残ったのです。この過程は太古に日本で縄文人がより高度な文明をもった弥生人によって塗り替えられた状況とも似ています。イギリスでのケルト人はまさに縄文人のような先住民でした。

イギリスでは、一時デーン人、すなわちデンマークからやってきた人々が王朝を建てたこともありましたが、基本的にはアングロ・サクソン系の王朝が11世紀まで継続します。その王朝は、ノルマン人が移住してくる中、彼らとの微妙な緊張関係を保ちながら、王権を維持していたのです。

時代
11世紀
欧州中世

地域
イギリス

分類
国家【民族】

キーワード
アングロ・サクソン朝・ノルマンコンクエスト・ウェールズ、スコットランドとの関係

However, following the death of the monarch Edward the Confessor, a dispute arose over who would succeed to the throne in Britain. During this controversy, William I, Duke of Normandy, who was related by blood to Edward the Confessor, landed in Britain and ultimately seized control. In 1066 at the famous Battle of Hastings, he gained a victory that was for all intents and purposes the English version of the Battle of Sekigahara.

Actually, the Duke of Normandy pledged allegiance to the Capetian dynasty which united the West Frankish Kingdom. The Capetians, after the lineage of the Carolingian dynasty died out, began with the influential Hugh Capet in 987 in Paris. In other words, a prominent feudal lord who had returned to France became the king of Britain. Therefore, during that time, French was used as the official language in England. Gradually the Normans mixed their own language with words from Anglo-Saxon languages and that mixture evolved into the English language. The invasion of Britain by the Normans is known as the Norman Conquest. The impact of the Norman Conquest on Ireland and Wales was not as significant as it was on England, and they followed their own distinct paths. Later, as Britain matured, Wales was annexed and Ireland was ruled as a colony.

At present, in the U.K. there is a separatist movement rising in Scotland. Even after Ireland became independent, with Northern Ireland still under the sovereignty of the U.K., Northern Ireland has opposed England on many issues due to the historical cultural rivalry and ethnic awareness resulting from having once been in a superior-subordinate relationship.

As an aside, in the 5th century Christianity was transmitted to Ireland by St. Patrick. On the anniversary of the death of that venerated figure credited with propagating the religion, both Ireland and the U.S., where many immigrants of Irish descent reside, celebrate the day—March 17—as a holiday.

しかし、エドワード懺悔王と呼ばれる王の死後、イギリスに後継者争いがおきます。その中で、フランスのノルマンディ公国の王で懺悔王とも血縁関係にあったノルマンディ公ウィリアムがイギリスに上陸し、最終的にはイギリスを支配したのです。1066年のことでした。その時の戦いとして有名なヘースティングスの戦いは、イギリス史にとっての関ヶ原の合戦ともいえるものでした。

　実はノルマンディ公国は西フランク王国の流れをくむカペー朝に忠誠を誓っていました。カペー朝は、カロリング朝の血統が絶えた後に、987年にパリの有力者ユーグ・カペーが開いた王朝です。言い換えれば、フランスに帰属する有力諸侯がイギリス王となったわけです。従って、当時のイギリスではフランス語が公用語として使われていました。それが次第にノルマン人やアングロ・サクソンの言葉などと混ざりながら、英語へと変化したのです。ノルマン人のイギリスへの侵攻をノルマンコンクエストと呼んでいます。このノルマンコンクエストの影響をそれほど受けることなく、イングランドとは異なる独自の道を歩んだのがアイルランドであり、ウェールズでした。その後イギリスが成長すると、ウェールズは併合され、アイルランドを植民地として支配します。

　現在、イギリスの中でスコットランドに独立運動がおき、アイルランドが独立したあとも、北アイルランドがイギリスの主権の中にありながら、イングランドと対立している背景には、こうした征服民族と被征服民族との民族意識と文化の対立があるのです。

　ちなみに、5世紀にはアイルランドにキリスト教が伝わります。伝道にあたった聖人とされる聖パトリックの命日は、アイルランドのみならず、アイルランド系移民の多いアメリカなどでも現在祝日となっているのです。

タペストリーに描かれたヘースティングスの戦い。左側にノルマンディ公ウィリアムの率いるノルマン騎兵、右側にイングランドの歩兵が描かれている。

The Battle of Hastings as depicted in a tapestry. The Norman cavalry led by William I, Duke of Normandy, is depicted on the left, and the English infantry on the right.

049 Central Asia becomes Islamic in the 10th century

During the time when the West Frankish Kingdom became France, and the Holy Roman Empire emerged as the foundation for Germany and Austria, and when the Norman Conquest shaped the formation of modern-day Britain, there were also significant changes taking place among the nomadic peoples in the area around Central Asia.

Before these ethnic groups grew into large nations, they often served as mercenaries rather than invaders, protecting the frontiers of previous great empires and accumulating strength. It is possible to see how they amassed power through their relationships with Germanic peoples and the Roman Empire. The Turkic people who moved west from Central Asia were active as mercenaries of the Abbasid Caliphate. Referred to as mamluks, they were bought and sold as slaves from childhood and eventually trained as soldiers.

The Seljuq Turks, who rose up in the southern region of the Aral Sea in Central Asia and then expanded their influence westward also made use of these Turkic mamluks. In 1038 the leading power among these increasingly powerful Turks, Tughril Beg, founded the Great Seljuq Empire. Following that, he advanced into the Middle East and was granted the title of sultan by the caliph of Baghdad. This parallels the way in which the Roman Catholic Church bestowed the title of emperor on Charlemagne and on Otto I. From the caliph's perspective, the Seljuq Turks were the protectors of Sunni Islam, and from the perspective of Tughril Beg, this bestowal gave official religious recognition to the territories that were under his control.

The Seljuq dynasty Turks maintained power over the entire area from Central Asia through the Middle East into the eastern provinces of present-day Turkey. They became a source of pressure upon the Eastern Roman Empire.

Further, in Turkestan, where some Turkic people became active, in the 10th century they brought about the Qarakhanid dynasty. These people believed in Islam and are one reason why Islam is so widespread across the western reaches of China today.

At the same time, another Turkic monarchy known as the Ghaznavid dynasty, under a former mamluk named Sabuktigin, created a country in what is now Afghanistan around 977. Descendants of this dynasty, the Ghurid dynasty,

10世紀に中央アジアはイスラム化した

時代
10世紀
イスラム中世

地域
中央アジア・中国

分類
民族【国家】

キーワード
トルコ民族の勃興・スルタンの授与・多数のイスラム王朝の成立・宋の建国

西フランク王国がフランスとなり、ドイツ、オーストリアの原点ともなる神聖ローマ帝国が発足し、ノルマンコンクエストによって、現代に繋がるイギリスが形成された頃、中央アジアを核にした遊牧民の間にも、変動がありました。

民族が大きな国家へと成長する以前、彼らは侵略者というよりも、それ以前の大国の辺境地域などを守る傭兵となり、力を蓄えていったことは、ゲルマン人とローマ帝国との関係からも見えてきます。中央アジアからさらに西進したトルコ系の人々も、アッバース朝などの傭兵として活躍します。彼らはマムルークと呼ばれ、幼少の頃に売買された奴隷で、その後軍人として育てられました。

中央アジアのアラル海南部におこり、西へと勢力を拡大していったセルジューク朝トルコも、同じトルコ系のマムルークを活用していました。その盟主トゥグリル・ベクが1038年にセルジューク朝を建国します。その後彼は中東に進出し、バグダードのカリフからスルタンの称号を与えられます。それは、ちょうどローマカトリックがカール大帝やオットー1世にローマ帝国の皇帝の称号を贈ったことと似ています。カリフの立場から見ると、セルジューク朝トルコはスンナ派の擁護者であり、トゥグリル・ベクから見れば、これによって自らの領土をイスラム教の盟主として正式に統治できることになるのです。

セルジューク朝トルコは中央アジアから中東地域、そして現在のトルコ東部までを支配し、東ローマ帝国を西から圧迫する存在となったのです。

また元々トルコ系の人々が活動していたトルキスタンには、10世紀になって同じトルコ系のカラハン朝がおこっていました。彼らもイスラム教を信奉し、現在の中国西域一体にイスラム教が拡大する原因の一つとなりました。

同時に、マムルークから身をおこしたサブクティ・ギーンにより、977年頃にもう一つのトルコ系の王朝ガズナ朝が現在のアフガニスタンに建国します。この流れをくむゴール朝が12世紀に北インドに侵攻

invaded northern India in the 12th century, disseminating Islamic teachings throughout the region.

From the 10th into the 11th century, in Eurasia, the basis was laid for the present-day international political confrontation between the Christian world and the Islamic world.

At the time when the Turkic people were active, in East Asia the chaos that followed the decline of Tang China was approaching a resolution. Zhao Kuangyin, an influential figure in the Later Zhou, the last of the monarchies known as the Five Dynasties and Ten Kingdoms, founded the Song state. That was in 960. When the Song was established, in the north, the Khitans and Mongol-related nomads were also active, putting pressure on China. We will discuss this later, but these are the direct forebears of the northern ethnic groups that would influence China for over 900 years.

050 When world religions merged with state power, there was a tendency toward confrontation

When one observes the history of the broad region stretching from Eurasia to North Africa, one encounters one significant fact. Over the course of five centuries, the majority of these regions have constantly experienced waves of ethnic migrations, reshaping the racial fabric. It was not simply a change of power. Ethnic groups have merged. At times a completely different ethnic group has redrawn the political map. Monarchies and empires have risen and collapsed, one after another.

At the same time, one must not forget that in the same period diverse religious authorities maintaining these individual ethnic groups were formed by the 10th century, dividing the world into different subgroupings. In Europe, the nucleus was Christianity; in the Middle East, it was Islam.

Ethnic group migration had a major impact on China.

However, there were always Han people in China. Whether they themselves were actually in control of administration or were under the control of another ethnic group, the Han continued to play the leading role in East Asian civilization. In Chinese society, there was no strong monotheistic religion that merged with secular power, as was the case in Europe and in the Middle East. As we have seen

したことが、インド世界にイスラム教が拡散する原因となるのです。

こうして、10世紀から11世紀にかけて、ユーラシア大陸では現在の国際政治にも直接関係するキリスト教世界とイスラム教世界との対峙の構図ができあがったのです。

トルコ系の人々が活発に活動していたこの時期は、東アジアでは唐の滅亡以来の混乱が収束に向かっていた頃にあたります。五代十国の最後の王朝であった後周の有力者、趙 匡胤が宋を建国したのです。960年のことでした。宋が建国する時期に、北方では契丹やモンゴル系の遊牧民が活動し、中国を北から圧迫します。後述しますが、彼らは中国がその後900年の長きにわたって様々な影響を受ける北方民族の直接の祖先にあたる人々でした。

趙匡胤
Zhao Kuangyin (927–976)

世界宗教が国家権力と融合したときに
対立へと傾斜した

ユーラシア大陸から北アフリカに至る広範な地域の歴史を紐といてゆくと、一つの事実に突き当たります。それは、五百年のスパンで見てゆくと、これら全ての地域の大半が常に新手の民族移動にさらされながら、人種模様を変化させてきたということです。単に権力が交代したのではなく、人種が融合し、時には新たな人種に塗り替えられながら、王朝や帝国が興亡を繰り返してきたのです。

同時に、そうした多様な民族を貫く宗教的権威が10世紀までに形成され、世界を色分けていったことも忘れてはなりません。ヨーロッパを核にしたキリスト教、中東を核にしたイスラム教がそれにあたります。

民族移動は、中国にも大きな影響を与えます。

しかし、中国では常に漢民族がそこにいました。彼らは、自らが為政者であったときも、他民族に支配されたときも、東アジア文明の牽引者であり続けました。中国社会には、ヨーロッパや中東にみられたような強力な一神教が国家権力と融合することはありませんでした。儒教はあくまで道徳規範であって、宗教ではないことは既に触れまし

時代
7～12世紀
欧州中世

地域
東アジア

分類
宗教【民族】

キーワード
漢民族の持続性と宗教的多様性 • 東アジアの文化浸透 • 東アジアの国際関係

earlier, Confucianism was simply a model of morals, not a religion. Furthermore, although Daoism and Buddhism matured in China, the Han people did not take up any one single religious belief.

This is also connected with the reason why Japan did not experience an invasion by people of different ethnic origins, as was the case in the Norman Conquest. While China was susceptible to political influence from other groups, the Han did not entirely replace other ethnic groups. China absorbed other ethnic groups like a sponge absorbs water. In other words, from the standpoint of Japan, China served as the last bulwark in the major ethnic migrations across Eurasia.

In Japan, in the Heian period Buddhism and Shinto, which can be called the religion of ancient Japan, subtly merged, cultivating a unique attitude toward religion. Even in China, Daoism, Confucianism, Buddhism, and diverse folk beliefs came together and through the ages influenced one another.

Buddhism originated in India, then took root in countries neighboring China, including Southeast Asia, Tibet, Mongolia, the Korean Peninsula, and Japan. In the 4th century, Kumarajiva transmitted Buddhist scriptures from Kashmir to China. Then during the Tang period, a large number of people risked their lives in the dangerous crossing between China and Japan to transmit these teachings, including Jianzhen, who reached Nara. As a result of their efforts, Buddhism was transmitted eastward. Within Japan, Buddhism was employed by the state authority to develop the country's system of government and to enhance its culture, but there was no attempt to force the people of the country to adopt it as their faith.

Nalanda University, established in northeastern India around the 5th century, played a significant role in the spread of Buddhism to the surrounding regions. Prominent examples include the Chinese monk Xuanzang, who studied there during the Tang Dynasty, and the Buddhist monks who embarked on missionary journeys from Nalanda, contributing to the propagation of Tibetan Buddhism. However, Nalanda University declined during the process of Islamization in northern India. Furthermore, as Hinduism gradually permeated Indian society from the 4th century onwards, the overall Indian society witnessed a decline in the number of Buddhist followers within India itself.

た。また、道教や仏教も、中国で熟成されてゆきますが、漢民族が全て一つの宗教に帰依したことはなかったのです。

　これは日本がノルマンコンクエストのような、大陸からの異民族の移動に見舞われなかった理由にも繋がりそうです。それは、中国が政治的影響を受けながらも、完全に漢民族が異民族に塗り変えられることなく、他の民族をスポンジのように吸収していった経緯が関係していたのです。つまり、中国がユーラシア大陸の壮大な民族移動の最後の防波堤の役割を果たしていたのです。

　日本では、平安時代に仏教と日本古来の宗教といえる神道とが、微妙に融合し、独特の宗教観が育ってゆきます。中国でも道教、儒教、仏教などが様々な民間信仰と重なり、時代を経てお互いに影響を与え合ってゆきます。

　仏教はインドで産声をあげ、インドを離れて東南アジアやチベット、モンゴル、朝鮮半島や日本といった中国周辺諸国にも根付いてゆきました。4世紀にカシミールから中国に仏典を伝えた鳩摩羅什。そして唐の時代に中国から奈良に渡ってきた鑑真和上など、多くの人が命がけの旅の末に、仏教を東へと伝播してゆきました。日本で仏教は国家権力によって国家の制度や文化の高揚に利用されますが、国民に信仰が強要されることはありませんでした。

　5世紀頃インド東北部に設立されたナーランダ学院は、仏教の周辺地域への拡散に大きな役割を果たします。その代表例が、唐の時代にそこで学んだ中国僧玄奘三蔵や、ナーランダ学院から逆に布教の旅にでた僧によって伝播していったチベット仏教です。そんなナーランダ学院も、北インドがイスラム化する過程で衰亡します。また、インド社会全体が、4世紀頃からヒンドゥー教がインド社会に浸透してゆくなかで、インド国内では仏教の信者そのものが減少していったのです。

051　Fear of the Eastern Roman Empire triggered the Crusades

Let us direct our attention once again to the antipathy between Islam and Christianity.

When one discusses medieval European history, one event that is inevitably brought forth is the Humiliation at Canossa in 1077.

In the medieval period, the clergy of the Roman Catholic Church enjoyed an independent tax revenue and exercised strong powers of jurisdiction over the peasants under their purview. When feudal lords or the emperor of the Holy Roman Empire sought to acquire such prerogatives, they themselves appointed these clergymen.

In response, the Roman Popes made fervent efforts to keep the churches under papal authority. The confrontation between the secular authority and the papal religious authority sparked major conflict regarding the investiture of the clerics. In opposition to this action by the pope, the Emperor of the Holy Roman Empire, Henry IV, was excommunicated by Pope Gregory VII. Feudal lords interfered in this confrontation, and surrendering to this pressure, the emperor ultimately went to Canossa, in Italy, to apologize to the pope.

Much was made of the incident thereafter for the purpose of enhancing the authority of the Roman Catholic Church. The story that was passed down among the people was that the emperor had been made to stand barefoot in the snow when asking for the pope's forgiveness. In fact, following this incident, Henry IV restored his regime, supported by a new pope, and ousted Gregory VII from Rome.

The events surrounding the Humiliation of Canossa serve rather as an indication of just how tentative the motives of the various feudal lords were in the Holy Roman Empire. In terms of Japanese history, the emperor of the Holy Roman Empire somewhat resembles the shogun during the Muromachi period, whose power base was not yet firm, and to a degree the daimyo resemble the feudal lords of Europe. If we take the analogy one step further and compare the Japanese emperor to the pope, the relationship of power is even easier to understand. Further, the feudal lords, corresponding to the daimyo, were attended by a band of knights. In the case of Europe, such knights were independent figures who had their own manors, and each of them was in a position to express their views to the king they served. Through the conflicts over investiture, the Pope capitalized

東ローマ帝国への脅威が十字軍の引き金になった

再びイスラム教とキリスト教との対立にスポットをあててみます。

ヨーロッパの中世史を語るとき、必ず取り上げられる事件に、1077年におきたカノッサの屈辱があります。

中世、教会の聖職者は独自の税収を享受し、傘下の農民への裁判権をも行使できるほどその影響力は甚大でした。諸侯や神聖ローマ帝国の皇帝は、そうした特権を獲得しようと、自らが聖職者を任命しようとします。

それに対してローマ教皇は、教会を自らの管理の下におこうと懸命でした。この世俗権力と宗教的権威であるローマ教皇との対立が、聖職者の叙任権をめぐり、火を吹いたのです。神聖ローマ帝国皇帝ハインリヒ4世が、ローマ教皇のこうした動きに反発したのに対し、当時の教皇グレゴリウス7世が皇帝を破門するという行動にでます。この対立に諸侯が介入し、その圧力に屈した皇帝が最終的にイタリアのカノッサで教皇に謝罪したのです。

この事件は、その後ローマカトリックの権威を高める目的で宣伝され、雪の中に裸足で立ち、教皇に許しを請うた皇帝の物語として、人々に語り継がれることになります。実際は、事件のあと、ハインリヒ4世は体制を立て直し、新しい教皇を擁立してグレゴリウス7世をローマから追い出します。

カノッサの屈辱の一件は、むしろ神聖ローマ帝国が様々な諸侯の政治的思惑に左右されている状況を印象付けたものでした。日本史で見るなら、神聖ローマ帝国皇帝は、まだ権力基盤がしっかりとしていなかった室町時代の征夷大将軍に、諸侯は大名にあたります。また、教皇が天皇であると思えば、その力関係がよくわかります。さらに、大名にあたる王、すなわち諸侯は、騎士団を従えていますが、ヨーロッパの場合、その騎士は荘園を持った独立した存在で、それぞれが王に対しても発言力を持っていました。聖職者の叙任権を巡る争いを経て、こうした世俗権力の政治的対立を利用しながら、ローマ教皇はヨーロッパ社会への影響力を高めていったのです。

時代
11世紀
欧州中世

地域
ヨーロッパ

分類
戦争【宗教】

キーワード
ローマ教会の優位・世俗権力との対立・トルコの発展と脅威・十字軍の開始

on these secular power struggles, thereby increasing the church's influence over European society.

During that time, the Roman pope, facing the threat of the Seljuq Empire, which was occupying the region of modern-day Turkey and pressuring the Eastern Roman Empire, received a plea for help from the Eastern Roman Emperor. At that time, the Eastern Roman Empire as a state possessed only present-day Greece and western Turkey. Upon receipt of this appeal, the Roman pope, Urban II, called a religious council at the French town of Clermont, urging participation in a fight against the followers of Islam. The year was 1095.

The next year, knights assembled by the feudal lords gathered at Constantinople, capital city of the Eastern Roman Empire, and from that point battles commenced against the Seljuq Turks. This was the beginning of the well-known Crusades, a series of attacks on Islamic society.

Over the following 200 years, a succession of Crusades involving all of European society created massive religious warfare. From the viewpoint of Islamic society, this was no less than a new ethnic movement by followers of a different religion pouring into their lands from Europe.

052 Discord between agricultural people and nomadic people stirs the world

At about the time when the might of Islam collided with that of Christianity, dividing the western half of Eurasia into two camps and leading to the strife of the Crusades, in the northern reaches of Asia, a large ethnic movement began that led to another period of history. We return our attention once again to another movement of ethnic groups between Central Asia and North Asia.

The pillars of world history are the agricultural people who engage in cultivating the land and nomadic peoples who migrate together with their domesticated animals. Needless to say, agricultural people support themselves by staying in one place, maintaining farmland, and building homes for their families. Always keeping harvests in mind, they form organized groups and bring about the development of towns and cities. The Japanese are seen as representative of these agricultural people.

そんなローマ教皇に、トルコ一帯を領有しながら東ローマ帝国を圧迫するセルジューク朝の脅威にさらされていた東ローマ皇帝から救援の依頼が届きます。当時、東ローマ帝国は、現在のギリシアとトルコ西部を領有するだけの国家になっていました。これを受けてローマ教皇ウルバヌス2世がフランスのクレルモンで宗教会議を開き、イスラム教徒との戦いへの参加を呼びかけます。1095年のことでした。

　翌年に諸侯によって構成される騎士団が、東ローマ帝国の首都コンスタンティノープルに集結し、セルジューク朝トルコとの戦いを始めます。世に名高い十字軍によるイスラム社会への攻撃の始まりです。

ギュスターヴ・ドレ
『コンスタンティノープルに入城する十字軍』
Gustave Doré —Entry of the Crusaders into Constantinople

　この一連の十字軍の活動は、その後200年にわたって、ヨーロッパ社会全体を巻き込んだ、宗教的軍事活動となってゆきます。それは、イスラム社会から見れば、ヨーロッパ社会から押し寄せてきた、異教徒による新たな民族運動に他なりませんでした。

農耕民族と遊牧民族の確執が世界を動かす

　イスラム勢力と、キリスト教勢力とが、ユーラシア大陸の西半分を二分し、十字軍の抗争へと繋がっていった頃、北方アジアでは次の時代に繋がる大きな民族活動がおきていました。何度か触れてきた、中央アジアから北アジアにかけての民族の動きに再び注目します。

時代
総合

地域
共通

分類
交流【侵略】

キーワード
農耕文化と遊牧文化の接点・富の蓄積と簒奪・民族対立と交流

　世界史の担い手には、農耕に従事する農耕民族と、家畜とともに移動して生活する遊牧民族がいます。農耕民族はいうまでもなく定住し、農地を持ち、そこに家を建てて家族を養います。彼らは常に収穫を念頭においた社会の仕組みを作り、都市を発展させます。日本人は代表的な農耕民族であるとされています。

In contrast, nomadic peoples are always on the move, domesticating livestock, and making skillful use of horses for transportation. Militarily, the nomadic people as highly mobile horse-riders, pose a constant threat to agriculturalists, whose movements are greatly restricted.

Agriculturalists, on the other hand, are able to maintain stable crops, their populations increase, and they are able to accumulate wealth. For these farming people, it was essential to sustain populations in order to maintain a labor force and to provide a sufficient military force to protect themselves. On the contrary, the nomads who are always on the move, travel on horseback over a wide area, led by a small elite, expanding the territories under their control. When nomadic people seize the wealth of the agriculturalists, a change occurs in the power of a state. When nomads become the new rulers, they assimilate into the civilization of the agriculturalists, gradually losing their nomadic lifestyle and merging with the agricultural people. Militarily as well, they are transformed from an aggressive people into a defensive people.

North Asia was a land of ups and downs for the nomads. Let us recall that the Xiongnu, Xianbei, Tujue, and others not only formed successive dynasties in China but also impacted events as far away as China's Western Regions, the Middle East, and Europe. Among those people, the Tungus were active in North Asia and also in northeastern China, the Korean Peninsula, and eastern Siberia, a wide area to be sure.

During the Tang period in China, Koguryo, which the Tungus-related nomads of the north had created in the Korean Peninsula, was overthrown. In 698 the people who migrated from Koguryo into what is now the east coastal region of Russia founded the state of Balhae. The country that Japan had connections with in the Nara and Heian periods was, from the perspective of present-day Korea, a large country founded by their ancestors. Dae Joyeong, the founder of that state, is so honored that it is the name given to a destroyer in the Korean navy.

The Balhae Kingdom was destroyed in 926 by the Khitan people, who are also said to have Mongol ancestry, and who were under the leadership of Yelu Abaoji. He established the Liao dynasty. Like Balhae, the Liao dynasty also grew into a powerful empire, encompassing various regions in North Asia.

The migrating nomadic nations aimed to expand southward into an agrarian civilization. That civilization was China. At the time, the Tang dynasty had given way to the Five Dynasties and Ten Kingdoms, and the Song dynasty had arisen. Descendants of these northern peoples had already in the past planted roots

それに対して、遊牧民族は移動を常とし、家畜をてなずけ、馬を巧みに操ります。軍事的にも遊牧民は騎馬民族として、機動性にたけ、農地にしがみつくことによって移動を縛られる農耕民族にとっては常に脅威となります。

　逆に農耕民族は、安定した農作物を得ることで、人口も増え、富を蓄積します。農耕民族にとって、人口を維持することは労働力を保ち、十分な兵力を養い、自らを防衛する上で必要なことでした。反対に、常に騎馬によって移動する遊牧民は、少数精鋭をもってより広域に活動することで、自らの領土を拡大します。そんな遊牧民が、農耕民族の富を纂奪するときに、国家権力の交代がおきました。そして、新たな支配者となった遊牧民は、農耕民族の文明に染まりながら、次第に遊牧民族としてのライフスタイルを失い、農耕社会に混ざりこみます。軍事的にも攻める民族から守る民族へと変化するのです。

　北アジアは、遊牧民族の興亡の大地でした。匈奴や鮮卑、突厥などが、中国の歴代の王朝のみならず、遠く西域から中東、そしてヨーロッパにも影響を及ぼしてきた様子を思い出しましょう。北アジアに活動していたツングース系の人々は、そんな遊牧民族の中でも現在の中国東北地方から朝鮮半島、そしてシベリア東部という広大な地域で活動した人々でした。

　唐の時代、そんなツングース系の北方民族が朝鮮半島に打ち立てた高句麗が滅びます。そして698年に高句麗から移動した人々が、現在のロシア東海岸一帯に渤海という国を築きます。奈良時代から平安初期にかけて日本とも交流していたこの国家は、現在の韓国から見ると、朝鮮族の祖先が打ち立てた大国でした。建国した大祚栄は、韓国海軍の駆逐艦の名前にもなっているほどです。

　渤海を926年に滅ぼしたのは、モンゴル系ともいわれる契丹人の耶律阿保機でした。彼の建てた国を遼といいます。遼も渤海と同様に北アジア一帯を領有する大国に成長しました。

　彼ら遊牧民族の国家が農耕文明を目指して南下してくるところ。それが中国でした。当時、中国は唐から五代十国を経て、宋が産声をあげていた時代です。すでに、過去の北方民族の末裔は中国社会に深く入り込み、漢民族と区別がつかなくなっているほどでした。しかし、

in Chinese society and were virtually indistinguishable from the Han Chinese. However, the Song, who once again united China, from the very beginning of the founding of that dynasty, had to face a new threat from the north.

053 China's Western Regions and the nomadic states mediated between the East and the West

In 960 when Zhao Kuangyin established the Song dynasty, the northern region was undergoing a transition. The global warming phenomena of the Middle Ages naturally stimulated activities among these northern people. There was undoubtedly an increase in the population as the northern ethnic groups, originally equestrian people, began to settle and take up agriculture within their states. Beginning in the Liao period, these northern groups were taking possession of the territories where the Great Wall was located, known as the Sixteen Prefectures of Yan and Yun. Following the establishment of the Song dynasty, in an effort to defend the state, it attempted to recapture these essential territories, but those efforts failed.

The Song, while placating the Liao, who were an immediate threat, constantly sought a way to unite the surrounding region and seize an opportunity to grasp control of the north. China was inevitably hemmed in by ethnic groups on three sides. To the west was Tufan in Tibet. To the north was the large developing state of Western Xia. This later state was established by Li Yuanhao who was entrusted with unifying that region as a tributary state of the Tang. Western Xia was a Tangut state, said to be made up of Burmese and Tibetan people.

The Song skillfully used the politics of Tufan, Western Xia, Liao and other people stretched across the north and the west in order to weaken them, allowing Song itself to remain stable.

Eventually, in 1125 Liao was overthrown by the Tungus-related Jurchens in the region the Liao had once controlled. The state that the Jurchens created became known as Jin. The Jin turned the tables on the political strategy of the Song, who worried about the menace of the neighboring groups, forming an alliance with the Song that destroyed the Liao.

At the time of the ruin of the Liao, its imperial clan fled westward. A member of the Liao was Yelu Dashi. With the help of the Mongols, he invaded Turkestan,

中国を再び統一した宋は、北の新たな脅威と建国当初から向き合わなければならなかったのです。

西域の遊牧国家が東西の橋渡しを行った

　趙匡胤が宋を建国した960年頃は、北方の変動期にあたりました。中世の温暖化現象は、当然これら北方民族の活動を盛んにしたはずです。元々騎馬民族であった北方民族が、国家の中で農耕を営み定住をも始める中で、人口も増えていったに違いありません。遼の時代から、北方民族は元々万里の長城がある地域にあたる燕雲十六州と呼ばれる領土を占有していました。宋は建国後、国家防衛のためにも重要なこれらの諸州の奪還に努めますが失敗します。

時代
10〜12世紀
中国中世

地域
中央アジア

分類
国家【交流】

キーワード
宋と辺境の国々の勃興・金の発展と遼の西走・多様な宗教の伝播・遊牧騎馬民族の活躍

　宋は、当面の脅威である遼を懐柔しながらも、常に周辺と組んで北方を平定する機会を狙っていました。そもそも中国は常に三方を様々な民族国家に囲まれています。西を見ればチベットに吐蕃があり、その北に大国に成長していた西夏という国がありました。西夏は、唐の時代に中央から節度使としてその地域の統治を任されていた李元昊が開いた国家です。西夏はビルマ、チベット系といわれるタングート族の国家でした。

　宋は吐蕃や西夏、そして遼など、北方から西域に至る国々の政治を巧みに利用し、お互いの力を削ぎ、自国の安定を図ります。

　やがて、遼は支配地で活動していたツングース系の女真族に1125年に滅ぼされます。女真族が打ち立てた国家を金といいます。金は周辺民族の脅威を気にする宋の政策を逆手にとって、宋と連携しながら遼を滅ぼしたのでした。

　遼が滅んだとき、遼の皇族が西へ逃れます。耶律大石という人物です。彼はモンゴル族を頼り、トルキスタンに攻め入ったあとそこを追われ、

was subsequently driven from there, and ultimately ended up in Central Asia, where he established a state called Western Liao.

One tends to imagine the Western Region as a frontier area, but in its various oases a number of city-states had absorbed various influences, including Islamic, as well as Chinese culture, through tributary missions during the heyday of the Tang period, and also, Buddhist culture. Western Xia and, further to the west, Western Liao were called Qara Khitai by the Islamic people on the western border. Both became especially prosperous states serving as valuable intermediaries in East-West exchanges.

In 431 under the leadership of the Roman Empire, the Nestorian off-shoot of Christianity was declared heretical by the council of Ephesus in Turkey. Over a long period of time, these Nestorian beliefs were transmitted along the Silk Road, ultimately reaching Tang China. As we have noted, in China it became Keikyo. As its teachings spread through Central Asia, it influenced the nomadic people of the region.

Among those who confronted the Western Liao were Nestorian followers. The Western Liao also confronted the Seljuq Turks to the west. Among the Crusaders that attacked the Seljuq Turks, rumors spread that there was a savior in the East who believed in Christianity.

In the North, there was a vacant area between nomadic states. This was the present-day Mongolia. It was a land of strong, unyielding horse-riding nomads. These were the Mongols, who would later build a world empire.

054 During the Crusades, the land and sea routes of the Silk Road transmitted civilization

The time when the Song dynasty was struggling with diplomacy with northern ethnic groups in East Asia corresponds exactly to the period when the Crusades were taking place in Europe.

The activities of the Crusades became bogged down in the Middle East, but as a result of the conflict, the transportation of goods flourished, and the Mediterranean world became a locus of merchant activity. Italian merchants centered in Venice became the main actors on this stage. Further, through the activities of the Crusades, when movement of people in Europe increased, a wave

最終的には中央アジアまで移動して西遼という国家を建国したのです。

　西域は辺境であるというイメージを抱かれがちですが、それぞれのオアシスには、イスラム文化や盛唐期の節度使などによる中国文化、さらには仏教文化などの多彩な影響を受けた都市国家がありました。西夏、そしてその西の西遼（イスラム側ではカラキタイともいわれています）は、その中でも特に栄えた国家として、東西交流の重要な中継点になったのです。

　431年に、当時ローマ帝国が主導してトルコで開いた、エフェソス公会議で異端とされたネストリウス派キリスト教が、この東西交流の道であるシルクロードを通り、長い年月を経て唐に伝わり、景教と呼ばれていたことはすでに記しました。伝播の途上、景教は中央アジアの遊牧民にも影響を与えます。

　西遼に対峙した人々にそうしたネストリウス派の人々がいたのです。そして西遼は、その西にあったセルジューク朝トルコとも対立していたため、セルジューク朝トルコを攻めた十字軍の間に、東にキリスト教を信奉する救世主がいるという噂が広まったとまでいわれています。
　そんな遊牧民の国家の空白地帯が北にありました。現在のモンゴル一帯です。そこにいた強靭な遊牧騎馬民族。それが、その後世界帝国を建設するモンゴル族だったのです。

十字軍の時代、海と陸にシルクロードが文明を運んだ

　東アジアで宋が北方民族との外交に苦しんでいた時代こそ、ヨーロッパで十字軍が活動していた時期にあたります。

　十字軍の活動は、中東地域を混乱に陥れますが、戦争により物資の運搬が盛んになり、地中海世界は商人の活躍の場へと変化します。ヴェネチアを中心としたイタリアの商人がその核となりました。また、十字軍の活動を通して、ヨーロッパでの人の動きが活発になると、商業活動の波は北ヨーロッパからバルト海、スラブ地域へと拡大します。

時代
11～13世紀 欧州中世

地域
ヨーロッパ・中東・日本

分類
経済【交流】

キーワード
東ローマによる古代文明の保存・戦争と運搬の発展・交易による商業発展・アフリカとの交流

of mercantile activity expanded from northern Europe into the Baltic Sea and into Slavic areas.

Due to this mutual exchange, the products of culture were transported eastward from Europe, and culture and institutions from the Chinese sphere flowed in the reverse direction. The stir caused by the Crusades and the nomads became evidence of the ironic truth that at the same time war brings destruction, it also contributes to the exchange of culture between different civilizations.

The western base of this commercial activity was Constantinople, capital city of the Eastern Roman Empire. The empire no longer had the expansive territory or military power that it once possessed, and most of its original territory had been absorbed by the Islamic world. However, the Eastern Roman Empire still preserved the culture and technology that had been handed down since the Greek period, and it had wealth. The activity of the Crusades played the role of spreading the civilization of the empire and that of the Mediterranean world, which was further cultivated by the Islamic world, even farther to the west.

At this same time, Japan was in transition between the Heian period and the Kamakura period. Enjoying a favorable environment as a result of being an island country, an indigenous culture developed in Japan. From the Yamato period through the Nara period, Buddhist culture that flowed in from China and the Korean Peninsula was assimilated into Japan's cultural climate.

The term *honji suijaku* refers to the theory that the Shinto gods are earthly manifestations of the heavenly buddhas and bodhisattvas. It refers to the shared religious beliefs within temples and other places between Shinto, which is the indigenous faith of Japan, and Buddhism, which was transmitted from the continent. They came to be regarded as religions with common roots.

Meanwhile, far away from Japan in Africa, Islam gradually penetrated deep into the hinterland of northern Africa, disseminating across the whole nomadic region of the Sahara Desert. One flow spread along the coastline of East Africa, and the bases Muslim merchants established to carry out their trade became city-states. The sea routes that these people developed later became sources of information that made possible Europe's Age of Discovery.

Merchants made use of the seasonal monsoon winds, traveling from Africa to the Arabian Peninsula in summer, and returning to Africa when the winds reversed in winter, trading gold, ivory, and other merchandise.

Thus, the artifacts brought from Africa became linked to trade routes that extended from India to Southeast Asia, creating a trade route that traversed the

こうした交流によって文物がさらに東へと伝わり、東からも中国世界の文物が流入してきたのです。戦争が破壊とともに文明の交流に貢献するという皮肉な現実が、十字軍や遊牧民の躍動によって証明された形になったのです。

　そんな商業活動の西の拠点となったのが、東ローマ帝国の首都コンスタンティノープルでした。東ローマ帝国には、以前のような広大な領土と軍事力はすでになく、元々の版図の多くはイスラム世界に編入されていました。しかし、東ローマ帝国にはギリシア時代以降の文物や技術が保存され、富があったのです。十字軍の活動は、そうした東ローマの文明、さらにはイスラム世界に育まれていた地中海文明を、改めて西へと伝播する役割を果たしたのです。

土佐光起筆『源氏物語画帖』より「若紫」。飼っていた雀の子を逃がしてしまった幼い紫の上と、柴垣から隙見する源氏。

Tosa Mitsuoki
—Ilustration of the *The Tale of Genji, ch.5-Wakamurasaki*. Young Murasaki no Ue, who has lost her sparrow, and Genji, who is watching the gap from the bush fence.

　この時期は、日本では平安時代から鎌倉時代にあたります。島国という恵まれた環境の中で日本では独自の国風文化が生み出されていました。大和時代から奈良時代にかけて、日本に流れ込んだ中国や朝鮮半島の仏教文化も、日本の風土に消化されてゆきます。

　本地垂迹という言葉があります。神道を中心とした日本固有の信仰と大陸から伝わった仏教とが、同じルーツを持つ宗教として寺院などの中で共有されるようになったのです。

　一方、日本から遠く離れたアフリカでは、イスラム教が次第に北アフリカ奥地に浸透し、サハラ砂漠一帯の遊牧民の間に拡散しました。その一部は東アフリカ沿岸にも広がり、イスラム商人の交流の拠点となる都市国家ができあがります。こうした人々が開拓した海路が、その後のヨーロッパの人々による大航海時代での航行を可能にした情報源となるのです。

　モンスーンにのって、商人は夏にはアフリカからアラビア半島へ、冬は風向きが変わることを利用して北アフリカ沿岸を南行し、金や象牙などの交易を行ったのです。

　そして、アフリカからもたらされた文物が、今度はインドから東南アジアに至る交易にリンクし、遥かインド洋から南シナ海を経て中国

vast Indian Ocean and South China Sea, and eventually reached China.

Italian merchants, who built wealth through the Crusades in bases like Venice, gathered information from other parts of the world from the sea routes of the Silk Road, as well as from the nomadic people who connected the land routes of the Silk Road. These wealthy merchants had great influence in the European world.

055 The riches of northern Africa reached the Mediterranean through the hands of Muslim merchants

At the time when the Crusades were heading east to regain Jerusalem, Andalusia in southern Spain was prospering under the rule of the Andalusian Umayyad dynasty. The great cathedral named Mezquita, which was built in Cordoba, the capital city of those times, still stands today. It is currently a Christian church, but in its early days the building was used as a mosque. Mezquita is simply the Spanish word for "mosque." Walking inside the massive structure, one is wrapped

メスキータの内部
Inside the Mezquita in Cordoba, Spain

in a mysterious atmosphere combining both Islamic and Christian culture.

The Andalusian Umayyad dynasty, as the guardian of western Islam, repelled the Normans. However, in the 11th century, when the Andalusian Umayyad dynasty collapsed due to infighting over power in the administration, Spain was divided among Islamic feudal lords called taifa. This discord provided an opportunity for the Christian monarchies of Castile and Aragon in northern Spain to expand their influence.

In reaction to this threat, an Islamic state called the Almoravid dynasty invaded Spain with the collaboration of the taifa. This dynasty was a monarchy formed by the indigenous Berbers of northern Africa in 1040.

The Berbers were originally desert people who were active in a wide area of northern Africa. Between the 7th and 8th centuries they were absorbed by the Islamic Empire, and they converted to Islam themselves. The domains of the Almoravids extended through present-day Algeria, Morocco, and southern Spain, and in their heyday it subjugated all of northwest Africa.

に至る交易ルートができあがったのでした。

　十字軍で富を築いたヴェネチアなどを基地にしたイタリア商人は、この海のシルクロードと、遊牧民族がつなぐ陸のシルクロードの双方から世界の情報を入手し、富裕な商人となり、ヨーロッパ世界に影響を与えるようになるのでした。

北アフリカの富はイスラム商人によって地中海に届けられた

　十字軍がエルサレムの回復へと東に目を向けていた頃、スペイン南部のアンダルシアは、後ウマイヤ朝の支配のもとで繁栄していました。今でも当時首都であったコルドバにはメスキータという大聖堂が残っています。現在はキリスト教の教会ですが、この建物はその昔イスラム教のモスクとして使用されていたのです。メスキータとはスペイン語でモスクのことに他なりません。壮大なメスキータの中を歩けば、イスラム文化とキリスト教文化とが折り重なった神秘的な風景に包まれます。

　後ウマイヤ朝は、西のイスラム教の守護神として、ノルマン人の侵入も退けます。しかし、11世紀になって後ウマイヤ朝が権力闘争の末に内部分裂をしたとき、スペインはタイファと呼ばれるイスラム教の諸侯によって分割されました。この混乱が、スペイン北部にあったカスティーリャやアラゴンといったキリスト教の王国が勢力を拡大する契機となったのです。

　その脅威に対して、タイファと連携しスペインに侵入したのが、ムラービト朝というイスラム国家でした。彼らは北アフリカの先住民ベルベル人が1040年に建国した王国です。

　ベルベル人は、元々北アフリカに広く活動していた砂漠の民でしたが、7世紀から8世紀にかけてイスラム帝国に吸収され、イスラム化してゆきました。ムラービト朝の版図は現在のアルジェリアとモロッコ、そしてスペイン南部に及び、最盛期には北西アフリカ一帯を支配下にいれます。

時代
11世紀
イスラム中世

地域
中東・アフリカ

分類
経済【国家】

キーワード
スペインのイスラム勢力・アフリカ王朝の興亡・商人の活躍・アフリカの国家

The long Niger River flows through northwestern Africa. It descends from the highlands of present-day Guinea through Mali, makes a large half-circle through Nigeria, and empties into the Gulf of Guinea. In the middle of the river's route, there was a kingdom called the Ghana Empire from the 4th century onwards. Because it was possible to extract gold dust there, Muslim merchants transported rock salt across the Sahara Desert to trade it for this gold. The Almoravid dynasty invaded Ghana in 1076 and took control. And for a century the Almoravids reigned over the entire area from Spain into Africa. In 1147, as a result of internal conflicts, it was destroyed by the feudal lords. From approximately that time, Christian forces began full-scale invasions of Islamic-controlled areas. In what was called the Reconquista, or warfare to return Spain to Christian domination, together with the Crusades in the east, set Islam and Christianity on a path of conflict that would be passed down through succeeding generations.

Meanwhile, after the Almoravid dynasty ended, an Islamic monarchy called the Mali Empire began to flourish in Ghana. The revenue from salt and gold dust and the agricultural products of its fertile lands along the Niger River became the source of Mali wealth. With this wealthy country as their destination, large numbers of merchants made the trek from the Mediterranean and crossed the Sahara in order to develop a regular trade there. Unfortunately, it is precisely the area where Mali once flourished that the present-day Islamic extremist organization Boko Haram has come to use as a base for its activities.

056　The Fourth Crusade drove the Eastern Roman Empire into a corner

When one pursues the history of the strife between Islam and Christianity, one can understand just how widespread and persistent it really was.

Following the incident of the Humiliation at Canossa, the Roman pope made every possible effort to establish his authority over secular government. Innocent III, who took over the papacy in the 13th century was, among others, a preeminent statesman.

Using the ultimate weapon of excommunication

インノケンティウス3世
Pope Innocent III (1161–1216)

北西アフリカにはニジェール川が流れています。それは現在のギニアの高地からマリを経て、半円を描くように大きく蛇行しながらナイジェリアからギニア湾に注ぐ大河です。その中流域には4世紀以降ガーナ王国という国家がありました。そこで砂金が採取されることから、イスラム系の商人はサハラ砂漠の岩塩を持ってガーナ王国にいき、黄金と交換していたといわれています。ムラービト朝は、1076年にそんなガーナ王国を攻略し支配します。こうして、ムラービト朝はスペインからアフリカに至る地域で百年にわたって君臨したのです。ムラービト朝が内部抗争の末に諸侯によって滅ぼされたのが1147年。その頃からスペインでもキリスト教勢力によるイスラム教支配地への侵攻が本格的に始まります。レコンキスタと呼ばれる、スペインでのキリスト教化闘争は、東の十字軍と並んで、イスラム教とキリスト教との対立の象徴として後世に語り継がれるようになるのです。

　一方、ガーナ王国からムラービト朝が去ったあと、そこにマリ王国というイスラム系の王国ができ繁栄します。塩と砂金、そしてニジェール川流域の肥沃な土地でとれる農作物がマリ王国の財源でした。この豊かな国を目指し、地中海からサハラ砂漠を越えて多くの商人が旅をし、交易ルートを整えていきます。残念なことに、その昔マリ王国が繁栄した地域こそが、現在はイスラム過激組織ボコ・ハラムの活動拠点になっているのです。

第4回十字軍は、東ローマ帝国を陥れた

　こうして、イスラム教とキリスト教の確執の歴史をおいかけると、それがいかに執拗で広範囲にわたっていたかが理解できます。

　あのカノッサの屈辱事件以来、ローマ教皇はその権威を世俗の政権の上に打ち立てようと努めます。13世紀に教皇となったインノケンティウス3世は、そうした中でも傑出した政治家でした。

　彼は、破門という伝家の宝刀を振りかざし、フランスやイギリス王、

時代
12, 13世紀
欧州中世

地域
ヨーロッパ

分類
戦争【経済】

キーワード
ローマ教皇権の優越・ヴェネチア商人の勃興・十字軍の脱線・東西教会の対立・十字軍の顛末

from the church, he intimidated not only the monarchs of France and England, but also the emperor of the Holy Roman Empire, and he has been known to later generations for stating that the pope is like the sun, which shines its own light, while the emperor is like the moon, which only reflects the light of the pope. He turned his gaze toward the Islamic world.

The Crusades were a series of events that mobilized the entire European world. Answering the pope's call, missionaries were mobilized in every region, and not only knights but ordinary people were caught up in the activity. Gathering ordinary, uneducated but zealous commoners and conveying the glory of God, the missionaries led people to blindly participate in the Crusader armies. There were armies of young Crusaders composed entirely of children, but along the way almost all of them met with mishaps, and it is said that from time to time they were sold as slaves.

Let us take a moment to gain an overview of the Crusade movement.

In the First Crusade, armies of feudal lords and knights occupied Jerusalem and set up the Kingdom of Jerusalem.

Indeed, due to the unstable situation and ongoing conflicts with the Muslims, the Second Crusade was launched in 1147. However, it did not achieve significant military successes.

In response to the situation, Saladin, the leader of the Ayyubid dynasty, who had overthrown the Shia-backed Fatimid Caliphate in Egypt in 1171, recaptured Jerusalem. This event led to the organization of the Third Crusade. This Crusade failed to recapture Jerusalem. Later the Kingdom of Jerusalem became the small monarchy of Palestine, and it was overthrown in the 13th century.

As things came about, Pope Innocent III called for the Fourth Crusade to attack the Ayyubid dynasty in Egypt. At this time, the merchants of Venice already had control of the Mediterranean in their grasp. The activities of this Crusade invigorated both marine transport and trade by land. At the instigation of these merchants, in order to procure funds for the expedition, the Crusades even attacked Christian cities. At that point, conflict over succession within the Eastern Roman Empire broke out. With that as a pretext the Crusaders attacked and plundered not only Egypt but Constantinople as well. In 1204 they completely devastated the Eastern Roman Empire and created a state called the Latin Empire.

As a result, the Orthodox Church and the Roman Catholic Church came to an absolute, permanent split. The Latin Empire was destroyed in 1261 by the royalty of the Eastern Roman Empire, who had fled into exile, and the

神聖ローマ帝国皇帝をも震え上がらせ、「教皇は太陽で、皇帝は月」という有名な言葉を残したことで知られています。そんな彼がさらにイスラム世界に目をやります。

　十字軍は、教皇の呼びかけで宣教師が各地に出かけて動員を行い、騎士団のみならず、民衆をも巻き込んだヨーロッパ世界の一大イベントでした。無知で狂信的な民衆を集め、神の栄光を伝え、人々は盲目的に十字軍に参加します。少年十字軍という子供たちで構成された十字軍まで現れますが、彼らのほとんどは途中で遭難し、時には奴隷として売られてしまったといわれています。

　ここで、改めて十字軍の動向を整理しておきましょう。
　第1回十字軍の時に、諸侯や騎士の軍団は、エルサレムを占領しエルサレム王国をうち建てます。
　しかし、情勢が安定せず、イスラム教徒との戦いも継続していたため1147年に第2回十字軍が遠征にでかけますが、大きな戦果はあげられません。
　その状況を見て、エジプトで1171年にシーア派のファーティマ朝を倒したアイユーブ朝の指導者サラディンがエルサレムを奪還。それが原因で第3回十字軍が組織されます。しかしエルサレムを取り戻すことはできませんでした。エルサレム王国は、その後パレスチナの小国になり13世紀に滅亡します。
　こうした経緯の中で、エジプトのアイユーブ朝を攻撃しようと、第4回十字軍の遠征をインノケンティウス3世が呼びかけたのです。このとき、すでに、ヴェネチアの商人が、地中海の制海権を握っていました。十字軍の活動が海運と交易を盛んにしていたのです。こうした商人の働きかけもあり、遠征の資金を調達するために、十字軍はキリスト教の都市までも攻撃します。そこに、東ローマ帝国の後継者争いがおこります。それを大義名分として、十字軍はエジプトではなく、コンスタンティノープルを攻撃し略奪します。彼らは、1204年に東ローマ帝国を潰し、ラテン帝国という国家を築いたのでした。
　このことは、正教会と、ローマカトリックとの決定的な対立を生みました。ラテン帝国は、亡命した東ローマ帝国の皇族によって1261年に滅ぼされ、東ローマ帝国が復活します。しかし、帝国が受けた損害

Eastern Roman Empire was restored. The damage that the empire had suffered, however, was serious. The Eastern Roman Empire's function as a bulwark against Muslim incursions from the east was stripped away. Down through succeeding generations, the actions of the Venetian merchants and the feudal lords of Europe, who laid claim to part of the spoils of war as their due reward for participating in the Crusades, have led observers to view the Crusades as a whole as meaningless at best.

057 The activities of the Crusades led to the downfall of the knight class

The Crusades were later treated in Western Europe with reverence as a symbol of the superiority of Christianity. The word "Crusade" itself came to be used as a catchword for carrying out reforms to expose and eliminate injustices. However, many people now point out that the truth of the matter is that as is represented by the Fourth Crusade, the Crusades were, overall, acts of slaughter and usurpation for the purpose of obtaining riches.

The disgrace of the Fourth Crusade later cast a subtle shadow over the authority of the Pope.

Of course, the Muslim states were not always benevolent entities either. These countries zealously expanded their own territories, and in the name of jihad, holy warfare, they aggressively sought the conversion of people in the territories they occupied. However, the massacres carried out by the Crusades were religious slaughters, and the victims were not all Muslim. The victims included Christians who subscribed to views that the Roman Catholic Church had declared to be heretical, and they also included Jews.

Louis IX of France used the organized Crusades to pursue an aggressive foreign policy, and these expeditions continued through the Seventh Crusade in 1270. During this period other expeditions, large and small, were launched.

In medieval Europe, large numbers of knights were active. Some were descendants of wealthy military families from the Roman period and others were prominent Germanic people.

The particularly strong members who were in positions of leadership became monarchs, to whom the knights pledged allegiance. Having said this, just as the

は深刻でした。東ローマはその後東から攻めてくるイスラム勢力の防波堤としての機能を失ってしまったのです。この十字軍は、ヴェネチア商人と、戦利品の見返りを求めるヨーロッパ諸侯による愚行としてその後語り継がれます。

十字軍の活動は騎士階級の没落へと繋がった

十字軍は、後世西欧世界でのキリスト教優越主義の象徴として神格化され、十字軍という言葉そのものも、不正を暴き改革を進める合言葉のように使用されるようになりました。しかし、十字軍の実態は、第4回十字軍で象徴されるように、富を求めた殺戮と簒奪行為であったと指摘する人も多くいます。

第4回十字軍の失態は、その後の教皇の権威にも微妙な影を落としたのです。

もちろん、イスラム教徒の国家が常に穏健であったわけではなく、それらの国家の多くが領土の拡張に熱心で、ジハード（聖戦）という名の元に、占領地の人々の改宗にも積極的でした。しかし、十字軍の行った殺戮は、宗教的な殺戮行為で、犠牲者にはイスラム教徒のみならず、ローマカトリックを信奉しない異端と呼ばれたキリスト教徒、ユダヤ教徒などが含まれていたのです。

組織的な十字軍は対外政策に積極的だったフランスのルイ9世が1270年におこした第7回十字軍まで継続しますが、そのほかにもこの時代には大小様々な十字軍が組織されました。

中世ヨーロッパには多くの騎士が活動していました。彼らは元々ローマ時代の富裕な軍人の子孫や、ゲルマン系の有力者でした。

その中でも特に力があり、指導的な立場にある者が王となり、騎士は王に忠誠を誓っていたわけです。とはいえ、騎士はいわゆる豪族と

時代
13, 14世紀
欧州中世

地域
西ヨーロッパ

分類
社会【政治】

キーワード
ローマ教皇権の動揺・騎士の没落・王権の伸張・商業都市の発生

powerful regional families pledged loyalty to a monarch, the knights pledged allegiance but at the same time were military leaders who managed their own lands and the people attached to those lands. The Crusades appealed to these knights, and they launched expeditions to far-away places like the Middle East and North Africa. In places such as Jerusalem, such groups of knights were stationed in strongholds for protecting pilgrims to the city. The military orders of the Knights Templar and the Hospitallers, the Hospital of St. John, are considered representative of these groups. On the other hand, due to the many knights who perished in the expeditions and the economic exhaustion that followed, it led to a relative increase in the position of monarchs.

In the Middle Ages, with the climate warming, agricultural lands expanded and populations increased. The activities of the Crusades also stimulated commerce, promoting the emergence of marketplaces as commercial hubs. Prominent merchants organized the craftspeople that gathered and formed alliances with other merchants, and gradually these marketplaces evolved into towns. The merchants who accumulated wealth joined together and received the protection of the local monarch. In fortified towns, they obtained the right of self-government and began to carry on their own businesses. As a result of the traders and monarchs being tied together, their wealth and security was guaranteed.

Freedom of navigation, whether in the Mediterranean Sea or the Baltic Sea, was a matter of life and death for prominent merchants, so they formed guilds, established trading firms in important towns, and gathered military forces to protect the transport of their valuable goods. The Hanseatic League, which was an exceptionally powerful guild, had its headquarters in Lubeck, but operated widely between Novgorod in Russia, Hamburg in Germany, and London.

Each of these towns had its own administration building and its own court house, and through these they guaranteed their autonomy. People who gathered in these towns and engaged in commerce and industry would, in the future, become the middle class.

同じで、王に忠誠を誓いながらも、自らの土地と民を束ねた軍団の長でした。十字軍は、そうした騎士に対して呼びかけられ、はるばる中東や北アフリカまで遠征を行ったのです。エルサレムなどでは、巡礼者の保護を目的に、そうした騎士団が城塞をつくり駐屯しました。テンプル騎士団、聖ヨハネ騎士団は、その代表的なものといえます。一方で、遠征により多くの騎士が戦死したり経済的にも疲弊したりしたため、そのことが相対的に国王の地位を高めてゆくことになりました。

　中世は気候が温暖で、農地も飛躍的に増えて人口も増加します。そして、十字軍の活動は、資金調達などの面からも商業を促進し、商業基地としての市場が生まれます。有力商人がそこに集まる職人などを束ね、他の商人とも連携し、市場は次第に都市へと変貌したのでした。富を蓄えた商人達は連携して国王の保護をもらい、城塞都市の中で自治権を得て活動を始めます。商人と国王とが結ばれることで、富と安全とが保証されることになったのです。

　地中海、バルト海など、海の自由な航行は有力な商人にとって生命線です。そこで、彼らはギルドをつくり、主要な都市に商館をおき、富の運搬を防衛する軍事力も持つようになります。ロシアのノヴゴロドからドイツのハンブルグ、そして西はロンドンに至る広範な商圏を持つハンザ同盟はそうしたギルドの中でも特に強大な組織で、ドイツのリューベックに本部がありました。
　これらの都市には裁判所や市庁舎があって、自治が保証されていました。都市に集まり、商工業に勤しむ人々。こうした人々が将来市民階級へと成長してゆくのです。

058 The Song principle of civilian government was inherited thereafter by China

A dramatic event occurred in China in 1127. As has already been mentioned, two years prior to this event, the Song had formed an alliance with the newly emerging country of Jin to overthrow the Liao. From the outset, threats from the north had been a foreign policy issue for the Song government.

The Song established their capital at Kaifeng, and the second Song emperor, Taizong, succeeded in unifying China. That was in 979. Initially, the Song expanded their power toward the end of the Tang dynasty, and through the Five Dynasties and Ten Kingdoms period, they revised the system of making their own territory in China their base and revived the system of tributary states. In order to prevent regional governments from becoming bloated, they set up a systematized military bureaucracy directly under imperial control, and reformed the civil service examination system for appointing capable people to important positions under the emperor. The emperor also established a group of scholar-officials called Shi daifu, consisting mainly of landed gentry, to serve under him. They constructed a country with an absolute monarch based on a pillar of parceling out landed estates to these bureaucrats. The policies of the Song dynasty were inherited by subsequent Chinese dynasties and continued to shape the political landscape of China until modern times.

The Song government continually maintained political power over external peoples via diplomacy rather than military force. They learned from previous dynasties that military rule led to their own downfall. In the Shanyuan Treaty of 1004 with the Liao government, they abandoned the northern regions that had innately been the territory of China, provided economic support to the Liao, and agreed to a nonaggression pact.

However, while these annual tributes toward other countries and the expansion of local bureaucracy did result in peace for the country, finances became strained. For that reason, the Song, while strengthening dependence on capable bureaucrats, also introduced through people like Wang Anshi a new law to implement a policy of constructing a rich country and a strong military. This became the cause of factional strife between bureaucrats who supported either the old law or the new law.

At that point, the Jin rose up. The Song had formed an alliance with the Jin in

宋の文治主義はその後の中国に
受け継がれる

　1127年、中国に異変がおきます。既に解説したように、その2年前に宋は北方の新興国金と同盟を結んで遼を滅ぼしました。もともと、北方からの脅威が宋にとっては外交課題だったのです。

　宋は首都を開封におき、2代目の太宗のときに中国の統一を果たします。979年のことでした。建国当初、宋の政権は唐末に力をつけ、五代十国に至るまで中国に割拠した節度使の制度を改めます。地方政権が肥大化しないように、皇帝直属の軍事官僚組織をつくり、優秀な人材を登用するための科挙制度も改革し、皇帝の元に士大夫と呼ばれる、地主を中心とした文人官僚をおきました。文治主義を柱にした皇帝独裁国家を造ったのです。この宋の政策は、その後近代まで中国の王朝に受け継がれ、中国の政治風土となってゆきます。

時代
11〜13世紀
中国中世

地域
中国

分類
国家【政治】

キーワード
北方民族国家の興亡・文治政策による統治・科挙による官僚と士大夫の登場・金の南下

　宋は対外的にも常に武力ではなく外交によって政権を維持します。過去の王朝が武断政治によって滅亡してきたことに学んだのです。遼とは1004年に澶淵の盟という約定を結んで、元来中国が領有していた北方の地域を放棄し、遼に経済的に援助をすることを盛り込んだ不可侵条約を結びます。

　しかし、こうした外国への歳幣や肥大化した官僚組織は、国家に平和をもたらしはしたものの、財政を圧迫します。そのため宋は、文治主義に徹しながらも、王安石などによって富国強兵策を目指した新法も導入します。これが旧法と新法とを支持する官僚の派閥争いの原因となってしまったのです。

　そんなときに金が台頭します。宋は金と同盟を結んで遼を滅ぼした

order to destroy the Liao and had felt relieved at being able to curb threats from the north. The reality was the exact opposite. When the Song were unable to meet the demands for the new annual tributes, the Jin launched a military action.

The Jin encircled the Song capital of Kaifeng in 1127 and apprehended the former emperor Huizong and Qinzong, and the Song all too easily collapsed. It was known as the Jingkang Incident. Following this, Qinzong's younger brother fled to southern China and established the Southern Song, but for many years thereafter a large part of China was controlled by the northern ethnic peoples.

During both the Liao and Jin dynasties, the territories that were originally under the control of China were governed by policies that combined the unique characteristics of the tribal system of the nomadic peoples' parent body with the state and district system of the Han Chinese. The Southern Song established their capital at Lin'an and attempted to recapture the territories that the Jin had taken from them. But there was internal strife and these attempts failed, so for approximately 150 years thereafter, they continued to rule as the government of southern China. The system of civilian government cultivated by the Song and the Southern Song, as a bureaucratic system in which intellectuals selected by the civil service examinations system supported the state, was passed down from one generation to the next.

The Song period was one in which Chinese civilization matured. Intellectuals of the Shi daifu class were active, and through the strict implementation of the civil service system, the study of Confucianism itself became the means for selecting persons fit for higher positions. A Confucian reformist movement also occurred. Among those neighboring states which digested the essence of that culture in its entirety was none other than Japan.

ことで、北の脅威をうまく抑え込めたと安堵します。しかし、現実は全く逆でした。新たな歳幣の要求に応えられない宋に対して、金が軍事行動にでたのです。

　1127年に金は宋の首都開封を包囲して、上皇徽宗と欽宗を捕縛し、宋はあっけなく滅亡してしまいます。この事件を靖康の変といいます。その後、欽宗の弟が華南に逃れて南宋を建国しますが、中国はその後長年にわたって北方民族にその国土の多くを支配されるようになるのです。

　遼も金も、元々中国の領土であった地域を支配するにあたって、遊牧民の母体となる部族制と、漢民族がつくりあげた州県制とを併用し、両者の特性を活かした政策を実施しました。一方、南宋は首都を臨安におき、金に奪われた地域の奪還を試みますが、内紛もあり失敗し、その後約150年間、中国の南部を支配する政権として存続したのです。宋と南宋によって育まれた文治政治は、その後科挙で選抜された文人が国家を支える官僚体制として代々受け継がれてゆくようになるのです。

　宋の時代は中国文明が円熟した時代でもありました。士大夫階級の知識人が活躍し、科挙制度の徹底により、儒教を学ぶことがそのまま人材登用に直結したことから、儒学の革新運動もおこりました。その文化のエキスをそのまま消化し、制度化していった周辺国家の代表が日本だったのです。

059 Song culture intact found its way into the minds of the Japanese

The Song and Southern Song periods were a time in which countries were constantly threatened by invaders from outside.

During this period of experiencing conflicts with external forces, people in China developed a strong sense of Chinese aesthetics and consciousness. Chinese thought sprouted, placing Chinese civilization at the center of its world view, and ethnic awareness of the Han Chinese began to be accentuated.

Where the culture of the Tang period was cosmopolitan in being open to the Western Regions and different ethnic groups, the culture of the Song period was more introspective in focusing on China itself. For example, in Buddhism at the end of the Tang period, the Zen school and the Jingtu, or Pure Land, school of Buddhism emerged and spread during the Song period. These new sects differed from the previous philosophical forms of Buddhism. The Zen school aimed at the cultivation of the mind and appealed to the Shi daifu class. The Pure Land school developed as a more practical form of Buddhism which provided salvation to the common people.

Also in the Song period, within Confucianism, the teachings of Zhu Xi were compiled and came to be referred to as Neo-Confucianism. Until then, Confucianism had placed emphasis on implementing heavenly or universal ethics in human affairs. Zhu Xi's interpretive studies, however, focused on reviewing the wisdom of four classic works, *The Analects of Confucius, Mencius, The Doctrine of the Mean,* and *The Great Learning*. Zhu Xi's new teachings aimed at spiritual elevation.

In Japan, the Zen and Pure Land schools spread during the Kamakura period.

The Zen school was adopted by the *bushi*, the warrior class, and it was patronized for its teachings regarding the spiritual improvement of the country's administrative class. The Pure Land sect gave rise to a number of schools that aimed their teachings at the salvation of the common people. Neo-Confucianism, or *Shushigaku*, became the school of learning advocated by the shogunate during the Tokugawa period, and it was held in esteem as the foundation of social order and as a philosophy of the warrior class. Further, people of culture in Japan for a long period of time had some degree of interest in the writings of Su Shi and others who were known as the Eight Great Prose Masters of Tang and Song.

宋の文化はそのまま日本人の心に 流れ込んだ

　宋、そして南宋の時代は常に国土が外敵の脅威にさらされていた時代です。

　外との対立を経験する中で、人々が中国人としての美学や意識を強く抱くようになったのもこの時代の特徴です。中国文明を世界の中心に位置づける中華思想が芽生え、漢民族という民族意識が強調され始めたのです。

　唐の文化が西域や異民族に開かれたコスモポリタンな文化であるとするならば、宋の文化はより内省的で、中国そのものを見つめたものでした。例えば、唐末に仏教界に禅宗や浄土宗が生まれ、宋の時代に広がります。これらの新しい宗派は、以前の哲学的な仏教とは異なり、禅宗は士大夫階級の心の修養を目指し、浄土宗は庶民に救いを与える実践的な仏教として発展しました。

時代
11～13世紀
中国中世

地域
中国

分類
文化【学問】

キーワード
漢人意識の発生・学問の発展・中国文化の昇華・日本の宗教・美術品の発展

　また、儒教は、南宋の朱熹によって朱子学として集大成されます。天や宇宙の理が人の営みにも取り込まれてゆくべきとして、『論語』『孟子』『中庸』、そして『大学』という四書を重んじ、過去の知識を復習するそれまでの訓詁学とは異なり、精神性を高めることを目的とした新たな儒教として発展しました。

　日本では、鎌倉時代に禅宗や浄土宗が広がります。

　そして禅宗は武士階級に受け入れられ、為政者の精神修養の宗教として保護されました。また浄土宗は、庶民を救済する宗教として様々な宗派を生み出します。一方、朱子学は、江戸時代になって官学となり、社会秩序の礎、武士の哲学として尊重されたのです。また、日本の文化人は、その後長きにわたって唐宋八大家といわれた、唐から宋にかけて活躍した蘇軾などの文章を嗜みました。

蘇軾
Su Shi (1037–1101)

There is a type of porcelain china called Song ware. It is famous for its celadon ware and a white porcelain known for its bluish or whitish glaze. Its combination of simplicity with depth appealed greatly to the Japanese desire for *wabi* and *sabi*, a simple austerity and a subdued refinement, from the Muromachi period onward. As the high-level bureaucrats became cultivated intellects, landscape painting and Southern painting—painting of the literati—which was popular in Southern Song China, was adopted in Japan in the form of ink painting, or *suiboku*, and Nanga Painting, a style adapted from the South China school.

At times we tend to forget that prior to the Heian period the Japanese placidly enjoyed dazzling, resplendent coloring. It was not until Song culture was imported that Japanese people developed a strong attachment to things that are somber and possess a subdued refinement. In Song China this evolved because, in contrast with the aristocracy, the prominent regional Shi daifu who became high-level bureaucrats became the nexus of the intellectual class.

Indeed, during that time, influential local figures in Japan also became rulers and warriors. The samurai class was educated to embody both military and literary skills, and they embraced the values of the Song culture, which favored simplicity over extravagance.

In this manner, the spiritual culture that was cultivated in Song China became, unchanged, the origins of Japanese culture. Emissaries sent to the Tang court during the Nara and Heian period absorbed knowledge from China. In contrast with that, what Japanese culture gained from China during the Song period led to a deepening of Japanese culture and cultural activity that to this day remains the key to Japanese aesthetic sensibility and moral sense.

060 The Mongol Empire conquered the world with its unique mobility and capacity for organization

The Song influenced the Western Regions in a variety of ways. During the Song era, these western peoples imitated Chinese written characters and created their own forms of writing. The Western Xia, the Liao, and the Junchens—the last of these stimulated by the Jin—each created their own way of writing. Both the Liao and the Jin, while attacking the Song, also skillfully put to practical use Song

宋磁といわれる陶磁器があります。それは青磁と白磁として知られていますが、そのシンプルな造りの中にある深みは、日本人が室町時代以降に求めた侘び寂びの精神にも通じます。また、士大夫階級が知識人として育ってゆく中で、山水画や南宋でもてはやされた南画は、日本でも室町時代以降水墨画、そして文人画として継承されたのでした。

　我々はともすれば忘れがちですが、平安時代以前の日本人は、きらびやかな色彩をおおらかに楽しんでいました。くすんだものや、寂びたものへの愛着が育っていったのは、宋の文化が日本に伝わった以降のことなのです。それは、宋でそれまでの貴族とは違い、地方の有力者が士大夫として官僚となり、知識層の中核となったことが影響しています。
　というのも当時、日本でも地方の有力者が武士として為政者になってゆき、武士は文武を備えた人格として教育され、華美なものではなく、質素なものを好む宋の文化が吸収されたからなのです。

　このように、宋の時代に育まれた精神文化は、そのまま日本文化の形成の源流となりました。それは、知識の吸収を中心とした奈良や平安初期の遣唐使の時代とは異なり、日本文化そのものの深化に影響を与え、その後現代に至るまで日本人の美意識や道徳観の中枢となった文化活動だったのです。

モンゴル帝国は独自の機動力と組織力で世界を席巻した

時代
13世紀
中国中世

地域
中国

分類
侵略【統一】

キーワード
モンゴルの登場・騎馬民族の機動性・金、宋の滅亡・ヨーロッパへの侵入

　一方、宋の文化は西域にも様々な影響を与えます。宋の時代に人々は漢字を模して独自の文字を作りました。西夏の西夏文字、遼の契丹文字、さらには金を興した女真族による女真文字などがそれにあたります。遼にしろ、金にしろ、宋を攻めながらも、宋の文化や政治制度を巧みに活用したのでした。

culture and systems of government.

The Jin, while themselves holding sway over northern China, also had to prepare themselves against possible threats from the north and from the Western Regions. At that time, the expanse of the Mongolian Plateau was an enormous power void. The tribes of Mongolian people made their own territories the bases of their activities, and the political conditions there remained unstable.

The Jin used the Mongol-related Tatars as a restraint against the other Mongolian peoples. However, out of the political strife that consumed the plateau rose a heroic figure named Temujin, who ironically unified the Mongolian peoples.

Temujin reorganized the affiliated groups into military corps and added organizational strength to the horse-riding peoples' unique mobility. Further, by taking along domesticated livestock when launching a military expedition, they devised a way to replenish their food supplies that did not require extensive time. Eventually, the Mongols defeated their Turkic rivals, the Tatars. Temujin took the title of Khan as the king of these ethnic peoples in 1206, and from that point onward he was called Genghis Khan. Thus was founded the Mongol Empire.

The army under Genghis Khan absorbed those who submitted to him into its own ranks, and as his conquests mounted, the numbers of his forces swelled. Each unit within the whole manifested impressive mobile power. He did not deploy these groups in tribal units. Instead, he assembled them in 1,000-men units, which would now be referred to as regiments, led by commanding officers who he himself chose. This method was called the mingghan system, and each unit functioned as both a shared community and a military group which displayed superb mobility. They defeated the Western Xia in 1209, the Western Liao in 1218, and went on to square off against the Islamic world. The first of these last states the Mongols ousted was Khwarazm on the Aral Sea in Central Asia, which it conquered in 1221.

When one thinks of a major migration of people across an entire continent, one tends to imagine a process that takes a century or more. But the expansion of the Mongol Empire occurred as quickly as the rapid pace of the horse-riding people themselves. They possessed the destructive power and speed of a tornado. Upon the death of Genghis Khan, Ogodei Khan succeeded him and used that speed to attack northern China. In 1234 the Jin were attacked from the south by the Southern Song, and when their capital city Kaifeng fell, they were destroyed.

From the viewpoint of the Southern Song, although their bitter enemy the Jin were gone, there was an even more powerful thread pressing down on them. At that time, it was impossible to command an overhead view of the world with any

そんな金は、自らが中国北部を統治するにあたり、逆に北方や西域からの脅威に備えなければならなくなります。当時、モンゴル高原一帯は権力の空白地帯でした。そこにはモンゴル族の部族が割拠し、政情は不安定でした。

　金はモンゴル系のタタールの人々を使い、同じモンゴル族を牽制させます。しかし、そうした草原での政争の中からテムジンという英雄が現れ、皮肉なことにモンゴル族をまとめたのです。

　テムジンは、傘下に加わった部族を軍団として再編成し、騎馬民族特有の機動性に組織力を付加しました。また遠征には家畜を伴うなど、食料の補給に時間をかけないように工夫します。やがて、モンゴル族はトルコ系やライバルであったタタール族を打ち破り、テムジンは部族の王として1206年にハンの称号を贈られ、以後チンギス・ハンと呼ばれます。モンゴル帝国の創立です。

チンギス・ハン
Genghis Khan (1162?–1227)

　チンギス・ハンの軍団は、服従する者は自らの軍団に取り込んでゆき、征服を重ねるごとに規模が膨らみますが、それぞれが見事な機動力を発揮します。彼は、部族を部族単位で機動させるのではなく、千人ずつの単位でまとめ、今でいう連隊とし、その指揮官に自らが信任した者をおきます。その方法は千戸制度と呼ばれ、生活共同体であると同時に軍事単位として抜群の機動力を発揮したのです。1209年には西夏を、1218年には西遼を滅ぼし、イスラム圏と対峙するに至ります。最初に駆逐されたのは、中央アジアからアラル海方面にあったホラズムという国でした。1221年のことでした。

　普通大陸規模での民族の大移動といえば、百年単位の動向です。しかし、モンゴル帝国の拡大は、騎馬民族そのものの速さを備え、あたかも竜巻のような破壊力を持っていました。チンギス・ハンの死後、そんな機動力をもってハンを継承したオゴタイ・ハンが華北に攻め入ります。金は南から南宋にも攻められ、1234年に当時首都としていた開封が落城し、滅亡します。

　南宋からしてみると、仇敵の金は去ったものの、そこにもっと強大な脅威が迫ったことになります。世界を迅速に俯瞰することが不可能であった当時にあって、それは仕方のないことかもしれません。ただ、

speed, so perhaps it could not have been helped, but surely the Southern Song must have been aware of the dilemma they faced: they would be pressured by either the Jin or by the Mongols.

The year following the sacking of the Jin, Ogodei Khan established his capital at Karakorum in Central Asia. From there he ordered his nephew Batu to lead troops further west. In 1241 a whirlwind of Mongols suddenly appeared in the European world. This was a speed that was absolutely unimaginable in an era when a journey across the Silk Road took several years.

061 The Yuan attempted invasions of not only Japan but also Sakhalin and Vietnam

The foundation of the growth of the Mongol Empire is not unrelated with the fact that frontier regions developed as a result of the military governors that established themselves during the Tang period.

When the Song established their state in the Western Region and in the southern areas that had been part of the Tang territories, military governors and regional clans remained independent, with their territories as the base of their administration. For example, in Yunnan, during the Tang period there was a country called Nanzhao, which at one time had allied itself with the Tang. Later, when Nanzhao fell, a state named Dali rose up. When the Mongol Empire subjugated China, that state was annexed by the Mongols.

The Mongols took control of northern China and established a capital at Dadu, near the city that is now called Beijing. As a result of internal conflicts, Kublai became the fifth Khan. Kublai Khan renamed the Mongol Empire in 1271 and thereafter it was known as the Yuan dynasty.

It is dangerous to consider international affairs of an earlier time from the perspective of the present-day sense of geography. Nonetheless, between the 1270s and 1280s, the Yuan made strategic inroads in East Asia. The dynasty annexed Koryo, which had unified the Korean Peninsula in 936. After the Jin collapsed, using the Jurchens and Koryo, the Yuan then attempted an invasion of Japan.

南宋にとっては金かモンゴル帝国かと選択を迫られること自体が、そもそもジレンマであったはずです。

金を滅ぼした翌年、オゴタイ・ハンは中央アジアのカラコルムを首都にします。そして甥のバトゥに命じて西へと兵をおくったのです。モンゴルという竜巻がヨーロッパ世界に忽然と現れたのは1241年のことでした。それは数年がかりでシルクロードを越えて旅をしていた時代としては考えられない速さでした。

オゴタイ・ハン
Ogodei Khan (1186–1241)

元は日本のみならず、樺太やベトナムにも侵攻した

モンゴル帝国が成長できた素地は、唐の時代に各地で自立した節度使によって辺境が開拓されていたこととも無縁ではないはずです。

やがて宋が建国しましたが、元々唐の版図にあった西域や南方の地域には、節度使や地方の部族が自立したまま割拠していました。例えば、現在の雲南省に唐の時代に南詔という国があり、一時は唐に恭順して

フビライ・ハン
Kublai Khan (1215–1294)

いました。その後南詔が倒れ大理という国がおこりますが、モンゴル帝国が中国を支配したあとは、モンゴルに併合されます。

モンゴルが北部中国を支配すると、首都を大都におきます。現在の北京にあたります。そして内部抗争の末に5代目のハンの地位についたフビライが、モンゴル帝国の国号を1271年に元とし、以後中国の王朝としてもこの名前が使用されます。

今の地理感覚で当時の国際情勢を考えることは危険です。とはいえ、1270年代から80年代にかけて、元は戦略的に東アジアを攻略します。936年以来朝鮮半島を統一していた高麗を恭順させ、金が滅びたあとは、金を打ち立てた女真族と高麗とを使って、日本への侵攻を試みました。

時代
13世紀
中国中世

地域
中国

分類
戦争【侵略】

キーワード
モンゴルのアジア征服・フビライが国号を元に・日本への侵攻と失敗・東南アジアへ侵攻

The Kamakura Shogunate, which patronized the Zen school of Buddhism that was introduced from China, promoted trade with the Southern Song using Hakata as the liaison port. The immediate goal of the Yuan was to overthrow all of the neighboring states connected with the Southern Song. The Mongol invasion of Japan in 1274, known as the Bun'ei War, ended in failure due to the timely occurrence of a typhoon in the area. Following that, the Yuan carried out a full-fledged assault on the Southern Song and ultimately destroyed it in 1279.

As a result, the Yuan then had two potential routes for invading Japan: through the Korean Peninsula and via the East China Sea. A second massive force was deployed against Japan using both of these routes in 1281. However, this assault, which turned the entire area around Hakata into a huge battlefront, was ultimately struck by another typhoon. With the assistance of this second timely typhoon, Japan was somehow able to overcome this second crisis.

The Yuan plotted subsequent attacks on Japan, but due to internal conflicts and the death of Kublai Khan, these plans were never carried out.

As it happens, immediately following the attack on Japan, the Yuan sent troops to Sakhalin and drove out the resident Ainu people.

In addition, after conquering Nan-zhao in the south, the Yuan on several occasions attacked the Chen dynasty of Vietnam. After repeated hard-fought battles, the Vietnamese succeeded in repulsing the Yuan in 1288, afterward becoming a tributary state instead. This victory over the Yuan later became bound with the stubborn resistance against American forces in the Vietnam War and became a source of pride among the people of Vietnam.

The Yuan also actively plotted attacks on other countries, including Burma and Java, but as was the case with Vietnam, differences in the climate and natural features of Southeast Asia made advances difficult, and ultimately the Yuan were militarily unsuccessful. Nonetheless, through this initial activity, trade between China and Southeast Asia became brisk.

062 The Mongol Empire beckoned the Europeans to Asia

The "Tatar yoke" is an expression that Russians are said to have used when referring to the period when they were under the subjugation of the Mongols.

鎌倉幕府は、中国から伝来した禅宗を保護し、博多を窓口にして南宋との貿易も促進させます。元の当面の目的は、そうした周辺国家ともつながる南宋を滅ぼすことでした。1274年の文永の役と呼ばれるモンゴル軍の日本への侵攻は、台風の影響で失敗に終わります。その後、元は南宋を本格的に攻略し、1279年についに南宋を滅亡させます。

　これで、元は朝鮮半島と東シナ海の二つのルートを通って日本を攻略できるようになりました。1281年に二度目の大軍がこの二つのルートを経由して日本に送られます。しかし、博多一帯が戦場になったこの侵攻も、最終的には再び襲ってきた台風に助けられ、日本はなんとか二度の危機を克服したのです。

　その後、元は再度日本の攻略を企てますが、元の内紛とフビライの死もあって計画が実行されることはありませんでした。
　実は、日本侵攻の直後、元は樺太にも兵を送り現地のアイヌを駆逐しています。
　さらに、南方方面では、大理国を従えたあと、元は数度にわたりベトナムの陳朝に侵攻します。何度かの激戦の末、1288年にベトナム側が元を押し返したのです。その後、陳朝は元に朝貢しますが、この元との戦いに勝利したことは、後年ベトナム戦争でアメリカに頑強な抵抗をしたこととも絡んで、ベトナム人の誇りとして語られるようになりました。
　元はさらにビルマやジャワなどにも積極的に侵攻を企てますが、ベトナム同様、東南アジアの気候や風土の違いもあり、軍事的には失敗しています。ただ、こうした活動を通して、中国と東南アジアとの交易がさらに活発になっていったのです。

時代
13世紀
欧州中世

地域
中国・中東・ヨーロッパ

分類
戦争【交流】

キーワード
モンゴルのヨーロッパ侵入・モンゴルの中東侵入・グローバル国家の成立・東西交流の促進

モンゴル帝国はヨーロッパの目をアジアにいざなった

　「タタールの軛」という言葉があります。これは、ロシアの人々が、モンゴルの支配に縛られた時代のことを語っているともいわれる用語です。

Genghis Khan's grandson Batu commenced a Mongol invasion in the west in 1236. From the perspective of the Russians, one day people they had never seen before suddenly appeared from the East and swiftly conquered their territories. Records show that the Russians had absolutely no idea who these people were nor where they might have come from.

Batu's expeditionary force destroyed the Kievan Rus, which was divided among prominent feudal lords, and progressed in 1241 as far as the arc between Poland and Hungary. At the Battle of Legnica, the allied forces of Germany and Poland were smashed. In part due to the report received of the death of Ogodei Khan, the Mongol army did not advance farther west, but the expeditionary force had a major impact on world history. This was the very first occasion when the European world became truly conscious of East Asia.

The area of southwest Russia which Batu conquered became the Kipchak Khanate, and a region in Central Asia became the Chagatai Khanate. As a result of the military expedition carried out by Hulagu—who like Batu was also a grandson of Genghis Khan—the Il Khanate was established in the Arabian world. Together these extensive territories formed the huge Mongol Empire.

As an aside, the Mongol troops led by Hulagu attacked and destroyed Baghdad in 1258, bringing an end to the Abbasid Caliphate both in name and in substance.

The Mongol Empire expanded with the Mongols and those who became subordinate to them. The Mongol army imposed the responsibility of paying taxes and were flexible in their dealings with those who pledged allegiance to them. But those who stood against the Mongols are said to have been mercilessly slaughtered. However, the Mongols did not massacre people they had not conquered. To the contrary, the Mongols expanded their territories through the use of prominent local figures who cooperated with them in conquering other peoples.

Because a large portion of the Eurasian landmass was subsumed under the Mongol Empire, in a single stroke East-West interchange accelerated. The empire was uniformly tolerant when it came to religious beliefs, so Christian missionaries and others headed east, and merchants from Europe initiated trade with Asia. It is well known that the Venetian merchant Marco Polo was taken into service by Kublai Khan and after returning home published *The Travels of Marco Polo*, originally titled in Italian as *Il milione*.

At first, when the Mongols suddenly appeared with swords drawn, the Roman pope and the political leaders of Europe all felt them to be a threat. Yet from the European perspective, the Mongol Empire also attracted attention because

チンギス・ハンの孫にあたるバトゥが1236年にモンゴルから西征を開始します。ロシア人から見ると、ある日東から見たこともない人々が現れ、瞬く間に領土を席巻されたのです。「彼らは誰なのか、どこから来たのか見当もつかなかった」と記録されています。

　バトゥの遠征軍は、有力諸侯によって分割されていたキエフ公国を滅ぼし、1241年には、ポーランドからハンガリーにまで軍を進め、ワールシュタットの戦いでドイツ、ポーランドの連合軍を打ち破っています。オゴタイ・ハンの訃報もあって、モンゴル軍はそれ以上西に兵を進めることはありませんでしたが、この遠征が世界史に与えた影響は大きなものでした。これこそが、ヨーロッパ世界がはじめて東アジアを本格的に意識した瞬間だったのです。

　バトゥの征服した南西ロシア一帯は、キプチャク・ハン国となり、中央アジアのチャガタイ・ハン国、そして、バトゥと同じくチンギス・ハンの孫にあたるフラグの遠征によってアラブ世界に打ち立てられたイル・ハン国と共に、モンゴル帝国の広大な領土を構成する国家となるのです。

　ちなみに、フラグが率いるモンゴル軍は、1258年にバグダードを攻め落とし、それによってアッバース朝が名実ともに滅んだのです。

　モンゴル帝国は、モンゴル人とそれに従う遊牧民族によって膨張しました。モンゴル軍は、恭順する者には納税等の義務を負わせ、柔軟に対応しましたが、抵抗した者は容赦なく殺戮したといわれています。とはいえ彼らは、被征服民族を抹殺したのではなく、征服した場所を協力してくれた現地の有力者に統治させる方式で、領土を拡大していったのです。

　ユーラシア大陸の多くがモンゴル帝国に帰属したことで、東西交流は一挙に促進されます。モンゴル帝国は一様に宗教に寛大であったこともあり、キリスト教の宣教師なども東へと向かい、ヨーロッパの商人もアジアとの交易に旅立ちます。ヴェネチア商人のマルコ・ポーロがフビライ・ハンに仕え、帰国後『東方見聞録』を発表したことは有名です。

　当初、いきなり剣をもって現れたモンゴルの軍団は、ローマ教皇にとっても、ヨーロッパの為政者にとっても脅威でした。しかし、ヨーロッパから見ると、敵対していたイスラム世界に楔を打ったモンゴル

it was driving a wedge in the Islamic world. As a matter of fact, in the domains occupied by the Mongols, Christian followers of the Nestorian sect lived under the control of Islamic nations. There were even Nestorian-sect Christians in the clan of Genghis Khan, and the Roman pope was made aware of that. On the other hand, the leaders of the Kipchak Khanate and the Il Khanate converted to Islam. In their world empire, various religious activities were promoted, and Islam and Christianity were propagated throughout East Asia.

063 Various Buddhist and Hindu states rose and fell in Southeast Asia

When one looks at the world's religious populations today, one finds approximately 2.4 billion Christians, 1.9 billion Muslims, 1.1 billion Hindus, and 490 million Buddhists. Of these religions, Christianity and Islam developed in the Middle Ages with strong ties to secular authority. As a result of this, from that period to the present, these two religions have been hostile toward each other.

In comparison, Hinduism, with the third largest population of followers, is primarily the state religion of India, and geographically its followers are concentrated in the region between India and Southeast Asia. Hindu and Buddhism were propagated through the state of Funan, which is thought to have controlled the coastal areas of Southeast Asia from the 1st through the 7th centuries, into Cambodia and Indonesia. Later, from the 9th century through the 13th century the Chola dynasty flourished in southern India, and Hindu culture was propagated throughout the Indian Ocean and the South China Sea. The people of Southeast Asia had worked diligently as agriculturalists from the era prior to the Common Era. In contrast with Christianity and Islam, which tended to spread more easily among hunting-gathering people and among nomadic peoples, Hinduism and Buddhism put down roots in Asia as religions of agricultural people.

A monarchy called the Shailendra dynasty ruled in Indonesia from the 8th through the 9th centuries. Still remaining from this dynasty are the Buddhist ruins at Borobudur in central Java. The Shailendra are also known for invading Zhenla, the state which took the place of Funan to rule over coastal Southeast Asia, subduing that region. The Shailendra were thought to be part of the Srivijaya Empire, which from the 7th through the 14th centuries, ruled the region from

帝国は興味のある存在でもあったのです。実際、モンゴルの占領した地域にはネストリウス派のキリスト教徒がイスラムの国々の支配のもとに生活していました。チンギス・ハン一族の中にもネストリウス派のキリスト教徒がいたほどで、ローマ教皇もそうした情報をつかんでいました。一方で、イル・ハン国やキプチャク・ハン国の為政者はイスラム教に改宗しました。世界帝国の中で、様々な宗教活動が促進され、東アジアにイスラムやキリスト教が伝播されていったのでした。

東南アジアでは多くの仏教、ヒンドゥー教国家が興亡した

　現在、世界の宗教人口を見ると、キリスト教徒が約24億人、イスラム教徒が約19億人、ヒンドゥー教徒が約11億人、仏教徒は約4億9千万人であるといわれています。中でも、キリスト教とイスラム教は中世に国家権力と強く結びつきながら成長しました。そのことが、その後の両者の現在にまで至る対立へと繋がっていったのです。

　一方、3番目に多くの人の信仰を集めるヒンドゥー教は、基本的にはインドの国民的宗教で、地理的にはインドから東南アジアに信者が集中しています。ヒンドゥー教、そして仏教は1世紀頃から7世紀にかけて東南アジアの南岸一帯を支配していたといわれる扶南国を通してカンボジアやインドネシアへと伝播してゆきました。また、9世紀から13世紀にかけては南インドにチョーラ王朝が繁栄し、インド洋から南シナ海一体にヒンドゥー文化を伝播しました。東南アジアの人々は紀元前から農耕にいそしんできました。キリスト教やイスラム教がどちらかというと狩猟民族、そして遊牧民族の間に拡大したのに比べ、ヒンドゥー教や仏教は農耕民族の宗教としてアジアに根付いたのです。

　インドネシアに8世紀から9世紀にかけてシャイレーンドラ朝という王朝がありました。シャイレーンドラ朝はジャワ島の中部にあるボロブドゥールの仏教遺跡などを残し、扶南国に変わって東南アジアの南岸を支配していた真臘にも侵入し、その地域を支配した国として知られています。また、7世紀頃から14世紀までインドネシアからマレー半島一帯を支配し、シャイレーンドラ朝もその一部だったのではない

時代
8〜17世紀
中世

地域
東南アジア

分類
宗教【国家】

キーワード
世界の宗教・インドのヒンドゥー教・東南アジアの宗教と文化・諸国家の興亡・交易の中継

Indonesia to the Malay Peninsula, and through this large territory Buddhism and Hinduism were widely embraced. Bordering the Srivijaya monarchy, the state which ruled large portions of Southeast Asia and is known for the construction of Hindu sites including the ruins of Angkor Wat was the Khmer Empire. This empire, which became independent of the Shailendra in 802, was originally a monarchy formed from Zhenla, a large state that existed until the 15th century across present-day Cambodia. Following the Yuan invasion of Southeast Asia, the Khmer monarchy became a Yuan tributary.

As for Vietnam, the northern part of the country was ruled by successive Chinese rulers until the Tang Dynasty. On the other hand, the Champa Kingdom flourished in the central part of the country for a long period of time from the 2nd century to around the 17th century. The country prospered as an intermediary in the sea-route trade between India and China.

Whether we are discussing the Middle East or Southeast Asia, we tend to think of history in terms of present-day borders between countries. However, a large number of present-day national borders are artificial lines drawn on maps by the Western world powers during the colonial period. When we look at the areas controlled by the earlier Khmer, Srivijaya, and Champa states, we see just how different they were from today's borders. And from this, we can grasp the cultural exchange across the seas from the Indian Ocean to the South China Sea to the Pacific Ocean.

ボロブドゥール
Borobudur

かといわれるシュリーヴィジャヤ王国でも、仏教やヒンドゥー教が
信仰されていました。そしてシュリーヴィジャヤ王国と国境を接し、
東南アジア一帯を広く支配した王朝がアンコールワットなどのヒン
ドゥー教の遺跡を築いたことで知られるクメール王国でした。802年
にシャイレーンドラ朝から独立したクメール王国は、元々真臘の流れ
をくむ王朝で、現在のカンボジア一帯に15世紀まで存続した大国です。
元の東南アジア侵攻後、クメール王国は元に朝貢したこともありまし
た。

　また、ベトナムはといえば、北部は唐の時代まで中国の歴代王朝の
支配を受けていました。その一方、2世紀から17世紀頃までの長期に
わたって、中部にはチャンパ王国が繁栄していました。チャンパ王国は、
インドから中国に至る海の道を通った海洋交易の中継地として栄えた
のです。
　我々は中東にしろ、東南アジアにしろ、現在ある国境をもって地域
の歴史を考えがちです。しかし、現在の国境の多くは、後年西欧列強
がこれらの地域を植民地にしたとき人為的にひいた線なのです。クメー
ル王国やシュリーヴィジャヤ王国、チャンパ王国などの支配地域を見
ると、東南アジアの国家のあらましが今といかに異なっていたかがわ
かってきます。そこからは、インド洋から南シナ海、太平洋に至る広
大な海の文化交流の姿が見えてくるのです。

アンコールワット
Angkor Wat

064 Southeast Asia was an "oasis" on the Silk Road sea routes

When we think of oceanic culture in a broad sense, starting with Southeast Asia, it is essential to know something about the people who speak Austronesian languages. Most of the people on Southeast Asia have roots among people speaking one of this category of languages.

As we observe their activities, we see these Austronesian-speaking people have a deep connection with the origin of Japan. Let us look back on Japan's past following the theme of Gauguin's painting: "Where did we come from? Who are we? Where are we going?"

The Austronesian-speaking peoples long ago crossed from the continent to Taiwan, and over thousands of years they scattered from various sub-regions of Southeast Asia to islands spread across the Pacific, including Hawaii and New Zealand. One group migrated by way of the Indian Ocean to Madagascar in Africa. Others crossed to Japan during the Jomon period, mixed with peoples from the North, and presumably became the roots of the Japanese people today.

Meanwhile other groups from the interior of China followed the flow of rice cultivation and migrated into Vietnam and Cambodia. The languages they spoke are referred to as Austroasiatic, and they are the ones that became pillars of the Khmer Empire and the Kingdom of Champa.

Additional groups belonging to other language categories migrated from the Chinese interior into Thailand and Laos.

As a result of this, East Asia became an area where various ethnic groups from the west and north flowed and mingled with one another. Even Japan, which is said by some to be monoracial, was no exception. Oceanic people and people migrating from the continent came together at a final destination we now call Japan.

From the last stages of the Jomon period through the Yayoi period which followed, rice culture was transmitted to Japan and, as we saw earlier, a wide spectrum of continental culture was also introduced.

Let us compare the history of Japan and Southeast Asia after that introduction occurred.

We have seen how ancient Japan absorbed civilization from China and formed an organized state system with Buddhism as a cornerstone. However, while

東南アジアは海のシルクロードの「オアシス」だった

　広く東南アジアをはじめ世界の海洋文化を考える時、オーストロネシア語族と呼ばれる海洋民族について知っておく必要があります。東南アジアの人々の多くが、オーストロネシア語族にそのルーツがあるのです。

　彼らの活動を見ていくと、オーストロネシア語族が日本の成り立ちにも深く関わっていることもわかってきます。あの「我々はどこから来たのか、我々は何者か、我々はどこへ行くのか」というテーマに日本を重ねながら、振り返ってみましょう。

　オーストロネシア語族は、昔大陸から台湾にわたり、その後数千年をかけて東南アジア各地からハワイやニュージーランドなどの太平洋の島々へ分散してゆきました。また、一部はインド洋を経由して、アフリカのマダガスカルへも移動しています。彼らが縄文時代に日本に渡り、北方系の人々と混ざり合ったのが現在の日本人のルーツではないかといわれているのです。

　一方、中国の内陸から稲作文化に乗るようにベトナムやカンボジアへと移動してきた人々がいます。彼らはオーストロアジア語族と呼ばれ、クメール王国やチャンパ王国の担い手がそうした人々でした。

　さらに、中国の内陸部からタイやラオスに入ってきた別の言語族に属する人の流れもありました。

　このように、東アジアは西や北から様々な民族が流れ込んできた地域なのです。単一民族の国といわれる日本の場合も、実は例外ではありませんでした。海洋民族と大陸を移動してきた人々とが、日本という終着点で出会います。

　かつ縄文時代末期から弥生時代にかけては、稲作文化が大陸から流入し、それと共に大陸の文明そのものも多彩な大陸文化が持ち込まれたことはすでに解説した通りです。

　その後の日本と東南アジアとの歴史を比べてみましょう。

　我々は、古代日本が中国から文明を吸収し、仏教を基軸にしながら国家体制を構築してきた様子を見てきました。しかし、一方で日本は

時代
総合

地域
共通

分類
交流【民族】

キーワード
オーストロネシア語族の世界・アジアの民族交流・文化、宗教の伝播

Japan became involved in the transitions within the monarchies on the Korean Peninsula, it also challenged China, seeking status as an equal state through political opposition.

Southeast Asia has tread a historical path similar to Japan's. Together with the introduction of rice culture, people from China came southward. Buddhism was transmitted early on, and it spread as the axis around which the countries evolved.

However, Southeast Asia lies between the three cultural nuclei of India, the Middle East, and China, and differs from Japan in that it has played the role of a relay point for exchange between them. Just like the towns that developed around the oases of Central Asia, the various areas of Southeast Asia played the same role along the maritime Silk Road routes.

This geographic location was also influential in that Islam was introduced in the 12th to 13th centuries and disseminated through Indonesia, Malaysia, and elsewhere.

065 Due to the Hundred Years' War, France and England parted ways

At about the time that East-West exchange invigorated the Asian world, in Europe a great groundswell was beginning to bring forth a new era.

Let's look at the relationship between France and England. Beginning in 1154, in England the Plantagenet dynasty maintained its political power. Originally this monarchy invaded England from France, where it also held a large amount of territory under its control. And these monarchs themselves were vassals of the king in France, to whom they pledged their loyalty. However, from time to time, rifts developed in these relationships. Retainers of domains that the French royal house directly administered became independent and maintained large domains in France as well. Out of this came conflicts of interest.

King John of England, as a result of conflicts with France, was dispossessed of his lands. Moreover, due to a confrontation with the Roman pope over the right of investiture of the priest of Canterbury Church, he was excommunicated. He sought a settlement and eventually straightened out the confusion. Due to his misrule, the problem of taxation due to warfare, and the opposition from

朝鮮半島での王朝の変遷などにも絡みながら、時には中国に挑み、対等な国家として政治的に対立したこともありました。

東南アジアも日本と似た歴史を歩んできました。東南アジアにも、稲作文化の伝来と共に中国から南下してきた人々がいました。仏教も早くから伝来し、国々の基軸となる宗教として広がりました。

ただ東南アジアは、インドや中東と中国という三つの文化の核の間にあって、その交流の中継地点の役割を担ってきたことは日本と異なっています。中央アジアのオアシスに発展した都市と同じような役割を海のシルクロードにおいて東南アジア各地がはたしてきたのです。

そうした地理的な位置も影響し、12世紀から13世紀にかけてイスラム教が伝わり、インドネシアやマレーシアなどに拡散したのです。

百年戦争でフランスとイギリスは袂を分かった

こうした東西交流が、アジア世界を活気づけていた頃、ヨーロッパでは次の時代に向けた大きなうねりがおこり始めていました。

フランスとイギリスとの関係に目を向けましょう。1154年以来イギリスではプランタジネット朝という王朝が政権を維持していました。元々彼らはフランスからイギリスに侵攻してきた王朝で、フランスにも多くの領地を持っていました。そして、フランスでの身分はというと、有力な家臣としてフランス王に忠誠を誓う立場をとっていたのです。しかし、時とともに、その関係に亀裂が入ります。フランスの王室は自らが直接管理できる地域の家臣がイギリスで自立し、さらにフランス国内に大きな領土を持っていることになります。そこに利害の対立が生まれたのでした。

イギリスのジョン王と呼ばれる人物は、このフランスとの抗争で土地を奪われます。そして、さらにカンタベリー教会の司祭の叙任権をめぐりローマ教皇とも対立し、破門され、最終的には和解を請い、混乱を収拾します。こうした失政と、戦争による課税問題、そして配下の騎士団との対立もあり、王は追い詰められていったのです。状況を

時代
12～14世紀
欧州中世

地域
イギリス・フランス

分類
戦争【政治】

キーワード
フランス出身のイギリス王室・ジョン王の失政・イギリス王権の制限・英仏の対立と百年戦争

the knights under his command, the king was driven into a corner. In order to improve the situation, the king and influential leaders in 1215 exchanged a written agreement that limited the authority of the monarch and recognized the authority of a legislative body to assist in government. This contract became known as the Magna Carta, an agreement that was the origin of the attempt to establish a parliamentary democracy in England in later years.

Following King John's reign, England and France once again came into conflict. In 1328 the lineage of the Capetian dynasty came to an end, so Philippe VI, of the House of Valois, became the French monarch. England's king Edward III asserted his own right to succeed to the throne. The English and French royal families had a blood connection at the time, as was a common practice among European powers to maintain diplomatic relations. As a result, many royal households are somehow related to one another.

The intervention of the English royal family in the affairs of the French royal family developed into an intermittent state of war between England and France that began in 1337 and lasted for more than a century. It was the outbreak of the Hundred Years' War. At the outset, England had the upper hand on the battlefields, and France found itself in desperate straits, but then a young girl in France named Joan of Arc suddenly appeared and announced that she had received a revelation from God telling her that she was to lead the French army.

Long ago even in Japan there were cases in which a child in whom a god was thought to dwell was held in esteem and was given support as a symbol in times of war. One cannot know just how much military and political prowess Joan of Arc possessed, but it is a fact that as a result of her appearance, the fighting spirit of the French armies increased, and they were able to drive the English out. However, Joan of Arc was captured by the English and, at the youthful age of 19, she was burned at the stake. As a result, she was for many years to come revered by the French as a national hero. Through the Hundred Years' War, England and France were transformed into the two independent sovereign countries that exist today.

改善するために、王と有力者との間で1215年に交わしたのが、課税（や戦争）などについての王の権限を制限し、議会の権限を認めたマグナカルタと呼ばれる誓約書でした。マグナカルタは、イギリスが後年議会制民主主義を模索する起点になった取り決めでした。

　ジョン王の後、再びイギリスとフランスとの間で抗争がおこります。1328年にカペー朝の血統が断絶したことで、ヴァロワ家のフィリップ6世がフランス王となりました。この王位継承を巡って、イギリスのエドワード3世がその権利を主張したのです。当時、イギリス王室とフランス王室には血縁がありました。これは両国のみならず、ヨーロッパ世界で外交関係を維持する上での一般的な慣習でした。多くの王室が親戚同士だったのです。
　このフランス王室へのイギリス王室の介入が、1337年以降、両国の100年間以上に及ぶ断続的な戦争状態へと発展します。百年戦争の勃発です。当初はイギリス側が有利に戦争を進めましたが、窮地にたったフランスに神の啓示を受けたとして、忽然と現れフランス軍を導いた少女ジャンヌ・ダルクが出現したのです。

　日本でも、昔子供に神が宿るものとして尊重され、戦争のときのシンボルに擁立されたことはありました。ジャンヌ・ダルクがどれだけ軍事的、政治的な能力があったかはわかりませんが、彼女の出現で、フランス軍の士気があがり、イギリスの勢力が駆逐されたことは事実です。しかしジャンヌ・ダルクは、イギリス側の捕虜となり、19歳の若さで1431年に火刑に処せられました。そのことによって、彼女はフランスの国民的英雄として末長く崇められるようになったのです。この百年戦争を経て、イギリスとフランスという二つの国家が、最終的に現在のような独立した別々の主権国家へと変化していったのです。

ドミニク・アングル『シャルル7世戴冠式のジャンヌ・ダルク』
Dominique Ingres —Joan of Arc at the Coronation of Charles VII

066 Europe in the 14th century entered the autumn of the Middle Ages

The Hundred Years' War, which began in 1337, was symbolic of the complex conflict between England and France. The war entangled surrounding regions, including Scotland and Flanders as well.

The war came to an end in 1453, when the French conquered the last English stronghold at Bordeaux. As a result of this defeat, England lost almost all of the territory it had held on to within France. The last English territory that remained was Calais, facing England across the North Sea, and it, too, was retaken by the French in 1558.

After the Hundred Years' War, England experienced a power struggle between the faction that wanted peace (the House of Lancaster) and the faction that wanted war, led by Richard, Duke of York (the House of York). These two influential noble houses, known for the white rose emblem of the Yorkists and the red rose emblem of the Lancastrians, continued their conflict involving the monarchy. The two houses enveloped the monarchy in continued warfare. For three decades beginning in 1455, England fell into a state of near anarchy known as the War of the Roses. Henry VII brought an end to the war, united the houses by marriage, and initiated the Tudor dynasty.

In the 14th century during the Hundred Years' War, Europe fell into complete chaos. A plague epidemic which first appeared in China was transmitted along the Silk Road and reached Italy. This was the beginning of the rapid spread of bubonic plague, which came to be known as the Black Death. It brought a succession of dark discoloration of the skin from internal bleeding, intense pain from swollen lymphatic glands, and a rapid, inevitable death.

Italian ports strengthened quarantine procedures but were unable to contain the spread of the epidemic. Particularly in the trading city of Venice, incoming ship crews were prevented from docking for 40 days after arrival, in order to determine whether the crew was free of the disease. In English, this period is called "quarantine"—from the Italian word for "40 days"—and it means inspection for a contagious disease. But the plague spread rapidly throughout all of Europe, as far north as England.

Given the scientific knowledge of those days, nothing short of burning an entire house or area where plague had appeared would stop it from spreading.

14世紀、ヨーロッパは中世の秋を
迎えていた

　1337年に始まった百年戦争は、イギリスとフランスとの複雑な確執を象徴したものでした。戦争は、スコットランドやフランドルといった周辺の地域をも巻き込みます。

　百年戦争は、フランス軍がイギリス側の最後の拠点であったボルドーを陥落させたことで1453年に終結します。これによって、イギリスは、フランス王国の中に維持していた領土のほとんどを失うことになります。ちなみに、フランスに最後に残ったイギリス領はイギリスの対岸にあったカレーという町ですが、ここも1558年にフランスが奪還します。

　百年戦争の後、イギリスでは、和平派（ランカスター派）とヨーク公リチャードを中心とした主戦派（ヨーク派）との権力抗争で、白バラの紋章をもつヨーク家と赤バラの紋章で知られるランカスター家という2つの有力諸侯が王室を巻き込んで抗争を続けます。1455年から30年にわたってイギリスを混乱状態に陥れた薔薇戦争の勃発です。この薔薇戦争を終結させた王がヘンリー7世で、彼が開いた王朝がテューダー朝でした。

　ところで、百年戦争最中の14世紀、ヨーロッパはパニックのどん底にありました。中国で発生した疫病が、シルクロードを経由してイタリアに上陸します。黒死病として知られるようになったペストの大流行の始まりです。内出血で全身に黒いあざができ、リンパ腺が腫れて苦しむ人々がばたばたと死んでゆきます。

　イタリアの港町では検疫体制を強化しますが追いつきません。特に交易都市ヴェネチアでは、入港する人を40日間海に止めて、ペストの発生の有無を確認していたといいます。この40日という言葉が、英語でquarantineとなりました。quarantineが検疫を意味するようになった背景です。ペストは、瞬く間にヨーロッパ全土からイギリスへと北上したのでした。

　当時の科学では発症した家や地域を焼き払わない限り流行を防げません。人々は恐怖に見舞われ神に祈ります。流言飛語も飛び交い、ユ

時代
14, 15世紀
欧州中世

地域
ヨーロッパ

分類
社会【戦争】

キーワード
百年戦争の終結・イギリスの混乱・ペストの流行・ユダヤ人迫害・中世秩序の崩壊

Struck by fear, people prayed to God. Groundless rumors spread regarding who might be responsible for the tragic epidemic, and Jews and people considered heretics by the Roman Catholics were massacred. Many persecuted Jews fled to Poland. In the 14th century the Kingdom of Poland was ruled by Casimir III, who opened the country's doors to them in order to encourage trade. As a result, the number of Jewish people in Eastearn Europe increased. Due to the chaos that resulted from the plague and this influx of people, more than one-third of the entire population of Europe died during the epidemic.

For the knights of the Middle Ages, the bubonic plague caused both anxiety about possibly contracting the disease and an economic predicament. Because agricultural villages became impoverished, the knights' income decreased markedly. Moreover, beginning in about the 14th century, the climate which had until then gradually been warming underwent a gradual cooling. Adding to the plague, this climatic change brought about a reduction in harvests of farm produce.

Due to this disaster and the period of warfare, the European social structure underwent a major change, and the feudal system collapsed. It was the beginning of the transition between medieval times and the early-modern era.

067 Central Asia was the epicenter of world history

Here we again focus our attention on the movements of the Mongol Empire. In the 13th century, Mongol forces advanced into the Middle East, conquering Baghdad and establishing the Il Khanate, but by the 14th century, in part due to conflicts over succession, that state fell into decline.

Central Asia was controlled by the Chagatai Khanate, and Russia was subject to the Kipchak Khanate. But under the descendants of Genghis Khan, these states were partitioned, and the people of these respective expansive territories became self-governing states under the umbrella of Han China.

It is extremely important to keep an eye on Central Asia throughout world history. Whoever has subjugated Central Asia has been able to link the eastern portions of the Eurasian landmass, centering on China, with European culture. In addition, the accumulated abundant civilization of the Islamic lands of the Middle East poured in, and to the south was the Indian civilization. It was only those who

ダヤ人やローマカトリックを信じていない異端と呼ばれた人々への殺
戮もおこります。迫害されたユダヤ人の多くはポーランドへと逃れま
した。14世紀のポーランド王国は、カジミェッシュ3世の時代でした。
彼は交易を奨励するために、ユダヤ人にも広く門戸を開けていたので
す。以降東欧のユダヤ人は増え続けます。ペストとそれと関連した社
会混乱で、ヨーロッパの人口の3分の1以上が犠牲になりました。

　中世の騎士にとって、ペストの大流行は自らが罹患するのではとい
う不安と共に経済的な苦境ももたらします。農村が疲弊することで、
彼らの収入が激減したのです。しかも、14世紀頃から、それまで温暖
であった気候が変化し、地球は寒冷化してゆきます。ペストに加えて、
この気候変動が農作物の収穫量をさらに押し下げたのでした。

　こうした災害や戦争を通して、ヨーロッパではそれまでの社会構造
が大きく変わり、封建制度が崩壊してゆきます。中世から近世へと脱
皮を始めたのです。

中央アジアは世界史の震源地であった

　ここで再びモンゴル帝国の動勢に目を向けてみます。13世紀に中東
に進出したモンゴル軍は、バグダードを陥落させイル・ハン国を建国
しますが、やがて後継者争いもあって、14世紀には衰退してしまいま
す。

　また、中央アジア、そしてロシアはそれぞれチャガタイ・ハン国と
キプチャク・ハン国によって支配されていましたが、それらの国家も、
チンギス・ハンの末裔によって分割され、それぞれの土地の人々がハ
ン国の傘下で自治国家を運営していました。

　世界史を通して、中央アジアに目を向けることはとても重要です。
中央アジアを制した者は、中国を核としたユーラシア大陸東部とヨー
ロッパ文明とをつなぐことができたのです。加えて、そこには中東か
らイスラム圏内に蓄積された豊かな文明が流れ込み、南に行けばイン
ド文明とも接触できます。中央アジアを震源地として繁栄できた者だ

時代
13、14世紀
イスラム中世

地域
中央アジア

分類
交流【民族】

キーワード
モンゴルの中央アジア・
東洋西洋の結節点・ティ
ムール帝国の成立

flourished in this epicenter of Central Asia who were within easy reach of the entire landmass of Eurasia.

In present-day Central Asia are the states of Turkmenistan, Tajikistan, Uzbekistan, Kazakhstan, and Kyrgyzstan. During the Union of Soviet Socialist Republics era, these states were self-governing republics under the control of Moscow, but following the collapse of the Soviet Union, they became independent countries. The suffix "-stan" in these countries' names means "the place where the ... people live," and the original Persian word has come to mean "country." The first half of each country's name refers to the nomadic peoples who lived and earned their livelihood there. In other words, the countries mentioned above are the lands of the Turks, Tajiks, Uzbeks, Kazakhs, and Kyrgyzs.

If we trace the roots of these countries, we can go back to the era of divide and rule within the Mongol Empire. Furthermore, it can be said that the foundation for their growth as modern-day states was established when they were under the rule of the nomadic tribes within the Mongol Empire. It need hardly be mentioned that the nomadic peoples such as the Xiongnu, the Tujue, and the Sogdians were strongly connected with China's Western Regions and with the northern territories.

中央アジア
Map of Central Asia

けが、ユーラシア大陸全体を鳥瞰できる位置に立てたのです。

　現在、中央アジアには、トルクメニスタン、タジキスタン、ウズベキスタン、カザフスタン、キルギスタンなどの国家があります。ソヴィエト連邦の時代には、これらの国々はモスクワの統制下の自治共和国でしたが、ソヴィエト連邦崩壊後は独立国となっています。これらの国々に共通している「スタン」という語尾は、「～が住むところ」というペルシア語が転じて「国」を意味する言葉となりました。そして、国名の前半がそこに住み活躍した遊牧民族の名称なのです。すなわち、これらの国家はそれぞれ、トルコ系、タジック系、ウズベク系、カザフ系、そしてキルギス系の人々の国ということになります。

　これらの国家のルーツをたどれば、モンゴル帝国の中での分割統治の時代へ遡れます。もっというならば、彼らが現代史に直接つながる国家として成長するその基礎となったのが、モンゴル帝国の支配下にあったときの遊牧民族の国家だったのです。これらの遊牧民族は、匈奴や突厥、ソグド人など中国の西域や北方の歴史と深く関わった人々にもルーツをたどることができることはいうまでもありません。

In the 14th century the lands ruled by the Chagatai Khanate in Central Asia fragmented. The Western Chagatai Khanate repeatedly sent military expeditions from Central Asia to regions in the Middle East and even into northern India. Then a heroic figure appeared who would establish a great empire, a man of Mongol descent named Timur, also known in English as Tamerlane. Skillfully manipulating the complex relations between the nomads, the descendants of the Mongol Empire who settled and dealt with complicated ethnic conflicts, Timur absorbed the virtually disintegrated Il Khanate, became conqueror of all of the lands between the Middle East and Central Asia, and in 1370 founded the Timurid Empire, which prospered like the Il Khanate before it as an Islamic country. Its capital was Samarkand in present-day Uzbekistan. It had been an important transit point from ancient times.

068 At the time the Mongol Empire declined, an important change of government occurred in the Far East

The Yuan dynasty, which was created by the Mongol Empire, devastated the Southern Song and united China in 1279. At that time, all of the functions of the entire Mongol Empire were in Karakorum in the western part of the Mongol territories. Prominent leaders from all over the empire came there for an assembly known as the Kurultai, where issues of great import were considered. Nevertheless, after the death of Genghis Khan, his descendants spread out all over Eurasia, and there were frequent power struggles among blood relatives.

In the midst of this, the Yuan made the city of Dadu, present-day Beijing, China's capital, and they ruled the country from there. The Yuan entrusted important roles to the Mongols and also to the Semuren, a people who were spread from Central Asia to the Near and Middle East. They directed their energies to trade, completed a system of post-stations, and aggressively pursued maritime trade through a port in Guangzhou.

Beginning with Kublai Khan, successive emperors became believers in Lamaism, known as Tibetan Buddhism, which of course was introduced from Tibet, but they were also tolerant of other religions as well. During this period, the Roman Pope dispatched John of Plano Carpini as an envoy to the Mongol

14世紀に、そんな中央アジアを統治していたチャガタイ・ハン国が分裂します。そして西チャガタイ・ハン国から、中央アジアから中東地域、さらには北インドにまで遠征を繰り返し、大帝国を築いた英雄が現れます。モンゴル系の血をひくティムールという人物です。遊牧民、そしてそこに定住していたモンゴル帝国の子孫など、複雑な民族抗争を巧みにかいくぐったティムールは、ほとんど分裂状態にあったイル・ハン国を吸収し、中東から中央アジア一帯の覇者となり、1370年にティムール帝国を開きます。ティムール帝国もイル・ハン朝と同様にイスラム教国として繁栄しました。首都は現在のウズベキスタンにあるサマルカンド。そこは古来東西交易の重要な中継地点だったのです。

モンゴル帝国が衰亡した頃、極東でも政変が重なった

　モンゴル帝国のおこした中国の王朝元は、1279年に南宋を滅ぼし中国を統一します。当時モンゴル帝国全体の本部機能は、現在のモンゴル西部にあったカラコルムに置かれていました。またモンゴル帝国全域の有力者はクリルタイと呼ばれる会合に召集され、そこで重要な意思決定がなされていました。とはいえ、チンギス・ハンの死後、その子孫はユーラシア大陸各地に拡散し、血族内での権力闘争も頻繁でした。

　そうした中、元は現在の北京にあたる大都を首都とし、中国を支配します。元では、モンゴル人と共に色目人と呼ばれる中央アジアから中近東にかけての人々を重用しました。交易に力を入れ、駅伝制などを整えると共に、広州などの港を通した海洋貿易にも積極的でした。

　フビライをはじめ、歴代の皇帝はチベットから入ってきたチベット仏教として知られるラマ教に帰依しますが、元王朝は他の宗教にも寛容でした。この時代ローマ教皇が、プラノ・カルピニを使者としてモンゴル帝国に派遣し、これと共にローマカトリックも中国に伝導され

時代
13, 14世紀 中国中世

地域
東アジア

分類
国家【政治】

キーワード
モンゴルの中国統治・カトリックの中国伝道・モンゴルの後退・明の成立・日本、韓国の政変

Empire, and with this, Roman Catholicism was also propagated in China. King Louis IX of France also sent a delegation.

In this way, for the first time in history, the European world officially recognized and began to interact with the Chinese world during the Yuan dynasty. This is because both the west and east of the Eurasian Continent were now under the control of a single empire, making it possible to travel back and forth more safely. However, in the 14th century, the Yuan would experience not only internal strife and economic disorder but also an insurgency.

Of special significance were the Red Turban Rebellions brought about by the White Lotus Sect, a sect of the Pure Land School, in 1351. At the forefront of this rebellion was a prominent leader with an extensive following named Zhu Yuanzhang, who expelled the Mongols from Dadu and forced them to withdraw to the Mongolian Plateau in 1368.

From that time forward, the capital of the state was relocated to Karakorum, and the dynasty came to be known as the Northern Yuan. This was two years before the Timurid Empire came under Mongol rule through Central and West Asia. China once again became a government under the Han Chinese, establishing the Ming dynasty.

Meanwhile, in Japan, following the failed Mongolian Invasions, the Kamakura Shogunate was overthrown in 1333, and a new administration under Emperor Godaigo also collapsed within three years. As a result, the country was split into two parts, with a Northern Court supported by the Muromachi Shogunate and the Southern Court under the successors of Emperor Godaigo. The Mongols were driven out of China in the same year that Ashikaga Yoshimitsu disentangled the chaos of the Northern and Southern Courts and became the third shogun.

At about the same time, a political disturbance arose in neighboring Korea.

Koryo, which had been occupied and governed by the Mongols, became independent upon their decline. The Koryo kingdom, however, continued to exist for a considerable period of time. Toward the end of the Koryo era, the Korean Peninsula suffered under attacks by pirates who were active in both China and Japan. These pirates are called *wako*, meaning Japanese pirates, but it is unclear whether they all originated in Japan or were from a variety of locations. Regardless, the prominent general Yi Seong-gye suppressed them and restored peace. In 1392 he destroyed the Koryo monarchy and intitiated the Joseon dynasty.

ます。実はフランス王ルイ9世も使節を派遣しています。

　このように、元の時代に、歴史上はじめてヨーロッパ世界が中国世界を正式に認識し、交流を始めたのです。それはユーラシア大陸の西と東とが一つの帝国の管理の元に、より安全に行き来ができるようになったからに他なりません。しかし、そんな元王朝も14世紀には内紛や経済的な混乱などに加えて、反乱に見舞われます。

　特に、1351年に浄土教の結社であった白蓮教による紅巾の乱がおきると、その乱に参加して頭角をあらわし、勢力を拡大した朱元璋によって、モンゴル人勢力は、大都を追われてモンゴル高原に退きます。1368年のことでした。

　以降、中国を去り、カラコルムを首都に展開した国家を、中国では北元とよんでいます。ティムール帝国が中央アジアや西アジアのモンゴル系の勢力にとってかわる2年前のことでした。中国に再び漢民族による王朝が生まれます。明の建国です。

　当時、日本では元寇の後、1333年に鎌倉幕府が滅び、後醍醐天皇によって打ち立てられた建武の新政も3年で瓦解。新たに成立した室町幕府が支持する北朝と、後醍醐天皇の後継者による南朝とに国が二分されました。元が中国を追われたのは、そんな南北朝の混乱を収拾した足利義満が3代将軍に就任した年のことでした。

　その頃、お隣の韓国でも政変がおこります。
　モンゴルによって占領統治されていた高麗が、元の衰退と共に自立します。しかし、その後高麗王朝は長くは続きませんでした。高麗の末期、朝鮮半島は日本や中国などで活動していた海賊の侵攻にも苦しめられます。こうした海賊を倭寇と呼びますが、倭寇の全てが日本からのものかどうかはわかりません。いずれにせよ、そうした混乱を平定し、台頭した軍人李成桂が、1392年に高麗王朝を滅ぼし、李氏朝鮮を開いたのでした。

李成桂
Yi Seong-gye (1335–1408)

069 Medieval Europe and the Ottoman Empire came to an end together

During the 14th century, a number of changes occurred in both Europe and Asia.

As we have already seen, with the bubonic plague raging across Europe and global cooling continuing, farming villages became impoverished. When that happened, people flowed into the towns and cities, and with that occurring, a commercial economy gained strength. As a result of the advance of the monetary economy, society underwent major changes. The monetary economy advanced into farming villages. Farmers bought and sold their own crops, and out of this population came some who developed into prominent farmers. At the same time, the knights who lost their economic base as a result of the rampant epidemic and cooling of the earth sought the protection of royal families, gradually transforming into nobles who were vassals of the kings, increasing the relative authority of the royal households. Where previously the kings had to request the cooperation of the knights whenever there was a war, the kings now had a standing army and they developed military capability as well. Moreover, prominent nobles became bureaucrats who carried out the administrative functions of the kingdoms, becoming involved in royal authority.

Royal families that grew stronger posed a challenge to the authority of the Pope. During this period, which is called the autumn of the Middle Ages, the delicate balance that had until then been maintained between the Roman Catholic Church, the kings, and the knights within the feudal system began to crumble at its very foundations.

At the time of the outbreak of the Hundred Years' War, faced with the trends of the times, the Holy See of the Roman Catholic Church was struck by a major incident. The king of France, Philippe IV, who opposed the pope's right of taxation, fought with the Holy See, and ultimately the Holy See moved to Avignon in France. The 77-year period beginning in 1309, during which this situation continued, has been called the Babylonian Captivity of the Papacy. The situation grew even more complicated thereafter as the Church split into two factions—one at Avignon and another in Rome—with the unprecedented appearance of two different popes. At times, there were even conflicts over the authority between multiple popes. This situation, which continued until 1417 is known as the Great Schism.

ヨーロッパの中世はオスマン帝国と共に
終焉を迎える

このように14世紀には、ヨーロッパでもアジアでも、社会に様々な変化がおきました。

すでに解説したように、ヨーロッパではペストの大流行や、寒冷化によって、農村が疲弊します。すると都市へと人が流れ、そこで台頭していた商業経済へと組み込まれます。貨幣経済の浸透によって社会が大きく変化したのです。貨幣経済は農村にも浸透します。農民は自らの作物を売買し、中には有力農民へと成長する者も現れます。同時に、寒冷化やペストの流行などで経済的基盤を失いつつあった騎士は、王室へ保護を求め、しだいに王の臣下として貴族となり、相対的に王の権力が強化されたのです。以前は戦争の度に騎士に助力を願っていた王も、常備軍を持つようになり、軍事的にも成長します。また、有力な貴族は王国の運営を司る官僚となり王権の中に組み込まれたのでした。

時代
14世紀
欧州中世

地域
ヨーロッパ

分類
社会【社会】

キーワード
貨幣経済の開始・世相の混乱・ローマ教皇権の衰退と王権の強化・トルコの伸張

力のついた王室はローマ教皇の権威にも挑戦します。中世の秋といわれるこの時代、ヨーロッパ世界ではそれまでのローマカトリックと王、そして騎士との微妙な緊張によって維持されていた封建制度が根底から崩れ始めたのです。

百年戦争が勃発した頃、この時代の流れを受け、ローマ教皇庁が大きな事件に見舞われます。ローマ教皇の課税権などに反発したフランス王フィリップ4世が教皇庁と争い、最終的に教皇庁をフランスのアビニオンに移したのです。1309年から77年まで続いたこの事件は、教皇のバビロン捕囚といわれています。そして、その後も教会はアビニオン派とローマ派とに分裂し、教皇が二人存在するという異常事態に陥ります。一時はさらに複数の教皇が権力を争ったこともありました。1417年まで続いたこの状況を教会大分裂といいます。

This series of incidents tells us just how the authority of the Roman Catholic Church wavered as royal authority strengthened. Needless to say, the religious reform that gave birth to Protestantism was an extension of this development.

As European society was undergoing this transformation, a particular tribe in present-day Anatolia in Turkey was gaining military power and gradually increasing its sway over the region.

The monarchy founded by the leader of this tribe, Osman I, founded the Ottoman Empire in 1299, one century after the departure of the Mongol Empire. Next it was the Ottoman Empire, which expanded as an Islamic country, which relentlessly put pressure on Europe from Turkey and the Mediterranean.

The Eastern Roman Empire, following the weakening of the Latin Empire established as a result of the Crusades, was no longer functioning as an effective barrier against threats from the east.

This threw a broad shadow over Europe, which had accumulated new wealth as a result of the development of cities.

From the perspectives of the Italian city-states, such as Venice, which had built their wealth from the Mediterranean world as well as that of the merchants of the Hanseatic League who connected trade across the Baltic Sea to the interior of Russia into the Eastern Roman Empire, the development of the Ottoman Empire became a serious force for change due to its very existence.

070 The Ottoman Empire led the world into modern times

During the 14th century, during the development of the Ottoman Empire, present-day Iran was under the rule of the Timurid Empire.

To the northeast, Turkic peoples continued to rise and fall. Active among these peoples were nomadic states including the Black Sheep Turkmen and the White Sheep Turkmen, who occasionally posed a threat to the Timurid dynasty. At that time, the Ottoman Empire had expanded toward the west and eventually had the whole of Eastern Europe under its umbrella. Due to the movements of these nomadic people, as well as internal conflicts within the empire, the Timurids collapsed in 1507. Then during the early years of the 16th century, the Safavid dynasty came to power in Rian, taking Shia Islam as the national religion. At present,

この一連の事件は、王権が強化される中で、いかにローマ教会の力が揺らいできたかを物語っています。こうした動きの延長に、新教（プロテスタント）を生み出す宗教改革があったことはいうまでもないことです。

ヨーロッパ社会がこのように変化していた頃、現在のトルコのアナトリア地方にあった一つの部族が軍事的に力をつけ、次第に勢力を拡大していました。

1299年に、その部族の長オスマン1世が開いた王朝が、オスマン帝国です。モンゴル帝国が去って1世紀。今度はイスラム教国として伸長してきたオスマン帝国がトルコや地中海からひしひしとヨーロッパに迫ってきたのです。

東ローマ帝国は、あの十字軍でのラテン帝国建国の事件以来衰弱し、すでに東からの脅威の防壁にはなりえませんでした。

これは、都市の発展によって新たな富を蓄積していたヨーロッパに大きな影を落とします。

地中海を舞台に富を築いたヴェネチアなどのイタリアの都市国家にとっても、ハンザ同盟によってバルト海からロシア内陸部を経て東ローマへと繋がっていた商人にとっても、オスマン帝国の成長は、活動のあり方そのものの変革を迫られる重大事となったのでした。

オスマン帝国は世界を近代へと導いた

オスマン帝国が成長途上にあった14世紀当時、現在のイランにはティムール帝国がありました。

その北東ではトルコ系民族の興亡が続いていました。黒羊朝、白羊朝といったトルコ系の遊牧国家がティムール帝国に挑みながら活動します。その時期にオスマン帝国は、西へと領土を拡張し、最終的には現在の東ヨーロッパ一帯を傘下に入れたのでした。ちなみに、ティムール帝国はこうした民族運動と内部の抗争の末に1507年に滅亡します。イランでは、その後16世紀初頭になってサファヴィー朝という王朝が興り、その核となる宗教集団によって、シーア派のイスラム教が国教となります。今ではイランはシーア派イスラム教の中心として、スン

時代
14～17世紀
イスラム中世～近世

地域
中東・東ヨーロッパ

分類
統一【宗教】

キーワード
シーア派とスンナ派・オスマン帝国のイスラム世界統一・東ローマ帝国の滅亡

Iran is the center of the Shia branch of Islam, while the Sunni branch is dominant in Saudi Arabia and its neighboring states, all of whom are opposed to Iran.

The Ottoman Empire bordered directly on the Safavid Kingdom and repeatedly threatened the latter. The Ottomans also invaded the Mamluk Sultanate, which had subjugated the southern Mediterranean centering around Egypt in 1250, and in 1517 it overthrew the Mamluks. Then to the west, it spread Islam through Eastern Europe and advanced into the Christianized world. The fact that there are many Muslims in Bosnia in Eastern Europe is due entirely to the influence of the Ottoman Empire. In 1453 the Eastern Roman Empire was at long last destroyed by the Ottoman Empire, and the Roman Empire ceased to exist in both name and reality. Constantinople was renamed Istanbul, and it became the capital city of the empire.

The growth of the Ottoman Empire began at the time of the Crusades, and from that time to the present, the confrontation between the Islamic world and the Christian world has deepened. That confrontation became a fuse that triggered the modernization of the European world.

Due to the fact that the Ottoman Empire commanded the eastern Mediterranean Sea, the world powers of Europe, which were blocked from using that maritime trade route, instead sought trade routes in the Atlantic and southward along the west coast of Africa. Of special importance was the attempt to advance westward across the Atlantic, which led to the discovery of the New World of the Americas. Moreover, tense relations with the Ottomans also played a role in the expansion of military capabilities and sovereign prerogatives in Russia, the Holy Roman Empire, France, and Spain. The Ottoman Empire's expansion into the Middle East meant that a vast Islamic realm came under the control of a single dynasty. It is this Islamic world that is the point of origin for today's Middle Eastern world.

The period from the 16th century through the 17th century was one which exerted various direct influences on contemporary society. People formed societies, which developed into states. As a result of a series of migrations and the merging of ethnic groups, monarchies rose and fell, and after long chaotic repetitions of these events, modern-day states came into being. Through conflicts between these states, the established power structure at the core of these states changed. In reaction to the suppression of people's individual beliefs and power, the time came when people began to search for individual rights such as freedom and human rights.

ナ派を信奉する人々が多数派となるサウジアラビアなどの周辺諸国と
対峙しています。

　オスマン帝国はこのサファヴィー朝と国境を接し、何度もサファ
ヴィー朝を圧迫します。また1250年以降エジプトを中心に南地中海を
支配していたマムルーク朝にも侵攻して、1517年にはこれを滅ぼしま
す。そして、西では東ヨーロッパをイスラム化しながら、キリスト教
世界に進出していったのでした。今でも、東ヨーロッパのボスニアな
どにイスラム教徒が多く居住するのは、オスマン帝国の影響に他なり
ません。1453年、ついに東ローマ帝国がオスマン帝国に滅ぼされ、ロー
マ帝国は名実ともに消滅します。コンスタンティノープルはイスタン
ブールと改名され、オスマン帝国の首都となったのでした。

　オスマン帝国の伸長は、十字軍の時代に始まり、その後現代まで続
くイスラム世界とキリスト教世界との対立をさらに深化させることに
なりました。そして、この対立が、ヨーロッパ世界を近代へと導く導
火線にもなったのです。

　オスマン帝国が東地中海の制海権をもつことで、商業活動の道を閉
ざされたヨーロッパ列強が、大西洋、そしてアフリカを南下するルー
トへと交易路を求めます。特に、大西洋を西に進もうとしたことが、
アメリカなど新大陸の発見に繋がったことはいうまでもありません。
また、オスマン帝国との緊張が、ロシアや神聖ローマ帝国、そしてフ
ランスやスペインでの軍事拡張や王権の伸長に繋がったことも事実で
す。また、オスマン帝国の中東への拡大は、広大なイスラム圏が一つ
の王朝の傘下に組み込まれることを意味します。このイスラム圏こそ
が、今の中東世界の原点となってゆくのです。

　16世紀から17世紀は、現代社会に直接影響を及ぼす様々なことがお
きた時代です。それは、人々が社会を作り、国家として発展し、民族
の移動と融合の連鎖によって王朝が興亡したそれまでの長い混沌の中
から、近代国家が生まれる時代にあたります。そして、近代国家の中
の確執を通して、国家の中枢となる権力構造が変化し、人々が個々の
信仰や権力による抑圧への反動から、自由や人権などの個人の権利を
模索し始める時代へと繋がってゆくのです。

071 We are absorbed in memories of a short history of only 500 years

We are captive to a belief that the European world has its origins in Christian civilization and that the civilization of that region is built on the tradition of Christian society.

To some degree this is true, but when we assume a bird's-eye view of Europe as a whole and direct our attention to the people who live there, we can comprehend that contemporary European civilization has been influenced not only by Christianity but by a blending of that faith with various others, including Judaism and Islam.

It is not merely because there never was a historical opportunity for Europe to become aware of itself as a Christian society and declare itself as such. Let us look at one such symbolic event that was such an opportunity.

First of all, there was the Battle of Kulikovo in 1380 in Russia.

This was a battle in which the Grand Duchy of Moscow, which was a vassal state of the Mongolian Kipchak Khanate, rebelled against Mongol rule. The victory of the Russians in this battle, known as the Battle of Kulikovo, marked the independence of Russia from the Kipchak Khanate, and it became a starting point for the flourishing of the Orthodox Church in Russia under imperial rule.

Secondly, in the Iberian Peninsula, Granada fell in 1492, and the Islamic Nasrid dynasty collapsed. This meant that since the Andalusian Umayyad dynasty took over the southern portion of the Iberian Peninsula and placed it under Islamic authority, for the first time the Islamic monarchy was ousted from the peninsula. From the perspective of the Christian side, this marked the recovery of territories that had been lost since the fall of the Visigothic Kingdom in 711, a process that took over 700 years. This recovery movement is known in Spanish as the Reconquista.

However, at the same time that a wedge was driven in the flow of ethnic groups from Asia in Russia and in the Iberian Peninsula, in the eastern Mediterranean the situation was the reverse, with the Ottoman Empire expanding its power. What stemmed this expansion from growing stronger and built a breakwater against a further inflow was the urgent business of stabilizing European society as a Christian one.

It was this process that served as an incentive for the political, religious, and

我々は、500年という短い歴史の記憶に
没頭する

　我々は、ヨーロッパ世界をキリスト教文明の源流ととらえ、この地域の文明がキリスト教社会とその伝統によって築かれてきたものと思っています。

　これは正しくもありますが、ヨーロッパ全域を俯瞰し、そしてそこに住む人々に目を向けたとき、単にキリスト教のみならず、ユダヤ教やイスラム教といった様々な宗教が溶け合い、影響しあって現代のヨーロッパ文明へと繋がっていることが理解できます。

　ただ、ヨーロッパがキリスト教社会であることを自覚し、それを断定してゆくような歴史的な契機がなかったわけではありません。ここにそんな契機となる象徴的なイベントを紹介します。

　まず、1380年にロシアでクリコヴォの戦いという戦争がありました。

　これは、モンゴル系のキプチャク・ハン国の属国となっていたモスクワ大公国が、モンゴル政権に反旗を翻した戦いでした。ロシア人がこの戦いに勝利したことは、ジュチウルスとも呼ばれるキプチャク・ハン国からロシアが独立し、皇帝の権力のもとで正教会がロシアで繁栄する出発点となりました。

　次に、イベリア半島では、1492年にグラナダが陥落し、イスラム教国であったナスル朝が滅亡します。これで後ウマイヤ朝以来イスラム勢力が支配していたイベリア半島南部から、最終的にイスラム王朝が駆逐されたことになります。キリスト教徒側から見れば、711年に西ゴート王国が滅亡して以来、700年以上をかけて失地回復をしたのです。この失地回復運動のことを、スペイン語でレコンキスタと呼んでいます。

　しかし、ロシアやイベリア半島でアジアからの民族活動の流れに楔が打たれたとき、東地中海では、オスマン帝国が逆に勢力を拡大したのです。この活動をさらにせき止め、防波堤を築くことが、ヨーロッパ社会をキリスト教社会として安定させるための急務となったのです。

　その過程こそが、近代に向かうヨーロッパでの様々な政治活動、宗教

時代
8〜15世紀
欧州中世

地域
ヨーロッパ

分類
社会【文化】

キーワード
ヨーロッパ文化・非キリスト教との対峙・スペインのレコンキスタ・中世の終わり

cultural activities that propelled Europe into the modern era.

It is about time for us to bring to an end to the first half of our History of Humankind. Although it is the first half, when one thinks of the history of humankind as lasting some 10,000 years, we have already covered the greater part of it. The older history is, the fewer sources are available and hints that might serve as evidence for the facts are even sparser. Despite this, we have on occasion portrayed the circumstances of the movements of ethnic groups across several hundred years as if they occurred in an instant.

In the latter half of this history, let us be strongly aware of those 500 years.

We have observed with considerable haste the events that served as the basis for the next, most recent 500-year period. Yet we cannot overlook the fact that despite the extremely short span that we are about to consider, it occupies the majority of our memory when it comes to contemplating the history of humankind.

活動、そして文化活動の動機となったのでした。

　さて、そろそろ「人類の歴史」の前半に終止符を打たなければなりません。前半といっても、1万年にも及ぶ人類の歴史の長さを思えば、すでにその大半をここに語ったことになります。歴史は古くなればなるほど資料も少なく、事実を証明するヒントも希薄になります。それだけに、我々は時には数百年にわたる民族移動の状況も、あたかも瞬時におきたかのように描いてしまいます。

　これから、後半で語られるのは、人類のたった500年の歴史であることを強く意識しておきましょう。
　その500年の人類の活動の土台となるそれ以前の動きを、我々は大急ぎで観察したのです。そして、これから語る500年という極めて短い時間が、我々人類の歴史という記憶の大部分を占めていることもまた事実なのです。

第四部

人間の世界が広がっていく時代（近世の世界）

Part Four:
The Expansion of the Human World
(The Early-Modern World)

　ヨーロッパで始まった新しい宗教活動は、宗教改革という嵐を巻き起こし、そこで育まれたヒトの意識は、教会に支配されていた世界常識を覆します。そして、ヒトは地球を観察し、科学し、技術革新を通して産業の発達を促しました。この新たな動きは、アジアと西欧という東西世界のバランスを壊し、天秤の水は西から東へと流れ始めたのです。

　西欧社会は、この動きによって複雑に分断され、度重なる戦争を経験しながらも、確実に科学技術を育み、進化させていったのです。そして大航海時代を経て、人々は新大陸を発見し、その富に貪欲な目を向けました。

　一方アジアでは、分断と統合を繰り返していた中国が、次第に大きな統一国家として成長します。同様の現象はインドや中東でも起こり、特にトルコ系の民族によって西欧社会が脅威にさらされたこともありました。

　しかし、中国と南アジア、中東の豊かな富はやがて、より洗練された技術に支えられるようになった西欧世界によって席巻され、その富は東から西へ、そして、その武力の矛先は西から東へと、ベクトルを変えていったのです。

072 The countdown to modern times began with the Reformation

From the 19th century into the 20th century, the West had a great influence on the rest of the world. Then from the final part of the 20th century into the present day, as a reaction against that world trend, a value system that is held to be somewhat Asian has come to be reconsidered, and in Islamic society an extreme movement toward excluding Western civilization has occurred.

The countdown to the present day commenced with the Reformation.

During the frequent conflicts which arose between the Pope and the kings who grew in strength in various parts of Europe, the Holy See was desperately trying to maintain its economic strength in order to safeguard its authority.

In response to these secularizing activities within the Church, a religious reformation movement arose which placed emphasis on returning to the Bible and religious faith. What came to be known as the Reformation was sparked by a German theologian named Martin Luther.

In order to raise money to build St. Peter's Basilica as the headquarters of the Roman Catholic Church, the Church issued indulgences, which forgave purchasers for sins that they had committed in the past, for a price. The origin of the Reformation was Martin Luther's nailing of his "Ninety-five Theses" on the door of the castle church in Wittenberg in 1517. They questioned this policy of selling indulgences under the directive of Pope Leo X.

Supporters of the actions of Martin Luther and supporters of Pope Leo X each gathered feudal lords as backers, and as a result, the European world, especially the Holy Roman Empire, was plunged into chaos. Conflict between members of the reformist group, known as Protestants, and members of the Catholic group lasted a long time thereafter and spread throughout Europe. We will consider the fine details of these events later, but suffice it to say that the conflict between the Protestants and the Catholics can be seen as having given birth to two

95カ条の論題
Ninety-five Theses

現代に至るカウントダウンは宗教改革に始まった

　19世紀から20世紀にかけて、西欧世界は世界に大きな影響を与えました。そして、20世紀の終盤から現代にかけて、そうした世界の流れへの反動として、アジア的とされる価値観が見直され、イスラム社会では極端な西欧文明への排除運動がおこりました。

　そんな現代へのカウントダウンはヨーロッパでの宗教改革に始まります。
　ローマ教皇とヨーロッパ各地で力をつけてきた国王との確執が頻発する中、ローマ教会もその権威を保全するため、経済力の維持に必死でした。
　そうした教会の世俗的な活動に対して、聖書と信仰への回帰を主張したのが宗教改革の動きでした。宗教改革は、ドイツの神学者マルティン・ルターによって始められたとされています。

　ローマ教会の総本山として、サンピエトロ大聖堂を建設するために贖宥状を発行し、それを買った者は過去の罪が許されるとしたローマ教皇レオ10世の政策にルターが抗議し、1517年にヴィテンベルグ市の教会に『95カ条の論題』を貼り付けたとされることがその発端でした。

　このルターの行為を支持する人々と、ローマ教皇を支持する人々とが、それぞれ諸侯と結びつきながらヨーロッパ世界、特に神聖ローマ帝国を混乱に陥れます。プロテスタントと呼ばれる改革派の人々と、カトリックとの確執はその後長期間にわたってヨーロッパ全域に広がりました。その詳しい経緯は後で解説するとして、我々はこのプロテスタントとカトリックとの対立が、現代に繋がる二つの大きな流れを生み出したことに注目しなければなりません。

ルーカス・クラーナハ
『マルティン・ルターの肖像』
Lucas Cranach the Elder
—Martin Luther

major trends that have come down to the present day.

One current is that in the midst of the confrontation between those who took the Protestant position and those who maintained the authority of the Catholic Church, people of both persuasions scattered throughout the world. Protestants seeking to escape persecution for their belief fled to places such as North America, where they settled. This later led to the founding of the United States of America. The Catholic side, countering the Protestants, advanced into Asia seeking new regions to proselytize their faith, transmitting it to Japan and elsewhere.

Another current, when all is said and done, is that the Western world, surmounting the conflict between these two religious groups, ultimately evolved into modern nation-states.

In France, for example, the state broke up as a result of the conflict between the Protestants known as Huguenots, King Henry III was assassinated, and the Valois dynasty died out. As a result, a distant relative of the royal house took the throne as Henry IV and founded the Bourbon dynasty. King Henry IV was a Protestant, and he issued the Edict of Nantes in 1598, which guaranteed tolerance to the Protestants. With this as a turning point, and after overcoming a number of ordeals, France went on to establish itself as a country, overcoming conflicts between the two religious groups.

It goes without saying that recognizing freedom of religion was a major factor behind the modernization of the Western world.

The process started by the Reformation which led to chaos throughout Europe and then overcame that confused situation in effect became the labor pains that led to modern society in Europe.

073 In response to the Reformation, the House of Habsburg looked to the New World

Religious activities criticizing the corruption of the Holy See had appeared throughout Europe prior to the arrival of Martin Luther.

From the 14th century into the 15th century, people such as John Wycliffe in England, Jan Hus in Bohemia, and Girolamo Savonarola in Italy advocated a return to the Bible and criticized the decadent state of the Roman Catholic hierarchy.

一つは、プロテスタントの立場をとる人々と、カトリックの権威を維持しようとする人々が、対立の中でそれぞれ世界に拡散していったことです。北アメリカなどには迫害を逃れるプロテスタントが移住し、後年にアメリカ合衆国の建国へと繋がりました。そしてカトリック側もプロテスタントに対抗するように新たな布教の地を求めてアジアに進出し、日本にもキリスト教を伝えました。

　そして、もう一つは、なんといっても西欧世界がこの両者の対立を乗り越えて、最終的には近代国家として成長したことです。

　例えば、フランスではユグノーと呼ばれる新教徒との戦いで国が分裂する中、アンリ3世が暗殺され、ヴァロワ朝が断絶します。その結果王家の縁戚にあたるアンリ4世が即位し、ブルボン朝を開きます。アンリ4世は新教徒で、1598年にナントの勅令を発布して、信仰の自由を保障します。これを契機にいくつかの試練を乗り越えたあと、フランスはプロテスタントとカトリックとの確執を克服した国家としてまとまってゆくのです。

　信教の自由を認めることが、西欧世界が近代化してゆく大きな背景となったことはいうまでもありません。
　宗教改革による、ヨーロッパの混乱と、それを克服するプロセスこそが、ヨーロッパの近代社会を生みだす陣痛となったのでした。

ハプスブルク家は宗教改革に対応するために新大陸に目を向けた

時代
16世紀
欧州近世

地域
ヨーロッパ

分類
宗教【技術】

キーワード
宗教改革の展開・ドイツ農民戦争・印刷技術の発展・ハプスブルク家の発展

　ローマ教皇庁の堕落を批判する宗教活動は、ルター以前からヨーロッパ各地でおこっていました。
　14世紀から15世紀にかけて、イギリスのジョン・ウィクリフ、ボヘミアのヤン・フス、そしてイタリアのジロラモ・サヴォナローラなどが、聖書への回帰を訴え、ローマ教会の現状を堕落したものとして批判したのです。

There was persistent persecution, with Hus and Savonarola being burned at the stake, and Wycliffe's tomb being desecrated and his remains burned.

However, Luther himself did not endure personal persecution. To the contrary, he received support from the general populace and feudal lords who were seeking independence from the Holy Roman Empire and the interests of the Pope, and his influence actually grew. Responding to this movement, a signal fire was lit under a new reform movement led by Huldrych Zwingli and John Calvin in Switzerland. In Germany, the German Peasants' War broke out among peasants who opposed taxation by the monasteries in 1524. The circle of opposition to the Roman Holy See, which had unified the European world through the authority of religion, began to expand throughout all of Western Europe.

Martin Luther translated the Bible into German, freeing it from the Latin language that was the privilege of the Roman Church. In doing this, he provided the means by which the Bible could reach the hands of the common people.

It should not be forgotten that what played a vital role in disseminating the various movements within the Reformation was the movable-type printing press invented in the mid-15th century by Johannes Gutenberg. Even Luther's "Ninety-five Theses," which became the inception of the Reformation, was printed by this advanced printing technology and rapidly transmitted throughout Europe.

The place where Luther was active was the Holy Roman Empire.

At that time, the empire received its emperor from the House of Habsburg.

In those days the royal families of the various states wove personal networks through marital relationships, and the center of those networks was the royal Habsburg family.

Originating in northeastern Switzerland, they later moved their base to Austria, and by means of a series of politically expedient marriages, they developed into the central royal house of Europe.

Maximilian I of the House of Habsburg, who was active in the first half of the 16th century, succeeded to the position of emperor of the Holy Roman Empire, while reigning as monarch in Austria and Germany. Despite this fact, since the Middle Ages, Germany had actually been under the rule of a large number of prominent, independent feudal lords, which meant that Habsburg rule was not absolute.

The Reformation gave rise to a political controversy within Germany. Following Maximilian I, Charles V of Flanders succeeded to the head of the Habsburg regime. In order to avoid being caught in the complex political affairs of Central Europe and to expand the influence of the Holy Roman Empire, Charles

フスやサヴォナローラは火刑に処され、ウィクリフも墓を暴かれ骨を焼かれるという執拗な迫害がありました。

　しかし、ルター個人はそうした迫害を受けませんでした。逆に彼は神聖ローマ帝国やローマ教皇の権益からの自立を模索する諸侯や一般大衆の支持を受け、影響力を拡大したのです。そんな動きに呼応して、スイスでツヴィングリやカルヴァンなどによって新たな改革の狼煙があげられます。また、ドイツでは1524年に修道院からの課税に反対する農民によってドイツ農民戦争がおこりました。ヨーロッパ世界を信仰という権威で統治してきたローマ教皇庁への反抗の輪が、西欧全体に拡大し始めたのです。

　ところで、ルターは聖書をドイツ語に翻訳しました。ラテン語というローマの特権から聖書を解放し、それを一般の人々の手元に届けるきっかけをつくったのです。

　こうした宗教改革の様々な動きを伝播する役割を担ったのが、15世紀中盤にグーテンベルクによって開発された活版印刷術であることを忘れてはなりません。宗教改革の発端となったルターの『95カ条の論題』も、印刷技術の進歩によって、ヨーロッパ各地に迅速に伝わっていったのでした。

　ルターが活躍した場所は、神聖ローマ帝国でした。

　当時、神聖ローマ帝国は、ハプスブルク家から皇帝を迎えていました。

　その頃、各地の王族は婚姻関係によってネットワークしていましたが、そのネットワークの軸の位置にあったのがハプスブルク家でした。

　スイス北東部におこったハプスブルク家は、その後オーストリアへ拠点を移し、政略結婚などを繰り返しながらヨーロッパの要となる王族へと成長します。

　16世紀前半に活躍したハプスブルク家のマクシミリアン1世は、神聖ローマ帝国の皇帝の地位を受け継ぎ、オーストリア、そしてドイツの王として君臨します。とはいえ、ドイツは中世以来、数多くの有力諸侯が自治を行っていたこともあり、ハプスブルク家の統治は絶対的なものではなかったのです。

　宗教改革は、そうしたドイツの政治的な状況に一石を投じたのでした。ハプスブルク家は、マクシミリアン1世のあと、フランドル出身のカール5世に継承されます。中部ヨーロッパの複雑な政治情勢をかいくぐり、神聖ローマ帝国の影響力を拡大するためにも、カール5世

V had to gain economic strength. Simultaneously succeeding to the Spanish throne—where he reigned as Charles I—he turned his attention to enterprises in the New World.

074 Influential figures tossed about by the Reformation became supporters during the Age of Discovery

When one listens to the flamenco, the folk music of Spain, one becomes aware that the melody brings to mind the call to prayer at a Muslim mosque. Considering that Spain was for a long period of time an Islamic monarchy, this is not surprising.

Until the 15th century, Spain consisted of the Kingdom of Aragon in the east and the Kingdom of Castile in the west, which together held out against the Islamic power in the south of Spain. When King Ferdinand II of Aragon and Queen Isabella I of Castile married in 1469, they effectively united their lands into a single monarchy, which became the precursor of present-day Spain.

In 1492 Ferdinand II drove the Muslims out of Spain. Immediately thereafter, Christopher Columbus, who had been granted the patronage of Queen Isabella, crossed the Atlantic Ocean and arrived in the islands of the Caribbean Sea.

About that time, Eastern Europe continued to be overwhelmed by the Ottoman Empire. The Islamic Empire essentially blocked the Europeans' trade routes to Asia. In response to this predicament, Columbus convinced the queen that he could reach India by going west instead, and then continue to Asia, with her support.

Founding colonies in the New World brought considerable riches to Spain. Within several decades of Columbus's discovery of the new continent, Spain set up bases in Central and South America and began to exploit the gold and silver that could be extracted there. Its means of operation in seizing the riches of the New World depended on extreme violence. Possessing neither advanced weapons nor immunity from the diseases that the Europeans introduced, the indigenous people were exterminated by military force and disease, and many of those who managed to survive were enslaved. The Spaniards then began to import slaves from Africa to work the mines of the new continent.

は経済力をつけなければなりません。そんな彼が、同時に継承したスペイン王室（スペインではカール1世となります）を通し着目したのが、新大陸の経営だったのです。

宗教改革に揺れる時の権力者が、
大航海時代の後ろ盾となった

　スペインの民族音楽、フラメンコを聴いていると、イスラム教のモスクから流れる祈りの呼びかけに通じた旋律があることに気付きます。スペインに長い間イスラム教の王国があったことを考えれば、それは容易に理解できるはずです。

　15世紀まで、スペインには東部にアラゴン王国と、西側にカスティーリャ王国とがあり、ともに南部のイスラム勢力と対峙していました。そしてアラゴン王国のフェルナンド2世とカスティーリャ王国の女王イサベル1世とが1469年に結婚したことで、事実上二つの王国は統合され、現在のスペインの前身となったのです。

　1492年に、フェルナンド2世がイスラム教勢力をスペインから追い払います。その直後に、イサベル女王の保護を受けて大西洋を渡り、カリブ海の島に到達したのが、クリストファー・コロンブスだったのです。

　その頃、東ヨーロッパは、オスマン帝国に席巻されつつありました。アジアへの交易路にイスラム帝国が立ちはだかったのです。そうした状況の中、コロンブスは、西へと航海を続ければインドへ、そしてアジアに到達できると女王を説き伏せ、船をだしたのです。

　新大陸に植民地を築いたことは、スペインに大きな収益をもたらします。コロンブスのアメリカ発見から数十年で、スペインは中南米各地に拠点を設け、金や銀の採掘を行います。彼らの新大陸経営は暴力による簒奪でした。進んだ武器をもたず、ヨーロッパの人々のもたらす病気への免疫もなかった現地の人々は、軍隊と疫病によって駆逐され、多くが奴隷となります。スペイン人はさらにアフリカからも奴隷を送り、新大陸での鉱山の採掘を進めていったのです。

時代
14, 15世紀
欧州近世

地域
ヨーロッパ

分類
交流【政治】

キーワード
イスラム教のスペイン撤退・オスマン帝国の東西交易独占・大航海時代の到来

Emperor Charles V was particularly interested in obtaining bounty from the New World. Charles V succeeded to the House of Habsburg through his maternal grandparents, Ferdinand II and Isabella I. As a result of this heritage, he inherited the position of King of Spain as well, where he became Charles I. Through promoting Spain's operations in the New World, he not only gained significant territory but also gained the economic power to become the preeminent monarch of Europe.

With the political ambitions of power holders in Europe, such as Charles V, following the discovery of the New World, adventurers began setting sail on the oceans of the world like water bursting from a broken dam. The Age of Discovery had arrived. Already in 1488 with the support of John II, who had unified Portugal, Bartolomeu Dias had sailed south along the west coast of Africa to the southernmost point at the Cape of Good Hope. Ten years later Vasco da Gama, by way of that cape, reached India. Then Ferdinand Magellan ventured out across the Pacific and by way of the southernmost tip of South America, reached the Philippines in 1521. Magellan himself was killed in an altercation with tribesmen in the Philippines, but members of his crew reached Spain the following year, completing the first circumnavigation of the globe.

At last Europe was beginning to make inroads around the world.

カール5世は新大陸からの富に特に興味を抱いた皇帝でした。ハプスブルク家を継承したカール5世の母方の祖父母は、フェルナンド2世とイサベル1世にあたります。このことから、カール5世はスペイン王の地位も継承し、スペインではカール1世と名乗ります。彼は、スペインを通した新大陸の経営を進めることによって、領土のみならず、経済的にもヨーロッパ屈指の王へと成長したのでした。

　カール5世に代表されるようなヨーロッパの権力者の政治的野心もあって、コロンブスの新大陸発見後、堰を切ったように探検家が航海に乗り出します。大航海時代の到来です。既に、1488年にはポルトガルを統一したジョアン2世の援助で、バルトロメウ・ディアスがアフリカの最南端である喜望峰に到達しています。その10年後にはヴァスコ・ダ・ガマが喜望峰を経由し、ついに海路でインドに至ります。さらにマゼランが南米から太平洋を渡りフィリピンに至ったのが1521年。そこでマゼランは部族との戦いで戦死しますが、その翌年には彼の部下がスペインにたどりつき、世界一周を成し遂げたのでした。
　ヨーロッパの世界への進出がいよいよ始まろうとしているのでした。

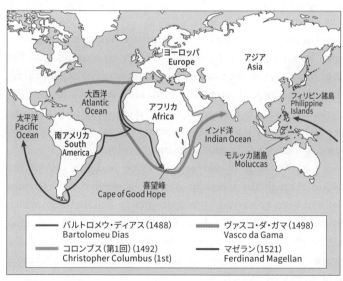

大航海時代の航路
Routes of the Age of Discovery

075 Stimulated by the inflow of knowledge from the Islamic world, the Renaissance began to bloom

In the blink of an eye, the impact of the Reformation was magnified by the invention of the moveable type printing press by Johannes Gutenberg. The Age of Discovery arrived and Magellan and his crew, as a result of their circumnavigation of the globe, proved that the world was round. With this and many other discoveries in the 18th century, common knowledge of the world expanded greatly.

The background for this development of science and technology was the Renaissance, which began in Italy in the 14th century. This is a good opportunity for us to examine how European civilization made the transition from the Middle Ages to the Renaissance.

In the process of turning Christianity into the state religion of the Roman Empire and to logically systematize Christianity, religious leaders and philosophers employed the logic that was created by the ancient Greek philosophers, such as Plato and Aristotle. St. Augustine, in particular, who was active from the 4th to the 5th century, integrated faith with a philosophical backing in the process of organizing the view of God.

Let us recall at this point the literary and scientific activities at Alexandria, where the existing knowledge of the ancient world was accumulated. The accomplishments of Aristotle, who is considered the founder of Greek philosophy, were influenced by Islam in the Mediterranean world centering in Alexandria. His philosophy was systematized not in Europe but in the Islamic Empire. In the same way that the faith of Christianity was logically examined by St. Augustine, Greek philosophy was used in the systematization of Islamic theology.

The commercial activity that developed in Venice and the rest of the Mediterranean world through the Crusades further accelerated the exchange of knowledge that had been preserved by Islamic society. Scholasticism which supported Christian thinking in the Middle Ages among people like Thomas Aquinas in the 13th century was, interestingly enough, greatly influenced by the logic cultivated within Islam. Knowledge from the Islamic world was reimported and continued to be employed thereafter.

Together with the inflow of Islamic culture, by the medium of the Islamic world, culture and technology from Eurasia also flowed into Europe. The technology of the East Asian world, such as the compass—invented in China during the Song

イスラム世界を通して流入した知識に
刺激されルネサンスが萌芽した

　宗教改革の波がグーテンベルクの発明した活版印刷で瞬く間に拡大していったこと。大航海時代が到来し、マゼランとその部下による世界一周の航海によって地球が球形であることが証明されたことなど、16世紀には世界の常識が大きく変化するようなことが多々おこりました。

　こうした科学技術の発展の背景にあったのが、14世紀にイタリアで始まったルネサンスです。ここで、ルネサンスに至る中世からのヨーロッパ文明の推移にスポットをあててみましょう。

　そもそもローマ帝国がキリスト教を国教としてゆく過程で、キリスト教を倫理的に体系づけようと、宗教家や哲学者がプラトンやアリストテレスなどに代表される古代ギリシア哲学で育まれた論理学などを活用します。特に4世紀から5世紀にかけて活動したアウグスティヌスなどが、信仰という課題を哲学的に裏付け、神のあり方についての見解をまとめてゆきました。

　ここで、古代の知識が集積されたアレクサンドリアでの文芸、科学活動を思い出してみましょう。ギリシア哲学の祖ともいわれるアリストテレスなどの業績は、アレクサンドリアを中心とした地中海世界がイスラム化してゆく中で、ヨーロッパではなく、イスラム帝国の中で体系づけられます。キリスト教での信仰のあり方がアウグスティヌスなどによって論理的に考察されたのと同様に、ギリシア哲学がイスラム神学を体系づけるために活用されたのです。

　中世の十字軍や、ヴェネチアなどが展開した地中海世界での商業活動は、イスラム社会に保存されていたこうした知識の交流をさらに促進させました。13世紀に活躍したトマス・アクィナスに代表される中世キリスト教を支えたスコラ哲学も、興味深いことにイスラムで培われた論理学などの影響を強く受けていたのです。このイスラム世界からの知識の再輸入は、その後も続きます。

　さらにイスラム文化の流入とともに、イスラム世界を通してユーラシア大陸の文化や技術がヨーロッパに流れこんできます。中国の宋の時代に発明された羅針盤や、元の時代に広く武器として使用された火

時代
16世紀
欧州近世

地域
ヨーロッパ

分類
学問【技術】

キーワード
印刷技術と大航海・ルネサンスの開始・学問や技術の復活・文芸復興・商業の発達

period—and gunpowder—used in weapons during the Yuan period—spread to the West by way of the Islamic domains.

The Reformation, which occurred in the 16th century, in addition to previously existing criticism of the Catholic world, also played a role in stimulating a reexamination of deep-rooted traditions and prejudices of the past. As a result, both well-educated people on the Catholic side and people supporting the Protestant side developed an interest in the revival of science, humanistic art, and literature. We refer to this cultural trend as the Renaissance.

The word Renaissance does not refer only to a movement in letters and pictorial arts. It includes everything from science to practical arts what would change the lifestyle of Europeans. The Renaissance refers to the totality of a broad cultural movement that extended from the end of the Middle Ages into early-modern times.

076 The confrontation between religious authority and the individual mind characterized the Renaissance

When we think of the artistic works of the Renaissance period, at the very beginning we think of Dante Alighieri's early 14th century *The Divine Comedy*, and a work produced by Giovanni Boccaccio titled *The Decameron*, which came several decades later. *The Divine Comedy* is an epic poem which portrays a migration from hell through purgatory to heaven. Significantly, it was not composed in Latin but in Tuscan, the language of one region of Italy.

The Decameron, in contrast, is a collection of allegories, including love tales, told by people who have secluded themselves in a grand residence out of fear of the plague that is raging outside the edifice. Influenced by this work, Geoffrey Chaucer in England composed a similar work in English under the title *Canterbury Tales*.

Until these works appeared, there had been no attempts at portraying in an interesting fashion the romantic entanglements and other affairs in the lives of ordinary people.

There were also epoch-making events in science as well. In the first half of the 16th century, Nicolaus Copernicus in Poland propounded his heliocentric theory on the basis of his own astronomical observations. Within close to a century,

薬など、東方世界の技術がイスラム帝国を経由して、さらに西へと伝播したのです。

そして、16世紀におこった宗教改革は、従来のカトリック世界に批判を加えることで、過去の因習や偏見を見直してゆくことに一役かいます。その結果、カトリック側の教養人も、プロテスタントを支持する人々も、共に科学的、人間的な文芸の復興に興味を持ちます。こうした文化的風潮のことを我々はルネサンスと呼んでいるのです。

ルネサンスとは単に文芸や絵画のみを指しません。後のヨーロッパの人々のライフスタイル自体を変えてゆく、科学から実学までを包含する、中世末期から近世にかけての幅広い文化活動こそがルネサンスの意味するところなのです。

宗教的権威と個人の意思との対立が
ルネサンスを特徴づけた

ルネサンス期の文芸作品といえば、真っ先に取り上げられるのが、14世紀初頭に執筆されたとされるダンテの『神曲』や、その数十年後に発表されたボッカチオの『デカメロン』などでしょう。神曲は地獄や煉獄、そして天国を旅する叙事詩ですが、ラテン語ではなくイタリアの地方の言語であるトスカーナ語で執筆されました。

一方、『デカメロン』はペストの大流行を恐れて邸宅にこもった人々が語る恋愛物語などの寓話集で、この影響を受けてイギリスのチョーサーが『カンタベリー物語』という同様の作品を英語で執筆したこともここに記しておきます。

色恋沙汰など、人間の生き様を面白く描くこうした試みは、それまでには見られないものでした。

科学の方面でも画期的なことがおこります。ポーランドのコペルニクスが16世紀前半に天体の観測から地動説を説き、それから100年近くのちにケプラーが惑星運動についての〈ケプラーの法則〉を発表し、

時代
16世紀
欧州近世

地域
ヨーロッパ

分類
文化【学問】

キーワード
文芸作品の開花・自国言語の使用・地動説の発展・キリスト教イデオロギーの後退

Johannes Kepler published his three laws of planetary motion, giving support to the heliocentric theory. Their works began to overturn the geocentric interpretation of the Bible that had been accepted as the common view up until that time.

At the end of the Roman Empire, due to the religious beliefs of Christianity, as we have already commented, the scientific way of thought in and of itself had been suppressed. From that point onward, people living in medieval European society interpreted their world with their beliefs in the Bible as a foundation.

Taking the commandments of God, who is the perfect creator of all nature, people established conventional wisdom and laid down the rules of how things on earth should be. Given authority over this, it was the Holy See in Rome that was to direct how people should live their lives. The Reformation sought to free people from the constraints of Roman Catholicism by connecting faith not to authority but directly to the hearts of individuals. A similar movement took place in scientific activities.

When scientists like Copernicus proposed theories such as heliocentrism, they still embraced the long-held "common understanding" that Roman Catholicism had put forth. Scholarship seeks to harmonize the activity of objective observation of natural phenomena and, borrowing mathematics and other intellectual tools, develop logical verification of theories. That being the case, it is clear that if one carries out scientific inquiry, one will come into direct confrontation with religious common understanding.

Scientists of those days confronted those inconsistencies, and this repeatedly gave rise to conflict. For example, Kepler thought that the orbit of the planets was elliptical. Galileo Galilei, who pursued the same geocentric theory more deeply, is said to have continued to believe that orbits were perfectly circular, because he was unable to free himself from the notion that the circle was the perfect form, which God had created.

However, the more one pursues scientific truth, the more likely it is that one will overcome these conflicting emotions, and the conscience of the individual scientist who is explaining natural phenomena will be able to overcome long-held conventions.

After having remained silent for a thousand years since the decline of the Roman Empire, individuals finally began to feel the desire to engage with science and seek its liberation.

This is precisely the reason why the revival of learning known as the Renaissance came about.

地動説をさらに裏付けます。常識とされていた聖書の解釈による天動説が覆され始めたのです。

　ローマ帝国末期にキリスト教という信仰によって、科学的思考そのものが弾圧されたことは既に解説しました。それ以来、中世ヨーロッパ社会に生きた人々は、聖書と信仰を基軸に世界を解釈していました。

　神という完璧な創造主の掟の中で、人々は常識を定め、天地のあり方を規定していたのです。そうした考え方を権威付け、人々の生活を統率していたのがローマ教皇庁でした。宗教改革は、信仰を権威ではなく、個人の心と直接つなぐことで、ローマカトリックのしばりから人々を解放しようとしたのです。これと同じような動きが、科学的な活動の中にもおこるのです。

　コペルニクスをはじめとした科学者が、地動説などを提唱するとき、まだ彼らの頭の中には長年のローマカトリックの「常識」が存在していました。科学は自然現象を客観的に観察する行為と、それを数学などの力を借りて論理的に証明する作業との調和を求める学問です。であれば、科学的探求を行えば、宗教的常識との間の矛盾に直面することは明白です。

　当時の科学者はその矛盾に直面し、葛藤を繰り返していたのです。例えば、ケプラーは、惑星の軌道が楕円であると考えます。しかし、同じ地動説を深化させたガリレオは、「円」は神が創造した完璧な形態であるとのこだわりから、なかなか脱却できなかったといわれています。

　しかし、科学的な探求を進めれば進めるほど、その葛藤を乗り越えて、自然現象を説明する科学者個人の良心が因習を乗り越えてゆきます。

　ローマ帝国末期以降1000年間沈黙していた個人が科学と向き合おうとする欲求が、やっと解放されようとしたのです。

　ルネサンスを文芸復興といった理由は、まさにそこにあったのです。

077 The Renaissance became the starting point for European culture thereafter

The background of the flowering of the Renaissance is closely related with the downfall of the Eastern Roman Empire in 1453. In the process of the downfall of Constantinople, which had inherited the culture of the Roman Empire, a large number of scholars and artists streamed into Italy. This was the reason why Roman civilization and ancient Greek civilization, which was its foundation, were completely reexamined.

Certain families played a major role in the advancement of artistic activities during the Renaissance period. Among those in Italy, the Medici in Florence accumulated great wealth through banking, which gave them enormous influence in the political world. The Fugger family, which established itself through mining operations during the Holy Roman Empire and developed ties with the Habsburg and the Vatican, flourished along with the Medici, and both became patrons of cultural activities.

Leonardo da Vinci, raised in the Tuscany region of north-central Italy, which was under the control of the Medici, is well-known as the artist who created the painting known as *Mona Lisa*. He also demonstrated genius in a number of different other fields, including science and medicine. He was a multi-talented genius of the latter half of the 16th century.

Michelangelo Buonarroti, also from Tuscany, is known not only as a painter but as an architect and poet, and he produced a huge mural painting for the Vatican. Raphael, a painter who was involved in the construction of St. Peter's Basilica, ranks with Da Vinci and Michelangelo as representatives of the Italian Renaissance.

The paintings of those days differed from medieval religious paintings. They portrayed humans as vividly as the sculpture of the ancient Greeks did. Although their motifs were from Biblical stories, the figures they produced exhibited physical beauty, bordering in some cases on eroticism. In the late 15th century this style of portrayal spread to France, the Netherlands, and into northern Europe. The Fugger family, for example, became patrons of Albrecht Durer from Nuremberg, who became one of the leading artists of the northern Renaissance.

ルネサンスはその後の西欧文明の起点となった

　ルネサンスが開花した背景には、1453年に東ローマ帝国が滅亡したことも深く関係しています。ローマ帝国の文化が継承されていたコンスタンティノープルの衰亡の過程で、多くの学者や芸術家がイタリアに流れ込みました。このことが、イタリアでローマ文明やその母体となった古代ギリシア文明が見直される原因となったのです。

　ルネサンス期の芸術活動を振興させるために大きな役割を果たしたファミリーがありました。イタリア、特にフィレンツェで銀行業によって繁栄し、政界にも大きな影響を与えていたメディチ家などの富豪です。神聖ローマ帝国の中で鉱山業から身をおこし、ハプスブルク家やローマ教皇庁とも繋がりのあったフッガー家もメディチ家と並ぶ文化活動のパトロンの一つでした。

　メディチ家が支配するイタリア中北部トスカーナ出身のレオナルド・ダ・ヴィンチは、絵画の世界では『モナ・リザ』の作者として有名ですが、その才能は広く科学や医学などにも発揮されました。彼は16世紀後半のマルチタレントでした。

　同じくトスカーナ出身のミケランジェロ・ブオナローティも、画家のみならず建築家や詩人としても知られ、ローマ教皇庁などで壮大な壁画を描きました。さらに、画家であると共にサンピエトロ大聖堂の建築にも携わったラファエロ・サンティも、ダ・ヴィンチやミケランジェロと共に、イタリアルネサンスを代表する人物でした。

　当時の絵画は、中世の宗教画とは異なり、古代ギリシア彫刻のように人間が生き生きと描写されています。聖書の題材が使われながらも、そこに描かれた人々は、肉体美を誇示し、エロチシズムをも漂わせます。こうした様式は、15世紀終盤にはフランスやオランダ、さらに北部ヨー

時代
16世紀
欧州近世

地域
ヨーロッパ

分類
文化【学問】

キーワード
東ローマ帝国からの学問の流入・豪商の出現・マルチタレントの出現・文芸、美術の発展

レオナルド・ダ・ヴィンチ
Leonardo da Vinci

ミケランジェロ・ブオナローティ
Michelangelo Buonarroti

ラファエロ・サンティ
Raphael Santi

One finds the impact of the Renaissance not only in painting and science but also in literary arts, music, and philosophy. Among the various creative figures of this broad flourishing period one should include William Shakespeare, the playwright who was active in the reign of Queen Elizabeth I. The current of the Renaissance lasted some 300 years from the 14th century into the early 17th century, and it became the starting point of the European world's humanities and the artistic activity that was to follow.

The novel *Don Quixote*, published by the Spanish writer Miguel de Cervantes in 1615, took a medieval knight as its subject and portrayed the dreaming protagonist as if he were living in an illusionary world completely divorced from reality. Cervantes himself had served in the Spanish navy and had fought at the Battle of Lepanto against the forces of the Ottoman Empire and with the Spanish Armada, which lost its battle against the English navy. Having seen with his own eyes the vicissitudes of Spanish power, Cervantes, living in the Renaissance era, portrayed in his novel the delusionary world of Don Quixote in which the medieval period was already in the remote past. The hands of time in Western Europe were steadily approaching the modern era.

078 The electors, the emperor, and the Pope were in a triangular deadlock

Under the stormy conditions brought about by the Reformation, conditions in Europe were chaotic. If one can grasp what these circumstances were like, it is extremely helpful for understanding what followed.

Let us briefly outline the political situation in Europe up to the appearance of Charles V of the Habsburg family.

Central Europe, centered around Germany, was divided into numerous duchies after the fragmentation of the Frankish Kingdom and the subsequent extinction of the royal lineage of the East Frankish Kingdom.

Ostensibly, the rulers of these various duchies were feudal lords who were unified by the Holy Roman Empire.

ロッパにも伝播します。フッガー家がパトロンをつとめたニュールンベルグ出身のアルブレヒト・デューラーなどは北方ルネサンスを代表する画家となります。

　ルネサンス期には絵画や科学のみならず、例えばエリザベス女王の時代に活動した劇作家ウィリアム・シェイクスピアなどの文学活動、さらには音楽や哲学に至る幅広い人々の活動を見ることができます。14世紀から17世紀初頭まで300年に及ぶルネサンスの潮流は、その後の西欧世界の人文科学や芸術活動の進化の原点となったのです。

　スペインの作家ミゲル・セルバンテスが1615年に発表した小説『ドン・キホーテ』は、中世の騎士を題材に、夢見る主人公が時代錯誤とも思われる妄想の世界を生きる様子を描きました。セルバンテス自身、スペイン海軍に勤務し、オスマン帝国と戦ったレパントの海戦や、イギリスにスペインが敗れるアルマダの海戦にも従軍しました。スペインの盛衰を目の当たりにしたセルバンテスは、ルネサンスという時代の中にあって、中世が既に遠い昔の、まさにドン・キホーテの妄想の世界であることを小説で暗示していたのかもしれません。西欧は近代へと徐々に時計の針を進めていたのでした。

選帝侯たちと皇帝、そして教皇は
三すくみの状態だった

　宗教改革の嵐が吹き荒れた時代のヨーロッパの情勢は極めて混沌としていました。その状況を理解すれば、その後のヨーロッパの政治の趨勢を知る上でも大変役に立ちます。

　ハプスブルク家のカール5世が登場するまでのヨーロッパの政治情勢を簡単にまとめておきましょう。

　ドイツを中心とした中部ヨーロッパは、フランク王国が分裂し、その後東フランク王国の王家の血統が途絶えて以来、多くの公国に分割されていました。

　もちろん、名目上はこれらの公国を治める者は神聖ローマ帝国によって統治される諸侯ということになります。

時代
13〜17世紀
欧州近世

地域
ドイツ

分類
国家【政治】

キーワード
ドイツの歴史・選帝侯による皇帝選出・有力諸侯の台頭・プロテスタントの保護

The Holy Roman Empire possessed the function of protecting Christianity as a representative of secular authority, and the emperor was the guardian of Roman Catholicism. This was all the more reason why the powerholders in Germany and Austria consistently sought that title and ruled the empire with one eye constantly on Rome. This was referred to as their Italian policy.

For that reason, from the 13th century onward, successors constantly participated in complex power struggles over the post of the emperor of the Holy Roman Empire. When this Great Interregnum followed, it was ultimately Charles IV, whose roots were in Bohemia, who regained control. His father Johann, who was monarch of Bohemia and simultaneously Duke of Luxemburg, was extremely bold and was deeply involved as a central figure in European politics. The year after his father died in 1346, Charles was recommended to assume the title of Emperor of the Holy Roman Empire.

Later, in 1356 Charles IV issued the Golden Bull, which was a document stamped with a golden seal. By means of this document, the emperor of the Holy Roman Empire selected four powerful duchies and three prominent clergy to form a body of seven electors who would establish the succession to the emperor's throne thereafter.

In due course, from the 15th century onward, the contemporary head of the House of Habsburg, who were descendants of Charles IV or related to that bloodline by marriage, would hold two posts concurrently—as monarch of Bohemia or Germany and as emperor of the Holy Roman Empire.

It is important to note the fact that the appointment of the emperorship of the Holy Roman Empire was entrusted to these electors. While the position of the emperor was actually hereditary, it was constantly under the constraints imposed by prominent feudal lords and princes. This situation proved advantageous to Martin Luther at the time of the Reformation. One of the prominent lords, the Elector of Saxony, opposed the view of Charles V, the contemporary emperor, and protected Luther.

The Pope, the Holy Roman Emperor and the leading elected German princes were all conscious of each other and tried to control European politics. In this sort of power game, neither Charles V nor the pope could strongly censure the Elector of Saxony.

It was the powerful Ottoman Empire in the East that sensed the political divisions in this power game in Germany and put pressure on the European world.

神聖ローマ帝国は、世俗権力を代表してキリスト教を保護する機能をもち、その皇帝はローマカトリックの庇護者であるとされていました。それだけに、ドイツやオーストリアの権力者は常にその座を求め、ローマを見ながら政治をします。イタリア政策と呼ばれるものでした。

　そのために、13世紀以降、後継者が途絶えた神聖ローマ帝国皇帝の椅子をめぐり、複雑な権力闘争が繰り広げられます。この時代のことを大空位時代と呼んでいます。大空位時代とその後の混乱を最終的に収拾したのが、ボヘミア（チェコ）にルーツをもったカール4世でした。ボヘミア王で、かつルクセンブルク公であった彼の父ヨハンは、極めて豪胆でヨーロッパの政治の中枢に深く関わっていました。そんな父親が1346年に他界した翌年に、彼は神聖ローマ帝国皇帝に推挙されたのです。
　その後、1356年にカール4世は金印勅書を発布します。それによって、神聖ローマ帝国の皇帝は、4つの有力な公国と3つの大司教が選帝侯となって選挙を行う形で選ばれることになりました。

　やがて15世紀から、カール4世の子孫と婚姻関係を結んだハプスブルク家の当主が、ボヘミアやドイツの王と神聖ローマ帝国の皇帝を兼務することになったのです。

　ここで注目したいのが、神聖ローマ帝国皇帝の地位が選帝侯に委ねられているという事実です。実際には皇帝の地位は世襲されてはいたものの、有力諸侯は常に皇帝に圧力を加えることのできる位置にいたのです。この状況が、宗教改革のときにルターに有利に働きました。有力諸侯の一人、ザクセン選帝侯が神聖ローマ帝国皇帝カール5世の意思に反してルターを保護したのです。

　ローマ教皇も、神聖ローマ帝国皇帝も、そしてドイツの有力な選帝侯も、お互いを意識しながら、ヨーロッパの政治をコントロールしようとしていました。そんなパワーゲームの中で、カール5世もローマ教皇も即座にザクセン選帝侯の動きを強く弾劾できなかったのです。
　このドイツでのパワーゲームによる政治的な分断を察知し、ヨーロッパ世界に圧力をかけてきた東方の大国がオスマン帝国だったのです。

079 The Ottoman Empire swept across the Balkan Peninsula

Emperor Suleyman the Magnificent of the Ottoman Empire played close attention to the political situation in Germany and Austria. Making adroit use of the conflict regarding succession in the Hungarian monarchy, he began to expand his influence westward. Ironically, the French king and others who were not kindly disposed to the growth of the House of Habsburg were said to be rather indifferent about the confrontation between the Ottoman Empire and the House of Habsburg, Europe's major powers. France, in particular, felt the threat of being attacked from both sides when Charles V, emperor of the Holy Roman Empire, became the king of Spain as well. Relations between the royal families of Europe were a complex network that resulted from the strategic marriages between them, so conflicts between family members could easily trigger political power struggles.

The great army of Suleyman the Magnificent set out from Istanbul in early summer of 1529, advanced along the Danube, and fought on successive fronts throughout Hungary. Reaching Vienna by the end of September, his forces besieged the city, stronghold of the House of Habsburg.

Because the response from the various European countries was noncommittal, the people of Vienna were forced to defend the city by themselves. Their opponent's great army numbered 120,000, and the offensive engineering corps attempted to attack the city by digging a tunnel into the castle grounds.

Fortunately for the Viennese, the supply lines needed to support the Ottoman forces were stretched so far that to continue to supply 120,000 troops required a military outcome within a short period of time. Small though they were in numbers, the Viennese soldiers defended the city well, accelerating the anxiety of their Ottoman opponents. Moreover, that year winter arrived earlier than usual. Ultimately after a two-month siege of the city, before the truly harsh winter weather arrived, the Ottoman forces gave up on taking Vienna by storm and the lifted the siege.

Vienna was in this manner relieved of the menace posed by the Ottomans, but the Balkan Peninsula continued to be under their influence.

From that point onward, the Balkan Peninsula continued to have a mingling of Islam and Christianity. The complex mosaic of ethnic groups and religions in the

オスマン帝国は、バルカン半島を席巻した

オスマン帝国のスレイマン大帝は、ドイツ、そしてオーストリアの政治的な状況を注視していました。そして、ハンガリー王国でおきた相続争いを巧みに利用し、西へと勢力の拡大を始めたのです。皮肉なことに、ハプスブルク家の伸長を快く思わないフランス王など、ヨーロッパの有力者はオスマン帝国とハプスブルク家との対立には冷淡だったといわれています。特にフランスは、カール5世が神聖ローマ帝国のみならず、スペインの王にもなり、フランスを挟み撃ちにすることに脅威を感じていました。ヨーロッパの王族は政略結婚によるネットワークが複雑で、そのことが逆に親族間の勢力争いの火種にもなっていたのです。

時代
16世紀
欧州近世

地域
トルコ

分類
戦争【宗教】

キーワード
**オスマン帝国の東欧支配
・ウィーン包囲・バルカ
ン半島の多宗教化**

スレイマン大帝の大軍は、1529年の初夏にイスタンブールをでて、ドナウ川に沿って進軍し、ハンガリー各地で転戦します。その後9月の下旬にはウィーンに至り、ハプスブルク家の本拠地であるウィーンを包囲するのです。

ヨーロッパ諸国の反応が曖昧だったことから、ウィーンの人々は自力で防衛しなければなりませんでした。相手は12万人という大軍で、工兵部隊はトンネルを掘って城内への侵攻を試みます。

幸い、オスマン帝国側は長い遠征で兵站も伸びきっており、12万人の兵士を支えるためにも短期間で勝敗をつけなければなりませんでした。寡兵ではあったもののウィーンの兵士はよく守り、そんなオスマン帝国軍の焦りを助長します。しかも、その年は例年になく冬が早く到来します。最終的に2カ月間の包囲の末、厳冬期になる前にオスマン帝国軍はウィーンの攻略をあきらめ、包囲を解いたのでした。

こうしてウィーンはオスマン帝国の脅威から解放されますが、バルカン半島は、そのままオスマン帝国の影響下におかれることになってしまいます。

以後バルカン半島はイスラム教とキリスト教とが混合する地域となりました。バルカン半島での民族、宗教の複雑なモザイクがそのまま

Balkan Peninsula became one cause of World War I, and in addition it became a remote cause of the conflict that erupted between Serbia and Bosnia in the 1990s, which also enmeshed Croatia.

Dubrovnik in Croatia is a beautiful fortified city facing the Adriatic Sea. It was once the base of the Republic of Ragusa. When the Ottoman Empire began to dominate the Balkan Peninsula, the Republic recognized Ottoman suzerainty and obtained autonomy by paying taxes. Competing with Venice and Genova, Dubrovnik by skillful diplomacy continued to exist as a Christian state, maintaining its activities as a commercial base on the Adriatic. Meanwhile, Bosnia, bordering it on the north, came under direct Ottoman rule, and the Muslim population continued to increase. Friction and discord between the Muslims and those who maintained their Christian or Judaic faith became chronic. The Ottoman Empire later besieged Vienna again in 1683. The tensions between Western Europe and the Ottoman Empire over the situation in Eastern Europe continued long term, becoming a source of instability in European affairs.

080 Navigators in the Age of Discovery were Muslims

While the Viennese were being threatened by the Ottoman Empire, what was the situation like on the eastern side of the empire?

As the Middle Ages drew to a close, giving rise to early-modern times, it became evident that the circumstances within the respective states were changing.

Previously countries obtained everything by conquest. A heroic figure would appear, unify an ethnic group, accumulate and increase economic and military strength through warfare, and form a state.

Within that state, systematic administrations would be established with bureaucratic and military structures. In countries such as China, for example, a civil service examination system was established early on which used a strict examination system to select highly talented personnel and a profound system of government administration was cultivated.

Monarchies such as these were, however, divided by conquerors or seized by powerful new figures time and time again.

第一次世界大戦の原因となり、さらには1990年代に勃発
したセルビアとボスニア、そしてクロアチアを巻き込ん
だ戦争の遠因にもなったのです。

ドブロブニク（クロアチア）
Dubrovnik, Croatia

　クロアチアにドブロブニクというアドリア海に面した
美しい城塞都市があります。ここはラグーサ共和国の拠
点でした。オスマン帝国がバルカン半島を席巻すると、
共和国はオスマン帝国の宗主権を認め、税金を納める形
で自治を認めてもらいます。ヴェネチアやジェノバと
いった都市と競合していたドブロブニクは、この巧みな外交でキリス
ト教国として存続し、アドリア海の商業拠点として活動を続けるので
す。一方、すぐ北に位置するボスニアは、オスマン帝国の直接支配を
受け、イスラム教徒の人口が増え続けます。そしてキリスト教の伝統
を守る人々、さらにユダヤ系の人々などとの摩擦や確執が慢性化しま
す。オスマン帝国は、その後1683年にもウィーンを包囲しています。
東ヨーロッパをめぐる西欧とオスマン帝国との緊張は、その後長きに
わたってヨーロッパ情勢の不安定要因となってゆくのでした。

大航海時代の水先案内人は、イスラム教徒だった

　ウィーンがオスマン帝国の脅威にさらされていた頃、オスマン帝国
の東側はどうなっていたのでしょうか。

　中世が終わり、近世へと時が流れるとき、国家のあり方が世界中で
変化しつつあることに気付かされます。

　以前、国家は多分に征服者の所有物でした。一人の英雄が現れ、民
族をまとめ、戦いの中で経済力と軍事力を蓄え、膨張して国家となり
ました。

　その国家の中には、組織もあり、官僚組織や軍事組織も存在しました。
中国などでは、早くから科挙制の元で、国民の中から選抜された優秀
な人材による重厚な行政組織が育成されていました。

　しかし、そうした王朝も幾度となく征服者によって分断され、新し
い権力者に簒奪されてきました。

時代
総合

地域
共通

分類
対立【交流】

キーワード
中国、インド、イスラム、
ヨーロッパの緊張関係・
文化は東から西へ

From the perspective of Europe, the usurpers and invaders were Islamic powers. From the perspective of China, in identifying the perpetrators we inevitably discover that they were horse-riding nomadic people from Central and North Asia.

Naturally enough, from the perspective of the Muslims or the horse-riding nomadic peoples, both Europe and China were serious menaces. Depending on one's point of view, therefore, the tense relationships were relative.

Similar to the Reconquista in Europe—in which the Spanish ousted the Moors—in East Asia it was the Mongols who were ousted from China and from the Korean Peninsula. That is, the Han Chinese pushed out the other ethnic groups and established the Ming dynasty. In response to these events, in the Korean Peninsula, Koryo was returned to Korean control and the Joseon dynasty succeeded to power.

Meanwhile, in India several monarchies succeeded to the Ghurid dynasty. Together they are referred to as the Delhi Sultanate. The last of these was the Lodi dynasty, which was overthrown by Babur of the Timurid Empire moving south from Afghanistan in 1526. This brought the establishment of the Mughal Empire. As a consequence, northern India continued under Islamic control.

India consistently felt the influence of advancing waves of government changeover from the north. But it was the sudden rise of the Mughal Empire which brought the impact of regime change even into southern India. If we examine the roots of the Mughal dynasty, which follows the lineage of Timur, it can be traced back to the Mongol Empire.

Whatever the case may be, to the east of the Ottoman Empire there remained an expansive sphere of Islamic culture. It actively expanded into the Indian Ocean and engaged in trade. When Vasco da Gama rounded the Cape of Good Hope and entered the Indian Ocean, he is said to have depended on Muslims who served his fleet as navigational pilots.

From the 15th century into the 16th century, culture still flowed from the East to the West. In the 17th century, however, the direction of that current would change.

ヨーロッパの視点で見た場合、篡奪の加害者はイスラム勢力だった
のです。そして、中国の視点で同様に加害者を特定しようとした場合、
そこにあったのは中央アジアや北アジアの騎馬民族だったのです。
　もちろん、イスラム教徒や騎馬民族の側から見るならば、ヨーロッ
パや中国こそが重大な脅威に他なりません。それは視点をどこにおく
かで常に変化する相対的な緊張関係だったのです。

　ヨーロッパにおけるレコンキスタと同様のことが、東アジアでもモ
ンゴルを駆逐した中国や朝鮮半島でおきました。つまり、漢民族が異
民族を排除して明をおこし、それと呼応するように、朝鮮半島でも高
麗が朝鮮民族の支配に戻り、李氏朝鮮へと受け継がれたのです。

　一方、インドでは、ゴール朝の後に続いたいくつかの王朝がありま
した。これらをまとめてデリー・スルタン王朝と呼びますが、その最
後の王朝ロディが、アフガニスタンから南下してきたティムール帝国
の流れをくむバーブルによって1526年に滅ぼされます。ムガル王朝の
成立です。これによって、インド北部ではイスラム王朝の支配がさら
に続くことになるのです。
　インドは常に北方から政権交代の波が押し寄せていました。そんな
北方からの政権交代の波が南インドまで飲み込んでいったのが、ムガ
ル王朝の勃興だったのです。ティムールの流れを引くムガル王朝であ
れば、そのルーツをずっとたどればモンゴル帝国にまで至ることがで
きます。
　いずれにしろ、オスマン帝国の東側には広大なイスラム教の文化圏
が控えていたことになります。インド洋にも彼らは積極的に進出し、
交易にいそしんでいました。ヴァスコ・ダ・ガマが喜望峰を周り、イ
ンド洋に入ったときも、航海の案内をしたのは、イスラム教の人々だっ
たといわれています。
　15世紀から16世紀にかけて、まだまだ文化は東から西へと流れてい
たのです。そうした流れに変化が起き始めるのが17世紀だったのです。

081 Portugal became the pioneer of maritime trade with Asia

The Ottoman Siege of Vienna occurred during Japan's Sengoku period.

Almost 200 years before that, the Kamakura Shogunate collapsed, in 1333. When Emperor Godaigo's attempted Kenmu Restoration failed, Japan was left divided between the Southern Court and the Northern Court. During that chaotic period, a group known as *wako* or "Japanese pirates" made inroads on the Korean Peninsula and the Chinese coast. Their activities fell into a decline around 1380 when the Muromachi Shogunate approached its golden age, but after that their activities revived once more.

They were called "Japanese pirates" with some justification, but as we have seen earlier, not all of them were Japanese. Throughout the Far East, not only in Japan but also in China and the Korean Peninsula, groups that lived apart from the control of any country sometimes engaged in piracy and sometimes acted as trading merchants, and they were referred to as wako. Active in trade with Muslim merchants in the Indian Ocean and at times serving as pilots for Spanish and Portuguese ships venturing into the Indian Ocean, these wako made their living on the seas between the East China Sea, Japan, and the Korean Peninsula. Because the Ming strictly regulated external trade, the wako actively engaged in smuggling. One Chinese merchant named Wang Zhi maintained a base in the Goto Islands and carried on trade between Hirado and present-day Zhejiang. It is said that Portuguese people aboard one of his ships drifted ashore on Tanegashima in 1543, leading to the introduction of Western-style firearms to Japan.

Meanwhile in Southeast Asia, in what is present-day Malaysia, the Islamic Malacca Sultanate flourished as a base for trade between China and India. Also active in this trade was the Ryukyu Kingdom. As a consequence, the Indian Ocean, the Arabian Sea, the South China Sea, and the East China Sea evolved into one enormous commercial sphere. This was what the Spanish and Portuguese made use of as they advanced into the East.

Vasco da Gama reached Calicut in India in 1498. In 1510 the Portuguese fleet made Goa its base of operations. The following year the Portuguese captured Malacca and commenced active trade in Southeast Asia.

Although they came from a remote region of the world, in an extremely short

ポルトガルがアジアとの海洋交易の先駆者になった

オスマン帝国がウィーンを包囲していた頃、日本はすでに戦国時代でした。

それより200年近く前、1333年に鎌倉幕府が倒れ、後醍醐天皇による建武の新政が失敗に終わったあと、日本は南北朝に分断されていました。この混乱期に海賊となって朝鮮半島や中国に進出していた集団がありました。倭寇と呼ばれる人々です。彼らの活動は室町幕府が最盛期を迎えた1380年頃には一時衰退しますが、その後再び活発になります。

もっとも、倭寇と呼ばれた人々が、全て日本人だったわけではなかったことは、すでに解説した通りです。日本のみならず、中国、朝鮮半島といった極東地域で、国家の統制から離れ、時には海賊行為を行い、時には貿易商として活動していた人々が倭寇と呼ばれたのでした。インド洋でイスラム教徒の貿易商が活発に活動し、ヨーロッパからインド洋に乗り込んだスペイン人やポルトガル人の水先案内も行っていたように、東シナ海から日本や朝鮮半島の沿岸までは、倭寇が海での活動の主体だったのです。中国の明が対外貿易を厳しく規制していたことから、中国への密貿易も盛んに行われました。王直と呼ばれる中国商人の場合、五島列島に本拠地をおき、平戸と現在の中国浙江省とを行き来して交易を行っていました。彼の船に乗っていたポルトガル人が1543年に種子島に漂着し、西洋式の鉄砲が日本に伝来したのではないかといわれているのです。

一方、東南アジアには現在のマレーシアにイスラム系のマラッカ王国があり、中国とインドとの交易の基地として繁栄していました。彼らとの交易には琉球王国も積極的で、このことによって、インド洋とアラビア海、そして南シナ海、東シナ海が巨大な交易圏を形成していたのです。この交易ルートをそのまま活用したのが、ポルトガル人やスペイン人だったのです。

ヴァスコ・ダ・ガマがインドのカリカットに着いたのが1498年。そして1510年には、ポルトガルの艦隊はインドのゴアに拠点をおき、翌年にはマラッカを占拠し、東南アジアでの交易を積極的に開始します。

彼らが遠隔地からやってきたのにもかかわらず、短期間でインドか

時代
15, 16世紀
日本中世

地域
日本・東南アジア

分類
交流【社会】

キーワード
倭寇の活躍・海上ルートの発達・東南アジアの中継貿易・ヴァスコ=ダ=ガマのインド航路の発見

period of time they made inroads in the belt from India to Southeast Asia. One reason they were able to accomplish this feat was that they possessed firearms. Gunpowder had naturally been used in China, where it was invented, and its use had spread to neighboring countries too. But in Europe during the first half of the 15th century, a portable firearm was invented: the matchlock musket.

In approximately 1557, Portugal was able to obtain Macao from the Ming to use as a settlement.

Trade routes between East and West, where exchanges between Muslims, followers of Hinduism, and others took place, were reorganized by the Portuguese into a single dominant trade route. And over this route the major European powers began competing for access to Asia.

By the time Japan entered the Sengoku period, it was the eastern terminus of this trade.

082 Zheng He reached Africa, and the Muromachi Shogunate took tribute to Ming China seeking trade

The wako engaged in smuggling, and both the Ming dynasty and the Joseon dynasty exercised strict control to prevent these activities. When the wako were active, the base of trade operations was in the islands of the East China Sea, such as Tsushima and in Hakata.

When Toyotomi Hideyoshi seized power in Japan, he attempted to gain control of overseas trade himself.

When seen from Southeast Asia and India, the Ryukyu Kingdom—otherwise called Okinawa—was a valuable base for contact with both China and Japan. Until the Meiji government incorporated Okinawa as part of Japan, Okinawa was an independent monarchy. During the Edo period, while under the influence of the Satsuma clan, the Ryukyu Kingdom maintained its own independent trade with China and Southeast Asia. It was the northernmost point in the trade route from the Kingdom of Champa, in today's Vietnam.

History advances through a succession of actions and reactions.

In the Eurasian continent, civilizations, such as Asia and Western Europe, and

ら東南アジアへと進出できた理由の一つに、彼らが鉄砲を所持していたことがあげられます。火薬はもともと中国で使用され、周辺国にも伝搬されていました。しかし、ヨーロッパでは、携帯用の火器、すなわち火縄銃が15世紀前半に発明されていたのです。

その後、ポルトガルは明に至り、1557年頃には明からマカオでの居留権を獲得したといわれます。

イスラム教徒やヒンドゥー教徒などによってバトンを渡すように海を経由した東西交流が行われていた状況が、ポルトガル人によって一本の強い交易ルートとして再編されたのです。そして、このルートにのって、その後ヨーロッパの列強が、競ってアジアへの進出を始めるのです。

戦国時代に日本は、そんな交易ルートの東のターミナルとなっていたのです。

明の鄭和はアフリカに、室町幕府は明へ交易を 求めて朝貢した

倭寇は、密貿易者であったこともあり、明や李氏朝鮮は厳しく取り締まっていました。倭寇が活動していた頃、対馬などの東シナ海の島々、そして博多などが交易の根拠地となります。

時代
15世紀
中国近世

地域
中国

分類
交流【経済】

キーワード
権力による交易コントロール・中国の大航海時代・朝貢貿易の発展・海上貿易の東西開通

やがて日本で豊臣秀吉が政権を握ると、海外との交易を自らのコントロールのもとにおこうとします。

一方、東南アジアやインド方面から極東をみた場合、中国や日本などと接触する重要な拠点として位置していたのが琉球王国、すなわち沖縄だったのです。明治政府が沖縄を日本に組み込むまで、沖縄には独立した王朝がありました。江戸時代には薩摩藩の影響下におかれながらも、琉球王朝は中国や東南アジアと独自の交易をしていました。現在のベトナムにあったチャンパ王国などからの交易ルートの北の拠点が琉球王朝だったのです。

歴史は「作用」とそれに対する「反作用」との繰り返しで進化します。

アジアと西欧、キリスト教文明とイスラム教の文明など、ユーラシ

Christian civilization and Islamic civilization, have been constantly interacting, merging and separating.

The seas have been a convenient space for people to venture into, where the forces of action and reaction do not easily escalate into large-scale wars. The Mediterranean, where people from Venice and Genoa operated, and the Indian Ocean and South China Sea, where the trade routes of Muslims and Hindus intersected, were such places. And farther to the north there was the Ryukyu Kingdom.

From the east end of this complex trade route, one man accomplished seven major voyages between 1405 and 1433. Admiral Zheng He, under orders of the Yongle Emperor of the Ming dynasty, led his fleet into the waters of the Middle East and East Africa. It is thought that he was a Muslim and a eunuch. Exactly why Zheng He was charged with carrying out these major voyages is unclear. The Yongle Emperor took the throne as a result of the political disturbance known as the Jingnan Campaign, which occurred in 1399. It may have been that the emperor, in order to stabilize Ming China as a country, thought it necessary to develop trade with areas to the south which promised bounty and thought it wise to develop relations with states that could become tributaries.

This occurred at the time when the Northern and Southern Courts in Japan were once again united and government administration was comparatively stable. From the time of Ashikaga Yoshimitsu, the third shogun of the Muromachi Shogunate, official trade was carried out with the Ming by way of Hakata.

Entering this Asian trade route from the west came Spain and Portugal. Seeking routes to Asia, they had accidentally discovered the New World. Until then, North and South America had remained outside the activity sphere of the people of all of Eurasia. And for that reason the sudden appearance of the Europeans had an enormous impact. The greatest "reaction" from Eurasia brought about by the New World was the arrival of America in world history.

In order to consider the circumstances leading up to that, it is important to consider the history of the discord and reconciliation that occurred in Europe between the Catholics and the Protestants.

ア大陸では常に、文明の交流が進み、融合と分離を繰り返していました。

　海は、そんな「作用」と「反作用」とが大規模な戦争に発展しない、人々にとっては進出しやすい場所でした。ヴェネチア、ジェノバといった人々が活動した地中海。そしてイスラム教徒の交易ルートとヒンドゥー教徒のルートが交錯したインド洋と南シナ海。そのさらに北に琉球王朝があったことになります。

　こうした交易ルートを東側から辿り、1405年から1433年にかけて7回にわたって大航海に挑んだ人物がいました。明の永楽帝の命令で中東から東アフリカまで艦隊をおくった鄭和という人物です。彼はイスラム教徒で宦官であったといわれています。鄭和が大規模な航海を行った理由は謎です。永楽帝は1399年におきた靖難の役という政変によって皇帝となった人物です。永楽帝にとって明を安定した国家にするためには、南方との交易から生まれる富、さらには各地からの朝貢による交流が必要だったのかもしれません。

　これは、南北朝時代を経て室町幕府が日本を統一し、政権としても比較的安定していた頃のことでした。室町幕府では、三代将軍の足利義満以来、博多を通して明と公式な交易を促進していたのです。

　こうしたアジアでの交易に西側から参入してきたのがスペインとポルトガルでした。彼らは、アジアへのルートを求めながら、偶然にも新大陸を発見しました。それ以前の南北アメリカは、ユーラシア大陸の人々の活動の外に置かれていました。それだけに、そこに忽然と現れた西欧の影響は甚大でした。その後、新大陸がユーラシア大陸に向けておこした最大の「反作用」こそが、アメリカの世界史への登場だったのです。
　そこまでの経緯を語るには、さらにヨーロッパでおきていたカトリックとプロテスタントとの確執と和解の歴史をみてゆかなければならないのです。

083 In the New World, a unique culture was formed during Japan's Jomon period

If the New World had not existed, the livelihood of Western Europe would be significantly different from what it is today. Tomatoes, corn, and potatoes, for example, would not have spread among Europeans as a staple in the diet, and people would not have smoked tobacco.

Together with the end of the glacial period some 10,000 years ago, the continents of North and South America separated from the Eurasian continent. Prior to that, our ancestors over a long period of time crossed from Asia into North America and subsequently migrated into South America. After the land mass divided, just like the people active in Eurasia, these migrants lived by hunting and gathering, and then by farming. They observed the stars. They created systems of social classes. They built villages and towns. Wherever humans went, they lived in the same way and established societies. Just as there are carved statues in ancient Greece, people carved human figures in the New World and cut temples and shrines from stone. In the same way they invoked the blessings of the gods for good harvests, and clans fought with one another to gain hegemony.

At the time known as the Jomon period in Japan, hunter-gatherer peoples called the Anasazi were active across a broad region of northern Mexico and the southwestern United States. They constructed settlements that came be called pueblos and began to practice agriculture. In present-day New Mexico there is an ancient site called Chaco Canyon. Enormous ancient structures still exist dating from about the 10th century, and the people who created them made astronomical observations, practiced hunting and gathering, and engaged in agriculture.

A similar civilization arose in Central America. In the southern part of present-day Mexico and Guatemala, Maya civilization appeared in the 13th century B.C. The Maya built pyramids, developed an extremely detailed calendar, and were ruled by a king.

Although there is no evidence that they used metals or raised livestock, they are thought to have developed advanced mathematics capable of calculating the orbits of the planets in the solar system. Due to the fact that the Mayan script is still not fully deciphered, there are still many things about them that remain unclear.

新大陸では縄文時代から独自の文明が創造された

　もし、新大陸が存在しなければ、西欧の生活習慣は今とは相当異なっていたはずです。トマト、トウモロコシ、ジャガイモなど、西欧の人々にとっては欠かせない食材も伝播しなかったでしょうし、人々がタバコを吸うこともなかったはずです。

　およそ1万年以上前の氷河期の終焉とともに、南北アメリカ大陸はユーラシア大陸から分離されます。それ以前に、長い年月をかけて我々の祖先がアジアから北米へ、さらに南米へと移動をしました。大陸が分離された後、彼らはユーラシア大陸で活動した人々と同様に、狩猟や農耕を営み、天体を観測し、階級制度をつくり、村や町をつくりました。人類はどこにいっても、同じように活動し、社会を作っていったのです。ギリシアに彫像があるように、新大陸でも人の姿を彫り、石を切り出して神殿をつくりました。そして同じように神に豊作を願い、部族同士は覇権をめぐって争いました。

　アナサジと呼ばれる狩猟民族が、日本では縄文時代にあたる時期にメキシコ北部からアメリカ合衆国の南西部にかけて広く活動をしていました。やがて彼らはプエブロと呼ばれる集落を形成し、農耕を始めます。現在のニューメキシコ州にはチャコキャニオンという遺跡があります。そこには10世紀頃から天体観測をしながら狩猟と農耕を営んでいた人々の巨大な遺構群が残っています。

　一方、中央アメリカにも同様の文明が生まれます。現在のメキシコ南部やグアテマラ周辺では、紀元前13世紀にはマヤ文明がおこり、ピラミッドを築き、極めて精緻な暦法をもとに、王が統治をしていました。

　マヤ文明では金属を使用することや家畜を飼育していた痕跡がみとめられない一方で、太陽系の惑星の軌道を計算するなどの高等数学を操っていたともいわれます。ただ、彼らの文字が完全には解読されていないだけに、様々な謎が残っているのも事実です。

時代
16世紀以前
アメリカ古代

地域
アメリカ大陸

分類
文化【社会】

キーワード
アメリカ古代文明・大規模帝国の成立・ヨーロッパとの出会い

マヤの最高神ククルカンを祀るピラミッド（通称「カスティーヨ」）。メキシコ南部のユカタン半島に残るマヤ文明の遺跡、チチェン・イッツァにある。
A pyramid dedicated to the supreme Mayan god Kukulcan (also known as "El Castillo"). It is located in Chichen Itza, an archaeological site of the Mayan civilization in the Yucatan Peninsula in southern Mexico.

In the central highlands of Mexico, from about the 13th century, the Aztecs established a large state. The name Mexico is said to come partly from the name Mexitli, a legendary leader and war god of the Aztecs, who were a strong and militant people.

In South America the famous Inca Empire developed. Among the ruins of the cities that date from before the Christian era is Cuzco, in present-day Peru, which was the base of the Quechuas, who unified the region. This was the Inca Empire.

They possessed bronze implements and constructed the huge Macchu Picchu complex in the mountainous region, where it remains today. They used unique technology to create a city with huge stones.

The first Europeans to appear before them were from Spain. The indigenous inhabitants of the New World, faced with the powerful weaponry and combat technology used by the Spanish and suffering from the diseases such as smallpox which these intruders introduced, declined within a short period of time and were absorbed into European culture.

084 With the Bible and the sword, the New World was conquered by Europeans

In present-day New Mexico in the southwestern United States, there is a settlement on a mesa called Acoma, which was built by Native Americans on the face of cliffs high above ground level. Their community settlement is generally referred to as a pueblo, from the Spanish, but the history of Acoma Pueblo dates back to before the 10th century. They lived above ground level and descended to the mesa in order to cultivate crops of corn.

In approximately the middle of the 16th century, people they had never seen before suddenly appeared. They were immigrants from Spain who explored the area around Acoma and began to subjugate the people there. The inhabitants of Acoma quickly rushed back to their mesa, harvested and collected their corn for emergency storage, and attempted to repulse the strange newcomers.

Before too long, large columns of Spaniards arrived, massacring the men of Acoma and abducting the women and children as slaves.

そして、メキシコ中央部の高原には、13世紀頃からアステカ人と呼ばれる人々が、巨大な国家を建設しています。メキシコという国名の由来は、強靭で軍事的な民族であるアステカの伝説的な指導者であり、戦いの神でもあるメシトリの名前から来ていると言われています。

さらに南米には有名なインカ帝国がありました。紀元前からいくつかの都市や国家の痕跡がみられる中、そうした人々は現在のペルーのクスコを本拠地とするケチュア族によって統一されます。それがインカ帝国でした。

彼らは青銅器を持ち、山岳地帯にマチュピチュに代表される巨大な遺跡を残します。巨石を見事に積み上げる独特な技術で都市を造っていったのです。

そんな彼らの前に現れたスペインからの来訪者。新大陸の人々は、来訪者の強力な武器と戦闘技術によって、さらに彼らが天然痘などの疫病を持ち込んだことによって、瞬く間に衰微し、ヨーロッパ文明に吸収されていったのでした。

剣と聖書によって、新大陸はヨーロッパに席巻された

現在のアメリカ合衆国の南西部にあるニューメキシコ州。そこのメサ（台地）の上に、アコマというネイティブ・アメリカンの天空の集落があります。彼らの集落は一般にプエブロと呼ばれていますが、アコマ・プエブロの歴史は、10世紀以前に遡るといわれています。集落の住人は、メサの下におりて、トウモロコシを育てながら生活をしていました。

16世紀の半ば頃、そんな彼らの前に見も知らない人々が現れます。スペインからはるばる入植し、アコマ近郊を探検しながら勢力下に治めていた人々です。アコマの人々は、メサの上のプエブロに逃げ帰り、備蓄用のトウモロコシを徴収しようとしたこの見知らぬ人々を撃退します。

それから、しばらくして、さらに多くのスペイン人が隊列を組んでやってきます。そしてアコマの男たちは惨殺され、女や子供たちは奴隷になりました。

時代
16世紀
欧州近世

地域
アメリカ大陸

分類
侵略【宗教】

キーワード
スペインのアメリカ侵入・インカ帝国、アステカ帝国の滅亡・ローマ・カトリックの新世界

Some 120 kilometers northeast of Acoma is the city of Santa Fe, now the capital of the state of New Mexico. In the 16th century, the Spanish established a base there and began to build a colony.

Known as conquistadors, Spanish troops conquered the New World and colonized the people. In Peru, Francisco Pizarro demolished the Inca Empire. In Mexico, Hernán Cortés became especially well known for devastating the Aztec Empire. And Francisco Coronado explored and conquered New Mexico, commencing with Acoma. Together these conquistadors in the first half of the 16th century with their armies of mercenaries used their military advantage of gunpowder and cavalry to crush the local people and place the New World under the thumb of Spain.

At the time, Charles I of Spain—who was also Charles V, emperor of the Holy Roman Empire—and his successor Philip II, facing the quake brought on by the Reformation, made Spain the base of Catholicism in Europe, seeking domination of Europe as a whole. As a source of funds to implement this domination, they were exceptionally keen on enterprises in the New World. The conquistadors made use of this state policy to gain profits there, bringing enormous wealth to Spain from operations such as the Potosi silver mines in Bolivia.

Slaves kidnapped in Africa were forced to work in these operations. As was the case with the Acoma people, many indigenous people were forced into submission as slaves with the savage warning of what would happen to them if they refused. Then once they became tractable slaves, they were forced to convert to Christianity.

The sword and the Bible. Conquistadors and missionaries. Spain and then Portugal employed both these methods in carrying out their respective global strategies.

Sent by Portugal, Francis Xavier arrived in Japan to spread Christianity in 1549, at about the same time that the Spanish appeared at Acoma Pueblo in the New World.

フランシスコ・ザビエル
Francis Xavier

アコマから北東に120キロほどのところに、サンタフェという町があります。そこはニューメキシコ州の州都です。16世紀、スペインの人々は、そこを拠点として、植民地の建設を始めたのです。

　コンキスタドールと呼ばれる、新大陸を征服し、植民地化するスペインの軍人たち。ペルーでインカ帝国を滅ぼしたフランシスコ・ピサロ。メキシコでアステカ帝国を滅ぼしたエルナン・コルテスは特に有名です。そして、最初にアコマなどがあるニューメキシコ州一帯を探検したコンキスタドールは、フランシスコ・コロナードでした。彼らは共に16世紀の前半に活躍した私兵団で、火器や騎馬戦術といった圧倒的に有利な戦力をもって現地の人々を駆逐し、新大陸をスペインの傘下に組み込んでいったのです。

　当時、スペインのカール1世（神聖ローマ帝国カール5世）、そしてその後帝位を継いだフェリペ2世は、宗教改革に揺れるヨーロッパの中でスペインをカトリックの拠点と位置づけ、ヨーロッパでの覇権を求めていました。その資金源として、新大陸の経営を極めて重視したのです。コンキスタドールたちは、そうした国策を利用して、利益をあげようと新大陸に乗り出したのです。ボリビアのポトシ銀山のように、彼らはスペインに莫大な利益をもたらします。

　新大陸の経営には、アフリカで拉致した奴隷も使用されます。アコマの人々のように、残虐な見せしめの上で、服従させられ奴隷として徴用された人々も多くいました。そして、従順になった人々はキリスト教に改宗させられます。

　剣と聖書。コンキスタドールと宣教師。この二つの方法を使い分けながら、スペイン、そしてポルトガルは世界戦略を遂行したのでした。

　日本に、ポルトガルから派遣されたフランシスコ・ザビエルがキリスト教を伝えたのも、アコマ・プエブロにスペイン人が現れたのとほぼ同じ時期、1549年のことでした。

085 Spain and Portugal divided and expanded their presence across the world map

The institutions that played major roles in propagating Christian education in the European world were the monasteries. These monasteries took the practical, ascetic life as their purpose for existing as a community that devoted itself to labor and prayer. The Benedictine Order, which was founded in the 6th century at Monte Cassino in Italy, is known for its large scale.

Among the monastic orders that criticized the bloated Benedictine Order, three became particularly well known. The Cistercian Order sought a return to the fundamentals of monastic life. The Franciscan Order and the Dominican Order placed emphasis on leading lives of honorable poverty, free of secular desires.

However, when it came to whether the people active within the monasteries actually cooperated with the Holy See, which was roiled by compromises and conflicts with the secular powers, that was not always the case. For example, within the Cistercian and Franciscan orders, there were many monks who criticized the secularization of the Holy See and were in turn persecuted for heresy.

Moreover, many monasteries took propagation of the faith as their central mission, and the Dominicans, among others, were ardent in proselytizing in Asia and the New World. However, it was the Society of Jesus who devoted themselves most strongly to missionary activities, making the greatest contribution to spreading the word throughout the world, including Japan.

Amid the expanding trend brought about by the Reformation, Ignatius of Loyola and others seeking to reform the Catholic Church from within founded the Society of Jesus in 1534. Commonly known as the Jesuits, they were earnest in their missionary work. Prominent among them was Francis Xavier, who, with the patronage of the King of Portugal, carried out missionary activities in Portuguese-controlled parts of Asia from Goa in India to Malacca in present-day Malaysia.

Xavier reached the Satsuma domain and traveled throughout Japan too. He laid the foundation for the propagation of Christianity, which would later waver in the chaotic period of Sengoku.

It is said that the Dominicans and the Franciscans did not approve of the exploitation of the indigenous people by the conquistadors; however they did not make their disapproval explicit. As a result, the ancient culture of the peoples of the New World was greatly changed by Christianity. What occurred in Cuzco in

スペインとポルトガルは世界地図を分割し進出した

　ヨーロッパ世界でキリスト教の教義を深化させてゆくことに大きな役割を果たしていたのは修道院でした。修道院は禁欲生活をモットーに、労働と祈りの日々を送る人々の組織です。中でも6世紀にイタリアのモンテカシーノに設立されたベネディクト会は、その規模の大きさで知られています。

　また、肥大化したベネディクト会を批判し、そこから分離し、修道活動の原点に立ち戻ろうとしたシトー会や、世俗欲にとらわれず清貧を重んじて活動するフランシスコ会やドミニク会などといった組織もよく知られた修道会です。

　ところで、修道院で活動する人々が、世俗権力との妥協や抗争に揺れる教皇庁と常に協調できたかというとそうではありません。例えば、シトー会やフランシスコ会の中には、世俗化する教皇庁を批判し、異端として迫害された修道士も多くいました。

　また、布教することを使命とした修道会も多く、ドミニク会などはアジアや新大陸での布教に熱心でした。しかし、こうした宣教活動を推進し、日本を含め、世界にキリスト教を拡大することに最も貢献した組織はイエズス会でした。

　イエズス会は、宗教改革の気運が拡大する中、カトリック教会を内部から改革し、強化してゆこうとイグナティウス・ロヨラを中心に1534年に設立しました。イエズス会は宣教活動に熱心で、特にフランシスコ・ザビエルは、ポルトガル王の庇護を受け、インドのゴアから現在のマレーシアにあるマラッカなど、ポルトガルが支配するアジアの拠点を中心に布教活動を行いました。

　ザビエルは薩摩に来航し、日本各地を訪れました。その後戦国時代の混乱に揺れる日本での布教の土台を築きます。

　ドミニク会やイエズス会は、新大陸ではコンキスタドールなどによるインディオへの収奪行為には必ずしも賛同していなかったといわれています。しかし、結果として新大陸にあった古来の文化はキリスト教によって大きく変貌しました。ペルーのクスコはその代表的な事例

時代
16世紀
欧州近世

地域
ヨーロッパ（世界共通）

分類
宗教【侵略】

キーワード
カトリックの修道院活動・カトリックの新世界布教・スペイン、ポルトガルの世界分割

Peru was a typical example. After the downfall of the Inca Empire, the existing city was demolished, and on top of those ruins, colonial buildings and churches were built, so that the previous appearance of Cuzco was completely lost. With the arrival of the 17th century, the country that exercised caution regarding the two sides of European colonization—propagation of religion and military power—was none other than Japan.

With the approval of the pope, Spain and Portugal signed the Treaty of Tordesillas in 1494 and the Treat of Zaragoza in 1529, by which they agreed on which lands each would lay claim to.

In accordance with these treaties, Brazil went to Portugal, the Philippines, discovered by Magellan, went to Spain, and Malacca and Macao were recognized as possessions of Brazil. Spain and Portugal's arrival in Japan came after these two agreements were concluded. However, while both Spanish and Portuguese visited Japanese shores during the latter country's Sengoku period, because Japan was already commanded by strong military forces and sengoku daimyo, the visitors were unable to colonize the country.

086 England organized a state church becoming independent of ties with Rome

Now let us turn our attention to England.

During the Hundred Years' War and the War of the Roses, there was great hostility between England and the Pope. However, in terms of religion, the royal family adhered to Catholicism and was unable to completely sever these ties out of regard for its ties with Rome.

But as was true elsewhere during the Middle Ages, the monasteries and the churches had their own system of taxation, in which it was difficult for the royal authority to intervene. England was no exception. In the case of England, territories were divided during the Hundred Years' War and the War of the Roses, and in the midst of all the destruction, it must not have been easy to control the clerics while extending royal prerogatives and rebuilding the economy.

Circumstances in England changed completely in 1509, when Henry VIII ascended the throne. Following the Hundred Years' War, England had continued to have a hostile relationship with France. As a result, Henry VIII married a woman

です。インカ帝国の滅亡後、それまでの町を破壊し、その上に植民地の施設や教会を建設したことで、クスコは以前の面影を失ってしまいます。17世紀になって、こうしたヨーロッパ勢力の布教と武力の双方による植民地化を警戒したのは、他でもない日本でした。

スペインとポルトガルとは、教皇の承認のもと1494年のトルデシリャス条約と1529年のサラゴサ条約によって、それぞれが獲得できる地域を取り決めました。

それによってブラジルはポルトガルに、マゼランによって発見されたフィリピンはスペインに、さらにマラッカやマカオはポルトガルに領有権が認められたのです。彼らが日本に至ったのはこれらの条約締結の後ではありました。しかし、戦国時代後期の日本にも、スペイン人とポルトガル人が共に来航してきたものの、すでに強い軍隊と戦国大名によって統率されていた日本を植民地にすることはできなかったのです。

イギリスは国教会を創立してローマの絆から独立した

ここで、目をイギリスに向けてみましょう。

イギリスは、百年戦争や薔薇戦争の時期に、ローマ教皇と激しく対立したこともありました。しかし、宗教的にはカトリックを信奉し王族もローマへの敬意と絆を完全に打ち切ることはありませんでした。

ただ、中世はどこでも同じでしたが、修道院や教会は独自の税制をもち、王権の介入が困難でした。イギリスも例外ではありません。イギリスの場合、百年戦争や薔薇戦争で国土が分裂し、荒廃する中で、こうした聖職者をも束ねながら王権を伸長させ、経済を復興させるのは容易なことではなかったはずです。

イギリスの状況が1509年に即位したヘンリー8世のときに一変します。百年戦争以来、イギリスは伝統的にフランスと対立関係にありました。従って、ヘンリー8世はフランスのライバルともいえるハプス

時代
16世紀
欧州近世

地域
イギリス

分類
宗教【政治】

キーワード
ヘンリー8世の離婚・イギリス国教会の成立・イギリス王権の強化

who was related by marriage to Charles V of the House of Habsburg, which was a rival of the French monarch. The origin of the problems was the attempt by Henry VIII to divorce that woman.

Marital relations within the royal houses were inevitably closely tied with the country's diplomatic relationships. England felt menaced by Scotland in the north and by France in the south, and was eager to maintain diplomatic relations with Spain and the Holy Roman Empire.

For the English monarch to divorce a relative of the emperor of the Holy Roman Empire was a momentous decision. The Pope opposed the divorce, and ultimately Henry VIII was excommunicated. In response to this, Henry VIII established the Church of England, an independent church that would not be subject to intervention from Rome, in order to strengthen his own political foundation.

From that point onward, Henry VIII repeatedly remarried and divorced and remarried, which left a messy series of relationships involving succession to the throne. In the middle of this messy situation there were always scheming feudal lords, leaving royal authority endangered. In the process of establishing this state religion, it was an essential policy to keep the churches and monasteries under the umbrella of monarchial power.

In addition to this confrontation with the papacy, Henry VIII faced another source of anxiety in the form of the strengthening of Protestantism in England. To deal with this issue, it was of major significance that the churches that had been under the control of the Holy See become subsumed under the Church of England. As a result, this allowed England to become an independent country that was the equal of both France and the Holy Roman Empire.

While the situation was complicated, Henry VIII survived the political strife and strengthened the power of the royal throne. Later on, this would exceed that of Spain, which claimed hegemony in the New World and in the Mediterranean, and would become the foundation upon which England would appear in world history as a strong European power. Further, England's significant participation on the stage of modern European history allowed it to have a major impact on the power balance in the New World.

ブルク家のカール5世と姻戚関係にあった女性と結婚します。その女性とヘンリー8世が離婚をしようとしたことが、問題の発端だったのです。

　王族の婚姻関係は、そのまま国家の外交戦略とも密接に絡んでいました。イギリスは、北にスコットランド、南にフランスという脅威を抱え、その向こう側にあるスペインや神聖ローマ帝国との外交戦略に熱心だったのです。

　そんなイギリスの王が神聖ローマ帝国皇帝の姻戚者と離婚することは、政治的にも大きな決断でした。ローマ教皇は離婚に反対し、最終的にはヘンリー8世を破門することになります。これを受けてヘンリー8世は自らの政治基盤を強化するために、ローマの介入を受けない独自の教会であるイギリス国教会を設立したのでした。

ハンス・ホルバイン『ヘンリー8世』
Hans Holbein —*Portrait of
Henry VIII*

　その後ヘンリー8世は、後継者問題も絡んだ複雑な人間関係の中で再婚と離婚を繰り返します。そこには常に有力諸侯の画策がみられ、王権の基盤を危うくしていたのです。国教会を設立する過程では、教会や修道院を傘下にいれるための戦略も必要でした。

　また、ローマ教皇との対立の中、イギリスにもプロテスタントの勢力が拡大してきたこともヘンリー8世にとっては新たな不安要因といえました。こうした課題を乗り越え、もともとローマ教皇庁の影響下にあった教会をイギリス国教会に組み込むことに成功した意義は大きなものです。結果として、それはイギリスが独立国として、フランスや神聖ローマ帝国と肩を並べたことになるのです。

　様々な経緯はあったものの、ヘンリー8世は、政争を乗り越え王権を強化します。これが、後年新大陸や地中海で覇権を唱えていたスペインを凌駕し、イギリスがヨーロッパの強国として世界史に登場する土台となったのです。さらに、ヨーロッパ近代史の舞台にイギリスが力強く参加することは、新大陸でのパワーバランスにも最終的に大きな影響を与えてゆくことになるのです。

The Puritans from within the Church of England crossed the Atlantic to America

The establishment of the Church of England was not merely the separation of a church from Roman Catholicism. In order to justify this separation, it also involved the work of establishing doctrines of faith that determined the relationship between the church and the monarch, and what made its teachings different from the Catholicism of the past. In that process, Protestant people also participated. In particular, the Calvinists become active in reform.

Just as had happened when Christianity became the state religion of the Roman Empire, controversy erupted regarding doctrine. During the controversy, a second split within the church occurred, and a new group broke off from the state religion, forming its own particular beliefs. Those known as Calvinists ultimately opposed royal authority and began searching for a way to break away from the established state church. One group of these separatists escaped government persecution by boarding the Mayflower and migrating to North America in 1620. These people came to be known as the Pilgrim Fathers. They are the initial group of Puritans who, in the following years, would develop the future United States of America.

At the time the Pilgrims set sail for America, James I reigned over England. James I was actually the eldest son of Mary Stuart, Queen of Scotland, and he had already succeeded to the throne. And because Mary continued the English blood line, when Elizabeth I died without leaving an heir, James succeeded to the throne of England.

The story is quite complex, but if we can grasp the circumstances in Scotland, we can absorb the fundamentals of the situation.

In Scotland, just prior to the Reformation, the clergy possessed strong authority, and it is said that people suffered under corruption within the church. In any event, the Calvinists, spread across unstable Scotland, and the country was caught up in the tempest of religious reformation. The Scottish royal family, which traditionally had strong connections with the French royal family, struggled to cope with this maelstrom. As a result of her father's death, the infant Mary succeeded to the throne, and until the age of 19, she was raised as a Catholic in France, her mother's home country. So when Mary returned to Scotland, where the Reformation was underway, she became caught up in the political strife there.

イギリス国教会の中から清教徒がアメリカに渡った

イギリス国教会の創立は、単にローマカトリックから教会が分離したことではありませんでした。それを正当化するためには、王と教会との関係、さらに従来のカトリックとは異なる信仰の基準を制定するという作業が必要だったのです。その過程の中には、プロテスタント系の人々も参加します。特にカルヴァン派の人々は、国教会の改革に熱心でした。

ちょうど、ローマ帝国がキリスト教を国教にしたときのような、教義をめぐる論争もおきました。論争の中で、再度国教会から分離し、独自の信仰に基づいて活動する集団も生まれたのです。カルヴァン派の人々の中にも最終的に王権と対立し、国教会からの離脱を模索する人々が現れます。そんな分離派の一部が、政府からの迫害を逃れようと、メイフラワー号に乗り、北アメリカに移住します。1620年のことでした。この人々のことをピルグリム・ファーザーズと呼びます。彼らこそが、将来アメリカ合衆国へと成長する種子となる清教徒と呼ばれる人々でした。

ピルグリム・ファーザーズが、アメリカに向かって旅立った頃、イギリスはジェームズ1世の治世でした。実は、ジェームズ1世は、スコットランド女王メアリーの長男で、既に彼はスコットランドの王となっていたのです。さらにメアリーがイギリス（イングランド）王の血も引いていたことから、子供のいないエリザベス1世が世を去ったときに、彼はイギリスの王位も継承したのでした。

複雑な話ですが、ここで改めてスコットランドの情勢について理解すれば、状況が飲み込めます。

宗教改革直前のスコットランドでは、聖職者の力が強く、教会の腐敗に人々が苦しんでいたといわれています。いずれにせよ、カルヴァン派はそうした不安定なスコットランドに浸透し、スコットランドは宗教改革の嵐に飲み込まれたのです。従来フランス王室と深い繋がりを持っていたスコットランドの王室はこの混乱への対応に苦しみます。メアリーは父親の死去によって幼児期に王権を受け継ぎますが、19歳までは母方の故郷フランスでカトリックの教育を受けて育てられていました。そんなメアリーが、宗教改革の進んだスコットランドに帰国すると、その政争に巻き込まれてしまい、結局イギリス（イングランド）

時代
17世紀
欧州近世

地域
イギリス・北アメリカ

分類
政治【宗教】

キーワード
スコットランドの混乱・国教会とカルヴァン派・メイフラワー号によるアメリカ移住開始・絶対王政へ

Eventually she took refuge in England, and her son James succeeded her.

However, in England, following Henry VIII, political turmoil continued, and after three more kings maintained power, Elizabeth I acceded to the throne. Because Mary was of royal blood, she became involved in political infighting which was aimed at taking the throne from Elizabeth I, and in 1587 Mary was executed.

Due to the Habsburg support of Mary and the English royal family's efforts to become independent of continental authority since the reign of Henry VIII, this incident let to great tension. In order to fully understand the situation, it is essential to examine the details of the reign of Elizabeth I.

088 Elizabeth's reign was buffeted by the politics of the continent

While Elizabeth I ruled England, Japan was passing through the Sengoku period and the Azuchi Momoyama period. The year 1603 was the year of Elizabeth I's death, and it was in exactly that year that the Tokugawa Shogunate was established.

In Europe in the 16th through the 17th centuries, there was a confrontation between those who promoted the Reformation and those who supported the Pope and the Holy Roman Empire, which sought to prevent the religious reformists' activities. Furthermore, Elizabeth's reign was characterized by a complex situation entangled with alliances between the aspiring Holy Roman Empire and Spain, as well as conflicts with France.

Meanwhile England tried to keep a distance from both parties, while it sought to establish its own church and become independent. In a sense this was a decision to follow a moderate separatism.

However, circumstances in neighboring countries did not allow that to happen. First, Catholic France, which had been England's rival since the Middle Ages, was rocked by confrontations with a Protestant offshoot known as the Huguenots.

In response to this series of disturbances known as the Wars of Religion, the Spanish King Philip II of the House of Habsburg, with the intention of weakening France itself, actively intervened and formed an alliance with the Catholic faction and the Catholic League in France. This league between prominent figures in France and the Habsburgs became a threat to England.

に亡命します。その後を継いだのが長男のジェームズだったのです。

　ところで、イギリスは、ヘンリー8世の後、政争が続き三人の王が政権を維持した後に、エリザベス1世が王位を継承します。そうした中で、メアリーはイギリスの王室の血を引く者として、エリザベス1世から王権を奪おうとする政争にのみこまれ、1587年にイギリス（イングランド）で処刑されたのです。

　この事件は、メアリーを支持していたハプスブルク家と、ヘンリー8世以来、大陸の覇権から自立しようとしていたイギリス王室とに大きな緊張を生み出します。その状況を理解するためにも、我々はエリザベス1世の治世をさらに詳しく見つめてゆく必要があるのです。

エリザベスの治世は大陸の政治に翻弄された

　エリザベス女王がイギリス（イングランド）を統治していた時代は、日本の戦国時代後期から安土桃山時代にあたります。そしてエリザベス女王の没年は、徳川幕府が成立した1603年にあたります。

　16世紀から17世紀のヨーロッパは、宗教改革を進めてゆこうとする人々と、それを阻止しようとするローマ教皇や神聖ローマ帝国皇帝との対立。さらには、覇権を目指す神聖ローマ帝国とスペインの同盟とフランスとの対立などが絡んだ複雑な状態にありました。

時代
17世紀
欧州近世

地域
イギリス・フランス

分類
対立【政治】

キーワード
プロテスタントとカトリックの対立・相次ぐ宗教紛争・絶対王政の確立・イギリスとスペインの対立

　イギリスは、その双方から距離を置きながら、自らの教会を打ち立てて自立していこうとします。それはある意味では穏健な孤立主義への選択のはずでした。

　しかし、隣国の状況がそれを許しません。まず中世以来イギリスのライバルであったフランスはカトリックとユグノーと呼ばれるプロテスタントとの対立に揺れていました。

　ユグノー戦争と呼ばれるこの一連の騒動に対して、フランスそのものの弱体化を意図したハプスブルク家のスペイン王フェリペ2世も積極的に介入し、フランスのカトリック勢力とカトリック同盟を結びます。フランスの有力者とハプスブルク家との同盟はイギリスへの脅威となりました。

In the meantime, turmoil continued in the Netherlands, where many Calvinist Protestants were active. In particular, when the Holy Roman Empire entrusted the governance of the Netherlands to the allied nation of Spain, many of the Protestants active in the Netherlands were Huguenots who had fled from France. This added to the tense situation. In response to this conflagration across the water, England began providing support to the Protestants.

This further enflamed the confrontation between England and Spain. The Holy See and the Holy Roman Empire, engaging in secret maneuvering seeking to topple the regime of Elizabeth I, who was trying to distance England from the continent. Under this threat, Mary Stuart, monarch of Scotland, which had friendly relations with Spain, was defeated in domestic political strife and took refuge in England. However, after Mary came to loggerheads with Elizabeth and was executed, relations between England and Spain became even tenser.

Tossed about by international chaotic affairs on the continent, military expenditures including support for the Netherlands put pressure on the finances of the English royal household. What assisted England in this case were the merchant vessels called privateers. In order to maintain and protect long, widespread sea routes during the Age of Discovery, a system was developed whereby states approved and even contracted with groups of private soldiers to serves as privateers. England employed such mercenaries to attack Spanish fleets operating in the New World to loot and plunder their riches. Typical of these privateers was the fleet of Sir Francis Drake, who advanced into the West Indies and caused great trouble for Spanish merchant fleets.

This string of confrontations led to the Anglo-Spanish War. Queen Elizabeth I, who led England to victory in that war, is lauded as the greatest monarch England ever had. However, a reaction against royal authority that resulted from the strengthening of her rule later proved to be the trigger that began the Puritan Revolution.

一方、プロテスタントのカルヴァン派の人々が多く活動するオランダでも騒乱が絶えませんでした。特に、オランダの統治を神聖ローマ帝国が同盟国のスペインに委ねると、オランダで活動するプロテスタントの多くがフランスから亡命してきたユグノーであったこともあって、状況は緊迫します。イギリスはこの対岸の火事に対して、プロテスタントへの支援を始めたのです。

　このことがイギリスとスペインとの対立を煽ります。大陸と距離を置こうとするエリザベス体制の転覆を図り、ローマ教皇庁と神聖ローマ帝国が暗躍します。こうした脅威の中、カトリック側につき、スペインとも親交のあったスコットランドの王メアリーが政争に敗れ、イギリスに亡命します。しかし、メアリーはエリザベスと対立した後に処刑され、このことがスペインとの新たな緊張関係へと発展しました。

　このような大陸での混沌とした国際情勢に翻弄される中、オランダへの支援などによる軍事費はイギリス王室の財政を圧迫します。そんなイギリスを助けたのが私掠船と呼ばれる商船でした。大航海時代に長く広大になった航路を維持し防衛するために、国家が承認し、契約した私兵団が私掠船のおこりです。イギリスはこの私掠船を使って新大陸経営を行うスペイン船団を攻撃し、その富を略奪し、イギリスにもたらしたのです。フランシス・ドレークなどに代表される私掠船は、遠く西インド諸島にまで進出し、スペイン船団を悩ませます。

　こうした一連の紛争が英西戦争へと拡大します。英西戦争を指導し勝利に導いたエリザベス1世は、イギリスで最も偉大な王と称えられます。しかしその治世を通して強化された王権への反発が、後にイギリスでおきた清教徒革命の導火線となっていったのでした。

089 The Protestants brought new ways of doing business to world history

When we consider history, we tend to focus only on changes in the relations that occur between states. However, when we look fixedly at the history of humankind, it becomes necessary to know not only about the states involved but also about how the people in those states thought, how they traded with one another, and how their lifestyles changed.

In the 16th century, Spain embarked on colonial administration in bases in the New World and the Philippines. Basically this amounted to dispossessing other people of their wealth and was an extension of the ancient activities of conquering, plundering, and looting other states and bringing that wealth home. Portugal proceeded into Asia early on, establishing its base in India at Goa and later at Malacca in present-day Malaysia. In 1517 the Portuguese commenced trade with Ming China, and took administrative control of Macao, out of which they commenced trade throughout East Asia. However, both Portugal and Spain, while they continued exporting the Catholic religion, were also carrying on trade as a means of offering wealth to their respective royal families.

It was England and Holland that introduced an entirely new variety of trade. In the Netherlands during the period when it was under Spanish control, a large number of Protestants lived in the northern region, where they sought independence from Spanish oversight. Through the efforts of influential figures such as William the Silent, the Union of Utrecht was formed as a regional alliance, and in 1581, they declared the establishment of the Dutch Republic, which corresponds to the present-day Netherlands. England supported the movement for independence, and due to England's victory over the Spanish Armada in 1588, the Netherlands effectively achieved independence.

Due to influence from the war with Spain and its Portuguese ally, the Netherlands found it hard to obtain resources. For that reason, in 1602 the Netherlands established the Dutch East India Company and set about importing spices and ceramic ware from Asia. The trading post established by them was initially located in Hirado, Japan, and later moved to Dejima in Nagasaki. Afterward, the Dutch expanded their presence to the New World and, as will be

プロテスタントは世界史に新たな
ビジネススキームを持ち込んだ

　我々は歴史を考察するとき、国家同士の変遷のみに焦点を当てがちです。しかし、人類の歴史を見つめるとき、国家ではなく、そこに生きる人々がどのように考え、交易をし、生活を変えていったかを知る必要があります。

　16世紀、スペインは新大陸やフィリピンに拠点をおいて、植民地経営に乗り出しました。それは基本的に他者の富を奪い、自国に持ち帰る古来の征服活動の延長でした。また、早くからアジアに進出したポルトガルは、インドのゴアに拠点をおき、その後現在のマレーシアにあるマラッカ、そして1517年には明と交易をはじめ、マカオを管理下において東アジアでの交易活動を始めました。しかし、ポルトガルもスペインと同様、カトリックという宗教の輸出を実行しながら、王室への富の献納という形での交易に専念します。

　そこに全く新しい形での交易のあり方を持ち込んだのが、イギリスとオランダだったのです。スペインが統治をしていたネーデルランドのうち、プロテスタントが多く住む北部地方が、カトリックの覇者であるスペインの支配からの独立を目指します。有力者オラニエ公ウィレムなどの活動で、ユトレヒト同盟という地域の連合体ができ、スペインのフェリペ2世に対し、1581年にネーデルランド連邦共和国の成立を宣言したのです。それが現在のオランダにあたります。この独立活動を支援したイギリスが、1588年にスペインの無敵艦隊アルマダと海戦をし、それを打ち破ったことなども影響して、オランダも実質上独立を勝ち得ることができたのです。

　オランダは、戦争の影響でスペインや1581年にスペインに併合されていたポルトガルからの物資が入りにくくなっていました。そこで、1602年に東インド会社を設立し、アジアからの香辛料や陶器などの輸入事業へ乗り出します。彼らが開いたオランダ商館は、日本では平戸に置かれ、後に長崎の出島へと移転

時代
16, 17世紀 欧州近世

地域
西ヨーロッパ

分類
経済【宗教】

キーワード
カトリック国家の植民地と布教 • 植民地経済の発展 • プロテスタント国家の優位 • 資本主義の萌芽

フィリップ・ジェイムズ・ド・ラウザーバーグ
『スペイン無敵艦隊の敗北』
Philip James de Loutherbourg —Defeat of the
Spanish Armada, 8 August, 1588

mentioned later, established a colony called New Amsterdam in present-day New York.

In the case of Spain and Portugal, their colonial administrations were always accompanied by a religious mission. In contrast, Protestants saw religious faith as a direct connection between the individual and God, so that being diligent in business was itself a means of maintaining one's faith in daily life. As a result, the Dutch separated business and social life, without the intermediary of a church authority. Colonies were not religious mission activities; they were just places for business operations.

Moreover, for the individual to devote himself to daily business was connected with purifying one's faith. It was this Protestant ethic that gave birth to industry within modern states. They did not seek colonies in order to convert people of other religious faiths. They cultivated an awareness of treating them solely as places to carry on business. In other words, they transformed the way people thought to adopting a business philosophy based on capitalism.

090 The introduction of Christianity affects Japan's strategy toward foreign countries

Christianity and firearms were introduced to Japan in the latter half of the Sengoku period.

This was a result of the activity of the Portuguese who reached East Asia via Goa and Malacca during the Age of Discovery.

In comparison with this, through the process by which England and Spain confronted each other, while the Protestants in the Netherlands fought for their own independence, a new power based on Protestantism began to spread from Europe throughout the rest of the world.

In the period of Oda Nobunaga, Portugal began to prosper from wealth attained in Asia, as Spain had done from the New World. It is well-known that Nobunaga was tolerant of the activities of the Protestant missionaries from Portugal. However, when Toyotomi Hideyoshi gained power after Nobunaga's death, stories of the pillage and plunder that colonies suffered under the Portuguese and the Spanish began to reach Japan. Further, Hideyoshi began to sense danger from stories regarding the process of conversion that the colonists carried out in the

しました。その後オランダは新大陸へも進出し、後述のように現在の
ニューヨークにニューアムステルダムという植民地を建設します。

　スペインやポルトガルの場合、彼らの植民地経営には常に宗教的ミッ
ションが伴いました。それに対してプロテスタントの人々は、神と個
人とが直接信仰という糸で結ばれていることから、勤勉でビジネスに
徹することは、そのまま自らの信仰を維持し、神と自らをつなげるこ
とに繋がりました。従って、オランダ人の場合、ビジネスと教会活動
とを切り分けて、教会の権威を間に挟むことなく、植民地でビジネス
を行えたのです。

　さらに、個人が日々ビジネスで自らを精進することが、信仰の純化
にも繋がったのです。このプロテスタントの倫理こそが、近代国家に
おいて産業を発展させ、植民地を宗教による異教徒への侵略ではなく、
ビジネス上の経営の対象として捉えてゆくという意識を育てます。つ
まり、資本主義的な経営理念を持った行動へと人々の意識を変化させ
ていったのでした。

キリスト教の新たなプレイヤーが日本の
外交戦略にも影響を与えた

　日本には戦国時代の後半に、キリスト教や鉄砲が伝来しました。

　これは、大航海時代にゴアやマラッカを経由して東アジアまで到来
したポルトガル人の活動によるものです。

　それに対して、イギリスとスペインとの対立、さらにオランダのプ
ロテスタントによる独立戦争といった経緯を経て、新教を軸とした新
な勢力がヨーロッパから世界に拡大を始めます。

　織田信長の時代、ポルトガルはアジアから、スペインは新大陸での
富によって栄えていました。信長が、ポルトガルやキリスト教の宣教
師の活動に対して寛容であったことはよく知られた事実です。しかし、
信長の死後政権を引き継いだ豊臣秀吉は、ポルトガルやスペインの植
民地での略奪行為の情報や、キリスト教への改宗の過程での仏教界と
の軋轢の中で、西欧との行き過ぎた交流に警戒感を抱き始めています。

時代
16, 17世紀
日本近世

地域
日本

分類
政治【交流】

キーワード
南蛮貿易の発展・戦国末
期の統一活動・ヨーロッ
パと日本の交流・カト
リック諸国が日本から後
退

Buddhist colonies and the general overzealous exchanges that the West brought about.

In 1596 the *San Felipe*, which departed from the Philippines bound for Mexico, encountered a storm and ended up drifting ashore in Tosa. From the information obtained by those on board, Hideyoshi became deeply suspicious that Spain was intending to invade Japan, and as a warning, he had a group of Catholic priests and converts in Nagasaki executed. They became known as the Twenty-six Martyrs of Japan. This was the first incident in a series that led the Tokugawa Shogunate to decide to close the country to the outside world.

In the year that Hideyoshi died, an English mariner was taken into service by a Dutch shipping firm, and he set sail from Rotterdam. This pilot had once served on an English privateer under Drake in the battle against the Spanish Armada. In the process of developing a strong naval power, the pilots and other mariners sailing on privateers pitted themselves against the Spanish and Portuguese ships and expanded English markets overseas.

The pilot mentioned above was William Adams. The fleet in which he served crossed the Atlantic Ocean, passed through the Straits of Magellan, and entered the Pacific Ocean. Along their route, many crew members were lost to conflict with local indigenous people and epidemic diseases, and only his ship barely escaped disaster when it was cast ashore in Bungo.

He and his fellow Dutch crewman Jan Joosten were detained by the authorities, and Portuguese missionaries called for the Japanese government to execute them. The conflict between the Catholics and the Protestants had reached Japan.

However, the two mariners were protected by the Tokugawa Ieyasu, who had become somewhat of a statesman, and were transported to Edo, where they were put into service as advisors to Ieyasu. William Adams was renamed Miura Anjin and Jan Joosten became Ya Yosu, and the two contributed to both the state-building of the Tokugawa Shogunate and the city-building of Edo. As an aside, the Yaesu district of present-day Tokyo Station derives its name from Ya Yosu.

In the transition among the participants in the Age of Discovery from the great Catholic powers to the enterprising Protestant countries, the foreign policies of Japan began to be influenced to a significant degree.

1596年に、フィリピンを出発しメキシコに向かおうとしていたサン・フェリペ号が嵐に遭い土佐に漂着します。その時に乗船していた者の情報から、秀吉はスペインの日本への侵略の意図を強く疑い、見せしめとして、日本で活動する神父と日本人の信者26名を長崎で処刑します。「26聖人の殉教」という事件です。これが、徳川幕府になって日本が鎖国へと傾斜してゆく最初の出来事となったのです。

　その秀吉が死亡した年に、一人のイギリス人航海士がオランダの船団に雇われ、ロッテルダムから海にでます。その人物は以前イギリスの私掠船を操ってスペインの無敵艦隊と戦ったドレークの傘下で仕事をしたこともありました。イギリスが強力な海軍国に成長する過程で、こうした無数の航海士や私掠船を操る船乗りがスペインやポルトガルに対抗し、イギリスの市場を拡大したのです。
　その人物の名前はウィリアム・アダムスです。船団は大西洋を渡り、さらにマゼラン海峡から太平洋に至りますが、途中でインディオの攻撃や疫病のため多くの船員を失い、彼の船だけが命からがら豊後に漂着したのでした。

　彼と同僚のオランダ人ヤン・ヨーステンが拘束されると、日本はポルトガル人の宣教師から彼らを処刑するようにという要請を受け取ります。カトリックとプロテスタントの戦いが日本に持ち込まれたのです。
　しかし、為政者となった徳川家康に保護された二人は、江戸に送られ、家康の顧問として活躍します。ウィリアム・アダムスは三浦按針、ヤン・ヨーステンは耶揚子と名前を変え、徳川幕府の国づくり、江戸の町づくりに貢献します。ちなみに現在東京駅のある八重洲は、ヤン・ヨーステンの名前からおこった地名です。

　大航海のプレイヤーが、旧教の大国から新興のプロテスタントたちへと変わってゆく中で、日本の外交政策も大きな影響を受け始めたのでした。

091 The expansion of the Ottoman Empire triggered discord with Russia

The fact that individuals from the great powers of contemporary Europe actually reached remote Japan in the closing years of that country's Sengoku period is indicative of how trade along the Silk Road, in which Central Asia was the focus of East-West exchange, was becoming outdated.

What this meant was that where Central Asia had long been the epicenter of the balance of power in the Eurasian world, it had now shifted to a new location: the vast oceans.

The Ottoman Empire, which arose in Central Asia because it maintained under its umbrella the western end of the Silk Road, effectively pushed the European world out into the oceans.

The Ottoman Empire actively sought control over the oceans. In 1571, shortly after the death of Suleyman the Magnificent, who contributed to the expansion of the empire, the naval forces of the empire fought against the Spanish Armada. The result, however, was a total defeat in the Battle of Lepanto.

The Ottomans were actively advancing in other regions as well.

They turned their attention from the Indian Ocean to Southeast Asia. For instance, they seriously threatened Portuguese-controlled Malacca in 1569.

Even after that, the Ottoman Empire maintained naval supremacy over the long coastline from the Black Sea to the eastern Mediterranean, seeking to deprive the Italian city-states of their vested interests. Especially in the region north of the Black Sea, the influence of the former Mongol Empire still remained, but the Ottomans defeated the Mongol remnants and extended their own influence.

As a result of this expansion of influence toward the north, the Ottoman Empire became a direct neighbor of the Russian world.

At that time, while being under the influence of the Mongols, in what was referred to as the "yoke" of Tartar rule, for more than 200 years Russia absorbed their culture while seeking to become independent from them.

Following the Battle of Kulikovo, conflict between the Grand Duchy of Moscow and the Kipchak Khanate continued. Out of this discord, it was the Grand Duchy which gradually increased its influence and became the nucleus of

オスマン帝国の拡大がロシアとの確執への
導火線となった

　当時のヨーロッパ列強の人々が、遠く戦国時代末期の日本にまで到達したことは、それまで東西交流の要となっていた中央アジアを核としたシルクロードの交易が廃れることを意味します。

　それは、中央アジアが震源地となっていた世界のパワーバランスの変遷の場が、より広範な海洋へと移行したことを意味します。

　中央アジアで産声をあげたオスマン帝国は、自らがシルクロードの西側を傘下に入れたことから、西欧世界を海へと押し出したのです。

　オスマン帝国も積極的に海洋での支配権を模索します。帝国の勢力拡大に貢献したスレイマン1世の死後まもない1571年に、地中海に進出したオスマン帝国の艦隊は、スペインの無敵艦隊と戦います。しかしこれには、大敗を喫してしまいます。レパントの海戦と呼ばれるものです。

　オスマン帝国は、その他の地域への進出にも積極的でした。

　彼らはインド洋から東南アジアにも目を向けます。例えば1569年にはポルトガルが支配していたマラッカを脅威に陥れたこともありました。

　オスマン帝国はその後も、長い間黒海沿岸から地中海東部での制海権をもち、イタリアの都市国家が持っていた既得権も奪ってゆきます。特に黒海から北にかけては、もともとモンゴル帝国の影響の残っていた場所ですが、オスマン帝国はそんなモンゴルの残滓となる国々を滅ぼして勢力を拡大したのです。

　そして、オスマン帝国はこの北方への勢力の拡大によって、ロシア世界と隣人になったのです。

　当時、ロシアは200年以上にわたって「タタールの軛」といわれるモンゴルの支配下におかれながら、その文明を吸収しつつ自立しようともがいていました。

　あのクリコヴォの戦い以来、モスクワ大公国とキプチャク・ハン国との確執が続きます。その確執の中から勢力を拡大し、次第にロシアの核となりつつあったモスクワ大公国は、イヴァン3世の時代に、「タ

時代
16, 17世紀
イスラム近世

地域
トルコ・ロシア

分類
政治【対立】

キーワード
シルクロードの衰退・オスマン帝国の海洋進出・ロシアの発展・ロシアとオスマン帝国の緊張

Russia. In the period of Ivan III, the Grand Duchy managed to cast off the yoke of Tartar rule, and, by merging with the Novgorodian Rus' to the north, created the archetype of the Russian world. This occurred in the final years of the 15th century.

Ivan III married Sophia, the niece of the last Emperor of the Eastern Roman Empire and declared himself to be the successor to the Roman Empire. This formed in Eastern Europe and was the same type of relationship that existed between the Holy See and the Holy Roman Empire. From that point onward, Russia reigned as the guardian of the Orthodox Church. Even in the present day, in every part of Russia, one finds Orthodox Church facilities and religious activities still being carried out.

As one can see from this outline of events, there were very complex and tense relations between the Ottoman Empire, which attempted to advance into territories north of the Black Sea, and the Grand Duchy of Moscow, which was in the process of unifying Russia centered around Moscow. For a long time to come, the Russian Empire would be the greatest rival of the Ottoman Empire.

092 The growth of the Ottoman Empire created the backdrop for contemporary international politics

Out of the tension and discord that developed between Russia and the Ottoman Empire, the southern region of Eastern Europe became the epicenter of friction in world affairs. Particularly after the 18th century, as the Russian Empire developed and the Ottoman Empire declined in inverse proportion, they confronted each other vigorously over rights and interests around the Black Sea.

One can find one source of tension between Slav and Islamic societies in modern and contemporary history by looking back to the 15th century.

International politics are complex.

When we look at the relationship between Slav and Islamic societies as one axis, we realize that there are a number of similar axes of conflict in Europe. When we observe relations between France and Germany, we count numerous times they fought each other and shed blood before and during World War II. We can see that the focal point of that relationship was the friction between the French

タールの軛」を克服し、北にあったノヴゴロド公国を併合して、ロシア世界の原型を作り上げました。15世紀終盤のことでした。

イヴァン3世は、ソフィアという東ローマ帝国最後の皇帝の姪と結婚し、自らをローマ帝国の後継者であると宣言します。ローマ教皇庁と神聖ローマ帝国と同様な関係が、東ヨーロッパでも成立したのでした。以後、ロシアは正教会の守護者として君臨することになるのです。今でもロシアには津々浦々に正教会の施設があり、宗教活動を行っています。

イヴァン3世
Ivan III

この図式からも見えてくるように、黒海以北へ進出をはかるオスマン帝国と、モスクワを核にロシア世界をまとめつつあったモスクワ公国との間には、微妙な緊張関係がありました。その後長年にわたって、ロシア帝国はオスマン帝国の最大のライバルになるのです。

オスマン帝国の成長が、現代の国際政治の背景を生み出した

ロシアとオスマン帝国との緊張と確執により、東ヨーロッパ南部は国際情勢の摩擦の震源地となってゆきます。特に18世紀以降、ロシア帝国が成長し、それに反比例するかのようにオスマン帝国が衰亡へと向かいだしたとき、両者は黒海での権益をめぐり激しく対立しました。

近現代史の緊張の一つの核であるスラブ社会とイスラム社会との対立の原点は、このように15世紀にまでさかのぼることができるのです。
　国際政治には微妙なところがあります。
　スラブ社会とイスラム社会との対立という一つの軸が見えてきたとき、ヨーロッパには同様の対立軸がいくつもあったことに気付かされます。第二次世界大戦まで、何度となく戦い、血を流してきたフランスとドイツとの対立軸を見ると、その原点には神聖ローマ帝国とその守護者であったハプスブルク家と、その勢力に挟まれていたフランス

時代
16世紀以降
欧州近世

地域
ヨーロッパ

分類
対立【政治】

キーワード
オスマン帝国の興亡・国、民族の対立の構図・対立のねじれ

monarchy and the House of Habsburg and the Holy Roman Empire which it protected.

The underlying cause of antagonism behind the fierce conflict that broke out between England and France in later years over the acquisition of colonies around the world was none other than the conflict between the two states during the Hundred Years' War.

It is said that "the enemy of my enemy is my friend," and indeed, such things are frequent in the European world. In Western Europe, France, which was in conflict with the Habsburg family, who ruled the Holy Roman Empire and Spain, had a close relationship with the Ottoman Empire, which exerted military pressure on Vienna, the stronghold of the Habsburgs.

Actually, the Ottoman Empire commenced a lenient policy including such things as recognizing extraterritoriality for French citizens within the empire. The delicate diplomatic relationship that emerged in Europe between the Ottoman Empire and the Kingdom of France had a lasting impact on the diplomatic strategies of the great powers in the 20th century.

Further, when one observes the current international situation, where the Middle East is of such significance, one can see just how deeply related the Ottoman Empire is. It expanded its influence into what is present-day Syria, Iraq, Egypt, and North Africa, areas which it ruled for a long period. The Mamluk Sultanate in Egypt perished in 1517, which meant that a monarchy of Turkic peoples came under the control of Arabic peoples. The Islamic holy sites of Mecca and Medina came under the control of the Ottoman Empire. In name and reality, the Ottoman Empire became an alliance of Islamic societies.

Circumstances in Eastern Europe were the same. As if responding to the collapse of the Eastern Roman Empire in 1453, the entire Balkan Peninsula, including Greece, and the entirety of Eastern Europe, came under the control of the Ottomans.

The place where Europeans could invest without being threatened by this empire from eastern Europe was the New World. Further, there was the maritime trade route from the New World across the Pacific to consider.

王室との対立が見えてきます。

　一方、イギリスとフランスとは後年世界での植民地の獲得をめぐり
激しく対立しますが、その対立意識の遠因は、中世のフランスとイギ
リスとの百年戦争に至るねじれの関係にあったことはいうまでもあり
ません。
　敵の敵は味方といいますが、ヨーロッパ世界ではまさにそうしたこ
とが頻繁におきています。西ヨーロッパで、神聖ローマ帝国やスペイ
ンを支配するハプスブルク家と対立していたフランスは、逆にそんな
ハプスブルク家の拠点であったウィーンに対して軍事的な圧力をかけ
るオスマン帝国とは親密だったのです。
　実際、オスマン帝国は、フランス人の帝国内での治外法権を認める
などの寛容な政策に終始しました。このヨーロッパでの微妙な外交関
係が生み出したオスマン帝国とフランス王国との関係は、そのまま20
世紀の列強の外交戦略にも影響を与えてゆくのでした。

　そして、現在の国際情勢を見てゆく上で欠かせない中東にも、オス
マン帝国は深く関係します。オスマン帝国は現在のシリアやイラク、
そしてエジプトから北アフリカへと勢力を拡大し、これらの地域を長
期間支配していたのです。エジプトにあったマムルーク朝が滅びたの
は1517年のことでした。このことは、トルコ系の民族王朝が、アラブ
系の人々を支配下においたことになります。メッカやメディナといっ
たイスラム教の聖地も、オスマン帝国の管理下におかれ、名実ともに
オスマン帝国がイスラム社会の盟主となったのです。
　状況は東ヨーロッパも同様です。1453年の東ローマ帝国の滅亡と呼
応するように、ギリシアを含むバルカン半島一帯、さらに東ヨーロッ
パ一円もオスマン帝国に支配されます。

　ヨーロッパの人々がこうした東からの脅威を受けずに投資できた場
所が新大陸であり、さらにそこからアジアへと向かう太平洋航路だっ
たのです。

093 Both the Ottoman Empire and the Mughal Empire were religiously tolerant

In its administration, the Ottoman Empire did not exert excessive pressure in terms of religion. In recent years, as European society has developed and came into conflict with the countries that were once part of the Ottoman Empire, it has come to seem as if that empire was a regressive, barbaric state, but that is nothing more than a prejudice cultivated in European society of the present day.

While the Ottoman Empire was an autocracy with a sultan at the top reigning in similar fashion to an emperor, it did establish a hierarchical system of local government and within its territories, believers in Christianity and Judaism were permitted to live alongside followers of Islam. These non-Muslims formed a special elite infantry called the Janissaries, who served as the sultan's standing army alongside the tribal cavalry that supported the empire. the members who were levied to form these infantry units were descendants of Christians in the realm who had converted to Islam. Further, there were also instances in which the knights of a conquered territory were reorganized and elevated to a military force within the cavalry.

In this way the empire was successful in inducting non-Muslims, and in the latter half of the 17th century, the domains of the Ottoman Empire remained as large as the Eastern Roman Empire was at its peak. This happened around the same time that Japan entered the Genroku period, which was the height of the Tokugawa Shogunate.

While the Middle East and the Islamic world were under the influence of the Ottoman Empire, in India another Islamic monarch was reigning over the Mughal Empire.

In 1556 under the third monarch Emperor Akbar, the empire entered a period of stability.

At that time various religions were appearing in India. Preaching a salvation that extended beyond the caste system, Nanak founded Sikhism slightly before Akbar took the throne.

Akbar is recognized for being aware of the diversity within Indian society, for adopting a policy of appeasement toward Hinduism, and for bringing the state together.

Government suppression of religion not only leads to social unrest but it also

オスマン帝国とムガル帝国はともに宗教に寛容だった

オスマン帝国は、その統治において、宗教を厳しく弾圧したわけではありません。近年、ヨーロッパ社会が成長し、オスマン帝国と対立し、それを圧迫するようになると、あたかもオスマン帝国が文明に逆行した野蛮な国家だったというイメージが広がりますが、これはあくまでも、近代ヨーロッパ社会に育まれた偏見にすぎません。

オスマン帝国は、皇帝にあたるスルタンを頂点とした専制君主国家ではあるものの、郡県制度を設け、領土内ではイスラム教徒とキリスト教徒、そしてユダヤ教徒などとの共存を認めたのです。彼らは、帝国を支える騎士団と共に、スルタンの常備軍としてイェニチェリという特殊な歩兵隊を組織します。構成員は領土内のキリスト教の子弟を徴発したものでした。また、征服された地域の騎士をも登用し軍事力として再編成した事例も多くありました。

時代
16, 17世紀
イスラム近世

地域
中東・インド

分類
宗教【政治】

キーワード
オスマン帝国とムガル帝国・イスラム国家の宗教政策・多様な宗教国家・宗教弾圧と衰退

こうした非イスラム教徒の導入にも成功し、17世紀後半にはオスマン帝国の領土は、東ローマ帝国の最盛期の版図をしのぐほどになったのです。それは、ちょうど日本が徳川幕府の最盛期である元禄時代に入った頃のことでした。

中東や東ヨーロッパのイスラム世界がオスマン帝国の影響下にあったとき、インドではムガル王朝がもう一つのイスラム教の盟主として君臨していました。

1556年に王位についた3代目の皇帝アクバルのとき、ムガル朝は安定期に向かいます。

当時、インドでは多彩な宗教が生まれています。カースト制を超越した人々の救済を説いたナーナクによってシーク教が成立したのも、アクバル帝が即位した少し前のことでした。

アクバルはそうした多様なインド社会を意識し、ヒンドゥー教との融和政策をとり、国家をまとめた皇帝としても知られています。

国家による宗教の弾圧は、社会不安のみならず、国家そのものの基

weakens the foundations of the state itself. During the reign of Emperor Akbar, vigorous religious activities in India laid the foundation for the diverse Indian society we see today. The reigns of Akbar and Shah Jahan, who followed him, were the golden age of the Mughal Empire. The Taj Mahal which Shah Jahan had built as a mausoleum in memory of his wife is beyond question symbolic of the prosperity of that era.

In both the Ottoman and Mughal Empires, decline came with the mistaken treatment of their respective religions and diverse ethnic groups, which incited discord within their territories. Especially within the Mughal Empire, under Aurangzeb, who succeeded Shah Jahan as emperor, that distortion began to appear. Aurangzeb promoted the supremacy of Islam and suppressed Hinduism, and it was this that divided the state. One might even say that he was the emperor who gave rise to the strife that has divided present-day India and Pakistan. It was during the late 17th century, precisely when the Ottoman Empire was at its peak, that the foundation of the Indian empire began to tremble.

094 When seen from the perspective of Asia Minor, a different view of modern history emerges

It is true that contemporary world history has predominantly revolved around Europe and the West.

However, if we change our point of view slightly, seeing world history from the perspective of the Ottoman Empire, we can see even more perceptively the process by which history led to the present.

The Ottoman Empire is the root of present-day Middle Eastern affairs. This is because the Middle East was controlled by the Ottoman Empire and was administered by Arabic people. In later years when the strong Western powers intruded upon the vested interests of the Ottoman Empire, it created the complex, unstable political situation that we see in the Middle East today.

In addition, the Ottoman Empire besieged Vienna twice, in 1529 and 1683, threatening certain territories, especially those ruled by the Habsburgs. This made the Ottoman Empire's rule in Eastern Europe especially complicated. Toward the

盤を脆弱にします。アクバル帝の時代、イン
ドでは活発な宗教活動によって、現在の多様
なインド社会の原点ができあがったのでした。
彼と、その後を継いだシャー・ジャハン帝の
時代が、ムガル朝の最盛期でした。シャー・ジャ
ハンが妃の墓として建立したタージ・マハル
は、当時の繁栄を象徴する建築物であること
はいうまでもありません。

タージ・マハル
The Taj Mahal

　オスマン帝国もムガル朝も、その衰亡期に
宗教や多様な民族への対応を誤り、領土内での混乱を煽りました。特に、
ムガル朝の場合、シャー・ジャハンの後を継いだアウラングゼーブ帝
のときに、そんな歪みがでてきました。アウラングゼーブがイスラム
至上主義をもって、ヒンドゥー教を弾圧したことが、国家の分断を招
いたのです。彼は現在のインドとパキスタンとの確執の導火線をつくっ
た皇帝ともいえるのです。17世紀後半、まさにオスマン帝国がその絶
頂にあった時代、インドでは大国の礎が揺らぎ始めていたのです。

小アジアから近代史を見れば異なる絵が
見えてくる

　近現代の世界史は、確かに欧米を中心に動いてきました。

　しかし、ここでちょっと視点を変え、オスマン帝国を世界史の中心
においてみると、現代に至る歴史の過程がさらによく見えてきます。

　オスマン帝国は、現在の中東問題のルーツとなりました。というの
も中東地域をオスマン帝国が支配し、アラブ人を統治したこと。そう
したオスマン帝国の利権に後年西欧列強が割り込んできたことが、中
東での複雑で不安定な政治情勢を作っていったからです。

　また、オスマン帝国は、1529年と1683年の二度にわたりウィーンを
包囲するなど、特にハプスブルク家の支配する地域の脅威となりまし
た。これは、オスマン帝国の支配する東ヨーロッパの事情を複雑にし

時代
16, 17世紀
イスラム近世

地域
トルコ

分類
政治【戦争】

キーワード
中東問題、バルカン問題
の原点・トルコ周辺の強
国・西欧とオスマン帝国
の複雑な関係

end of the 20th century, a large number of Bosnian Muslims suffered persecution at the hands of Serbian forces. The epicenter of the confrontation between followers of Islam and followers of Christianity in Eastern Europe was this territory under the control of the Ottomans.

The same is true of the situation in Russia. When Russia became a powerful country, in order to maintain its military might, it was essential to expand its influence from the Black Sea to the Mediterranean. It was the Ottoman Empire that became an obstacle to Russia's strategy for southward expansion. As a result, Russia and the Ottoman Empire engaged in hostilities repeatedly, with repercussions in later years across the Far East.

Another target of the Russian measures to extend farther south, which were obstructed by the Ottoman Empire, was the seas of the Far East. This also led to the Russo-Japanese War at the beginning of the 20th century. Japan, albeit indirectly, entered the network of Western diplomatic strategies that viewed the Ottoman Empire as a focal point, and this had a significant impact on Japan's contemporary history.

Looking at the East, on the side of the Ottoman Empire was the Mughal Empire in India, and Islam began to spill forth from both of these major powers and penetrate Indonesia and Malaysia. Along with the Middle East, the political situation in Southeast Asia was greatly influenced by followers of Islam.

The history of the region from present-day Western Europe to the Middle East is a repetition of "hot wars" and "cold wars" between Ottoman control and the major European powers who sought to overthrow it. When the Ottoman Empire and the Mughal Empire went into decline, it was the Western powers that penetrated the grooves in the cracks, enjoying the rights and interests of those areas.

In the 17th century, for the newly emerging country of England, the Ottoman Empire was a remote entity. However, France was already intent on checking the House of Habsburg, so it approached the Ottoman Empire. In the era of Ivan IV, who succeeded Ivan III and is known as Ivan the Terrible, Russia constructed a centralized government and solidified its base for developing into a powerful state. It put pressure on the residue of Mongolian control in Crimea by pressuring the Crimean Khanate, which was allied with the Ottoman Empire.

The world commenced complicated strategies for dealing with the Ottoman Empire.

ました。20世紀の終わり頃、ボスニア系のイスラム教徒がセルビア人勢力に大量に迫害されるという事件がおきました。こうしたイスラム教と、キリスト教との東ヨーロッパでの対立の震源地も、旧オスマン帝国の支配地でおきたのです。

ロシア情勢も同様です。ロシアが強国になり、その軍事力を維持するためには、黒海から地中海に至る海への勢力拡大が必須でした。このロシアの南下政策の壁になったのがオスマン帝国でした。したがって、ロシアとオスマン帝国とは何度も戦火を交えますが、その影響は後年極東にも影を落とします。

オスマン帝国に阻まれたロシアの南下政策のもう一つのターゲットが極東の海だったのです。これが20世紀初頭の日露戦争の原因にもなりました。日本が間接的とはいえ、オスマン帝国を視点に据えた西欧の外交戦略のネットワークの中に入っていったことが、日本の近現代史に大きな影響を与えたのです。

東を見れば、オスマン帝国の横にインドのムガル王朝があり、さらにこの2大勢力から溢れ出るように、イスラム教はインドネシアやマレーシアに浸透してゆきます。中東と並んで東南アジアの政治情勢に大きな影響を与えるイスラム教の人々のルーツをここに見ることができるのです。

現代の西欧から中東に至る歴史は、このオスマン帝国の支配と、それを覆そうとしたヨーロッパ列強との「熱い戦争」と「冷たい戦争」との繰り返しでした。オスマン帝国、そしてムガル王朝が衰退したときに、そのひび割れた溝に浸透し、やがてそれらの地域の利権を享受したのが西欧列強だったのです。

17世紀、新興国イギリスにとっては、まだオスマン帝国は遠い存在でした。しかし、フランスはすでにハプスブルク家への牽制の意図から、オスマン帝国に接近していました。ロシアは、イヴァン3世の後を継いだイヴァン雷帝ことイヴァン4世の時代に、中央集権国家を作り上げ、強国に成長する基礎を固めます。クリミアにあったモンゴルの残滓で、オスマン帝国と同盟関係にあるクリミア・ハン国へ圧力をかけたのです。

世界が「オスマン帝国対策」の中で複雑に動き始めたのです。

095 The West comes into contact with Ming China, and people actually experience global interchange

At exactly the same time that the Ottoman Empire began to expand toward the European sphere, the Ming dynasty appeared in China.

The Ming dynasty, established in 1368, like the ancient Qin, reinforced the Great Wall and developed it even further. This was due to the menace posed by the Mongol state of the Northern Yuan in the north. The Ming managed to suppress the external threats and entered a period of stability as a state around the time of the Yongle Emperor, who took power after a fierce struggle for supremacy. The Ming Dynasty developed with Nanjing as its base, but the Yongle Emperor moved the capital to Beijing, renovated the original royal palace, and designated it as the imperial residence. This is the Forbidden City, which remains to this day.

Once again, however, the Ming were exposed to threats from wako, so-called Japanese pirates, and people in the north. In the Tumu Crisis in 1449, they experienced an unprecedented incident in which Ming Emperor Yingzong was taken prisoner by a group of Mongols called the Oirats. This period of Ming history is recalled in the phrase "Mongols to the north and Japanese pirates to the south." It is of particular importance to note here that among the threats along its borders was the invasion of the Korean Peninsula by Toyotomi Hideyoshi. In order to support the Joseon dynasty, which paid tribute to the Ming, the Ming joined in battles with Toyotomi Hideyoshi on two occasions, between 1592 and 1598, when Hideyoshi invaded the peninsula. This put substantial pressure on national finances.

The strength of the Ming weakened in the 17th century, and finally it collapsed when the Li Zicheng Rebellion broke out in 1644. Immediately thereafter, as a result of a full-scale invasion by the Manchus, China once again came under the control of people from the north.

The Ming dynasty was the first government by the Han Chinese in a long time. It was also a time when China and Japan came into contact with the West. By way of Goa, the Portuguese base in Asia, the Italian missionary Matteo Ricci, a member of the Society of Jesus, arrived in China, became naturalized, and devoted himself to propagating Christianity. This occurred right when Toyotomi Hideyoshi invaded the Korean Peninsula.

明に西欧が接触し、人々はグローバルな交流を実感した

　ちょうど、オスマン帝国がヨーロッパ世界に向けて膨張を始めた頃、中国では明王朝が生まれました。

　1368年に建国した明は、古代王朝の秦と同様に万里の長城を補強し、さらに整備しました。それは、北に追いやったモンゴル民族の国家、北元への脅威によるものです。明は、激しい権力闘争の末に政権を奪取した永楽帝の頃に、外憂をなんとか押さえ込み、国家として安定期に入ります。南京を拠点として成長した明ですが、永楽帝は北京に遷都し、元の王宮を改修して皇居に定めます。それが今でも残る紫禁城です。

時代
14〜17世紀
中国・日本近世

地域
中国・日本

分類
国家【交流】

キーワード
漢民族の国明の興亡・周辺諸国との対応・西欧世界からのコンタクト・徳川幕府の鎖国政策

　しかし、再び明は倭寇や北からの脅威にさらされます。1449年には土木の変といって、明の皇帝英宗がモンゴル族の一派であるオイラートの捕虜となる前代未聞の事件もおきています。この倭寇や北方の脅威のことを、明では北虜南倭と呼んでいました。中国にとっての辺境の脅威の中でも特筆したいのが、豊臣秀吉の朝鮮半島への進攻です。明に朝貢をしていた李氏朝鮮を支えるために、1592年から98年まで二度にわたって朝鮮半島に侵攻した豊臣秀吉軍と明は交戦し、そのことで国家財政も圧迫されたのです。

　17世紀に入ると明の国力は衰え、ついに1644年におきた李自成の乱によって滅亡します。その直後に満州族の本格的進攻によって、中国は再び北方からの民族に支配されるようになったのでした。

　明は久しぶりの漢民族の王朝です。そして、この時代に日本と同様に明にも西欧からのコンタクトがありました。イタリアからポルトガルのアジアの拠点となったゴアを経由し、明にやってきたイエズス会の宣教師マテオ・リッチが、中国に帰化し、キリスト教の布教に専念したのです。ちょうど豊臣秀吉が朝鮮半島を侵略した頃のことでした。

マテオ・リッチ
Matteo Ricci

Due to the Society of Jesus's activities, the distance between the European world and the Far East narrowed rapidly. In particular, Matteo Ricci showed great respect for local culture and enthusiastically embraced Eastern philosophies, such as Confucianism, gaining acceptance from Chinese society. At the time, the Age of Discovery had occurred, and intellectuals in the West were beginning to get a broader view of the world. On the basis of that knowledge, Matteo Ricci produced a map of the world which is known as *Kunyu Wanguo Quantu*. This map depicted detailed information about the New World and Africa. It marked the beginning of the global sharing of a "worldview" as the knowledge of the world became more widely disseminated.

The influence of this was also felt in Japan. From the Azuchi Momoyama period to the beginning of the Edo period, a large number of Japanese advanced into Southeast Asia, creating areas where Japanese lived and participated in trading activities. There were even cases such as Hasekura Tsunenaga, who traveled as an envoy in the service of the daimyo Date Masamune through Mexico to Spain and Rome.

What threw a wedge in this Japanese participation in global interchange was the Tokugawa Shogunate policy of national seclusion. In the background of this change of policy was the discord between the newly rising European powers England and the Netherlands and the Catholic powers Spain and Portugal.

096 The signing of the Peace of Westphalia brought about a new European order

Let us turn our attention once again to the situation in Europe. From the Reformation onward, discord in Europe split the Holy Roman Empire, and conflicts between feudal lords supporting the Protestants and those supporting the Catholics continued without end. The situation grew especially strained in 1618, when the Emperor of the Holy Roman Empire, Ferdinand II, considered the guardian of the Catholic faith, suppressed the Protestants in Bohemia.

The politics of Central Europe at that time were strongly influenced by confrontations between the House of Habsburg and the rising powers of France

彼らの活動は、西欧世界と極東との距離を急速に縮めます。特にマテオ・リッチは、現地の文化を尊重し、儒教などの東洋思想の受容にも熱心で、中国社会からも歓迎されました。当時、すでに大航海時代を経て、西欧の知識層には世界の全貌が見え始

坤輿万国全図
Kunyu Wanguo Quantu

めていました。『坤輿万国全図』はその知識をもとに、マテオ・リッチが明に紹介した世界地図です。その地図には新大陸やアフリカの詳細も描かれています。「世界観」がグローバルに共有され始めたのです。

この影響を日本も受けることになります。安土桃山時代から江戸時代の初期にかけて、多くの日本人が東南アジア方面に進出し、各地に日本人街を作り、交易を行いました。また、伊達政宗に仕えた支倉常長のように、新大陸を経由してスペイン、そしてローマを訪問した使節もありました。

そうしたグローバルな交流への日本の参入に楔を打ったのが、徳川幕府のいわゆる鎖国政策です。この政策転換の背景にあったのが、ヨーロッパの新興勢力であるイギリスやオランダと旧教国であるスペイン、ポルトガルとの確執だったのです。

ウェストファリア条約の締結がヨーロッパに新たな秩序をもたらした

再び、ヨーロッパ情勢に目を向けます。宗教改革以降、ヨーロッパにおきた混乱は神聖ローマ帝国を分断し、プロテスタントを支持する諸侯と、カトリック派の諸侯との争いが絶え間なく続いていました。特にカトリックの守護神ともいえる神聖ローマ帝国皇帝フェルディナント2世が、1618年にボヘミアでプロテスタントを弾圧した騒乱が拡大した時、事態が緊迫したのです。

当時の中部ヨーロッパの政治は、ハプスブルク家と、その台頭に脅威を抱くフランス、そして新興国として北から勢力を拡大してきたス

時代
**17世紀
欧州近世**

地域
ドイツ

分類
戦争【国際】

キーワード
ヨーロッパ最大の宗教戦争・神聖ローマ帝国の解体・国際法の登場と新しい国際関係

and the expanding, strengthening northern powers of Sweden and Denmark. France was a Catholic country, but in the uprising in Bohemia, it sided with the Protestant forces within the Holy Roman Empire against the Habsburgs.

In addition, Christian IV of Denmark and Gustavus Adolphus of Sweden also entered the fray. The rebellion which erupted in Bohemia developed into a full-scale war between the great powers of Europe. This intermittent conflict later came to be known as the Thirty Years' War.

As a result of the Thirty Years' War, the Holy Roman Empire weakened as an entity and began to disintegrate. Germany also became politically and economically exhausted. This cast a subtle shadow over the Habsburg House, which was the leading power of the Holy Roman Empire.

It is important to recognize that where the previous configuration of European conflicts had been along religious lines, there was now a new factor involved: the power balance between the strong powers. This meant a breakaway from religious control. This disengagement would fundamentally change the history of Europe thereafter.

In 1648 the peace agreement called the Peace of Westphalia was reached to terminate the Thirty Years' War. This accord became the foundation for the order of the European world thereafter. It was the first multilateral peace treaty in history. In the middle of the Thirty Years' War, Spain had attempted to thwart the Netherlands from gaining independence, but in this treaty the Netherlands was officially recognized as an independent country. Ironically, the Netherlands and Spain thereafter remained on good terms. The motivation for this was the threat posed by England and France. And more than anything else, as a result of this treaty, the separate states that had been allied with the Holy Roman Empire achieved individual sovereignty. The empire had in effect become a mere shell of its former self.

From that point onward, too, friction over religious differences led to conflicts throughout Europe. However, following the end of the Thirty Years' War, within the individual states, the active intervention of religion diminished. Religious authority and state authority began to disconnect. And further, Catholicism and Protestantism began to coexist. This is what provided a springboard for the next development in European society.

ウェーデンやデンマークといった北欧の国々との対立に左右されていました。フランスはカトリックの王国ですが、ボヘミアでの反乱ののち、神聖ローマ帝国内のプロテスタント派と組んでハプスブルク家に挑みます。

　また、デンマークのクリスチャン4世、そしてその後はスウェーデン王のグスタフ・アドルフが戦争に介入したのです。こうしてボヘミアで勃発した反乱は、ヨーロッパの列強を交えた大規模な戦争へと発展したのです。これが後に三十年戦争と呼ばれる断続的な戦乱なのです。

　三十年戦争の結果、神聖ローマ帝国という国家自体が求心力を失い、分裂状態に陥ります。そしてドイツは政治的にも経済的にも疲弊してしまいます。このことは、神聖ローマ帝国の盟主でもあったハプスブルク家の影響力にも微妙な影を落とすことになったのです。

　また、以前は旧教対新教という図式で捉えていたヨーロッパの騒乱が、三十年戦争の頃から宗教のみではなく、大国のパワーバランスというもう一つの動機に左右され始めたことも注目すべきです。宗教の支配からの離脱。これはヨーロッパのその後の歴史のあり方を本質的に変えてゆくことになるのです。

　1648年、この三十年戦争を終結させるために、ウェストファリア条約と呼ばれる和平条約が締結されます。この条約は、その後のヨーロッパ世界の秩序の土台となった、史上初の多国間による和平条約です。三十年戦争の最中にはオランダの独立を阻止しようとしていたスペインですが、この条約でオランダは正式に独立国として承認されます。以後、不思議なことに、オランダはスペインと友好関係を維持します。新たなライバル、イギリスやフランスへの脅威がその動機でした。そして、何よりもこの条約で神聖ローマ帝国内の領邦国家がそれぞれ主権を持つことができるようになり、神聖ローマ帝国は事実上形骸化することになるのです。その後も宗教の違いによる摩擦はヨーロッパ各地で火をふきます。

　しかし、国家の中で権力が宗教に介入する事態は三十年戦争以降希少になってゆきました。宗教と国家権力とが分離し始めること。そしてカトリックとプロテスタントとが共存を始めること。これこそが、西欧社会の次の発展への大きなバネとなったのです。

097 The Dutch invested in what became New York

At about the time the Peace of Westphalia was concluded, in the Far East, the Qing yielded the reins of Chinese power to the Ming, and in Japan, following the Shimabara Rebellion, the closing of the country to outsiders brought a period of stability during the Edo period.

A Dutch warship cooperated in the suppression of the Shimabara Rebellion. Those Christians who participated in the rebellion had become followers as a result of the efforts of Portuguese and Spanish missionaries. It is said that these Christian converts found it difficult to grasp why they were bombarded by a ship belonging to the Netherlands, which was supposedly a Christian country.

During the time when the Netherlands sought to gain independence from Spain as a maritime nation, it clashed fiercely with the Catholic powers in various parts of Asia. The Dutch East India Company, with its base in Indonesia, dispossessed Catholic Portugal of Malacca and actively advanced into Asia. Elsewhere, the Dutch joined forces with the Tokugawa Shogunate in expelling Spain and Portugal from Japan. Meanwhile, in the New World, Spain had already placed the southwestern region of North America under its umbrella. The Dutch engaged in frequent hostilities with Spain in the Caribbean and elsewhere, while establishing its own colony in present-day New York.

Manhattan is the center of the world's business activities. The first European to set eyes on this island was an Italian under the employment of the French king named Giovanni da Verrazano, who reached it in 1524. Eighty five years later, in 1609, another explorer guided the sailing ship *Half Moon* into the same waters. His name was Henry Hudson, an Englishman in the employment of the Dutch. The Hudson River, which is named after him, flows on the west side of the island of Manhattan, and he explored the river northward.

Later, in 1624, colonists from the Netherlands came ashore in this new land. They were people who fled to the Netherlands to escape from religious persecution in France. One year later, the first governor-general arrived, and he is sometimes said to have made a deal with local indigenous people for land in Manhattan. The colony came to be named New Amsterdam, and it was only a small settlement on the southernmost tip of Manhattan Island. On the north edge of this settlement, the colonists constructed a wall of stakes to protect it against

オランダ人は、現在のニューヨークに投資をした

ウェストファリア条約が締結された頃、極東では明から清へと政権が交代し、日本は島原の乱から鎖国を経て、江戸時代の安定期へと入っていました。

島原の乱の鎮圧には、オランダの軍艦も協力しました。反乱に参加したキリスト教徒たちは、ポルトガルやスペインの布教活動によって信者となった人々でした。彼らは、キリスト教国のはずのオランダの船がなぜ自分たちを砲撃したのか理解に苦しんだといわれています。

海洋国家としてスペインから独立しようとしていた頃のオランダは、アジア各地でも旧教国と激しく対立していました。オランダ東インド会社は、インドネシアを拠点に、マラッカを旧教国のポルトガルから奪い、積極的にアジアに進出します。日本でも徳川幕府と組んで、スペインやポルトガルを追い出します。一方、新大陸ではすでにスペインが北米南西部までを傘下にいれていました。オランダはカリブ海などでスペインなどと戦闘を繰り返しながら、現在のニューヨークに植民地を拓きます。

世界のビジネスの中心マンハッタン。この島を最初に目にしたヨーロッパ人はフランス王に雇われたイタリア人探検家、ジョヴァンニ・ヴェラッツァーノでした。1524年のことでした。85年後の1609年の春。ハーフムーン号という帆船を操って、この地に現れた探検家がいました。彼の名前はヘンリー・ハドソン。イギリス人でしたが、オランダに雇われて海を渡ってきたのです。マンハッタンの西を流れるハドソン川は、彼が探検をし、北上した川だったのです。

その後、1624年になってこの新天地に、オランダから入植者が上陸します。彼らはフランスでの迫害を逃れてオランダにやってきた人々でした。そして、その1年後に、初代の植民地総督が着任し、マンハッタン島を先住民であるネイティブ・アメリカンと取引したと言われることもあります。植民地の名前はニューアムステルダム。それはマンハッタン島の南端に築かれた小さな入植地だったのです。入植地の北端には、木の杭を使って外敵の侵入を防ぐ壁（ウォール）を作りました。

時代
17世紀
欧州近世

地域
オランダ

分類
交流【経済】

キーワード
オランダの世界進出・オランダの日本貿易独占・ニューヨークの登場・商業国家オランダの発展

attacks by foreign enemies. This wall later became the source of the name Wall Street, which developed into the financial center of the world.

The Netherlands later developed into a mercantile country at a dizzying pace.

In order to promote uninterrupted commercial activity, the Netherlands supported the colonists' freedom of action and encouraged migration. New Amsterdam also welcomed migration and trading activities by Jewish people and people from England and France. The fur of beavers which flourished along the Hudson River sold for high prices for the making of hats, and the fur trade brought many people to Manhattan. One traveler of the time, as he concluded the long voyage to New York, wrote upon approaching the harbor, "The fragrant smell of the land reached us from across the waters. The reflection of the land appeared on the vast water, gradually transforming into a beautiful harbor surrounded by forests. Deep in the mouth of the river was a small hillock on an island." According to one immigrant, that was how Manhattan appeared.

098 The English Revolution was caused by the gentry

Meanwhile, facing the Netherlands across the English Channel, England was divided into two parties at the time of the Thirty Years' War.

During that period people belonging to a social class called the gentry became quite active. Many members of the gentry were prominent figures who had lived in England since the distant past. When England became a Norman state following the Norman Conquest, they acceded to the wishes of the monarchy's noble classes, and from the period of the War of the Roses, they began to enter the English upper class.

Included among the gentry were affluent farmers. Many of these farmers, known as yeomen, were self-employed and liberated from the feudal system of landownership. It is said that they experienced a polarization, where some succeeded as gentry while others faced decline due to the impacts of war and economic fluctuations. In addition, under the influence of the Thirty Years' War and as a result of the religious conflicts between the Church of England and Scotland and Ireland, England in the first half of the 17th century was visited by

それが後年ウォール・ストリートとなり、世界の金融の中心地へと発展してゆくのです。

　オランダは、その後商業国家としてめまぐるしく発展します。

　商業活動を円滑に進めるため、オランダは人々の自由な活動、移動を奨励します。ニューアムステルダムでも、ユダヤ系の人々やイギリスやフランスからの移住者も商業に勤しんでいました。ハドソン川に生息するビーバーの毛皮が帽子の材料として高く売れたのが、人々がマンハッタンにやってきた理由だったのです。「海の向こうから香ばしい土の香りが漂ってきた」と当時ニューヨークへとはるばる航海をしてきた人が、新大陸に近づいてきたときのことを書き残しています。やがて平たい陸地の影が海原の向こうに浮かんで見え、次第に森に覆われた美しい湾に至ります。その奥の河口にあった小高い丘の島。ある移民の記録によると、それが当時のマンハッタンだったのです。

ハドソン川河口部にあるマンハッタン島
Manhattan Island in the Hudson River estuary

清教徒（ピューリタン）革命は「ジェントリ」によっておこされた

　一方、オランダと海峡を挟んで対峙するイギリスは、三十年戦争の時期に国家を二分する騒乱がおきていました。

　当時のイギリスには、ジェントリという階層に属する人々が活動していました。彼らの多くは、古くからイギリスに住んでいた有力者ですが、ノルマンコンクエストによってイギリスがノルマン人の国家となると、王朝の貴族階級に従い、次第に地方の有力者となり、薔薇戦争の頃から彼らは地方行政を司るイギリス上流階級の仲間入りを始めたのです。

　こうしたジェントリの中には富裕な農民も含まれていました。ヨーマンと呼ばれた彼ら農民の多くは、封建時代の領主制の枠から解放された自営農で、ジェントリとして成功する者と、戦争や経済変動の影響で没落する者との二極分解がおこっていたといわれています。しかも、三十年戦争の影響や、イギリス国教会とスコットランドやアイルランドとの宗教的な対立による内戦などによって、17世紀前半のイギリスは極度の財政難に見舞われていました。

時代
17, 18世紀
欧州近世

地域
イギリス

分類
社会【革命】

キーワード
ヨーマンの格差拡大・イギリスの社会・絶対王政と地方貴族の相克・宗教対立・市民革命

extreme financial troubles.

Following the death of Queen Elizabeth, King James VI of Scotland became king of England too, and he was succeeded by his son, who became Charles I. In passing let us mention that the unification of Scotland and England as the Kingdom of Great Britain formally occurred with the accession of Queen Anne in 1707.

Let us return to the era of James VI and Charles I. Taking the Church of England as their own church, they set forth their right to rule under the theory that came to be known as the divine right of kings. They sought to establish an autocracy which could be called an absolute monarchy. Charles I, in particular, imposed taxes without consulting with Parliament to cope with financial troubles and ended up in conflict with the gentry, who were influential in that legislative body. Parliament passed a bill known as the Petition of Right in 1628 against the arbitrary actions of the monarch, but by dissolving Parliament the following year, the king basically ignored the legislation.

This confrontation between the king and the Parliament, especially the gentry which had a base in the provinces, gradually developed into an armed struggle. The leader who rose to the head of the gentry was Oliver Cromwell.

Cromwell was an ardent Puritan. He excelled as a military strategist. In the end, he defeated the Royalists in 1648. The following year, Charles I was executed, and England transformed into a republican form of government. This change of government is referred to in Japan as the Puritan Revolution, and is known elsewhere as the English Revolution. This revolution was the first of many that would arise between early-modern times and modern times and the first to overthrow monarchal rule and autocracy.

Cromwell became Lord Protector, and he dispatched troops to Ireland, the stronghold of Catholic followers, and to Scotland, stronghold of the Royalists. He cracked down on the resistance with military force. Meanwhile, the gentry who controlled Parliament sought to protect the rights and interests of English overseas trade and in 1651 establish the Navigation Acts, which excluded vessels of other national registrations from England and its colonies. This process in due course led to conflict with the Netherlands, which were rising as a maritime power.

エリザベス女王の死後、スコットランド王ジェームズ6世がイギリス王を兼ね、その子供のチャールズ1世が後を継ぎます。ちなみに、スコットランドとイングランドとが同じ王の元に正式に統一され、大英帝国となったのは1707年、アン女王のときでした。

　話をジェームズ6世とチャールズ1世の時代に戻します。二人の王は、イギリス国教会を自らの教会として、王の権威は神に授かったものという「王権神授説」を唱えました。絶対君主制と呼ばれる専制政治を模索したのです。特にチャールズ1世は議会を無視して課税を行い、財政難に対応しようとしたために、議会に影響力を持つジェントリと対立したのです。1628年には「権利の請願」と呼ばれる、国王の専制体制への抗議が議会で可決されますが、王はそれを無視するかのように、翌年には議会を解散します。

　こうした対立が次第に王と議会、特に地方に地盤を持つジェントリとの武力抗争へと発展します。そんなジェントリの筆頭として台頭したのが、オリバー・クロムウェルだったのです。
　彼は熱心な清教徒、すなわちピューリタンでした。そして彼は卓越した軍略家でもありました。最終的に1648年にクロムウェルは王党派を打ち破り、その翌年にチャールズ1世を処刑、イギリスは共和政に移行したのです。この政変を主に日本では清教徒革命と呼んでいます。清教徒革命は、近世から現代にかけて、王政や専制政治に対して人々が立ち上がり、それを打倒してゆく最初の革命となりました。

　クロムウェルは護国卿となり、カトリック教徒の地盤ともいえるアイルランドや、王党派の地盤でもあったスコットランドなどに派兵し、武力で抵抗勢力を弾圧します。一方、議会を制していたジェントリは、イギリスの対外貿易での権益を守ろうと、1651年にイギリスとその植民地から他国籍の船舶を排除する航海条例を制定します。このことがやがて、海運国として台頭していたオランダとの対立へと繋がったのです。

099 England created a parliamentary cabinet system through the Glorious Revolution

Under the Tokugawa government, Japan established a policy of national seclusion in 1639. During this same general period, a chain of events occurred in Europe, including the end of the Thirty Years' War and the Puritan Revolution in England. From that point onward, Japan was, for close to 200 year, left in the dark about the West becoming the supreme ruler of the outside world.

During this period, the major European powers devoted their energies to overseas trade, actively advancing into Asia and the New World. This policy is known as the mercantile system, and England and the Netherlands were its leading enactors.

The first of the Anglo-Dutch Wars between England and the Netherlands broke out in 1652. Out of a need to oppose the overwhelming superiority of the Dutch in trade between every region of Europe and Asia, England, having transitioned to a republican form of government, enacted the Navigation Acts. On the basis of these regulations, English ships seized Dutch ships that passed along the English seacoast, and this led to warfare.

This conflict continued for two years, and with England gaining the upper hand, the two countries signed a peace treaty in 1654.

In the midst of these circumstances, when Cromwell passed away and the Royalists regained power, the son of Charles I became King Charles II in 1660, and monarchal government was restored. The monarchy and Parliament worked in concert to maintain mercantile policies.

In 1664 a British fleet sailed into New Amsterdam and called upon Peter Stuyvesant, the Dutch governor-general, to surrender the city. Stuyvesant advocated resistance, but placing priority on its international commerce, New Amsterdam capitulated without resistance. This led to the second of the Anglo-Dutch wars. This conflict ended in a reconciliation despite ongoing rivalry, and under that treaty, the Dutch colonies in North America were incorporated into those of the English, and New Amsterdam was renamed New York.

As a result, British rights and interests on the eastern coast of North America expanded, and thereafter, those vested interests would take the form of the thirteen British colonies that would eventually form the foundation of the United States.

イギリスは名誉革命を経て責任内閣制度を
作り上げた

　日本が徳川政権のもと、鎖国政策を確立させたのは1639年のことでした。三十年戦争の終結、イギリスでの清教徒革命など、一連のヨーロッパでの動きは、まさにこの前後におこっています。以後日本は西欧が世界の覇者となるに至る重要な200年を「かやの外」で過ごすことになったのです。

　この時代、ヨーロッパの主要国は海外との交易に力を入れ、アジアや新大陸に積極的に進出します。こうした政策を重商主義政策といい、イギリスやオランダがその先駆けとなったのです。

　1652年にイギリスとオランダとの間に第一次英蘭戦争が勃発します。ヨーロッパ各地からアジアにかけての交易で圧倒的に優位に立っていたオランダに対抗する必要から、共和政に移行したイギリスが航海条例を制定したのです。この条例に基づいて、イギリス沿岸を通るオランダ商船を、イギリスが拿捕し始めたことが戦争の原因となりました。

　2年続いたこの戦争は、イギリスが戦争を有利に進め、1654年には講和条約を結びます。

　こうした状況の中、イギリスでクロムウェルが没すると、王党派が勢力を挽回し、1660年にチャールズ1世の子供がチャールズ2世となり、王政が復活します。王制はイギリス議会と協調する形式をとり、重商主義政策を維持したのです。

　1664年、新大陸のニューアムステルダムにイギリスの艦隊が現れ、オランダの総督ピーター・ストイフェサントへ降伏を勧告します。総督は抗戦を主張しますが、通商を重んずる有力者が戦争を嫌ったことから、ニューアムステルダムは、イギリスに無血開城したのです。これが、第二次英蘭戦争の原因となりました。戦争は拮抗したまま講和となりますが、そのときの条約によって、北米のオランダの植民地はイギリスに編入され、ニューアムステルダムは、ニューヨークと改名されたのでした。

　これで、アメリカ東海岸でのイギリスの権益は拡大し、その後のアメリカ合衆国の母体となる13の植民地が形成されたのでした。

時代
17、18世紀
欧州近世

地域
イギリス

分類
革命【政治】

キーワード
英蘭戦争のイギリス勝利
・王政復古と再革命・王
権の制限と議会の発展・
責任内閣制度の成立

The English Parliament conducted affairs by way of the Tory party, which was composed of Royalists, and the Whig party, which asserted the rights of the Parliament in making decisions. However, after James II succeeded Charles II, when the king sought absolute control, Parliament invited another king from the Netherlands, and eventually James II was forced into exile. This change in political power in 1689 is referred to as the Glorious Revolution, and this bloodless revolution led to the constitutional monarchy that continues to the present. According to the Declaration of Rights (later the Bill of Rights), which was enacted that same year, the monarch's authority was seriously restricted, and it declared that Parliament would be responsible for making the major decisions for the country. In the end, Robert Walpole of the Whig party would, in 1721, become head of the Cabinet, making the responsibility for administration lie not with the monarch but within the Parliament, giving birth to a cabinet system.

100 By looking at the system of taxation, one can understand the form of a state

Americans often refer to "the taxpayers' money" when referring to reforming the way that the government operates. The administration uses the taxpayers' money to provide services as a nation, and the allocation of these funds is approved by the legislature. Of course, it is the citizens who select the legislative representatives. Initially it was only citizens of a special status who possessed the right to vote. Over a period of 300 years, the state has expanded that right to include all citizens.

The system of parliamentary democracy was first codified in the Bill of Rights enacted in England during the Glorious Revolution. This idea was later used as the legal basis for opposition to taxation by England in the British colonies in North America. That is, colonists were not allowed to send representatives to the British Parliament, yet they were required to pay taxes. They were one-sidedly taxed by the mother country. While opposition to taxation led to the American Revolution, the idea of representation found in the original Bill of Rights was passed down through the generations and developed as a starting point by democratic societies as a fundamental part of their system of values.

When the power to collect taxes belongs to a monarch or other rulers, their

イギリス議会は、王党派のトーリー党と、議会の権利を主張するホイッグ党の2大政党によって運営されました。しかし、チャールズ2世のあとを継いだジェームズ2世の時に、王が専制政治を求めたことから、議会がオランダから新しい王を招き、最終的にジェームズ2世は海外に亡命してしまいます。1689年におきたこの政変を名誉革命といい、イギリスはこの無血革命で現在も続く立憲王制を確立したのです。同年に制定された「権利の章典」には、王の権利が厳しく制限され、議会によって国の重要な決議がなされることがうたわれています。やがてイギリスでは、1721年にホイッグ党のウォルポールが首班となる内閣が発足し、王ではなく議会に対して責任をもって行政活動を行う、責任内閣制が誕生したのでした。

税金の制度を見ると、その国家の形態が理解できる

　アメリカ人はよく「納税者のお金」という表現で行政のあり方を正します。行政は国民の税金を使用して国としてサービスをおこない、その税金の使い道を議会が承認するというのが、近代国家の基本的な構造です。もちろん、議員を選ぶのは市民です。当初は参政権を持つ市民は特別な身分の人たちでした。以後300年かけて、国家はその市民の枠を全ての人々に拡大してゆくのです。

　この議会制民主主義の制度を最初に明文化したのが、イギリスで名誉革命のときに制定された「権利の章典」でした。この思想は、後にアメリカにあったイギリスの植民地がイギリスからの課税に対して立ち上がった法的根拠にもなりました。つまり、植民地の人々はイギリス議会に議員を送っていないにもかかわらず、一方的に本国から課税されたのです。この課税への抗議が独立革命へと繋がったように、「権利の章典」の精神は時と共に受け継がれ、現在の民主主義社会の原点となる価値観へと磨かれます。

　税金の徴収権限が王などの権力者に属する場合、戦争や築城など、

時代
17, 18世紀
欧州近世

地域
イギリス・オランダ・アメリカ

分類
政治【経済】

キーワード
議会制民主主義の確立・税制の確立・資本主義の発展・列強の萌芽

actions, such as war and castle-building, unilaterally affect the lives of the people. However, when a cabinet designated by a legislative body whose members are elected by citizens makes use of tax revenues, peoples are able to form their own wealth with greater stability, and citizens are able to enjoy the infrastructure of their country. The country's citizens are not subjects of a lord but are sovereign beings who choose legislators, and who can freely engage in economic activities. the leader in enacting this type of system was England, and it became a dynamic source of power throughout the world thereafter. The prominent figures such as the gentry became financiers, and with that capital, industrial activity was enhanced. In this fashion, Britain began its development as a modern state.

By the end of the 17th century, in terms of industrial strength, Britain surpassed the Netherlands. Interestingly enough, because these two countries each gave free rein to economic activity, even the Dutch became active in investing not only in their own country but also in London.

Meanwhile on the continent, the French monarchy was under the rule of Louis. From the remains of the fragmented Holy Roman Empire, the monarchy of Prussia arose. This structure of co-existence and rivalry between Germany, France, and Britain became the foundation of international politics in the West. Also, previously strong countries such as the Netherlands, Spain, Poland, and Lithuania came to be tossed about between the three aforementioned countries and Russia, which was developing on its own.

The cycles of peace and conflict that began between the great powers in the 17th century over political vested interests would lead to the great tragedy of two world wars in the 20th century. Europe overcame the confrontation between Catholicism and Protestantism, and over a period of 300 years, it brought up its own superpowers, which then competed for dominance.

The great waves of their ambitions spilled forth in Asia, Africa, and the American continents.

権力者によるあらゆる行為が国民の生活に一方的に影響を与えるのです。しかし、国民の選挙による議会によって指名される内閣が税金を使用するなら、人々はより安定して自らの資産を形成でき、国家のインフラも国民が享受できるようになるわけです。国民は王の臣民ではなく、議員を選ぶ主権者として、自由な経済活動ができるようになるのです。こうした制度を先駆けて制定したことが、イギリスがその後世界に向けて発展してゆく原動力となりました。ジェントリなどの有力者が資本家となり、その資本による産業活動が活性化します。こうしてイギリスは近代国家として成長を始めるのです。

　17世紀終盤には、イギリスは経済力においてオランダを凌駕します。面白いことに、この二つの国家は経済活動を自由にしたことから、オランダ人も自国ではなく、ロンドンで積極的な投資活動を行ったのです。

　一方、大陸にはルイ王朝によるフランス王国がありました。また、分裂した神聖ローマ帝国の中からは、プロイセンが王国として台頭してきます。このドイツとフランス、そしてイギリスの共存と対立の構図が、欧米の国際政治の基軸となってゆくのです。そして、オランダやスペイン、ポーランドやリトアニアといったかつての強国は、この3つの大国と、当時東で成長したロシアを交えた西欧列強の政治の駆け引きに翻弄され始めます。

　17世紀からの列強の政治的な利害関係による戦争と平和の繰り返しの向こうにあった大きな悲劇が20世紀の二つの世界大戦でした。ヨーロッパは、カトリックとプロテスタントとの対立を克服し、300年の年月をかけて、自らの国家を超大国へと育て上げようと、覇権を争ったのです。

　その欲望の波をかぶってゆくのがアジアやアフリカであり、初期のアメリカ大陸だったのです。

101 In the first part of early-modern times, there was "Golden Liberty" in Poland

Let us return our attention now to Eastern Europe.

From the 18th century until the last phase of the Cold War in the 20th century, there was incessant foreign intervention in Poland.

Squeezed between the great Eastern European powers of Russia and Prussia, and the Austrian Empire of the Habsburgs in the south, the country suffered repeatedly from territorial fragmentation.

However, even earlier than England, Poland was the first state to introduce a parliamentary democracy. From early times, the northern part of Eastern Europe was a region in which various ethnic groups intermingled, and out of this blend, in the 10th century came the Kingdom of Poland. The Mongol Empire, however, dealt a decisive blow to it. In the 13th century, the Mongol army led by Batu thoroughly destroyed Poland. To achieve a revival, Poland accepted migrants from Germany. Furthermore, Jewish people, who were liable to suffer persecution in Christian countries, migrated in, and as a result of the economic activities of these diverse populations the state was reconstructed.

One example of those of German descent was Copernicus, who set forth the heliocentric theory.

The aristocracy who possessed serfs, like the gentry in England, administered a legislature by which the policies of the country were approved. This assembly was extremely tolerant of religion and ethnic groups, and although the monarch reigned as a symbol of unity, the monarch's powers were quite restricted. This lenient system served Poland afterward as the driving force of its prosperity.

From the Middle Ages onward, Poland and the neighboring Duchy of Lithuania were ruled by the same monarch, and in 1569 the countries merged into the Polish-Lithuanian Commonwealth. From that point onward, a unique situation continued through which the monarchy was not hereditary but was chosen by election. This period was called the period of "Golden Liberty."

Needless to say, this freedom was guaranteed by specific aristocratic families. However, it is also said that groups such as merchants within the citizenry were able to rise into the privileged classes. It is ironic that this "Golden Liberty" was unable to develop into a democratic country like that which exists today or into

近世初期、ポーランドには「黄金の自由」があった

　ここで、東欧に目を向けてみます。

　18世紀から20世紀終盤の冷戦の終結に至るまで、ポーランドは常に他国の干渉下にありました。

　東欧の覇者であるロシアやプロシア、そして南からはハプスブルク家のオーストリア帝国に挟まれ、国家は何度も分裂の憂き目をみたのです。

　しかし、そんなポーランドはイギリスなどよりも早く初期の議会制民主主義を導入した国家でした。東ヨーロッパ北部は古くから様々な民族が交錯する地域で、ポーランド王国もそういった多様な民族の中から10世紀に王国として成長します。しかし、モンゴル帝国がポーランドに決定的な打撃を与えます。13世紀に突如侵入してきたバトゥ率いるモンゴル軍は、ポーランドを徹底的に破壊したのです。この復興のため、ポーランドはドイツからの移民を受け入れました。また、キリスト教国でとかく迫害の対象となったユダヤ系の人々も移住し、多様な人々の経済力によって、国家が再建されたのでした。

　例えば、地動説を唱えたコペルニクスは、ドイツ系の血を引いた人物でした。

　そして、農奴を所有する貴族階級がちょうどイギリスでのジェントリのように議会を運営し、その議会の承認によって国政が運営されたのです。議会は宗派や民族に対しては極めて寛容で、国王は統合の象徴のような存在として君臨はしても、権限は厳しく制限されていました。そうした柔軟な制度がその後のポーランドの繁栄の原動力になりました。

　ポーランドは中世以来隣国のリトアニア公国と共通の王を抱いていましたが、1569年に両国は一緒になり、ポーランド・リトアニア共和国となります。その後、王も世襲ではなく貴族によって選挙で選ばれるという特異な状態が続きます。「黄金の自由」と呼ばれた時代でした。

　もちろん、自由は特定の貴族等に保障されたものでした。しかし、例えば商人などの市民層が特権集団に昇進することもあったといわれています。この「黄金の自由」がさらに現代の民主主義国家、あるいは立憲君主国に進化できず、王を選定する選挙制度が、後年になって

時代
10〜18世紀
欧州中世・近世

地域
ポーランド

分類
国家【社会】

キーワード
東欧の強国ポーランド・多様性と経済力の発展・議会の導入と自由の萌芽・列強による分割

a constitutional monarchy. The system of electing the monarch later evolved into one in which neighboring powers schemed to capture monarchal power and use it for their own interests.

In the 17th century, these powers intervened in the process of selecting the monarchs, and this developed into civil war. Under pressure from Russia and from the conflict with both the Crimean Khanate to the southeast and Sweden over domination in the north, the state gradually grew impoverished. As a result, in the 18th century, Poland was divided among its neighbors, Russia, Prussia, and Austria.

The destiny of Poland was an event symbolic of how the supreme powers of Europe passed through the chaotic period of the 17th century and declined during the power struggles between the newly risen powers.

102 The collapse of the Holy Roman Empire became the driving force for the development of European society

That the Holy Roman Empire became emasculated meant that its authority to serve as the protector of the Roman Catholic Church was destroyed.

These circumstances, which evolved in the 17th century, were of great significance.

Prior to this, it was possible for religion to rule over the law. Ultimately, it was Roman Catholic discipline that imposed restraints on and delivered judgments on the people. However, when the secular power which guaranteed that authority broke apart, religion began to fall under the control of the state, and further, fall under the control of the law.

That was not all. Due to the Reformation, people were able to detach religious discipline from secular legal discipline. This meant that in the secular world, it became possible to promote reason and rationality. Through the promotion of science and industry, people became free to pursue secular well-being. Further, religious authority resided in the mind and heart of the individual. To have social influence without reigning made it possible for the individual self to be free from social restraints and to be independent. This change ultimately made the Industrial Revolution possible, and that in turn altered world history. It also

王権の奪取を目論む周辺列強に利用されたことは皮肉な成り行きでした。

　17世紀には列強が王の選挙に干渉し、それが内戦にも発展します。さらに、ロシアの圧力や南東部でのクリミア・ハン国との戦い、北方での覇権をめぐるスウェーデンとの戦いなどを経て、国家は次第に疲弊していったのです。その結果、ポーランドは18世紀に隣国のロシア、プロイセン、そしてオーストリアによって分割されてしまいます。

　ポーランドの運命は、旧時代の西欧の覇者が17世紀の混乱期を経て、新たに登場した列強による覇権争いの中で衰亡していったことを象徴する出来事だったのです。

神聖ローマ帝国の崩壊がヨーロッパ社会の発展の原動力になった

　神聖ローマ帝国が形骸化したことは、ローマカトリックの守護神となりうる権威が崩壊したことを意味しています。
　17世紀ヨーロッパでおきた、この状況は極めて大切です。

　それ以前は、宗教が法の上に君臨することが可能でした。ローマカトリックの規律こそが最終的に人を拘束でき、裁くこともできたのです。しかし、その権威を保証していた世俗の権力が崩壊したことで、宗教は国家の権威の下、さらには法の権威の下に位置するようになり始めたのです。
　それだけではありません。宗教改革の影響で、人々は心の中の宗教的な規律と、世俗の法的規律とを分離させることができたのです。これは、世俗の世界において合理主義を推し進めることを可能にしたことを意味します。科学や産業の振興を通して世俗の幸福を追求する自由を人々は獲得したのです。また、宗教の権威が個人の心の中に宿り、社会上の権威として君臨しないことは、自我、個人の社会的な束縛からの自立も可能にします。この変化が、やがて世界の歴史を変革する産業革命を可能にし、アメリカなどでの富の追求を背後から支援する

時代
17, 18世紀
欧州近世

地域
西ヨーロッパ

分類
社会【宗教】

キーワード
キリスト教権力の衰退・政教分離の始まり・近代的自我の目覚め・個人的自由の始まり

supported, behind the scenes, the pursuit of wealth in places such as the Americas.

The Discourse on Method, a work by the philosopher René Descartes, who was active in the 17th century in France and in his later years in Sweden, contains the famous passage "I think, therefore I am." It is precisely this consciousness of the self that became the driving force behind the social revolution that occurred in Europe. The activity that aimed at the creation of a society which guaranteed the rights of freedom, equality, and the pursuit of happiness became the foundation for the social revolution for everything that began with the English Revolution and continued through the American War of Independence and the French Revolution.

Meanwhile, in another world, this separation of religion and society did not proceed. In many Islamic countries, religious authority continued to supersede secular authority. In East Asia, although one cannot say that secular power and religion were always inseparable, up until the 20th century, the authority of the emperor of monarch continued to be the authoritative standard of the respective societies. This became a negative force in terms of the cultivation of industry, and the enhancing of the social system.

And yet a certain problem remains. The awareness of the self that began in the West took at least another 200 years before it developed to the point where it evolved a corollary concept of respecting other selves. It took that long to grasp the fact that one's own happiness is dependent upon treating the happiness of others as being of equal value. Until that occurred, it was not taken as problematic to oppress others in the pursuit of prosperity for one's own society, and in particularly disturbing cases, to exploit others as slaves. Reforms came later, but even now that issue remains in the form of economic disparity and social discrimination. Needless to say, humankind is still confronting these problems.

After the 17th century, Western society, armed with a sense of self-awareness, began to expand into Asia and Africa under the guise of commercial activities, without invoking the name of God as Spain and others had done in the past.

ことになります。

　17世紀にフランスで、晩年はスウェーデンで活動した哲学者
デカルトの名著、『方法序説』の中に記された、「我思う、ゆえ
に我あり」という言葉はあまりにも有名ですが、こうした自我
の自覚こそが、その後の西欧の社会変革の原動力となりました。
自由と平等、人々が幸福を追求する権利が保証される社会づく
りを目指した活動が、イギリスの清教徒革命に始まり、アメリ
カの独立革命やフランス革命など、あらゆる社会変革の土台と
なったのです。

フランス・ハルス『ルネ・デカルト
の肖像』
Frans Hals —*Portrait of René
Descartes*

　一方、他の世界ではこの宗教と社会との分離が進みませんでした。
イスラム社会においては、多くの国で宗教的権威が世俗の権威を凌駕
し続けました。東アジアでは、宗教と常に一体ではないとはいえ、20
世紀に至るまで皇帝や王の権威が社会規範そのものの権威であり続け
ました。これが産業の育成、社会制度の整備にとって負のベクトルと
なったのです。

　ただし、ここに課題が残ります。それは、西欧で始まった自我の自
覚が、他の自我の尊重という概念に発展してゆくのに、さらに200年
以上の年月がかかったことです。自らの幸福と他者の幸福とを同等の
価値の上におく必要性に人類が気付き、自己の社会の繁栄のために他
者を支配し、ひどいときには奴隷として酷使したりしてきた行為にメ
スが入ったのはずっと後年のことだったのです。そして、この課題は
現在でもまだ、格差の問題や差別の問題として、人類に問いかけられ
ていることはいうまでもありません。

　17世紀以降、自我の自覚という武器を手にした西欧社会は、商業行
為の名の下に、過去のスペインなどのように神の名前を振りかざすこ
となく、アジアやアフリカに進出を始めたのです。

Discord and political maneuvering in the royal houses led to a succession of conflicts in Europe

As the Holy Roman Empire split into pieces, major changes occurred in the circumstances surrounding the electoral princes who selected the emperor of the Holy Roman Empire.

Among the changes, the House of Hohenzollern, which was the Elector of Bandenburg ruling eastern Germany, at the time of Frederick I was allowed to take the throne as a reward for collaborating with the Habsburgs. In the western extremity of Russia, Konigsberg—present-day Kaliningrad—which merged with the State of the Teutonic Order during the Crusades, unified the Kingdom of Prussia. The House of Habsburg, while maintaining its influence within the Holy Roman Empire, had to give tacit approval to this move in order to counter the rapid rise of France.

During the late 17th century to the early 18th century, France was in the era of Louis XIV.

The Bourbon dynasty in France overcame the conflicts between the Protestants and the Catholics through the strategy of Cardinal Richelieu, councilor to the previous monarch, Louis XIII. Richelieu is noted in history as the one who established the foundation of French authority. But it was King Louis XIV, building upon that foundation, who developed France into a first-rank country.

As we have noted repeatedly, the royal families of Europe were always aware of discord between countries, and at the same time they maintained complex networks of kinship relations with strategic intentions. Louis XIV was no exception, and his queen came from the Spanish Habsburgs. This meant that if the royal house of Spain produced no heir, both Austria and France would have the right to succeed to the throne. As things turned out, Spain's King Carlos II had no children.

ルイ 14 世
Louis XIV

王家の確執と政治的駆け引きが西欧での紛争の連鎖をつくった

　神聖ローマ帝国が分断されてゆく中で、もともと神聖ローマ帝国の皇帝を選定する権利のあった選帝侯の状況も大きく変化します。

　中でも、東部ドイツを領有するブランデンブルク選帝侯であったホーエンツォレルン家は、フリードリッヒ1世のときに、ハプスブルク家との協調の見返りに、王を名乗ることを許されます。そして、現在のロシア西端ケーニヒスベルク（現在のカリーニングラード）にあって、十字軍の時代からドイツ騎士団領であったプロイセンを合併させ、プロイセン王国としてまとめます。ハプスブルク家は、神聖ローマ帝国内に自らの影響力を維持しながら、当時急成長していたフランスと対抗しなければならず、こうした動きを黙認します。

　17世紀後半から18世紀初頭にかけてのフランスは、ルイ14世の時代です。

　フランスのブルボン王朝は、プロテスタントとカトリックとの確執を先王のルイ13世の宰相として知られるリシュリューの軍略で乗り越えます。リシュリューは、フランスの覇権の基礎を築いた宰相として歴史に名を残しますが、ルイ14世は、リシュリューの築いた地盤の上に立って、フランスを一大強国として成長させたのです。

　何度か触れてきたように、ヨーロッパの王室は国家同士の確執を常に意識しながら、同時に政略上の思惑もあって複雑な縁戚関係を持っていました。ルイ14世も例外ではなく、王妃はスペインのハプスブルク家出身でした。これは、スペインの王家にもし跡継ぎが絶えたときは、オーストリアとフランスの双方が王位継承権を持てることを意味します。そして実際にスペイン王のカルロス2世には子供がなかったのです。

1668年のヴェルサイユ宮殿。最初はルイ13世の狩猟の館として建てられ、ルイ14世が1661年からおよそ四半世紀を費やして宮殿と庭園を完成させた。

The Palace of Versailles in 1668. Originally built as a hunting lodge for Louis XIII, it took Louis XIV almost a quarter of a century from 1661 to complete the palace and gardens.

時代
17, 18世紀
欧州近世

地域
西ヨーロッパ

分類
国際【戦争】

キーワード
プロイセンとハプスブルク家の発展・フランスの国力充実・絶対王政下の戦争・列強の勢力均衡

At that time, France had formidable power, and King Louis XIV ruled with such absolute power that he became known as the Sun King. After the Netherlands became independent from Spain, Louis attempted to extend France's influence into present-day Belgium, which was seen as a threat by not only the Habsburgs but also the Netherlands. Further, expansion by France was surely undesirable to neighboring England. This friction eventually developed into the War of the Spanish Succession in 1701. This war inevitably turned into a conflict that involved France and England within the New World, and even the indigenous peoples of the New World became caught up in the fighting between the English and the Spanish. As a result of the war, the Peace of Utrecht led to the Spanish throne being inherited by the French side, establishing the Bourbon dynasty that continues to this day.

In contrast with East Asia, where China served as a single nucleus around which significant events tended to occur, in Western Europe frequent wars broke out as a result of conflicts over succession and over political and economic interests between various monarchies.

In due course, as a result of these countries seeking rights and interests overseas, the conflicts that were initiated in Europe eventually spilled over into the colonies of the respective European powers, with repercussions felt in all parts of the world. Let us just note here that the two world wars of the 20th century were extensions of these conflicts.

104 In the 17th century, Russia joined the world powers

At about the time Europe was experiencing the Thirty Years' War and the War of the Spanish Succession, in the East, Russia was expanding its territories and becoming a major power too.

As has already been mentioned, Ivan III had united Russia into a single country. Under his son Ivan IV, the Grand Duchy of Moscow grew rapidly as a state. This occurred during the 16th century.

Ivan IV first occupied the Mongol-derived countries who posed a threat in the east. He then turned his attention to oppose threats from the northwest, first Poland and Lithuania, who were ruled by the same monarch, and then the

当時、フランスは国力が充実し、ルイ14世は太陽王といわれたほど
に絶対君主として君臨していました。ルイ14世は、もともとオランダ
が独立した後もスペインの影響下にあった現在のベルギーへも勢力を
拡大しようとします。これはハプスブルク家のみならず、オランダか
ら見ても脅威です。また、フランスの伸長は隣国イギリスから見ても
望むところではないはずです。この摩擦が1701年にスペイン継承戦争
へと発展したのでした。スペイン継承戦争は、新大陸でもフランスと
イギリス、さらにイギリスとスペインの間で先住民族をも巻き込んだ
戦争に発展します。戦争の結果、ユトレヒト条約によって、スペイン
王家はフランス側に継承され、ブルボン王朝として現在に至ります。

　東アジアが中国という一つの核を中心に動いていたこととは対照的
に、西欧は王国同士の血縁や政治的経済的な利害の対立による戦争が
頻発します。

　やがて、西欧が利権を求め海外に影響力を及ぼすに従って、そうし
た紛争がそれぞれの国の植民地同士の戦争へと拡大し、世界各地に飛
び火をするようになるのです。その延長に、20世紀の二つの世界大戦
があったことを、ここで前もって記しておきます。

17世紀にロシアが列強の仲間入りをした

　ヨーロッパが三十年戦争やスペイン継承戦争などを経験している頃、
東ではロシアが国土を拡大し大国として膨張を始めました。

　すでに解説したように、ロシアを一つの国家として統一したイヴァ
ン3世、そしてその子供のイヴァン4世の時代に、彼らの治めるモスク
ワ公国が国家として急成長したのです。16世紀のことでした。
　イヴァン4世は、まず東側の脅威であるモンゴル系の国々を占領し
ます。さらに、北西を見るとポーランド、そしてポーランドと同じ王
を抱くリトアニアといった国々、さらにはスウェーデン王国の脅威に

時代
15〜18世紀
欧州近世

地域
ロシア

分類
国家【政治】

キーワード
イヴァン4世によるロシ
アの発展・農奴制の強化
・西欧文化の輸入・不凍
港を求めて

Kingdom of Sweden.

In this process, Ivan seized the city-state of Novgorod, which was under the influence of Lithuania, in 1570, carrying out a major massacre there.

Such heavy-handed politics earned him the sobriquet Ivan the Terrible.

Out of concern for maintaining his own economic base, Ivan was intent on trading with England. He developed a sea route that reached the Arctic Sea by way of the North Sea. It is said that he was aggressive in seeking not only trade with Queen Elizabeth's England but also in endeavoring to secure an alliance with it.

By prohibiting the movement of farmers and binding them to the lands they cultivated, he aimed at obtaining a stable tax revenue. This was the origin of Russia's later system of serfdom.

For a short period following the death of Ivan the Terrible, Russia was in political chaos. In 1613 Mikhail Romanov, to whom the wife of Ivan the Terrible was related by marriage, gained power, took the title of Tsar—Russian for emperor and ultimately derived from the word Caesar—and established the Romanov dynasty.

At the beginning of the Romanov dynasty, Russia was threatened by Poland and the Crimean Khanate to the south. It was Peter the Great, who ruled from the 17th century into the 18th century, who elevated the monarchy into a great European power. Peter the Great made himself emperor of all of Russia, establishing the Russian Empire.

Peter the Great himself visited England and the other powers of Europe in an effort to absorb the civilization of Western Europe, very much like the Japanese did during the Meiji Restoration period.

At that time, Russia did not have a harbor that was ice-free throughout the year. Peter allied the country with Poland to stand against the Kingdom of Sweden in the Great Northern War, which broke out in 1700. As a result of its victory in this war, Russia was able to expand into territories along the Baltic Sea. By reclaiming land at the entrance to the Baltic, he began constructing a port city on the sea in 1703, naming it after himself. This evolved into the present-day economic hub city of St. Petersburg.

As a result, Russia not only established a foothold in Europe but also expanded its presence in the world. Eventually a royal palace was built in the city, and it became the capital of the Russian Empire. As if in inverse proportion to the Westernization and growth of Russia, Poland and Sweden, which had conquered the countries of Northern Europe, began to wane. The 17th century was a period of major change in the balance of power in Europe.

対抗してゆく必要がありました。

　その過程の中で、1570年にリトアニアの影響を受けていた都市国家ノヴゴロドを簒奪し大虐殺を行ったこともありました。

　こうした強権政治がイヴァン4世に雷帝のあだ名をつけたのです。

　一方、イヴァン4世は、自らの経済基盤の維持のため、イギリスとの交易にも熱心でした。北海を経由し北極海に至る航路を開発し、エリザベス女王統治下のイギリスとの交易、さらには同盟に積極的だったといわれています。

　また、農民の移動を禁止し、土地に縛り付けることによって、税収の安定を目指します。これがその後のロシアの農奴制のおこりとなったのでした。

　イヴァン雷帝の死後、ロシアはしばらく政治的に混乱しますが、1613年に、雷帝の妻と姻戚関係にあるミハイル・ロマノフが台頭し、ロシア語で君主を意味するツァーリとなり、ロマノフ王朝を開きます。

　ロマノフ王朝初期も、ロシアはポーランドや南方のクリミア・ハン国などの脅威にさらされます。王朝をヨーロッパの強国に育て上げたのは、17世紀から18世紀にかけて君臨したピョートル大帝でした。大帝は、自らを全ロシアの皇帝とし、ロシア帝国を開いたのです。

　ピョートル大帝は自らもイギリスなどヨーロッパの列強を訪問し、まさに日本の明治維新のように、西側の文明の吸収に努めます。

　当時、ロシアには不凍港がありませんでした。大帝は、ポーランドと同盟してスウェーデン王国に対抗し、1700年に大北方戦争を起こし勢力をバルト海へと拡大します。そして、1703年にバルト海の入り口を埋め立てて自らの名前をつけた港湾都市の建設を始めます。これが、今ロシアの経済拠点となっているサンクト・ペテルブルクです。

　これによって、ロシアはヨーロッパのみならず、世界に向けて進出する拠点を築いたことになります。サンクト・ペテルブルクには、その後王宮が建設され、ロシア帝国の首都となります。ロシアの西欧化とその伸長と反比例するように、ポーランド、そして北欧世界を席巻していたスウェーデンの衰退が始まります。17世紀は西欧でのパワーバランスに大きな変化がおきた時代でもあったのです。

105 The great powers of Western Europe took note of the stability of Qing China

In 1616, three years after the founding of the Romanov dynasty in Russia, a new country appeared in North Asia. Nurhaci unified the Jurchen people in Manchuria and founded the Later Jin. The militaristic Yuan, who organized their armies into eight basic elite units called the Eight Banners, were followed by the Later Jin, who were Mongols, and then the Han Chinese. In due course his son Hong Taiji dominated the territory north of the Great Wall in northeast China and took the throne of emperor as a Han. These people referred to themselves as Manchus, and they became the predominant northern ethnic group. The first expansion since the Yuan by the northern people had begun.

Shortly after the death of Hong Taiji, the Li Zicheng Rebellion occurred and the Ming were destroyed. Taking advantage of this opportunity, at long last the Manchus crossed over the Great Wall and reached Beijing, suppressed Li Zicheng, and commenced the Qing unification of China. The emperor who followed Hong Taiji took the title Shunzhi Emperor, making it fit the Chinese style. Zheng Chenggong, who opposed the Qing from a base in Taiwan, and kin of the Ming emperor who fled to South China continued their resistance, but military leaders such as Wu Sangui, who left the side of the Ming and turned to support the Qing, hunted them down and killed them.

In this manner, the Qing established their country and the Han people had military power. However, Emperor Kangxi, who followed Shunzhi, chipped away at the power of the military clique that the Han had created in their domestic territories. Wu Sangui and others who rebelled against this policy raised the Revolt of the Three Feudatories in 1673, but they were suppressed by Kangxi in 1681, and he ruled as the Chinese emperor. During his reign, the Qing expanded into neighboring territories. That became the prototype of the extent of the domains of present-day China.

In 1689, just prior to the commencement of Peter the Great's Russian autocracy, Russia signed the Treaty of Nerchinsk with Qing China. The Qing, in response to Russia's expansion of its domains from Siberia into the Far East, extracted from Russia a compromise that established the border between the two states at the Stanovoy Range.

The Qing actively promoted the Han people, carrying out an appeasement

清の安定は、西欧列強にも注目された

ロシアにロマノフ王朝が成立した3年後の1616年、北アジアに一つの国家が生まれました。満州で女真族を統一したヌルハチという人物が、後金を建国したのです。八旗と呼ばれる軍制のもと、後金はモンゴル族、さらには漢民族も従えてゆきます。やがて、息子のホンタイジは、万里の長城以北の中国東北地方を領有し、ハンとして皇帝を名乗ります。彼らは自らのことを満州族と呼び、北方民族の支配者となったのです。元以来の北方民族の膨張が始まります。

【時代】
17世紀
中国近世

【地域】
中国

【分類】
国家【政治】

【キーワード】
満州族による清帝国の成立・ロシアとの和解・中国の発展と安定・ヨーロッパ諸国の注目

ホンタイジの死後まもなく、李自成の乱がおき明が滅びます。この機会に乗じ、ついに満州族は万里の長城を越えて北京に至り、李自成を討伐、清による中国統治が始まったのでした。ホンタイジの後を継いだ皇帝は名前を順治帝と中国風に改めます。清に対し台湾を拠点にした鄭成功や華南に逃れた明の皇帝の親族などが抵抗を続けますが、明を離れ清に協力した将軍呉三桂などに追討されます。

康熙帝
Emperor Kangxi

このように清は建国にあたり、漢民族の軍事力に依存していました。しかし、順治帝のあとを継いだ康熙帝は、国内に藩を形成していた漢民族の軍閥の力をそぎ落とします。この政策に反発した呉三桂などが1673年に三藩の乱をおこしますが、康熙帝は1681年に乱を平定し、中華帝国の帝王として君臨したのでした。康熙帝の時代に清は領土を周辺に拡張します。それが現在の中国の領土の原型となったのです。

ポール・ドラローシュ『ピョートル大帝』
Paul Delaroche —Peter the Great

1689年に、ピョートル大帝が親政を開始する直前のロシアと清とは、ネルチンスク条約を締結します。シベリアから極東へと領土を拡大していたロシアに対応した清は、外興安嶺（スタノヴォイ山脈）を中国との国境としてロシア側の妥協を引き出したのでした。

清は、漢民族を積極的に登用し、制度上も人事上も宥和政策を実施

policy involving both the system of government and the selection of personnel. At the same time, however, the Manchu actively maintained their queues, or pigtails, which was their traditional hairstyle. In the 17th and 18th centuries, while absolute monarchs like Peter the Great and Louis XIV reigned in Europe, the Qing dynasty, under the emperors Kangxi, followed by Yongzheng and then Qianlong, emerged as a formidable nation, exerting pressure on its surrounding regions.

In Japan at that time, under the government of the Tokugawa Shogunate, the country closed its gates to the outside world and stabilized the nation, and during the Genroku period, the culture of Edo and Osaka flourished.

Indeed, this stability in Asia drew the attention of the West.

During that time, the Western European powers invited philosophers and intellectuals to cultivate their own education, particularly among the royal families. Such monarchs came to be referred to as enlightened despots, and exemplars included Prussia's Frederick II, known as Frederick the Great. It is particularly well-known that Frederick was on friendly terms with the French intellectual Voltaire. It is said that Voltaire, among others, extolled the Chinese system of autocracy. This Chinese government by means of royal administration was introduced as an ideal model for absolute monarchal rule in Europe.

106 The growth of Russia had a subtle impact on international politics in the Far East

In East Asia, from ancient times many states paid tribute to the governments that developed in China. In exchange, they sought Chinese wealth and culture, as well as protection under China's military power. Typical examples of these tributary states were the Ryukyu Kingdom, which ruled what is now Okinawa, and the Joseon dynasty, which ruled the Korean Peninsula.

In passing, let us note that in English the countries on that peninsula are referred to as "Korea," which derives from the name of an early state known as Koryo.

In contrast with the way in which the Mongols and the Manchus moved about and from time to time controlled China, the Korean peoples consistently resided in the Korean Peninsula. The states that evolved there did not attempt to expand widely.

It is said that the foundation of the Joseon dynasty was solidified in the first half of the 15th century by the fourth-generation monarch Sejong the Great.

します。しかし、同時に満州族のヘアスタイルともいえる弁髪を強要し、自らの伝統の継承にも積極的でした。17世紀から18世紀にかけて、ヨーロッパでピョートル大帝やルイ14世といった絶対君主が君臨していた頃、東アジアでは康熙帝やその後を継いだ雍正帝、さらにその次の乾隆帝といった皇帝のもとで、清は強大な国家として周囲を威圧していたのでした。

それは、徳川幕府の統治下、日本が海外との門戸を閉ざしながらも国家として安定し、江戸や大阪に元禄文化が開花した頃のことでした。

実はこのアジアの安定は、西欧の注目するところともなりました。

当時、西欧列強は、多くの王族が自らの教養を育成するために、哲学者などを招いていました。こうした王のことを、啓蒙専制君主と呼び、プロイセンのフリードリッヒ大王と呼ばれたフリードリッヒ2世などは、その典型でした。大王とフランスの思想家ヴォルテールとの親交は特に有名です。そんなヴォルテールなども、中国の専制君主制度を賛美していたといわれています。中国の王朝がヨーロッパでの絶対王政の理想的なモデルとして紹介されていたのです。

ロシアの成長は極東の外交にも微妙な影響を与えていった

東アジアには、昔から中国に成立した政権に朝貢し、中国の富と文明、さらには軍事力の傘下にはいる国家が多くありました。現在の沖縄にあった琉球王国、そして朝鮮半島を支配していた李氏朝鮮などは、そうした国家の典型でした。

ところで、韓国や北朝鮮のことを、英語でコリアといいますが、この語源は高麗に由来しています。

モンゴル民族や満州族が移動しながら、時には中国をも支配した状況とは対照的に、朝鮮民族は常に朝鮮半島に居住し、そこで成立した国家から広く膨張を試みることはありませんでした。

李氏朝鮮は、15世紀前半の4代目の王世宗の時代に国家基盤が整ったといわれています。国家の運営の基軸として儒教を奨励し、逆に高

時代
17, 18世紀
中国近世

地域
日本・朝鮮・ロシア

分類
国家【対立】

キーワード
李氏朝鮮の成立・日朝の対立・日本の鎖国政策・ロシアのアジア登場と南下政策

Confucianism was promoted as the ideological backbone of the state, while Buddhism, which had prospered during the Koryo era, was suppressed. It was also during this period that hangul script was devised and employed. Relations between Korea and Japan grew frigid due to the activities of so-called Japanese pirates, or wako, in the Muromachi period and even more so due to the Invasion of Korea during the Keicho period under Toyotomi Hideyoshi. It was the Tsushima domain that became the liaison with the Joseon dynasty and that attempted to restore diplomatic relations.

During the Edo period, due to the fact that Japan adopted a policy of national seclusion, from the Joseon dynasty's perspective, it was no longer essential to feel Japan to be a threat. Moreover, because the Joseon maintained their status as a Chinese tributary state, thereby being guaranteed protection, despite some tension as a result of the transition from Ming to Qing, the Joseon maintained good relations with the Qing thereafter.

It was against this background that Russia advanced into the Far East. Because the Joseon were originally friendly with the Ming, when the Qing became a stronger state, the Joseon could not have helped feeling somewhat apprehensive. However, under the circumstances resulting from Russia's advance into the Far East, things changed completely. Russia sought an ice-free port in the Far East. To put things another way, Russia began looking for an opportunity in the Far East to advance southward. This presented a threat to both the Chinese and the Koreans.

This is an appropriate occasion to lay out the basic scheme of the international relations in East Asia between the 18th and 20th centuries. How one should deal with Russia was problematic for all of the countries in the region, including Japan. In Japan's case, the Korean Peninsula was essential for mitigating this menace, as was the northeastern region of China.

Unfortunately, when Japan became a powerful country following the Meiji Restoration, the Joseon dynasty was left with no alternative but to somehow deal with the dual threats from Russia and Japan at the same time.

In the 18th century, Qing China still wielded power as a strong state. However, as it later began to decline, a significant shift occurred in the power balance within the Far East.

From the 17th century into the 18th century, Joseon Korea, unaware of the future tragedy that would befall it, continued as a Qing tributary state, one which had continued to absorb Chinese culture since the Ming dynasty, and it maintained its pride in doing so.

麗の時代に繁栄した仏教は弾圧されました。また、ハングルを発明し、使用し始めたのも当時のことでした。韓国と日本との関係は、室町時代の倭寇、さらには文禄慶長の役と呼ばれる豊臣秀吉の侵攻によって冷え切ってしまいます。そうした李氏朝鮮との窓口となり、国交回復に尽力したのが対馬藩だったのです。

　江戸時代、日本は鎖国政策をとったことで、李氏朝鮮から見れば日本に対して以前のような脅威を抱く必要はなくなりました。また、中国に対しては朝貢を続け国家としての保護を受けていたため、明から清への政権が交代するときには緊張があったものの、あとは概ね清とも良好な関係を維持しました。

　その背景にあったのが、ロシアの極東への進出でした。李氏朝鮮は、元々明との和親を国家の基本政策にしていたために、清が強大な国家になることへの抵抗感がなかったわけではありません。しかし、極東へのロシアの進出が状況を一変させました。ロシアは極東で不凍港を求めていました。別の言い方をすれば、ロシアは極東で南下する機会をうかがうことになります。それが、李氏朝鮮と清にとっての共通の脅威となったのです。

　ここに、18世紀から20世紀にかけての東アジアの国際関係の基本的な図式ができあがったことになります。ロシアへの対応こそが日本を含む極東の国々の課題となってゆくのです。日本の場合、その脅威を緩和するために必要だったのが朝鮮半島であり、中国の東北地方であったということになります。

　不幸にして、明治維新を経て日本が強国として成長したとき、李氏朝鮮はロシアと日本という二つの脅威への対応を余儀なくされたのです。

　18世紀にはまだ、清が強国として君臨していました。しかし、その後清が衰亡へと向かったとき、極東のパワーバランスに大きな変化がおきたのです。

　17世紀から18世紀にかけての李氏朝鮮は、この未来の悲劇をまだ知ることなく、清への朝貢国として、さらに明以来の中国文明を吸収した国家として、そのプライドを維持してゆくことができたのでした。

107 Slaves supplied from Africa carried on the operations of the New World

Let us cross the Pacific Ocean. From a bird's-eye view of 18th-century world history, as Russia advanced into Northeast Asia, the European states expanded colonies in North America, which would later have a significant impact on history.

The newly risen powers of the Netherlands and England, as well as France, which was flourishing under King Louis XIV, were aggressively investing in North America. France claimed a broad colonial territory stretching from eastern Canada, along the Mississippi River, and across the Caribbean. The present-day state of Louisiana, in the United States, was administered by the French monarchy and took its name from the king.

Elsewhere, the British, rivals of the French, maintained their own colonies on North America's eastern coast in New England and Virginia.

As the clearing of forests progressed in the New World, colonists needed a workforce. It was this that accelerated the supplying of enslaved people from Africa.

At the outset, with the exception of the regions of Africa that faced the Mediterranean Sea and the broad sweep of North Africa which had come under Islamic influence during the Middle Ages, connections between Africa and Europe were minimal at best. For example, during the Roman period, one branch of Christianity known as the Coptic Church spread through Egypt and Ethiopia. In successive Ethiopian monarchies, under this influence, believers followed an offshoot known as the Orthodox Church. Christian branches they were, but these faiths had very little connection with the European world.

Following the Age of Discovery, however, the west coast of Africa gained importance as a source of slaves that could be sent to work in the Caribbean and in the Americas. For example, in present-day Nigeria, beginning in the 14th century the monarchy of the Kingdom of Benin prospered. In order to maintain the country's military force, it purchased guns from the Portuguese, and in return it supplied subjugated people as slaves.

The Dutch and the English actively followed along in pursuing this slave trade. It need hardly be pointed out that the descendants of these enslaved people now make up a majority of the African Americans now in the United States.

Slaves were acquired through conflicts that broke out between tribes in Africa, and they were transported to the New World on British and Dutch slave ships.

新大陸の経営に奴隷がアフリカから供給された

　ここで太平洋を渡りましょう。18世紀の世界史を鳥瞰したとき、ロシアの東北アジアへの進出と、北アメリカにある西欧の植民地の拡張は、その後の歴史に大きな影響を与えることになります。

　北アメリカには、新興勢力となったオランダやイギリス、そしてルイ14世の元で繁栄したフランスが積極的に投資します。フランスはカナダ東部からミシシッピ川に沿ってカリブ海に至る広大な植民地を経営することになります。現在アメリカにあるルイジアナ州は、ルイ王朝下のフランスによって経営されたルイジアナ植民地の名前を受け継いでいるのです。

　一方、フランスのライバルのイギリスは、ニューイングランドやバージニアといった植民地を東海岸に維持します。

　新大陸の開墾が進む中で、入植者は安価な労働力を求めます。このことが、アフリカからの奴隷の供給を促進したのでした。

　元々、アフリカは地中海に面した地域や、中世にイスラム教の影響を受けた北アフリカ一帯を除けば、西欧世界との接点は希薄でした。例えばエジプトやエチオピアには、ローマ時代にキリスト教の一派であるコプト教などが広がり、エチオピアの歴代の王朝では、その影響を受けたエチオピア正教会が信奉されますが、西欧世界と深く関わったわけではありません。

　しかし、大航海時代を経た後には、アフリカ西海岸がカリブから南北アメリカへの奴隷の供給地として注目されるようになります。例えば、現在のナイジェリアには14世紀以降ベニン王国という王朝が繁栄していました。ベニン王国は自国の軍事力を維持するために、ポルトガルなどから銃を購入し、その見返りに被征服民族などを奴隷として輸出していたといわれています。

　こうした奴隷貿易は、オランダやイギリスなどにも積極的に受け継がれます。その子孫が現在アメリカ合衆国の主要な構成員となっているアフリカ系アメリカ人であることはいうまでもありません。

　奴隷はアフリカでの部族の対立を利用して獲得され、イギリスやオランダなどの奴隷船によって新大陸に送られます。奴隷といえば、ア

時代
18世紀
欧州近世

地域
アフリカ・北アメリカ

分類
社会【対立】

キーワード
ヨーロッパ人のアメリカ入植・新大陸の開発と発展・奴隷貿易の開始・アメリカでの英仏対決

When one hears the word slave, one tends to imagine slaves forced to cultivate and harvest cotton in the fields of the American South. In actual fact, however, slaves were traded in every region of America. As one example, until the end of the 18th century, there was an active slave market in New York City, and there are records of a number of slave uprisings in that city.

It was only in the 19th century that the system of slavery came to be seen as a humanitarian issue. Until then, slaves served as a valuable labor resource for the rapid economic growth of North America.

Eventually, whenever the European countries clashed over expansion of their territories, the colonies in North America—sources of wealth for the respective mother countries—became entangled. Especially in the frequent conflicts between England and France over territories, they engaged in hostilities in the colonial areas as well.

It was this that triggered the movement for independence within the thirteen British colonies.

108 The struggle for hegemony turned into the American Revolution

Let us return our attention to Europe.

In 1740, when Frederick the Great of Prussia ruled as an enlightened despot, a war over succession broke out between Maria Theresa, empress of Francis I and co-ruler of the Holy Roman Empire, over the right of dominion over Silesia. This War of Austrian Succession pit Prussia against the House of Habsburg in Austria.

The Silesia region straddled present-day Poland and Czech Republic.

An extension of this discord between the two powers occurred in 1756 with the outbreak of the Seven Years' War. As a result of that conflict, Silesia eventually became Prussian territory. Needless to say, the war involved not just the two parties; other European powers were also participants in the fighting. England and Prussia formed an alliance, and France took the side of the Habsburgs. This resulted in the French and Indian War in America. England and France entangled the indigenous Iroquois in their competition for dominance. In the end, England was

メリカ南部での綿花畑で農作業に従事させられていた人々のことが知られていますが、実際はアメリカ各地で取引されていたのです。例えば、ニューヨークでも18世紀の終わり頃まで奴隷市場があり、奴隷による反乱も何度か記録されています。

　奴隷制度の人道的な問題が表面化してくるのは19世紀になってからです。それまでは、アフリカから運ばれた奴隷こそが、急速に経済成長をしてゆく北アメリカの貴重な労働資源となったのです。
　やがて北アメリカの植民地は、ヨーロッパ本国にとっての富の供給源として、国家同士が衝突するたびに、新大陸にも戦火が広がり、領土拡張の試みがなされるようになります。特にイギリスとフランスとは領土問題で何度も植民地で戦火を交えます。

　このことがアメリカの独立運動への導火線となってゆくのでした。

列強の覇権争いがアメリカの独立革命へと発展した

　再びヨーロッパに目を向けます。
　プロイセンのフリードリッヒ大王が啓蒙専制君主として君臨していた1740年に、神聖ローマ帝国の皇帝フランツ1世の皇后で、共同統治者であったマリア・テレジアが継承したシュレジェン地方の領有権をめぐって、プロイセンとオーストリアのハプスブルク家との間にオーストリア継承戦争がおきてしまいます。
　シュレジェン地方は現在のポーランドとチェコとにまたがった地域のことです。
　さらにその延長として両国は1756年に再び衝突し七年戦争が勃発します。戦争の結果、シュレジェン地方は最終的にプロイセンのものとなりました。もちろん戦争には、当事者となる二つの国家のみならず、ヨーロッパの他の列強も参戦します。イギリスとプロイセンとが同盟し、フランスはハプスブルク側につきます。それが、新大陸ではフレンチ・インディアン戦争となり、イギリスとフランスとがイロコイ族と呼ばれる先住民族をも巻き込んで覇権を争いました。最終的にはフ

時代
18世紀 欧州近世

地域
西ヨーロッパ・北アメリカ

分類
戦争【革命】

キーワード
ヨーロッパの絶対王政戦争・戦争のアメリカへの波及・アメリカへの重税・アメリカ合衆国の成立

victorious in the conflict, and it acquired an enormous expanse of land east of the Mississippi River.

Warfare requires a huge amount of money. It puts a country's finances under pressure, and heavy taxes on the people of the country causes a backlash. This backlash ignited the American Revolution against Britain in the New World and the French Revolution in the Old World.

Dissatisfaction with the Stamp Act that England imposed on its American colonies in 1765 led to protests by the colonists. Also, in 1773, in an effort to save the British East India Company, which was threatened with financial collapse, Britain passed the Tea Act. This legislation gave the company a monopoly on tea sold in the colonies, which led to further opposition from the colonists. This resulted in a group of colonists attacking an East India Company boat loaded with tea in Boston Harbor and dumping the tea overboard. This came to be known as the famous Boston Tea Party.

In the background of this act of protest was resentment over the one-sided imposition of regulations and taxation on the people of the thirteen colonies, who were not given representation in the legislature. "No taxation without representation!" became the slogan that led to calls for independence. The year after the Boston Tea Party, the thirteen colonies held a Continental Congress and acted in unison to petition the British crown for a redress of grievances. In response, Britain attempted to suppress the colonies with military force. The ultimate outcome was the outbreak of armed conflict between the British and the colonists in 1775 in Lexington and Concord, on the outskirts of Boston.

The thirteen colonies decided upon full-scale resistance with George Washington as commander in chief. Hastily assembled groups of citizen-soldiers called militia confronted the regular, trained troops of the British.

In 1776 representatives of the thirteen colonies assembled in Philadelphia, and Thomas Jefferson and others presented a draft of the Declaration of Independence from Britain. For a period of six years thereafter, fierce fighting spread across the continent. The thirteen British colonies rose up, banded together, and sought to withdraw from British rule, and for that reason, this war of independence is known as the American Revolution.

This was the birth of the United States of America, which by the 20th century would become a world superpower.

レンチ・インディアン戦争はイギリス側の勝利に終わり、イギリスは
ミシシッピ川以東の広大な植民地を獲得したのです。

　戦争は莫大な経費を必要とします。それは国家の財政を逼迫させ、
国民へは重税となってはね返ってきます。この重税への反発が、新大
陸ではイギリスに対する独立革命を、ヨーロッパではフランス革命へ
と引火してゆくのです。

　1765年にイギリスが新大陸に押し付けた印紙税
への不満が、新大陸の13州の植民地での抗議行動
へと発展します。そして1773年には財政破綻に
苦しむイギリスの東インド会社を救済しようと、
同社に紅茶の独占販売権を与えた茶条例に人々が
反発します。その結果、ボストンで東インド会社
の船舶を人々が襲い、積載された紅茶を海に投棄
したのです。有名なボストン茶会事件です。

1773年のボストン茶会事件を描いたリトグラフ
A lithograph depicting the 1773 Boston Tea Party

　これらの抗議行動の背景には、議会に代表を送
ることができない13州の人々への一方的な課税や
条例の設定への憤りがありました。「代表なくし
て課税なし」という言葉が独立へ向けたスローガンとなるのです。ボ
ストン茶会事件の翌年に大陸会議が開催され、13州は一致団結してイ
ギリスへ抗議を行います。それに対してイギリスは武力での制圧を試
み、ついに1775年にボストン郊外のレキシントンとコンコードでの武
力衝突へと発展したのでした。

　13州側はジョージ・ワシントンを総司令官として徹底抗戦を決意し
ます。ミリシアと呼ばれる民兵を急遽組織し、イギリスの正規軍に対
抗したのです。

　1776年に、13州の代表はフィラデルフィアに集まり、トマス・ジェ
ファソンをはじめとする人々が独立宣言を起草し発表します。以後6年
間にわたって新大陸では激しい戦闘が繰り広げられます。イギリスに
所属する13州が、イギリスの主権から離れようと立ち上がったことか
ら、この独立戦争を人々は独立革命と呼んだのでした。

　20世紀に世界の超大国へと成長するアメリカ合衆国が産声をあげた
のでした。

第五部

自由と革命、混乱と植民地化の時代（近代の世界）

Part Five:
Freedom and Revolution, Chaos and Colonization (The Modern World)

　長い間、ヒトの歴史はユーラシア大陸を中心に展開してきました。ユーラシア大陸の西と東に、中央で活動していた騎馬民族が影響を与え、東にある中国社会、西にある西欧社会はそうしたヒトの動きを触媒に、文明の交流を行いました。

　そのエネルギーが飛び火したのが、アメリカでした。新大陸に向けたヨーロッパ諸国の進出は、ユーラシア大陸とはまったく異なる、広大な大地への投資へとヒトを駆り立てます。その源流となった西欧社会は、産業革命を経て、さらに新大陸はもとより、ユーラシア大陸の他の地域やアフリカなど、地球の隅々に向けて今までにない進出を繰り広げたのです。

　その過程で、ヒトは自らの社会も変革させます。階級社会のあり方も、市民革命を通して、国家の構造を大きく変革させてゆきました。

　一方、産業の発展は市場をめぐる激しい競争をもたらし、その過程で多くの戦争も起こります。ヒトの血が流れるとき、新たな革命が起こり、社会構造や階級構造そのものもさらに大きく変化を遂げていったのです。

109 With American independence, humankind acquired rights that they had never had before

The people who lit the signal fire of independence in America were those who fostered a consciousness of their rights as citizens, rights which were cultivated in England during the Glorious Revolution.

The way of thinking that denied the theory of the divine right of kings and held individual rights to have precedence over monarchial rights was advocated by such thinkers as John Locke and philosophers who lived through the Glorious Revolution. This way of thinking was incorporated into the American Declaration of Independence in the phrase asserting that humankind has the rights of freedom and equality, and the right to pursue happiness.

One of the prominent thinkers of contemporary America was Thomas Paine.

His pamphlet *Common Sense* criticized the British monarchial system and strongy incited public opinion by making the case for freedom and independence for the American colonies. One year earlier, in 1775, in the colony of Virginia, Patrick Henry called for independence in a speech declaring, "Give me liberty or give me death!"

The Declaration of Independence was a groundbreaking document that articulated the spirit of individual independence and freedom, which had not yet fully taken root in the Old World. The achievement of such a claim could only have been carried out by those who had escaped the restraints of the Old World and, relying only upon their individual abilities, had crossed the Atlantic Ocean and with self-reliance established their own way of life.

The Declaration of Independence specifies two ideas that had never appeared before.

One is the belief that all people are equal. At that time, however, those who this applied to were those adult males who possessed property, and in fact many of them owned slaves. Close to 200 years would pass after gaining independence before the concept of equality would be expanded to include all people.

The second was the assertion that if the government infringed upon the fundamental rights of those people, they had the right to overthrow that government. This was the right of the citizens to revolt.

In order to overthrow a government, of course, people had to possess weapons.

アメリカの独立によって、人類は今までにない権利を獲得した

　アメリカで独立の狼煙をあげた人々は、元々名誉革命などを通してイギリスに培われてきた市民としての権利意識を抱いた人々でした。

　王権神授説を否定し、王権よりも個人の権利を優位におく発想は、ジョン・ロックなど、名誉革命期を生きた哲学者などによって既に唱えられていました。そうした発想が人間には自由、平等、幸福を追求する権利があるのだという表現で、アメリカの独立宣言に織り込まれました。

　当時のアメリカを牽引した思想家にトマス・ペインがいます。
　彼の『コモンセンス』という著書は、イギリスの君主制を批判し、アメリカの自由と独立を主張して世論を強く刺激したのです。その1年前（1775年）には、バージニア植民地で、パトリック・ヘンリーがバージニアの独立を説き、有名な「自由を。しからずんば死を与えよ」という演説を行っています。
　独立宣言は、旧大陸にはまだ十分に根づいていなかった個人の自立と自由を求める精神を明文化した画期的な内容でした。それは旧大陸の束縛を逃れて移住し、個人の力に頼りながら、大西洋の反対側で黙々と自らの生活を築いてきた自立心旺盛な人々であればこそ成しえた快挙だったのです。

　独立宣言には今までにはない二つの思想が明記されています。

　一つは、全ての人は平等であるという考え方です。ただし、当時平等とされた人は、資産を持つ成人男性に限られていて、彼らの多くは奴隷の所有者であったこともまた事実です。アメリカは、独立以降200年近くの年月を経て、この「平等」という概念を全ての人々に普遍化していったのでした。
　二つ目は、もし政府がこうした人々の基本的な権利を蹂躙した場合は、人々はその政府を倒す権利があると明記していることです。革命権を市民の権利であるとうたっているのです。
　政府を倒すためには、人々は武器を持たなければなりません。この

時代
18世紀
近代

地域
アメリカ合衆国

分類
革命【政治】

キーワード
絶対王政の否定・自由と平等の獲得・権利意識の顕在化・市民革命の幕開け

This right to "bear arms" is still held as important among many Americans, and there is a nation-wide controversy over whether there should be a system of gun control to deter crime involving weapons.

Initially the Continental army was repeatedly put to rout. The British troops, in order to suppress the guerrilla activities of the revolutionaries, requisitioned colonists' residences and carried out thorough search operations to locate and detain those who advocated revolution. As a result of this experience, once America did become independent, it was established in the modern legal system that no public authority could enter an individual's private property without a search warrant. It was also established that the army was prohibited from requisitioning citizen's houses.

The parliamentary democracy which began in Britain and which placed emphasis on the rights of the citizens, as a result of the attainment of independence by the Americans, progressed as an even further refined system.

Moreover, the new concept of a national system, which was given concrete expression in the New World, was thereafter imported back to Europe.

110 The U.S. Constitution encouraged compromise between the rights of the local areas and the central government

The American Revolutionary army was a resistance movement composed of miscellaneous militias.

For that reason, they were regularly punished by the well-trained, well-equipped regular troops of the British. At the beginning, British troops seized the main cities, such as New York and Philadelphia, and the American army was in danger of being totally destroyed. By 1777, however, they rallied, and the war became a sequence of advances and retreats.

Meanwhile, for Britain's rival France, the North American conflict was a perfect opportunity for reducing British influence everywhere. Obtaining cooperation from France was an extremely important strategy for the Continental army. Together with Thomas Jefferson, Benjamin Franklin, known as an advocate of American independence, proceeded to Paris once the war with Britain began and led the diplomatic negotiations there.

武器を持つ権利は、現在でもアメリカ人にとって大切な権利とされ、銃による犯罪を抑止するために銃規制を行うべきかどうか、国をあげての論争になっているのです。

　革命軍は、最初は敗走を続けました。イギリス軍はゲリラ活動を抑止するために、植民地の人々の家屋を接収し、革命を唱える人々に対して徹底的な捜索活動を展開しました。この経験から、独立後のアメリカでは公権力が捜査令状なしに個人の不動産に立ち入ること、あるいは軍隊の都合で家屋を接収することを禁止しようという近代的な法制度が整えられます。

　イギリスで始まった市民の権利を尊重した議会制民主主義は、アメリカが独立するにあたり、さらに洗練された制度へと進化したのです。

　また、新大陸で具現化された新たな国家体制への考え方は、その後ヨーロッパにも逆輸入されることになるのです。

合衆国憲法は地方の権利と中央政府との妥協を促した

　独立革命軍は、寄せ集めの民兵による抵抗運動です。

　それだけに、訓練をつみ、優秀な装備をもったイギリスの正規軍に彼らは苦しめられます。当初はニューヨークやフィラデルフィアといった主要都市をイギリス軍に奪われ、革命軍は壊滅の危機に見舞われますが、1777年になるとようやく体制を立て直し、戦争は一進一退を繰り返すようになりました。

　一方、イギリスのライバルであるフランスにとっては、新大陸での混乱はイギリスの影響力を削ぐための絶好の機会となりました。独立革命軍にとっても、フランスの協力を得ることは極めて重要な戦略です。トマス・ジェファソンと共に、独立革命の論客として知られるベンジャミン・フランクリンはイギリスとの戦争が始まるとパリに赴き、外交交渉をリードしました。

時代
18世紀
近代

地域
アメリカ合衆国

分類
独立【革命】

キーワード
独立革命の進展・フランスの介入・独立の宣言・中央と地方の対立と妥協・合衆国憲法の制定

As a result, France joined the war on the American side. Britain's rivals Spain and the Netherlands declared a pro-American policy. The war on the North American continent enlarged into an international network opposed to Britain.

With such support from other countries, the revolutionary army gradually gained ground on the battlefield. Then in October 1781, the revolutionary army and the French, acting in concert, forced the capitulation of the British army at Yorktown. American independence was formally recognized by the Treaty of Paris in 1783.

When the American colonies achieved their independence, the issue remained as to how to unite them.

The people who stood in opposition to oppressive British rule developed the land in their respective colonies and created their own unique rules for living together. At the conclusion of the war, they returned to their own towns and villages scattered across the land and resumed their previous daily lives. They assembled in the town square or in the church in the square in order to make decisions important to the local community. They possessed guns and other weapons that they use to protect themselves. Anything that was not of common concern to the community they left as much as possible to the discretion of the individual.

In considering this uniquely American way of life, following independence, some people asserted that all of the former colonies should unite together as a single country. From that time to the present, this has been a principal theme in American politics. The debate is whether the central government should be strong, or whether there should be a small government and greater power should be left to the local regions and the individual. Alexander Hamilton, the first Secretary of the Treasury, asserted that the powers of the federal government should be strengthened. In opposition, people like Thomas Jefferson, the first Secretary of State, called for a smaller, less powerful federal government.

The Constitutional Congress, held in Philadelphia in 1787, compromised on this issue by recognizing the local powers and specifying that the federal government would administer the country as a whole and leave other decisions to the local governments. The United States Constitution was adopted, and in 1789 George Washington became the new country's first president.

その結果、フランスがアメリカ側について参戦。スペインやオランダといったイギリスのライバルも親米政策を表明します。新大陸での戦争は、イギリスに対抗する国際的な包囲網へと拡大したのでした。

　こうした外国の支援もあって、独立革命軍も次第に有利に戦闘を進めます。そして、1781年10月に革命軍とフランスとの連携によって、ヨークタウンでイギリス軍を降伏させたのです。アメリカの独立が正式に承認されたのは、1783年に締結されたパリ条約でのことでした。

　アメリカの植民地が独立したとき、いかに13州をまとめてゆくかという大きな課題が残りました。

　イギリスの圧政に対して立ち上がった人々は、それぞれの入植地で土地を開拓し、独自のルールを作って生活をしていた人々です。独立戦争が終結すると、人々は、広大なアメリカ大陸にある自らの町や村に戻り、今までの生活を続けるのです。町の広場やそこにある教会で地元の重要なことを決議し、それぞれは身を守るために銃や武器を所持し、共通の利害に関係のないことは、できるだけ個々人の判断に任されました。

　こうしたアメリカならではのライフスタイルに対して、独立後はアメリカ合衆国という一つの国家に全てをまとめてゆくべきだと主張する人々がいました。この対立は、その後現代に至るアメリカの政治の主要なテーマとなります。強い政府か、地方や個人の権利を大切にした小さな政府かを選択する論争です。初代財務長官になったアレクサンダー・ハミルトンは連邦政府の権限強化を主張。それに対して初代国務長官となったトマス・ジェファソンに代表される人々は小さな政府を主張します。

　その妥協の上に、1787年にフィラデルフィアで憲法制定会議が開催され、地方の権限を認めた上で、連邦政府が国家を管理することを明記した合衆国憲法が採択され、89年にジョージ・ワシントンが初代の大統領となったのでした。

1776年7月4日、13州の代表はフィラデルフィアで独立宣言を発表した。中央の5人が起草委員で、うち一番左が第2代大統領のジョン・アダムズ。右から二番目が第3代大統領のトマス・ジェファソンで、一番右がベンジャミン・フランクリン。

On July 4, 1776, representatives of the thirteen states issued the Declaration of Independence in Philadelphia. The five members of the drafting committee are in the center, the leftmost of whom is John Adams, the second president. Second from the right is Thomas Jefferson, the third president, and on the far right is Benjamin Franklin.

ジョージ・ワシントン
George Washington

Revolution spread from America to France

The United States Constitution is characterized by its Executive Branch, the Senate, the House of Representatives, and the Judicial Branch. The U.S. Constitution set a precedent by introducing the principle of the separation of powers, which has since been adopted by many countries around the world.

Since its enactment, the Constitution has been amended, and regulations and ordinances have been added. Of particular note are the ten amendments added to the Constitution which were added by 1791, which stipulated the powers of the individual and the states vis-à-vis the federal government, completing the framework of the Constitution.

The first ten amendments, like the Bill of Rights established in 1689 in Britain, are known in America as its own Bill of Rights. Including these ten, a total of 27 amendments have been added to the Constitution.

During the American War of Independence, volunteer armies of Europeans joined the Americans. Among the famous figures are Marie-Joseph La Fayette, a French nobleman, and Tadeusz Kosciusko, a Polish military leader. These Europeans made enormous contributions to the American side and for a long period of time thereafter, they were lauded as heroes in America. What is important to note here is that it was through these figures that the spirit of revolution was conveyed to Europe.

Ironically enough, the first to be affected by this was the monarchy of France, which had supported America.

Contemporary France was ruled under a system of an absolute monarch referred to as the Ancien Régime. This political and social system since the Middle Ages concentrated power in two classes: the clergy and the nobility. Unless they were able to obtain aristocratic status through the purchase of court titles or through the obtaining a government appointment, the general citizenry, known as the third estate, remained subject to taxation.

The absolute monarchy was supported by a bureaucracy and a standing army. Following the Middle Ages, many of the knights who had been reduced to financial ruin became court nobles, and while they served the monarch, they maintained their own domains.

The monarchs maintained this regime, and in order to accumulate wealth, they

革命はアメリカからフランスに伝染した

合衆国憲法の特徴は、大統領制と、上院と下院の議会があり、司法権を独立させるといった三権分立の原則を世界にさきがけて打ち出したことです。合衆国憲法はその後修正が加えられ、条項が付加されています。

特に憲法の本文と共に1791年までに、連邦政府に対して、個人や州の権利を明記した10か条の修正条項が付加され、憲法の骨格ができあがりました。

この10か条は、1689年にイギリスで制定された「権利の章典」と同様、アメリカ版の「権利の章典」と呼ばれています。この10か条を含み、現在までに27の修正条項が加えられています。

ところで、アメリカの独立革命には、ヨーロッパからの義勇軍も参加しました。有名なのは、フランスの貴族ラファイエットやポーランドの軍人コシューシコですが、実際に彼らは独立戦争に多大な貢献をしたことで、アメリカでは長年英雄として扱われました。大切なことは、こうした人々を通して、独立革命の精神がヨーロッパに伝えられたことでした。

皮肉なことに、アメリカを応援したフランスのルイ王朝が、その最初の影響を被ることになります。

当時のフランスは、「アンシャン・レジーム」という絶対君主制の元で、中世さながらに聖職者と有力貴族の二つの階級に権限や特権が集中し、第三身分と呼ばれる一般の市民は資金のあるものが買位や売官によって貴族の身分を得ない限り課税の対象となっていました。

絶対君主制は、官僚と常備軍に支えられています。中世以降没落した騎士の多くは宮廷貴族となって、君主に仕えながら自らの領地を維持していました。

君主はこの体制を維持し、富を蓄積するために重商主義政策をとっ

時代
18世紀
近代

地域
アメリカ合衆国・フランス

分類
革命【政治】

キーワード
アメリカ合衆国の理念と政治体制・重商主義の矛盾・フランスの矛盾蓄積・国民会議の結成

adopted the mercantile system, venturing into the operation of overseas colonies. This, however, resulted in confrontation between the egos of different countries, and in order to restrain competitors' desire for domination, the great powers repeatedly went to war with one another. The prosecution of warfare required the commitment of enormous sums of money and large numbers of competent people, as well as complex bureaucratic structures. Due to the fact that these countries suffered from chronic financial troubles while their bureaucracies grew ever more cumbersome, the power of the monarchy itself weakened in relative terms.

This tendency can be observed in Britain in the period between Queen Elizabeth I's reign and that of King Charles I. Similarly, this also occurred in France in the more than century-long period that passed between the reigns of Louis XIV and Louis XVI.

Louis XVI, who was suffering from financial troubles, hoped to impose taxation on the privileged aristocracy, but this met with resistance from them. Accordingly, an assembly referred to as the Estates General was called to bring together the clergy, the aristocracy, and prominent citizens, but this had the reverse effect of stirring up antagonism between the three groups.

The parliamentary democracy that had evolved since the Glorious Revolution in Britain and the democratic ideology that had been cultivated by the Revolutionary War in America reached France as well. A group of prominent citizens, using these two precedents from overseas as points of reference, formed the National Assembly to oppose the privileged classes in 1789.

112 Amidst the confusion of the French Revolution, King Louis XVI is executed by radicals

In truth, the French government was going bankrupt.

Despite the fact that the people were suffering under heavy taxation, Louis XVI supplied support for the American War of Independence. In addition, in about 1783, as a result of a volcanic eruption in Iceland, Europe was struck by cold temperatures. France also suffered from a steep rise in prices of agricultural products, and resentment increased as people were no longer able to buy bread.

In order to overcome these circumstances, the National Assembly sought to

て、海外の植民地経営などに乗り出します。しかし、それが結局は国家間のエゴの対立となって、列強はお互いの覇権を牽制するために戦争を繰り返すことになったのです。戦争の遂行維持には、莫大な資金と有能な人材や官僚組織の投入が必要です。国家は慢性的な財政難に苦しめられ、同時に国の組織も複雑になったために、王個人の権限は相対的に脆弱になっていったのです。

　この傾向は、イギリスでエリザベス女王からチャールズ1世に至るまでの間にみられた現象です。そして、同様の傾向がルイ14世からルイ16世に至る100年強の間にフランスでもおきたのです。

　財政難に苦しむルイ16世は、特権貴族への課税を意図しますが、彼らの反抗にあってしまいます。そこで、聖職者と貴族、そして有力な市民による三部会という会議を招集しますが、逆にこれが市民と貴族や聖職者との対立を煽ってしまうのです。

　名誉革命以来のイギリスでの議会制民主主義と、アメリカの独立革命を通して育った民主化思想がフランスにも上陸します。有力な市民グループは、そうした海外での事例を参考にしながら、1789年に特権階級に対抗する国民議会を結成したのでした。

フランス革命の最中、急進派によってルイ16世は処刑された

　実際、当時のフランスの国家財政は破綻していました。
　人々が重税に苦しんでいたにもかかわらず、ルイ16世はアメリカの独立革命を支援します。加えて、1783年頃、ヨーロッパはアイスランドの火山の噴火の影響もあって、冷害に見舞われます。フランスでも穀物の値段が高騰し、パンを買えなくなった人々の怨嗟がつのりました。
　国民議会はこうした状況を打破するために、王や特権階級の利権を

時代
18世紀
近代

地域
フランス

分類
革命【政治】

キーワード
フランス革命の勃発・人権宣言の採択・列強の動揺・ジャコバン派の伸長と国王の処刑

control the vested interests of the monarch and the privileged classes, holding an assembly on the tennis court at the Palace of Versailles with the aim of establishing a written constitution. This event became known as the Tennis Court Oath.

Due to the fact that the monarch and the conservative faction of the aristocracy attempted to suppress this movement, the masses abandoned this attempt and instead, on July 14, 1789, they stormed the Bastille. This was the outbreak of the French Revolution. People rose up in every region, and the territories of the nobility and the clergy were raided. In August, the National Assembly adopted the Declaration of the Rights of Man and of the Citizen.

This declaration followed in the footsteps of the spirit of the American Revolution and took things even further. It held liberty and equality to be the fundamental rights of the people of the country and that was the right of the people to stand against an oppressive regime. It prohibited any infringement or trespass upon the rights of private property and stipulated that sovereignty resided in the people themselves.

In an attempt to wrest the king back from the privileged classes, the people moved him and his family from Versailles to Paris, where they decisively implemented various administrative reforms. At this point, the populace still retained confidence in the king and sought to find a way to bring about reforms under him. However, frightened by the developing circumstances, Louis XVI attempted to flee Paris. As a result of this event, which became known as the Flight to Varennes, the monarch and the masses drifted apart.

The political disturbance in Paris came as a shock to the powers of Europe. Austria, the homeland of Louis XVI and his wife Marie Antoinette and a perennial rival of France, feared that revolution might spread and sought to extend the circle of support for Louis XVI. Austria formed an alliance with its archrival Prussia and put pressure on France. Britain, which was ahead of France in terms of the establishment of a parliamentary democracy and which had various strategies for dealing with its French rival, followed suit in counter-revolutionary activities. Following the Revolutionary War, America remained independent and unallied with European powers as it worked assiduously at national development, adopting a wait-and-see policy.

Within this tense international environment, in Paris, in opposition to the faction supporting a constitutional monarchy, a faction known as the Girondins, a group of prominent citizens calling for a republican government, seized power. However, the general populace, which was agitated by the threat of counter-

抑制しようと、憲法制定を目指してヴェルサイユ宮殿のテニスコートで集会を開きます。テニスコートの誓いと呼ばれる出来事です。

この動きを国王や保守派の貴族が弾圧しようとしたことから、民衆が蜂起して1789年7月14日にパリのバスティーユ牢獄を襲撃します。フランス革命の勃発です。各地で民衆が反乱を起こし、貴族や聖職者の所領が襲撃されます。そして国民議会は同年8月に人権宣言を採択しました。

人権宣言はアメリカの独立革命の精神を踏襲し、深化させました。自由と平等が国民の基本的な権利であるとし、市民は圧政に抵抗する権利を持つとされました。そして私有財産への権力の侵害を禁止し、主権在民も明記されます。

人々は特権階級から王を奪還しようと、王とその一族をヴェルサイユからパリに移し、様々な行政改革を断行します。この時点では、まだ民衆は王を信頼し、王のもとでの改革を模索していたのです。しかし、状況を恐れたルイ16世はパリからの逃亡を試みます。ヴァレンヌの逃亡といわれるこの事件によって、王と民衆は離反してしまうのです。

パリでの政変は、ヨーロッパの列強に衝撃を与えます。ルイ16世の妻マリー・アントワネットの故郷であるオーストリアは代々フランスのライバルとして活動していましたが、革命の波及を恐れ、ルイ16世への支援の輪を広げようとします。オーストリアは宿敵であるプロイセンとも同盟し、フランスに迫ります。議会制民主主義という点では先輩格にあたるイギリスも、フランスというライバルに対する戦略もあって、反革命の動きに同調しました。独立革命後ヨーロッパに対して非同盟中立政策をもって国づくりにいそしむアメリカだけが状況を静観します。

緊迫した国際情勢のなか、パリでは立憲君主派に対抗していた、有力市民による共和政を主張するジロンド派が政権を握ります。しかし、反革命勢力の脅威に刺激された民衆はついに王権をも停止した形で、共和政の樹立を宣言します。これを第一共和政と呼んでいます。共和

revolutionary power, had already suspended monarchial authority and declared the establishment of a republican government. This is known as the First Republic. The parent administrative body of this republican government was the National Convention, which was composed of adult males chosen by election. With the power of the people, a voluntary army was organized in order to prevent other European powers from attempting to intrude into France. Those who sought to expand the political power of this National Convention were radicals who came to be known as Jacobins. In 1793, by a decision made by the Convention, King Louis XVI was executed.

113 The chaos of the Revolution and anxiety among the populace gave rise to the heroic Napoleon Bonaparte

The execution of Louis XVI proved to be a major stimulus to the European powers.

Led by Britain, the anti-French First Coalition was formed, creating a blockade around France. The major powers collaborated with conservative factions within France to strategize regarding counter-revolutionary movements. On the basis of such suspicions, a large group of people who were assumed to have carried on secret communications with overseas entities were massacred in September 1792, and Paris was beset with social unrest. The Jacobins, centered around Robespierre, in order to weather this crisis carried out the Reign of Terror to silence opposition factions and the conservative factions. Marie Antoinette, who had communicated secretly with Austria and other countries, was sent to the guillotine in October 1793.

However, the Reign of Terror turned the citizenry into its enemy. The coup d'état known as the Thermidorian Reaction occurred during this period. This revolt against the Reign of Terror was named after the French word for "summer," which was introduced in the unique calendar that the revolutionary government created when it abolished the conventional calendar. (The coup was initiated on July 27, 1794, or 9 Thermidor in the revolutionary calendar.)

The moderate faction, which ousted Robespierre, experienced difficulties in establishing a presidential government. However, France, facing looming counter-

政の運営母体は、選挙で選ばれた成人男性による国民公会でした。こうして民衆の力によって義勇軍が組織され、列強のフランスへの侵入を押しとどめたのでした。この国民公会で勢力を伸ばしたのが、ジャコバン派と呼ばれる急進派の人々です。1793年に、ルイ16世はついに国民公会の議決によって処刑されたのでした。

ルイ16世の処刑
The Execution of Louis XVI

革命の混乱と民衆の不安が、ナポレオンという英雄を生み出した

ルイ16世の処刑は、ヨーロッパの列強を強く刺激しました。

イギリスを中心に、対仏大同盟が結成され、フランス包囲網ができあがります。列強はフランス国内の保守派と連携して反革命運動を策謀しました。こうした猜疑心から、1792年9月には海外と内通している疑いをかけられた多数の人が虐殺される事件もおき、パリは社会不安に見舞われました。ジャコバン派は、この危機を乗り切るために、ロベスピエールを中心に反対派や保守派の人々を粛清し、恐怖政治を断行します。オーストリアなどと内通していたとしてマリー・アントワネットも1793年10月には断頭台にかけられました。

しかし、恐怖政治は市民層を敵にまわしてしまいます。テルミドール9日のクーデターと呼ばれる政変は、こうした中でおこります。テルミドールとは、革命政府が従来の暦法を強引に廃止して作った革命暦での夏にあたる言葉です。（クーデターは1794年7月27日、革命暦ではテルミドール9日に始まりました。）

ロベスピエールを倒した穏健派は、総裁政府を樹立して難局にあたろうとします。しかし、迫り来る海外の反革命勢力や、経済的な不安

時代
18世紀
近代

地域
フランス

分類
革命【戦争】

キーワード
列強のフランス包囲・ジャコバン派の恐怖政治・ナポレオンの登場・ヨーロッパを席巻・帝政に

revolutionary forces from abroad and economic anxieties, required strong leadership. That is how Napoleon Bonaparte, who during the French Revolution exhibited military genius in warfare against various countries, came to center stage in the political world.

Napoleon's immediate problem was how to counter Austria and Britain, which were the central figures in the Coalition against France. In the south, he invaded Austria in 1797. As a result, Napoleon succeeded in reaching an accord with Austria. In 1798, he sent an expeditionary force to Egypt to cut off the supply route of goods from Asia to Britain, effectively blocking it.

In European history, Napoleon ranks with Julius Caesar of the ancient Roman Empire as an unsurpassed strategist.

When Napoleon invaded Egypt, Britain crushed the French navy and used its maritime superiority to oppose France. Using this opportunity, the second Coalition was formed to encircle France. The people lost confidence in the ability of the impotent Directoire, the presidential government, to deal with the emergency. When Napoleon returned from Egypt, he was given an enthusiastic welcome by the populace. He took control of the government, replacing the Directoire, and succeeded in effecting what was in essence a coup d'état.

Napoleon led his troops across the Alps and initiated a surprise attack on Italy, dealing a blow to the Austrian army. Then by means of another peace agreement with Austria, he ultimately reached an accord called the Treaty of Amiens with Britain. This was the agility of true genius.

For some time thereafter, Napoleon concentrated on domestic affairs. He founded the Banque de France, reconstructed the national economy, and cultivated commerce and industry. Following a reform of the education system, in order to provide the basis for putting the country under the rule of law, in 1804 he promulgated the Napoleonic Code.

In that same year, Napoleon was elected emperor by a national referendum, and he commenced his reign as Napoleon I.

におののくフランスは、強力な指導力を必要としていました。フランス革命での諸外国との戦争で軍事的才能を発揮したナポレオン・ボナパルトは、このようにして、政界の表舞台に出てきたのです。

　ナポレオンの当面の課題は、対仏大同盟の中心となったオーストリアやイギリスの排除でした。1797年には、南からオーストリアへ侵攻します。この結果、ナポレオンはオーストリアとの講和に成功し、1798年にはイギリスへのアジアからの物資の供給路を断つためにエジプトに遠征してそれを遮断したのです。

　ナポレオンは古代ローマ帝国のジュリアス・シーザーと共に、ヨーロッパ史の中でも卓越した軍略家として歴史に名を残します。

　ナポレオンがエジプトに侵攻しているときに、イギリスはフランス海軍を打ち破り、制海権を獲得して対抗します。これを契機に、第二次対仏大同盟と呼ばれるフランス包囲網が再び形成されたのです。こうした危機に対応できなかった総裁政府の無力さに国民は失望しました。ナポレオンはエジプトから帰還すると国民に熱狂的に迎えられます。彼は、総裁政府に代わって政権を握り、事実上のクーデターを成功させたのです。

　ナポレオンはアルプスを越えてイタリアを奇襲し、オーストリア軍に打撃を与えます。そしてオーストリアと再び講和を結び、イギリスとも最終的にアミアンの和約という和平協定を締結したのです。それは天才的な俊敏さでした。

　以後しばらくナポレオンは内政に集中します。フランス銀行を設立して、財政を立て直し、商工業を育成します。教育改革に続いて、法治国家としての基盤を整備するために、1804年にはナポレオン法典を発布します。

　同年にナポレオンは国民投票によって皇帝となり、ナポレオン1世としてフランスに君臨することになるのです。

ジャック＝ルイ・ダヴィッド
『アルプスを越えるナポレオン』
Jacques-Louis David
―Napoleon Crossing the Alps

114 After the revolutions, as the West modernized, conflicts spread in Asia

We have considered the English Revolution and the Glorious Revolution which occurred in Britain, the War of Independence in America, and the French Revolution.

We have also seen that they are closely connected phenomena, not isolated events.

Each of these revolutions occurred in the process of making the individual self independent of blind obedience to either religion or to an absolute monarch. The term citizen for the first time came to connote respect for and self-awareness of the rights of the individual. Beginning with the Reformation and continuing through the Renaissance, the individual came to be highlighted more than religious authority. There is no more cogent ideal than the way of thinking that the person should be the subject of attention. In addition to the West's pursuit of this easily comprehended, easily acceptable theme, the world followed suit in learning this from European culture.

Meanwhile, European culture gave rise to discrimination in Asia and Africa. By liberating the individual, as the logic of capitalism rapidly advanced, the pursuit of wealth came to supplant morality. Ironically, from the viewpoint of Asia and Africa, it was as if they were being taken hold of by a new absolute monarch called the West.

Having undergone their own revolutions, the more modernized the Western countries became, the more apparent this contradiction became in the colonies that the Europeans founded.

For example, following the War of American Independence, ironically Asia came to be viewed as a new colonial market. Due to the changes of governance in the New World following American independence, Britain was obliged to escalate the pace of its advance into India.

Britain handed over its domination of Southeast Asia to the Dutch in the 17th century. The Dutch East India Company constructed the Batavia Castle in Indonesia, which became the predecessor of present-day Jakarta, turning it into the base for their Asian trade in 1619. Following the 1623 Amboyna Massacre of Britons by the Dutch in Indonesia, Britain withdrew from Indonesia. In the same year, the British trading house in Hirado was shut down. From then on,

革命を経て欧米が近代化すれば、
紛争がアジアに蔓延した

　我々はイギリスでおきた清教徒革命と名誉革命という一連の革命、アメリカでの独立革命、そしてフランス革命という3つの出来事を見てきました。

　そして、それぞれが孤立したものではなく、密接に関係した現象であることも理解しました。

　これらの革命は、宗教や絶対君主への盲従から自我を自立させる過程でおこりました。市民という言葉は、個々人の権利への尊重の意識があってはじめて活性化されます。宗教革命に始まり、ルネサンスを経て、宗教的権威より個人がクローズアップされてきます。人を主体におこうという考え方ぐらい説得力のある理想はありません。この解りやすく納得しやすいテーマを西欧が追いかけたがゆえに、その後ヨーロッパ文明を世界が学習することになるのです。

　一方で、ヨーロッパ文明はアジアやアフリカでの差別も生み出しました。個人を解放することで、資本主義の論理が躍進する中、モラルよりも富の追求が優先されたのです。それが皮肉にもアジアやアフリカから見るならば、西欧という新たな専制君主を抱かなければならなくなったのです。

　これらの革命を経て、西欧が近代化すればするほど、その矛盾は西欧が植民地とした地域で顕在化しました。

　例えばアメリカの独立革命以降、皮肉にもアジアが新たな植民地市場として注目されます。アメリカの独立で新大陸経営の変更を余儀なくされたイギリスがインドへの進出を加速させるのです。

　イギリスは、17世紀に東南アジアでの覇権をオランダに渡していました。オランダ東インド会社がインドネシアに現在のジャカルタの前身となるバタヴィア城を築き、交易の拠点としたのは1619年のことでした。1623年におきたアンボイナ事件と呼ばれる、インドネシアでのオランダによるイギリス人虐殺事件以来、イギリスはインドネシアを放棄し、同じ年に平戸にあったイギリス商館も閉鎖します。以後、イ

時代
18世紀
近代

地域
ヨーロッパ（世界共通）

分類
社会【侵略】

キーワード
ヨーロッパでの市民革命と資本主義の発展・アジアが植民地ターゲットに

Britain shifted its focus toward expanding into India. The government-controlled corporation that monopolized Asian trade, the British East India Company, established its base in Chennai in 1639. In addition, from the 1670s into the 18th century, the corporation advanced into Bombay—present-day Mumbai—and Calcutta—present-day Kolkata.

At that time, India was under the control of the Mughal Empire, but in the 18th century prominent regional figures became independent, and a number of small monarchial states were established. Friction deepened as a result of attacks from Iran and Afghanistan and discord among domestic Hinduism and Sikhism. Britain skillfully expanded during the twilight of the Mughal Empire.

Contemporary Europe was shaken by the War of Austrian Succession and the Seven Years' War. These wars had repercussions in India, and as a result, Britain ousted French influence from India. Immediately thereafter, America gained its independence. At the time Britain was speeding up its investments in India, Napoleon I deployed his military expedition to Egypt, seeking to blockade the trade route between India and Britain.

115 Napoleon I became the origin of the conflict between two sets of values: democracy and nationalism

We enter the 19th century with the appearance of Napoleon I.

With Napoleon ascending the imperial throne, Britain and Austria, worried that France might expand its influence within Europe and outside as well, sought a coalition with Russia and formed the third Coalition against France in 1805.

At the famous Battle of Trafalgar, Britain destroyed the French fleet, seeking to defeat the French attempt at establishing an economic blockade.

However, Napoleon invaded Austria, and in the Battle of Austerlitz he defeated the united armies of Austria and Russia and established the League of the Rhine, putting various states of southwest Germany under his protection. At this point, the Holy Roman Empire, which existed in name only and was devoid of substance, to all intents and purposes disintegrated, disappearing from history. In name and reality, the Middle Ages had come to an end.

ギリスはインドへの進出へと方針を転換します。アジア貿易を独占していた国策会社であるイギリス東インド会社は、1639年に現在のチェンナイに拠点を設けます。さらに、1670年代から18世紀にかけてボンベイ(現在のムンバイ)やカルカッタ(コルカタ)にも進出しました。

　当時のインドはムガル朝が支配していましたが、18世紀には地方の有力者が自立し、幾つもの小王国が形成されていました。また、イランやアフガニスタンからの侵攻や、国内でのヒンドゥー教、シーク教などとの摩擦も深刻でした。イギリスは、衰退期のムガル朝にたくみに進出したのです。
　当時のヨーロッパは、オーストリア継承戦争と、その後の七年戦争に揺れていました。この戦争はインドにも飛び火をし、その結果イギリスはフランス勢力をインドから駆逐します。その直後にアメリカが独立したのです。ナポレオンはイギリスがインドへの投資を加速させていた頃に、エジプトに遠征し、インドとイギリスとの通商ルートを断とうしたのでした。

ナポレオンは民主主義と民族主義の二つの価値の対立の源泉となった

　ナポレオンの登場とともに、我々は19世紀へと入ってゆくことになります。
　ナポレオンが帝位につき、フランスがヨーロッパ内外で勢力を拡大することを恐れたイギリスやオーストリアは、ロシアを誘って3回目の対仏大同盟を結成します。1805年のことです。
　イギリスは、有名なトラファルガーの海戦でフランス軍を破り、フランスの目論む経済封鎖を打破しようとします。
　しかし、ナポレオンはオーストリアに侵入し、オーストリアとロシアの連合軍をアウステルリッツの戦いで破り、西南ドイツの国々を保護下におきライン同盟を結成します。この時点で有名無実になっていた神聖ローマ帝国は事実上崩壊し、歴史から姿を消したことになります。中世が名実ともに終焉したのです。

時代
19世紀序盤
近代

地域
ヨーロッパ・ロシア

分類
戦争【革命】

キーワード
ナポレオン戦争の展開・革命理念の輸出・ナショナリズムの成立・ナポレオンの没落と革命の挫折

The series of conflicts that came to be known as the Napoleonic Wars gave rise to two different phenomena. One was the export of the ideology of the French Revolution by way of Napoleon.

Many European intellectuals expressed misgivings about long-established regimes, and this had a major impact on the movements for democratization in European countries. The second phenomenon was the awakening of nationalism as a backlash against French occupation. In various regions in Germany and Russia, ethnic awareness sprouted, and that in turn caused Napoleon distress.

In 1812, Napoleon invaded Russia, which antagonized France by exporting goods such as grain to Britain. Discouraged by the defensive war against Napoleon's ambitions, the French army, which once occupied Moscow, was inevitably forced to withdraw.

This state of affairs is portrayed in the famous Russian author Tolstoy's *War and Peace*. Also portrayed vividly in that work is how the reaction to Napoleon's actions resonated in the democratization movement and the nationalist fervor that sought relief for Russia. From the 19th century into the 20th century, discord as a result of the contradiction between democracy and nationalism constantly shook the world.

With Napoleon routed from Russia, the European powers went on the offensive. During this war between France and the Fifth Coalition in 1814, Paris surrendered, and Napoleon was exiled to the island of Elba.

In the following year, Napoleon escaped and returned to France, where he once again raised an army to fight against the coalition powers. At what later became known as the Battle of Waterloo, the tone was set for what would occur throughout all of Europe and even beyond.

Defeated in war, Napoleon was exiled to Saint Helena in the South Atlantic, an isolated, distant island where he died at the age of 51 in 1821. Under the supervision of the major powers, the monarchy of France was restored, and the brother of Louis XVI took the throne as Louis XVIII. However, France did not return to the old system of the Bourbon monarchy. Instead, by a continuation of trial and error, France advanced along the path toward democratization.

ナポレオン戦争と呼ばれるこの一連の戦いは、ヨーロッパに二つの異なる現象を引き起こします。一つは、ナポレオンによるフランス革命の理念の輸出です。

　ヨーロッパの多くの知識人は、旧来の体制に疑念を呈し、それがヨーロッパ諸国の民主化運動に大きな影響を与えることになります。そして二つ目が、フランスに占領されたことへの反発から芽生えたナショナリズムです。ドイツやロシアなど各地で、民族意識が芽生え、それが逆にナポレオンを苦しめることになったのです。

　イギリスへの穀物などの輸出によってフランスに対抗するロシアにナポレオンが侵攻したのは、1812年のことでした。このナポレオンの野望が国家をあげた防衛戦争によってくじかれ、フランス軍は一度占領したモスクワからの撤退を余儀なくされます。

　その模様は、有名なロシアの作家トルストイの小説『戦争と平和』に描かれています。そして、そこには、ナポレオンによってもたらされた民主化運動に共鳴しながらも、ロシア救済への民族主義に燃える人々の模様が生き生きと描かれています。19世紀から20世紀にかけて、この民主主義と民族主義の矛盾と確執が常に世界を揺り動かすことになるのです。

　ナポレオンがロシアから敗走したことで、ヨーロッパの列強はフランスへの攻勢に転じます。諸国民戦争と呼ばれるこの戦争ののち、1814年にはパリが陥落し、ナポレオンはエルバ島に流されました。

　翌1815年のこと、ナポレオンは一旦フランスに戻り、列強を相手に再び戦いを挑みます。後世ワーテルローの戦いで知られるこの戦争は、まさにその後の「天下」の趨勢を決めるものでした。

　戦いに破れたナポレオンは、南大西洋のセントヘレナ島に流され、1821年に絶海の孤島で51年の生涯を閉じたのでした。列強の管理の中、フランスはルイ16世の弟にあたるルイ18世によって、王政復古が行われます。しかし、すでにフランスは過去のルイ王朝のフランスに戻ることはなく、民主化への試行錯誤が継続することになるのです。

116

The Industrial Revolution advanced the motive power revolution which transformed human lifestyles

Just before and after the French Revolution and its aftermath another kind of revolution was about to make major changes in Western Europe. This was the motive power revolution which brought about dramatic changes in history. Historians refer to this upheaval as the Industrial Revolution. With the advance of motive power, industry as a whole became greatly modernized.

Traditionally humankind depended on oxen or horses for traction capacity or on the power of nature, such as wind power.

People continuously innovated technologies, such as the design of wheels, to reduce friction with the ground and effectively harness the power of these pulling forces.

In ancient times, people discovered iron, and they developed sturdy vehicles by using parts made of iron and steel. Be that as it may, these technologies were still dependent on power provided by animals, wind, or water currents, and people were still devising more efficient technologies within those restricted boundaries.

Beginning with the Reformation and individuals gradually becoming aware of the independent self, it took from 300 to 400 years for that historical energy to lead to the French Revolution. In a similar process, it took almost the same length of time for people in the Renaissance to reawaken to Greek civilization and to begin to observe nature once again, which is what led to the revolution in motive power.

During the Renaissance, the natural sciences were reexamined, and through the work of prominent figures such as Isaac Newton, who was active in Britain between the 17th and 18th centuries, dramatic advances were made in mathematics and astronomy. Newton's discovery of universal gravitation is well-known, but he is also known for the employment of mathematical theory in reforming Britain's monetary system.

In this way, science was removed from the realm of the divine, and by merging it with practical applications, they together had both direct and indirect impacts on the Industrial Revolution.

In Britain and elsewhere during this period, an agricultural revolution occurred, and large-scale management of agricultural lands evolved. Additionally,

産業革命は人類の生活を変えた
動力革命へと進化する

　フランス革命とその余波がヨーロッパ中を襲っていたその前後、もう一つの革命が西欧世界を大きく変えようとしていました。それは歴史の大きな転換点をつくった動力革命でした。歴史家はこの革命のことを産業革命と呼びます。動力が進化したことで、産業全体が大きく近代化したからです。

　古来人類は動力を牛馬の牽引力や風などの自然の力に頼ってきました。

　これらの牽引力に頼りながら、いかに地面との摩擦を減らして力を有効的に活用しようかと、車輪の構造などの技術革新を繰り返してきました。

　古代には、人々は鉄を発見し、鉄製の部材を用い強靭な乗り物を開発することができるようになりました。とはいえこれらの技術は、常に動物や風、海流などの力を借り、それをいかに有効的に活用しようかという工夫の域をでていなかったのです。

　ちょうど宗教改革に始まって、人々が個々人の中に自我を目覚めさせ、その歴史のエネルギーがフランス革命につながるのに300年から400年を要したように、人々がルネサンスでギリシア文明を呼び起こし、そこから改めて自然を観察するようになって以来、それが動力革命へと導かれるには、同様な年月が必要でした。

　ルネサンスの時代に、自然科学が見直され、それが17世紀から18世紀にイギリスで活躍したアイザック・ニュートンなどによって、数学や天文学を飛躍的に進歩させます。ニュートンは、万有引力の発見で知られていますが、数学の理論をもってイギリスの通貨制度を改革した人としても知られています。

　このように、科学が神の手を離れ、実学と融合したことが、産業革命にも直接、間接の影響を与えたのです。

　イギリスなどでは、こうした時期に、農業革命がおこり、農地の大規模経営が進みます。また、そうした時代の流れの中で、小規模の農

<table>
<tr><td>時代</td></tr>
</table>

時代
18, 19世紀
近代

地域
西ヨーロッパ

分類
技術【経済】

キーワード
科学の発展・科学と技術の融合・農業の大規模化・産業構造の変化・蒸気機関による動力革命

as a result of these changes, unemployed peasants who had relied on small-scale agricultural management left rural areas and became laborers in towns and cities. This created a supply of industrial workers.

Further, inexpensive cotton was imported from America, and Britain used the workers who gathered in the factories and the new technologies that were being developed to produce great amounts of cotton fabric, as well as weapons. Britain exported these to Africa and other markets. Particularly in the case of Africa, however, commerce involving the export of slaves as a labor resource for the cultivation of cotton in America boomed in the form of the triangular trade.

In order to coordinate with this change in industrial structure by raising production capacity, practical science was also employed in the actual production process. In 1733 John Kay invented the flying shuttle, and this is often pointed to as the beginning of the Industrial Revolution. This flying shuttle was an epoch-making technological innovation in the manufacturing of fabric, greatly improving production volume.

Following this, several varieties of manufacturing machinery using hydraulic power were developed. As a result of a long process of development from the 17th through the 18th centuries, in 1769 James Watt made a major improvement in the building of the steam engine, which was the start of the full-blown motive power revolution.

業経営に依存していたために失業した農民は、農村を出て都市で労働力となりました。工場労働者を供給する下地がこうしてできあがります。

　さらに、アメリカ大陸から安価な綿花が輸入され、イギリスでも工場に集まった労働者と新技術によってより大量の綿布や武器などが、アフリカなど各地に輸出されます。そして特にアフリカからは、奴隷がアメリカに輸出用綿花栽培の労働資源として輸出されるという三角貿易も盛んになります。

　こうした産業構造の変化に対応して、生産効率を上げようと、生産現場などで実学に応用されるのです。1733年にジョン・ケイが飛び杼を発明したことが、産業革命の始まりといわれています。飛び杼は機織りの技術を画期的に進化させ、生産量が向上します。

　その後水力を使った製造機器がいくつも開発されます。そして、もともと17世紀から18世紀にかけて開発されていた蒸気機関をジェームス・ワットが1769年に大きく改良したことが、本格的な動力革命の起点となったのでした。

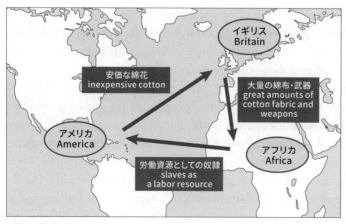

大西洋三角貿易
Atlantic Triangular Trade

117 The Vienna system attempted to turn back the clock in Western Europe

In 1814 George Stephenson succeeded in putting the steam engine to practical use. The steamship had already made its debut in America thanks to Robert Fulton. As a result of the use of a machine that could power its own locomotion, people were able to use it to move from one place to another. The conversion of fuel into power through combustion, known as the internal combustion engine, has since become the main means of transportation for humanity, even to this day.

The history of humankind underwent a major change after the invention of the steam engine (later internal combustion). The fact that mass production and large-scale production became possible allowed the evolution of capitalism, and it also became the reason why the West became dominant and conquered the rest of the world.

The Industrial Revolution spread thereafter through the main countries of Europe, eventually creating major changes even in Japan, which had just undergone the transition from the Bakumatsu period to the Meiji Restoration.

Affluent people invested in industry, and investments went into technological innovation. Machinery that was invented and subsequently improved was put to use in production inside large-scale factories. Laborers who had until then been farmers tied to agricultural villages went to work in factories. This shift in occupation fostered a growing sense of themselves as workers, aligning with the more liberal mindset prevalent in cities. This lead to the socialist movements that sought rights and better working conditions for laborers.

Especially in the early period of the Industrial Revolution, those who were wrapped up in the pursuit of profits actively expanded the use of inexpensive child labor and involved themselves in the slave trade. In response to these developments, social movements aiming to improve labor conditions emerged in countries like Britain, considering them from a human rights perspective. From the latter half of the 18th century into the 19th century, activists like Robert Owen became known for their efforts in obtaining education for workers and in prohibiting child labor.

From the second half of the 18th century onward, Britain became the first to succeed in the Industrial Revolution. It succeeded in becoming the world's factory and in administering colonies around the world. As the world's leader after the

体制は西欧の時計の逆行を試みた

1814年になると、ジョージ・スティーヴンソンがついに蒸気機関車の実用化に成功します。当時すでにアメリカではロバート・フルトンによって蒸気船がお目見えしていました。これによって、自力で走行する機械を利用して人々は移動することができるようになったのです。燃料を燃焼させ動力に変換する内燃機関は、現代まで人類の移動手段の主力となっているのです。

この蒸気エンジン（後の内燃機関）の発明の後、人類の歴史は大きく変化します。大量生産と大規模輸送が可能になったことは、資本主義を進化させ、欧米が圧倒的なパワーをもって他の世界を席巻する原因ともなります。

産業革命はその後ヨーロッパの主要国に伝播し、最終的には幕末を経て明治維新を経た日本をも大きく変化させることになるのです。

裕福な人間は、産業に投資し、技術革新に資金が投下されます。発明され改良された機械は大規模な工場での生産に活用され、工場には今まで農村に縛られていた農民が労働者として働くことで、労働者としての意識が芽生え、都市の自由な考え方にもそまってゆきます。それが、労働者の権利や待遇改善を求める社会主義運動へも繋がってゆくのです。

特に、産業革命初期には、利益の追求に走る人々が、低賃金での少年労働や奴隷貿易を拡大させてゆきます。こうした動きに人権擁護の観点から労働条件へメスを入れようとする社会運動がイギリスなどでおこります。18世紀後半から19世紀にかけて活動したロバート・オーウェンなどは、労働者への教育活動や少年労働への反対運動などを通して社会改革を目指した人物として知られています。

18世紀後半以降、いち早く産業革命を成功させたイギリスは、世界の工場として成長し、世界各地で植民地を経営します。ナポレオン戦争後の世界のリーダーとして、文字どおり世界はイギリスの世紀を迎

時代
19世紀序盤
近代

地域
西ヨーロッパ

分類
技術【国際】

キーワード
産業革命の進展・大量生産と大量輸送・資本主義の発展と矛盾・政治の反動化（ウィーン体制）

Napoleonic Wars, the century that followed was the British Century.

As the industrial world was achieving this remarkable reformation, the governments of Europe, in order to maintain the old regime in the face of the influence of the French Revolution were, to the contrary, attempting to turn back the clock. After the death of Napoleon, the Coalition powers assembled in the Congress of Vienna, and with Austria's Foreign Minister Klemens Metternich as chairman, they discussed a postwar settlement. France and Spain restored the Bourbon dynasty, German-speaking states were organized into the German Confederation, and Russian domination of Poland was recognized. Together, this meant that the old order, the Ancien Régime, was to be restored. Known as the Vienna system, these policies aimed at resurrecting the earlier European order.

Running counter to this system were new causes of discord in France and elsewhere. Charles X succeeded Louis XVIII, and because he leaned even more strongly toward the old regime, in 1830 the July Revolution erupted. The monarch was exile, and Louis-Philippe, a relative of the Bourbon family, was then chosen as the new king.

118 As a result of the Spring of Nations, the Vienna system collapsed

France, which had eliminated the threat of strong monarchial power as a result of the July Revolution, aggressively pressed forward with promoting industries under capitalists. This brought the full-scale Industrial Revolution to France.

However, in France, as was true in Britain, the sudden wave of the Industrial Revolution brought about great social disparity, and anxiety and dissatisfaction became rampant. As a result, the populace rose up in 1848, calling for universal suffrage, Louis Philippe abdicated, and France once again proceeded to become a republic. This political upheaval during called the February Revolution.

In observing this upheaval in the first half of the 19th century, we want to pay special attention to the placement of France and Austria in the overall scheme of things. Austria, under the House of Habsburg, ruled as the leading power of the Holy Roman Empire from the late Middle Ages, governing the countries of Eastern Europe and exerting powerful influence in Italy as well. After the French Revolution, popular movements spread throughout Europe, and France played a

えるのです。

このように産業界が目覚ましい変革を遂げているとき、ヨーロッパの政治はフランス革命の影響から旧体制を守るために、むしろ時代の針を押し戻そうとしていました。ナポレオンの没落後、列強はウィーンに集まり、オーストリアの外相メッテルニッヒが議長となって戦後処理について話し合います。フランスとスペインでブルボン王朝が復活し、ドイツの小国がドイツ連邦としてまとまり、ロシアのポーランド支配が認められるなど、旧体制の復活が定められました。ウィーン体制と呼ばれるヨーロッパの秩序の復活を目指したのです。

この時代に逆らう動きが、フランスなどで新たな混乱の火種を作ってゆきます。特に、ルイ18世の後を継いだシャルル10世が旧体制へとさらに傾斜しようとしたことから、1830年にパリで七月革命と呼ばれる革命がおき、王は追放され、ブルボン家の縁者からルイ・フィリップが新国王として迎えられたのです。

「諸国民の春」によって、ウィーン体制は崩壊した

七月革命によって王の強権への脅威を拭い去ったフランスは、資本家による産業の振興を積極的に推し進めます。これが、フランスに本格的な産業革命をもたらすのです。

しかし、フランスでもイギリスと同様、産業革命の急激な波は社会に格差を生み、不安や不満が蔓延します。その結果1848年に普通選挙を求めた民衆による暴動でルイ・フィリップは退位、フランスは再び共和政へと移行したのです。二月革命と呼ばれる政変です。

19世紀前半のこうした動乱を見るときに注目したいのが、フランスとオーストリアとの図式です。オーストリアは、ハプスブルク家の下、中世末期から神聖ローマ帝国の盟主として君臨し、東欧諸国をも傘下におさめ、イタリアにも強い影響力を持ってきました。そして、フランスで革命がおきた後は、革命による民衆運動がヨーロッパ各地に広まる中で、自らが古きヨーロッパの秩序の要として常にフランスでの

| 時代 |
| 19世紀中盤 |
| 近代 |

| 地域 |
| 西ヨーロッパ |

| 分類 |
| 革命【社会】 |

| キーワード |
| フランス2月革命・ウィーン体制の崩壊・民主化の進展と民族自立・ドイツ統一運動の開始 |

pivotal role in the confrontation with the old European order.

Klemens von Metternich, who created the Congress of Vienna system and worked tirelessly to maintain it, played the role of preserving this order.

When revolution occurred again in France in 1848, its impact instantaneously spread to Austria. A sudden uprising of the populace in Vienna occurred in March of that year and Metternich was brought down.

From the outset, the financial affairs of the Austrian Empire were on the brink of collapse due to military expenditures for maintaining the Vienna system, and the domestic economy was exhausted. Meanwhile, within the empire, a movement for democratization developed into nationalistic movements in the region that were still under control of the empire. As if in response to the fall of Metternich, disturbances broke out in the same year in Italy. Hungary and what later became Czechoslovakia called for democratization and national independence.

These nationalist movements throughout Europe in 1848 are collectively referred to as the Spring of Nations. As a result of the crises in Vienna and surrounding regions, Emperor Ferdinand I abdicated. He was succeeded by Francis Joseph I. With assistance from Russia, Austria then was able to somehow overcome the discord and return things to normal. However, as a result of these nationalist movements, the Vienna system completely collapsed.

This nationalist independence movement which occurred in the Austrian Empire was later connected with the political instability that occurred in the Balkan Peninsula. One ought not forget that it later triggered World War I.

Germany meanwhile, from 1848 into the following year, held the Frankfurt National Assembly in an effort to come to grips with a new order for Germany. It was an attempt to establish a new constitution and a democratic, unified nation-state.

This attempt, however, was suddenly checked by resistance from countries including Austria and Prussia. The birth of the German Empire nation-state would not come until 22 years thereafter.

動向に対峙してきました。

　その役割を担ってきたのが、ウィーン体制をつくり、その維持に奔走してきた宰相クレメンス・メッテルニッヒでした。

　1848年に、フランスで再び革命がおきると、その影響はまたたく間にオーストリアにも拡大し、3月にはウィーンでも民衆の蜂起があり、メッテルニッヒが失脚します。

　もともと、ウィーン体制の維持のための軍事費などで、オーストリア帝国の財政は破綻寸前で、国内経済も疲弊していたのです。一方、帝国内での民主化運動は、そのまま帝国の支配を受けていた地域の民族運動へと発展します。メッテルニッヒの失脚に呼応するように、イタリアやハンガリー、そして後のチェコスロバキアなどで同じ年にたて続けに民主化と民族の自立を求めた騒乱が勃発します。

　こうした1848年にヨーロッパ各地でおきた民族運動を人々は「諸国民の春」と呼んでいます。ウィーンや帝国周辺を見舞った危機で、皇帝フェルディナンド1世は退位します。帝位を継承したのはフランツ・ヨーゼフ。彼によって、ロシアなどの力も借りながら、オーストリアはなんとか混乱を収束させたのでした。しかし、こうした民族運動の結果でウィーン体制は、完全に崩壊してしまうのです。

　また、ここでおきたオーストリア帝国内の民族自立運動が、その後バルカン半島での政情不安に繋がり、最終的には第一次世界大戦への導火線となったことは忘れてはなりません。

　一方ドイツでは1848年から翌年にかけて新しいドイツでの秩序を模索したフランクフルト国民会議が開かれます。それは新たな憲法を制定し、民主的な統一国家を作ろうという試みでした。

　しかし、この試みはオーストリアやプロイセンなどの反発で頓挫します。ドイツ帝国という国民国家が誕生するのは、その22年後のことでした。

119 Following the Industrial Revolution, the West turned its attention to Asia

Great changes occurred in Russia, too, during the Industrial Revolution. The spirit of freedom and equality was exported by Napoleon I to all parts of Europe. Russia was no exception.

In the middle of the 18th century, Russia was under the rule of the famous empress Catherine II. She was the daughter of a prominent German noble family and was not actually Russian. After she arrived in Russia as the empress of Peter II, however, she cast aside her incompetent husband and took the throne herself.

Catherine II, like Frederick the Great of Prussia, is known for being an enlightened despot. She aggressively pressed onward with policies of southward expansion, and through the Russo-Turkish Wars obtained control of the Crimean Peninsula from the Ottoman Empire. She aggressively participated with Prussia and Austria in the partitioning of Poland and launched an advance through Siberia into the Far East. In the later years of her reign, she encountered the shock wave emitted by the French Revolution.

During the Napoleonic Wars, Paul I, who succeeded Catherine II, was caught up in political strife and was assassinated. When Alexander I ascended the throne, Napoleon I invaded Moscow.

Later, toward the end of the Napoleonic Wars, many Russian commissioned officers were posted in Paris, among other cities, and there they underwent a baptism in the movement toward democracy.

Meanwhile Alexander I maintained a leading position in supporting the Vienna system. Russia's active involvement in the international politics of Europe began with it.

Alexander I died in December 1825. In that same month, the commissioned officers who were dissatisfied with the political order which had remained unchanged for such a long period of time finally revolted, in what is known as the Decembrist Revolt. This rebellion was suppressed, but during the 92 years that passed between it and the Russian Revolution, discord repeatedly surfaced in Russia between the conservatives who supported the old system and the forces who sought democratization.

At the same time that Russia was making its presence felt in Europe, it also

産業革命の後、欧米列強はアジアの市場に注目した

産業革命の時期、ロシアでも大きな変動がありました。フランス革命の自由と平等の精神は、ナポレオンによってヨーロッパ各地に輸出されます。ロシアも例外ではありませんでした。

18世紀中盤、ロシアは女帝として有名なエカチェリーナ2世の治世にありました。エカチェリーナ2世はドイツの有力貴族の娘で、ロシア人ではありません。ピョートル3世の妃としてロシアにきた後に、非力であった夫を廃して自らが帝位についたのです。

エカチェリーナ2世は、プロイセンのフリードリッヒ大帝などと同様、啓蒙専制君主として知られています。彼女は積極的に南下政策を推し進め、オスマン帝国との露土戦争を経てクリミア半島をロシアに組み入れます。また、プロイセンやオーストリアとポーランド分割にも積極的に参画し、シベリアを経て極東への進出にも乗り出します。そんな彼女が晩年に直面したのが、フランス革命の衝撃波だったのです。

ナポレオン戦争時、エカチェリーナ2世の後を継いだパーヴェル1世が、政争に巻き込まれて暗殺されるという事件がおきました。そのあとを継いだアレクサンドル1世の時に、ナポレオンがモスクワに侵攻したのでした。

その後、ナポレオン戦争末期には、多くのロシア人将校がパリなどに駐屯し、そこでヨーロッパにおきている民主化運動の洗礼を受けました。

一方アレクサンドル1世は、ウィーン体制では指導的な立場を維持しようとします。ロシアが西欧の国際政治に積極的に関わり始めたのは、このウィーン体制からなのです。

アレクサンドル1世が世を去ったのが1825年12月。その同じ月に旧態依然とした体制に不満をもつ将校たちが蜂起します。デカブリストの乱と呼ばれる出来事です。乱は鎮圧されますが、この乱から92年後のロシア革命まで、ロシアでは旧体制を維持しようとする保守派の人々と、民主化を求める勢力との確執が顕在化するのでした。

ロシアはヨーロッパでのプレゼンスを誇示すると同時に、シベリア

時代
19世紀序盤
近代

地域
ロシア・中国

分類
政治【侵略】

キーワード
ロシアの発展・クリミア半島領有・シベリア進出・保守派と民主派の対立・清の全盛と典礼問題

エカチェリーナ2世
Catherine II

actively advanced from Siberia into the Far East.

During this period, China was midway through the Qing dynasty.

In the 17th century, under Emperor Kangxi, the Qing were at their peak, and when they were expanding their territories, it was Russia that they confronted. Once the Emperor Qianlong succeeded Emperor Yongzheng, Russia came from the north, and Britain and France came from the south, seeking access to the enormous Chinese markets.

During the Ming dynasty, China had contact with Europe through missionaries, but when the Qing dynasty arrived, among the missionaries there occurred the Chinese Rites Controversy, a debate over whether to recognize ancient Chinese Confucian morals. Wary of this, the Qing government attempted to maintain a certain distance from Europeans. As was the case with Japan, the countries of the Far East which had shut their doors to the outside world were later forced to make major concessions.

120 Markets underwent a cruel transformation from ceramics to tea, and eventually to opium

The first Asian cultural product that the Europeans showed an interest in was porcelain china.

The history of pottery and porcelain in the Far East reflected the East-West interchange and the region's political circumstances.

From ancient times into the Middle Ages, as the production of receptacles progressed from unglazed pottery pots to ceramic ware, and kilns were built in various places, successive Chinese dynasties also supported their production.

During the Song dynasty, a new method was developed that made vessels with a glass-like glaze by firing them at higher temperatures. The result was the development of porcelain. Beautiful chinaware called white porcelain and blue porcelain spread throughout European society during the period of East-West exchange and especially upon the arrival of the Age of Discovery.

This technology was transmitted to Korea as well, and during the Ming period, when Toyotomi Hideyoshi invaded Korea from Japan, both pottery technology and actual potters were brought to Japan. The entire Far East region began to draw attention for its production of ceramics.

から極東へも積極的に進出をしました。

　当時の中国は清朝の中期にあたります。

　17世紀、康熙帝の頃に清はその最盛期を迎え、領土を拡張したとき
に対面したのがロシアでした。その後雍正帝を経て乾隆帝の時代にな
ると、北方からはロシアが、南方からはイギリスやフランスが、広大
な中国の市場を狙うようになりました。

　中国は明の時代に宣教師を通して西欧とのコンタクトを持ちますが、
清になると、宣教師が中国への布教に対して中国古来の儒教道徳を認
めるかどうかという課題をめぐる典礼問題という対立が宣教師の間で
おこり、それを警戒した清朝政府は、西欧と距離をおくようになった
のです。日本と同様、海外との門戸を閉ざしていた極東の国々は、そ
の後大きな代償を強いられるのです。

陶磁器からお茶、そしてアヘンへと市場は
残酷にも変化した

　西欧の人々が、最初にアジアの文物に興味を持ったのは陶磁器でし
た。

　極東の陶磁器の歴史は、東西交流やその地域の政治情勢を反映した
ものでした。

　古代から中世にかけて、素焼きの壺から陶器へと器が進化すると、
各地に窯ができ、中国の歴代王朝も積極的にその制作を支援しました。

　宋の時代に、より高温でガラス化した器を作成する手法が開発され
ます。磁器の誕生です。白磁、青磁と呼ばれる美しい陶磁器は、東西
交流の時期、さらに大航海時代の到来によって西欧社会にも伝播され
ました。

　この技法は韓国にも伝わり、明の時代に豊臣秀吉が日本から朝鮮半
島に侵攻すると、多くの製陶技術が陶芸家と共に日本にも伝わりまし
た。極東全体が、陶磁器の産地として注目されるようになったのです。

（時代）
16〜19世紀
近代

（地域）
ヨーロッパ・東アジア

（分類）
交流【経済】

（キーワード）
東アジアの製陶技術の向
上・陶磁器、茶、胡椒の
貿易・産業革命による市
場としてのアジア

The Ming opened direct government-operated kilns, and in these sites pottery motifs and technologies from both East and West were integrated. Motifs such as arabesques and aspects of technology were transmitted to the Chinese world from the Islamic sphere that was contiguous with China. When these were fused with motifs from ancient China's ink painting tradition, a large number of beautiful ceramic vessels were produced. Further, from the Ming period into the Qing period, technology for applying color progressed. In addition, through the missionaries, artisans learned methods of making pottery with making use of enamel, and during the Qing period, under the influence of Western art, they produced porcelain ware that was even more colorful.

Following Toyotomi Hideyoshi's invasions of Korea, Japanese pottery technology, particularly in Kyushu, made dramatic strides, and a large number of pottery producers began to create porcelain ware. At first, it was Jesuit missionaries and later it was Dutch and British merchants who introduced this earthenware from China and Japan to the aristocracy in Europe. Now these pieces exhibited in European museums, such as the those of the Habsburg family, are highly prized articles.

There were, however, other Asian products that captivated the Western world: pepper and tea. Pepper reached the West from Indonesia, and tea came from China and India, causing a revolution in the eating habits of Europe.

At the outset, it was the Dutch and British who amassed fortunes by introducing Asian products to Europe. Dejima in Nagasaki harbor is a typical example of how they would establish a trading house in the locale and lay in stocks of ceramic ware. In Indonesia and India, they established plantations, cultivated pepper and tea, and loaded the harvested goods on ships. What occurred in these locations was part of the Industrial Revolution.

The Industrial Revolution dramatically expanded the output of Europe. When that occurred, Europeans began looking at Asia as a market for selling these manufactured goods. They accumulated wealth by importing products of culture from Asia, and then exporting the goods they produced to Asia. They created a complex trade network through which they purchased inexpensive products from the local area, and then exported them to places around the world. Representative of this intricate trading system was the British "triangular trade." They imported tea from China, sold cotton fabrics to India, and, in order to raise more funds, exported Indian opium to China.

明は、官窯と呼ばれる政府直営の製陶所を経営し、そこに東西から取り入れた様々なモチーフや技術も集約させました。中国世界が接するイスラム圏からも唐草模様などのモチーフや製陶技術の一部が伝達され、そこに中国古来の水墨画などのテーマが融合し、たくさんの美しい陶磁器が作成されます。さらに明から清にかけて、彩色の技術も進化します。加えて、宣教師を通してエナメルを使用した製陶法なども西欧から伝わったことで、清の時代になると、西欧美術の影響も受けた一段と華やかな陶磁器が制作されるようになったのです。

　一方、日本でも豊臣秀吉の朝鮮出兵後、九州を中心に製陶技術が飛躍的に進歩し、数多くの窯元が陶磁器の制作を始めます。中国や日本のそうした焼き物が、当初はイエズス会の宣教師、後にはオランダやイギリスの商人によって欧米の貴族社会に紹介されたのでした。それらは、今ではハプスブルク家などの宝物として西欧の博物館に展示されています。

　ところで、アジア圏には西欧を魅了した別の産物がありました。それが胡椒とお茶でした。胡椒はインドネシアから、お茶は中国やインドから西欧に伝わり、彼らの食生活に革命をおこします。

　当初、オランダやイギリスは、こうしたアジアの商品を西欧に紹介することで富を築きます。長崎の出島に代表されるように、現地に商館を開き、陶磁器を買い付け、インドネシアやインドなどではプランテーションを開いて胡椒やお茶を栽培して船で運びました。そこにおきたのが産業革命です。

　産業革命は、西欧の生産力を飛躍的に伸ばします。すると西欧は生産した商品の市場としてもアジアに注目するようになったのです。彼らはアジアからの文物の輸入による富の蓄積から、アジアへ製品を輸出し、現地からはより安く産品を仕入れ、再び世界へと輸出する複雑なネットワークによる貿易網を作り上げました。その代表が、中国から茶を輸入し、インドに綿織物を売り、さらなる資金調達のために中国にインド産のアヘンを輸出するという、イギリスによる三角貿易だったのです。

アヘンを巡る三角貿易
Triangular Trade
over Opium

イギリス
Britain

茶
tea

清
Qing

綿織物
cotton fabrics

アヘン
opium

インド
India

121

Civilian government and the policy of national seclusion drove the countries of the Far East into a corner

Already by the end of the 18th century, Britain was making repeated demands for China to open its doors to trade. At that time, Guangzhou was serving in the role of liaison to the outside world, just as Nagasaki had functioned under orders from the Tokugawa Shogunate. Britain was hoping for the opening of ports in addition to Guangzhou and was pressing the Qing government for full-scale trade.

Meanwhile, having achieved a major aim with the Qing government regarding territory, Russia switched its focus to Japan as a base for sea routes from the Pacific into Asia. In the 18th century, under the administration of the Tokukugawa Shogunate, Japan enjoyed a long period of peace, and prosperous Edo and Osaka ranked among the foremost large cities of the world, while their merchant class culture reached full bloom. However, the shogunate itself had fallen behind in implementing economic policies as the monetary economy spread, and it found itself in chronic financial trouble. In 1792, at about the time when Matsudaira Sadanobu carried out the Kansei Reforms in an effort to reconstruct the financial situation of the shogunate, which was facing financial pressures, Russia dispatched a mission led by Adam Kirillovich Laksman to Nemuro in Hokkaido seeking the return of some castaways and the establishment of commercial relations.

The shogunate, steadfastly maintaining its policy of national seclusion, rejected the request.

Meanwhile, Britain was scheming to establish economic inroads into China from the south. In due course, opium, which was the driving force behind this maneuvering, would undermine Qing society. Britain, which had purchased tea from China from the beginning, was troubled by a trade deficit. Through the sale of opium, however, Britain was able to gain a huge flow of silver from China, resulting in enormous profits.

The impoverishment of society and the outflow of silver posed a serious threat to the Qing government. At the time, Qing China was expanding its territory, and its population was rapidly increasing. However, in the provinces, poverty was spreading and farming villages were falling into decay. Due to the lack of development of a middle class as was found in Western Europe, the wealth of the privileged classes did not go into investing in industrial development.

文治政治と鎖国政策が、極東諸国を
追い詰めた

既に18世紀末から、イギリスは中国に対して門戸を開くように再三
要望していました。当時、徳川幕府にとっての長崎のように海外との
窓口の役割を果たしていたのは広州でした。イギリスは広州以外の港
も開港し、清との本格的な交易を進めることを望んでいたのです。

一方で、清との領土交渉を一段落させていたロシアは、太平洋から
アジアに向けての航路の拠点として日本に着目します。18世紀は徳川
幕府の統治のもとで平和が続き、江戸や大坂は世界有数の大都市とし
て繁栄し、町人文化が花開いていました。しかし、幕府自体は貨幣経
済が浸透してゆくなかで経済政策が後手にまわり、慢性的な財政難に
苦しんでいました。松平定信が、逼迫する幕府の財政を立て直そうと
寛政の改革を行っていた頃の1792年に、ロシアはラクスマン率いる使
節を北海道の根室に派遣し、漂流民の引き渡しと共に、通商を求めて
きたのです。

しかし、鎖国政策を堅持していた幕府はそれを拒絶します。

そんなときに、イギリスが南方から中国に対して経済進出を画策し
ていたのです。やがてその牽引役となったアヘンは清の社会を蝕みま
した。一方で、もともと中国からお茶を購入し、貿易赤字に悩んでい
たイギリスには、アヘンの販売によって中国から大量の銀が流れ込み、
莫大な利益を生み出したのです。

アヘンによる社会の疲弊と銀の流出は、清朝に深刻な脅威を与えま
す。当時の清朝は領土も拡大し、人口も急増していました。しかし、
地方では貧困が蔓延し、農村は荒廃します。西欧のように市民階級が
育たなかったことで、一部の特権階級の富が、産業の育成への投資に
回らなかったのです。

時代
18, 19世紀
近代

地域
中国・日本

分類
外交【社会】

キーワード
鎖国政策・西欧列強の通
商要求・アヘンの流入・
清の動揺・迫りくるヨー
ロッパの脅威

In the midst of this, in a movement similar to the Ikko uprisings that frequently broke out in the Sengoku period in Japan, in China at the end of the 18th century followers of the White Lotus Sect, a millenarian faction of Pure Land Buddhists, gathered displaced people and created an uprising. The Qing invested huge amounts of money in suppressing these uprisings.

Traditionally China administered the country by means of a civilian government. In the background was a lengthy dependence on the influential civil service examination system. Bearing responsibility for the conduct of state affairs were the civil service officials who had been selected by these examinations. These civil officials were supporters of traditional Chinese values. The Qing were not an exception to the pattern of actively introducing this system of functionaries. Because there was too much bias in favor of civilian government, the mounted troops of the northern nomadic people called the Eight Banners became obsolete in terms of their equipment and their military operations during the 19th century. This process was the equivalent of the way in which the bushi, or samurai, became bureaucrats during the Edo period.

As long as a country enjoys peace and stability, a civilian government ought to be able to contribute to the advance of a rich culture. In both the Genroku period and the Bunka Bunsei period during the Edo era, due to such social circumstances, the culture of the common people of Japan flourished. However, as a result of the need for markets brought about by the Industrial Revolution, leading the European powers to advance overseas, such an affluent land must have appeared like a delicacy to a lion. The issues of opium and silver exposed to the world this disparity in power.

そうした中、18世紀末には日本でいえば戦国時代まで盛んにおきた一向一揆にあたる、浄土教の一派白蓮教徒が流民を糾合し、反乱をおこします。この乱の鎮圧にも、清朝は莫大な資金を投じたのです。

　中国は伝統的に文治政治を国家経営の軸にしています。その背景には長年にわたる科挙制度が大きな影響を与えていました。国政を担うものは科挙を経て採用される文官だったのです。そうした文官は中国の伝統的価値観の担い手でもありました。積極的に伝統的な中国の統治機能を導入した清も例外ではありません。文治政治に偏りすぎたことで、八旗と呼ばれる北方民族の騎馬隊も、19世紀になれば装備も軍隊の運営力も老朽化します。これは、江戸時代に武士が官僚化した過程に通じるものがあるようです。

　平和を享受できれば、文治政治は芳醇な文化の振興に寄与できたはずです。江戸時代の元禄や文化文政時代もそんな背景で庶民の文化が花開いたのです。しかし、産業革命による市場のニーズによって海外への進出を図る西欧列強には、そんな豊かな土地は、ライオンにとっての脆弱な餌に見えたはずです。アヘンと銀の問題が、その力の差を世界に露呈することになるのです。

122 The Opium War was a turning point in the balance of power in world history

During the 1840s in Japan, not only the shogunate but also the assorted feudal domains that supported the administration of the government were under financial stress. The internal affairs of the Qing were in the same situation.

In an effort to somehow cope with the insidious influence of opium, the bureaucrat Lin Zexu, who was sent to Guangzhou, strictly clamped down on the opium imports by the British. In 1840 the two countries clashed, and the Opium War commenced.

Britain dispatched a fleet from India, and by means of its overwhelming modern equipment, the fleet won repeated encounters with the Chinese, devastating the country's fortified cities.

The Opium War was a decisive turning point in the power balance between the Western world and the Asian world. For the Qing, it was the starting point of a social upheaval, just as Commodore Matthew Perry's arrival in Japanese waters thirteen years later would lead to social turmoil.

There was a fundamental difference, however, between the fifteen year period between Perry's arrival and the Meiji Restoration and the more-than seventy year period between the Opium War and the collapse of the Qing. In China's case, the impact was a definitive decline in its image as a great country.

As a result of the Treaty of Nanjing in 1842, Qing China ceded Hong Kong Island and opened five ports, including Guangzhou, to British trade. In addition, China was forced to agree to a number of unequal treaties, which included the abandonment of tariff autonomy and extraterritorial rights. Following in Britain's wake, other European powers forced China to agree to similar treaties. When Japan abandoned its policy of national seclusion, it, too, was forced into signing similar unequal treaties.

In the first half of the 19th century, as the expanding Western world grew, three former powers spanning from Asia to North Africa began to decline in inverse proportion to the West's growth. This decline appeared in the Ottoman Empire, the Mughal Empire, and the Qing Empire in China.

We can also see how these problems—Middle Eastern discord, confrontations between Hindu society and Muslim society, unrest in the Far East, and China's revival—directly affected current world affairs. In the vast ocean of human history,

アヘン戦争は世界史のパワーバランスの
転換点だった

1840年代、日本では、幕府のみならず、江戸時代の権力を支えていた諸藩の財政も逼迫していました。清も内情は同じでした。

なんとかアヘンの弊害に対処しようと、広州に派遣された官僚林則徐が、イギリスから輸入されるアヘンを厳しく取り締まったのはまさにそうしたときのことでした。1840年、ついに両国が衝突します。アヘン戦争の勃発です。

イギリスは、インドから艦隊を送り込み、圧倒的に近代化された装備によって、各地で連勝し、清の城塞都市を蹂躙しました。

アヘン戦争は、欧米世界とアジア世界とのパワーバランスが決定的に変化する転換点になりました。また清にとっては、ちょうどその13年後におきるペリーの日本来航のように、中国社会の変革の起点にもなりました。

ただ、ペリー来航から明治維新までの15年間という時間と、アヘン戦争から清の滅亡に至る70年以上の年月の差こそが、その後の中国という大国のプレゼンスの低下の決定的な原因になりました。

1842年に南京条約によって、清は香港島を割譲し、広州を含め5つの港を開きます。さらに、関税自主権の放棄や治外法権の承認など、様々な不平等条約を押し付けられます。西欧列強はイギリスに追随するように同様の条約を締結します。そして、こうした不平等条約は、日本が鎖国を放棄したときにも導入されたのでした。

19世紀の前半、膨張する西欧世界に反比例して、アジアから北アフリカにかけて、かつての3つの勢力が衰亡に向かい始めます。オスマン帝国、ムガル王朝、すでに解説した清が牽引してきた中華帝国というパワーです。

そして、それらが中東問題、ヒンドゥー社会とイスラム社会との対立、極東の混乱と中国の再生など、現在の世界情勢に直接影響を及ぼしていることが見えてきます。人類の長い歴史という大海原の彼方に、

時代
19世紀中盤
近代

地域
アジア

分類
戦争【侵略】

キーワード
清のアヘン取り締まり・アヘン戦争の勃発・不平等条約と香港の割譲・アジアの大国の衰退

the faint image of our existence in the present starts to emerge.

The countries of the West made use of the conveniences of modern civilization provided by the Industrial Revolution. However, the methods of utilizing this civilization were inherited from ancient human practices. In other words, they funneled unprecedented transportation capacity, destructive power, and productivity into the domination of other ethnic groups and countries by force, for the sake of reaping profits from it. The 19th century, in particular, witnessed a state of indigestion within the human "stomach" caused by the clash between old traditions and the new civilization. The global fever and collapse resulting from this indigestion manifested as the two World Wars in the 20th century. For the principal region of Asia, from the Opium War to the end of World War II, after which ethnic groups began the process of obtaining independence and revival, the dark tunnel lasted a full hundred years.

123 Political instability in the Old World supplied a labor force for America

In addition to Britain, two other superpowers had a major impact on Asia during the second half of the 19th century: Russia and America.

After the Industrial Revolution, when European powers were beginning to make serious inroads into Asia, America, having established itself as an independent country, was focused on nation-building. Under the third president, Thomas Jefferson, policy debates over whether the powers of the federal government should be strengthened or whether local autonomy should be maintained were temporarily settled, and the outward form of the country was complete.

However, the French Revolution and the state of affairs that followed it in Europe cast a shadow over America. For a time, because America opposed the post-Revolution French government, there were frequent incidents in which French privateers attacked American merchant vessels, which brought about major damage to the newly formed U.S.

In 1812, conflict intensified between British-occupied Canada and the American settlers regarding land ownership rights of the indigenous peoples. In the end, the War of 1812 broke out. The conflict lasted two years and peace

今を生きる我々の姿がかすかに見え始めてくるのです。

　西欧諸国は、産業革命を通して手に入れた新たな文明の利器を使用します。しかし、その文明の使用方法は古代からの人類の手法を継承します。つまり、力による他民族や他国の支配と、それによる利益の享受のために、過去にはない輸送力や破壊力、そして生産力の全てを注ぎ込んだのです。19世紀は、特に古い伝統と、新しい文明が人類という胃袋の中で消化不良をおこしていました。その消化不良による地球規模での発熱と昏倒が20世紀におきた二つの世界大戦だったのです。アジアの主要な地域は、アヘン戦争を境に、第二次世界大戦後に始まる民族の自立や再生への道のりに至るまで、まさに100年間にわたる暗いトンネルへと入ってゆくのでした。

旧大陸の政情不安がアメリカへ労働力を供給した

　イギリスの他に19世紀後半以降アジアに大きな影響を与えるようになる二つの超大国。一つはロシア。そしてもう一つはいうまでもなくアメリカです。

　産業革命を経た西欧諸国がアジアに本格的に進出を始めた頃、アメリカはまだ建国後の国づくりに注力していました。アメリカ合衆国は、3代目の大統領トマス・ジェファソンの時に、連邦政府の権限を強化するか地方分権をしっかりと維持するべきかという政策論争も一段落し、国家としての体裁も整ってきました。

　しかし、フランス革命とその後のヨーロッパ情勢は、アメリカに影を落とします。一時、革命後のフランスの政権に敵対しているとして、アメリカの商船がフランスの私掠船に襲われる事件も頻発し、新生間もないアメリカ経済に大きな損害をもたらしました。

　そして1812年になると、カナダを領有するイギリスと、アメリカの入植者との間で先住民の土地の所有権をめぐる争いが激化。ついに米英戦争が勃発します。2年間に及ぶ戦いの後、ガン条約によって和平が

| 時代 |
| 19世紀序盤 近代 |

| 地域 |
| 北アメリカ |

| 分類 |
| 政治【社会】 |

| キーワード |
| アメリカ合衆国の発展・ヨーロッパ勢力の後退・移民の流入・飢饉や迫害からの解放地アメリカ |

was restored by the Treaty of Ghent. Thereafter, however, America traditionally pressed forward with policies that drew a line between itself and European upheavals, choosing to focus on improving its own national strength. Known as "isolationism," America's foreign policy retained this traditional stance toward the outside world.

However, we have seen how France maintained a large colonial territory in the New World: Louisiana. This territory stretched from the Gulf of Mexico in the south to the Great Lakes in the north. Following the French Revolution, Napoleon I was preoccupied with rebuilding France, and in 1803 he agreed to sell this vast territory to the U.S. for the exceptionally low price of $15 million. With this purchase, it became possible for the U.S. to extend its territories westward.

Having acquired this enormous new land, America needed a massive labor supply to develop it. This need was filled in the 19th century by waves of immigrants who were forced out of Europe by political instability.

During the period when the tempest of the Spring of Nations raged, primarily centered around Austria, Ireland, which had long suffered under the oppressive colonial rule of Britain, was struck by the potato famine. The famine impoverished the farming villages of Ireland, and the population of Ireland shrank by some 20%. One reason for the decrease was the large number of Irish who were crossing the Atlantic for the U.S.

Also among those fleeing Europe were Poles and Jewish people fleeing the czarist oppression in Russia, and Armenians escaping persecution by the Turks.

Just as Western Europe was gathering inexpensive laborers from agricultural villages and colonies, some laborers were taking the initiative in making passage to America. It was the influx of these industrious immigrants who worked hard to start new lives from scratch in the New World who became the driving force in building America into a superpower in the 20th century.

実現しますが、その後アメリカは伝統的にヨーロッパの騒乱とは一線を引く政策を推し進め、国力の充実に専念しました。孤立主義と呼ばれるアメリカの外交政策は、その後もずっとアメリカ外交の伝統として維持されます。

ところで、フランスは新大陸にルイジアナと呼ばれる広大な植民地を維持していたことはすでに解説しました。それは、南はメキシコ湾から北は五大湖に至るものでした。革命後の国家再建に忙しいナポレオンは、1803年にこの広大な土地を1500万ドルという破格値でアメリカに売却します。これで、アメリカ合衆国は西へ向けて領土を拡張することが可能になったのです。

新天地を獲得したアメリカの発展には膨大な人手が必要です。それを担ったのが、19世紀のヨーロッパでの政情不安に押し出されるようにして大西洋を渡ってきた移民でした。

「諸国民の春」の嵐がオーストリアを中心に吹き荒れていた頃、イギリスの植民地として圧政に苦しむアイルランドをジャガイモ飢饉が襲います。この飢饉は、アイルランドの農村を疲弊させ、アイルランドの人口は20％も減少したといわれています。こうした人々が、海を渡ってアメリカにやってきたのです。

ロシアからは、皇帝の弾圧に苦しむポーランド系やユダヤ系の人々、トルコからは迫害を逃れたアルメニア系の人々など、旧大陸での矛盾が、移民を海の向こうに押し出したのです。

西欧世界が安価な労働力を求めて農村や植民地から人々を集めていた頃、アメリカには労働者が自らの意思で渡航してきたのです。新大陸で一から生活を立て直そうと働く勤勉な移民の流入こそが、20世紀になってアメリカが超大国へと発展する原動力となったのでした。

アイルランドから旅立つ移民を見送る人々
Seeing off emigrants leaving Ireland

124 During the Oregon Trail era, people headed west

In the year 1825, the United States opened the Erie Canal, which connected the Hudson River in New York City to the Great Lakes. As a result, not just the inland areas but also the Midwest benefited from improved distribution networks, and the movement of people became much easier.

Once one reaches the Midwest by the combination of river and canal, the Mississippi River divides the continent into two parts. Halfway down the river is the city of St. Louis, located near the confluence of the Missouri River and the Mississippi River. The early pioneers started their journey toward the west from St. Louis, along the river.

They gathered in groups in a town called Independence, Missouri, at the gateway to what is now the state of Kansas, where they secured supplies for their long journey west. From that point onward, they had to either walk or ride in covered wagons over rough, unpaved roads. In the mid-19th century, the U.S. government encouraged westward settlement and aimed to effectively incorporate the Oregon Territory, located near the current states of Oregon and Washington, particularly close to the border with Canada. For that reason, the federal government approved grants of land free of charge to those who settled in Oregon Territory. Upon departing from Independence, it took these pioneers six months to cross the Rocky Mountains and the deserts to reach Oregon. One out of ten ancestors of Americans today traveled over the Oregon Trail or one like it, and the passage was so perilous that of those who started out, one in ten died along the way.

They departed from Independence in the spring in order to reach Oregon before the harsh winter weather set in. These migrants, who often didn't speak the same language, formed impromptu groups to travel west together. They could not ship heavy possessions, such as furniture. Along the way, they had to cope with not only threats from natural phenomena but also attacks by indigenous people.

Immigrants who had come from Ireland, Eastern Europe, and the Middle East aimed for locations which dotted the American West where earlier settlers from their homelands had already established villages. In addition to the Oregon Trail, migrants carved out several other routes and settled the remote western region— the frontier.

オレゴントレイルの時代、人々は西に向かった

1825年のことです。アメリカはニューヨーク市の横を流れる大河ハドソン川と五大湖を結ぶエリー運河を開通させます。これで内陸、さらに中西部との物流が改善され、人々の移動も楽になります。

中西部に行けばミシシッピ川が大陸を縦断しています。その中流域にセントルイスという町があります。そこはミズーリ川がミシシッピ川に合流する地点です。このセントルイスからミズーリ川に沿って開拓者は西に進みました。

カンザス州の入り口にあるインディペンデンスという町に彼らは集結し、そこで物資を調達します。そこからは幌馬車か徒歩で悪路を進まなければなりません。19世紀中盤、アメリカ政府は西海岸への入植を奨励し、特にカナダとの国境に近い現在のオレゴン州とワシントン州に位置するオレゴンテリトリーの開拓をすることで、そこを実質的にアメリカに組み込もうとしていました。そこでオレゴンに入植した人に無償で土地を与えることを承認したのです。人々はインディペンデンスから6カ月かけて、ロッキー山脈や砂漠を越えてオレゴンに向かいました。アメリカ人の祖先の10人に1人が、このオレゴントレイル、あるいはそれに似た開拓路を通って西に向かいました。それは、さらに10人に1人が途中で死亡するという命がけの旅でした。

春にインディペンデンスを発ち、厳しい冬が訪れる前にオレゴンに到着しなければなりません。言葉も通じない移民たちは即席のグループを作って西に向かいます。家具などの重たいものは輸送できません。また、途中自然の脅威のみならず、先住民の攻撃にも対応しなければなりませんでした。

アイルランドや東ヨーロッパ、中東などから移住してきた人々は、アメリカ西部各地に点在する自らの先輩がすでに開墾した村落をも目指します。こうしてオレゴントレイル以外にも、いくつもの開拓ルートが切り開かれ、西部の辺境、すなわちフロンティアに入植していったのです。

時代
19世紀序盤～中盤
近代

地域
アメリカ合衆国

分類
移動【社会】

キーワード
運河、河川による交通の発達・フロンティアの開始・内陸の開発・ゴールドラッシュ

This great migration, rare in world history, ranks with that of the Germanic peoples and the Normans in ancient history. Through the experience of this great migration, these people came to hold in common the frontier spirit, taking risks to carve out a new livelihood. Further, they cultivated a spirit of self-government and self-reliance through administering the land and the villages they and their cohorts settled and defended. These people who had gathered from all over the world, developed a shared consciousness as Americans.

When gold deposits were discovered in California in 1848, a large number of these pioneers along the Oregon Trail headed south into California instead. Thus began to Gold Rush. By means of the California Trail the opening of present-day California made rapid headway.

When the settling of the West Coast progressed and the population along the Pacific Coast began to increase, Americans began to cast their gaze upon the vast market of Asia in the distance.

125 As a result of the Mexican–American War, American territory increased

Let us now consider South America. The Napoleonic Wars and the uneasiness in Europe that followed them had a significant impact on the colonies of the European powers. Especially after Spain became embroiled in warfare due to the invasion of Napoleon I, independence movements occurred throughout Central and South America.

In these movements for independence, it was people of Spanish descent who were born in South America, known as criollos, who played a central role. The movement, which began in Venezuela, was led by Simón Bolívar, who came from an elite criollo background. As a result of a series of battles with Spanish forces, the region that includes today's Venezuela, Colombia, Panama, Ecuador, Bolivia and Peru gained independence from Spain around 1825. Several of these became a federal republic called Gran Colombia.

However, due to internal conflicts, each region eventually became independent, and the prototype of today's South America came into being. A similar type of activity occurred in Argentina, and it gained its independence from Spain too.

In this connection, as a result of Napoleon I's invasion of Portugal, and

これは古代のゲルマン人やノルマン人の大移動に匹敵する世界史で
も稀な民族の大移動です。大移動の経験を通して、人々はリスクをとっ
て生活を切り開くフロンティア・スピリットを共有します。また、自
らや仲間が切り開いた土地や村落を運営し、防衛するという自治独立
の精神も培います。世界各地から集まった人々に、いわゆるアメリカ
人としての共通の意識が育まれてゆくのです。

　1848年にカリフォルニアで金鉱が発見されると、多くの開拓者がオ
レゴントレイルの途中からカリフォルニアへと南下します。ゴールド
ラッシュです。カリフォルニアトレイルによって、現在のカリフォル
ニアの開拓も進むのです。
　こうして西海岸へ入植が進み、太平洋岸の人口が増え始めた時、ア
メリカ人の目の向こうにアジアという広大な市場が見えてきたのです。

米墨戦争によって、アメリカの国土は膨張した

　ここで南米を見てみます。ナポレオン戦争とその後のヨーロッパの
動揺は、列強の植民地にも大きな影響を与えました。特にナポレオン
の侵攻によってスペインが戦火に巻きこまれると、中南米では各地で
独立運動がおこります。

　独立運動には、クリオーリョと呼ばれる、南米生まれのスペイン系
の人々が中心的な役割を果たしました。運動はまずベネズエラで始ま
り、それをクリオーリョの名門の生まれであるシモン・ボリバルが指
導します。スペイン軍との攻防の末に1825年頃までに現在のベネズエ
ラ、コロンビア、パナマ、エクアドル、ボリビア、そしてペルーにあ
たる地域が独立し、コロンビアという連邦共和国が成立しかけました。

　しかし、その後の内部分裂により、それぞれの地域が独立。現在の
南米の原型が生まれたのです。同様の活動はアルゼンチンなど南部の
地域でもおこり、スペインの支配から独立してゆきます。
　ちなみに、ナポレオンのポルトガル侵攻によって、一時ブラジルに

時代
19世紀序盤～中盤
近代

地域
中南アメリカ

分類
独立【社会】

キーワード
中南米国家のスペイン、
ポルトガルからの独立・
先住民との対立・米墨戦
争・アメリカ大陸の安定

beginning with the establishment of the provisional government in exile in Brazil, an independent Portuguese-connected group sought to establish independence and in 1822 established the Empire of Brazil.

What was common throughout South America was the economic control maintained by the elite white classes. Due to the rift between the indigenous populations, descendants of slaves, and those who were forced into harsh living conditions, and the affluent criollos, the society in Central and South America was fragmented. In addition, there were conflicts within the criollos between those who sought a republican form of government and those sought a monarchy ruling a centralized nation-state.

In Mexico in 1808, the Creole Mexican priest Miguel Hidalgo led a revolution against Spain which involved Indians and mestizos, but it was defeated, and he was executed in 1811. Following this, the war for independence continued, and at one point Mexico came under the rule of prominent Creole leaders, but that collapsed within two years. In 1836 the Mexican Republic was formed. It was in this northern region of Mexico that immigrants from the United States settled, and they declared independence from Mexico that same year, forming the Republic of Texas. Eventually Texas was annexed by the U.S. and then became a state.

The Mexican-American War later broke out over territorial borders, and in 1848 this war ended in the defeat of the Mexicans. As a result, the U.S. succeeded in cutting away a huge swath of territory from Mexico that included land from the Rocky Mountains to California. In contrast with the poverty and government paralysis in Central and South America, the U.S. steadily expanded its own territories, and the labor force of immigrants poured in.

Due to the stability of the U.S., the colonial aspirations in North America by European powers, such as Britain and France, miscarried. Fortunately for the U.S., in the first half of the 19th century, due to political discord in both the Old World and Central and South America, it was able to expand its territories dramatically.

亡命政権がおかれたことを皮切りに、ブラジルでは独自にポルトガル系の帝政を維持しようと、ブラジル帝国が1822年に成立したこともありました。

そんな南米に共通したのは、白人系富裕層による経済支配です。先住民族や奴隷の子孫など、過酷な生活を強いられる人々と、富裕なクリオーリョとの亀裂によって、中南米の社会は分断されていました。そして、クリオーリョの中でも共和政を目指す者と、専制君主、あるいは強力な中央集権国家を目指す者との間で、様々な確執があったのです。

メキシコではクリオーリョの神父ミゲル・イダルゴが1808年に、先住民も巻き込んで革命をおこしますが結局失敗し、1811年に処刑されてしまいます。その後独立戦争は継続し、メキシコは一時クリオーリョの有力者による帝政に移行しましたが2年で瓦解。1836年になってメキシコ共和国が成立します。そんなメキシコが領有していた北部地方にアメリカ合衆国から移民が入植し、その年にメキシコからの独立を宣言したのです。テキサス共和国の成立です。やがてテキサス共和国はアメリカに併合されます。

その後アメリカとメキシコは領土をめぐって米墨戦争をおこしますが、1848年にメキシコの敗北で戦争は終結します。その結果、アメリカはロッキー山脈周辺からカリフォルニアに至る広大な領土をメキシコから切り取ることに成功したのです。中南米に続く政治の停滞と貧困とは対照的に、アメリカは着実に領土を拡大し、そこに移民という労働力を注ぎ込んだのです。

アメリカが安定したことで、イギリスやフランスといったヨーロッパの列強が北アメリカに抱いた植民地的な野心も挫折することになります。アメリカは19世紀前半に、幸運にも旧大陸と中南米での政治的混乱によって国土を大幅に拡大できたのです。

126 Seeking raw material for candles, America pressed Japan to open its doors

Within world history, the year 1848 has a special place. The Spring of Nations, the Irish Potato Famine, and the conclusion of the Mexican-American War, enabling American expansion westward were all events that occurred in that year.

The European movement toward democratization which followed the French Revolution and led to continued instability in Europe caused large numbers of people to migrate out of Europe to America in the years immediately before and after 1848.

In America during this period, whaling became a major industry for the collecting of whale oil to use as material for producing candles. Whaling ships carried on activities all around the Pacific Ocean. For these whalers, there was an urgent need to obtain a supply route with a stable source of fuel and provisions during whaling operations. Geographically, Hawaii was the first place that drew their attention. Not only America but also Britain and France maneuvered to take possession of this small group of strategically located islands.

The next place that the Americans turned their attention to was Bakumatsu Japan. In 1853 Commodore Matthew Calbraith Perry, leading a fleet of ships, appeared in the offing at Uraga. Under this pressure, two years later Japan abandoned the policy of national seclusion it had long maintained and opened the country again.

Japan had closed its doors to the outside world during the Thirty Years' War which followed the Reformation in Europe. Following the initiation of that policy, Japan had been left behind as the West advanced. At the time, the Japanese were aware of the events surrounding the Opium War, which was threatening Qing China. They were also aware of the pressure being put on the Qing after the war, not only by Britain but also by France and Russia. In 1858 through the Treaty of Aigun, Russia received from Qing China the territory north of the Amur River, and in 1860, through the Convention of Beijing, China was forced to cede Primorsky Krai, the Maritime Territory. As a result, Russia was able to gain Vladivostok, a key port in the Far East, which was ice-free. This, in turn, posed a direct threat to Japan.

By the middle of the 19th century, the distribution of European power in Asia was for the most part complete. The Netherlands had colonized Indonesia, while Britain expanded its colonial rule from India to Myanmar and the Malay

ろうそくの原料を求めて、アメリカは日本に開国を迫った

1848年という年は世界史の上でも大切な一年でした。諸国民の春、アイルランドの飢饉、アメリカの西への拡大を容易にした米墨戦争の終結、これら全てのことが1848年におこっています。

フランス革命以来のヨーロッパでの民主化運動に始まり、その後の不安定な政情が続くヨーロッパからアメリカに移民が大量に流出し始めたのも1848年前後からのことでした。

時代
19世紀中盤
近代

地域
アジア

分類
外交【侵略】

キーワード
太平洋の分割・日本の開国・ロシアの南下・アジアの植民地化・オスマン帝国の衰退

そんなアメリカではろうそくなどの原料となる鯨油を採取するための捕鯨が一大産業となっていました。捕鯨船は太平洋各地で活動します。彼らにとって、捕鯨船の燃料や食料の安定した補給ルートを確保することは急務だったのです。地勢的にまず注目されたのがハワイでした。アメリカのみならず、イギリスやフランスなどもこの小さな諸島の領有を目論見ます。

そしてアメリカが次に注目したのが幕末の日本でした。1853年にペリー提督率いる船団が浦賀に現れ、その圧力のもと、翌年に日本は長年続いた鎖国政策を放棄し、開国します。

マシュー・ペリー提督
Commodore Matthew Perry

日本が鎖国したのは、ヨーロッパが宗教改革の後の三十年戦争に揺れている頃でした。以後の西欧の発展から日本は取り残されていたのです。当時、日本はアヘン戦争に苦しむ清の情勢をつかんでいました。また、アヘン戦争の後にイギリスのみならず、フランスやロシアが清に圧力をかけていたこともつかんでいました。ロシアは1858年にアイグン条約で清から黒龍江以北を、60年には北京条約で沿海州を割譲させています。その結果、ロシアはウラジオストックという不凍港を極東で手に入れたのです。これは日本への直接の脅威でした。

19世紀の中盤までに、西欧のアジアでの勢力地図は大方完成していました。オランダがインドネシアを領有し、イギリスはインドを植民地経営の拠点としてミャンマーやマレー半島へと進出し、シンガポー

Peninsula, establishing a base in Singapore.

France used the Nyugen dynasty, which it set up and supported, to carry out commercial operations in Vietnam and Cambodia.

In West Asia, the Ottoman Empire had declined.

The Ottomans had possessed enormous territories in Eastern Europe, but as a result of conflict with Austria, the Ottomans lost Hungary and Romania.These changes had a major impact on nationalist movements in the Balkan Peninsula.

In particular, the independence movement in Greece, which directly experienced the effects of the Napoleonic Wars, had a significant influence on the Ottoman Empire. Needless to say, the independence movement in Greece was entangled with the intentions of Russia, Britain, and France. Greece became independent in 1830. Rather than being just a conflict between the Ottomans and the Greeks, this involved a gamble over various interests among the powers of Western Europe, and it would not be going too far to say that it ended with the Ottomans being made fools of. The decline of the Ottoman Empire and China led to an era in which the West dominated the East.

127 The Crimean War was a world war that engaged the great powers

In the mid-19th century, the Ottoman Empire was unable to sustain either the political power or the military strength to maintain its expansive territories.

Despite being the leader of Islam, the Ottoman Empire faced challenges from Arab peoples of the same faith who sought national independence in various parts of the Middle East.

It was Britain that sought to gain advantages by making use of these nationalist movements.

In addition, Russia placed pressure on the Ottomans from the north. Seeing this, Britain, France, and Austria also intervened to gain advantages for themselves.

When these powers came into confrontation with the Ottoman Empire, large-scale hostilities broke out in 1853. This was the Crimean War.

The Crimean War started with the movement for self-determination by ethnic groups within the domains of the Ottoman Empire, particularly in the Balkan

ルにも拠点をおきました。

　フランスは、自らが支援して建てた阮朝という王朝を通し、現在のベトナムやカンボジアの経営に集中します。

　そして、西アジアでは、オスマン帝国が衰退していました。

　オスマン帝国は、東欧に広大な領地を持っていましたが、オーストリアとの抗争の末にハンガリーやルーマニアを失います。こうした動きは、バルカン半島での民族運動にも大きな影響を与えました。

　特に、ナポレオン戦争の影響を直接被ったギリシアでの独立運動はオスマン帝国に大きな影響を与えます。ギリシアの独立運動にはロシアやイギリス、そしてフランスなどの思惑も絡んでいたことはいうまでもありありません。ギリシアが独立したのは1830年。それはオスマン帝国とギリシア人の抗争というよりは、西欧列強の利害をめぐる駆け引きに、オスマン帝国が翻弄された結果といっても過言ではなかったのです。オスマン帝国や中国の衰退は、世界史を西高東低の時代へと導いたのでした。

クリミア戦争は列強をまじえた世界大戦だった

　19世紀中盤、オスマン帝国は広範な領土を維持するだけの政治力、軍事力を保てなくなっていました。

　イスラム教の盟主であったオスマン帝国ですが、中東各地では、同じイスラム教を信奉するアラブ系の人々の民族独立運動に悩まされることになります。

　そうした民族運動を利用して利権を獲得しようとしたのがイギリスでした。

　加えて、ロシアが北からオスマン帝国へ圧力をかけます。それを見たイギリスやフランス、そしてオーストリアが、自国の利益のために介入します。

　オスマン帝国を軸に列強の利害が対立したとき、1853年に大規模な戦闘が始まりました。クリミア戦争です。

　クリミア戦争は、オスマン帝国の領内、特にバルカン半島でおきた民族自決運動がその端緒でした。

時代
19世紀中盤
近代

地域
ロシア・トルコ

分類
戦争【民族】

キーワード
オスマン帝国の衰退・ロシアの南下・バルカン問題の顕在化・グレートゲームの始まり

Peninsula.

The background of the war involved the Slavs in the Balkan Peninsula who were responding to the Russian policy of pushing southward, and countering the intentions of France and Britain, who were eager to contain Russia's expansion.

Jerusalem, which was under Ottoman control, was also a holy place in Christianity, and because Russia acknowledged itself to be the guardian of the Greek Orthodox Church, Jerusalem was one place where it wanted to have a degree of political influence.

Meanwhile, in the Balkan Peninsula, there was incessant economic and political friction between the ruling Muslims and the ruled Christians. This unstable situation came to be referred to as the Eastern Question.

Later, after World War I, the conflict that broke out between Serbia, Croatia, and Bosnia at the end of the 20th century was nothing less than an extension of this Eastern Question.

In 1853, Russia declared war on the Ottoman Empire.

The pretext was to protect the Slavic Christians within Ottoman territories. In response, Britain and France allied themselves with the Ottomans and joined the conflict. As a result the conflict spread from Eastern Europe to the coast of the Black Sea, with repercussions reaching the Baltic Sea and the remote Russian Far East. The war came to a temporary end with the 1856 Treaty of Paris, dealing a blow to Russia's policy of southern advance.

The Crimean War was the first true world conflict following the Industrial Revolution in which the combatants employed modern weaponry. And as was true of the later Russo-Japanese War, which was fought in a third nation, the Crimean War was fought within the sovereign territories of the Ottoman Empire. Availing itself of this opportunity, Britain blatantly asserted hegemony over the present-day territories from the Middle East to Egypt. France similarly laid claim to territory from Morocco to Algeria. While Russia gave up its political policy of southward advance, as a result of the Crimean War, it thereafter engaged more actively in the Far East. This had a major impact on Japanese foreign policy following the Meiji Restoration.

クリミア戦争の背景には、南下政策をとるロシアと、それに呼応するバルカン半島のスラブ系の人々と、ロシアが強大になることを牽制したいフランスやイギリスの思惑がありました。

　オスマン帝国が支配するエルサレムは、キリスト教の聖地でもあり、特に正教会の保護者を自認するロシアにとっては面目上もなんらかの形で政治介入したい場所でもありました。

　一方、バルカン半島は、支配層のイスラム教徒と被支配層のキリスト教徒との間に、経済的、政治的な摩擦が絶えませんでした。こうした不安定な状況を人々は「東方問題」と呼んだのです。

　その後、第一次世界大戦を経て、20世紀終盤におきたセルビアやクロアチア、そしてボスニアを巻き込んだ紛争なども、「東方問題」の延長に他なりません。

　1853年にロシアはオスマン帝国に対して宣戦を布告します。

　名目はオスマン帝国領内にいるスラブ系のキリスト教徒を保護することにありました。これに対して、イギリスとフランスがオスマン帝国側に立って参戦したことで、戦争は東欧から黒海沿岸、さらにはバルト海や遠く極東ロシアにまで飛び火する大規模なものとなったのです。1856年のパリ条約によって戦争は一段落して、ロシアの南下政策には楔が打たれました。

　クリミア戦争は、産業革命を経て近代化した兵器を使用した初めての本格的な国際紛争でした。そして、この戦争は後年、第三国が舞台となった日露戦争などのように、オスマン帝国という主権国家の領土の中で他の列強が争った戦争でもありました。これを契機にイギリスは現在の中東からエジプトにかけて、フランスはモロッコからアルジェリアにかけて露骨に覇権を主張するようになったのです。一方、クリミア戦争で黒海を経由した南下政策を断念したロシアは、以後極東への進出に積極的になります。このことが、明治以降の日本の外交政策に大きな影響を与えるようになるのでした。

フローレンス・ナイチンゲール：イギリスの看護師。1854年、クリミア戦争にイギリスが参戦すると、38名の看護団を率いて前線に赴いた。劣悪な衛生状況のなか、敵味方の区別なく負傷兵を看護した。

Florence Nightingale (1820–1910)：British nurse; when the British entered the Crimean War in 1854, she led a team of 38 nurses to the front line. In poor hygienic conditions, she nursed wounded soldiers, friend and foe alike.

In the latter half of the 19th century, in Europe, modern nation-states came into existence one after another

Following the revolutions of 1848 in France, Louis Napoleon, nephew of Napoleon I, came to power and, after a coup d'état in 1851 and a popular referendum, he became the emperor Napoleon III. This imperial regime is known as the Second Empire.

During the era of Napoleon III, the Industrial Revolution permeated France even further, and France advanced aggressively into China and Indonesia.

Within Germany, an economic alliance centered around Prussia was established to distance itself from Austria.

In eastern Germany, landowner elites known as Junkers, aristocrats with roots among the knights of the Middle Ages, were highly influential. Among these Junkers was Otto von Bismarck, who was appointed prime minister in 1862.

Bismarck actively promoted military expansion in Prussia and won a war against Denmark over Schleswig-Holstein, forcing Denmark to surrender that province. Prussia took the province under its control and later annexed it. In response to pressure from Austria, which was displeased by Prussia's rise to power, in 1866 war broke out between the two states in 1866. This Austro-Prussian War resulted in the surrender of Austria.

The expansion of territory by Prussia created a sense of potential danger in France, which bordered directly on Germany. On the pretext of a confrontation between the two states over succession to the Spanish throne, Prussia led a coalition of German states against France in 1870 in the Franco-Prussian War.

Originally, Prussia was a monarchy in eastern Germany. However, with Bismarck's strategy of building a wealthy country and a powerful army, combined with excellent diplomatic maneuvering, Prussia brought Bavaria in southern Germany and other states onto the Prussian side and crushed the French army. Prussia seized and occupied Paris in 1871. At the same time, the Second Empire in France collapsed. Prussia's Wilhelm I assumed the imperial throne at the Palace of Versailles, and the German Empire was established, with Bayern, Saxony, and Prussia allied with other states.

As a result, for the first time since the Holy Roman Empire, the complicated international relations that had existed between Germany and Austria came to

19世紀後半に、西欧に近代国家が続々と成立した

1848年の革命の後、フランスはナポレオンの甥にあたる、ルイ・ナポレオンが政権をとり、51年のクーデターと国民投票を経て、皇帝となります。ナポレオン3世の登場です。この帝政のことを第二帝政と呼んでいます。

ナポレオン3世の時代、フランスは産業革命がさらに浸透し、中国やインドシナにも積極的に進出しました。

一方ドイツ内部では、オーストリアと距離をおいた形で、プロイセンを中心とした経済同盟が成立します。

ドイツ東部では、中世の騎士にルーツを持つユンカーと呼ばれる地主が大きな影響力を持っていました。1862年にプロイセンの首相に任命されたビスマルクもそんなユンカーの出身でした。

ビスマルクは積極的な軍備拡張を推し進め、デンマークとの間のシュレスヴィッヒ・ホルシュタイン州の帰属をめぐる国境紛争に勝利して、これらの州を管理下におき、後に併合します。さらにプロイセンの台頭を嫌うオーストリアの圧力に抵抗し、1866年に勃発したプロイセン－オーストリア戦争によって、オーストリアを屈服させたのでした。

プロイセンの領土拡張は、ドイツと国境を接するフランスにも警戒感を与えます。両国は、スペイン王の継承権をめぐる対立を名目として、1870年についに普仏戦争をおこします。

もともとプロイセンは、ドイツ東部の一王国でした。しかし、ビスマルクのとった富国強兵策と卓越した外交手腕で、ドイツ南部のバイエルンなどの州もプロイセン側につき、フランス軍を圧倒したのです。プロイセンは、1871年にはパリを占領。同時に第二帝政は崩壊します。その折に、プロイセンのヴィルヘルム1世は、ヴェルサイユ宮殿で帝位につき、バイエルンやザクセンなども含めたドイツ帝国が成立したのです。

これによって、神聖ローマ帝国以来、複雑な国際関係を生み続けてきたドイツとオーストリアとは、正式に別の国家になったことになり

時代
19世紀中盤
近代

地域
西ヨーロッパ

分類
統一【対立】

キーワード
列強が近代国家として確立・プロイセンの躍進・独仏の対立・ドイツ、イタリアの統一

an end, with the two officially becoming separate states. And this is how the new Germany came into existence, a country that would have enormous influence in the world in the 20th century.

At the same time, the humiliating defeat in the Franco-Prussian War (and the harsh indemnity France was forced to pay) resulted in bitter strife between the two countries that continued through World War II.

Meanwhile, unification movements arose in Italy, too, which since the Middle Ages had been strongly influenced by Austria. Victor Emmanuel II, monarch of Sardinia, allied with Napoleon III to defeat the Austrians. Once that occurred, the unification movement by Giuseppe de Garibaldi of the Young Italy party brought together a collection of smaller states that had been divided since the Middle Ages and presented them to Victor Emmanuel II. So in 1861 these unified states became a single country: the Kingdom of Italy. From the 1860s into the 1870s, the many countries that form present-day Western Europe replaced the old ones, and the modern nation-state began to appear on history's stage.

129 Countries in the Far East were forced to take various measures to deal with the threats posed by Western powers

As Europe reconfigured itself into national states and nation power became more substantial with the advance of the Industrial Revolution, Asia and Africa were hard-pressed to deal with the threat they presented. One notable example of this was China.

After witnessing the enormous losses and the carnage of the Opium War, the Qing dynasty, after concluding the Treaty of Nanjing, failed to make effective domestic reforms and was forced to constantly deal with the strategies of the Western powers.

Becoming economically impoverished as a result of the domestic disorder resulting from the opium trade and the inequity of the Western powers' control of tariffs on trade, internally China was caught in a whirlpool of discontent. It was against this backdrop that Hong Xiuquan, under the influence of Christianity, launched the Taiping Rebellion in 1851.

ます。20世紀に世界に甚大な影響を与える新生ドイツはこのようにして世界史に登場します。

　同時に、普仏戦争での屈辱的な敗北は、第二次世界大戦に至るまで、ドイツとフランスとの間に感情的な軋轢を生み出すことになったのです。

　一方、中世以来オーストリアが強い影響力を持っていたイタリアでも統一運動がおこります。サルデーニャ王エマヌエーレ2世がナポレオン3世と組んでオーストリアを駆逐します。それを受けて、統一運動の中核として活動していた青年イタリア党から身をおこしたガリバルディが、中世以来分断されていた国家群を統一し、エマヌエーレ2世に献上したのです。こうして1861年にイタリア王国が誕生しました。このように1860年代から70年代にかけて、現在の西ヨーロッパの主要国が次々と新陳代謝を行い、近代国家として歴史の表舞台に登場することになったのでした。

ヨーロッパ列強への脅威に極東諸国は様々な対応を迫られた

　ヨーロッパが国民国家として再統合され、産業革命の進行と共に国力を充実させるに従って、その脅威がアジアやアフリカを見舞うことになります。その代表的な事例が中国でした。

　アヘン戦争で多大な痛手と殺戮を目の当たりにしながらも、清王朝は南京条約を締結したあとも、効果的な国内改革を怠り、同時に欧米列強にも対処療法的な戦略に終始していました。

　アヘンによる国内の混乱と、欧米列強が関税をコントロールする不公正な貿易活動による経済の疲弊は、中国国内に不満の渦を巻きおこします。そうしたときに、洪秀全がキリスト教の影響を受けながら1851年におこしたのが、太平天国の乱でした。

時代
19世紀中盤
近代

地域
中国・日本

分類
国家【戦争】

キーワード
清の国内改革の遅滞・戦乱によるの混乱と弱体化・日本の開国と近代国家へ進展

This rebellion served as the catalyst for China's transformation into a modern nation. Hong Xiuquan, in response to the challenges faced by the Qing government both internally and externally, advocated for the slogan "Overthrow the Manchus, Restore the Han" and promoted the idea of national liberation from Manchu rule. The insurgency rapidly grew, taking hold across southern China. Nanjing was renamed Tianjing and was established as the capital of a new state.

Under these tense circumstances, as a result of the seizure of the Arrow, a ship of British registry, the British—and the French who responded to a British appeal—formed an allied force and commenced warfare with the Qing. As a result, Beijing was occupied by the Europeans and the Qing were forced to agree to the 1860 Convention of Beijing. Consequently, freedom to trade in opium was granted, foreigners were permitted to carry out various activities including the propagation of Christianity, and further, a large number of Chinese ports were opened to foreign ships. In addition, the Chinese ceded the Kowloon region north of Hong Kong to the British.

Once the Convention of Beijing was concluded and their mutual aims had been achieved, Britain and France then joined in cooperating with the Qing government in dealing with the troublesome Taiping Rebellion by providing military support. Together with this support from the Western powers, the Qing introduced a volunteer army under the leadership of two Han Chinese, Zeng Guofan and Li Hongzhang, to cope with the Taiping Heavenly Kingdom. The collapse of this latter entity came in 1864. The activity of the Han consolidated dissatisfaction with the Qing, and it took close to 50 years for the Xinhai Revolution to overthrow the Qing, finally succeeding in 1912.

The plight of China being trampled upon by the Western powers posed a significant threat not only to China but also to neighboring countries.

However, in Korea, which shared a border with the Russian-occupied Primorsky Krai, the Joseon dynasty, as a tributary state of China, continued to keep its doors closed to the Europeans and the Americans.

In contrast, as if sensing an impending crisis due to the actions of the Western powers, in Japan the Tokugawa Shogunate was overthrown in 1868, and the Japanese, by trial and error, began to join the ranks of international political powers. The disparity between the Qing, the Joseon, and the reborn Japanese in coping with international affairs had a major impact on the situation in the Far East in the years that followed.

And immediately prior to Japan's reawakening, an upheaval occurred in

この乱は、中国が近代国家へと生まれ変わる導火線となった乱でした。洪秀全は、国内外の課題に対応できない清朝政府に対して、「滅満興漢」をスローガンに、満州民族による支配からの脱却という民族主義を掲げます。反乱はみるみる拡大し、華南一帯を占領します。南京を天京と名付け、首都として国家を樹立しようとしたのでした。

　緊迫した情勢の最中、清朝政府は、再びイギリス船籍のアロー号を拿捕したことから、イギリスと、その呼びかけに応じたフランスとの連合軍を相手に戦争を始めたのです。結果は北京を占領され、1860年に北京条約を押し付けられます。その結果、アヘン販売の自由化や外国人の国内での活動やキリスト教布教の自由などを認めさせられ、多くの港を開港します。さらにイギリスには、香港北部の九龍地区を割譲させられたのでした。

　一方、北京条約を締結したことで、一応の目的を達成したイギリスとフランスは、その後太平天国の乱に悩む清朝政府に協力し、軍事力を提供します。清朝は、列強の支援と共に曾国藩や李鴻章といった漢民族の官僚による義勇軍を導入して、太平天国に対応します。太平天国が滅亡したのは1864年のことでした。こうした漢民族の動きが、清朝への不満へと統合され、辛亥革命によって1912年に清朝政府が滅亡するには、さらに50年近い年月がかかったのです。

　列強に蹂躙される中国の状況は、近隣の諸国にも大きな脅威と映りました。
　しかし、沿海州を占領されロシアと国境を接した李氏朝鮮では、未だに中国への朝貢政策の元で欧米に対しては門戸を閉ざした王朝を維持していました。
　逆に、欧米の危機感に煽られるかのように、日本は1868年に徳川幕府を倒して明治維新となり、国際政治のプレイヤーに加わろうと試行錯誤を始めたのです。清朝と李氏朝鮮と新生日本とのこの国際政治への対応の差が、その後の極東の情勢に大きな影響を与えるようになるのです。

　そして、日本が新しい国家に生まれ変わる直前に、アメリカでもそ

America that would have a decisive impact on what would happen in that country and elsewhere in the following years. The Civil War broke out.

130 Economic disparity between the North and the South was an important factor in bringing about the Civil War

Prosecuting a war requires enormous resources and power.

With the arrival of the modern era and the development of industry, iron, coal, ships, and railroads became indispensable. It was the disparity in availability of resources that enabled Bismarck to achieve overwhelming victory in the Franco-Prussian War and allowed the vast territories of China to be overrun.

Ironically, outside areas that are devastated by warfare, war actually stimulates industrial production. Especially as a result of the plundering of resources of colonized territories, the great powers were able to expand their colonial possessions further. Moreover, when weapons were exported to the battlegrounds, things got even better.

In the United States, industrial and financial activities were concentrated in the North, while the South was dominated by large-scale agricultural operations. Southern plantation owners, in order to convert cotton cultivation into money, depended on the inexpensive labor of black slaves, and they had to sell cotton to markets in the North or to factories in Britain.

The North advocated the abolition of the system of slavery that formed the foundation of the southern economy. Further, as America expanded its territories from east to west, there was vociferous public controversy regarding whether the future states that would be created in the West should allow slavery or not.

The United States was originally a federalist nation with strong state autonomy. Controversy between the two regions ignited over the expansion of slavery. When Abraham Lincoln, who stood against the system, was elected president of the country, the states that sanctioned slavery seceded from the United States of America and established the Confederate States of America. They established their own capital at Richmond, Virginia. The Civil War, which took place in 1861, was the conflict that occurred to reunify the divided United States.

Like the Crimean War, the Civil War was one of the earliest wars of mass

の後のアメリカの歴史に決定的な影響を与える動乱が発生します。南北戦争の勃発です。

南北の経済格差が南北戦争を引き起こす重要な要因だった

戦争を遂行するには、莫大な資源と動力を必要とします。

近代になり、産業が発達すると、鉄と石炭、そして船舶と鉄道が戦争遂行にとって必須の条件となります。ビスマルクが普仏戦争に圧勝したのも、中国が広大な国土を蹂躙されたのも、こうした資源の動員力の格差によるものでした。

戦争は皮肉にも被災地以外の産業を活性化させました。特に列強は植民地からの資源の収奪によって、さらに植民地を拡大できました。また、武器は戦地に輸出され、時と共に改良を加えられました。

時代
19世紀中盤
近代

地域
アメリカ合衆国

分類
戦争【制度】

キーワード
戦争の近代化・南北の経済制度の齟齬・南北戦争の勃発・黒人奴隷の解放・産業界の進展

アメリカでは北部にそうした産業や金融活動が集中し、南部は大農経営が中心でした。南部のプランテーションのオーナーが綿花を栽培して資金化するためには、安い労働力である黒人奴隷に頼り、製品を北部の市場や、イギリスの工場に売らなければなりませんでした。

南部が経済基盤として維持しようとする奴隷制度に対し、北部はその廃止を唱えます。また、アメリカが東から西へと領土を拡大するごとに、そうした地域にできた州を奴隷制度を認める州にするかどうかで世論が対立します。

もともと、アメリカは連邦制をとる国家で、州に強い自治権があります。この奴隷制度をめぐる議論が発火し、奴隷制に批判的なエイブラハム・リンカーンが大統領に選ばれたとき、奴隷を認める州は、アメリカ合衆国を脱退して、アメリカ連合国という国家をつくったのです。バージニア州のリッチモンドが首都となりました。分断されたアメリカを再統一するために1861年におきたのが、南北戦争だったのです。

南北戦争はクリミア戦争と同様、歴史が経験する極めて初期の大規

slaughter in human history. The army of the South, led by generals like Robert E. Lee, clashed violently with Northern armies under commanders like Ulysses S. Grant. In New York, indigent immigrants from Ireland rebelled against the system of conscription into the northern army, and there were lynchings of blacks in the city.

In 1863, President Lincoln issued the Emancipation Proclamation, and the North won the crucial Battle of Gettysburg. With these events as turning points, the army of the North, which had greater economic strength, continued to gain advantage on the battlefields, and the South surrendered in 1865. However, after the war ended, poverty in the South and the economic disparity between blacks and whites remained a social problem in America.

Weapons that were left over after the Civil War were imported by Japan and employed in the fighting that occurred before and after the Meiji Restoration. Once America was reunited, the West was opened further, and in 1869, the First Transcontinental Railroad was completed. Chinese who struggled against poverty in their own country immigrated to America, where they were employed as laborers in constructing railroads. At the time when American territories expanded as far west as the Pacific Ocean, when Asian immigrants such as these began to stream in in large numbers, they became the target of discrimination among immigrants from Europe who had previously settled in the West.

エイブラハム・リンカーン
Abraham Lincoln (1809–1865)

模な殺戮戦争でした。リー将軍らが率いる南軍に対して、グラント将軍らが率いる北軍が激しくぶつかります。ニューヨークでは徴兵に反対する貧しいアイルランド系移民などが反乱をおこし、黒人をリンチする事件もおきました。

　1863年に、リンカーン大統領は奴隷解放宣言を出し、ゲティスバーグの戦いに勝利します。これを契機に、経済力に勝る北軍が戦争を有利に進め、65年に南軍は降伏しました。しかし、その後も南部の貧困と、黒人と白人との格差は、アメリカの社会問題として残ったのです。

　一方、南北戦争の終結で余った武器は、日本に輸出され、明治維新前後の戦いに使用されました。さらに、再統一されたアメリカは、西部開拓を進め、1869年には大陸横断鉄道も開通します。貧困にあえぐ中国からの移民が鉄道建設の労働力として活用されたのです。アメリカの領土が太平洋に至った頃、こうしたアジアからの移民も流入し、それが先に西部を開拓したヨーロッパ系移民による差別にも繋がっていったのです。

ゲティスバーグの戦い（1863年7月1日-7月3日）
南北戦争はアメリカで最大の犠牲者を出した戦争であり、この戦いでも多くの戦死者を出した。同年11月にリンカーンは戦場跡での追悼式で演説を行い、有名な「人民の、人民による、人民のための政治」を主張した。

Battle of Gettysburg (July 1–3, 1863)
The Civil War was the largest war in U.S. history, and the Battle of Gettysburg claimed enormous casualties. In November of that year, President Lincoln spoke at a memorial service at the site of the battle and famously argued for "government of the people, by the people, for the people."

131 The birth of communism became the spark that ignited the 20th century

In the 1870s, the German Empire came into existence, and the United States was reunified following the Civil War. In Japan, the Meiji Restoration was carried out, and Britain and Russia aggressively advanced into the Far East.

With these developments, discord sprang up between the conquerors and the conquered, and through the unification of countries, nationalism arose.

The concentration of population in the cities as a result of the Industrial Revolution and the broadening of the working population aroused in people a certain degree of distrust regarding the disparity between the rich and the poor and regarding the lack of social welfare. As we have seen earlier, people such as Robert Owen in Britain were aiming for improvement of the rights of laborers.

Karl Marx and his friend Friedrich Engels theorized about labor movements and analyzed past revolutions and the Napoleonic Wars. In their 1848 publication *The Communist Manifesto*, they predicted that the capitalist society led by the bourgeoisie, which had already overturned the era of kings and aristocrats, would eventually be overthrown by the working class. This concept was based on the idea of class conflict.

This movement merged with nationalism in Europe and America and provided new ideas for refoming of the social system. It provided the foundation for socialist societies envisioned in the 20th century by the Russian Revolution and the establishment of the People's Republic of China, and nation-building based upon communism.

Poland, divided between Prussia, Russia, and Austria, became a symbol of both the nationalist and socialist movements of the time. The intense nationalist movement, particularly against Russia, became one of the underlying causes of events such as the assassination of Russian Emperor Alexander II in 1881. The assassination of the emperor by Polish anti-establishment activists using a bomb had a significant impact on imperial Russia. When these nation-building activities and nationalist movements merged, the history of the 20th century was set in motion.

Among those that are generally placed within the category of communists appeared people, such as Mikhail Bakunin, who were anarchists who rejected the existing government and religion. Christianity could be said to have been both the

共産主義の誕生は20世紀への導火線になった

　1870年代、ドイツ帝国が誕生し、アメリカも南北戦争を経て再統一されました。また、日本では明治維新がおき、イギリスとロシアは積極的に極東地域に進出しました。

　こうした動きは、征服民族と被征服民族の確執、さらには国家の統一という作業を通した民族主義を萌芽させます。

　一方で、産業革命による都市への人口の集中と労働人口の拡大は、貧富の差や社会福祉の欠如についての疑念を人々に投げかけます。イギリスでは労働者の権利向上を目指すロバート・オーウェンなどによる活動があったことはすでに記しました。

　カール・マルクスと彼の友人のフリードリッヒ・エンゲルスは、こうした労働運動を理論化し、過去におきた革命やナポレオン戦争などを分析します。そして王侯貴族の時代を覆した市民による資本主義社会も、やがて労働者によって打ち倒されてゆくことを予測した『共産党宣言』を1848年に発表します。階級闘争という考え方です。

　この動きは、その後の欧米列強での民族主義とも融合しながら、社会体制に新たな改革のヒントを与えます。20世紀におきるロシア革命や中華人民共和国の成立などに繋がる社会主義、そして共産主義に立脚した国家建設への動きがそれにあたります。

　当時の民族運動と社会主義運動の象徴として語られるのが、プロイセンとロシア、そしてオーストリアに分割されたポーランドでした。特にロシアに対する激しい民族運動は、1881年におきたロシア皇帝アレクサンドル2世暗殺事件などの遠因ともなりました。ポーランド系の反体制活動家の爆弾によって皇帝が暗殺されたことは、帝政ロシアに大きな影響を与えます。この国家建設の動きと民族運動とが融合したとき、20世紀に繋がる歴史の針が回り始めるのです。

　共産主義に母体を置く人々の中には、ミカエル・バクーニンのように、既存の政府や宗教を完全に否定する無政府主義者も現れました。キリスト教はヨーロッパ社会の支柱ともいえる道徳律でもあり心のよりど

【時代】
19世紀中盤
近代

【地域】
ヨーロッパ

【分類】
社会【革命】

【キーワード】
植民地化と民族主義・産業化と貧富の格差・共産主義運動の始まり・パリコミューンの成立

ethical code, as well as the source of emotional support, in European society. The anarchists challenged the validity of that fundamental value system.

In Russian and numerous other countries, in response to social unrest, underground movements began, stimulated by the theories of communism as well as anarchism. Socialists gathered together in London in 1864 and formed the First International.

At precisely that time, the Franco-Prussian War broke out. As a result of the war, Paris fell, and during the chaos that followed, the populace of Paris, together with laborers, established a government known as the Paris Commune.

The Paris Commune was a short-lived government, lasting only from March through May 1871, but it embodied what Marx had predicted, carving itself indelibly into the minds of the people.

Ultimately, the Paris Commune was quelled by the republicans, and France then transitioned to the Third Republic. With this, the country was finally able to break out of a period of disorder that had continued since the French Revolution and was beginning to develop as a nation-state.

132 India and China became subordinate to Britain through cotton and opium

Following the Industrial Revolution, in the 19th century technology advanced further, and the pace of technological innovation increased. At the same time, with the rise of the middle class, society began to move according to the logic of capital. People who were bounced out of rapidly changing European society emigrated to America. There they became pioneers, or they started up new businesses and gradually built America's wealth.

When the West had power to spare, that energy gushed forth into Asia and Africa. Colonial rivalries emerged in the quest for securing raw materials and expanding markets. As a result, in the rapidly evolving societies this produced, there was an increase in the number of people who were left in poverty, and, in colonized areas, people who were unfairly discriminated against as subjugated people. This inconsistency in society first came to people's attention in the 19th century. Not only the communist movement, but also the concept of human rights, which focused on the rights of individuals who were treated unfairly, began to sprout.

ころでもありました。彼らはそうした価値観に疑問符を突きつけたことになります。

　ロシアをはじめ多くの国々で、社会不安に対して、無政府主義者も含め、共産主義の理論による地下活動が始まります。1864年には、社会主義者がロンドンに集まり、第1インターナショナルも結成されました。

　そうした時に勃発したのが普仏戦争でした。戦争によってパリが陥落し、無政府状態になったとき、パリの民衆は労働者と共にパリ・コミューンという政府を樹立したのです。

　パリ・コミューンは1871年3月から5月に至る短期間の政権でしたが、まさにマルクスの予言を具現化したものとして、人々の心に刻み込まれました。

　結局、パリ・コミューンが共和派に鎮圧され、フランスは第三共和政へと移行します。フランスは、これでフランス革命以降の混乱期からようやく脱皮して、国民国家として成長を始めたのです。

インドと中国は綿花とアヘンでイギリスに従属した

　産業革命の後、19世紀になると、技術はさらに進歩し、技術革新に加速度がつきました。同時に市民階級の台頭によって、資本の論理で社会が動き始めました。激変するヨーロッパ社会にはじき出された人々は、アメリカへ移民としてわたり、そこで開拓者となり、あるいは新しいビジネスにチャレンジして次第にアメリカの富を築いていきました。

　西欧の力があり余ったとき、そのエネルギーはアジアやアフリカへも噴出しました。原料の確保や市場の拡大を求めた植民地の争奪戦がおきたのです。その結果、あまりにも急速に変化した社会の中で、貧困の中で取り残されたり、植民地での被征服者として不当に差別されたりする人々も増えてきました。こうした社会の矛盾に人々が注目をし始めたのも19世紀でした。共産主義運動のみならず、不当に取り扱われる人の権利、すなわち「人権」という発想が芽吹いたのです。

時代
19世紀中盤～終盤
近代

地域
ヨーロッパ・インド

分類
社会【経済】

キーワード
資本主義と帝国主義・人権意識の向上・ムガル帝国の衰退・イギリスのインド統治の強化

This movement also began to reform the activity of buying and selling people, based on capitalist notions, that turned human beings into slaves. In addition, attention came to be paid to nationalist movements in colonized regions.

Over a period of roughly 90 years beginning in the middle of the 19th century, a certain country began its own progress along the path of nationalism. That country was India.

Let us briefly outline the advance of Britain into Indian society.

From the outset, it was through the chartered British East India Company that Britain expanded India's economic activity. Indian-produced cotton cloth and tea rapidly spread throughout European markets.

Initially Britain obtained privileges from prominent local Indian figures, skillfully expanding Britain's own rights and interests. In 1757, Britain joined together with the governor of the state of Bengal in the Mughal Empire to drive out France, which was maneuvering to increase its own interests in the region, at the Battle of Plassey. As a result of its victory in this conflict, not only was Britain able to drive its European rival out of India, but it was able to gradually put pressure on the Mughal Empire as well.

Before long, having become an industrial power as a result of the Industrial revolution, Britain, instead of importing cotton fabric from India, began to import the unprocessed cotton itself. Britain had developed the ability to mass-produce finished products on its own. This change was a direct blow to the Indian economy. In the 19th century, Britain gained economic control over India, securing taxation rights throughout the region and effectively taking over administration of the nation.

Ironically, what helped the stagnant Indian economy was the export of Bengal-grown opium to China. Furthermore, it was British merchants who facilitated the opium trade.

The British domination in India was fueled by the promotion of opium exports, and as a result of the Opium Wars that ensued, Britain gained the opportunity to expand aggressively into China.

The overwhelming industrial power of Britain—the world's factory—eventually sought to incorporate India as a directly controlled market system.

それは、資本主義の論理で人を売り買いしていた奴隷制度にもメスを入れることになります。また、植民地での民族運動にも注目が集まり始めました。

　19世紀中盤から90年の年月をかけて、そんな民族運動の道を独自に歩み始めた国家がありました。インドです。

　ここでインドへのイギリスの進出のあらましを整理してみます。

　もともと東インド会社という勅許会社を通して、イギリスはインドでの経済活動を拡大していました。インド産の綿布やお茶などが、ヨーロッパの市場にどんどん浸透していったのです。

　イギリスは、最初は地方の有力者から特権を得るなどして、巧みに自らの利権を拡大します。1757年にイギリスは、ムガル王朝のベンガル地方の太守と組んで権益の拡大を目論むフランスをプラッシーの戦いで駆逐します。その結果、イギリスはフランスというライバルをインドから追い出しただけでなく、次第にムガル王朝をも圧迫するようになったのです。

　やがて、産業革命によって、工業大国となったイギリスは、インドから綿布を輸入するかわりに、その原料の綿花を輸入し始めます。イギリス本国で繊維製品を大量に生産できるようになったのです。この変化はインド経済を直撃します。19世紀になると、イギリスはそんなインドを経済的に支配して、インド各地での収税権も確保し、インドを実質的に管理するようになったのです。

　皮肉なことに、インドの沈滞した経済を助けたのは、ベンガル産アヘンの中国への輸出でした。しかもアヘンの交易は、イギリスの商人によって担われたのです。

　イギリスのインドの支配はアヘンの輸出を促進させ、それが原因でおこったアヘン戦争でイギリスは中国にも積極的に進出することができるようになったのです。

　世界の工場となったイギリスの圧倒的な工業力は、やがてインドという市場を直接管理できる仕組みを求めるようになるのでした。

133

In the year that Japan was shaken by the Satsuma Rebellion, India became a territory of Britain

When Britain became the world's factory, it collected cotton from America and India, and as has been mentioned, that became a cause of the Opium War and the Civil War. Originally, the great powers of Western Europe that had undergone the Industrial Revolution were smaller than either China or India in terms of population and territory. However, by harnessing the progress of technology brought about by the Industrial Revolution and efficiently conducting economic activities, even small territories could acquire vast colonies. The key to colonial management was for small nations to invest in large territories. This was especially true in the various parts of Asia, where there was already an abundance of industry and manpower.

Admittedly, the West trifled with China, but they could not break down the enormous power structure of the Qing dynasty. To start with, because other European rivals besides Britain had gained access to China, it was simply not possible for one country to consolidate everything.

How about Japan? At the end of the Edo shogunate, like Qing China, Japan was unfamiliar with the economic mechanisms of the West, and Japan lost the right of tariff autonomy. With large quantities of raw materials, such as silver and manufactured products, flowing to the West, Japan was on the brink of falling under its economic control. Following the Meiji Restoration, the rapid domestic reforms that were carried out and the rapid introduction of Western technologies enabled Japan to pull through the crisis. They enabled it to resist attempts by the Western powers to colonize it.

However, different as it was from China and Japan, India and the surrounding territories fell completely under the control of a single country: Britain. Britain's rivals France and Russia were almost entirely out of the picture, and the newly emerging powers of America and Germany were too remote. Britain was easily able to control India all by itself.

In 1857, a rebellion led by sepoys, who were mercenaries of the British East India Company, erupted in India. They utilized the figurehead Emperor of the fading Mughal Empire to oppose British rule, and the rebellion spread throughout the country.

日本が西南戦争に揺れていた年に、インドはイギリス領になった

イギリスが世界の工場になったとき、アメリカやインドから綿花が集められ、それがアヘン戦争やアメリカでの南北戦争の原因となったことは既に解説しました。もともと、産業革命を経た西欧列強は中国やインドなどと比較すれば、人口も国土も小さかったのです。しかし、産業革命による技術の進歩を活用し、機能的に経済活動を遂行すれば、領土は小さくても、広大な植民地を獲得することができるようになったわけです。小さい国家が大きな領土に投資を行うことこそ、植民地経営のうまみであったというわけです。特に、アジア各地はもともと産業もあり、労働力も豊富でした。

もっとも、欧米は中国を翻弄しますが、清王朝という巨大な権力構造を崩壊させることはできませんでした。そもそも、イギリスのみならずライバルとなる他の西欧諸国が中国への進出を伺ったために、一国の利権の元に中国を統合することはできなかったのです。

日本はどうでしょう。日本は江戸時代末期に、西欧の経済の仕組みへの不案内から清と同様に関税自主権を失いました。そして、銀に代表される大量の原料や産品が西欧へ流れ、欧米の経済支配を受け入れる寸前に陥りました。明治維新を経て、急速に国内を改革して西欧の技術を取り入れたのは、そうした危機を乗り切り、欧米の植民地化の動きに対抗するためだったのです。

しかし、日本や中国とは異なり、インドとその周辺地域は完全にイギリス一国の支配を受けていました。ライバルのフランスやロシアが不在に近い状態にあったこと、アメリカやドイツといった新興勢力からも遠い位置にあったことが、イギリス単独でのインド支配を容易にしたのです。

1857年に、インドで東インド会社の傭兵であったシパーヒーが、ほとんど形骸化していたムガル朝の皇帝を利用して、イギリスに対して反乱をおこします。反乱は、インド大反乱と呼ばれ、全土に拡大しました。

時代
19世紀中盤
近代

地域
東アジア・インド

分類
国家【侵略】

キーワード
中国、日本の植民地化回避・ムガル帝国の滅亡・インド帝国(イギリス領インド)の成立

In the process of suppressing this uprising, Britain banished the Mughal monarch, completely destroying the empire. The upheaval was suppressed in 1859 and India became, in substance, entirely under British administration. Neighboring Ceylon and Myanmar were already under Britain's umbrella and Nepal had become a British protectorate.

In 1877, Britain finally established the British Raj, with Queen Victoria assuming the title of Empress of India. In name and substance, India was a British colony. This developed immediately after the Meiji government abolished the former feudal domains and implemented laws that ordered the cutting off of the topknots of the samurai and banned them from wearing of swords. And then the former samurai, who had lost these special prerogatives, joined in the Satsuma Rebellion. Surviving this rebellion accelerated the modernization of Japan.

Meanwhile, from the founding of the Indian Empire, India faced a long history of struggle for independence that continued until 1947.

134 Chinese pride brought new tension to East Asia

At about the time the Indian Empire was founded, China was in the midst of a trial and error effort to deal with the same menaces from the Western powers.

As a major country in East Asia, China had repeatedly expanded and contracted due to the activities of different ethnic groups. From the perspective of China, it may have seemed that its struggles in dealing with the British and the Russians were basically similar to dealing with the invasions of the Xiongnu and Mongols during ancient times, and during the Middle Ages whenever the Chinese monarchy was experiencing a weak period.

Qing China was a Manchu empire. However, the system of government itself was based on Chinese traditions. From the viewpoint of the Qing, despite the fact that the Western powers came fully equipped with modern technology, these external forces were a modern version of the horse-riding savage tribes that long ago advanced deeply into the Chinese homeland. The Qing would deal with them in the traditional manner. While accepting these outsiders as tributary entities, they would continue to take pride in their Chinese homeland, which they saw as the center of the world.

これを鎮圧する過程で、イギリスはムガル王朝の皇帝を流刑にし、王朝を完全に滅ぼしたのです。1859年には反乱も鎮圧され、インドは実質上イギリスの統治下におかれることになりました。既に、周辺のセイロンやミャンマーもイギリスの傘下となり、ネパールも保護国となっていたのです。

1877年、イギリスはついにヴィクトリア女王をインドの皇帝として、インド帝国を樹立します。インドは名実ともにイギリスの植民地となったのです。それは、明治政府が旧来の藩を廃止し、断髪令や廃刀令を施行した直後のことでした。そして特権を奪われた旧士族が西南戦争を起こしたときのことでした。西南戦争を乗り越えたことが、日本の近代化をさらに促進させます。

そして、インドではインド帝国ができた瞬間から、1947年に至る独立運動への闘争の歴史が始まったのです。

ヴィクトリア女王
Queen Victoria of England, Empress Victoria of India (1819–1901)

中国のプライドが東アジアでの新たな緊張をもたらした

インド帝国が成立した頃、同じ西欧列強の脅威にさらされていた中国は試行錯誤の只中にありました。

中国という東アジアの大国は、常に異民族との関係で膨張と縮小を繰り返していました。そんな中国から見れば、古代や中世に匈奴やモンゴル民族が衰えた中国の王朝に侵攻してきた状況と同様のものを、イギリスやロシアに見ていたのかもしれません。

清は満州族の帝国です。ですが、制度そのものは中国の伝統を引き継いでいました。清から見れば、いかに近代的な技術で武装した西欧諸国が侵攻してきても、あたかも騎馬に長けた「蛮族」が中国深く侵入してきた過去と同様の対応を考えていたはずです。朝貢を許すという対応で面子を保ちながら、中華というプライドを維持しようと懸命だったのです。

時代
19世紀全般
近代

地域
東アジア

分類
制度【国家】

キーワード
清末の混乱・清の近代化への模索・日本の近代化・朝鮮、ベトナムの危機

Having said that, in order to confront the European powers, it was urgent to modernize the nation-state. Among those who advanced such policies were Han Chinese bureaucrats who suppressed the Taiping Rebellion, such as Li Hongzhang and Zeng Guofan. While steadfastly maintaining a China-centered view of the world, their reforms aimed at introducing Western technology was called the Self-Strengthening Movement.

However, for the Industrial Revolution to occur in Europe, it was necessary for European society to undergo a transformation to a civil society. Because China did not have such a society, it had to try to introduce technology into society without altering the traditional way of thinking or the long-established systems.

Meanwhile, in Japan, as a result of the Meiji Restoration, the Tokugawa Shogunate was completely abolished, the Meiji government established a constitution, and the Imperial Diet was founded. As a result of the mutually essential systematic reforms and technological innovation, the nation-state was modernized. However, even in Japan there was no cultivation of a European-type civil society. The transformation resulted from reforms implemented by members of the former samurai class elite who supported the Meiji government. The disparity between Asian countries, represented by Japan, and Western countries in the process of modernization became the origin of the subsequent ideological conflict between Asian and Western societies.

How about the periphery of China? The Joseon dynasty which controlled the Korean Peninsula was a long-term Qing tributary state. In the latter half of the 19th century, even while it was conscious of changes overseas, within the Joseon dynasty, Daewongun, father of the monarchy, stuck firmly to the traditional system's anti-foreign stance. It was Japan, which had implemented the Meiji Restoration, that earnestly knocked at its firmly closed gate.

In the south, Vietnam continued to be controlled by France.

Vietnam, which was in a state of domestic conflict, was opened in 1802 by a member of the royal family named Nguyen Phuc Anh, who established the Nguyen dynasty. Supporting it was France.

Later France intervened in the Nguyen suppression of Christianity, causing Nguyen to surrender. This movement led to the development of conflict between France and China, which insisted that Vietnam was a Chinese tributary. As a result of the Sino-French War, which broke out in 1884, Qing China was forced to abandon all authority pertaining to Vietnam. Hence, Vietnam came under the control of France.

とはいえ、西欧列強と対峙するには、国家の近代化は急務です。それを推し進めたのが、太平天国の乱を平定した漢民族の李鴻章や曾国藩といった官僚達でした。中華思想を堅持しながらも、西欧の技術を取り入れようとした彼らの改革を洋務運動と呼んでいます。

　しかし、西欧で産業革命がおこるには、西欧社会が市民社会へと脱皮していった過程があったのです。そうした市民社会をもたない中国は、あくまでも思想や制度は旧来のままにした状況で技術の導入を試みます。
　一方、日本は明治維新によって徳川幕府が壊滅し、明治政府は憲法を造り、帝国議会も開きます。制度の改革と技術革新の両輪によって国家を近代化させていったのです。ただ、そんな日本ですら西欧流の市民社会が育ったわけではありません。それはあくまでも明治政府を支えていた旧士族エリートによる改革でした。日本に代表されるアジアの国々と欧米諸国との近代化の過程でのこの差異が、その後のアジア社会と西欧社会との意識対立の原点となってゆくのです。

　中国の周辺はどうでしょう。朝鮮半島を支配していた李王朝は長年清を宗主国としてきました。19世紀後半になって、海外での変化を意識しながらも、李王朝は、国王の父親にあたる大院君によって、従来の制度に固執した排外主義を貫こうとします。朝鮮半島の頑なに閉ざした門戸を本格的にたたいたのが、明治維新を遂行していた日本だったのです。
　南方では、ベトナムがフランスによって支配されつつありました。
　内乱状態にあったベトナムは、1802年に王族の一人であった阮福映（げんふくえい）によって統一され阮王朝が開かれます。それを支援したのがフランスでした。
　その後、阮によるキリスト教の弾圧などにフランスが介入し、阮朝を屈服させます。そうした動きは、ベトナムの宗主国であると主張する清とフランスとの対立へと発展するのでした。1884年におきた清朝とフランスとの戦争の結果、清はベトナムに対する権利を放棄します。これで、ベトナムはフランスの支配下におかれるようになったのです。

135 Britain hemmed in Africa from the north and the south

By 1899 France formed French Indochina, controlling present-day Vietnam, Cambodia, and Laos. Southeast Asia was in this manner partitioned among the European powers and deprived of its sovereignty. Thailand alone was able to maintain its independence. Making use of its location between the British-controlled region from India to Burma and the French-controlled region in the eastern part of Southeast Asia, it was able to implement the diplomatic policies of an enlightened monarchy.

Similar movements occurred in Africa.

In North Africa, which had been under the control of the Ottoman Empire until the latter deteriorated, powerful figures in the various regions created independence movements. Egypt was no exception. From the period of Napoleon I, France actively made inroads into Egypt and in 1869 opened the Suez Canal. This was a major reform in transportation between Asia and Europe. As an unprecedented construction project, it placed a heavy economic burden on France and Egypt. It was Britain that made the project possible. In 1882, by purchasing the concession rights to the Suez Canal and amassing authority, England suppressed the anti-British movement that arose in Egypt and made it a protectorate.

Moreover, within the Vienna system, present-day South Africa was transferred from the Netherlands to Britain. The British traveled across the African continent, manipulating the tribal states of the interior from Egypt to South Africa. It was during this period that explorers, such as David Livingstone and Henry Morton Stanley, introduced the products of African culture to their home country.

From the outset, once Bartolomeu Dias discovered the Cape of Good Hope in 1488, the Dutch advanced into every part of South Africa. In the same period, Protestants including the French Huguenots also migrated there to escape persecution in their homelands. These people, known as Boers, brought indigenous people from Dutch-controlled regions including Indonesia as slaves.

With the French Revolution as an opportunity, Britain extended its power and essentially held any potential French advances in check. The British confronted the Boers. On one side were the British, who opposed the system of slavery, and on the opposite side were the Boers, who stood to suffer economic damage if

イギリスはアフリカを北と南から挟んでいった

　フランスは、1899年までに、現在のベトナムを中心に、カンボジア
やラオスを支配し、フランス領インドシナ連邦を形成します。このよ
うにして東南アジアは列強によって分割され、主権を奪われてゆきま
す。ただタイだけが独立を保つことができました。インドからビルマ
を支配したイギリスと、東南アジアの東部を支配したフランスの中間
に位置していることを利用した、開明的な国王による外交政策がそこ
にあったからです。

　この動きは、アフリカでも同様でした。

　劣化したオスマン帝国が支配していた北アフリカは、地方地方で有
力者が独立運動を起こしていました。エジプトも例外ではありませ
ん。エジプトには、ナポレオンの時代以降フランスが積極的に進出し、
1869年にはスエズ運河を開設します。これはアジアとヨーロッパとを
結ぶ交通の大改革になりますが、この未曾有の公共工事はフランスに
もエジプトにも経済的な負担として重くのしかかります。そこに進出
してきたのがイギリスでした。スエズ運河の利権を買収し、力を蓄え
たイギリスは、1882年には、エジプトで起きた反英運動を鎮圧し、同
地を保護国化したのです。

　さらに、ウィーン体制の中で、イギリスはオランダから現在の南ア
フリカを譲り受けます。イギリスはエジプトと南アフリカから、内陸
の部族国家を操りつつ、アフリカ大陸を縦断していったのです。リヴィ
ングストンやスタンリーといった探検家が、アフリカの文物を本国に
紹介したのもその頃のことです。

　もともと南アフリカ一帯には、1488年にバルトロメウ・ディアスが
喜望峰を発見したのち、オランダ人が進出していました。同時に、フ
ランス系のユグノーなどに代表される新教徒各派も、本国での迫害を
逃れて移住してきます。彼らはボーア人と呼ばれ、オランダ領インド
ネシアなどから現地の人々を奴隷として送り、使役していました。

　そこにフランス革命などを契機に、フランスの進出を牽制するかの
ようにイギリスが勢力を伸ばしてきたのです。イギリス人はボーア人
と対立します。奴隷制度を否定するイギリス側と、その廃止によって
経済的ダメージを被るボーア人。それにも増して、長年開墾してきた

時代
19世紀終盤
近代

地域
アフリカ

分類
侵略【外交】

キーワード
アジア分割の完了・スエ
ズ運河利権がイギリスに
・アフリカの分割・イギ
リスの南アフリカ支配

slavery were to be abolished. Intensifying this was the Boers' fear that the rights to the lands that they had spent years reclaiming would be taken from them. When South Africa was officially transferred from the Netherlands to Britain in the 19th century, the Boers, who were under pressure, migrated into the interior and attempted to attain independence. Toward the end of the 19th century, the British and the Boers engaged in two wars in what is known as the Boer Wars. The outcome was that Britain obtained an enormous colony, which stretched from present-day South Africa through Zimbabwe. Incidentally, earlier, Zimbabwe was called Rhodesia, and it was named after Cecil John Rhodes, a British politician who sought to expand Britain's rights and privileges in Africa through the Boer War.

136 Public opinion, education, and the development of media raised the curtain on a new era

The remarkable emergence of Britain on the world stage in the 19th century brought about an unprecedented phenomenon to humankind.

This was the sharing of English as a common language. Not only was English used in the colonies that Britain acquired, but with the later advance of America around the world, English became the language of business everywhere around the globe. Due to the fact that humankind possessed a common language, the transmission of culture and information became swifter, and people were able to share a view of the world and practical wisdom more easily.

In order to maintain civil society, it was essential for people to carry on business and to share information in order to raise profits. In order to maintain market prices and healthy markets, people sought various kinds of information about political affairs across the globe, and that subtly influenced people's way of life. This contradicts the last sentence. Suggest deleting. At the same time, one certainly cannot overlook the development of mass media in the transmission of information to the populace.

In an earlier epoch, it was the movable-type printing of Johannes Gutenberg which played a role in spreading the Reformation throughout Europe. In the 19th century, in addition to printing technology, methods of transmitting information also progressed. It became possible to rapidly transmit information in the form

土地と利権を奪われる恐怖もボーア人にはありました。19世紀になって、南アフリカが正式にオランダからイギリスに譲渡されると、それに押されたボーア人は内陸へと移住して独立をはかります。やがて19世紀終盤に、2度にわたって、イギリスとボーア人は戦闘を交えます。ボーア戦争と呼ばれるこの戦いを通して、イギリスは最終的に現在の南アフリカからジンバブエに至る広大な植民地を入手するのです。ちなみに、ジンバブエは昔ローデシアと呼ばれていました。その名前は、ボーア戦争でイギリスの権益を拡大した政治家セシル・ローズにちなんだ国名だったのです。

世論と教育、メディアの成長が新たな時代の幕をあけた

　19世紀のイギリスの世界へのめざましい進出は、今までにない現象を人類にもたらしました。

　それは、英語という言語の共有化です。英語はイギリスが獲得した植民地で使用されるだけではなく、その後世界に進出するアメリカと共に、世界各地でのビジネス用語として活用されるようになりました。人類は共通の言語を持ったことで、文化や情報の伝達がより迅速になり、人々は世界観や様々な常識を共有できるようになったのです。

　市民社会を維持するためには、人々がビジネスをし、利益をあげるための情報共有が欠かせません。相場や市場を健全に維持するためにも、世界各地の政情などに関する様々な情報が求められ、それが人々の生活を微妙に左右するようになったのです。この情報の共有に英語が果たした役割は計り知れません。同時に情報を市民に伝達するマスメディアの発展も無視するわけにはいきません。

　その昔、宗教改革の波がヨーロッパ中に拡散する役割を果たしたのがグーテンベルクの活版印刷でした。19世紀には、印刷技術に加え、情報の伝達手段もさらに進化しました。書簡や大量に印刷された媒体が迅速に輸送されるようになったのです。さらに1875年には、アメリ

時代
19世紀全般
近代

地域
共通

分類
文化【社会】

キーワード
英語の国際語化・印刷、電信の発達・出版の隆盛・教育の向上・世論の形成

of written correspondence and mass printed material. Furthermore, in 1875, Graham Bell invented the telephone in America, enabling instant transmission of voice communication.

Supported by its citizens, nations developed, and in order to receive the benefits of industrial activities, it became necessary to raise the educational levels of the laborers who engaged in production. From the 19th century onward, in the powerful nations, efforts were made on a national scale to raise literacy rates, and to provide opportunities for education and access to information.

As a result, people were stimulated like never before to take an interest in society, the economy, and political issues. With the improvement in literacy rates, anyone could read newspapers, and it was possible to come into direct contact with the arts. People encountered information and in response developed opinions concerning it. The concept of public opinion came forward. And nations and authority figures paid attention to the fact that public opinion was a dynamic that could greatly alter society.

The rise of English as a mutually shared, worldwide language, and the evolution of media that could affect public opinion started to have a major impact on society, one that began in early-modern times and has continued to the present day.

The advance of European powers in Asia and Africa can be seen, in a sense, as a migration of the people of Europe. In the same way that the Germanic peoples, the Normans, and the Mongols participated in great migrations, they became a great historic ground swell that influenced every corner of the world. That influence— one page, one scene at a time—reached every part of society. Nationalism and socialist movements are intrinsically related to the diffusion of printed matter and the elevation of the education levels of the citizenry. They have become an intangible infrastructure upon which present society is dependent.

カでグラハム・ベルが電話を発明し、音声が瞬時に伝えられるように
なりました。

　また、市民に支えられた国家が発展し、産業活動の恩恵を受けるた
めには、生産活動に従事する労働者の教育レベルの向上も求められま
す。19世紀以降、列強では国をあげて国民の識字率の向上、教育や情
報へのアクセスの機会均等への取り組みがなされていったのです。

　このことは、人々の社会への関心、政治や経済への関心を今まで以
上に刺激することになりました。識字率の向上で、誰もが新聞を読む
ことができ、芸術に接することも可能になりました。人々は情報に接
し、それに対する意見を持ちます。世論という概念ができあがるのです。
そして、社会を大きく変化させる原動力となる世論の力に、国家も権
力者も注目するようになったのです。

　英語という世界共通の言語の登場と、世論を左右するメディア活動
の成長が、近世から現代にかけて、社会に大きな影響を与え始めたの
でした。

　ヨーロッパ列強によるアジアやアフリカへの進出は、ある意味でヨー
ロッパ市民の民族移動とも捉えられます。それはゲルマン人やノルマ
ン人、モンゴル民族の大移動などと同様に、大きな歴史のうねりとなっ
て世界各地に影響を与えました。そんな影響の1コマ1コマが、新聞な
どによって、社会の隅々に伝えられます。ナショナリズムも、社会主
義運動も、こうした文字媒体の普及と国民レベルでの教育水準の向上
と無縁ではありません。それらは現代社会の基礎となる無形のインフ
ラとなってゆくのです。

137 The Dreyfus Affair questioned the state of public opinion under imperialism

We refer to the period of struggle between the European powers for hegemony over colonies between the second half of the 19th century and the 20th century as the Age of Imperialism. During this period, against the backdrop of the enlarged economy that resulted from the Industrial Revolution, nations deployed their citizens overseas, rival countries clashed with one another, and by rousing a sense of patriotism, countries sought to conquer new lands.

In implementing such national strategies, in the West, those people who sought to give precedence to the benefit of their own countries came into conflict with those who saw in the colonized territories the inconsistencies of capitalist society that led to poverty and social disparity. Both parties made use of media, such as newspapers, to influence public opinion.

In France, under the Third Republic, which was established after the Paris Commune, the Dreyfus Affair occurred in 1894.

As a result of its defeat in the Franco-Prussian War, France was suffering psychologically, as well as economically. During this troubled period, a French army officer of Jewish descent named Alfred Dreyfus was accused of disclosing military secrets to the Germans. Right-wing newspapers portrayed this as a "Jewish

ドレフュスの不名誉な除隊を描いた挿絵（官位剝奪式で剣を折られるドレフュス）

Illustration depicting Dreyfus' dishonorable discharge from the army (Dreyfus' sword is broken at the ceremony to deprive him of his rank)

ドレフュス事件は、帝国主義下での国民世論のありかたを問いかけた

　19世紀後半から20世紀にかけての西欧列強の植民地をめぐる覇権争いの時代を、我々は帝国主義の時代と呼んでいます。それは産業革命で肥大化した経済を背景に、国家が国民をあげて海外に進出し、ライバルとなる国との確執を、愛国心を鼓舞することで克服しようとした時代でした。

　国家戦略を遂行する中で、欧米では国家の利益を優先させようとする人々と、植民地での差別や、資本主義社会の矛盾の中で育まれた貧困や格差に目を向ける人々との間に対立がおこります。そして、そのどちらもが、世論を誘導しようと新聞などの媒体を活用したのです。

　パリ・コミューンの後に成立した第三共和政下のフランスで、1894年にドレフュス事件という出来事がおこります。
　フランスは、普仏戦争での敗北によって精神的にも経済的にも苦しんでいました。そこに、軍事機密が漏洩され、犯人としてユダヤ系の将校アルフレド・ドレフュスが訴追されたのです。右翼系の新聞が、この事件を「ユダヤ人の陰謀」として書き連ねます。ヨーロッパには、

時代
19世紀終盤
近代

地域
西ヨーロッパ

分類
世論【社会】

キーワード
国民国家と帝国主義の進展・ユダヤ人問題の顕在化・メディアの発達と世論

1898年1月13日発行の新聞「オーロール（英語版）」に掲載された、エミール・ゾラによる公開状。「私は弾劾する」という記事を発表して、ドレフュスを支援した。

An open letter by Emile Zola, published in the newspaper "L'Aurore (English Edition)" on January 13, 1898. He supported Dreyfus by publishing an article entitled "J'Accuse...! (I accuse...!)"

conspiracy." In Europe, there was a long tradition of discrimination against Jews who did not convert to Christianity, and from the Middle Ages this persecution of Jewish people had resulted in considerable bloodshed. Even in the modern era, this persecution continued in places such as Russia. Large numbers of those who were persecuted and discriminated against flowed to places like America as immigrants. France was no exception to this treatment of Jewish people. Dreyfus became a suitable target for promoting this prejudice against people of Jewish descent.

Pressured by public opinion, the French military put Dreyfus on trial, found him guilty as charged, and sentenced him to life imprisonment. In response to this, among others, Emile Zola, a leading writer of this period, denounced the military's actions, claiming the trial was unjust. Public opinion in France over whether Dreyfus was guilty was split into two groups, and there was a furious controversy in the newspapers.

Ultimately the charges brought against Dreyfus were shown to be false, and he was released from prison. But this incident came to symbolize the conflict within public opinion over nationalism under imperialism and those who opposed it.

Within the history of humankind, it was initially the monarchs, the nobles, and the wealthy merchants who possessed the privilege of employing written language and receiving education. By pledging loyalty to those in power, these people were able to maintain these privileges for themselves. With no connection to this spirit of allegiance and fidelity, ordinary people were simply kept under control.

Following the Industrial Revolution, however, education extended to all levels of society, and the ruled began to develop ideas regarding what the state should be like. This led to the national awareness that evolved between the modern period and the present in what we call nationalism.

Politicians manipulated this consciousness in order to benefit their own interests. They did this by placing emphasis on the menace posed by outsiders and other countries and on a sense of their own ethnic superiority. The extension of this relationship between the politicians and the people of the same country evolved into Nazism and militarism in the 20th century.

キリスト教に改宗しないユダヤ系の人々に対する差別が伝統的にあり、中世以来多くの血が流れてきました。近代になっても、ロシアなどを中心に差別は続いていました。差別や迫害を受けた人々の多くは、アメリカなどに移民として流出したのです。フランスも例外ではありません。ドレフュスはそんなユダヤ系の人々への偏見を助長するための格好の標的となったのです。

軍部は世論に押され、ドレフュスを有罪として終身刑に処します。それに対して、当時を代表する作家エミール・ゾラなどが、裁判の不正を主張して軍を弾劾します。ドレフュスが有罪かどうか、フランスの世論は二つに分かれ、新聞などを通して激しい論戦が展開されたのです。

最終的にドレフュスの冤罪が認められ彼は釈放されますが、この事件は帝国主義下でのナショナリズムとそれを批判する人々との世論の対立を象徴した事件となったのです。

人類の歴史において、文字を操り、教育を受けていたのは王侯貴族や富裕な商人など特権を持った人々でした。こうした人々は、権力者に忠誠を誓うことで、自らの特権を維持します。そして一般の人々は、そうした忠誠心とは無縁の存在として、ただ支配を受けていたのです。

しかし、産業革命以来、教育が社会の隅々にいきわたったとき、こうした支配を受けていた人々にも国家観が芽吹いたのです。これが、近代から現代にかけてのナショナリズムという国家意識へと繋がったのです。

この意識を為政者がうまく自らの利益へと誘導するためになしたこと。それは、他国の脅威や民族的な優越感を強調することでした。この為政者と国民との関係の延長に、20世紀でのナチズムや軍国主義の悲劇があったのです。

138 While maintaining imperial rule supported by serfs, Russia competed with Western Europe

At the time of the Dreyfus Affair in Europe, Japan was in the midst of the Sino-Japanese War.

This was after the promulgation of the Constitution of the Empire of Japan and the opening of the National Diet, whereby Japan joined the ranks of the modern nation-states as a constitutional monarchy. Within an imperialist world, the greatest threat to Japan was none other than Russia, which continued its policies of southward expansion. In order to mitigate the threat from Russia, Japan wanted to place the Korean Peninsula under its own influence. Because Qing China had powerful influence over the Joseon dynasty on the peninsula, the struggle between Japan and Qing China for supremacy there led to the Sino-Japanese War.

The Sino-Japanese War ended in a Japanese victory. Although Japan as a victorious country acquired the Liaodong Peninsula from China, Russia called for France and Germany to put pressure on Japan to renounce its rights and interests there. Under the international pressure of this Triple Intervention, Japan relinquished its concessions in China.

However, as a result of this, a major rift developed between Japan and Russia. From its own perspective, Japan was eager to eliminate the threat of Russian incursion into East Asia from the north. At this juncture, England, which was anxious about Russian activities in Turkey and North Asia, initiated an approach. As a result of their shared interests, in 1902 the two nations joined in the Anglo-Japanese Alliance.

So what was the situation in Russia?

The only Western power which remained an autocratic empire without a civil society, Russia was unable to catch the wave of the Industrial Revolution.

The Russian economy continued to be dependent upon the productivity of the people in a fief whose freedom was taken away and who were known as serfs. As happened in the 17th century Rebellion of Stenka Razin and the 18th century Pugachev Rebellion, while there were uprisings and social instability originating in the system of serfdom, under which people suffered from poverty, the imperial Russian state remained reliant on that system, making no attempts at reforming the nation by itself. In the 19th century, within the nobility an increasing number of people began to think that as long as Russia was dependent on the system of

ロシアは農奴に支えられた帝政を維持しながら西欧と対抗した

　ドレフュス事件がおきた頃、日本は日清戦争の只中でした。

　それは、大日本帝国憲法が発布され、国会が開催されたことによって、日本も立憲君主国として近代国家の仲間入りをした後のことです。帝国主義下の世界にあって、日本にとっての最大の脅威は、南下政策を続けるロシアに他なりません。ロシアへの脅威を緩和するため、日本が影響下におきたかったのが朝鮮半島だったのです。日清戦争は、そんな朝鮮半島に君臨する李氏朝鮮に大きな影響力をもつ清との覇権争いが原因でした。

　日清戦争は日本の勝利に終わります。しかし、戦勝国の日本が獲得した中国の遼東半島での利権を放棄するようにと、ロシアはフランスとドイツを誘い日本に圧力をかけます。この三国干渉と呼ばれる国際的な圧力によって、日本は中国での利権を断念したのです。

　しかし、このことは、日本とロシアとの関係に大きな亀裂を入れることになりました。日本としては、北から東アジアを伺うロシアの脅威をなんとか排除したいのです。ここに、トルコや北アジアへのロシアの行動に懸念を持つイギリスが歩み寄ってきます。日本とイギリスの利害関係が一致した結果、1902年に両国は日英同盟を締結したのでした。
　では、ロシアの情勢はどうだったのでしょうか。
　欧米列強の中で、唯一皇帝による専制政治が続き、市民社会の育っていなかったロシアは、産業革命の波に乗ることはできませんでした。
　ロシアの経済は、依然として農奴と呼ばれる自由を奪われた領民の生産によって支えられていたのです。17世紀のステンカ・ラージンの乱や、18世紀におきたプガチョフの乱のように、貧困にあえぐ農奴制度に起因する反乱や社会不安はあったものの、その制度自体に依存していた帝政ロシアという国家に、自浄作用はなかったのです。19世紀になって、貴族の中にもロシアが農奴制度に依存する以上、近代化は進められないと思う人も増えてきます。特にナポレオン戦争以後、人々が西側諸国の思想や文化を積極的に取り入れる中で、多くの人が農奴

時代
19世紀終盤
近代

地域
日本・ロシア

分類
制度【社会】

キーワード
日本の近代国家化・日清戦争と三国干渉・日本の軍事大国化・旧体制の中のロシアの矛盾

serfdom, it was impossible to implement modernization. Particularly after the Napoleonic Wars, as people began to actively introduce the ideas and culture of the West, more people began to call for reform of that system.

Their voices and the need to reform Russia's impoverished economy led Alexander II to issue the Emancipation Reform of 1861. However, because this did not improve the actual conditions in the agricultural villages, he was criticized by reformist groups of Russian populists called Narodniks. Then, in 1881, the emperor was assassinated by a person of Polish descent who felt oppressed by Russia. The result was that Russia retained its system of heavy-handed politics in which the tsar stood at the top of the pyramid of the aristocracy, a phenomenon which went in the opposite direction from the norms of the period.

While continuing to face the inconsistencies of the domestic economy and social instability, Russia took part in the imperialist struggle for power as a means of dealing with its economic adversity.

Threatened by these measures were the Ottoman Empire and its previous domains to Russia's west, and Qing China, Joseon dynasty Korea, and Japan to its east.

139 When America reached the Pacific Ocean, strife with Japan began

In our own day, when it comes to the nations that have the greatest impact on the world, we would probably begin our list with the United States, China, and Russia.

In the background of the growth of America into a superpower was the inflow of immigrants from various parts of Europe and elsewhere, who brought with them varieties of knowledge and energies.

The immigrants who crossed the oceans to reach America developed the frontier in the 19th century, turning endless plains into a broad land that supplied grains and cattle.

In the 1890s, America's frontier, as its undeveloped lands were called, rapidly disappeared. Supported by inexpensive immigrant labor, industrialization increased in the East and productivity eclipsed that of the major European powers.

As a result, America, like England, began to seek out overseas markets for products from its own industries. America took economic control of Cuba, where

制度の改革を叫ぶようになります。

こうした人々の声と、疲弊するロシア経済の改革に迫られたアレクサンドル2世は、1861年に農奴解放令をだしますが、農村の貧困は改善されず、ナロードニキと呼ばれる改革派の人々の批判にさらされます。そして1881年に皇帝は、ロシアに蹂躙されたポーランド系の人物に暗殺されてしまいます。この結果、ロシアでは貴族社会のピラミッドの頂点に立つロシア皇帝による強権政治が温存されるという、時代に逆行した現象がおきるのです。

ロシアは、こうした国内の経済的な矛盾や社会不安を抱えたまま、経済的困窮を解決する手段として帝国主義の覇権争いに参加したのでした。

西ではオスマン帝国やその旧領、東では清や李氏朝鮮、そして日本がそうした脅威にさらされていたのです。

アメリカが太平洋に達したとき、日本との確執が始まった

現代、我々の生きる世界に大きな影響を与えている国家といえば、まずアメリカ合衆国、そして中国やロシアといった国々でしょう。

アメリカ合衆国が超大国へと成長した背景には、ヨーロッパなどからの多彩な移民の知恵やエネルギーがこの国に流れ込んだことにあります。

アメリカに渡ってきた移民は19世紀に辺境を開墾し、荒野を穀物や家畜の一大供給地へと変えてゆきました。

1890年代には、アメリカからフロンティアと呼ばれる未開の地が消滅します。そして、移民の安価な労働力に支えられて、東部の工業化も進み、その生産力はヨーロッパの列強をしのぐまでになりました。

その結果、イギリスと同様に、アメリカは自国の産業の市場を海外に求めるようになったのです。アメリカはスペインの凋落により独立

時代
19, 20世紀
近代・現代

地域
アメリカ・ロシア・中国

分類
社会【外交】

キーワード
フロンティアの終了・アメリカの大国化・中国の弱体化・矛盾強まるロシア・中国の半植民地化

a movement for independence from a declining Spain took place.

In 1898, under pressure from public opinion, American president William McKinley initiated the Spanish-American War. In the conflict, America drove the Spaniards out, and as a result of the Treaty of Paris that followed, America established supremacy in the Caribbean Sea. Puerto Rico became an American territory. Spain also surrendered the Philippines, where an independence movement had arisen, and also Guam, in the Pacific.

In the same year, having annexed Hawaii, America actively maneuvered its way into Asia. Particularly in regard to China, where European powers were jockeying for concessions, and Japan, Secretary of State John Hay pressed for the opening of trading ports with the same rights for America that the other Western powers had obtained. This move on the part of America invited confrontation with Japan, which was also seeking to place China under its own influence.

Let us now turn to the situation involving Russia and China.

At the beginning of the 20th century, China and Russia were both under imperial rule. In these two nations, the emperor or tsar and those who surrounded him monopolized education and information.

Interestingly enough, in the 20th century, both experienced a revolution by which the imperial regime was overthrown.

This common feature thereafter influenced the confrontation between America and Russia, and later, America and China. On the one side was America society, which had developed through the War of Independence, the Civil War, and the inflow of countless immigrants. On the other side were Russia and China, where new regimes were established through imperial rule and communist revolution to form a new kind of leadership.

The differences between the two sides exceeded just the differences in their systems of government. They include marked gaps between the self-awareness of the people and the societies themselves.

Having said this, in the 19th century China had weakened, and the Qing were under the thumb of the Western powers, who were looking for rights and privileges. Meanwhile, Russia kept an eye on the movements of Japan and other countries, while also staying alert to ways of making inroads into China.

運動がおきたキューバを経済的に支配していました。

　1898年にアメリカのマッキンリー大統領は、世論に押され米西戦争をおこします。戦争はアメリカがスペインを駆逐し、パリ条約によってアメリカのカリブ海での覇権が確立します。プエルト・リコはアメリカ領となり、アジアでは独立運動がおきていたフィリピンや太平洋のグアム島がスペインから譲渡されました。

　同年にハワイを併合したアメリカは、積極的にアジアへの進出を試みます。特に中国への利権の獲得に奔走するヨーロッパ列強や日本に対して、当時の国務長官ジョン・ヘイはアメリカにも平等に市場への進出を求める門戸開放宣言を行います。このアメリカの動きは、その後中国を自らの影響下に置こうとする日本と利害の対立を招くのです。太平洋戦争への導火線が19世紀終盤にすでに設置されたことになります。

　次にロシアと中国の状況に目を向けます。

　20世紀のはじめまで、中国もロシアも共に皇帝が君臨していました。これら二つの国家では、皇帝とそれをとりまく人々が教育も情報も独占していました。

　そして、面白いことに、この二つの国は共に20世紀に革命を経験し、こうした体制を覆しています。

　この共通項が、その後のアメリカとロシア、そして中国との対立の背景となるのです。独立革命から南北戦争、そしてそこに流れ込む無数の移民によって育成されたアメリカという社会と、帝政から共産主義革命を通して新たな指導体制が樹立され統制されてゆくロシアや中国。

　そこには単なる体制の違いを越えた、人々の意識の違い、社会そのもののあり方の違いがあるのです。

　とはいえ、19世紀の時点ではまだ中国は弱体化し、西欧列強に利権をあさられていた清朝の支配下にありました。一方のロシアは、日本などの動きを注視しながら、そんな中国への進出を試みていたのです。

第六部

戦争と自由・グローバルの時代（現代の世界）

Part Six:
The Age of War, Freedom and
Globalization (The Contemporary World)

　文明は常に一つの拠点で発生し、波のように世界に拡散します。波は時には交差し、摩擦を起こし、そして戦争を引き起こしてきました。その動きは、我々の記憶する時代に入ってもとどまることはなく、ついにヒトは大量破壊兵器を携え、世界中で戦争を起こしてしまいました。

　当然、ヒトはそんな社会制度に疑問も持ちました。階級の重圧を打破して新しい理想を掲げる社会主義国家も成立しました。しかし、その試みが新たな戦いの原因になったのも事実です。

　現在、ヒトは戦争の記憶を引きずりながら、それでも武器を捨てず、同時に通信や交流などの分野で新しい手法を開発しています。ヒトの社会はネット社会へと変化を始めました。また、AIやバイオテクノロジーの発展で、ヒトが動物の一つの進化形であるという状況を超えて、さらにどう進化してゆくのかという課題にも直面しています。

　ナショナリズムとグローバリズムの振り子に翻弄されながら、先端技術という新たな道具を活用し、次の進化をどう成し遂げるのか。現在は、人類の次の500年に向けたルネサンス活動の最中にあるのです。

140 In the Russo-Japanese War, Japan and Russia waged war in a third country, China

The 20th century began with a maelstrom in the Far East.

In the last years of the 19th century, the Boxer Rebellion broke out in China. The Boxers were a religious group that sought to eliminate Christianity and other Western influences from China. Under the slogan "support Qing, destroy the foreign," the movement sought to strengthen Qing rule. The Qing were half-hearted about suppressing the movement, and the uprising spread from Tianjin to Beijing.

Two years prior to the rebellion, Kang Youwei and others were concerned about the decline of the Qing administration, which was being suppressed by outside powers, and they formed a reformist movement. At the time, Empress Dowager Cixi, the aunt of Emperor Guangxu, was the real power behind the throne. Fearing that the reformist movement might lead to her own downfall, the Empress Dowager initiated a coup. As a result, the emperor was imprisoned, and the reformist faction called bianfa was purged. This incident is known as the Hundred Days of Reform. As a result of not having a reform like the Japanese had in the Meiji Restoration, the Qing became embroiled in the Boxer Rebellion.

西太后
Empress Dowager Cixi
(1835–1908)

The Empress Dowager supported the Boxer Rebellion and declared war on the great powers, but seven Western countries, including England and Russia, together with Japan suppressed the movement. According to the Peking Protocol of 1901, Qing China was once again burdened with the payment of enormous reparations.

In the suppression of the Boxer Rebellion, Japan, which felt a strong sense of impending crisis, made a major contribution. However, once the incident was concluded, Russia did not withdraw its own troops. England and America were openly wary of Russia's blatant advances into China. At the time, England was heavily involved in administering its interests in Africa and the Middle East. This was the reason for the rapid rapprochement between Japan and England. Equally cautious of Russian advances into the Far East, America also supported their actions.

As a result, with the arrival of the 20th century, Japan, supported by England, ended up confronting Russia in China.

日露戦争では中国という第三国で日本とロシアが交戦した

20世紀は極東での混乱で始まりました。

19世紀の終盤に、中国で義和団事件がおきました。義和団はキリスト教や西欧の影響を排除しようとする宗教団体です。扶清滅洋というスローガンのもと、清朝を盛り上げようとしたこの運動の鎮圧には清朝も消極的で、騒乱は天津から北京へと広がります。

義和団事件の2年前、列強に蹂躙され、衰退した清朝をなんとかしようと、康有為などによって刷新運動が展開されました。当時、清朝は皇帝であった光緒帝の伯母にあたる西太后が実権を握っていました。刷新運動が自らの進退に発展しかねない状況に対抗し、西太后がクーデターをおこしたのです。これによって皇帝は監禁され、変法派と呼ばれた改革派の人々が粛清されました。この事件は戊戌の政変と呼ばれ、その結果清朝は日本が経験した明治維新のような改革の機会を経ないまま、義和団事件へと巻き込まれたのです。

西太后は義和団を支持し、列強に宣戦布告をしますが、イギリスやロシアなど欧米の7カ国に日本を加えた国々によって乱は鎮圧され、1901年に締結された北京議定書によって、清朝は再び多額の賠償金を支払わされることになったのです。

ところで、義和団事件の鎮圧に、ロシアの南下への強い危機感を抱いていた日本は大きく貢献しました。しかし、ロシアは事件以降も軍隊を撤退させません。イギリスもアメリカも、中国へ露骨に進出するロシアに警戒感をあらわにします。当時のイギリスはアフリカや中東の経営に忙しかったこともあり、極東に強い同盟国が必要でした。日本とイギリスとはこうして急激に接近したのです。同じくロシアの極東進出を警戒していたアメリカもそうした動きを支持します。

この結果、20世紀に入って、イギリスに後押しされた日本とロシアとが中国で対峙することになったのです。

時代
20世紀1900年代
現代

地域
日本 • 中国 • 朝鮮 • ロシア

分類
外交【戦争】

キーワード
清末の混乱 • 義和団の乱と列強の介入 • 日本とイギリスの接近 • 朝鮮の動揺 • 日露戦争勃発

1900年に共同出兵した8カ国連合軍の部隊
左から順に、イギリス、アメリカ、オーストラリア（当時は大英帝国の植民地）、インド（当時は大英帝国の植民地）、ドイツ（当時はドイツ帝国）、フランス、オーストリア＝ハンガリー帝国、イタリア、日本。

Troops of the eight nations alliance of 1900 in China.
Left to right: Britain, United States, Australia (British Empire colony at this time), India (British Empire colony at this time), Germany (German Empire at this time), France, Austria-Hungary, Italy, Japan.

During the Sino-Japanese War, in the Joseon dynasty in Korea, which lost its backing from Qing China, Gojong established the Korean Empire and took power as Emperor Gwangmu. This meant that Korea, which had long been paying tribute to China, ceased to do so and declared itself an independent sovereign nation.

The Korean Empire, which was at the point of making a new start as a modern nation-state, needed to decide whether to side with Japan or form an alliance with Russia, leaving Japan and Russia in a tug-of-war.

Finally, in 1904, Japan and Russia plunged into the Russo-Japanese War. Japan and Russia engaged in hostilities regarding rights and interests in Korea and China in battles in northeast China. In that sense, it was a war based on imperialistic motives.

For Japan, which had to turn to England and America to obtain funding to prosecute the war, it was like fighting with its back to a wall, trying to avoid financial collapse while taking on the powerful nation of Russia. From the Russian point of view, this war was a chance to acquire the huge Chinese market and reestablish the long-unstable dynasty of the Romanovs.

141 The world was at the mercy of the great powers' diplomacy and maneuvering

At the beginning of the Russo-Japanese War, Japan had a tough time raising funds overseas. Most countries believed that Japan would not be able to sustain warfare against Russia due to the overwhelming disparity in national power between the two. Domestically, however, Russia was in a state of turmoil. Political instability continued, with farmers rebelling against economic disparity and autocratic rule, and with the outbreak of strikes in the factories. Once conflict began, Japan put up a good fight and a war-weary mood spread throughout Russia. In January 1905 in the capital St. Petersburg, a demonstration broke out calling for a peace settlement and relief from poverty. The armed forces fired on the protestors in what became known as the Bloody Sunday incident, and the domestic state of affairs grew even more strained.

At the stage where Japan had achieved victories in the Battle of Mukden and the Battle of Tsushima, American president Theodore Roosevelt interceded, and Japan concluded a peace agreement with Russia. By playing a part in the peace negotiations between Japan, which had fought desperately given the limitations of

一方、日清戦争で清という後ろ盾を失った李氏朝鮮は、1897年に高宗が光武帝として大韓帝国を樹立しました。これは、長年李氏朝鮮が行っていた中国への朝貢をやめ、主権国家として独立したことを意味します。

近代国家として再出発しようとした大韓帝国が日本側につくか、それともロシア側と同盟するのか、日本とロシアとは綱引きを続けます。

1904年に、日本とロシアとはついに日露戦争に突入します。日露戦争は、日本とロシアが朝鮮半島や中国での利権をめぐって、中国東北部で戦闘を交えるという、帝国主義の論理による戦争でもありました。

日本にとっては、戦争を遂行するための資金調達をイギリスやアメリカで行い、辛うじて財政破綻を回避しながら強国ロシアを相手にするという「背水の陣」での戦いでした。そしてロシアからしてみれば、この戦争は中国という巨大な市場を獲得し、政情不安の続くロマノフ王朝を立て直す機会でもあったのです。

列強の外交政策とその駆け引きに世界は翻弄された

日露戦争の初期、日本は海外での資金調達に苦労します。多くの国が、国力に圧倒的な差があるロシアとの戦争を日本が継続できないと思っていたのです。しかし、ロシア国内も混乱状態にありました。経済的格差や皇帝の専制政治に苦しむ農民の反乱や、工場などでのストライキが頻発し、政情不安が続いていたのです。開戦後日本が善戦すると、ロシア国内では厭戦ムードが広がります。1905年1月に、首都ペテルブルクで平和と貧困からの救済を求めるデモに軍隊が発砲するという血の日曜日事件がおきると、国内情勢はさらに緊迫してゆきました。

奉天会戦や日本海海戦で日本が勝利した段階で、アメリカのセオドア・ルーズベルト大統領の仲裁で、日本はロシアと講和します。アメリカは国力の限界の中で必死に交戦していた日本と、政情不安に悩まされたロシアとの講和に一役買うことで、極東への影響力を強めよう

時代
20世紀1900年代
現代

地域
日本・中国・朝鮮・ロシア・アメリカ

分類
戦争【外交】

キーワード
ロシア第一革命と日本の勝利・アメリカの仲介・韓国の植民地化・三国協商・三国同盟の成立

its national power, and Russia, which was troubled by political instability at home, America maneuvered to increase its own influence in the Far East.

Immediately prior to the end of the Russo-Japanese War, Japan's prime minister, Katsura Taro and America's special envoy William Taft held a meeting in the Philippines. The outcome of their discussions was that America approved Japan's advance into the Korean Empire, and Japan approved America's control of the Philippines. This Katsura-Taft Agreement, together with the Anglo-Japanese Alliance, became a mutual understanding regarding Japanese, English, and American vested interests in the Far East. On the basis of this common assumption, America interceded in the peacemaking process.

Beginning during the Russo-Japanese War, Japan actively intervened in the Korean Empire. The Korean emperor Gojong sent a secret envoy to the International Peace Conference held in The Hague in an attempt to effect some kind of a breakthrough, but the great powers refused to accept the participation of the secret envoy in their deliberations.

To take responsibility for the envoy incident at The Hague, Gojong abdicated the throne. In 1910 Japan officially annexed Korea.

As the 20th century dawned, the world found itself entangled in the web of diplomatic strategies pursued by the great powers.

Following the Franco-Prussian War, out of fear of Germany, which had become a powerful state, France and Russia established close relations with one another, and in 1894 they formed the Franco-Russian Alliance. However, once the Russo-Japanese War ended and the Russian threat in the Far East was diminished, England and Japan agreed to a peaceful settlement with Russia. In order to check German advances into the Middle East, England and Russia concluded the Anglo-Russian Entente. Together with the Franco-Russian Alliance, the Triple Entente came into effect.

Meanwhile, after the downfall of Germany's Otto von Bismarck, Kaiser Wilhelm II, who held the reins of actual power, undertook aggressive policies to dominate a broad region. It included construction of railroads tying together Berlin, Byzantium (later Istanbul), and Baghdad, using this so-called "3B Strategy" to expand its economic and military influence. With this as a statement of its foreign policy, Germany clashed with the foreign policies of Russia and England. In this connection, England was pursuing its own "3C Strategy", which aimed at linking Cairo, Calcutta, and Cape Town. The conflict between England and Germany in their respective pursuits of rights and interests would lead to World War I.

と目論んでいたのです。

　日露戦争終結直前に、当時の日本の総理大臣桂太郎と、アメリカの特使ウィリアム・タフトとがフィリピンで会合を持ちました。その結果、アメリカは日本の大韓帝国への進出を是認した上で、日本はアメリカのフィリピン支配を認めるという協定を結びます。この桂タフト協定は、日英同盟と共に、極東での日本、イギリス、そしてアメリカの利権を相互に承認した取り決めになります。その前提でアメリカは日露戦争の調停に立ったのです。

　日露戦争中から日本は大韓帝国に積極的に介入します。大韓帝国の皇帝高宗はハーグで開催されていた万国平和会議に密使を送り、事態の打開を図りますが、列強は密使の会議への参加を認めませんでした。

　高宗は、ハーグ密使事件の責任をとって退位します。そして1910年に日本は同国を正式に併合したのでした。日韓併合です。
　20世紀初頭、世界はこのように列強の外交戦略の網の目の中にありました。
　普仏戦争を経て強国となったドイツへの脅威から、フランスとロシアは接近し、1894年には露仏同盟が締結されました。しかし、日露戦争が終結し、極東でのロシアの脅威が軽減されると、イギリスと日本はロシアと和解します。1907年には中東への進出を目論むドイツを牽制するために、イギリスはロシアと英露協商を締結。露仏同盟と合わせて、三国協商が成立します。

　一方、ドイツはビスマルク失脚後に実権を握っていた皇帝ヴィルヘルム2世が積極的な対外進出を企てていました。特にベルリン（Berlin）からビザンティウム（Byzantium、のちのイスタンブール）、そしてバグダード（Baghdad）を鉄道で結び、経済的にも軍事的にも影響下におこうとする3B政策は、皇帝の外交政策の看板として、ロシアやイギリスの対外政策と衝突するようになったのです。ちなみに、イギリスはカイロ（Cairo）とカルカッタ（Calcutta）、そして南アフリカのケープタウン（Cape Town）とを結ぶ3C政策を推進していました。イギリスの権益と、それを打ち破ろうとするドイツとの確執が、その後第一次世界大戦へと繋がってゆくのです。

142 With the Xinhai Revolution, China parted from thousands of years of dynastic government

On the eve of World War I, the powers of the West sought to protect their respective interests through assorted treaties and secret agreements. These agreements, such as the Triple Entente and the Triple Alliance, were so complex that suspicions arose about who was allied with whom.

Ironically, in the Far East, it was Japan's prevention of Russian attempts at southward advance that brought about a new menace to the Ottoman Empire. Russia turned the aim of its attacks from the Far East to the Middle East and Eastern Europe.

Meanwhile Qing China, like the Ottoman Empire, was like a patient on the verge of death, and in October 1911, an upheaval broke out that became known as the Wuchang Uprising. There was widespread discontent with the Qing as a result of its surrendering to the great powers during the Boxer Rebellion and its inability to do anything about the fighting in China during the Russo-Japanese War.

By this time, the Qing government had already abolished the civil service examinations in 1905 and made a strict promise that it would establish a legislative body, but in the final analysis, there was no actual change in policy. In order to maintain its already weakened economic circumstances, the Qing government nationalized the railroads, but this ended up generating opposition from financiers in the provinces.

Toward the end of the Qing period, the armed guard directly under the command of the emperor, which was called the Eight Banners, became a shell of its former self, and the true military power was supported by prominent provincial figures. An example of this was the Beiyang Army, which had its roots in the Huai army established by Li Hongzhang to suppress the Taiping Rebellion.

Within this army, there was widespread distrust of the Qing. Further, among Han Chinese, there were many who wanted to take government out of the hands of the Manchus and return it to the Han people. In response to this sentiment, political organizations advocating for democracy, such as the Revive China Society, led by Sun Yat-sen, merged with the movement. With the support of Chinese people living abroad, Sun Yat-sen united the revolutionary forces dispersed throughout China to form the Chinese Alliance in 1905. This took place in Tokyo. Sun Yat-sen took as their slogan the Three Principles of the People, referring to nationalism,

中国は辛亥革命で数千年の王朝政治に訣別した

　第一次世界大戦の前夜、西欧列強は様々な条約や密約によって自らの権益を守ろうとしていました。それは三国協商、三国同盟など、どこがどこと結ばれているか疑心暗鬼に陥るほどの複雑なものでした。

　皮肉なことに、極東で日本がロシアの南下を妨げたことが、オスマン帝国に新たな脅威をもたらしました。ロシアの矛先が極東から中東や東ヨーロッパに向いたからです。

　一方、オスマン帝国と同様に瀕死の重病人であった清では、1911年10月になって武昌蜂起と呼ばれる反乱がおこります。義和団の乱での清の列強への屈服、日露戦争が中国国内で行われたことに清朝政府が無策でいたことへの反発など、中国では清への不満が蔓延していたのです。

　すでに、清朝政府も1905年には科挙を廃止し、議会開催の確約などを行っていましたが、結局政策に目立った変化はありませんでした。清朝はさらに弱体化した経済体制を維持するために鉄道を国有化しますが、これは逆に地方の資本家の反感を買うことになってしまいます。

　清朝末期には、八旗と呼ばれる皇帝直属の軍隊は形骸化し、実際の軍事は地方の有力者が担っていました。李鴻章が太平天国の乱を平定したときに設立した淮軍をルーツにもつ北洋軍などはその代表でした。

　そうした軍隊の中にも、清への不信感が蔓延したのです。また、漢民族の中には、満州族を中心とする清を漢民族の手に取り戻そうと思う人々も多くいました。この流れに、孫文を中心に結成された民主化を求める政治結社興中会などが合流します。海外在住の中国

孫文
Sun Yat-sen (1866–1925)

人の支援も受けながら、孫文は中国に分散した革命勢力を一つにまとめ、1905年に中国同盟会を結成したのです。東京でのことでした。「民族、民権、民生」、すなわち、中国民族の自立、そして人民が政治に参

時代
20世紀1910年代
現代

地域
中国

分類
革命【制度】

キーワード
ロシア南下が東欧、中東へ・清の半植民地化・清末の改革の失敗・軍閥の跋扈・辛亥革命の成立

democracy, and livelihood. This meant the independence of the Chinese people, the right of the people to participate in governing the country, and economic equality in earning a livelihood.

The sudden uprising that occurred against this background in Wuchang instantly spread through other regions, and the provincial armies declared their independence from the Qing administration. The Qing ordered Yuan Shikai, who was in charge of the Beiyang forces, to regain control over the situation. Sun Yat-sen had already returned to China, and in January 1912, he assembled the revolutionary forces and declared the establishment of the Republic of China, taking the office of president himself. This series of events is called the Xinhai Revolution.

During the Xinhai Revolution, Yuan Shikai turned against the Qing Dynasty and forced the abdication of the last emperor, Puyi, who became known as Emperor Xuantong.

The imperial government that had continued unbroken in China since ancient times came to an end.

The Republic of China became the first republic in Asia that was not headed by either an emperor or a monarch. However, its future was full of difficulties. China had just begun to pass through a long tunnel leading to stability and regeneration.

143 Antagonism between the haves and the have-nots came to light at the beginning of the 20th century

When we look at the 20th century in the context of the world's long history, we can observe a shift in a major trend. It was a shift where, in response to Western expansion that had been going on since the 17th century, nationalist movements emerged in Asia and began to exert influence as a new centripetal force in the world.

The beginnings of this movement in the Far East were the rise of Japan, the Xinhai Revolution in China, and the movement for independence in India. Prior to this change, power had tended to move from the West to the East, but that power was gradually stemmed, and the vector shifted to a force that moved from the East to the West. Unfortunately, when that movement began, Japan followed the path toward imperialism in the Far East.

Japan hastily followed the path that Britain and France had pursued in the 19th

加する権利、そして人々の生活が経済的な平等の上に営まれるべきという三民主義が孫文のスローガンとなりました。

　こうした背景の中でおきた武昌での蜂起は、瞬く間に地方に広がり、地方の軍隊が清からの独立を宣言したのです。それに対して、清朝は北洋軍を率いる袁世凱に事態の収拾を命じます。すでに孫文は中国に帰国し、1912年1月には、革命勢力を結集して中華民国の建国を宣言、自ら大総統となりました。この一連の動きを、辛亥革命と呼んでいます。

袁世凱
Yuan Shikai (1859–1916)

　この、辛亥革命の最中、袁世凱は清朝に反旗を翻し、最後の皇帝となった宣統帝溥儀を退位させます。1912年2月のことでした。

　古代から脈々と続いた中国の帝政はここに終焉しました。

　中華民国は、アジア初の皇帝や王を抱かない共和国として産声をあげたのです。しかし、その前途は多難でした。中国は安定と再生へ向けて長いトンネルをくぐり始めるのでした。

持てる国と持たざる国との対立が20世紀初頭にあぶり出された

　世界の長い歴史の中に20世紀をおいたとき、一つの潮流の変化を見ることができます。それは17世紀頃から続いていた西欧の世界への進出に対して、アジアを中心に民族運動がおこり、新たな求心力として世界に影響を与え始めたことです。

　その原点となったのは、極東での日本の台頭と、中国での辛亥革命、そしてインドの独立運動でした。今まで、西から東へと動いていた力が次第に食い止められ、東から西へのベクトルが生まれ始めたのです。残念ながら、そうした動きが始まったとき、日本は極東で帝国主義への道を追随しました。

　イギリスやフランスが19世紀にたどった道を日本は急ぎ追いかけよ

時代
19, 20世紀
近代・現代

地域
共通

分類
政治【経済】

キーワード
新興列強の日独、既得権を持つ英仏・民族主義の高まり・植民地獲得の飽和状態・ロシアの矛盾

century. Germany followed a similar route. Unlike America and Russia, neither of these two nations possessed large territories. Similarly, neither had a significant inflow of migrants to count on for increasing new domestic demand. Eventually both countries, under the influence of domestic nationalism, began to confront Britain, America, and France over vested interests abroad.

Actually, the imperialist competition for the acquisition of colonies had already reached a saturation point by the end of the 19th century. For example, in Africa, France had extended its influence from western Africa eastward along the Sahara Desert. In contrast, in Egypt and in Cape Town, the British army had sought to expand British interests and rights along a north-south axis, confronting the French at Fashoda in the present-day Republic of South Sudan in 1898. The two narrowly averted conflict in what is known as the Fashoda Incident. While they succeeded in avoiding armed conflict, as a result of the tension created by such imperialist activities, the great powers began to seek new pathways to reconcile their differences by means of international treaties.

Following the Industrial Revolution, in the West, the major powers made use of the abundant resources of the colonial territories, and through technological innovation, they were able to cultivate large-scale industries. In this way, mass production became possible, and financial capital to support industry developed on a global scale. These countries achieved the development of electric power and communication technology, called the Second Industrial Revolution, and cultivated basic national industries, including the steel industry and heavy industries. Especially prominent was America's progress, which at the start of the 20th century made it the strongest industrialized country in the world, making it a major mover in international politics.

うとしたのです。似た状況はドイツにもありました。両国には、アメリカやロシアのように、広大な領土がありませんでした。さらに、移民の流入による新たな内需も期待できませんでした。やがて両国とも、国内ではナショナリズムを煽りながら、対外的には、こうした既得権益を持つイギリスやアメリカ、フランスなどと対峙するようになるのです。

　実際、帝国主義による植民地獲得競争は、19世紀終盤にはすでに飽和状態になっていました。例えば、アフリカでは西アフリカからサハラ砂漠に沿って東へと影響力を拡大していたフランスがありました。それに対してエジプトとケープタウンを軸にアフリカを縦断しながら権益を拡大しようとしていたイギリスの軍隊が、1898年に現在の南スーダンにあるファショダで遭遇したことがありました。あわや紛争寸前となったこの事件を、ファショダ事件と呼んでいます。武力衝突はなんとか回避され、逆にこうした飽和状態での緊張を経て、列強は国際条約を軸にした融和の道を模索し始めたのです。

　また、欧米では産業革命後、植民地からの豊富な原料を使用し、さらなる技術革新によって巨大産業が育成されます。これによって大量生産が可能になり、産業を支える金融資本も世界規模で成長します。第二次産業革命と呼ばれる電力や通信技術が発展し、鉄鋼業などの重工業も国家の基幹産業として成長を遂げていました。特にアメリカの進歩は著しく、20世紀に入った段階で、世界一の工業国として国際政治にも大きな影響を与えるようになったのです。

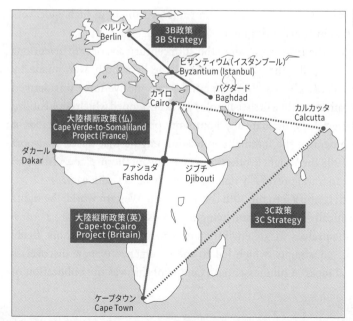

アフリカ分割
Scramble for Africa

In contrast with this cultivation of industry, one cannot overlook the active socialist movements that sought rights for laborers. Particularly in Russia, which had maintained its distorted social structure under imperial rule, the Russian Social-Democratic and Labor Party was formed in an effort to overturn autocratic rule, and the Bolsheviks, a communist political party, emerged under Vladimir Ilich Lenin. During the Russo-Japanese War, Nicholas II, sensing an impending crisis as a result of this socialist movement, established a national legislature and set about implementing an agricultural reform, but these efforts failed.

So at the beginning of the 20th century the world situation was a complex mixture of the national destinies of the haves and the have-nots.

144 The advance of industry confronted the issues of people's culture and morals

In order to succeed in the Second Industrial Revolution, a merging of science and technology was indispensable.

Conventional logic and mathematics were applied to practical science, and the results were utilized in improving people's daily lives.

Such practical applications were a splendid opportunity for investments. The combination of technological innovation and investment in such endeavors further nurtured industrial development.

From the end of the 19th century into the 20th century, a variety of inventions employing electricity, like the phonograph and the light bulb, were made by Thomas Edison. Times changed from a period when motive force was derived from coal and steam to one in which technology was developed which could utilize petroleum and electricity, dramatically improving productivity. In particular, it was the improvement of the internal combustion engine that raised transport capacity, and in 1903 the Wright brothers used it to invent the airplane. With that, people were able to travel previously unimaginable distances with ease.

From the 19th century into the 20th century, in the Western world, the rights of citizens dramatically improved, and living standards became more prosperous. People found themselves in an environment where they could think freely without religious constraints, which led to the emergence of new discoveries and philosophical ideas. A quintessential example of this was the publication of

こうした産業の育成に対して、労働者の権利を求める社会主義運動が活発になったことも見逃せません。特に帝政という歪んだ社会構造をそのまま維持していたロシアでは、専制政治を覆そうと、ロシア社会民主労働党が結成され、そこからレーニンによってボリシェヴィキと呼ばれる共産主義政党が生まれました。日露戦争の最中、こうした社会主義活動に危機感を覚えた皇帝ニコライ2世は国会を開設し、農村改革にも取り組もうとしますが挫折します。

　このように、持てる国と持たざる国との様々な運命が交錯したのが20世紀初頭の世界情勢だったのです。

産業の振興は、人々に文明とモラルという課題を突きつけた

　第二次産業革命を成功させるには、科学と技術の融合が必要不可欠でした。
　古来の論理学や数学などが実学に応用され、人々の日々の営みを向上させるために活用されたのです。
　この活用は金融資本にとって絶好の投資の対象となります。技術革新と、その試みへの投資の両輪が産業をさらに育成してゆきます。

　19世紀後半から20世紀にかけて、トーマス・エジソンによって、蓄音機や電球など、電気を使った様々な発明がなされました。石炭と蒸気を原動力とする時代から、石油と電気によって動力を生み出す技術が開発されたことで、生産力は飛躍的に向上したのです。特にこうした新しいエネルギーを使用した内燃機関の改良は輸送力を改善し、1903年にはライト兄弟によって飛行機も発明されます。人々は以前では考えられないほど容易に長距離を移動することができるようになったのです。
　19世紀から20世紀にかけて、欧米では市民の権利が飛躍的に向上し、生活も豊かになりました。人々は宗教的な束縛を受けることなく自由に思考できる環境が整ったことで、今までにはない発見や哲学的な発想が育まれます。典型的な例は、チャールズ・ダーウィンが1859年に発表した『種の起源』でした。そこで語られた進化論は、それまでの

時代
19, 20世紀
現代

地域
西ヨーロッパ・アメリカ合衆国・日本

分類
技術【文化】

キーワード
科学と技術の融合・第二次産業革命・芸術の隆盛・娯楽の発達・文明とモラルのバランス

Charles Darwin's *On the Origin of Species by Means of Natural Selection* in 1859. The theory of evolution presented though this work fundamentally overturned the religious view that contended humans were created in the image of the deity, and therefore it discredited the entire value system based on that premise.

The same was true in the world of the arts. They ceased to be devoted to embellishing religious rituals and the facilities used by the politicians. A particular characteristic of the 19th century was that the arts became more devoted to activities focused on individuality. Artistic activity became the object of investment, and creative activities aimed at amusement of the masses evolved. That has evolved into the performing arts and sports businesses of the present day.

Simultaneously, as the West advanced into Asia and Africa, folklore studies and cultural anthropology made strides, and conversely, a greater number of people were strongly influenced by the non-Western cultures. The story of how the Impressionists became fascinated by the colored woodblock prints, or ukiyo-e, from Japan is well-known.

Unfortunately, it is also a fact that industry and technology produced new instruments for inflicting harm on humankind. Warfare serves as a prime example of this. Airplanes enabled air raids. Developments in chemistry created poison gas. Dynamite, invented by Alfred Bernhard Nobel, was employed in wartime destruction and carnage. Examples like these are endless. Industrial technology and military technology both became recipients of investments on a national scale.

That science and technology could be employed in destroying life and property in warfare is now one of the most important issues humankind has to deal with. It involves how we are to balance culture and morals. Humanity faced this dilemma from the very beginning of the process.

145 The conflict and contradictions between the old and new sets of values framed contemporary history

Accompanying the progress of industry and standards of living between the 19th and 20th centuries was a change in the values themselves.

In the West, following the establishment of Christianity as the state religion of

人は神の姿を借りた存在だという宗教観、そして価値観を、根本から覆したのです。

　芸術の世界も同様でした。宗教的儀式や為政者の施設を装飾する目的を離れ、芸術がより個性を重んじた活動へと変わっていったのも19世紀の特徴でした。資産家は技術革新と同様、芸術活動へも注目します。芸術活動が投資の対象となったことで、大衆の娯楽などを意図した積極的な創作活動が展開されるようになったのです。それが現在のパフォーミングアートやスポーツ興行などへと進化してゆくのです。

　同時に西欧世界がアジアやアフリカへと進出するにつれて民俗学や文化人類学も進歩し、逆にそうした非西欧的な文物に強い影響を受ける人々も増えてきました。印象派の画家たちが日本の浮世絵に魅了されたことは有名な話です。

　一方、残念なことに、産業や技術が人類を苦しめる新たな道具を製造するようになったことも事実です。戦争はその代表的な事例でした。飛行機による空襲、化学の発展による毒ガスなどの開発、ノーベルが発明したダイナマイトなどが戦争での破壊と殺戮に転用されたことなど、事例をあげればきりがありません。産業技術と軍事技術は、共に国家規模での投資の対象となったのです。

　科学技術が戦争での生命や財産の破壊を目的として活用されたことは、文明とモラルとのバランスへの問いかけとして、今なお我々人類の最も重たい課題となっています。そんな問いかけが始まったのも、当時のことなのです。

ダーウィンを猿に見立てた風刺画。『種の起源』の刊行で進化論は一躍脚光を浴びたが、当時の宗教観に反するその理論は、教会から激しい非難を浴びた。

Caricature depicting Charles Darwin as an ape. The theory of evolution was thrust into the spotlight with the publication of *The Origin of Species*, but its theory, which was contrary to the religious views of the time, was heavily criticized by the church.

新旧の価値観の対立と矛盾が現代史を綴ってゆく

　19世紀から20世紀にかけての産業や生活水準の進化に伴って人類の価値観自体が変貌しました。

　欧米では、ローマ帝国が国教として以来、西欧世界の背骨として培

the Roman Empire, Christian ethics and religious views formed the backbone of the Western world. That changed greatly. The morals, ethics, value systems, and belief in life after death that had been embraced until then suddenly ceased to have meaning. Human beings no longer followed ethics that depended on the existence of God, but instead began to stress the importance of individual self-awareness and personal desires. Friedrich Nietzsche, a philosopher known for his work in the late 19th century, depicted the figure of the Übermensch (superman) who lives with a strong individual will beyond the collapse of these values. Nietzsche became known to succeeding generations as an intellectual who actively embraced nihilism, a philosophical stance that held all existing value systems to be meaningless. In the same way that Nietzsche challenged existing common sense, Charles Darwin's theory of evolution, and Karl Marx and Friedrich Engel's communism also evolved out of the conclusion that the previously existing Christian way of thinking had been proven false through scientific reasoning.

In the East, a searching inquiry was initiated in the ethical view based on the Confucian spirit that had become intertwined with the state during the Earlier Han period. With the inflow of logical Western civilization, in Japan and China, where modern nation-states were inevitably constructed, the traditional social order which had been continually cultivated over a period of some 2,000 years was consigned to oblivion, and the value system which had served as its pillar was called into question.

Within the alteration of consciousness that occurred both in the East and the West, people somehow continued to clasp the value system of the past as an inherited DNA, even while they had begun to seek a new, practical lifestyle following the Industrial Revolution. Within the same country—and even within the same individual—a new way of thinking emerged, in which people were conscious of their own roots, in which they leaned toward a modern material culture and toward a nationalism that sought spiritual and cultural independence, while seeking a more abundant, enjoyable way of life. While people clung to traditions, they also introduced the conveniences of culture, such as electrical goods, into their daily lives. The spread of material culture standardized the world. However, while people utilized these conveniences, they also advocated for recognition of their own identity.

In the Meiji period, Japan actively reformed the former system and introduced Western culture. At the same time, it was affected by a nationalist sentiment to confront the Western powers as a country, and it was fixated on its own traditional

われてきたキリスト教の倫理観、宗教観が大きく変化しました。それまで信じられていた道徳律、価値観、そして来世観などが無意味に思われ、神の倫理に従う人間ではなく、個人個人の意識や欲求がより重んじられるようになりました。19世紀後半の哲学者として知られるニーチェは、こうした価値観の崩壊の向こうに強い個人の意志をもって生きる超人の姿を描きます。彼はそれまでの価値観が無意味なものとされるニヒリズムを積極的に捉えた人物として後世に名を残しました。ニーチェが哲学者として既存の常識に挑んだのと同様に、ダーウィンの進化論も、マルクスやエンゲルスの説く共産主義も、それまでのキリスト教的な考え方の崩壊を科学的に裏付ける中で芽生えた帰結だったのです。

時代
19, 20世紀
近代・現代

地域
共通

分類
学問【文化】

キーワード
既存の権威の崩壊・価値観の変化・合理主義の進展・民族意識の高まり

東洋では、前漢の頃に国家と結び付いた儒教精神に基づく倫理観にメスが入りました。合理的な西欧文明の流入によって、近代的な国家建設を余儀なくされた日本や中国などの中で、2000年近く育まれ続けた伝統的な社会秩序が葬られ、その支柱となってきた価値観が問われたのです。

洋の東西でおきた社会や意識の変化の中で、人々は過去の価値観を遺伝子として個人の奥に抱きながら、生活の中では産業革命以降の合理主義に基づいたライフスタイルを求め始めたのです。自らのルーツを意識することで、精神的、文化的自立を模索する民族主義と、近代の物質文明に傾斜し、より豊かで恵まれた生活を目指そうとする考え方が、同じ国家の中に、そして個人の中に同居するようになったのです。人々は、伝統に回帰しながらも、家電製品などの文明の利器を生活に取り入れました。物質文明の浸透は、世界をより画一化してゆきます。しかし、同時にその利器を利用して人々は自らのアイデンティティを世界に訴えようともしたのです。

明治時代、日本は積極的に旧体制を改革し、西欧の文明を取り入れました。同時に国家として列強に対抗するために民族意識を煽り、自らの伝統的な価値観にも強くこだわりました。人は自らと異なる者に

value system. When people come into contact with people who are different, they take a fresh look at themselves. The same occurred when Asia encountered Western civilization. Moreover, among the Western powers, for example when France and Germany encountered one another, through this confrontation both parties began to feel a strong sense of nationalist awakening.

The same has occurred in present-day Islamic society. Through this process of action and reaction, human society as time passes will in all likelihood continue to change. The past 200 years, which directly connect to our contemporary lives, have been precisely the era when such changes were set in motion and began to gather momentum.

146 Together with the change in sense of values, the arts progressed

Since the 19th century, together with the shift in conventional values, there has been a major change in artistic activities.

Following the Renaissance, in the West, science has advanced and natural phenomena have been observed in minute detail. Therefore, the previously held notions that had been bound by a belief in divine providence have been reexamined. Following that, through revolutions and ethnic movements, with the freedom of the individual as a citizen being taken seriously, individuality has come to be considered important. In the art world, too, individuality has been freed from the restraints of religion, allowing for greater freedom and diversity in artistic expression.

In order to obtain the skills for expressing that originality, people have become more scientific in viewing sound and color. In the 19th century, music developed through thinking scientifically about logical methods of expression and instilling individuality. Ludwig van Beethoven, Johannes Brahms, and Gustav Mahler, among others, composed magnificent symphonies this way. The same applies to painting. While inheriting motifs and themes from religious art of the past, the people depicted in these paintings became more human, and the artifacts of the real world were observed and expressed with precision.

In Asia, meanwhile, traditions from the past had been passed down in an unbroken flow. In that carrying on of tradition, a unique Asian style of beauty

接したとき、改めて自らを見つめようとします。西欧文明に接したアジアにもそうした作用がありました。また、西欧列強の間でも、例えばフランスと対抗したドイツなどのように、対立を通して双方に強い民族的自覚が芽生えました。

　それは現在のイスラム社会などでも同様です。こうした作用と反作用を経て、人類の社会は時間をかけて一歩一歩未来へと変化してゆくのかもしれません。我々が生きる現代に直結するこの200年は、まさにそうした変化が始動し、うねりとなり始めた時代だったのです。

価値観の変化と共に、芸術も進化した

　19世紀以降、伝統的な価値観の変化と共に、芸術活動も大きく変化します。
　ルネサンス以来、欧米では科学が振興し、自然現象を精緻に観察することで、それまでの神の摂理で縛られていた考え方が見直されてきました。その後革命や民族運動などを経て、市民としての個人の自由が重んじられると、個性も尊重されるようになりました。芸術の世界でも、宗教的な束縛から個人が解き放たれ、表現方法もより自由で多様になったのです。

時代
19, 20世紀
近代・現代

地域
共通

分類
文化【交流】

キーワード
宗教から個性へ・音楽美術の発展・日本のアートが欧米で評価・民族土着的文化の見直し

　そんな個性を表現するノウハウを得るために、人々はより科学的な目で音や色を考えます。19世紀に音楽は合理的な表現方法を科学しながら、そこに個性を注入して発展したのです。ベートーベンやブラームス、マーラーなどの壮大な交響曲もこうして作曲されました。絵画も同様です。過去の宗教画のモチーフやテーマなどを受け継ぎながらも、そこに描かれる人々はより人間的になり、現実の世界の文物が精密に観察され、表現されるようになりました。

　一方、アジアでは、古くからの伝統が脈々と継承されていました。その継承の中から、アジア独特の様式美が生まれ、写実の世界とはか

arose. Through the generations an accumulated sense of beauty that sought something completely separate from the objective world evolved.

In the 19th century, this Asian art became widely known in Europe and North America, and for the Western world of art, which tended toward structure and realistic portrayal resulting from a scientific perspective, this Asian form proved a major stimulus. If we take Japanese art as an example, the eyes of a statue of Buddha are portrayed in the same style used to depict an Edo period courtesan in ukiyo-e. The only difference is that the former is an expression of quiet enlightenment, while the latter is an expression of secular pleasure. Within the portrayal is a very slight difference that indirectly expresses the heart of the person being depicted. This had a powerful impact on the artists of the West, who were used to portraying everything in a lively, natural fashion. Oriental art was to the Western artist the ultimate abstract art.

Artists who were captivated by works of art like the woodblock prints called ukiyo-e, as a result of this fresh stimulus, attempted to break away from the forms that has existed in the West to that point. Artists such as the Impressionists began to portray scenes that they imagined in their minds with complete abandon, no longer bound by the need for realistic portrayal. This tendency became the precursor of a reform movement that led to the abstract conceptions and images expressed on canvases in the 20th century. The same was true in the music world.

This was not only a result of the stimulus of Oriental arts but also a response to attention being paid to ethnic, native traditions. The rhythms and verse patterns that had been passed down from one generation to the next among African Americans evolved into jazz, an archetype that had a significant impact on many musicians. Especially in the early 20th century, when Western society was devastated by warfare, some people began to embrace doubts about Western science and rationality. At least partially as a result of this, more attention was given to the lifestyles and expressive forms that had traditionally been handed down in Asia, Africa, and South America.

As we have seen earlier, from the 19th into the 20th centuries, the current of civilization that flowed from West to East, becoming a precursor of artistic activity, began to change slightly, and a phenomenon of reverse-flow began to appear.

け離れた美への探求が世代を超えて堆積してゆきました。

　19世紀にそうしたアジアの芸術が欧米に伝わると、科学の目によってより構造や写実に傾斜していた西欧美術の世界が、大きな刺激を受けるのです。例えば、日本のアートを例にとれば、仏像の目も浮世絵の遊女の目も同じような様式で描かれています。ただ、前者には静かな悟りが、後者には世俗の愉悦が表現されています。様式の中に微妙に異なる人の心を埋め込み表現した究極の婉曲がそこにあります。それが、物事を生き生きとありのままに表現してきた欧米の芸術家に強い印象を与えたのです。東洋芸術は彼らにとって、究極の抽象芸術だったのです。

フィンセント・ファン・ゴッホ『花魁』
Vincent van Gogh
—The Courtesan (after Eisen)

　浮世絵などの美術に魅せられた画家たちは、その新鮮な刺激によって、それまでの西欧の型を打ち破ろうと試みます。心に抱いた風景を思い切って表現しようとする印象派などの活動が始まるのです。その傾向は、20世紀にさらに抽象的な思考やイメージをキャンバスに表わそうとする様々な改革運動の先駆けとなりました。それは音楽の世界でも同様でした。

　東洋芸術だけでなく、それまで忘れ去られていた民俗的、土俗的な伝統にも光があてられました。アフリカ系アメリカ人の中に伝わっていたリズムや節回しがジャズとして進化し、多くの音楽家に影響を与えたのはその典型でした。特に20世紀になって欧米社会が戦争で破壊されると、西欧の科学や合理性に疑問を持つ人も現れます。そうした影響もあって、アジアやアフリカ、そして南米などに受け継がれてきたライフスタイルや表現形式が、着目されたのです。

　既に解説したように19世紀から20世紀にかけて、西から東へと流れていた文明の潮流が、芸術活動などを先駆けとして、微妙に変化し、逆流現象がおき始めていたのです。

147 In two Balkan wars, the Ottoman Empire lost Europe

We return again to international affairs.

In order to obtain the vast resources of Siberia, Russia constructed the Trans-Siberian Railway. It was completed in 1904. During the same period, as a new policy following the Russo-Japanese War, Russia actively made inroads into the Balkans. Needless to say, it was the Ottoman Empire and Austria that opposed Russia's incursions. From the Middle Ages onward, these two empires had exerted enormous influence in Europe, but they were on the decline. Independence movements in these territories played a direct role in the conflicts that developed thereafter in the Middle East and Eastern Europe. Taking advantage of the decline of the Ottoman Empire, Russia supported the nationalist movements of the Slavic peoples in the Balkan Peninsula.

The Austrian Empire felt a sense of crisis in response to this development. Following the nationalist movements called the Spring of Nations, the Austrian Empire was troubled by the independence movements of ethnic groups within its territories. The Germanic people who controlled Austria eventually joined forces with the Magyars, who held sway over Hungary, established the Austro-Hungarian Empire in 1867, and attempted to stabilize the nation. Reacting against this activity on the part of the Germanic peoples were the Slavic peoples, who were supported by Russia.

Meanwhile, also within the Ottoman Empire, there was a group of people who felt a sense of crisis as a result of the accompanying advance of the British and Russians into Turkish domains. This group organized a political entity called the Young Turks. In 1908 they brought about the Young Turk Revolution, and the Ottoman Empire transitioned into a constitutional monarchy. In northern Africa, meanwhile, Italy deprived the Ottomans of Libya, thereby presenting itself as a competitor for African territories. Within this context, the Balkans became an area of conflict between those who supported and those who resisted the Austro-Hungarian Empire, while nationalist movements within territories under Ottoman control made the situation even more complex, making the entire region the "powder keg of Europe."

In 1912, Bulgaria, Serbia, Montenegro, and Greece—which had already achieved independence from the Ottoman Empire—with backing from Russia

二度のバルカン戦争で、オスマン帝国は
ヨーロッパを失った

再び、国際情勢に戻ります。

ロシアはシベリアの広大な資源を獲得するためにシベリア鉄道を敷設します。完成は1904年。同時に日露戦争後の新たな政策として、バルカン地方へも積極的に進出します。ロシアの動きと対立したのは、いうまでもなくオスマン帝国とオーストリアです。中世以来、ヨーロッパを左右してきたこの両帝国が衰退し、その領土で独立運動がおきたことが、その後の中東問題や東欧での紛争に直接影響を与えます。ロシアは、オスマン帝国の衰退に乗じてバルカン半島で自立したスラブ系の民族主義運動を支援します。

時代
20世紀序盤
現代

地域
オーストリア・トルコ

分類
戦争【独立】

キーワード
ロシアの南下とオーストリア、トルコの動揺・バルカン戦争の勃発・バルカン諸国の独立

これに危機感を持ったのがオーストリア帝国でした。あの「諸国民の春」と呼ばれる民族運動以来、オーストリア帝国は領土内での民族自立の動きに悩まされてきました。オーストリアを支配するドイツ系の人々は、最終的にハンガリーの支配層であるマジャール人と組んで、1867年にオーストリア・ハンガリー帝国を建国し、国家の安定を図ります。こうしたドイツ系の人々の動きに反発したのが、ロシアに支援されたスラブ系の人々だったのです。

一方、オスマン帝国国内でも、帝国の衰退と、それによるイギリスやロシアのトルコ領への進出に危機感を抱いた人々が、青年トルコという政治団体を結成します。彼らは、1908年に青年トルコ革命をおこし、オスマン帝国は立憲君主制へと移行したのです。また、北アフリカでは、イタリアがオスマン帝国領のリビアを奪い、アフリカでの領土獲得競争に名乗りをあげます。そうした状況の中で、バルカン半島は、オーストリア・ハンガリー帝国の支配と、それに反発する人々、さらにオスマン帝国の支配地域での民族運動などが複雑に入り乱れた「ヨーロッパの火薬庫」と呼ばれる紛争地域となったのです。

1912年、すでにオスマン帝国から独立を達成していたブルガリアやセルビア、モンテネグロ、そしてギリシアといった国々が、ロシアの

entered into conflict with the Ottomans. This became the First Balkan War. In the cease-fire agreement that was signed that same year, the Ottoman Empire surrendered its considerable sway over the Aegean Sea and the Balkan Peninsula. However, following this, disagreement arose over these territories, and Bulgaria and related states fell into conflict. War broke out again in 1913, becoming the Second Balkan War. The people of Macedonia and Kosovo were suppressed by Serbia, Montenegro, and Greece. This ethnic conflict not only shaped the course of the First World War but also became an ongoing political issue in the region to this day.

As a result of the Second Balkan War, the Ottoman Empire lost virtually all of its territories in the peninsula and retreated from the European world. In the maelstrom of the Balkan Peninsula, Austria came under threat from Russia. It is ironic that the Ottomans and the Austrians, long-term rivals, during this great decline both shared common interests.

148 The Balkan Peninsula chaos became linked to World War I

When people are controlled or under the threat of becoming controlled, they awaken to nationalist sentiments.

At times nationalism transforms into anti-foreign thinking. A classic example of this occurred during the Bakumatsu period in Japan with the movement calling for revering the Emperor and expelling the foreigners. In Turkey, that is exactly what happened with the Young Turks movement. And when that movement became overheated, the energy that powered it developed into a movement that denounced the government of its own country, which had remained unchanged.

In the 20th century, independence movements occurred in a large number of colonial territories. The winds of reformist movements swept over states in which people were tormented by outmoded customs and where the government was undermined. In Russia and China that turned into revolutions.

In the Balkan Peninsula, alongside ethnic tensions, there were intense rivalries between Austria and Russia, as well as between Russia and the Ottoman Empire.

Following the Franco-Prussian War, because Germany had a heavy industrial area on its border with France, it was constantly edgy about a possible French

後ろ盾を元にオスマン帝国と戦争状態に突入します。この戦争は第一次バルカン戦争と呼ばれ、同年の休戦協定でオスマン帝国はエーゲ海やバルカン半島での支配権の多くを放棄します。しかし、その後の領土問題をめぐりブルガリアと関係国が対立。1913年には再び戦争がおこります。第二次バルカン戦争の勃発です。マケドニアやコソボなどの人々がセルビアやモンテネグロ、そしてギリシアなどによって蹂躙されます。この民族同士の対立は、その後の第一次世界大戦のみならず、現在に至るまでこの地域の政治問題となりました。

　第二次バルカン戦争の結果、オスマン帝国は、バルカン半島のほとんどを失い、ヨーロッパ世界から後退したのです。また、オーストリアもバルカン半島の混乱の中でロシアからの脅威にさらされます。長年のライバルであったオスマン帝国とオーストリアは、その衰亡の渦の中で、皮肉なことに共通の利害を共有するようになったのです。

バルカン半島の混乱が第一次世界大戦へと繋がった

　支配されたり、支配の脅威を受けたりしたとき、人々は民族主義に目覚めます。
　民族主義は、時には排外的なナショナリズムに変化することもありました。日本の幕末の尊王攘夷運動などはその典型でした。トルコでは、青年トルコの運動がまさにそれにあたります。そしてこうした運動が過熱したとき、そのエネルギーは、旧態依然とした自国の政権への弾劾運動へと発展するのです。

　20世紀には、数多くの植民地で独立運動がおこりました。また、長年の因習に苛まれ、統治能力が蝕まれた国家でも改革運動の嵐が吹き荒れます。ロシアや中国ではそれが革命となりました。

　バルカン半島では、民族的な緊張に加えて、オーストリアとロシア、さらにロシアとオスマン帝国とが鋭くにらみ合います。
　ドイツは普仏戦争以降、フランスとの国境に重工業地帯があったこともあり、フランスの反撃に神経をとがらせます。そして、そのフラ

時代
20世紀1910年代
現代

地域
ヨーロッパ

分類
民族【戦争】

キーワード
民族主義とバルカンの緊張・三国同盟と三国協商の対立・第一次世界大戦の勃発

counterattack. And then there was a disturbing alliance called the Triple Entente, which was formed by Russia, France, and Britain.

To counter this, Germany joined hands with Austria, and Austria, in order to avoid conflict in the Balkans, moved toward a rapprochement with the Ottoman Empire.

As a consequence, the countries of Western Europe separated into two camps: the Triple Entente of Britain, France, and Russia, and the Central Powers of Germany, Austria, and the Ottoman Empire. Moreover, Italy, in order to protect its interests in North Africa, joined in a Triple Alliance with Germany and Austria, seeking a means of confronting the Triple Entente countries who had interests not only in North Africa but also in the Middle East.

What changed this chaotic situation in Europe was an incident that occurred in Sarajevo, the capital of Bosnia, which was part of the Austro-Hungarian Empire. In June 1914, a Serbian nationalist assassinated Austrian Archduke Franz Ferdinand and his wife.

Following this incident, Austria declared war on Serbia. Russia, which supported Serbia, entered a state of hostilities with Austria, and Russia's allies, Britain and France, joined in the fighting. Naturally, the German Empire and the Ottoman Empire joined on the Austrian side. Bulgaria, which reached a peace agreement with the Ottoman Empire following the Balkan Wars, joined the side of the German alliance. Italy, which had territorial issues with Austria, established close relations with Britain and France, and ultimately the Triple Entente collapsed.

And so it was that World War I began.

As a result of the Anglo-Japanese Alliance, Japan participated in the conflict on the British side. Warfare also extended into the European colonial territories in Africa. Through these four years of war, in many areas, the previously existing regimes collapsed.

World War I came to be remembered through the generations as the first use of modern science on a worldwide scale for appalling slaughter.

ンスはロシア、イギリスと三国協商という同盟関係にあったのです。

　ドイツは、これに対抗するためにオーストリアと手を結び、オーストリアは、バルカン半島の混乱を回避する意味からもオスマン帝国に接近します。

　この結果、西欧諸国はイギリス、フランス、ロシアという三国協商側とドイツ、オーストリア、そしてオスマン帝国の陣営とに分かれることになるのです。さらに、イタリアは北アフリカでの利権を獲得し維持するために、ドイツやオーストリアと三国同盟を結び、同じく北アフリカや中東での利権を争うイギリスやフランス、さらにロシアと対抗していました。

　混沌としたヨーロッパの状況が変化したのは、オーストリア・ハンガリー帝国の一部であったボスニアの州都サラエボでの事件でした。1914年6月にセルビア系の民族主義者が、オーストリア大公フランツ・フェルディナントとその妻を暗殺したのです。

　オーストリアは事件を受けてセルビアに宣戦布告。セルビアを支援していたロシアがオーストリアと戦闘状態になり、ロシアと同盟していたイギリスやフランスも参戦しました。ドイツ帝国とオスマン帝国は当然オーストリア側につきます。バルカン戦争の後にオスマン帝国と講和していたブルガリアもドイツなど同盟

サラエボ市庁舎を出て車に戻るオーストリア大公夫妻。この数分後に暗殺されてしまった。

The Austrian Archduke and his wife leave Sarajevo City Hall and return to their car. They were assassinated a few minutes after this.

国側について参戦したのです。オーストリアとの領土問題を抱えるイタリアはイギリスやフランスに接近し、最終的には三国同盟は崩壊します。

　こうして第一次世界大戦が始まりました。

　日本は日英同盟によってイギリス側について参戦します。戦争は、列強が支配していたアフリカなどの植民地にも拡大し、文字どおり世界中が戦火に巻き込まれることになったのです。そして、この4年間の戦争を通して、多くの地域ではそれ以前の国家体制そのものが崩壊してしまうのです。

　第一次世界大戦は、近代科学を駆使した世界規模での凄惨な殺戮の記憶として人々に受け継がれることになるのでした。

149 Seeking to fill the void left by the upheaval among the great powers, Japan invaded China

Once World War I began, Germany invaded neutral Belgium and advanced into French territory. However, there the Germans encountered resistance from the allied powers, and the fighting became a deadlock.

Along the border between France and Germany, both armies dug long trench works, and the fighting continued utilizing new weapons, including poison gas and armed aircraft. Along the Russian front, conditions were quite similar. The First World War resulted in over 20 million casualties, including noncombatants, and every part of Europe fell into ruin. The First World War was more brutal than any that had previously occurred in history.

International politics of modern Europe can be seen as based on confrontations between the two axes of Germany and France. Following the breakup of the Holy Roman Empire, as the German Empire gradually developed into a powerful nation, the most cautious nation close by was France. Losing the Franco-Prussian War in 1870, France armed itself against future German aggression, constructing a line of defense trenches several hundred kilometers in length along its entire border with Germany. In the Second World War, as well, the most severe fighting repeatedly occurred along this line of defense.

The Allied Powers carried out an economic blockade on the seas against the enemies in the Central Powers. In response, Germany deployed submarines to attack Allied merchant ships.

The economic blockade dealt a heavy blow to Germany. In Russia the fighting strained the national finances. Resentment against the existing poverty and socio-economic disparity spread among the populace. As the fighting dragged on, rather naturally, the dissatisfaction with the government exploded.

Meanwhile in Britain, because the fighting continued, a general mobilization was carried out in order to protect the country's overseas interests. First, in order to obtain economic and human cooperation, Britain promised the establishment of independent countries in the Middle East, a long-desired goal among Arabs and Jews. Colonized India also sent soldiers to the front, hoping to gain some advantage as a result of its cooperation.

Britain's response in the Middle East had a direct impact on the independence movement in Palestine for both Arabs and Jews. As a result, until the present day,

列強の動乱の空白を狙って日本は中国に進出した

　第一次世界大戦が始まると、ドイツは中立国であったベルギーに侵攻し、さらにフランス領内に進軍します。しかし、そこで連合国側の抵抗にあい、戦争はこう着状態へと陥ります。

　フランスとドイツとの国境周辺に、両陣営共に長い塹壕を掘り、毒ガスや戦闘機といった新しい兵器を使用して戦闘を継続したのです。ロシアとの戦線においても状況は同様でした。第一次世界大戦は、非戦闘員を含め2000万人以上の犠牲者をだし、ヨーロッパ各地は戦争によって荒廃します。第一次世界大戦は、過去に例を見ない残酷な戦争だったのです。

　近代ヨーロッパの国際政治は、ドイツとフランスとの対立を軸にして見ることができます。神聖ローマ帝国の解体後、次第に成長し、強国となったドイツ帝国を最も警戒したのはフランスでした。1870年の普仏戦争で敗戦国になったフランスは、その後もドイツの侵攻に備えて、国境一帯に数百キロにも及ぶ防衛ラインを構築していました。第二次世界大戦でも、この防衛ラインで最も過酷な戦闘が繰り広げられたのです。

　連合国は、同盟国に対して海上から経済封鎖を行いました。ドイツはそれに対抗して潜水艦によって連合国の艦船を攻撃しました。

　経済封鎖はドイツにとっては大きな痛手だったのです。ロシアでも戦争の継続が国家財政を逼迫させます。なんといっても以前から貧困と格差による怨嗟が民衆に広がっていたロシアです。戦争が長引くにつれて為政者への不満が噴出したことはいうまでもありません。

　一方でイギリスは、戦争の継続のために、自らの海外での利権を総動員します。まずは経済的、人的な協力を求めて、アラブ系やユダヤ系の人々の悲願であった中東での独立国家建設を約束します。また、植民地であったインドからも兵士を送り、戦闘を少しでも有利に展開しようとしたのです。

　このイギリスの中東での対応が、ユダヤ系、アラブ系双方のパレスチナでの独立運動に直接の影響を与えます。その結果、現代に至るまで、

【時代】
20世紀1910年代
現代

【地域】
ヨーロッパ・日本・中国

【分類】
戦争【技術】

【キーワード】
独仏戦線の膠着・新兵器の開発・国民の総動員・日本の中国進出・ユダヤ、アラブの独立運動

there has been an unending, frequent series of conflicts between the two in the Middle East.

Japan suffered no direct damage as a result of World War I. Germany dispatched troops to China's Shandong province, where it had interests. While the powers of North America and Europe concentrated on warfare, Germany maneuvered to expand its interests in China.

Following the Xinhai Revolution in China, Yuan Shikai, who had directly overthrown Qing rule, held the reins of power, and he squared off against the forces of Sun Yat-sen.

Japan confronted Yuan Shikai with its Twenty-one Demands, and the German interests in Shandong were transferred to Japan. Japan's advance into China in World War I would eventually become the source of new tension in the Far East from that point onward.

150 World War I demolished the existing imperialistic regimes

After a period of meandering in the 20th century, the world became steeped in the ideas of capitalism.

We return for a moment to 1776, the year in which America declared its independence from Britain. In that year, Adam Smith published a book titled *The Wealth of Nations*. It was the world's first true publication about economics, and it became read around the world.

According to Smith's thesis, capitalism supported by a free economy would bring abundance to the world as a whole. By means of the motive power of supply and demand, economies would grow and many nations and individuals would obtain wealth.

From that time onward, within the great powers, citizens have gone out into the world in pursuit of wealth. In the process through which the old social system has broken down and citizens have obtained rights and privileges, Smith offered a vision of freedom, equality, and benevolence. However, in the process of securing wealth, there were many excuses for rationalizing the pursuit of wealth.

Nineteenth-century Britain, for example, made advances in China through the sale of opium, under the premise that markets should be open and that there should

中東では両者の確執が拭えないまま紛争が多発するようになったのです。

　日本は第一次世界大戦では直接被害を受けることはありませんでした。ドイツが権益を持つ中国の山東省に出兵し、欧米列強が戦争に集中している間に、自らの中国での利権の拡大を目論んだのです。

　中国は、辛亥革命の後に、清朝を直接倒した袁世凱が実権をにぎり、孫文率いる勢力と対立していたのです。

　日本は、そんな袁世凱に対華21カ条の要求を突きつけ、山東省にあったドイツの利権を日本に引き渡させます。第一次世界大戦での日本の中国への進出こそが、その後の極東の新たな緊張の原因となったのでした。

第一次世界大戦でそれまでの帝国主義体制が崩壊した

　20世紀は、紆余曲折の後に、世界が資本主義という考え方に染まっていった時代でした。

　ちょうどアメリカが独立宣言をおこなった1776年に遡ります。その年にアダム・スミスが一冊の書籍を出版します。『諸国民の富』というその書籍は、世界初の本格的な経済書として世界中で読まれることになったのです。

　そこでは、自由経済に支えられた資本主義によって、世界が豊かになってゆく法則が示されました。需要と供給との双方の牽引力によって、経済は発展し、多くの国や個人が豊かになるのだと彼は説いたのです。

　以来、列強では市民レベルで富を求めて世界に進出します。社会で旧体制が壊され市民が権利を獲得した過程では、自由、平等、そして博愛といったビジョンが語られました。しかし、富を求める過程では、まず富を獲得し、それを合理化するためにビジョンが言い訳のように語られたことも多々ありました。

　例えば19世紀のイギリスは、アヘンを売って中国に進出しながら、市場進出の機会均等、ビジネスをする自由を主張しました。20世紀に

時代
20世紀1910年代
現代

地域
ヨーロッパ・日本・アメリカ合衆国

分類
戦争【革命】

キーワード
帝国主義の行き詰まり・アメリカの参戦・ロシア、ドイツ、オスマン帝国の終焉

be equality of access to those markets. In the 20th century, America appealed to international society that it should be given equal access to markets everywhere.

The egos of such powerful countries brought forth criticism at home and abroad. Because it came from a particularly large country and there were many countries where the development of civil society was precarious at best, within the impossible logic of competition, a magma-like pool of dissatisfaction welled up against the political class of impoverished societies.

Amidst such inconsistencies, World War I broke out. It is only natural that this magma erupted when there was a war. The war served as a trigger for the revision of how capitalism had worked when it was supported by imperialism. Nevertheless, when World War I occurred, America, which had invested in Britain and France, was cautious about a German invasion. America's economic world was urgently concerned with how to bring the war to a close so that American investors could collect on the debts in Europe under beneficial conditions.

Moreover, the state of the world became even more chaotic with war in the background. Already, on the eve of the war, the Xinhai Revolution had broken out in China.

In addition, in 1917 the Romanov dynasty was overthrown in Russia. Toward the end of the war, a revolution occurred in the German Empire, and just after the war ended, the Ottoman Empire ceased to exist. For many of the major countries of the world, the old system, which had tended toward becoming sheer memories of the past, were finally destroyed, in both name and substance. World War I brought many of the changes that the participating countries were undergoing to a conclusion.

Under these conditions, America, which had maintained neutrality until then, declared war on Germany in April 1917. Its deployment of a major military force greatly altered how the war was going. At the time, a revolution was underway in Mexico, and Germany was carrying out secret operations on behalf of Mexico, which was in a tense confrontation with America. Then when a German submarine attacked and sank a passenger ship with a large number of Americans aboard, America used that as the immediate excuse for declaring war on Germany. However, the true underlying reason mentioned above was the desire to protect its economic interests overseas.

With the worsening of the war situation and a destabilized domestic political situation to deal with, Germany, the main ally among the Central Powers, agreed to an armistice in November 1918.

なると、アメリカも世界の市場に対して自分たちにも平等な機会をと国際社会に訴えます。

こうした強国のエゴは内外に批判を生みます。特に大きな国でありながら、市民社会の発展がおぼつかなかった国々では、無理な競争原理の中で社会が疲弊し、為政者への不満がマグマのように溜まってゆきます。

こうした矛盾の中で、第一次世界大戦がおこりました。であれば、この戦争を契機に、マグマが吹き出したのも当然の成り行きといえましょう。第一次世界大戦は、それまでの帝国主義に支えられた資本主義のあり方を修正するきっかけとなったのです。とはいえ、第一次世界大戦がおきると、イギリスやフランスに投資をしていたアメリカはドイツの侵攻を警戒します。いかにして、戦争を終わらせ、アメリカに有利な状況で債権を回収できるかはアメリカの経済界にとって喫緊の課題となったのでした。

しかも世界情勢は戦争を背景にますます混沌としてきます。すでに中国では大戦前夜に辛亥革命が起こりました。

そして、1917年にはロシアでロマノフ王朝が打倒されます。さらに、戦争末期にはドイツ帝国にも革命がおき、世界大戦直後にはオスマン帝国も消滅します。世界の主要国の多くにおいて、この時期に過去の遺物になりつつあった旧体制が名実ともに崩壊したことになるのです。第一次世界大戦は、これら参戦していた国家の状況の変化によって終結に向かいます。

こうした状況の中で、当初中立を保っていたアメリカが1917年4月になってドイツに対して宣戦布告し、大軍を送り込んできたことが戦局を大きく変化させました。当時メキシコで起きていた革命運動で、ドイツはメキシコと緊張関係にあったアメリカに対し、メキシコ側に立って工作活動をしていました。それに加えてドイツの潜水艦によってアメリカ人が多数乗船していた旅客船が沈められたことが宣戦布告の直接の原因でした。しかし、アメリカの本音は先に解説した経済的利権を守ることにあったはずです。

戦況の悪化と国内の政情不安によって、同盟国側の主役であったドイツが休戦に応じたのは、1918年の11月のことでした。

151 The Russian Revolution became a model for the colonial territories in Asia and Africa

We now turn our attention to the Russian Revolution, which occurred during the Great War.

In order for a revolution to succeed, an anti-government movement has to spread among the police and the army, who are on the side trying to suppress the rebellion.

In Russia prior to World War I, there were political activities centered around the Soviets, organizations supporting laborers. Composed of Bolsheviks, who sought a communist revolution, and Mensheviks, who advocated a more democratic revolution, these organizations led a mass movement against the Romanov dynasty.

When World War I broke out, these people's dissatisfaction changed into a struggle that involved both the military and the police. In March 1917, in the capital Petrograd, demonstrations and strikes arose in protest over the ongoing war and over poverty. More people in the military and police forces began to side with the protestors, and protest movements in major cities of Russia began to increase. As a result, Nicholas II abdicated, and the Romanov dynasty ceased to exist.

Eventually, the Provisional Government was formed by the Mensheviks headed by Alexander Kerensky. While continuing the war, they sought to stabilize the government, but the protests did not subside. In the end, in November of that year, the Bolsheviks, led by Vladimir Ilich Lenin, overthrew the Provisional Government, and the communist revolution occurred. Hence a communist country arose with the soviets as its foundation.

Lenin, together with his comrade Leon Trotsky, emancipated the peasants from under the control of the landowners and declared a withdrawal from the fighting, actualizing a separate peace with Germany in the Treaty of Brest-Litovsk.

Previously a communist movement called the Second International had occurred in 1889, in which labor unions from various parts of the world attempted to form an alliance. Following the precedent of that movement, once Lenin attained political power, he called for a worldwide revolution through a "dictatorship of the proletariat," the laboring class. As a result, in 1919, the Third International, also known as the Comintern, was established. After that, the Soviet government

ロシア革命はアジアやアフリカの植民地の
ビジョンとなった

　ここで、大戦の最中におきたロシア革命にスポットをあてます。

　革命が成功するためには、革命を鎮圧する側にある警察や軍隊にも
反政府運動が波及しなければなりません。

　ロシアでは、第一次世界大戦以前からソヴィエトという労働者によ
る組織を支持母体とした政治活動がありました。彼らは、共産主義に
よる革命を模索するボリシェヴィキと、より民主的な革命を唱えるメ
ンシェヴィキによって、ロマノフ王朝を批判する大衆運動を先導した
のです。
　第一次世界大戦がおきると、そうした人々の不満が軍隊や警察をも
巻き込んだ闘争に変わります。1917年3月に、首都ペトログラードで
戦争の継続や貧困に抗議するデモやストライキがおきると、軍隊や警
察からも同調する人々が増え、ロシアの主要都市に抗議運動が拡大し
ました。これによって、ニコライ2世は退位し、ロマノフ王朝は滅亡
したのです。

　やがて、ケレンスキーを首班としたメンシェヴィキによ
る臨時政府が発足します。彼らは、戦争を継続しながら政
情を安定させようとしますが、抗議活動は収まりません。
結局同年11月に、ウラジミール・レーニンの率いるボリシェ
ヴィキによって、臨時政府が打倒され、共産主義革命がお
こるのです。こうしてソヴィエトを基盤とした共和国が誕
生します。
　レーニンは盟友トロツキーと共に、農民の地主からの解
放と戦争からの離脱を宣言し、ドイツとはブレスト・リト
フスク条約によって単独講和を実現します。

ウラジミール・レーニン
Vladimir Ilich Lenin
(1870–1924)

　既に1889年には第2インターナショナルと呼ばれる共産
主義運動がおき、そこで世界各地の労働組合などの連携が試みられま
した。レーニンはその動きを踏襲して政権を獲得すると、プロレタリ
アート、すなわち労働者の独裁による世界革命を呼びかけます。これ
によって1919年に第3インターナショナルとも呼ばれるコミンテルン

時代
20世紀1910年代
現代

地域
ロシア

分類
革命【制度】

キーワード
戦争継続への不満増大・
二度の革命による共産化
・国際主義の進展・列強
の干渉・独立運動への波
及

joined together with the communist governments of neighboring countries to form the Union of Soviet Socialist Republics in 1922, its formal appearance in international society.

This action had a significant impact on the territories that had been colonized through imperialism, and communism became a slogan of their movements for independence.

At present, when one talks about communism, it seems to symbolize a powerful government under a dictator. For many people at that time, however, communism signified a vision of emancipation from the exploitation of imperialism.

All the more because of this, the appearance of the strong country called the Soviet Union was seen as a threat to the various countries of Western Europe. They supported the remnants of resistance within Russia, and to bring about a defeat of the Russian Revolution, they dispatched troops through Vladivostok into Siberia. In response, the Soviets formed the Red Army to engage in the conflict.

The country that suffered the greatest sacrifices as a result of this Siberian Expedition was Japan. By the time the Soviet Union stabilized and the Siberian Expedition was defeated, Japan had mobilized more than 70,000 troops.

152 China struggled to free itself from the negative legacy of the end of the Qing

World War I was a conflict that became a turning point in the world's transition from the modern period to the contemporary era.

Several events that occurred just before and after World War I shook the society in which we now live because they served as the causes of various political problems that humankind still needs to solve.

The First World War resulted in unprecedented casualties and the use of modern weapons, such as poison gas and aerial bombings, in the combat zones, causing widespread devastation across the world. While this conflict bore the inconsistencies of the 19th century, the tragedy that was brought forth by the enormous progress of Western civilization later had a great influence on international politics.

While Europe was suffering devastation as a result of the conflict, America came to the fore as a world leader. Furthermore, as the great powers became

が創設されました。その後、ソヴィエトは近隣の共産主義政権と共に1922年にソヴィエト社会主義共和国連邦（ソ連）として国際社会に正式に登場したのです。

この動きは、帝国主義によって植民地化されていた人々にも大きな影響を与え、その後の独立運動のスローガンともなってゆきます。

現在、共産主義といえば、独裁者による強権政治の象徴のように思われています。しかし、当時の人々の多くにとって、共産主義は帝国主義によって収奪された国々を解放するビジョンとなったのです。

それだけに、ソ連という強力な国家の出現は、西欧諸国にとっては脅威となりました。彼らはロシア内に残った抵抗勢力を支援し、ロシア革命の挫折のために、ウラジオストックなどからシベリアにも出兵しました。これに対してソヴィエト側は赤軍を組織して戦います。

このシベリア出兵で最も大きな犠牲を払ったのが日本でした。日本はソ連が安定し、シベリア出兵が失敗に終わるまで、7万人以上の兵士を動員したのでした。

中国は清末の負の遺産からの脱却にもがいていた

第一次世界大戦は、世界が近代から現代に移行する転換点となった戦争でした。

第一次世界大戦前後の様々なイベントが、現代我々が生きる社会を揺るがし、人類に解決を迫っている政治問題の原因となったからです。

第一次世界大戦は過去に類を見ない犠牲者を生み、戦闘地域では毒ガスや航空機による爆撃など、近代兵器が使用され、被害の規模は全世界に及びました。この戦争は、19世紀に矛盾を抱えながらも、飛躍的に伸長した欧米の文明そのものが導き出した悲劇として、その後の国際政治に大きな影響を与えます。

ヨーロッパが戦争によって壊滅的な被害を受けている中、アメリカが世界の指導者として台頭します。さらに、戦争によって列強が疲弊

時代
20世紀1910年代
現代

地域
ヨーロッパ・中国

分類
戦争【侵略】

キーワード
ヨーロッパの荒廃・アメリカ合衆国の台頭・日本の中国進出・五・四運動・中国共産党の成立

impoverished as a result of the fighting, independence movements became active in colonial territories in Asia and the Middle East. It was this rise of the United States and the surge of nationalistic movements in the Middle East and Asia that acted as significant wedges against the previous international political order established by Western imperialism.

We turn our focus now to China before and after the First World War.

In China, following the Xinhai Revolution, Yuan Shikai, who overthrew the Qing, attempted to become emperor himself, and the Chinese Nationalist Party, led by Sun Yat-sen, was violently opposed to this. In the end, Yuan Shikai's scheme failed, but as the Qing dynasty collapsed, in the midst of the resulting chaos, the military slit into cliques. Simultaneously, Outer Mongolia declared its independence, and in Tibet, the 13th Dalai Lama, head of Tibetan Buddhism, took power in the independent regime that was created.

Before long, in Europe, World War I broke out, and while the European powers were constantly occupied in that conflict, China was confronted by the new menace posed by the inroads made by Japan. Originally, Germany had interests in the region surrounding Qingdao. In World War I, Japan, which joined the Allied Powers, sought to eliminate that German influence and, as explained earlier, demanded the continuation of those rights and interests for itself. The pressure of the Twenty-one Demands was too great for the weak political base of Yuan Shikai to reject, but they stimulated the nationalist movement within China.

Moreover, following the conclusion of World War I, at the Paris Peace Conference held in 1919, the great powers supported Japan's position. In response to that, Beijing became hugely anti-Japanese, and the Chinese nationalist movement developed.

This mass movement was named after the day it arose: the May Fourth Movement. This movement became the starting point of anti-Japanese sentiment in China.

For Chinese intellectuals who had been suppressed by the Western powers, the communist government that arose in Russia as a result of the Russian Revolution there appeared as an ideology that freed them from the spell of capitalism. Following the May Fourth Movement, out of this mass movement the Chinese Communist Party was launched in 1921 by Chen Duxiu and Mao Zedong. This marked the beginning of China's journey toward becoming a giant that would re-enter world history as a superpower in the 21st century, aiming to settle the turmoil that had plagued China since the late Qing dynasty.

する中、アジアや中東地域などの植民地での独立運動が活発になります。このアメリカの台頭と中東やアジア各地での民族運動こそが、過去の欧米列強の帝国主義による国際政治のあり方に大きな楔を打つことになるのです。

　第一次世界大戦前後の中国に目を向けてみましょう。
　中国では辛亥革命のあと、清を倒した袁世凱が皇帝となろうとしたために、孫文が率いる国民党と激しく対立します。結局袁世凱の目論見は挫折しますが、中国は清朝末期の混乱で台頭した軍閥によって分断されてしまうのです。同時に外モンゴルが独立を宣言し、チベットもチベット仏教の頂点に立つダライ・ラマ13世による独立政権が誕生します。

　間もなく、ヨーロッパで第一次世界大戦が勃発し、ヨーロッパ列強が戦争に明け暮れている間に、中国は日本の進出という新たな脅威に直面します。中国の青島を中心とした地域には、もともとドイツが権益を持っていました。第一次世界大戦で連合国側に立って参戦した日本は、そんなドイツの影響力を排除し、中国に対してその権益の継承を要求したことはすでに解説しました。この対華21カ条の要求と呼ばれる圧力を政権基盤の弱い袁世凱が受け入れたことが、中国での民族運動を刺激することになったのです。
　しかも、第一次世界大戦が終結したあと、1919年に開かれたパリ講和会議で、列強は日本の立場を支持します。それに対して北京などで大々的な反日、民族主義運動が展開されたのです。

　この大衆運動は、その発生した日付をとって五・四運動と呼ばれています。そして、この運動が、その後の中国の反日運動の出発点となったのです。
　一方、西欧列強に蹂躙されていた中国の知識人にとって、ロシア革命で誕生した共産主義政権は、資本主義の呪縛から自らを解き放つ理想として映りました。五・四運動の後、1921年に大衆運動の中から陳独秀や毛沢東らによって中国共産党が発足します。21世紀に超大国として再び世界史におどり出る中国という巨人が、清末以来の混乱の清算に向けて始動したのでした。

153 The League of Nations failed to apply the lessons of World War I

How then did the Paris Peace Conference become a factor in the occurrence of the May Fourth Movement in China? Many politicians recognized the discord and the twists and turns of imperialism involved in World War I. American President Woodrow Wilson, in particular, criticized secret diplomacy and undemocratic colonial policies and envisioned a liberalist economy based on a new international order.

President Wilson presented the Fourteen Points proposal for the creation of a new world order. As a result, the League of Nations was established, with its headquarters in Geneva, Switzerland, as an international body aimed at establishing a permanent peace. At the same time, the Permanent Court of International Justice was established at The Hague in the Netherlands as an agency of the League of Nations, whose purpose was to legally decide cases of international conflict.

However, excepting these results, the Paris Peace Conference was conducted according to the egotistic motivations of the victorious nations for the purpose of containing the defeated nations, particularly Germany.

First of all, Britain and France maintained their vested interests in their own colonial territories, and in the Treaty of Versailles, signed in 1919 after the Paris Peace Conference, they imposed burdensome reparations upon Germany and began negotiating the amount. Further, Germany's colonies and overseas interests were divided among the victorious nations.

Areas including Alsace-Lorraine, the possession of which had been a source of conflict, were restored to France, and German armaments were seriously reduced.

Also reduced were Austria's territories, and the independence of ethnic groups in those territories was recognized. The various Middle Eastern countries which had once been controlled by the Ottoman Empire were placed under the administration of France or Britain.

At the Paris Peace Conference, one additional nation besides Germany was excluded from participation. That was the Soviet Union, which had recently been established by the revolution. Absorbed in protecting capitalist economies, the nations at the conference and in the League that was later established did their best to isolate the Soviet Union. These actions inadvertently stimulated communist

国際連盟では第一次世界大戦の教訓が
活かされなかった

　では、中国で五・四運動がおきた原因となったパリ講和会議とはどのようなものだったのでしょうか。第一次世界大戦という、帝国主義の確執と捻れがもたらした不幸に多くの政治家は注目しました。特にアメリカのウィルソン大統領は、西欧列強の秘密外交や、非民主的な植民地政策などを批判し、新たな国際秩序のもとに自由主義経済を発展させようと目論見ます。

　ウィルソン大統領は、世界の新たな秩序を創造しようと14カ条の提案を行い、その結果、恒久平和を目指す国際機関として国際連盟が1920年にスイスのジュネーヴに本部をおいて発足します。同時に国際連盟の機関の一つとして、国際紛争を法的に裁くための常設国際司法裁判所もオランダのハーグに開設しました。

　しかし、これらの成果を除けば、パリ講和会議は第一次世界大戦で敗戦国となった同盟国側、特にドイツの力を封じ込めようとする戦勝国のエゴに従って運営されます。

　まずイギリスやフランスは、既得権益である植民地を維持し、講和会議の後1919年に調印されたヴェルサイユ条約ではドイツに高額な賠償金を課すことが定められ、その金額の交渉が始まりました。さらに、ドイツの植民地や海外での権益は戦勝国側に分配されたのです。

　また、アルザス・ロレーヌなど、フランスと領有権をめぐって争っていた地域はフランスに返還され、ドイツの軍備は大幅に削減されました。

　さらにオーストリアも領土が縮小され、その地域での民族の独立が承認されました。現在の東欧諸国が誕生したのです。そして、オスマン帝国の支配していた中東諸国はフランスやイギリスの管理下におかれます。

　パリ講和会議では、ドイツ以外に排除しようとしたもう一つの国がありました。革命によって成立したソヴィエト連邦です。パリ講和会議もその後に成立した国際連盟も、いかにソ連を国際社会から孤立させ、資本主義経済を守るかというテーマに没頭します。その動きが、中国などでソ連の成立に呼応しておきた共産主義運動を逆に刺激しま

時代
20世紀1910年代
現代

地域
共通

分類
和平【制度】

キーワード
パリ講和会議・ヴェルサイユ条約締結・国際連盟の成立・ドイツ、ソ連の排除

movements that sympathized with the formation of the Soviet Union, particularly in countries like China. The Soviet Union openly opposed the efforts of Western powers to maintain their colonial empires and sought alliances with movements advocating for self-determination in regions such as Asia.

In sum, from the very beginning of its existence, the League of Nations excluded the Soviet Union and prohibited participation by the defeated nations altogether. Further, the League of Nations possessed no means of imposing by military force the restraints on nations that suppressed peace, and ultimately in America, which contributed to the establishment of the League, Congress did not ratify membership, and therefore America did not become a member of the League.

The weak points of the League of Nations after World War I became a cause of the descent of the whole world into new upheavals.

154 With the appearance of Mahatma Gandhi, India took the path toward independence

If any single country in Asia symbolizes colonization by the imperialist policies of the great powers, it is India. In order to incorporate this extensive country into its economic bloc, Britain sometimes employed the strategy of pitting Hindus against Muslims, sometimes promised Indians the right to participate in the government, and overall attempted complex strategies for administering the country.

In order to continue uninterrupted rule over India, in 1885 the Indian National Congress was established with the aim of obtaining advice from the Indian people.

Under British rule, India witnessed the development of various types of infrastructure, including railways, and the promotion of industries like cotton production, which had positive economic impacts. Britain, as a leading industrial power in the world, left its influence on India.

Ironically, however, following the spread of British influence throughout India, intellectuals in India began to develop a racial self-awareness. As things go in world history, when a strong country controls a weaker country, the people of the subjugated country absorb the culture of the subjugator country, and with that as a lever, nationalist movements develop.

す。欧米列強の植民地を維持しようとする動きに、ソ連は真っ向から対立し、アジアなどでの民族自決運動との連携を図ってゆくのです。

このように、国際連盟は当初からソ連を除外し、敗戦国も参加できませんでした。さらに国際連盟には平和を蹂躙した国家への軍事的制裁力もなく、その設立に貢献したアメリカも、議会での承認を得ることができなかったために連盟に参加しなかったのです。

こうした国際連盟の弱点が、第一次世界大戦後の世界が新たな騒乱へと傾斜する原因にもなったのです。

1919年5月27日、パリ講和会議における「四巨頭」
左から順に、ロイド・ジョージ首相（イギリス）、オルランド首相（イタリア）、クレマンソー首相（フランス）、ウィルソン大統領（アメリカ）。

Big Four at the Paris Peace Conference, May 27, 1919. Left to right: Prime Minister David Lloyd George (Great Britain), Premier Vittorio Emanuele Orlando (Italy), Premier Georges Clemenceau (France), President Woodrow Wilson (USA).

ガンディーが現れ、インドは独立への道を歩みだした

アジアで列強の帝国主義政策によって植民地化された象徴的な国といえばインドです。イギリスは、この広大な国家を自らの経済圏に組み込むために、時にはヒンドゥー教徒とイスラム教徒との対立を利用し、時にはインド人に政治への参加を約束するなど、様々な戦略をもって統治を試みました。

インドの統治を円滑に進めるために、インド人の諮問を受けることを目的としたインド国民会議も1885年に開設しました。

世界の産業をリードしたイギリスに管理されたことにより、インドでは鉄道をはじめ様々なインフラが整備され、綿花生産などの促進により、経済的な好影響があったことも事実です。

しかし、皮肉なことに、イギリスの影響がインドに浸透するに従って、インドの知識層に民族意識が高まってゆきます。世界史の常として、一つの強力な国家が他国を支配したとき、逆に征服国の文明を吸収した被征服国の人々が、それをテコとして民族運動を展開してゆきます。

時代
19、20世紀
近代・現代

地域
インド

分類
独立【民族】

キーワード
イギリスによる植民地統治・インド国民会議の開設・民族運動の高揚・ガンディーの登場

At the same time, many nations with multiple religions and ethnicities that had previously lacked a sense of national consciousness were consolidated into unified entities and saw a surge in ethnic identity upon becoming conquered nations.

In a broader sense, it was a worldwide trend of that time when the Western powers overwhelmed Asia. Asians learned from Western culture, and what they learned energized nationalist movements. India was a typical example of that evolution.

At the end of the Mughal Empire, the respective regions of India were ruled by princes called maharajas, and India as a unified country collapsed. Britain took advantage of that internal state of affairs to advance the colonization of India.

However, in response to the racial discrimination and various restraints resulting from colonial policies, Indian intellectuals who participated in the Indian National Congress rebelled. At the same time, as a result of their influence, with the arrival of the 20th century, the call for sovereign independence of the Indian people began to take hold.

After the end of World War I, a charismatic leader appeared named Mahatma Gandhi. The first half of his life was symbolic of the changes that occur in the consciousness of a subjugated people. In his youth, Gandhi went to Britain to study law as an attorney, absorbing Western culture. However, while he was residing in South Africa, he experienced racial discrimination. Through this emotional turmoil, he began to search for a way by which India could become independent, and he settled upon an Asian sense of values in order to turn that ideal into a reality.

Casting aside his Western suit and necktie, dressing himself in simple Indian clothing, and adopting a path of non-violence and civil disobedience, he developed a resistance movement against Britain.

He endeavored through this movement to overcome the antagonism between Hindus and Muslims and enhance a nationalist movement that surmounted the complexities of multiple religious beliefs.

His leadership in the independence movement not only influenced the colonial power, Britain, but also had an impact on intellectuals in Europe and the wider Western world.

同時に、今まで人々が統率されることなく、国家という意識を持ちにくかった多宗教、多民族国家が、被征服国家となることで一つにまとまり、民族意識が高揚してゆくことも多々ありました。

　大局的にいうならば、西欧文明がアジアを席巻したとき、その文明を学びながら、アジアの人々がそれを民族運動のエネルギーへと進化させていったのが当時の世界の動向でした。インドはその典型的な事例の一つとなったのです。

　ムガル王朝末期のインドは、地方の権力者がそれぞれ藩王（マハラジャ）として君臨し、インドという統一国家は事実上崩壊していたのです。イギリスはそうしたインドの内情を利用し、植民地化を進めました。

　しかし、まず植民地政策による人種差別や様々な抑圧に対して、インド国民会議に参加していたインドの知識人が反発します。同時に、彼らの影響を受け、20世紀になるとインド人という民族としての自主独立運動が芽生えるのです。

　第一次世界大戦後、それを指導するカリスマ的な人物が現れました。マハトマ・ガンディーです。彼の前半生はまさに被征服民族の意識の変化を象徴したものでした。若き日のガンディーは弁護士として、イギリスの法律を学び、西欧文明を吸収します。しかし彼は南アフリカに滞在中に差別を体験します。その葛藤の中で、インドの独立を模索したガンディーは、アジアの価値観をもってその実現に取り組もうとしたのです。

　背広とネクタイを捨て、質素なインドの衣装をまとい、非暴力と不服従をモットーに、イギリスへの抗議運動を展開したのです。

　彼は、その抗議運動を、ヒンドゥー教とイスラム教の対立を克服し、複雑で多様な宗教意識を乗り越えた民族運動に高めようと努力しました。

　彼の指導する独立運動は、宗主国イギリスのみならず、広く欧米の知識人にも影響を与えていったのです。

マハトマ・ガンディー
Mahatma Gandhi
(1869–1948)

155 The tragedy of war and the pursuit of convenience were created by the development of the same culture

Here let us consider the cultural conveniences employed in World War I.

As we have already touched on, in the 19th century, humankind developed new forms of convenience through the use of electricity. It conquered darkness, and telegraphic communication enabled accurate, rapid transmission of people's thoughts. In the 20th century, Henry Ford, who greatly admired Thomas Edison, developed the assembly line for the mass production of automobiles. When the Wright brothers invented the airplane in 1903, the world began to become a smaller place. As a result of their accomplishments, people were able to travel long distances quickly and safely.

Lands in the Siberian forest were cleared for the construction of a railroad, and when the Siberian Railroad was completed, it linked Europe and Asia, making it possible to travel from Europe to the Atlantic in a single week. The surplus time that resulted from this could be used for further production or commercial activity, stimulating the economy.

However, as civilization progresses, people drift away from nature. Humankind lost the sense of smell they had possessed when walking through the dark forests and their ability to predict the arrival of a storm by sensing the humidity carried on the winds. Listening carefully, they had sensed the movements of herds of buffaloes. Smelling the soil, they could tell when the herds had passed and head out to hunt them. All of these skills were lost.

At the beginning, people were oblivious to the loss of the sensitivities that they had originally possessed. They became more interested in the rapid development of technology, and they obtained the self-confidence that, for the first time, humankind had truly conquered nature. It was that self-confidence that led them to the massacres of two world wars.

It was in the 20th century that humankind, through the tragedies of the destruction wreaked by these conveniences of civilization, began to question the pros and cons of this conquering of nature by civilization. World War I in particular seriously challenged the established norms of the Western world. The wounds of war and the societal inconsistencies and absurdity that created them led numerous artists, philosophers, and psychologists to endeavor to understand why it happened.

戦争の悲劇と利便性の追求は同じ文明の発展が生み出した

　ここで第一次世界大戦で使用された文明の利器について考えてみます。

　すでに解説したように、19世紀に人類は電気というエネルギーを利用し新たな利器を開発します。闇を克服し、電信が人々の意思疎通を正確に、そして迅速にしました。20世紀になって、エジソンに憧れていたヘンリー・フォードが開発した自動車が大量生産できるようになり、ライト兄弟が1903年に飛行機を発明したとき、世界はさらに小さくなり、人々は生命の危険なく、遠い距離を早く移動できるようになったのです。

　シベリアの森林が切り開かれ、ヨーロッパとアジアとを結ぶシベリア鉄道ができ、大西洋も一週間もあれば横断できるようになりました。人々はそこで生まれた余剰の時間をさらに生産や商業活動にあて、経済を活性化することができるようになったのです。

　しかし、文明が進歩すれば、人々は自然から遠のきます。人類は森を覆う闇を歩く嗅覚や、風がもたらす湿気から嵐を予知する能力を失ってゆきました。耳をすませてバッファローの群れの移動を察知し、土の香りから、それが遠ざかりつつあることを感知して狩猟に向かうノウハウを失いました。

　当初人々はそうした人類がもともと獲得していた感性の損失には鈍感でした。むしろ、技術の飛躍的な発展で、人類ははじめて本格的に自然を克服できるのではという自信を得たのです。その自信が人々を殺戮へと駆り立てたのが二つの世界大戦だったのです。

　20世紀は、人類が文明の利器を使った破壊の悲劇を通し、文明で自然を克服することの是非が本格的に問われるようになった時代といえるのです。特に第一次世界大戦は、西欧世界の常識に大きな疑問符を投げかけました。戦争の傷とそこに至った社会の矛盾や不合理に、数多くの芸術家や哲学者、心理学者が答えをだそうともがきました。

時代
20世紀1920年代
現代

地域
ヨーロッパ・アメリカ合衆国

分類
文化【技術】

キーワード
自動車の普及・飛行機の出現・鉄道網の発展・アメリカの繁栄・工業都市の発展・商業の発展

However, the country that benefited the most from civilization was the United States, which emerged as the world's leading creditor nation after the First World War and took on the responsibility of the global economy. In the major cities, tall buildings stood together in large numbers, and immigrants from the world over flowed into its harbors in hopes of enjoying its abundance. Industrial cities like Pittsburgh and Cleveland produced steel, sending it on to cities which produced automobiles on automated assembly lines. Chicago was home to the headquarters of Sears, Roebuck and Company, which in order to satisfy the desires of the populace for consumer goods began to advertise its wares through the famous Sears catalogues. Through the consumer network based on these catalogues, the spotlight fell on a new form of commerce that sold goods to customers in remote areas through catalogues and the postal delivery system.

The spread of these modern conveniences into the ordinary household also brought about a major change in the arts. Commercial art and advertising art emerged to make products more appealing, and in the world of architecture, the influence of commercial art known as Art Deco brought about streamlined architectural art that adorned skyscrapers.

The world following World War I consisted of a peculiar balance between the suffering that had been imposed by the war and the dreams of enjoying the products of modern civilization that mesmerized the people.

156   The political affairs of the world underwent major changes at the beginning of the 1920s

In the 1920s, the leader of the Young Turks in Turkey, who later became known as Mustafa Kemal Atatürk, established the Republic of Turkey, and the country forged ahead with modernization.

Austria had already been reduced to a small country in Central Europe.

Thus collapsed the enormous power that had shaken the Western world since the Middle Ages and swept the world throughout the Reformation and the Age of Discovery.

The Middle East, under the powerful influence of Britain, was exposed to complex nationalist movements among Muslims. In what is present-day Algeria and Morocco, in the western part of North Africa, France retained influence. In the central part of North Africa, Italy was influential.

一方、最も文明の恩恵にあずかったのが、第一次世界大戦後に世界一の債権国として世界の経済を担ったアメリカでした。主要都市には高層ビルが林立し、富を享受しようと港には世界中から移民が押し寄せました。ピッツバーグやクリーブランドといった工業都市で鉄が生産され、オートメーション化した生産ラインによって自動車が市場に送り出されます。シカゴに本社のあったシアーズでは、豊かになった市民の消費意欲を満たそうと、シアーズカタログを通したネットワークで遠隔地に商品を販売する商法が脚光を浴びました。

こうした文明の利器の家庭への浸透は、芸術の上でも大きな変化をもたらします。商品をより魅力的に見せるための商業芸術や広告芸術が芽生え、建築の世界ではアールデコと呼ばれる商業芸術の影響を受けた無駄を省いた建築アートが高層ビルを彩ったのです。

第一次世界大戦後の世界は、戦争が生み出した苦悩と、文明の利器の享受に夢中になる人々との間の微妙なバランスの上に成り立っていたのです。

世界の政治は1920年代初頭に大きく変化した

1920年代になると、トルコでも青年トルコを率い、後にケマル・アタテュルクと呼ばれた指導者によって、正式にトルコ共和国が成立し、トルコは近代化を推し進めます。

すでにオーストリアは中部ヨーロッパの小国となっていました。

こうして、中世以来西欧世界を揺るがし、宗教改革から大航海時代を経て、世界を席巻した巨大な権力が崩壊したのです。

中東はイギリスの強い影響下のもと、イスラム教徒の複雑な民族運動にさらされます。そして、現在のアルジェリアやモロッコといった北アフリカ西部はフランスの、北アフリカ中部はイタリアの影響下におかれたのです。

時代
20世紀1920年代
現代

地域
世界

分類
国家【民族】

キーワード
ヨーロッパの凋落・アメリカ、ソ連、日本の発展・大衆文化の発展・民族国家の出現

After the Russo-Japanese War, Japan acquired rights and interests in China and expanded its influence, particularly through the construction of the South Manchuria Railway and its growing presence in the northeastern region. Opposed to this development were America and Britain. However, China itself remained effectively divided among the military cliques. Reunifying the country became their major concern in revitalizing the country.

The situation in postwar Germany was grave. The reborn Germany attempted to rebuild itself in the mold of what was, for its day, the most democratic constitution in Europe: the Weimar Constitution. However, as a result of the enormous reparations imposed on Germany and postwar economic disorder, severe inflation arose and the German mark crashed.

America, meanwhile, prospered. In major cities, such as New York, people enjoyed American-born arts like jazz, and America not only led the world in economics and military strength but also in the fields of art and architecture.

By 1922 Russia had defeated the forces that resisted the Russian Revolution, and it officially established the Union of Soviet Socialist Republics. After Vladimir Lenin died in 1924, following a struggle for supremacy, Joseph Stalin built a dictatorial regime, had Leon Trotsky assassinated in Mexico, and implemented ideological and economic control over the country. This became the initial stage of transforming a nation founded on socialism into a dictatorship.

Britain faced independence movements in every region. This was not limited merely to India. It also occurred in Ireland, which Britain had long kept under colonial rule. A nationalist independence movement arose there under the Sinn Fein party. A war for independence broke out, and as a result, with the exception of six counties in the north, in 1922 Ireland gained independence from Britain.

The old European world declined, just as America and the Soviet Union were rising. In that narrow interval, the expansion of Japan in the Far East became another cause of conflict in the world. Then there was Germany, which had become impoverished as a result of the defeat. This was the situation of world affairs at the start of the 1920s. Britain and France, the main victorious European powers had borrowed enormous sums of money from America to prosecute the war. France, in particular, stubbornly pressed Germany for reparations in order to repay its debts. Under that heavy pressure, the German economy was on the brink of bankruptcy.

中国では、その後日露戦争で獲得した利権のもと、日本が南満州鉄道を敷設し、東北地方を中心に影響力を拡大していました。それを嫌ったのがアメリカ、そしてイギリスでした。しかし当の中国は、軍閥により実質分断されたままでした。国家の再統一こそが中国再生の大きな課題だったのです。

　戦後のドイツの状況は深刻でした。新生ドイツはワイマール憲法という当時としては最も民主的とされた憲法の元で再生を図りますが、多額の賠償金と戦後の経済混乱で激しいインフレがおこり、通貨のマルクが暴落したのです。

　アメリカは繁栄します。ニューヨークなどの大都市では、人々はジャズやミュージカルといった、アメリカ生まれの芸術を楽しみ、経済や軍事のみならず、アートや建築の分野でも世界をリードしました。

　ロシアは1922年までにロシア革命に反抗する勢力を駆逐し、正式にソヴィエト社会主義共和国連邦（ソ連）が成立しました。レーニンが1924年に他界すると、権力闘争の末、スターリンが独裁体制を築き、ライバルのトロツキーをメキシコで暗殺するなど、強力な思想経済統制を実施します。これが、その後誕生する社会主義国家が独裁国家へと変貌する端緒となりました。

　イギリスは、各地で独立運動に見舞われます。それはインドだけではありませんでした。長年イギリスの統治下におかれていたアイルランドでも、シン・フェイン党による民族自立運動がおき、独立戦争が勃発し、結局1922年に北部の6州を除く地域がイギリスから独立します。

ヨシフ・スターリン
Joseph Stalin (1878–1953)

　ヨーロッパという旧世界の凋落、そしてアメリカやソ連の台頭。その狭間で世界の新たな火種となる極東での日本の伸長。敗戦により疲弊したドイツ。それが1920年代はじめの世界の状況でした。ヨーロッパの主要戦勝国であるイギリスやフランスも、戦費調達のためにアメリカから多額の資金を借り入れていました。特にフランスはその返済の原資としてドイツから強硬に賠償金を獲得しようとします。ドイツ経済はそんな重圧の中、破綻状態に陥ったのでした。

157 In the 1920s, the world was shaken by an imperfect understanding of democracy

Globally, it was an era marked by independence movements and nationalist movements in colonial territories dominated by countries like Britain. These movements would connect with the Asian and African nations that would gain independence after the Second World War.

Such movements also occurred in the domestic affairs of the great powers. Through universal suffrage and the extension of political rights to women, a larger number of citizens were able to participate in government. In America in 1920, suffrage for women was officially recognized, and in Britain in 1928, women over the age of 21 were given the right to vote. In Germany as well, under the Weimar Constitution, universal suffrage regardless of gender was put into effect.

In Japan, in 1925 males aged 25 and over were granted suffrage, but women would not be granted that right until after World War II.

However, with the increasing reflection of popular opinion in politics, it cannot be denied that politicians began to exploit the anxieties of the people and inflame national and ethnic sentiments. It is said that Adolf Hitler was elected in accordance with the law, but then established a dictatorial regime. In fact, without the people realizing the threat, Hitler used the media and populism to stimulate the masses and gain power. Populism denies complex notions and leads people with simple, easy-to-grasp language and ideas.

The conflation of nationalism and hatred toward other ethnic groups, as well as the distortion of labor movements into totalitarianism or nationalism, resulted in new, aggressive wars and ironically became the trigger for World War II.

Despite politics becoming more open to the entire citizenry, the know-how, institutions, and people's consciousness to sustain democracy did not catch up, leading to this imbalance that resulted in new misfortunes.

In America and elsewhere, too, while the nation was a democracy, there was still a deep-rooted prejudice against black people even after they were emancipated from slavery through the Civil War. Despite the influence of socialism and the increased awareness of human rights, to the contrary, white supremacists who rebelled against such movements frequently carried out violent acts against black people, even lynching them. It was not until the 1960s that steps were taken to end official racial discrimination.

20年代、世界は民主主義への消化不良に揺れていた

　1920年代は、世界的に見れば、イギリスなどが支配する植民地での独立運動や民族運動が各地でおこった時代でした。それが第二次世界大戦後のアジアやアフリカの国々の独立へと繋がったのです。

　こうした動きの一方で、列強の内部でも、普通選挙や婦人の参政権など、より多くの市民が政治に参加できるようにもなりました。1920年にはアメリカで女性の参政権が認められ、28年にはイギリスでも21歳以上の女性に選挙権が付与されます。ドイツでもワイマール憲法のもと、性別に関係なく普通選挙が実施されるようになりました。

　日本は、1925年に25歳以上の全ての男子に選挙権が付与されますが、女性に参政権が与えられるのは戦後のこととなりました。

　しかし、このように民意が政治に強く反映され始めたことで、政治家が国民の不安を煽り、国家意識や民族意識を扇動するようになったことは否めません。ヒトラーは合法的に選ばれ、独裁体制を確立したといわれています。実際国民がその脅威に気付く間も無く、ヒトラーはマスメディアなどを利用し、大衆を刺激するポピュリズムによって、政権を獲得したのです。ポピュリズムは、複雑な概念を否定し、よりシンプルでわかりやすい言葉で人々を先導します。

　民族主義と他民族への憎悪が混同されたり、労働運動が全体主義や国家主義へと変質したりした結果、新たな侵略戦争が勃発し、第二次世界大戦の引き金になったことは皮肉な事実です。

　政治が市民全体に対して開かれていったにもかかわらず、それを民主的に維持してゆくノウハウと制度、そして人々の意識が追いつかず、そのアンバランスが新たな不幸へと繋がったのです。

　アメリカなどでは、民主主義国家でありながら、南北戦争で奴隷の束縛から解放された黒人への差別も根強く残っていました。社会主義の影響もあり、人権意識が高まる中で、逆にその動きに反発するように白人至上主義者による黒人への暴行やリンチも頻発しました。公的に人種差別を撤廃する措置がとられたのは1960年代になってからのことでした。

時代
20世紀1920年代
現代

地域
共通

分類
政治【制度】

キーワード
民主主義の進展と不徹底・民族主義の高揚・ポピュリズムと全体主義・スターリンの独裁

In the Soviet Union, which remained isolated from the international community, under the name of communism, Joseph Stalin strengthened a dictatorial regime, strictly enforcing discipline on anyone who opposed him. Stalin promoted industrialization, and beginning in 1928, implemented five-year plans for economic development. Under the one-party system of the Communist Party, a planned economy was pressed forward.

Stimulated by the movement in the Soviet Union, nationalist movements in Asian countries, such as China and Vietnam, also became active.

In sum, the decade of the 1920s, during which people awoke to a new awareness of human rights and democracy, was also a period in which a dramatically changing society produced new trends that shook the world that was unable to fully process everything.

158 The Great Depression changed all of the prosperity that had come after World War I

Following the war, France, which remained insistent on retaliating against and remained distrustful of Germany, in 1923 on the pretext that Germany had failed to pay its reparations occupied the Ruhr region, Germany's industrial belt. This act by France suffered a setback as a result of opposition from the international community, but as a result Germany's industrial productivity was dealt a severe blow.

Amid the turmoil in Germany, communist forces and nationalist movements emerged. When the nation became impoverished, people tried to overcome their animosity through nationalism. In 1919, Adolf Hitler joined the German Workers' Party, which was a precursor of the National Socialist German Workers' Party, known commonly as the Nazi Party.

In 1923, Gustav Stresemann, who had become German chancellor, in an effort to restore the German economy, issued the Rentenmark. Due to the collapse in the value of the currency due to inflation, the idea was to change over to a new currency. As a result of this, the German economy was somehow able to avoid collapse and head in the direction of regeneration. After resigning as chancellor and becoming foreign minister, Stresemann, with the mediation of America, sought to negotiate with French Foreign Minister Aristide Briand in reducing the amount of reparations.

一方、国際社会から孤立状態にあったソヴィエト連邦では、共産主義の名の下に、スターリンによる独裁体制が強化され、反対する者への厳しい粛清が続いていました。スターリンは工業化を推し進め、1928年から五カ年計画を実施します。共産党の一党独裁体制による計画経済を推進したのです。

こうしたソ連の動きに刺激され、中国やベトナムなどアジアでの民族運動もさらに活発になります。

このように、1920年代は、人々が人権や民主主義への意識に目覚めつつも、激変する社会の新たな潮流への消化不良に揺れていた時代だったのです。

世界恐慌が戦後の繁栄の全てを変えた

戦後もドイツへの報復と警戒を怠らなかったフランスは、1923年に賠償金支払いの不履行を理由にドイツの工業地帯であるルール地方を占領します。このフランスの行為は国際社会の反発で挫折しますが、この行為でドイツの工業生産は大きな打撃を受けます。

混乱するドイツで台頭したのが、共産主義勢力と国粋主義運動でした。国家が疲弊したとき、人々はその憎悪をナショナリズムによって克服しようとしたのです。ナチスという通称で知られる国家社会主義労働者党の前身となるドイツ労働者党にアドルフ・ヒトラーが入党したのは1919年でした。

1923年にドイツの首相となったグスタフ・シュトレーゼマンは、ドイツ経済を立て直すため、レンテンマルクを発行します。インフレによって価値の下落した通貨を新しい通貨に切り替えたのです。これによって、ドイツ経済はなんとか破綻から再生に向かいます。首相辞任後、外務大臣となったシュトレーゼマンは、アメリカの仲介のもと、その後協調外交を推進しようとしたフランスの首相ブリアンなどとも交渉を進め、賠償金の軽減にも取り組みました。

時代
20世紀1920年代
現代

地域
ヨーロッパ・アメリカ合衆国

分類
経済【政治】

キーワード
戦後ドイツの苦難と復興
● グローバル経済の萌芽
● 復興景気によるバブル
● 世界恐慌

It would not be going too far to say that the world economy in the 1920s was a harbinger of the global economy we deal with today, in that the economic conditions in different regions were closely connected to one another and affected one another.

However, there is doubt as to whether people were aware of this change in the world's economic environment. It takes time, and people have to learn the lessons of change.

At the time of World War I, every part of Europe was economically impoverished. And after the war ended and those countries sought to rebuild, meeting their demands simulated the economies of America and Japan. Japan grew from being a chronic debtor country into a creditor country, and America became the driving force behind the global economy. However, when the European economy began to recover as a result of Germany's economic reforms, as a result of its fragile economic foundations, within a short period of time, Japan began to encounter headwinds.

Meanwhile America moved the profits it had gained as a creditor nation into financial investments, stock prices rose, and a favorable economy, resembling an economic bubble, came into play. However, in reality, nonperforming loans resulting from overinvestment and dead stocks began to eat away at the financial environment.

Having said that, America was carried away by the opulence known at the Jazz Age. The author who symbolized this colorful epoch was F. Scott Fitzgerald. His novel *The Great Gatsby* portrayed the flamboyant, fashionable circles of New York City, scrupulously depicting people caught up in the bubble of extravagence.

However, bubbles inevitably burst. And it did in 1929, starting the Great Depression. October 24, 1929, is remembered as Black Thursday. On that day stocks on the New York Stock Exchange went into a serious free fall, pressing a sudden brake on postwar reconstruction, and an economic depression spread throughout the world.

Two countries were particularly impacted. One was Germany, which was just beginning to progress toward recovery. The other was Japan, which was troubled by a slowdown of the economy due to stagnation of demand. Both nations suffered a direct blow from the worldwide financial recession.

20年代の世界経済は、既にグローバル経済の先駆けと言っても過言
ではないほど各地域の経済状況が密接に影響し合い、リンクしていま
した。

　しかし、そうした世界の経済環境の変化を、人々が意識していたか
といえば、疑問です。変化に人間がついてゆくには時間と教訓が必要
なのです。
　第一次世界大戦当時、ヨーロッパ各地が経済的に疲弊し、その後復
興を目指すと、その需要がアメリカや日本の経済を刺激します。日本
は慢性的な債務国から債権国へと成長し、アメリカは世界経済の牽引
車となりました。しかし、ドイツでの経済改革などによってヨーロッ
パ経済が回復すると、もともと経済基盤が脆弱だった日本は瞬く間に
逆風にさらされます。

　一方のアメリカは、債権国として潤った資金が金融投資に回され、
株価が上昇、いわゆるバブル経済に酷似した好景気に踊っていました。
しかし、実際は過剰投資による不良債権や不良在庫が金融環境を蝕ん
でいたのです。

　とはいえ、アメリカはジャズエイジと呼ばれる豊かな時代に浮かれ
ていました。そんなアメリカを象徴した作家がスコット・フィッツジェ
ラルドでした。彼がニューヨークの華やかな社交界を描いた『グレート・
ギャツビー』には、そうしたバブルに浮かれた人々の様子が克明に描
かれています。
　しかし、バブルはいつかはじけます。それが1929年の世界恐慌でし
た。1929年10月24日は暗黒の木曜日として人々に記憶されます。こ
の日のニューヨークでの株価の大暴落によって、戦後の復興に急ブレー
キがかかり、恐慌が世界に波及したのです。

　特に、やっと復興へと進みだしたドイツや、需要の停滞で景気の鈍
化に悩んでいた日本は、世界規模での金融恐慌の波をまともに被って
しまったのです。

159 The remaining egotism of the great powers undermined efforts for peace

Ironically enough, the Great Depression occurred at the very moment when the major Western powers, as a result of their wretched war experiences, were just beginning to move toward a general trend toward reconciliation. In 1922 at the Washington Naval Conference an arms reduction agreement was concluded. In 1925 the Locarno Pact delineated the boundaries of Germany. And in 1928 in Paris, the Kellogg-Briand Pact, advocated by France and America, was brought to fruition, stunning the entire world.

In this treaty, it was stipulated that war would be abandoned as a means for settling international disputes. Further, the year following the stock market crash in New York, America, Britain, and Japan concluded the London Naval Treaty, in which limitations were placed on the number of support ships each nation was allowed to possess.

Why then was it that these disarmament and peace efforts failed, ultimately leading the world toward World War II?

One reason is the self-centeredness of the related countries. Whether it was the League of Nations or the London Naval Treaty, if each country wanted to construct a system that was faithful to the original intention of the cosigners, that would infringe on the vested interests of the large nations.

For example, Britain maintained colonial territories around the world. America was actively advancing into South America and the Pacific region. Japan, too, was maneuvering to expand its sphere of influence in China.

When these countries attempted to renounce war for anything other than self-defense, they inevitably encountered an insurmountable barrier regarding what exactly was included within "self-defense." Britain asserted that deploying troops overseas to defend its colonies was an exercise of its rights to defend itself. America similarly claimed that its economic advances into South America were "self-defense" in terms of protecting the country's assets and interests. Japan meanwhile contended that it was taking the stance of "self-defense" in sending troops into China, where there was political instability, to protect its own position.

The League of Nations lacked the ability to impose sanctions against taking the interpretation of "self-defense" this far. The powers that agreed to the renunciation of warfare and this treaty asserted irrational flexibility in interpreting the contents

列強に残ったエゴの根が平和への取り組みを破綻させた

　皮肉なことに、世界恐慌は、戦争の悲惨な体験から、西欧の主要国が融和ムードへと向かいつつあった最中におきました。1922年にワシントン会議で締結された海軍軍縮条約や、ドイツの国境を画定させた1925年のロカルノ条約、さらに1928年にフランスやアメリカが提唱して実現したパリ不戦条約など、平和への努力が結実したときに世界を見舞ったショックだったのです。

　不戦条約では、国際紛争を解決する手段として戦争を放棄することも条文化されました。さらに、ニューヨークで株価が暴落した翌年には、アメリカとイギリス、そして日本との間に、補助艦の保有を制限するためのロンドン軍縮条約も締結されました。

　では、なぜこうした軍縮や平和を求める努力が結実せず、第二次世界大戦へと世界が傾斜していったのでしょうか。
　理由の一つは関係国のエゴにあります。国際連盟にせよ、不戦条約にせよ、本来の目的に忠実な制度を作ろうとすれば、それが当時の大国の利害を侵害することになったのです。

　例えば、イギリスは世界中に植民地を維持していました。また、アメリカは南米や太平洋地域に積極的に進出していました。そして日本も中国での利権の拡大を目論んでいました。
　これらの国々が、自衛以外の戦争を放棄しようとした場合、そもそも「自衛」とは何かという壁にぶつかります。植民地を守るために、海外に軍隊を送ることは自衛権の行使であるとイギリスは主張します。南米への経済的な進出に対して、アメリカは自国の資産や権益を守ることは「自衛」にあたると主張します。日本は、政治的に不安定な中国で自らの地位を維持するために、軍隊を送ることも「自衛」であるという立場をとろうとします。

　国際連盟は行き過ぎた「自衛」への制裁能力が欠如していました。不戦条約でも、条約を締結した列強がその条文を自国の都合によってどうとでも解釈できる不合理な柔軟さがあったのです。

時代
20世紀1920年代
現代

地域
ヨーロッパ・アメリカ合衆国

分類
外交【経済】

キーワード
協調の時代・不戦条約と軍縮会議・列強の利権への固執・恐慌による経済混乱・ブロック経済

according to their respective country's convenience.

While sensibly talking about the tragedies of warfare, the great powers' real intentions were to obstinately pursue their respective vested interests, and those intentions caused peace efforts to fail.

The imperialism that seemed to have collapsed in the aftermath of World War I had continued to take root within the consciousness of these nations, ultimately becoming the fuse for the next tragedy.

The catalyst for the great cracks in the asphalt of peace was the Great Depression.

It was during this time that Adolf Hitler most acutely exploited this catalyst, seeking to transform his own country. The tensions between Japan, which aimed to expand its sphere of influence in China, and the United States and Britain, who harbored strong concerns about this expansion, also became a significant cause of fracture.

Less than 15 years after the tragedy of World War I, the world began to slide once more toward catastrophe.

160 Fascism is a distortion of the socialist movement that transformed states

People often say that World War II was a war against fascism. But what exactly does fascism mean?

The term fascism derives from the name of the Fascist political party led by Benito Mussolini in Italy. The term refers to solidarity, unity, or a united front. It contains the meaning that citizens ought to come together as a united whole in support of the nation.

ベニート・ムッソリーニ
Benito Mussolini
(1883–1945)

Let us make something very clear here.

It is essential to grasp the difference between nationalism and fascism.

First, let us examine the personal history of Mussolini. Needless to say, he formed an alliance with Germany and Japan as the political leader of Italy in World War II. He was born in 1883 in northern Italy, and his father was an ardent admirer of socialism. Benito was strongly influenced by this as he was growing up.

建前では戦争の悲惨さを語りつつも、したたかに自国の利益を追求しようとした大国の本音が、こうした平和への努力を破綻させたのです。

　第一次世界大戦で崩壊したかに見えた帝国主義が、これらの国々の意識の中で「根」を張り続けていたことが、次の悲劇への導火線となったのです。

　世界恐慌は、そうした「根」が平和というアスファルトに大きなひびを入れる触媒になったのです。

　この触媒を最も敏感に利用し、自国を改造しようとしたのがヒトラーでした。そして、中国での利権拡大を目指す日本と、それに強い危機感を抱いたアメリカやイギリスとの確執も、大きなひび割れの原因となりました。

　世界は第一次世界大戦という悲劇から15年足らずで、新たな破局へと転落を始めたのです。

ファシズムは社会主義運動が変質して国家を蝕んだ

　よく人々は第二次世界大戦をファシズムとの戦いであったといいます。そもそもファシズムとはどのようなものなのでしょう。

　ファシズムは、イタリアのムッソリーニの政党「国家ファシスト党」に由来する言葉です。その語源を探れば、「結束」という言葉にいきあたります。国民が国家のために結束しようという意味が込められているのです。

　ここで、注意したいことがあります。

　民族主義とファシズムとの違いは何かというテーマです。

　まずムッソリーニの来歴に注目します。ベニート・ムッソリーニは、いうまでもなく、ドイツや日本と同盟し、第二次世界大戦を指導したイタリアの政治家です。彼は1883年にイタリア北部に生まれました。父親は社会主義に傾倒し、彼はその影響を強く受けて育ちます。

時代
20世紀1920年代
現代

地域
ヨーロッパ

分類
政治【制度】

キーワード
社会主義と民族主義・ファシズムの登場・民族至上主義と全体主義

As an adult, he participated in socialist movements and was on close terms with Vladimir Lenin.

Rebelling against the fact that Italy was strongly influenced by the Austro-Hungarian Empire, which was under the authority of the Pope, Mussolini called on Italians to unite and build a nation-state for the people. This led to the thesis of the National Fascist Party.

Put in different terms, in the background of the Nationalist Fascist Party was the idea that socialism was a foundation and through the process of class conflict it was possible to free people from the suppression exerted by great authority and the state.

Socialism and nationalism are often joined to form a whole. The Chinese Communist Party, which resisted the invasion of the Japanese, was a typical example. Similarly, the Vietnamese, who gained independence from France after World War II, opposed pressure from America with an ideology that combined socialism and nationalism.

However, on behalf of that ethnic nationalism, people were required to completely surrender their individual rights and freedom of thought. The distinguishing characteristic of fascism was that the state was placed above the people, who were forced to serve the state. In Mussolini's case, while he stood on the side of the Allies in World War I, and was on the victor's side, his vision appeared in the postwar when Italy faced chaos in the economy and in politics. He organized the Blackshirts, broke away from the leftist forces, and by carrying out a big demonstration called the March on Rome in 1922. Then after the government fell, he seized power.

Mussolini then aimed at creating an autocratic regime, suppressing opposition forces with strict suppression of freedom of speech. He further attempted an advance into Africa. He suppressed the nationalist movement in Libya, which was already an Italian colony, and in 1936 he took control of Abbysinia, which later became Ethiopia. The special character of fascism was its merger with a sense of racial superiority, and its lack of any hesitation at all to invade any opposing country that resisted its grand cause.

While fascism was based on socialism, it grew like cancer cells, transmuting into ultra nationalism.

成人してからも社会主義運動に加わり、レーニンとも親交がありました。

　ムッソリーニは、イタリアがローマ教皇の権威の下でオーストリア・ハンガリー帝国の影響を強く受けてきたことに反発し、イタリア人が民族として結束し、民族のための国家を作ることを訴えます。これが国家ファシスト党のテーゼに繋がってゆくのです。

　言葉を変えれば、社会主義を土台として、社会主義のテーマである階級闘争の過程として、民族主義をもって人々を抑圧する大きな権力や国家から解放しようという考え方が、国家ファシスト党の背景にあったのです。

　社会主義が民族運動と合体することはよくあることです。日本の侵略に対抗した中国共産党も、戦後にフランスから独立し、アメリカの圧力に対抗したベトナムも、社会主義と民族主義とを融合させて抵抗運動を繰り広げました。

　ただ、その民族主義のために、個々人の権利や自由な発想を認めず、人々の上に国家をおき、国家への奉仕を強制したことが、ファシズムの特徴です。ムッソリーニの場合、彼は第一次世界大戦では連合国側に立ち、戦勝国となったものの、経済的にも政治的にも混乱していたイタリアの中で台頭しました。黒シャツ隊を組織し、左翼勢力とも決別し、1922年には「ローマ進軍」という実力行使によってイタリア王国の国王を動かして政権を奪取したのです。

　その後、ムッソリーニは独裁政権を目指し、厳しい言論統制をもって対抗勢力を弾圧します。さらに、アフリカへの進出も試み、すでにイタリアの植民地になっていたリビアの民族運動を弾圧し、1936年にはエチオピアも支配します。ファシズムの特徴は、民族至上主義とも融合し、その大義のために他国に対する侵略も躊躇しないことにありました。

　社会主義を土台にしながらも、そこからがん細胞のように、超国家主義へと変質したのがファシズムだったのです。

161 A rift deepened between Japan, America, and Britain over China's fate

Let us shift our focus back on the Far East.

While Sun Yat-sen carried out the Xinhai Revolution and established the Republic of China, he lost in the struggle with the military factions and was at one point compelled to seek refuge in Japan.

Later with the rise of nationalist movements including the May Fourth Movement, Sun Yat-sen collaborated with the Chinese Communist Party in resisting the military factions. He accepted members of the Chinese Communist Party into the Kuomintang. The Soviet Union played a mediating role in this alliance. In 1924, the Kuomintang and the Communist Party formed an alliance known as the First United Front.

While Sun Yat-sen advanced as far as Beijing, he left behind the famous words "The revolution is not yet accomplished" before he died in 1925. Chiang Kai-shek became the successor to Sun Yat-sen. He advanced into conflict against the military factions called the Northern Expedition. After Yuan Shikai lost power, he took on Zhang Zuolin, who rose to prominence in the military clique of the northeast and drove Zhang out.

During this Northern Expedition, Chiang Kai-shek carried out a coup d'état in Shanghai.

The purpose was to expel the Chinese Communist Party. For Chiang Kai-shek, who formed a collaboration with the Zhejiang conglomerate, communism was unacceptable. Needless to say, America and Britain, which maintained economic interests in China and wanted to eliminate the influence of the Soviet Union and Japan from China, strongly supported these actions by Chiang Kai-shek.

While Japan was wary of Chiang Kai-shek, it was focused on the strengthening of interests in China's northeastern region, which it had obtained as a result of the Russo-Japanese War. In an attempt to eliminate the influence of Zhang Zuolin, who had been defeated by the Northern Expedition, he was assassinated. As a result, because Zhang Xueliang, Zuolin's son, got involved with the Kuomintang, China was reunited under Chiang Kai-shek. Consequently, American and British support of the Kuomintang put them in opposition to Japan.

In 1931 the Japanese army in aiming to strengthen its control over China's northeast territory touched off the Liutiaohu Incident, also called the September

中国をめぐり、日本とアメリカ、イギリスの溝は深まった

ここで極東に目を向けましょう。

中国では、孫文が辛亥革命を成し遂げ、中華民国が成立したものの、軍閥との抗争に敗れ一時日本に亡命を余儀なくされました。

その後、五・四運動などの民族運動が高揚すると、孫文は中国共産党と協調し、軍閥勢力に対抗したのです。共産党員が国民党に入ることも容認します。そこにはソヴィエト連邦による仲介もあったのです。こうして1924年に、国民党と共産党とは第一次国共合作と呼ばれる同盟関係を築いたのでした。

孫文は北京まで進軍したものの、「革命は未だ成功せず」という有名な言葉を遺して1925年に他界します。孫文の後継者となったのは蒋介石でした。彼は北伐と呼ばれる軍閥との戦争を展開し、袁世凱の失脚後に内部抗争を通して頭角を現していた東北地方の軍閥、張作霖を駆逐します。

この北伐の途上、蒋介石は上海でクーデターをおこしました。

それは中国共産党の排除が目的でした。浙江財閥と呼ばれる財閥と組んでいた蒋介石にとって、共産主義は容認できなかったのです。中国での経済的な権益を維持し、ソ連や日本からの影響を取り除きたいアメリカやイギリスも、蒋介石のこうした動きを積極的に支援したことはいうまでもありません。

日本は、蒋介石を警戒する一方で、日露戦争で得た中国東北地方の権益強化に注力します。そして、北伐で敗退した張作霖の影響力の排除を目論み、彼を暗殺します。その結果、張作霖の息子の張学良が国民党に走ったことで、中国は蒋介石のもとで統一されることになったのです。アメリカとイギリスが支援する中華民国と、日本との対立軸がこれでできあがります。

1931年、日本軍は中国東北地方の支配強化を目指し、柳条湖事件を引き起こします。柳条湖は現在の瀋陽（当時は奉天と呼ばれていました）

蒋介石
Chiang Kai-shek
(1887–1975)

時代
20世紀1920年代
現代

地域
中国・日本

分類
外交【侵略】

キーワード
中国の民族意識・軍閥の勃興と蒋介石・日本の権益への固執と満州事変・日本と米英との対立

18 Incident. Liutiaohu was the name of a place in Fengtian, which is present-day Shenyang. The incident involved an explosion on the Japan-owned South Manchurian Railway. On the pretext that this explosion was carried out by the Chinese, Japanese troops intervened with the stated intention of restoring normal conditions. This was the outbreak of the Mukden Incident. As a result of this conflict, Japan established a puppet regime in northeastern China. In 1932 Manchuria broke off from China and became independent, taking the last Qing emperor, Puyi, as its leader and becoming Manchukuo. Also in that same year, Japan ordered troops into Shanghai, an essential city of the Chinese economy, in the Shanghai Incident.

These actions by Japan brought condemnation from Europe and America. China initiated proceedings in the League of Nations against Japan's establishment of the puppet government in Manchuria. The League dispatched the Lytton Commission to investigate. While the Commission ultimately recognized the Japanese interests in that region, it denied recognition of Manchuria as a state. Japan hardened its position. It withdrew from the League of Nations in 1933.

After this, Japan and China became bogged down in the quagmire of a conflict that lasted until 1945.

162 Three nations isolated from the world began to draw closer to one another

Japan's military actions toward the region posed a great threat to the Republic of China led by Chiang Kai-shek. At that time, while Chiang Kai-shek confronted Japan, he was also engaged in fierce battles against the Chinese Communist Party within the country.

As a result of the coup d'état in Shanghai in 1927, the Chinese Communist Party, which was ousted from the administration, moved the base of its operations to Ruijin in southern China.

However, upon being attacked by the Nationalist army, in 1934 the Communist army moved further inland. This was the beginning of a two-year action that continued to Yan'an and became known as the Long March. The distance covered is said to have been some 12,500 kilometers. On the way, the Communist army suffered major casualties from attacks by Kuomintang forces. During this harsh march, Mao Zedong became leader of the Communist Party.

近郊の地名です。ここで日本が所有する南満州鉄道が爆破されたのです。これを中国が行った爆破事件として、日本軍が正式に事態収拾へ向けて介入します。満州事変の勃発です。この戦争によって、日本は中国東北地方に傀儡政権の樹立を企てます。1932年に満州を切り離し独立させ、清朝最後の皇帝溥儀を擁立して、満州国を建国したのです。さらに同年に、日本は中国経済の要である上海にも軍隊を投入し、上海事変を起こしました。

こうした日本の動きは欧米の批判にさらされます。中国は、満州国は日本の傀儡国家であると国際連盟に提訴します。その結果、国際連盟からリットン調査団が派遣されました。リットン調査団は日本の中国東北地方での権益については理解を示したものの、最終的に満州国の存在は否認します。日本は硬化し、国際連盟を脱退したのです。1933年のことでした。

その後、日本と中国との間では1945年まで泥沼の戦闘が続くのでした。

世界から孤立した３つの国家が接近を始めた

中国に対する日本の軍事行動は、蒋介石率いる中華民国に大きな脅威となりました。当時蒋介石は日本と対立しながら、国内では中国共産党と激しい戦いを繰り広げていたのです。

1927年の上海でのクーデターによって政権から排除された中国共産党は、中国南部の瑞金に拠点を移しました。

しかし、中華民国政府の攻撃を受け、1934年にさらに内陸へ移動します。長征と呼ばれる延安までの2年にわたる行軍の開始です。移動距離は1万2500キロに及ぶといわれています。途上中華民国軍の攻撃によって共産党軍が受けた被害は甚大でした。この厳しい行軍の中で共産党の指導者となったのが毛沢東だったのです。

時代
20世紀1930年代
現代

地域
ヨーロッパ・中国・日本

分類
侵略【戦争】

キーワード
中国の内戦・日中戦争・ヒトラーの出現・イタリアのエチオピア侵略

Mao called for a joining of forces with the Kuomintang government in a common front for nationalist unity.

In the midst of these events, Zhang Xueliang, son of Zhang Zuolin, and others took action. Chiang Kai-shek reached a reconciliation with the Communists and they established a second United Front. This resulted in an all-out war against the Japanese in 1937.

As warfare grew ever more fierce between Japan and China in the Far East, in Germany Adolf Hitler was rising to prominence. Germany, suffering from the aftermath of the Great Depression, saw public opinion swaying toward a powerful political authority capable of overcoming the existing situation. In 1933 the Nazi Party led by Hitler became the leading political party, and leftist parties including the communists were also expanding their influence. The latter were suppressed after they were framed as the perpetrators of the Reichstag Fire, the burning of the national assembly building. Through this process, the Nazi Party was able to establish itself as a single autocratic power under the Enabling Act of 1933.

The Nazis denied the Versailles system and strengthened the process of rearmament. They also instituted merciless suppression of opposition forces domestically. From the very outset they carried out policies driving out Jews, sending large numbers to concentration camps.

In 1934 President Paul von Hindenburg, who had served under the Weimar Constitution, died. Hitler combined the authority of the prime minister and the president and took the reins of power as Germany's Führer. The model that Hitler embraced was fascism, as advocated by Mussolini. Germany then began to seek an alliance with Italy.

Attempting to get back on its feet after suffering the blows of the Great Depression, Italy invaded Ethiopia, exposing itself to international criticism. Japan meanwhile found itself the target of greater resistance from America and Britain over its support of the Manchu Empire. Meanwhile Hitler was consolidating his autocratic regime in Germany. At these three countries became ever more isolated from the rest of the world, they began to approach one another.

In 1937, the Nationalist army and the Japanese army clashed in the outskirts of Beijing in what is known as the Marco Polo Bridge Incident. This event brought the two nations into full-scale war. For Japan, controlling the entirety of the vast Chinese landmass was an impossibility.

When the Republic of China's capital city of Nanjing was occupied, the Nationalists moved first to Wuhan, then further inland to Chongqing, maintaining the resistance against Japan.

毛沢東は国民党政府に民族統一戦線の結成を呼びかけます。

こうした情勢の中で、張作霖の息子の張学良などの活動もあり、蒋介石は最終的には共産党と和解し、第二次国共合作が成立します。これで中国は総力で抗日戦争を展開することになったのです。1937年のことでした。

東アジアで日本と中国との戦争が激しさを増してゆくなか、ドイツではヒトラーが頭角を現します。世界恐慌の余波に苦しむドイツでは、強力な政治権力による状況の打破へと世論が傾斜したのです。1933年にヒトラー率いるナチスは第一党となり、当時同じく勢力を拡大させていた共産党などの左翼勢力を、国会議事堂放火事件の犯人に仕立てて弾圧します。そうした過程を踏んだ上で、ナチスは全権委任法を通すことで一党独裁体制を確立したのです。

ナチスはヴェルサイユ体制を否定し、再軍備を強行します。さらに反対勢力には容赦のない弾圧と言論統制を行いました。また、当初から主張していたユダヤ人の排斥を政策として実行し、多くの人々を強制収容所へと送り込んだのです。

1934年にワイマール憲法のもとで大統領を務めていたヒンデンブルクが死去すると、ヒトラーは首相と大統領の権限を合わせ、総統してドイツに君臨したのです。ヒトラーがモデルにしたのはムッソリーニの標榜するファシズムでした。ドイツはイタリアとの連携を模索します。

世界恐慌の痛手から立ち直ろうと、エチオピアに侵攻し、国際的な非難を浴びたイタリア。そして、満州国を擁立してアメリカやイギリスと対立が深まった日本。そしてヒトラーの独裁体制を確立したドイツ。この3国が世界から孤立するにつれ、接近を始めたのです。

1937年、日本軍と中華民国軍とは、北京郊外の盧溝橋で軍事衝突をおこし、以後両国は全面戦争へと突入しました。日本にとって、広大な中国を面で制圧することは不可能なことです。

中華民国の首都南京が占領されると、中国は首都を武漢、さらに内陸の重慶へと移し、抗日戦線を維持していったのです。

163 The "have-not" countries again become a menace to the world

At this point let us turn our attention to America following the Great Depression.

The Great Depression significantly changed the destinies of countries, distinguishing between "have" nations with colonies, vast territories, and populations, and the "have-not" nations that lacked them.

America was a major creditor vis-à-vis the European economy. That was all the more reason why the weakening of the European economy due to the spread of the Great Depression was an economic threat to America. President Herbert Hoover implemented relief measures known as the Hoover Moratorium, which temporarily suspended European debt repayments. In 1932, America's industrial output shrank to almost half of what it had been before the beginning of the Depression.

Amidst this crisis, Franklin Delano Roosevelt, a Democrat, was elected president. He implemented economic recovery policies known together as the New Deal. By putting a stop to free competition, approving adjustments of production and price agreements, and supporting the activities of labor unions, the New Deal reduced people's anxiety. At the same time, the government invested in public works projects and increased public expenditures. As a result, the American economy bottomed out in 1932 and slowly began to recover. While maintaining a distance from the turmoil in Europe, America utilized its own vast resources and sought ways to emerge from the crisis.

Britain and France made use of their respective colonial territories. They blocked off their colonial territories by imposing tariffs, and endeavored to revive their economies within their respective spheres. In addition, America, Britain, and France avoided unnecessary confrontations with the Soviet Union, promoting a good-neighbor policy, while strengthening vigilance against the current threat of fascism.

Initially Britain sought to break through the stalemate with Germany using a policy of appeasement. From the standpoint of capitalist societies, fascist regimes were seen as a bulwark against the threat of the Soviet Union. The same tendency was apparent in America's financial world. Some people, including Henry Ford, founder of the major automobile manufacturer Ford Motors, actually showed initial support for the Nazi regime.

「持たざる国」が再び世界の脅威を
生み出した

　ここで、世界恐慌後のアメリカに目を向けます。

　世界恐慌は、植民地や広大な領土、そして人口を有する国家（持てる国）とそうでない国家（持たざる国）との運命を大きく変えました。

　アメリカは、ヨーロッパに膨大な債権を維持していました。それだけに、恐慌の伝染によるヨーロッパ経済の劣化は、アメリカにとっての新たな経済的脅威となったのです。フーヴァー大統領はフーヴァー＝モラトリアムといわれる、ヨーロッパの債務返済を一時停止するなどの救済策を実施しますが効果はなく、1932年にはアメリカの工業生産高は恐慌以前の半分近くにまで落ち込んだのです。

　この危機の中で民主党から大統領に選ばれたのがフランクリン・ルーズベルトでした。彼はニューディール政策と呼ばれる経済復興策を断行します。自由競争にブレーキをかけ、生産調整や価格協定などを容認し、労働組合の活動もサポートし国民の不安を取り除きます。同時に公共事業に投資して消費の拡大に取り組んだのです。その結果、アメリカ経済は1932年を底に、少しずつ回復し始めます。アメリカはヨーロッパの混乱とは距離をおきながら、自国の広大な資源を活用して危機からの脱却を図ったのです。

　イギリスやフランスは、世界に拡散する自国の植民地を活用します。植民地を関税などでブロックし、自らの経済圏の中で経済の再生を図ったのです。そして、アメリカもイギリスもフランスも、ソヴィエト連邦との無用な対立を避け、善隣外交を進めながら当面の脅威であるファシズムに対する警戒を強めます。

　とはいえ、イギリスは当初はドイツに対しては宥和政策による事態の打開を目指しました。資本主義社会にとって、ファシズム政権はソ連の脅威に対する防波堤と捉えられたのです。その傾向はアメリカの財界にも見られました。実際に自動車大手フォードの創業者ヘンリー・フォードなどは、当初ナチス政権への支持を表明していたのです。

時代
20世紀1930年代
現代

地域
アメリカ合衆国・ヨーロッパ・中国・日本

分類
政治【経済】

キーワード
アメリカの経済復興・英仏のブロック経済・スペイン内乱・日本、ドイツ、イタリアの孤立

ハーバート・フーヴァー
Herbert C. Hoover
(1874–1964)

フランクリン・ルーズベルト
Franklin Delano Roosevelt
(1882–1945)

Among people whose livelihoods were destroyed by the Depression, socialist ideology actually spread. In Spain in 1936 socialist supporters called the Popular Front government took power after the collapse of the monarchy and established a cabinet supported by the whole nation.

In response to this, the land-owning class, the wealthy, and people hoping for a restoration of the monarchy backed General Francisco Franco and sought to recover control of the government. As a result, the Spanish Civil War that broke out developed into an international conflict that enmeshed intellectuals of the day.

The Spanish Civil War concluded with General Franco's gaining control of Madrid in 1939, but the boost given to socialist movements not only in the Soviet Union and China but also in various European regions set nerves on edge in the various powers.

Making use of this mentality in the countries of Western Europe, Germany, Italy, and Japan formed the Anti-Comintern Pact to oppose the communist movement in 1937. This pact strengthened into the Tripartite Pact in 1940. These three "have-not" nations, which were not able to deal with the Depression through their own powers alone, sought to break through the realities facing them by new acts of aggression, which triggered World War II.

164 World War II began with Germany's invasion of Poland

Sigmund Freud, who analyzed human reactions due to instincts and consciousness, and revolutionized the world of psychology, is one of the leading psychologists of the 20th century. Influenced by him, Erich Fromm wrote *Escape from Freedom*.

In this volume, Fromm explains that people can attain security by placing themselves in an intermediate position between those who strongly dominate them and those whom their sense of superiority leads them to dominate. It is this psychology that gave birth to fascism. Placed in a position of submission to the strong authority of the state and embracing a sense of superiority over other peoples by acts of aggression, the individual is relieved of the anxiety that arises from economic and social activities.

Prior to this war, many Japanese were filled with a sense of superiority

実際、恐慌によって生活を破壊された人々の間には社会主義思想が浸透していました。スペインでは1936年に人民戦線と呼ばれる社会主義を支持する人々が、王政が崩壊したあと政権を獲得し、挙国一致内閣を樹立しました。

　それに対して、地主層や資産家、さらに王政復古を望む人々は、フランコ将軍を押し立てて、政権を奪還しようとします。これによっておきたスペイン内戦は当時の知識人をも巻き込んだ国際紛争へと発展しかけます。

　スペイン内戦は、フランコ将軍が1939年に首都マドリードを制圧して終結しますが、ソ連や中国のみならず、ヨーロッパ各地でのこうした社会主義運動の高揚に列強は神経をとがらせていたのでした。

　そうした西欧諸国の心理を利用し、ドイツ、イタリア、日本は1937年に共産主義運動に対抗することを名目に三国防共協定を締結します。この協定が、三国同盟へと強化されたのは1940年のことでした。恐慌に対して、自力で対処できなかった3つの「持たざる国」が、新たな侵略行為によって事態を打破しようとしたことが、第二次世界大戦への直接の引き金となったのです。

ドイツのポーランド侵攻で
第二次世界大戦が始まった

　人間の本能と意識の反応を分析し、心理学の世界を変革したジークムント・フロイトは20世紀を代表する心理学者です。彼の影響を受けたエーリッヒ・フロムの著書に、『自由からの逃走』があります。

　その中で、人々は強く自らを支配する者と、自らが優越感をもって支配できる者との中間におかれることで、安心を手に入れることができると解説します。その心理が、ファシズムを生み出したのです。国家という大きな権威に自らを服従させ、侵略行為などにより他の人々に優越感を抱くことが、人々の経済活動や社会活動に起因する不安を取り除いたのです。

　戦前、多くの日本人は、天皇制への服従と、朝鮮半島を植民地にし、

時代
20世紀1930年代
現代

地域
ヨーロッパ・中国・日本

分類
戦争【外交】

キーワード
全体主義の進展・ユダヤ人弾圧・宥和政策の破綻・第二次世界大戦の勃発

by submitting to the emperor system, colonizing the Korean Peninsula, and advancing into China. The Nanjing Incident, in which Japanese forces conquered Nanjing and massacred a large number of Chinese civilians, became the cause of the change in the Western world's view of Japan from one of caution to one of animosity.

In Italy, the glorification of the Roman Empire combined with prejudice toward the invaded African countries. In Germany, glorification of the nation and the Germanic peoples combined with cruelty toward the Jewish people. All followed this pattern. Believers in Judaism had traditionally been the target of persecution in heavily Christian-influenced Europe. In recent years, Jewish people had become prominent in the financial and industrial worlds, and feelings of prejudice changed to animosity and hatred.

Under the Nazi regime, that hatred was systematically stimulated, and Jewish people were persecuted. The slaughter of Jews in the Holocaust is the worst large atrocity in recorded history.

As a result of this German policy, large numbers of Jewish people fled Germany and took refuge in the United States. Prominent figures, such as Albert Einstein, who discovered the theory of relativity, were representative of this wave of immigrants and refugees, resulting in the concentration of intellectual assets in America.

Moreover, Hitler, who emphasized the unification of the Germanic peoples, asserted that all areas neighboring Germany in which Germanic peoples resided should also be incorporated into Germany. In 1938 he incorporated Austria and demanded the cession of the territory of the Sudetenland in Czechoslovakia, where many Germans resided.

Prime Minister Neville Chamberlain of Britain joined with France, Italy, and Germany in Munich, seeking an appeasement policy to resolve tensions. However, Germany thereafter broke up Czechoslovakia, and further demanded that Poland return the region around Danzig, which had once been part of Prussian territory.

Seeing these circumstances, the Soviet Union embraced a strong distrust of these Western European countries who were placating Germany, a country the Soviets were strongly wary of. Sensing the Soviet Union's moves, Germany held talks with the USSR and in 1939 concluded the Molotov-Ribbentrop Pact between itself and the USSR. On the basis of this agreement, Poland was invaded.

中国へと進出していったときに抱く優越感にひたりました。そんな日本が中国の南京を陥落させたときに多数の中国市民を虐殺した南京虐殺事件などが、西欧世界が日本への警戒心を敵愾心に変化させる契機になりました。

　イタリアではローマ帝国への賛美と、侵略したアフリカ諸国への偏見が、ドイツでは国家とゲルマン民族への賛美と、ユダヤ人への虐待行為が、この図式を作りました。ユダヤ教を信奉する人々は、キリスト教の影響の強いヨーロッパでは伝統的に迫害の対象となっていました。そして、近年ユダヤ系の人々が金融や産業界に進出することが、そうした偏見を憎悪へと変えていったのです。

　ナチス政権下のドイツでは、その憎悪を組織的にあおり立て、ユダヤ系の人々への迫害を行ったのです。ホロコーストと呼ばれるこのユダヤ人への大虐殺は、世界史の中でも最悪の大量殺戮として記録されることになります。

　こうしたドイツの政策によって、多くのユダヤ系の人々がアメリカに移民として亡命します。相対性理論を発表したアルベルト・アインシュタインなどはその代表でした。この移民や難民によって、アメリカに知的資産が集中することになります。

　さらにドイツ民族の統合を主張するヒトラーは、ドイツ人の居住するドイツ周辺の地域も自国に編入すべきだと主張します。1938年にはオーストリアを併合し、ドイツ系の人々の多く住むチェコスロバキアのズデーデン地方の割譲を要求したのです。

　当時のイギリスの首相チェンバレンは、フランスやイタリアを交え、ドイツとミュンヘンで会談し、宥和政策によって事態の打開を模索します。しかし、ドイツはその後チェコスロバキアそのものを解体し、ポーランドに対しても元々プロシアの領土であった地域との間にあったダンツィヒの返還を要求したのです。

　この情勢を見たソヴィエト連邦は、西側諸国のソ連を意識したドイツへの宥和政策に強い不信感を抱きます。ソ連の動きを察知したドイツはソ連と会談、1939年に独ソ不可侵条約を締結し、その上でポーランドに侵攻したのです。

As a result of this action, Britain and France, which had supported Poland, declared war on Germany, thereby initiating World War II.

165 During the initial stages of World War II, Germany stormed across Europe

While hardly enough time had passed to allow humankind to forget the horrific tragedies of World War I, they foolishly brought about a second world war. We ought not overlook the fact that in a mere 20 years, humankind forgot the past tragedy and once again started a large-scale conflict, one that was unprecedented in world history.

When we look at the flow of events of World War II in Europe, we tend to place Germany in the center of the stage. However, what we cannot ignore is the moves made by the Soviet Union.

As a result of the Molotov-Ribbentrop Pact, the Soviet Union obtained a bulwark to protect itself from discord with the countries of Western Europe. When Germany invaded Poland from the west, the Soviet army invaded Poland from the east, and the two countries split Poland between themselves. The Soviets further annexed Finland and the three Baltic states, and aggressively advanced into Eastern Europe, taking over neighboring countries.

These actions, however, eventually gave birth to a conflict of interests between Germany and the Soviet Union.

While the Soviets had concluded a treaty with the Germans, the German advance eastward set Soviet nerves on edge. When the two countries went to war, in the background was an attempt to establish ties with Japan in order to secure safety in the Far East. The result was the Soviet-Japanese Neutrality Pact, which was concluded in 1941. To secure its operations in Manchukuo, Japan had hoped to remove the threat posed by the Soviet Union.

Immediately thereafter, Germany abandoned its agreement with the Soviet Union. It began an invasion of the Soviet Union, with Moscow as its goal.

Prior to this, in 1940 Germany invaded Denmark, Norway, the Netherlands, Belgium, and France. In June 1940 Paris fell, and France surrendered to Germany. After that, Germany occupied northern France, while in southern France, Vichy France under Philippe Petain maintained an appeasement policy with Germany.

この行為によって、ポーランドを支援していたイギリスやフランスがドイツに宣戦を布告。こうして第二次世界大戦が始まったのです。

大戦初期にはドイツはヨーロッパを席巻した

人類は愚かにも、第一次世界大戦の惨劇を忘れる暇もなく、再び世界大戦をおこしてしまいました。たった20年という年月で、人類が過去の悲劇を忘れ、再び歴史上類を見ない大規模な殺戮を繰り返してしまった事実を我々は忘れてはなりません。

我々はヨーロッパでの第二次世界大戦の趨勢を見るとき、ドイツを中心におきがちです。しかし、忘れてはならないのはソヴィエト連邦の動きです。

ソ連は、独ソ不可侵条約で西欧諸国との確執から自らを守る防波堤を得たことになります。ドイツがポーランドに侵攻すると、ソ連も東からポーランドを攻め、両国でポーランドを分割したのです。また、フィンランドやバルト海沿岸のバルト三国も併合し、東欧にも積極的に進出します。こうしてソ連も近隣の地域を接収していったのです。

しかし、この動きが最終的にはドイツとソ連の利害の対立を生んだのです。

ソ連はドイツと条約を結びながらも、ドイツの東進政策には神経をとがらせていました。そこで、ドイツと戦争状態になったときに背後となる極東の安全を担保しようと日本に接近します。その結果1941年に締結されたのが、日ソ中立条約だったのです。日本も満州国を安全に経営するためには、ソ連の脅威を取り除きたかったのです。

そしてこの直後、ドイツはソ連との条約を破棄。モスクワを目指して侵攻を始めたのです。

それ以前、1940年にはドイツはデンマークやノルウェー、オランダ、さらにベルギーを経てフランスに侵攻していました。1940年6月にはついにパリが陥落し、フランスはドイツに降伏します。以後フランスは、北部をドイツに占領され、南部にドイツとの融和政策をとって国家の

時代
20世紀1940年代
現代

地域
ヨーロッパ

分類
侵略【戦争】

キーワード
独ソ不可侵条約とポーランド分割・独ソの対立・日ソ中立条約・ドイツのヨーロッパ席巻

France retained its identity as a sovereign state under considerable duress.

With France's defeat, Britain came under direct threat of German invasion, and London was assaulted by air raids. Charles de Gaulle left France and took refuge in Britain, where he established the government in exile of Free France, leading a resistance movement within France itself.

Further, Germany with its ally Italy extended the war front into North Africa and the Balkan Peninsula. As a result of his successful occupation of large areas of Europe, Hitler was enthusiastically supported by the people of Germany. However, as Germany continued its offense against the Soviet Union, it encountered stubborn resistance, and its situation grew tenuous. Germany was able to procure resources and personnel from the regions it occupied and was able to continue fighting, but it was harassed by resistance movements. As time passed, the Soviet Union went on the offensive, and Germany began to come under pressure.

166 Japan's and Germany's hopes for a short war crumbled

When the Tripartite Pact between Germany, Italy, and Japan was concluded in 1940, Japan was already exhausted from in warfare with China. While Japan was occupying the urban areas, it was unable to push farther into the vast inland regions.

In the case of resource-poor Japan, it was an all-important issue to obtain a supply of resources, such as petroleum, in order to continue fighting. Therefore, Japan carried out a strategy for advancing southward toward resource-rich Southeast Asia. First, with Germany occupying France, Japan advanced into the former French colony that is present-day Vietnam and occupied that region.

America responded strongly to this action. America repudiated the U.S.-Japan commercial treaty and together with Britain and the Netherlands, who possessed colonies in Southeast Asia, America began an economic blockade.

Japan initiated negotiations with the United States, but talks in which the

運営をはかったフィリップ・ペタンによるヴィシー政権が成立します。フランスはかろうじて主権国家として存続したのです。

　フランスの敗北によって、イギリスはドイツの侵攻の脅威にさらされ、ロンドンなどは空襲に見舞われます。そんなイギリスにフランスからシャルル・ド・ゴールが亡命し自由フランスという亡命政権を樹立し、フランス国内でのレジスタンス（抵抗運動）を指揮したのでした。

　さらに、ドイツは同盟国のイタリアとともに北アフリカ、バルカン半島へと戦線を拡大していったのです。ヨーロッパの広大な地域を占領したことで、ヒトラーはドイツ国民に熱狂的に支持されます。しかし一方でソ連との戦線ではドイツは攻勢を続けながらも、執拗な抵抗にあい苦戦を強いられます。ドイツは占領地から資源や人員を調達し、戦闘を維持しますが、占領地でも人々の抵抗運動に苦しめられます。そして、時と共にソ連側が攻勢に転じ、ドイツを圧迫し始めるのです。

シャルル・ド・ゴール
Charles de Gaulle (1890–1970)

短期決戦を望む日本とドイツの思惑が崩れていった

　1940年に日独伊三国同盟が締結されたとき、日本は中国との戦争で消耗していました。都市部は占領できても、内陸の広大な地域まで押さえ込むことは不可能でした。

　資源のない日本の場合、戦争を継続するための石油などの物資の調達は必須の課題でした。そこで日本は資源の豊富な東南アジアに向け、南進政策を実施しようとしたのです。まずドイツがフランスを占領すると、フランスの植民地であった現在のベトナムに侵攻して占領したのです。

　こうした動きにアメリカは強く反発します。アメリカは日米通商条約を破棄し、東南アジアに植民地を持つイギリスやオランダと共に、経済封鎖を始めます。

　日本は日米交渉を始めますが、中国や東南アジアからの撤退を強く

| 時代 |
| 20世紀1940年代 現代 |

| 地域 |
| 日本・中国・アメリカ合衆国 |

| 分類 |
| 侵略【戦争】 |

| キーワード |
| 泥沼の日中戦争・日本のインドシナ進駐・日米交渉の決裂・日本と英米の海戦・同盟国の劣勢 |

United States strongly demanded a withdrawal from China and Southeast Asia hit an impasse.

Moreover, at home, the military faction, who pressed strongly for a continuation of the war, took control of the government, abolished government by political parties, and strongly influenced public opinion toward war.

Among the leadership there were some who asserted that it would be ill-advised to confront America while continuing the war with China. However, while the whole country was being swept toward war, no one was able to stop the flood of opinion.

At length in December 1941, Japan launched a surprise attack on America's naval base in Hawaii. America immediately declared war on Japan. Warfare expanded across the globe.

Both Germany and Japan were from the outset resource-lacking "have-not" countries. Therefore, they hoped to carry out surprise attacks, obtain an advantage on the battlefields in a short period of time, and then reach an armistice. However, Germany lost its footing in the Russo-German War, and with Japan's participation, America became involved in the conflict as well. In the early stages of the war, the Japanese army advanced into Southeast Asia and the islands of the South Pacific, and continued on the offensive. In the areas that Japan occupied, it imposed compulsory education in Japanese culture and Japanese language, and the military carried out tight restrictions on freedom of speech. Needless to say, this led to anti-Japanese actions in the respective regions.

Eventually, as a result of its overwhelming quantity of supplies and resources, America's methodical counteroffensive, and China's stubborn resistance, Japan began to give way due to inferior strength.

The Soviet Union, with its security in the Far East guaranteed by its treaty with Japan, began to gain advantage through its alliance with Britain and cooperation with America.

At the stage when America gained the advantage in the war against Japan, America was able to distribute its military strength, which had been focused on Europe as the main priority. Under pressure from the Allied Powers, which America had joined in 1943, Mussolini fell from power and Italy collapsed. The following year, the Allied armies of America and Britain launched an offensive by landing at Normandy, and in August of that year, they liberated Paris.

求めるアメリカとの話し合いは暗礁に乗りあげます。

　さらに、日本国内でも戦争継続を強く主張する軍部が政権をとり、政党政治を解体し、世論を戦争へと強く誘導していました。

　中国と戦争を継続させながら、さらにアメリカと対立することの無謀さを主張する人が指導層の中にいなかったわけではありません。しかし、国家全体が戦争に押し流される中で、誰もそれを押しとどめることはできなかったのです。

　1941年12月に、ついに日本はハワイのアメリカ海軍基地を奇襲します。こうして、アメリカは即刻日本に対して宣戦を布告。戦争は文字どおり世界へと拡大したのです。

　ドイツも日本も、もともとは資源の乏しい「持たざる国」でした。ですから、戦争を電撃的に行い、短期で有利に矛を収めたかったのです。しかし、ドイツは独ソ戦でつまずき、日本の参戦でアメリカとも戦闘状態になってしまいました。日本も緒戦は東南アジアや南方の島々へと軍隊を進め、攻勢を続けていました。日本は占領した地域で日本の文化や日本語教育を強制し、軍隊により厳しい言論統制も行います。これがそれぞれの地域での反日活動へと繋がったことはいうまでもありません。

　やがて、圧倒的な物量によるアメリカの組織的な反撃と、中国での執拗な抵抗の前に、日本は次第に劣勢を強いられてしまいます。

　ソヴィエト連邦は、日本との条約で極東での安全が保証されると、イギリスと同盟し、アメリカとも協力して戦争を有利に展開します。

　アメリカは、対日戦争で優位に立った段階で、もともとプライオリティの高かったヨーロッパへも戦力を振り分ける余裕がでてきます。アメリカも加わった連合軍に圧され、1943年には、ムッソリーニが失脚し、イタリアが降伏します。そして翌年にはアメリカやイギリスの連合軍がフランスのノルマンディに上陸し、8月にはパリも解放されたのです。

167 With the surrender of Japan, World War II came to an end

In 1943 U.S. President Franklin D. Roosevelt, Britain's Prime Minister Winston Churchill, and China's President Chiang Kai-shek held talks in Cairo, ultimately issuing a proclamation calling for the unconditional surrender of Japan.

Following this, in the Pacific region, America overpowered the Japanese army, and in 1945 after Japan had already lost command of the skies, America intensified its air raids on the Japanese mainland. In June, the American forces occupied Okinawa, but the Japanese continued their desperate resistance.

Meanwhile on the American side, circumstances called for an early end to the conflict. One factor was the concern that overcoming the stubborn resistance of the Japanese military would lead to an increase in the number of casualties. A second factor was that before the Soviet Union's declaration of war on Japan, America intended to defeat Japan and place it under its own influence. It was essential to American interests to prevent the Pacific region from being overtaken by an expansion of communist influence.

In order to resist such moves by America, the Japanese government tentatively approached the Soviet Union, with whom it had a neutrality agreement, regarding a reconciliation offer. The Soviet Union simply ignored the issue.

The reason for this lack of any response whatsoever was that in February 1945, Roosevelt, Churchill, and the Soviet Union's Joseph Stalin had met in Yalta in the U.S.S.R., and had agreed that the Soviet Union would later declare war on Japan.

At the end of April that same year, Hitler took his own life, and on May 7, Berlin fell. The world then began to change course dramatically toward the creation of a postwar world order. On July 26, the Potsdam Declaration was issued by America, Britain, and China. It warned that if Japan did not agree to the abandonment of militarism and did not agree to accept occupation and punishment for war crimes, its homeland would be completely destroyed.

The Japanese government, however, remained completely silent in response to this declaration.

As a result, the world's first atomic bomb was dropped on Japan. The bomb, which was dropped into the skies over Hiroshima on the morning of August 6,

日本の降伏で、第二次世界大戦は終結した

時代
20世紀1940年代
現代

地域
世界

分類
戦争【外交】

キーワード
連合国のカイロ、ヤルタ
会談・ドイツの降伏とポ
ツダム宣言・原爆投下と
ソ連参戦・日本敗戦

　1943年に、アメリカのルーズベルト大統領とイギリスのチャーチル首相、そして中国の蒋介石総統とがカイロで会談し、日本に無条件降伏を求める宣言を発表します。

　その後、太平洋ではアメリカが日本軍を圧倒し、1945年になると既に制空権を失った日本本土への空襲も激化してきました。6月には沖縄がアメリカ軍に占領されますが、日本政府は絶望的な抗戦を継続したのです。

　一方、アメリカ側には戦争を早期に終わらせたい事情がありました。その一つは日本軍の執拗な抵抗を抑え込むことで、さらに犠牲者が増えることへの懸念でした。そして、ソヴィエト連邦が対日宣戦に踏み切る前に、日本を降伏させ、自国の勢力下に日本を抱え込みたいというアメリカの目論見もあったはずです。太平洋地域に共産主義勢力が拡大することを防ぐ必要があったのです。

　日本政府は、そうしたアメリカの動きに対抗するために、中立条約を締結していたソ連に対して講和を打診しますが、ソ連はそれを黙殺します。

　というのも、既に1945年2月にルーズベルト、チャーチル、そしてソ連のスターリンによってソ連のヤルタで行われた会談で、ソ連の対日宣戦が約定されていたからです。

　同年4月末にヒトラーは自ら命を絶ち、5月7日にはベルリンが陥落。世界は戦後の秩序のありかたに向けて大きく舵を切り始めていたのです。7月26日、アメリカ、イギリス、そして中国の名前で、ポツダム宣言と呼ばれる対日降伏勧告が発表され、軍国主義の解体と占領、戦犯の処罰などを受諾しない限り、国土が徹底的に破壊されるという警告を行います。

　しかし、日本政府はその宣言に対して沈黙を続けたのでした。

　その結果、日本に世界で初めて原子爆弾が投下されることになりました。8月6日朝、広島の上

ヤルタ会談に臨む（前列左から）チャーチル、ルーズベルト、スターリン
Churchill, Roosevelt and Stalin (front row, from left) at the Yalta Conference.

created a fireball some 500 meters in circumference, with a temperature of nearly 3,000 degrees, which incinerated everything nearby, destroying buildings and instantly killing people. Within three months of the bombing, the death toll rose to over 100,000. On August 9, a second nuclear bomb was dropped on Nagasaki. Then the U.S.S.R. joined the war, and the Soviet army began moving southward into Manchuria, which the Japanese occupied and on to Sakhalin.

On August 14, 1945, the Japanese government decided to accept the conditions of the Potsdam Declaration. On the following day, the voice of the Emperor announced over the radio to the nation that Japan had agreed to surrender.

And so it was that World War II came to an end.

The war was the largest in scale in world history in terms of not only combatant casualties but also civilian casualties in areas where ordinary citizens were the direct victims of the fighting. And together with the ending of the war, the actual proof of massacres having been carried out in various parts of the world became known to the whole world. It is believed that if one includes all of the victims of the war around the world, the number would exceed 100 million people.

168 Humanity was met with repercussion for a series of conflicts and deep-seated hatreds

Let us here take stock by reflecting on the past.

First there were the hostilities between countries and ethnic groups beginning with the Reformation in Europe. As a result of these conflicts in which there was considerable bloodshed, modern nation-states came into existence. Following this, the Western powers, which grew stronger as a result of revolutions and the Industrial Revolution they experienced, launched forth into competition to acquire colonial territories in Asia and Africa, and imperialism became rampant. With World War I, in which these strong countries opposed one another, it seemed that the books would be closed on those rivalries.

Within these movements in history, at each critical junctur, a new international order came into being. Among these, following the Napoleonic Wars, it was the Vienna system. Following World War I, it was the Versailles system. These were attempts at restoring some order to the chaotic situation and realizing a lasting peace.

空から投下された原爆は、周囲500メートルを3000度近い高温で焼き尽くし、その周辺も含め、建物は倒壊、多くの人が即死しました。被爆後3カ月以内の死亡者は10万人を超えたのです。8月9日には長崎が2度目の原爆攻撃にさらされました。そしてソ連が参戦。ソ連は北から日本軍が占領していた満州地区、そして樺太南部へと南下を始めます。

1945年8月14日。日本政府はついにポツダム宣言の受諾を決定。翌日、全国に天皇の声で発表したのです。

こうして、第二次世界大戦は終結しました。

この戦争は、戦闘員のみならず、非戦闘員である市民をも直接犠牲にした、史上最大規模の戦争となりました。そして、戦争終結と共に、世界各地で行われた殺戮行為の実態が明らかになってきたのです。そうした全ての犠牲者を世界規模で見た場合、その数は1億人を超えるのではないかといわれています。

確執と怨念の連鎖の代償に人類は見舞われた

ここで改めて、過去を振り返ってみましょう。

ヨーロッパでの宗教改革に始まった国家や民族の対立。そしてその対立によって多くの血が流された末に、近代国家が産声をあげたこと。その後それぞれの国家でおきた革命や産業革命によってさらに力のつけた西欧列強が、アジアやアフリカなどへの植民地獲得競争に乗り出し、帝国主義が横行したこと。そして、そうした強国の勢力の対立が第一次世界大戦によって一度清算されたかのようにみえたこと。

これらの歴史の動きの中では、節目ごとに新たな国際秩序が生まれました。ナポレオン戦争後のウィーン体制、第一次世界大戦後のヴェルサイユ体制などがそれにあたります。それらは混乱した秩序を取り戻し、和平を実現させようという動きでもありました。

時代
16世紀以降
近世・近代・現代

地域
共通

分類
社会【国際】

キーワード
宗教、民族の対立から国家対立へ・ヨーロッパの植民地主義・民族弾圧・巨大な殺戮

As a result, some states that had until them held supremacy either disappeared or shrank, and new states appeared. Ironically enough, the weakening of these states and the antagonism between them would bring forth new tensions.

This was also the history of the vicissitudes of the Habsburgs' Holy Roman Empire, the Ottoman Empire, England, France, Russia, and Prussia. Within the powerful surges of history, there was frequent merging and breaking away between neighboring states and peoples. Through this process, Russia became the Union of Soviet Socialist Republics and, in the New World, America became a new player on the world stage.

Meanwhile in Asia, China greeted a new era through the painful struggles of escaping its past. During this transition, Japan rose up and opposed the Western powers who possessed vested interests in Asia. The various countries of Asia spent the first half of the 20th century fighting with countries of the West with the aim of gaining independence and contending with the advances being made by Japan.

Through World War II, the great waves of human activity and the contradictions of discord over those several centuries were absorbed, and the world brought forth a new order. Therefore, in this major conflict, the numerous intentions, deep-seated hatreds, and contradictions that have resulted from previous eras burst forth, causing an enormous eruption across the face of the globe.

Germany, both in its homeland and in the areas it had occupied, systematically slaughtered some 6 million Jews in gas chambers, in human experimentation, and in harsh forced labor. The Japanese army inflicted harm on non-combatants in China and other parts of Asia during the war.

However, one ought not forget that the Allied Powers who opposed the menace of militarism also supported or took part in the indiscriminate bombing of the German city of Dresden and the civilian districts of Tokyo and other major cities, and dropped nuclear bombs on Hiroshima and Nagasaki, acts of carnage that would leave scars on future generations. When humanity struggled to overcome the accumulated resentments and contradictions of the past, the fact that such sacrifices spread worldwide serves as a profound lesson.

People focused on the causes of the Versailles system, which was a direct cause of World War II, and on the contradictions in the Weimar Constitution, the League of Nations, and the Paris Treaty for the Renunciation of War. What was formed as a result was the United Nations.

その結果、それまで覇権を握ってきた国家が消滅あるいは縮小し、そのたびに世界に影響を与える新たなプレイヤーが生まれました。皮肉なことに、そうした国家の衰亡と対立がさらなる緊張を生み出してゆきました。

　それはハプスブルク家の神聖ローマ帝国、オスマン帝国、イギリスやフランス、そしてロシアやプロシアという国家の盛衰と対立の歴史でもありました。この歴史のうねりの中で、周辺国家や民族が融合と分離を繰り返しながら、ロシアはソヴィエト社会主義共和国連邦に、そして新大陸からはアメリカという新たなプレイヤーが世界史に登場しました。

　一方、アジアでは、中国が新しい時代に向けて脱皮するための生みの苦しみを味わっていました。その過渡期に日本が台頭し、アジアに利権を持つ西欧勢力と対立しました。アジア諸国は、欧米への独立を目指す闘争と、日本の進出への対応に揺れながら、20世紀前半を過ごしたのです。

　こうした数世紀にわたる人類の活動と確執の矛盾を津波のように飲み込み、世界に新しい体制をもたらしたのが、第二次世界大戦だったのです。ですから、この大戦では、それまでの時代の生み出した無数の思惑、怨念、そして矛盾が吹き出し、地球上のあちこちで巨大な噴火をおこしました。

　ドイツが占領地域をも含めた地域で組織的に行ったユダヤ人の虐殺では600万人がガス室や人体実験、過酷な労働で殺害されたといわれています。日本軍も、中国やアジア各地で戦争の加害者となりました。

　ただ、軍国主義の脅威に対抗した連合国側も、ドイツのドレスデンや、東京などでの市民を巻き込んだ無差別爆撃、広島や長崎への原爆投下など、後世に禍根の残る殺戮行為に加担したことも忘れてはなりません。人類全てが過去に積もった怨念と矛盾を払拭しようともがいたとき、これだけの犠牲が世界中に拡散した事実は、大きな教訓となりました。

　人々は、まず第二次世界大戦の直接の原因となった、ヴェルサイユ体制の崩壊の原因に注目し、ワイマール憲法、国際連盟、そしてパリ不戦条約などの矛盾点に注目します。こうして結成されたのが国際連合だったのです。

169

The United Nations became the core of the postwar order

The fundamental idea for the formation of the United Nations emerged from the Atlantic Charter, which was a joint declaration by American president Franklin Roosevelt and British prime minister Winston Churchill in August 1941. Based on this declaration, the United Nations was formed at the San Francisco Conference held in April 1945.

In line with the stipulations in the United Nations Charter, the UN Security Council was established as an organ of the highest level of decision making in adjucating international disputes. Within the UN Security Council, permanent seats possessing the right to veto were given to the United States—which had played a major role in bringing the war to a close—and the Soviet Union, Britain, France, and China. Together with the nonpermanent member nations elected every two years, the Security Council deliberates on how to settle disputes that arise in various parts of the world.

A system is provided whereby all the member nations of the UN can, through the General Assembly of the UN, advise the Security Council regarding matters of human rights and international disputes, drawing on lessons learned from two world wars. In the earlier League of Nations, when a conflict arose, there were no armed measures for resolving issues. Reflecting on that insufficiency, the United Nations forces were given authority and enabled to carry out activities to bring resolutions to areas in dispute throughout the world.

国際連合紋章
Emblem of the United Nations

国際連合は戦後の秩序の核となった

　国際連合は、1941年8月に、アメリカのルーズベルト大統領と、イギリスのチャーチル首相が大西洋で発表した大西洋憲章で発芽した構想をもとに、1945年4月から開催されたサンフランシスコ会議を経て発足しました。

　国際連合のあり方を示した国際連合憲章に従い、国際連合では安全保障理事会をおき、国際紛争の解決に注力する最高意思決定機関としました。安全保障理事会では、世界大戦の終結に大きな役割を果たしたアメリカ、ソヴィエト連邦、イギリス、フランス、中国が拒否権を有する常任理事国となりました。そして、2年ごとに選挙で選ばれる理事国と共に、世界各地でおこる紛争などの問題を協議することになったのです。

　さらに加盟国全てが参加する国連総会を通して、二つの世界大戦を教訓にした人権問題や国際紛争の課題について安全保障理事会に勧告をする制度も整えました。過去の国際連盟では紛争がおきても、それを解決する武力的手段を持ちませんでした。その反省から、国連軍の活動をみとめ、世界各国の紛争地の終結のために活動できるようにしました。

時代
20世紀1940年代
現代

地域
世界

分類
和平【国際】

キーワード
国際連合の発足・広範な国連の領域・戦争犯罪の処罰・戦後秩序の成立・分断国家の出現

ニューヨークにある国連本部ビル
United Nations Headquarters in New York City

The UN further established affiliated agencies that contribute to world stability through education, culture, medical treatment, and economics. Familiar ones include UNESCO, which contributes to the promotion of educational and cultural activities; UNICEF, which promotes human rights, education, and the health of children; and the WHO, which works on issues regarding medical treatment and public health.

Running parallel with the founding of the UN, the main countries of the world supported a post-fascist world order.

Japan and Germany were placed under occupation. Germany was occupied by a strategy of divided administrations by the United States, Britain, France, and the Soviet Union.

Within the policies of occupation were the establishment of courts in each country to judge war crimes by the two nations: the Nuremberg International Military Tribunal and the International Military Tribunal for the Far East in Tokyo. In these respective courts, leaders who were held by the victor nations to have committed war crimes and people who carried out inhumane actions during the war were tried.

It is a fact that there was criticism that the victor countries were one-sidedly sitting in judgment on the defeated countries. It is also true that some victorious countries, such as the Soviet Union, interned German and Japanese officers and men for long periods of time and subjected them to hard labor, and that soldiers were tried in various places where battles had taken place without sufficient evidence.

However, it is also a fact that, within this new order, major countries around the world have managed to avoid conflicts with each other for over 70 years.

On the other hand, in Asia, the Middle East, and African countries that were colonies of Western powers for many years, there are regions still plagued by serious conflicts due to subsequent independence movements and the twisted relationships with their former colonial powers.

Whether the new world order that was created following World War II will be no more than another system that was created by humankind and then failed is a question we are still unable to answer.

また、国際連合は教育、文化、医療、経済など、世界の安定に寄与するための付属機関を設けています。身近なところでは、教育文化活動の促進に貢献するユネスコや、子供達の人権と教育、健康の促進を担うユニセフ、さらには、医療や保健活動に従事するWHO（世界保健機関）などがそれにあたります。

　国際連合の発足と並行して、世界の主要国はファシズムが崩壊した後の秩序の維持にもあたりました。
　日本やドイツは占領下におかれます。特にドイツはアメリカ、イギリス、フランスとソ連によって、国家が分割統治されました。

　そして、占領政策の中で、ドイツと日本の戦争犯罪を裁くために、ニュールンベルク国際軍事裁判所と極東国際軍事裁判所がそれぞれの国に設けられ、戦勝国によって戦犯とされた指導者、戦争で非人道的行為を行った人物への裁判がおこなわれました。

　これらの裁判は、戦勝国が敗戦国を一方的に裁いたのではないかという批判があったことは事実です。また、ソ連など一部の戦勝国がドイツや日本の将兵を長期間抑留し重労働を課したり、充分な証拠を揃えないまま、戦闘の起こった各地で敗戦国の将兵が裁かれたりした事実もありました。

　とはいえ、こうした新たな秩序の中で、少なくとも世界の主要国の間では戦後70年以上にわたって国家同士の戦争が回避されてきたこともう一つの事実です。
　反面、長年にわたって西欧列強の植民地であったアジアや中東、アフリカ諸国では、その後の独立運動と旧宗主国との関係のねじれなどから、現在でも深刻な紛争に見舞われている地域もあるのです。

　第二次世界大戦を経てできあがった新たな秩序が、何度も人類が作っては壊してきた秩序の一つに過ぎないのかどうか、その答えは今もでていないのです。

170 Following the war, many Asian and African nations became independent

The end of World War II greatly altered the circumstances of the major European nations, which, since the Industrial Revolution, had dominated Asia and Africa.

In various parts of the world, colonies became independent. In Asia, even prior to the war, independence movements had arisen. For example, in Vietnam, the Indochinese Communist Party led by Ho Chi Minh, and in Myanmar, a nationalist movement led by General Aung San, sought independence from their respective colonizer nations, France and Britain.

Similar movements developed in Indonesia and other territories under Dutch control.

During the war, the major powers made use of these independence movements in Asia and elsewhere to prosecute their wars. As an illustration, Japan, employing the slogan of the Greater East Asian Co-prosperity Sphere, supported independence movements in Vietnam, Indonesia, the Philippines, and Myanmar in order to oppose Britain and the United States.

Following the war, these countries accelerated their movements toward gaining independence. Ho Chi Minh declared the independence of Vietnam, but France, the suzerain state, sought to suppress it, resulting in the opening of the Indochina Wars. As a result, according to the Geneva Agreements of 1954 France recognized Vietnamese independence. One year before that, Cambodia obtained independence from France.

India gained independence in 1947.

However, once it gained independence, India split apart. Mahatma Gandhi had sought to establish rapport between the Hindus and the Muslims, but he failed. India and Muslim-dominant Pakistan split, and each became a sovereign state. Ironically, the following year Gandhi was assassinated by a Hindu extremist.

In virtually every part of Africa, independent states rose up. Due to the fact that 17 countries on the continent became independent in 1960, that year came to be known as the Year of Africa. However, due to the conflicts between ethnic groups within many of these countries and an inability to overcome economic challenges, the reality is that many areas remain troubled by poverty and political instability.

戦後アジアやアフリカで多くの国々が独立した

　第二次世界大戦の終結は、産業革命以来アジアやアフリカを席巻してきたヨーロッパ主要国の状況を大きく変えました。

　世界各地で植民地が独立します。アジアでは戦前からすでに独立運動がおこっていました。例えば、ベトナムではホー・チ・ミンが率いるインドシナ共産党が、ミャンマーではアウンサン将軍などによる民族運動がそれぞれ宗主国のフランスやイギリスに対して独立を求めていました。

　こうした動きはオランダに支配されていたインドネシアなどでも同様でした。

　戦争中、世界の主要国はアジアなどでの独立運動を、自らの戦争遂行のために利用しました。例えば、日本はベトナムやインドネシア、さらにはフィリピンやミャンマーなどで、独立運動を支援するために、大東亜共栄圏をスローガンに、イギリスやアメリカに対抗しようとしていました。

　そして戦後、そうした国々が独立へ向けて活動を加速します。ホー・チ・ミンはベトナムの独立を宣言しますが、宗主国のフランスはそれを抑えようと、インドシナ戦争が始まります。結局1954年に、フランスはジュネーヴ協定によってベトナムの独立を認めます。その1年前にカンボジアもフランスから独立を果たしました。

　インドが独立したのは1947年のことでした。

　しかし、インドは独立後分断されてしまいます。ガンディーが求めていたヒンドゥー教徒とイスラム教徒との融和が失敗し、インドはイスラム教徒が主体となったパキスタンと決別し、それぞれが主権を獲得したのです。皮肉なことに、ガンディーはその翌年にヒンドゥー教の過激派に暗殺されてしまいます。

　アフリカでも各地で独立国家が生まれます。1960年には17もの国家が誕生したことから、その年は「アフリカの年」と呼ばれました。ただ、アフリカの多くの国々の中には部族間の対立や、経済問題を克服できず、未だに貧困や政情不安に苦しんでいる地域があることもまた事実です。

時代
20世紀1940～60年代
現代

地域
世界

分類
独立【対立】

キーワード
植民地の独立運動・インドの分断独立・アジア、アフリカ諸国の独立・中華人民共和国の成立

With the end of World War II, for the first time since the Opium Wars, China overcame advances by foreign nations. However, conflicts between the Communists and the Nationalists intensified, and in 1949 due to numerical inferiority, Chiang Kai-shek was forced to flee to Taiwan, where he sustained the Republic of China. In that year, Mao Zedong declared the establishment of the People's Republic of China in Beijing, with himself as the leader of the state.

Hence with the Second World War as a turning point, the world map was extensively redrawn. Within independent nations, such as India and Pakistan, North and South Vietnam, and on the Korean Peninsula, the Democratic People's Republic of Korea and the Republic of Korea, the path to independence involved a separation of ethnic groups. And in the background of these separations stood the rivalry between communist forces centered around the U.S.S.R. and the capitalist forces centered around the U.S. It was this rivalry that caused strife throughout the world in the postwar era.

171 The Korean Peninsula gained independence from Japan but was subsequently divided

In the early stages of World War II, America and Britain were trying to find a way to form a postwar order. In World War II, in order to remove the cancer of fascism that sprang up within capitalist societies, the main capitalist countries tentatively compromised with socialist forces centered around the Soviet Union in prosecuting the war. As a consequence, as the fighting began to turn to the disadvantage of Germany and Japan, America sought to bring the conflict to an end as soon as possible, return Germany to its original affiliation in the Western camp and bring Japan under its own umbrella as a nation opposed to socialist influences.

Toward the end of the war against Germany, the Soviet Union had already invaded Berlin. As a result, Germany was divided into two parts. The western part was under the control of the capitalist countries, including America, and the eastern part was under the rule of the Soviet Union. Japan was fortunate in that regard. Before the Soviet Union reached the islands of Japan itself, Japan was occupied under American initiative, and democratization was being enforced. Ironically, in the Far East, the land that was split into two parts was on the Korean Peninsula.

中国は第二次世界大戦終結をもって、アヘン戦争以来の外国の進攻を克服します。しかし、その後共産党と国民党の対立が激化し、1949年に劣勢に立たされた蒋介石は台湾に逃れ、そこに中華民国を維持します。その年に毛沢東は北京で中華人民共和国の成立を宣言し、自ら国家主席となりました。

　このように、第二次世界大戦を契機に、世界地図は大きく塗り替えられました。そして、独立した国家の中にはインドとパキスタン、南北ベトナム、朝鮮半島に建国した朝鮮民主主義人民共和国と大韓民国のように、その独立の経緯の中で民族が分断されたままになった地域があったのです。分断の背景には、ソヴィエト連邦を中心とする共産主義勢力とアメリカを中心とする資本主義勢力の対立がありました。その対立こそが戦後世界各地で起こる紛争の原因となったのです。

朝鮮半島は日本から独立したあと国家が分断された

　第二次世界大戦の初期段階で、アメリカやイギリスは戦後の体制作りを模索していました。第二次世界大戦はファシズムという資本主義社会の中に発生したがん細胞を除去するために、主要な資本主義国がソヴィエト連邦を軸とした社会主義勢力と一時的に妥協しながら展開した戦争でした。従って、戦況がドイツや日本に不利に進み出すと、アメリカは一刻も早く戦争を終結させ、元々「西側」に属していたドイツや日本を社会主義勢力に対抗する国家として、自国の傘下におこうと考えます。

　対独戦の末期、すでにソ連軍はベルリンに侵攻していました。その結果、ドイツはアメリカなど資本主義国が管理する地域と、ソ連が管理する東側とに分断されて統治されることになってしまいます。日本は幸運でした。ソ連が日本本土に到達する前に、日本はアメリカの主導で占領され、民主化が断行されました。皮肉なことに、極東で分断の憂き目にあったのは朝鮮半島だったのです。

時代
20世紀1940〜50年代
現代

地域
朝鮮半島

分類
戦争【民族】

キーワード
東西(社会主義と資本主義)冷戦・朝鮮半島の分断・朝鮮戦争の勃発

With the surrender of Japan, the Soviet army moved southward into the peninsula, and the American army moved northward from the opposite direction, effectively splitting the country at the 38th parallel. America, the Soviet Union, and Britain intervened in the independence movement in the Korean Peninsula. While trial-and-error efforts to achieve unification continued, in 1948, at America's suggestion, a general election was held under UN supervision. The result was the establishment of the Republic of Korea (ROK, South Korea) under President Rhee Syngman in the southern half of the peninsula, but there was a backlash from the Soviet Union. Subsequent to that, Kim Il-Sung, supported by the Soviet Union, established the Democratic People's Republic of Korea (DPRK, North Korea) as a socialist nation in the northern part of the peninsula. In the chaos, due to conflict between the communist forces and ROK forces, many inhabitants of Jeju Island were slaughtered.

In 1950 in an effort to unite the Korean Peninsula, North Korea invaded South Korea, resulting in the outbreak of the Korean War. Warfare continued until 1953, and the recently established People's Republic of China joined in the fray. When the forces reached a standoff against each other along the 38th parallel, they eventually reached a cease-fire agreement. The cease-fire came after enormous casualties and heavy damage. And as a result, even today the peninsula is divided between North Korea and South Korea. This is how, amidst the ongoing nuclear armament issue, the tensions between Japan, South Korea, and North Korea have continued to worsen today.

While the livelihoods of people on the peninsula were laid waste by the Korean War, the economic activity of Japan, which served as a supply base for the American forces prosecuting the war, enabled it to recover from the damage it had incurred during World War II. In the midst of the Korean War, in 1951, Japan recovered its sovereignty by way of the Treaty of San Francisco. And as a result of the Security Treaty between the United States and Japan, Japan was placed under America's military umbrella. Then during the 1960s, having recovered economically, Japan developed through a period of high economic growth into an economic superpower.

As partners in the ranks of the capitalist nations, Japan and South Korea provided the motive power of the economies of the Far East, normalizing relations in 1965.

朝鮮半島は、日本が敗北すると、南下してきたソ連と、南から進駐してきたアメリカ軍とによって、北緯38度線で分断されました。アメリカとソ連、そしてイギリスによる朝鮮半島の独立運動への介入と、統一への試行錯誤が続く中、1948年にアメリカの提案で国連の管理下で総選挙が実施されます。その結果、李承晩大統領のもとで朝鮮半島南部に大韓民国が発足しますが、ソ連はそれに反発。その結果、ソ連に支援された金日成が朝鮮半島北部に、社会主義国として朝鮮民主主義人民共和国（北朝鮮）を建国したのです。この混乱の中で、済州島では社会主義勢力と大韓民国との対立の結果、島民の多くが虐殺される事件もおこりました。

　1950年、北朝鮮が朝鮮半島の統一を目指し、大韓民国へと侵攻します。朝鮮戦争の勃発です。53年まで、朝鮮半島で展開された朝鮮戦争は、建国したばかりの中華人民共和国の参戦で、北緯38度線付近で両勢力が対峙したまま休戦協定が結ばれました。それは、甚大な犠牲者と破壊の末の休戦でした。その結果、今でも朝鮮半島は朝鮮民主主義人民共和国（北朝鮮）と大韓民国（韓国）とに分かれているのです。現在、核武装を進める中、韓国や日本に脅威を与えている北朝鮮との緊張と対立が、こうして始まったのでした。

　朝鮮戦争によって朝鮮半島の人々の生活が破壊される中、日本は戦争を遂行するアメリカへの物資の供給基地として経済界が活性化し、戦災から復興してゆきます。朝鮮戦争の最中の1951年に、日本はサンフランシスコ平和条約で独立を回復します。そして、日米安全保障条約によって、アメリカの軍事的な傘下におかれることになったのです。その後、経済的に立ち直った日本は60年代以降の高度経済成長を経て経済大国として成長します。

　日本と韓国とが極東地域の経済を牽引する資本主義陣営のパートナーとして、国交を正常化したのは1965年のことでした。

172

The Cold War between East and West facilitated the economic recovery led by the United States

Let us return again to Europe. Soon after the Second World War came to an end in Europe, tensions rose between the communist camp and the capitalist camp. Winston Churchill, who was the prime minister leading Britain during the Second World War, in a speech after he resigned that position became known for describing the division between East and West as the Soviet Union's having lowered an "iron curtain" between the two.

From the American perspective, it was essential to achieve the economic recovery of Europe at the earliest possible time and to oppose communism. In fact, due to the economic chaos of the postwar period, people who had grown disenchanted with capitalist society turned to supporting communism, and there were threats to the continued existence of liberal regimes, even in countries such as Italy and France. Particularly in severely impoverished Greece, opposition against socialist forces intensified. However, Britain, which had originally supported Greece, no longer had the leeway to continue to support that nation. Turkey, too, was under additional stress due to the Soviet Union's attempts to advance from the Black Sea into the Mediterranean Sea.

Faced with this situation, in March 1947, U.S. president Harry Truman put forth the Truman Doctrine, which promised full-fledged support in solving issues in Greece and Turkey. Further, in June of that same year, Secretary of State George C. Marshall presented the European Recovery Program, commonly known as the Marshall Plan, to implement the economic recovery of Europe. The realization of peace by means of American economic assistance on a worldwide scale is referred to as the Pax Americana, comparing it to the Pax Romana, the period of peace in Europe under the Roman Empire.

Naturally enough, the Soviet Union opposed this. In order to strengthen unity in Eastern Europe, in 1947 the Soviet Union created an intelligence exchange organization called the Cominform (Communist Information Bureau), and in 1949 set up COMECON (the Council for Mutual Economic Assistance) for the nations of Eastern Europe, aimed at the economic recovery of socialist countries.

The world was divided into two camps, East and West, pivoting around, respectively, the Soviet Union and America, which stood glaring at each other. Learning the lessons of the world wars, they competed with one another in

東西冷戦は、アメリカによる戦後の経済復興を促進させた

　再びヨーロッパに注目します。ヨーロッパでは戦後早々に共産主義陣営と資本主義陣営との緊張が高まります。第二次世界大戦を指導したイギリスの首相ウィンストン・チャーチルは、首相を退任した後の演説で、東西分断の状況を、ソヴィエト連邦によって鉄のカーテンが下ろされていると表現し、話題になりました。

　アメリカとしては一刻も早く、ヨーロッパの経済復興を成し遂げ、共産主義に対抗する必要に迫られます。実際、戦後の経済混乱の中で、資本主義社会に幻滅した人々が共産党を支援し、イタリアやフランスなどでも自由主義政権の存続が脅かされる事態となっていたのでした。特に経済的疲弊の激しかったギリシアで、社会主義勢力との対立が激化します。しかし、もともとギリシアを支援していたイギリスも、援助を継続する余裕はありませんでした。また、トルコも黒海から地中海へと進出を狙うソ連との新たな緊張に見舞われていました。

　こうした状況を受けて、1947年3月に当時のアメリカ大統領トルーマンは、トルーマン・ドクトリンを発表し、ギリシアやトルコの問題の解決を目指し、本格的な支援を約束します。さらに同年6月に当時の国務長官ジョージ・マーシャルが欧州復興計画、通称マーシャル・プランを発表し、ヨーロッパへの経済援助が実行されたのです。アメリカによる世界規模での経済支援による平和の実現を、人々はローマ帝国で続いた平和「パクス・ロマーナ」になぞらえ、「パクス・アメリカーナ」と呼びました。

　当然ソ連も対抗します。東欧での結束を強めるために1947年にコミンフォルムという情報交換機関を結成し、49年には東ヨーロッパ各国と経済相互援助会議（コメコン）を創設し、社会主義に基づいた経済復興を目指します。

　こうして、世界はアメリカとソ連を軸に、東西両陣営に分かれてにらみ合ったのです。世界大戦の教訓から、それは経済、諜報、外交上のつば競り合いとなりました。東西冷戦と呼ばれた対立です。しかし、

ハリー・トルーマン
Harry S. Truman
(1884–1972)

ジョージ・マーシャル
George C. Marshall
(1880–1959)

時代
20世紀1940～50年代
現代

地域
ヨーロッパ

分類
対立【経済】

キーワード
鉄のカーテン（東西冷戦）
●アメリカによる西欧復興●ソ連による東欧復興
●ドイツの分断

economics, intelligence, and diplomacy. This was referred to as the Cold War between the East and the West. However, there were cases, such as the Korean War and the Vietnam War, in which the conflict between communist powers and capitalist powers transformed from cold war to hot war.

Symbolic of the Cold War was the division of Germany. At the end of the war, Berlin was under the control of both camps. From 1948 into 1949, the Soviet Union blocked the supply route of the Western powers into the city, in what is known as the Berlin Blockade. The Soviet Union then declared the portion of Germany it controlled to be an independent German Democratic Republic, or simply East Germany, in 1949. The western part of Germany under the control of Western powers became the Federal Republic of Germany, and in 1954, it was officially returned to the status of a sovereign state.

The Cold War had a major impact not only on the economy but also on the military balance of the world. In 1949 Western countries established the North Atlantic Treaty Organization (NATO) to strengthen their military alliance. To counter NATO, the Soviet Union formed the Warsaw Treaty Organization in 1955.

173 The ideals of peace and human rights were inconsistent with the concept of nation-states

Following the war, despotic rule under Joseph Stalin continued.

The Soviet Union put energy into the development of nuclear capacity. It successfully created an atomic bomb in 1949 and a hydrogen bomb in 1953, intensifying the nuclear-testing competition with the U.S. The ironic state of affairs in which peace was supposedly protected by the threat of nuclear power continued for a long time. America pursued military agreements, such as NATO, with nations around the globe and sought ascendancy in nuclear development.

For all that, the lessons of two world wars were still valid. Just one step away from war, people made use of the United Nations and made efforts to resolve prickly situations by means of negotiation. Particularly in Europe, which had suffered enormous devastation through armed conflict, the repeated conflicts over centuries between France and Germany progressed toward a reconciliation.

A significant institution was established in the Treaty of Paris in 1951. Based

例えば朝鮮戦争や、後年のベトナム戦争のように、実際に共産主義勢力と資本主義勢力とが戦争をおこし、冷戦が熱い戦争に変化したことも多々ありました。

　冷戦の象徴は、ドイツの分断でした。戦後東西両陣営によって管理されていたベルリンで、1948年から49年にかけて、西側が管理する地域への物資の供給がソ連側によって遮断されるという事態がおきます。ベルリン封鎖という事件です。その後、ソ連の管理下におかれていたドイツはドイツ民主共和国（東ドイツ）として49年に独立します。一方、西側に管理されていた地域は、ドイツ連邦共和国として、1954年に正式に主権を回復したのです。

　冷戦は経済のみならず、軍事的なバランスにも大きな影響を与えました。1949年に、西側諸国は北大西洋条約機構（NATO）を結成し、軍事同盟を強化します。それに対してソ連は、55年にワルシャワ条約機構を結成して、NATOと対抗したのでした。

平和と人権という理想は国家という概念と矛盾した

　戦後、ソヴィエト連邦ではスターリンによる独裁体制が続いていました。
　ソ連は核開発にも力を入れます。1949年には原子爆弾を、53年には水素爆弾の開発に成功し、アメリカとの核実験競争が激化します。核での威嚇によって平和が保たれるという皮肉な情勢が、その後長く続くことになったのです。アメリカは、NATOと同様な軍事協定を世界各地で推し進め、こうした核開発競争でも優位に立とうとしてゆきました。
　とはいえ、二つの世界大戦の教訓はいきていました。人々は戦争の一歩手前で国連などを利用して、交渉によって事態を打開しようと努力していたのです。特に、戦争で甚大な被害に見舞われたヨーロッパでは、数百年にわたって対立を繰り返してきたフランスとドイツの融和が進みました。
　1951年に締結されたパリ条約で一つの機関が誕生します。フランス

時代
20世紀1950年代
現代

地域
ヨーロッパ

分類
経済【統一】

キーワード
ソ連の核保有・西欧の経済統合（後のEU）・平和と人権

on a concept by Jean Monnet, a French diplomat and entrepreneur, French foreign minister Robert Schuman called for a European Coal and Steel Community. In order to prevent France and Germany, which had fought frequently with each other, from ever doing so again, this proposed cooperative entity would cooperate in managing coal mining and steel production, which were essential for fighting a war.

This community expanded, stimulating the economic activities of Europe as a whole, and has continued to function to the present day. This is now the European Union (EU). Following the Marshall Plan, the European Coal and Steel Community became a focal point of development for recovery.

Through two world wars, people learned how priceless peace was. They also developed an awareness of the need to defend the human rights that are trampled on in war and other conflicts. In contemporary society after World War II, we constantly confront the issues of how we can preserve peace and human rights.

Nonetheless, in ethnic conflicts and movements for independence in places throughout the world, these ideals are crushed time and time again. In ancient times, people who were active in regions surrounding large nations that developed in such places as Rome and China alternated between invading and carrying out trade in order to absorb the vitality of the civilizations of these great powers. Gradually, the idea of what a state should be began to sprout in their own regions as well. That vision merged with nationalistic movements, and those people began to build their own countries, imitating the superpowers of the day. Among the examples of this evolution we can include the Roman Empire and the Germanic peoples, as well as China and the northern ethnic peoples, and Japan.

Centuries passed, and in the 20th century, numerous sovereign states emerged and established borders through independence movements from colonial powers in various regions. In delineating some national boundaries, the boundary lines are decided by the lines that the great powers established when they set up their colonies. So the planet now has a larger number of countries than have ever existed before. However, these countries were sometimes manipulated by the Cold War and experienced the rule of dictators before democracy could flourish. And to the present day, many countries have been unable to overcome tensions between ethnic groups, poverty, and economic disparities.

の政治家で実業家としても知られていたジャン・モネの構想に基づいて、フランスの外務大臣ロベール・シューマンが提唱してできあがった欧州石炭鉄鋼共同体です。欧州石炭鉄鋼共同体は、フランスとドイツが幾度となく繰り返してきた戦争を二度と行わないように、戦争に必要な石炭と鉄を、両国を中心とした当事国同士で共同管理するための機関です。

この共同体が拡大し、ヨーロッパ全体の経済活動を活性化し、現在に至りました。それが欧州連合（EU）なのです。ヨーロッパ経済は、マーシャル・プランの後、この欧州石炭鉄鋼共同体の発展を軸にしながら回復していったのでした。

二つの世界大戦を通して、人々は平和の尊さを学びました。そして戦争などで踏みにじられる人権を擁護する意識も芽生えました。第二次世界大戦後の現代社会では、この平和と人権をいかに大切にするかというテーマが常に問いかけられてきたのです。

しかし、そうした理想は世界各地での民族紛争や独立運動などの中でしばしば蹂躙されます。古代、人々はローマや中国などに生まれた巨大国家の周辺で活動をし、巨大国家の文明のジュースを吸収しようと侵略や交易を繰り返していました。次第にそうした地域にも国家観が芽生え、民族運動と融合しながら、当時の超大国を模倣した国づくりが始まります。ローマ帝国とゲルマン人、中国と北方民族や日本などの事例がそれにあたります。

それから長い年月が経ち、20世紀になり、各地での列強からの独立運動を通して、数多くの主権国家が成立し、国境を持ちました。国境はときには列強が植民地を獲得したときに策定した境界線を継承します。こうして地球は過去にはない多数の国家で埋め尽くされたのです。しかし、これらの国々は時には冷戦に翻弄され、民主主義が育つ前に、独裁者が君臨することもありました。また、部族間の緊張、貧困、そして格差を克服できないまま現在に至っている国々も多くあるのです。

174 The Cold War, which gave birth to the Berlin Wall, led to nuclear proliferation

In 1961 a wall was constructed in Berlin as a physical boundary between the eastern half, occupied by the Soviets, and the western half, controlled by the countries of the West. The Berlin Wall thereafter served as a symbol of the Cold War.

Another symbol of the Cold War was the proliferation of nuclear weapons. During the Cold War, America and the Soviet Union used nuclear armaments as a deterrent while carrying out other diplomatic strategies.

Following the construction of the Berlin Wall, the development of nuclear weapons evolved into the actual threat of nuclear warfare during the Cuban Missile Crisis. A revolution occurred in Cuba, a short distance from American waters, and in 1962 evidence showed that the Soviet Union, which supported the revolution, had brought missiles mounted with nuclear weapon into Cuba. The relationship between the U.S.S.R. and the U.S. became highly volatile. We will examine these circumstances in detail momentarily.

It should at all times be emphasized that following the Cuban Missile Crisis, although there were heated diplomatic confrontations between the two countries, there was always an endeavor to avoid actual warfare.

This was the commencement of the so-called thaw in relations. However, both sides continued nuclear development. And, as a result, nuclear armaments proliferated. In 1964 China tested nuclear weapons, and in the 1960s France repeatedly tested its nuclear armaments.

The most serious crisis involving the potential use of nuclear arms arose between India and Pakistan, both of which possessed such weapons, over religious confrontations and territorial issues. Both countries became involved in hostilities over the independence of Bangladesh, and they confronted one another three times in Kashmir in northern India. India became a nuclear power in 1974, and in 1998 Pakistan announced that it had nuclear weapons in order to counter India.

To mitigate the nuclear threat, in 1968, 62 members of the United Nations signed the Treaty on the Non-Proliferation of Nuclear Weapons (NPT).

However, this initiative itself was not perfect. The agreement included no provisions regarding the reduction of nuclear weapons that nations already possessed. There were also states that possessed nuclear weapons without

ベルリンの壁を生み出した冷戦は、核の拡散をもたらした

　1961年にベルリンでは東ドイツから西側への人の流出を食い止めるために、東西の境界線に壁が作られ、人の行き来を厳しく制限します。その後、ベルリンの壁は冷戦の象徴として記憶に残ることになったのです。

　冷戦時代のもうひとつの象徴は核兵器の拡散でした。冷戦時代、アメリカとソヴィエト連邦は核を抑止力とし、相手を威嚇しながら外交戦略を遂行しました。

　ベルリンの壁の建設の後、核開発が実際の核戦争の脅威へと繋がったのが、キューバ危機でした。アメリカの隣国キューバで革命がおこり、1962年に革命を支援するソ連が、核弾頭を搭載したミサイルをキューバに搬入していた事実が判明したのです。アメリカとソ連が一触即発の状態になったのです。この状況については後でさらに詳しく説明します。

　キューバ危機の後、アメリカとソ連とはお互いに外交上は激しく衝突しながらも、戦争を回避するという点では常に協調してゆきます。

　いわゆる「雪解け」の始まりでした。しかし、双方とも核開発は継続します。その影響もあって、核は拡散し続けます。1964年には中国が、フランスも60年代に何度も核実験を繰り返しました。

　そして、現実の核戦争の危機という意味でいうならば、宗教的な対立に加え、領土問題も抱えていたインドとパキスタンの双方が核を保有したことがあげられます。両国は、パキスタンからのバングラデシュの独立をめぐる争いや、インド北部のカシミールの領有権問題で3度も戦争を起こしています。インドは1974年に核武装します。パキスタンがインドに対抗して核の保有を宣言したのは98年のことでした。

　核の脅威を緩和するために、1968年に国連加盟国62カ国によって調印されたのが核拡散防止条約です。

　しかし、この条約自体完璧なものではありませんでした。条約は既存の核保有国の核軍縮に対して効果を発揮できないのです。また、インドやパキスタンのように条約の批准を拒否したまま核を保有してい

時代
20世紀1960年代
現代

地域
世界

分類
対立【国際】

キーワード
冷戦の進化とベルリンの壁・キューバ危機・インドとパキスタンの対立・核兵器の拡散

ratifying the treaty, such as India and Pakistan, and there was no effective means for preventing the proliferation of nuclear technology.

One also should not forget that there are countries in highly contested regions of the world that are suspected of possessing nuclear weapons. Suspicions regarding the possible possession of nuclear arms in countries such as Israel and Iran are one factor resulting in the instability of the Middle East.

It is known that at present, North Korea, which has withdrawn from the agreement, has tested both nuclear weapons and missiles capable of carrying them.

Humankind is still unable to extract itself from the temptations of employing nuclear threats as weapons of mass destruction in diplomatic relations. Japan, which experienced exposure to radioactivity in the bombings of Hiroshima and Nagasaki, can surely be called the nation most sensitive to nuclear threats. The proliferation of nuclear armaments during the Cold War, even now that more than 30 years have passed since the collapse of the Berlin Wall, remains the ultimate weapon for the destruction of the world.

175 Antagonism between Israel and the Arabic nations has given rise to new discord in the Middle East

Humanity has yet to solve the dilemma of ethnic self-determination versus maintaining nation-states, and the Middle East has repeatedly suffered tragedies while this issue remains unresolved.

We refer to believers in Judaism as the Jewish people. Over their long history, they have been persecuted by Christian societies. Therefore, from the beginning of the 20th century, in response to the call to return to the holy city of Jerusalem and form a country of their own, a large number of Jewish people migrated to the Middle East.

The Middle East was a region where Arabs lived, seeking independence from the Ottoman Empire.

At the same time that the weakening of the Ottoman Empire accelerated, in order to drive a wedge into Germany's efforts to advance into the region, as already mentioned, Britain was promoting the independence of both the Jewish

る国家が存在し、核技術の流出にも有効な手段が打てないのです。

　さらに、核を保有しているのではという疑惑を投げかけられている国家が紛争多発地域にあることも忘れてはなりません。イスラエル、イランなどへの核保有疑惑は、中東の不安定要因の一つでもあるのです。

　そして現在、核拡散防止条約から脱退した北朝鮮は、核兵器と核の搭載が可能なミサイルの発射実験を行っていることは周知の通りです。

　大量破壊兵器である核を外交の威嚇として使用する誘惑から、人類は未だに抜け出せないのです。広島と長崎での被爆を経験した日本は、核の脅威に最も敏感な国といえましょう。冷戦時代に拡散した核は、ベルリンの壁が崩壊して30年以上経った現在でも、世界を破壊する最終兵器となっているのです。

「原爆ドーム」の名で知られる広島平和記念碑
The Hiroshima Peace Memorial, also known as the Atomic Bomb Dome

イスラエルとアラブ諸国との対立が新たな混乱を中東にもたらした

　実は人類は、民族の自立か国家の維持かという課題を未だ解決できないでいます。この問題を解決できないままに、悲劇を繰り返してきたのが中東です。

　ユダヤ教を信奉する人々を我々はユダヤ人と呼んでいます。彼らは長い間キリスト教社会の中で迫害を受けてきました。そこで、聖地エルサレムに帰還し、自らの国を作ろうというスローガンのもと、20世紀初頭から多くのユダヤ人が中東へ移住したのです。

　中東は、オスマン帝国からの独立を目指すアラブの人々の住む地域でした。

　オスマン帝国の弱体化を促進すると同時に、当時中東への進出を狙っていたドイツに楔を打ちたかったイギリスは、ユダヤ系、アラブ系双方の人々に民族の自立を促していったことは既に述べました。

時代
20世紀全般
現代

地域
中東

分類
戦争【民族】

キーワード
ユダヤ人の聖地回復運動・イスラエル建国・アラブ諸国の独立・中東戦争の勃発

people and the Arabs.

Following the end of World War I, when the Ottoman Empire collapsed, Britain was appointed by the League of Nations to administer the Middle East. During this period, migration of Jews was expedited, as was the Arab movement for independence. In 1921 with Britain's backing, Iraq became the Kingdom of Iraq. The following year Egypt achieved independence as a constitutional monarchy.

Just before and after World War II, Iraq and Egypt both attempted to divest themselves of British influence.

In the middle of this regeneration of Arab peoples, the Jewish people who settled in Palestine began to establish a state. In 1948 Israel was established as a nation-state. In the background of this development was the Holocaust perpetrated by Nazi Germany. The actions of the Jewish people developed into discord with the Arabic people who were already living in Palestine.

The year Israel was established, the First Arab-Israeli War broke out between the Arab states and Israel. Israel emerged victorious and gained control over the Palestinian territories, becoming a nation-state. Arabs who had lost their homes and lands as a result of this conflict ended up as Palestinian refugees, and they thereafter bitterly opposed Israel. That is one source of the various problems in the Middle East today.

In 1956 Egypt under the leadership of President Gamal Abdel Nasser declared the nationalization of the Suez Canal to oppose Britain and France. In 1958 Nasser briefly succeeded in forming the Arab Union with Syria, seeking to unify the Middle East.

During the depths of the Cold War, the Soviet Union immediately offered support to this movement. The Soviets supplied weapons. However, the United Arab Republic was opposed by Iraq, and there was opposition to Egypt within Syria, so the Republic collapsed within three years.

During this period, the Ba'ath Party, embracing socialist ideology and Arab nationalism, rose to power in Iraq and Syria. They advocated for the resolution of the Palestinian refugee problem through the elimination of Israel and sought to unify the Middle East as an Islamic society.

第一次世界大戦後、オスマン帝国が崩壊すると、イギリスは国際連盟から中東の統治を委任されます。その中で、ユダヤ人の移住の促進と、アラブ諸国の独立運動が共に推し進められます。1921年にイラクがイギリスの支援でイラク王国を建国。翌年にはエジプトもエジプト王国として独立します。

　第二次世界大戦の前後、イラクもエジプトもイギリスの影響力からの離脱を試みながら共和政に移行します。

　こうしたアラブの再生の中、パレスチナ地域に入植してきたユダヤ系の人々が国家建設を始めたのです。1948年にイスラエルが建国します。背景にはナチスドイツでのホロコーストもありました。ユダヤ系の人々の動きは、そこに居住していたアラブ人との摩擦へと発展します。

　イスラエル建国の年、アラブ諸国とイスラエルとが第一次中東戦争をおこします。それを戦い抜き、軍事力をつけたイスラエルは、国家としてパレスチナ一帯を統治したのです。戦争によって家と土地を失ったアラブ系の人々がパレスチナ難民となり、その後イスラエルと厳しく対立したのです。これが現在の中東での様々な問題の原因のひとつとなりました。

　1956年、エジプトではナセル大統領の指導のもとで、スエズ運河の国有化を宣言し、イギリスやフランスに対抗します。そしてシリアと共同して58年にアラブ連合を発足させ、中東地域の統一を目指したのです。

　冷戦のさなか、ソヴィエト連邦は即座にこの動きに呼応。武器の供与を行いました。しかし、アラブ連合はイラクの反発と、シリア内部のエジプトへの反抗から3年で崩壊してしまいます。

　こうした中で、社会主義の理念を取り入れ、アラブ民族主義の元、中東地域をイスラム社会で統一してゆこうというバース党がイラクやシリアで台頭します。彼らは、イスラエルを排除することで、パレスチナ難民の問題の解決を提唱したのです。

176 The pivot of the Middle East problem moved from Palestine to Iraq

Let us continue our consideration of the situation in the Middle East.

At the end of World War II, the independence movement in Algeria, which was under French control, grew more intense. Fearing that it would lose its rights and interests in North Africa due to the rise of Arabic society, France supported Israel. In reaction to Egypt's nationalization of the Suez Canal, Britain also supported Israel. Receiving this support and wanting to eliminate the threat of the Arab states, Israel invaded Egypt in 1956. This was the Suez crisis, also known as the Second Arab-Israeli War. In this conflict, America, fearing that an isolated Egypt might turn to the Soviet Union, interceded in order to bring the fighting to an end. As a result, Egypt officially nationalized the Suez Canal. And in passing we note that Algeria became independent in 1962.

In 1967, however, Israel once again carried out a lightning invasion against the Arabs. As a result of the Six-Day War, or the Third Arab-Israeli War, Israel completely took over Palestine. Egypt and Syria carried out a reprisal against Israel in 1973. The Fourth Arab-Israeli War is widely referred to as the Yom Kippur War. Upon the commencement of this war, nations in the Middle East implemented harsh restrictions on the export of petroleum to nations supporting Israel, confronting the nations of the West with an economic crisis referred to as the oil shock.

In order to bring a solution to the bogged-down Middle East affairs, President Jimmy Carter intervened, and in 1979 Egypt and Israel reached a peace agreement. However, the issue of the Palestinian refugees came to symbolize anti-Western sentiments among Arabic peoples. From that point onward, Yasser Arafat led the Palestine Liberation Organization (PLO) in a deeply rooted resistance movement against Israel.

In Iran, the Iranian Revolution carried out by the Shia faction in 1979 overthrew the Western-leaning monarchy. Neighboring Iraq, led by Saddam Hussein of the Ba'ath Party of the Sunni faction established a dictatorial regime. In addition to the religious conflict between Iraq and Iran, there was also a confrontation over territory. In 1980 Iraq took up arms against Iran. Fearing a spread of the Iranian Revolution to other countries, the U.S. and the U.S.S.R. supported Iraq. That in turn increased resentment in Syria and Libya, which opposed their support. The resulting Iran-Iraq War continued until 1988 ending in a stand-off.

中東問題はパレスチナからイラクへと
その軸を移していった

　さらに中東の情勢を追いかけます。

　第二次世界大戦が終わると、フランスが支配していたアルジェリアでの独立運動が激化します。フランスは、アラブ社会の台頭によって北アフリカでの利権を失うことを恐れ、イスラエルを支援します。イギリスも、エジプトがスエズ運河を国有化したことに反発し、イスラエルへ援助を行います。この支援を受け、アラブ諸国の脅威を排除したいイスラエルは、1956年にエジプトに侵攻します。これが第二次中東戦争です。この戦争は、エジプトが孤立しソヴィエト連邦側に走ることを恐れたアメリカの仲介で終結します。これによって、エジプトは正式にスエズ運河を国有化したのです。ちなみに、アルジェリアは1962年に独立しました。

　しかし、1967年に、イスラエルは再び電撃的にアラブ側に侵攻します。第三次中東戦争と呼ばれるこの戦闘で、パレスチナは完全にイスラエルに掌握されることになったのです。エジプトやシリアによるイスラエルへの報復が行われたのは1973年のことでした。第四次中東戦争です。この戦争にあたって、中東諸国がイスラエルを支援する国家への石油の輸出を厳しく制限し、西欧諸国はオイルショックと呼ばれる経済危機に見舞われたのです。

　泥沼化した中東問題を解決するために、当時のアメリカの大統領ジミー・カーターが再び調停を行い、1979年にエジプトとイスラエルとの和平協定が成立します。しかし、パレスチナ難民の問題は、アラブの人々の反西欧意識の象徴となりました。そして、その後もヤセル・アラファト率いるパレスチナ解放機構は、イスラエルへの根強い抵抗運動を展開していったのです。

　一方、イランでは1979年にシーア派のイラン革命がおき、西欧よりの王政が打倒されます。隣国イラクはスンナ派でバース党を指導するサダム・フセインが独裁政権を打ち立てていました。宗派対立に加え、イラクとイラン間には領土問題がありました。1980年にイラクがイランに対して戦端を開きます。イラン革命の伝播を恐れるアメリカやソ連はイラクを支持。それに反発したシリアやリビアなどとも緊張が高まります。イラン・イラク戦争は、その後硬直状態に陥ったまま、1988年まで続いたのです。

時代
20世紀後半
現代

地域
中東

分類
戦争【国際】

キーワード
アルジェリア独立・度重なる中東戦争・イランのシーア派革命・イラン・イラク戦争

Through the Iran-Iraq War, Saddam Hussein, who received American support, became a strong military presence in the Middle East as head of a military dictatorship. It became known that under his regime ethnic Kurds had been massacred, and in 1990 Iraq carried out a military action aimed at realizing a long-held desire to annex Kuwait. This triggered America's estrangement from Iraq.

The Middle East situation shifted greatly from a focus on discord between Egypt and Israel over the establishment of the latter to a focus on conflict between America and Iraq.

177 The Vietnam War became a turning point for the Pax Americana

Whereas the Middle East before World War II was basically a competition for interests and rights between the powers of the West, after the war, following the first impact of the Cold War between East and West, there were complex, frequent changes.

Both before and after the war, the region of Central and South America, including the Caribbean, continued to be influenced by the United States. When the Cold War began, the Organization of American States (OAS) was formed under the leadership of the United States in 1951.

In Central and South America, there was resistance against long-term political instability, and in fact there were frequent anti-American movements. And as has already been touched upon, a communist administration came into existence in Cuba in 1959, led by Fidel Castro.

It came as a big shock that a communist government sprang up so close to the United States. Not only that, but Cuba actively dispatched people like Ernesto Che Guevara to South America to export the revolution to countries there. America broke off relations with Cuba and initiated an economic blockade of the island nation. The Soviet Union's support of Cuba in response to this gave rise to highly volatile relations between America and the Soviet Union.

In the case of the Cuban Missile Crisis, American President John F. Kennedy and Russian Premier Nikita Khrushchev negotiated and were somehow able to prevent warfare from breaking out.

イラン・イラク戦争を通して、アメリカの支援を受けたサダム・フセインは軍事独裁政権として中東に強いプレゼンスを持つようになったのです。そして、その政権下で実施されたクルド人虐殺事件などが国際社会に暴かれる中、イラクは1990年に宿願であったクウェートの併合を目指し、軍事行動をおこしたのです。これがアメリカのイラクからの離反の引き金になりました。

中東情勢は、イスラエル建国をめぐるエジプトとイスラエルの確執から、アメリカとイラクの対立へと、混迷の軸が大きく変化していったのです。

ベトナム戦争はパクス・アメリカーナの転換点となった

このように、中東は戦前の西欧列強の利害の対立、戦後の東西冷戦の洗礼を受けながら、複雑に変化を繰り返してゆきました。

一方、カリブ海を含む中南米は、戦前戦後を通してアメリカの強い影響下におかれていました。冷戦が始まると、アメリカが主導して1951年には米州機構が結成されます。

中南米では、長引く政情不安や封建的な地主制度に反発し、反米運動が頻発していたのも事実です。そしてすでに解説したように、1959年にキューバにフィデル・カストロによって共産主義政権が誕生したのです。

アメリカのすぐそばに共産主義政権が誕生したことは大きな衝撃でした。しかもキューバはチェ・ゲバラなどを南米に派遣して、革命の輸出にも積極的でした。アメリカはキューバと断交し、経済封鎖を行います。これに対してソヴィエト連邦がキューバを支援したことが、アメリカとソ連とに一触即発の緊張を生み出しました。

キューバ危機の場合、アメリカのケネディ大統領と当時のソ連の指導者フルシチョフ首相との交渉もあり、戦闘はなんとか回避されました。

時代
20世紀後半
現代

地域
キューバ・ベトナム

分類
対立【戦争】

キーワード
キューバ危機・ベトナム戦争の勃発・北ベトナムの勝利とアメリカ撤退

On the contrary, tensions during the Cold War did lead to war elsewhere—in Vietnam. Upon achieving independence from France, Vietnam became divided into the Democratic Republic of Vietnam (North Vietnam) under the leadership of Ho Chi Minh and the State of Vietnam, supported by France. When France withdrew from Vietnam, with American support the anti-communist forces in the south established the Republic of Vietnam (South Vietnam) in 1955.

In response to this, within the territory of South Vietnam the National Front for the Liberation of the South (NLF) was formed for the reunification of Vietnam, and it began a guerrilla war to achieve that goal. America then began introducing serious military support to protect South Vietnam. In 1965 the American air force commenced a bombing campaign in North Vietnam. Deploying ground troops as well, America joined in the actual fighting alongside allies from Korea and elsewhere. American devoted all of its energies toward protecting South Vietnam from falling into the hands of the communists.

However, with support from the Soviet Union and China, the army of North Vietnam and the NLF put up determined resistance, much to the consternation of the Americans. With the war in a quagmire, anti-war public opinion in America strengthened. Further, when massacres of civilians by American troops on the battlefields were made public in the media, America became the target of international criticism. From the 1960s into the 1970s, the Vietnam War became a symbol of American hegemony, criticized around the world by intellectuals, students, and political figures.

Faced with strong public disapproval of a war with no exit, America signed the Paris Peace Accords in 1973 and withdrew from Vietnam. Saigon fell in April 1975, Vietnam was reunified in 1976, and the Socialist Republic of Vietnam came into existence. The human and economic sacrifices America had made were enormous.

America's withdrawal from Vietnam led to the establishment of socialist governments in Cambodia and Laos thereafter. And from that point forward, it was China that developed great influence in the Asian region.

反対に、冷戦下の緊張が実際の戦争となったのがベトナムでした。フランスからの独立にあたって、ベトナムはホー・チ・ミン率いるベトナム民主共和国（北ベトナム）と、フランスの支援を受けたベトナム国とに分断されてしまいます。その後フランスがベトナムを放棄すると、アメリカの支援で反共政府として南部にベトナム共和国（南ベトナム）が建国します。1955年のことでした。

　これに対して、ベトナムの統一を求めて南ベトナム領内に成立した南ベトナム解放民族戦線がゲリラ戦を展開すると、アメリカは南ベトナムを防衛するために本格的な軍事介入を行ったのです。1965年にアメリカ軍は北爆と呼ばれる北ベトナムへの空爆を開始。地上軍も展開させ、アメリカと同盟関係にある韓国なども戦争に参加します。アメリカは総力をあげてベトナムの共産化を防ごうとしたのです。

　しかし、ソ連や中国に支援された北ベトナム軍とベトナム民族解放戦線は頑強に抵抗し、アメリカ軍を悩ませます。泥沼化した戦争にアメリカ国内でも反戦を求める世論が高まります。また、戦場でのアメリカ軍の残虐行為などが報道され、国際的な非難の対象ともなりました。60年代から70年代にかけて、ベトナム戦争はアメリカの覇権を象徴する戦争として、世界中の知識人や学生、さらには政治家による批判にさらされたのです。

　出口の見えない戦争に抗議する強い世論に押され、アメリカは1973年にパリ和平協定に調印し撤退します。そして、1975年4月のサイゴン陥落を経て、1976年にベトナムは統一され、ベトナム社会主義共和国が誕生します。アメリカが払った人的経済的犠牲は莫大でした。

　ベトナムからのアメリカの撤退は、その後カンボジアやラオスなどでの社会主義政権誕生の原因にもなりました。そうしたアジアでの情勢に大きな影響を与え始めたのが、中国だったのです。

178 Awareness of "civil rights" changed American society

Humankind has undergone countless wars to date. Among them, World War II, which brought about the greatest wide-scale slaughter and damage, left behind the moral lesson that it is important to protect the dignity of human beings. That lesson has been passed down through various systems and international laws. As one example, it can be said that one legacy is the Japanese Constitution, which set great value on fundamental human rights, the sovereignty of the people, and the negation of wars of aggression.

Following World War II, America assumed a position of leadership in the world, becoming the standard-bearer of the community of free nations. However, in domestic affairs, America continued to tolerate racial discrimination, and socio-economic inequality was commonplace.

Particularly in the American South, discrimination against Black people remained uncorrected. Slaves were freed as a result of the Civil War, but once the war came to an end, Black people suffered from poverty and endured obvious discrimination in the workplace and in public facilities. This treatment was not limited to people of African descent. People of color who immigrated to the United States—including people of Japanese heritage—as well as Native American peoples were also discriminated against.

In World War II, non-white people also fought on the American side. But even after the war, social conditions remained unimproved.

In December 1955, in the southern city of Montgomery, Alabama, a Black woman who had boarded a city bus refused to surrender her seat to a white person who got on the bus. The Black woman was subsequently arrested for breaking a local law over seating on the bus. With this incident as a spark, demonstrations strongly protesting racial discrimination spread throughout America. In particular, Reverend Martin Luther King Jr., inspired by Mahatma Gandhi, the father of Indian independence, launched a nonviolent movement of civil disobedience and garnered significant support.

Demanding that all people be treated equally under the law, their movement is called the civil rights movement. The movement met with various obstructions, including violence and murder by lynching, by people who reacted against their

「公民権」という意識がアメリカ社会を変革した

　人類は、数えきれない戦争を経験して、現在に至っています。中でも最も大規模な殺戮と破壊が行われた第二次世界大戦は、我々に人間の尊厳を守ることの大切さを教訓として残しました。その教訓は、さまざまな制度や国際法などによって受け継がれようとしています。例えば、基本的人権の尊重や国民主権を明記し、侵略戦争を否定した日本国憲法もそうした遺産の一つといえます。

　戦後、アメリカは世界に対してリーダーシップをとり、自由主義陣営の旗手となりました。しかし、アメリカ国内はというと、まだまだ人種差別が黙認され、社会的な不平等が横行していたのです。

　特に南部を中心に、アフリカ系アメリカ人への差別が是正されずにいました。アメリカでは南北戦争で奴隷は解放されましたが、その後もアフリカ系の人々は貧困に苦しみ、職場や公共施設などでの歴然とした差別に苦しんでいたのです。さらに黒人に限らず、アメリカに移民してきた日系移民などの有色人種、加えてネイティブ・アメリカンなども同様の差別を受けていました。

　第二次世界大戦では、非白人系の人々もアメリカのために戦いました。しかし、戦後も社会の状況は改善されなかったのです。

　1955年12月に、南部の都市モンゴメリーで、市営バスに乗車していた黒人女性が白人系の人に席を譲らなかったことで逮捕される事件がおきました。これを皮切りに、全米で人種差別に対する強い抗議行動が巻きおこったのです。特に、マーティン・ルーサー・キング牧師はインドの独立の父マハトマ・ガンディーにならい、非暴力と不服従による運動を展開し、多くの支持を集めます。

　全ての人が法の下での平等に扱われるように求めた、彼らの運動を公民権運動と呼んでいます。公民権運動は、それに反発する人々の暴力やリンチ事件など、様々な妨

時代
**20世紀後半
現代**

地域
アメリカ合衆国

分類
人権【社会】

キーワード
自由の国アメリカでの差別・公民権運動の開始・ベトナム反戦運動

1963年8月28日、ワシントン大行進で「I Have a Dream（私には夢がある）」と演説するマーティン・ルーサー・キング牧師。

Martin Luther King Jr. giving his "I Have a Dream" speech during the March on Washington in Washington, D.C., on 28 August, 1963.

demands. Dr. King was himself assassinated in 1968. Having said this, successive presidents showed at least a degree of support for the aims of the civil rights movement, including presidents Dwight Eisenhower, John F. Kennedy, and Lyndon Johnson. The Civil Rights Act of 1964 officially abolished systematic racial discrimination.

After that, expanding anti-war demonstrations against the chronic Vietnam War and protest demonstrations on behalf of eliminating racial discrimination across the nation led to a social movement that questioned exactly what kind of nation America should be.

Without question, the Vietnam War was a serious defeat for America. At home, American cities were impoverished and crime reached epidemic proportions. While their civil rights were being safeguarded, African Americans found it difficult to improve their economic circumstances. The social division between the wealthy and the poor—economic disparity—remains a serious issue even today. Having said this, American society attempted to reduce racial discrimination with the enactment of the Civil Rights Act, and as a result of the expansion and penetration of systems thereafter, major changes have been implemented. That various races are able to coexist with far less discrimination has become the origin of a new American strength.

179 The civil rights movement created the foundation of a society that values diversity

With the establishment of the Civil Rights Act in America and the establishment of a social system that accepts various races and cultures, humankind attained a new form of wisdom. Through 10,000 years of history, the human species has fostered and merged numerous cultures, and now people recognize anew that an infinite number of different cultures exist around the world.

Immigrants from around the world come to America. They came from the Old World, bringing their individual lifestyles, traditions, and wisdom. There people became one in the modern nation called America, and by blending together, they cultivated new wisdom and new culture. That is, when they became conscious of something that was different, they accepted the culture that they themselves did not already possess, recognizing that by accepting it, they would build an even

害にさらされます。キング牧師自身も1968年に凶弾に倒れました。とはいえ、アイゼンハワー、ケネディ、ジョンソンといった歴代の大統領が公民権運動を支持。1964年に、人種差別を制度上撤廃した公民権法が制定されたのです。

その後、慢性化したベトナム戦争への広範な反戦運動と、人種差別を改善してゆこうとする抗議行動によって、アメリカという国家のあり方そのものに疑問を投げかける社会運動が各地で展開されたのです。

確かにベトナム戦争の挫折は深刻でした。都市は疲弊し、犯罪も多発。公民権に保護されながらも、アフリカ系アメリカ人が経済的に立ち直ることはなかなかできませんでした。そうした貧富の差などの社会的分断は、現在も深刻な課題となっているのです。とはいえ、アメリカ社会は公民権法の制定で人種差別の撤廃を試み、その後その制度を拡大浸透させることで、大きく変化しました。多様な人種がはるかに少ない差別で共存できるようになったことが、アメリカの新たなパワーの源泉となったのです。

公民権運動は、その後の多様性を尊重する社会の下地を作った

アメリカでの公民権法の導入と、多様な人種や文化を受容する社会システムの導入は、人類に新たな知恵を与えました。この1万年の歴史を通じて人類が様々な文化を育て、融合させ、異なる文化がこの地球に無数に存在することを、人々に再認識させたことです。

アメリカには世界から移民がきます。彼らはそれぞれのライフスタイルや伝統、知恵をもって旧大陸からやってきたのです。こうした人々がアメリカという近代国家で一つになり、溶け合うことで新たな知恵や文化が育まれます。つまり、異なることを認識したとき、人々はその異なることからお互いに無い文化を受容しあい、より強い文明を築けるのだということを改めて理解したのです。

時代
20世紀後半〜21世紀
現代

地域
アメリカ合衆国・ヨーロッパ

分類
人権【社会】

キーワード
移民の国アメリカ・多様性の承認・自由と人権

stronger one.

Humankind recognized this in the past as well. There are any number of examples of countries that became wealthy through the abilities of various peoples coming together, such as the consecutive dynasties in China, which were administered by the gathering together of nomadic peoples and the Han Chinese, and the Kingdom of Poland in the Middle Ages being tolerant of Jewish people. However, for the most part, these benefits were not put to use in a systematic manner. Rather than doing that, differences between people gave rise to pathways leading to confrontation and exclusion.

America was the first country that was clearly able to envision the possibility that by overcoming discrimination in society, the diversity of humankind could create the future.

In places like Silicon Valley that lead the high-tech industry in the United States, various ideas from Asia, Latin America, Africa, Eastern Europe, and other parts of the world come together, refining new concepts that shape the future of humanity. This culture which sets store by diversity, since the enactment of the Civil Rights Act became accepted practice in America, and through the coming and going of immigrants, has spread throughout the world.

This way of thinking has also become rooted in the EU, in which the countries of Europe have become united. Newly rising countries like Canada and Australia have also cast aside their past views that white culture is superior to any other kind.

In fact, these countries are even more actively accepting diverse cultures than America has been.

In Australia, an independent nation in the Pacific which was discovered in early-modern times and became a member of the Commonwealth of Nations, there was long-lasting antagonism between the Aboriginal Peoples and South Pacific culture on the one side, and white settlers from Britain on the other side. In the present day, based on the fundamental belief in civil rights, attempts at achieving reconciliation between multiple cultures have been pursued more actively. In fact, in recent years the number of immigrants from Asia to Australia has increased.

Human beings have only recently started this experiment. This idea has only been a topic for consideration since the 19th century, and it may be the sole means by which nationalism and democracy can be harmonized.

Currently, many countries and regions are continuing the process, by trial and

人類は、過去にもこのことにうすうす気付いていました。遊牧民族と漢民族が集まり運営した歴代の中国の帝国や、ユダヤ系に寛容だった中世のポーランド王国など、多様な人々の力で国家が豊かになった事例はいくつもあります。しかし、多くはその効用を制度上で活用できませんでした。むしろ、人と人とが異なることは、対立と排除のベクトルをも生み出していました。

　アメリカは、社会での差別を乗り越えたとき、その向こうに人類の多様性が未来を作ることをはっきりとビジョン化できた最初の国になったのです。
　アメリカのハイテク産業を牽引するシリコンバレーなどには、アジア各地、中南米、アフリカ、東欧など世界中の知恵が集まり、人類の未来をつくる新たな発想を磨いています。この多様性を尊重する文化が公民権法の制定以来、アメリカでは常識となり、それが移民の行き来を通して世界に拡散していったのです。

　ヨーロッパの国々が手を結んだEUの中にもこうした発想が根付いてきました。カナダやオーストラリアなど、新興の国家でも白人の文化のみに優越性を見ることは過去のこととして捨て去られました。

　実際、これらの国ではアメリカよりも、多様な文化への受容に積極的です。
　近世に発見され、イギリス連邦の一つとして自立した太平洋の国家オーストラリアは、先住民や南太平洋の文化と、イギリスから移住してきた白人系の人々とが長年対立していました。今では公民権の発想の元で、そうした多文化の融和の試みに積極的です。加えて、アジアからの移住者も近年増え続けたのです。

　人類のこうした新たな試みは、まだ始まったばかりです。この発想は19世紀以来の課題であった、民族主義と民主主義との融和につながってゆく唯一の方途かもしれません。
　現在、人種や肌の色のみならず、性別や年齢、疾病の有無や、同性

error, in order to grant equal rights not only based on race or skin color but also in terms of gender, age, presence or absence of illness, and sexual orientation, among others. There is also a growing focus on the cultural differences in communication of people from diverse cultural backgrounds. With World War II, society first began to make a change by overcoming the negative cycle created by fear and hatred of anything and anyone that was different.

180 After the Great Proletarian Cultural Revolution, China became a giant

While America was being shaken by the civil rights movement and troubled by the Vietnam War, China was experiencing a social movement that overturned everything that had been conventional until then.

Following the establishment of the People's Republic of China (PRC) in 1949, the country's most urgent task was to revive the economy, which had been impoverished by all the international wars and civil wars it had experienced to that time.

In the 1950s Mao Zedong deployed the Great Leap Forward, aiming to increase production on a nation-wide scale. The campaign completely rejected capitalism and, under the system of a socialist state, emphasized only numerical targets, pushing forcefully for economic reforms. It failed. Farming villages were ruined, and it is believed that tens of millions of people died of starvation.

During that time, China invaded Tibet and annexed it. The 14th Dalai Lama, the religious leader of Tibet, took refuge in India, and relations between India and China became strained. In the Soviet Union, in 1953, Stalin died, and after the Cold War between the Soviet Union and America grew colder, steps toward the acceptance of some sort of coexistence began to appear.

This in turn led to antagonism between the Soviet Union and China, the latter aiming at a heavy-handed form of communism. The Soviet Union then cut off all economic and technological support for China.

In order to avoid political responsibility for these internal and external disruptions and to maintain the political base, the Cultural Revolution, which began in 1966, was developed with Mao Zedong as its leader.

Through the Cultural Revolution, Mao concentrated his power within the

愛者などへも平等に権利が与えられるよう、多くの国や地域で試行錯誤が続いています。また、異なる文化背景を持つ人々のコミュニケーション文化の違いにもスポットがあてられるようになりました。第二次世界大戦で人類が目の当たりにした異なる者への憎悪が生み出す負のサイクルを克服すべく、社会が変化を始めたのです。

中国は文化大革命を経て巨人へと成長を始めた

アメリカが公民権運動に揺れ、ベトナム戦争に苦しんでいた頃、中国でもそれまでの常識を覆す、社会運動がおこっていました。

1949年に中華人民共和国が建国して以来、中国はそれまでの戦争や内戦で疲弊した経済の立て直しが直近の課題となっていました。

50年代になると、毛沢東は大躍進運動を展開し、全国規模での生産力の向上に取り組みます。しかし、この試みは資本主義を完全に否定し、社会主義国家の制度のもとで、数値目標のみを重視し強引に経済改革を推し進めたことで、失敗します。農村は荒廃し、数千万人とよばれる餓死者をだしたのです。

当時中国は、チベットに侵攻し中国に取り込みます。チベットの宗教的指導者であったダライ・ラマ14世はインドに亡命し、中国とインドとの緊張も高まりました。また、ソヴィエト連邦は1953年にスターリンが死去し、冷戦でのアメリカとの対立が深刻化する中で、次第に米ソ共存の道を模索し始めます。

この路線は、強権的な共産主義化を目指す中国との対立を生み、ソ連は中国への経済、技術支援を中止します。

こうした内外での混乱による政治責任を回避し、政治的基盤を維持するために、毛沢東を指導者として展開されたのが、1966年から始まった文化大革命だったのです。

文化大革命を通し、中国共産党は毛沢東に権力を集中し、政敵を資

時代
20世紀1950〜70年代現代

地域
中国

分類
革命【政治】

キーワード
社会主義中国・チベット動乱・中ソ対立・文化大革命による混乱・改革開放路線へ

Chinese Communist Party, enforcing discipline over political adversaries and labelling those who sought compromise with capitalism "capitalist roaders." The base supporting this revolution was composed of youth groups called the Red Guards. Affirming the use of violence and vigorously seeking to exclude all remnants of capitalist thought and activity, their activities escalated and even exceeded Mao's original intentions. In workplaces and educational institutions, administrators were harshly condemned. The deep-rooted traditions of ancient cultural heritage were destroyed and lost forever.

The Cultural Revolution negated and demolished the traditional value system and moral sense that had been cultivated in China, including that of Confucianism.

In 1976 Mao died, and the Cultural Revolution, which had lasted over a decade, came to an end. Following this, Deng Xiaoping led economic reforms in China that introduced capitalism, and the Chinese economy made rapid strides. China has since grown into a superpower, and it can now boast of being the world's second-largest economy.

However, in China, traditional values that were lost during the Cultural Revolution have not been fully regained, and the country has continued to undergo growth and development. At present, China as a country is still at a loss over what kind of values it should uphold in dealing with the rest of the world. Just as America underwent major changes following the establishment of the Civil Rights Act, the Cultural Revolution greatly impacted China, now another superpower.

181 The post-war period witnessed the recovery of the Far East and Europe, which also had an impact on the presence of the United States

Following the Korean War, Korea was troubled by an economic slump. As a result of a democratization movement, the administration of Rhee Syngman collapsed. In 1961 Park Chung-hee led a military coup d'état and set up an autocratic regime.

Park strengthened the country's military alliance with America, and in 1965 he normalized diplomatic relations with Japan, which had been a pending issue, through the conclusion of the Treaty on Basic Relations between Japan and the Republic of Korea.

本主義に妥協しようとした「走資派」として粛清してゆきます。改革を底辺で担ったのは紅衛兵と呼ばれる青年団でした。暴力を肯定し、資本主義を徹底的に排除しようとした試みは、現場にいけばいくほどエスカレートし、毛沢東の意図を超えて暴走します。職場や教育施設などでも管理者が厳しい糾弾を受け、膨大な文化遺産が旧来の因習として破壊され、失われました。犠牲者の数は今でも特定できません。

　文化大革命は、それまで中国に培われてきた儒教をはじめとする伝統的な価値観、道徳観を否定し、破壊したのです。
　1976年に毛沢東が死去したことで、10年以上に及ぶ文化大革命は終息します。その後、中国は鄧小平による資本主義を導入した経済改革が進み、中国経済は飛躍的な成長を遂げます。今では、中国は世界第二の経済力を誇る超大国に成長しました。

　ただ、中国では、文化大革命によって失われた伝統的な価値観を取り戻せないまま、その後成長を続けました。現在中国は、国としてどういった価値観をもって世界と対応してゆくべきか、模索が続いているのです。アメリカで公民権法が制定されたことが、その後のアメリカを大きく変えていったように、文化大革命は現在のもう一つの超大国、中国を大きく変貌させたのです。

戦後に極東とヨーロッパが復興し、アメリカのプレゼンスに影響を与えた

　韓国は、朝鮮戦争のあと、経済的な低迷に苦しんでいました。民主化運動によって李承晩政権が倒れ、その後朴正煕が1961年に軍事クーデターをおこし、独裁政権を打ち立てます。
　朴正煕は、アメリカとの軍事連携を強め、懸案であった日本との国交も1965年に締結した日韓基本条約によって正常化しました。

時代
20世紀1960〜70年代
現代

地域
日本・韓国・ヨーロッパ

分類
経済【国際】

キーワード
韓国の独裁政権と経済発展・日本の高度経済成長・ヨーロッパの統合と発展・アメリカの影響力の低下

In the 1960s, under America's military umbrella, Japan experienced a period of high economic growth, becoming one of the world's few economic superpowers. In Japan's case, economic policies were driven by collaboration between the bureaucracy, the government, and the business community.

Korea, on the other hand, plotted out its own economic revival under an autocratic administration, achieving economic growth known as "the miracle on the Han River." However, the Park administration was dictatorial and thoroughly enforced anti-communist policies, and there was no prospect of thawing relations with North Korea.

In Europe, the recovery of West Germany, which was divided from East Germany following World War II, was impressive. As the central government promoting the transition from the European Coal and Steel Community to the European Economic Community (EEC), it contributed to the economic unification of Europe.

France adopted a new constitution in 1958, establishing the Fifth Republic, and Charles de Gaulle was elected president. While seeking economic and military independence from America, with strong government leadership de Gaulle made every effort possible to pull France out of the postwar chaos. In this way, France and Germany, despite their contrasting styles of government, did not oppose each other after the war but instead worked together to become the motive power for the recovery of Europe.

Later the ECC expanded the number of its member nations and reformed its organizational structure, evolving in 1967 into the European Community (EC). Further, through the adoption of a unified currency and other policies in 1993, the member nations formed the European Union (EU).

With the exception of Britain, each member state adopted the euro as its currency, making it one of the key currencies of the world, alongside the U.S. dollar.

Through this process, development in Europe and the Far East had the impact of causing America's presence to recede to some degree. Especially in economic terms, America transitioned from a patron nation to an economic rival. Further, as in the Middle East, the number of countries who no longer had to listen to America began to increase.

This impatience became a regular factor in American politics, especially in the campaigns for the presidency. President John F. Kennedy, who overcame the Cuban Missile Crisis and showed strong leadership in calling for support of the

日本は、1960年代にアメリカの軍事的な傘の下で高度経済成長を経験し、世界有数の経済大国へと成長します。日本の場合は、官僚と政府と財界の協調による経済政策が推し進められたのです。

　一方の韓国でも、独裁政権のもとで経済の立て直しが図られ、「漢江の奇跡」といわれるほどの経済成長を遂げたのです。とはいえ、朴政権はその独裁色と反共政策を徹底させます。北朝鮮との雪解けのめどは立ちません。

　ヨーロッパでも、第二次世界大戦後分断されていた西ドイツの復興が目覚ましく、欧州鉄鉱石炭共同体から進化した欧州経済共同体（EEC）の中核としてヨーロッパの経済統合に貢献するようになりました。

　フランスは、1958年に新憲法を採択し第五共和政の元、シャルル・ド・ゴールが大統領に就任します。シャルル・ド・ゴールは、アメリカからの経済的、軍事的な自立を模索しながら、政府の強力なリーダーシップで戦後の混乱からの離脱を試みました。このようにフランスとドイツとは政治色は異なるものの、戦後は対立することなく、ヨーロッパの復興の牽引車となったのです。

　その後ECCは、1967年に加盟国を増やしながら組織を改変し、ヨーロッパ共同体（EC）へと成長し、1993年には加盟国の通貨統合などを伴った欧州連合（EU）が成立したのです。

欧州連合旗
The Flag and Emblem of the
European Union (EU)

　イギリスなど一部の例外を除き、各国の通貨はユーロとしてまとめられ、アメリカのドルとともに、世界の主要基軸通貨となったのです。

　このように、ヨーロッパと極東の成長は、相対的にアメリカのプレゼンスを後退させることになります。特に経済面では、アメリカは援助者から競争競合相手へと変化してゆくことになるのです。また、中東のように、「アメリカのいうことを聞かなくなった国々」も増えてきます。

　この焦りが、アメリカの大統領選挙などにも常に影響を与えるようになるのです。アメリカでは、キューバ危機を乗り越え、公民権運動を支持しながらアメリカの強いリーダーシップを唱えていたジョン・F・

civil rights movement, was assassinated in 1963. He was followed by Lyndon Johnson, and then Richard Nixon, during whose presidency America withdrew from the Vietnam War. Nixon, however, was enmeshed in a wiretapping scandal known as the Watergate scandal during the presidential election, and in 1974, he was forced to resign.

From the 1960s into the 1970s, America's presence on the world stage underwent a subtle change.

182 The Soviet Union failed in attempting to introduce socialism in Afghanistan

Six years after America withdrew from Vietnam, another military superpower, the Soviet Union, invaded Afghanistan.

The aim was to strengthen the socialist regime of destabilized Afghanistan. Since the 17th century, Afghanistan had seen the recurrent rise and fall of governments between the Safavid dynasty in Iran and the Mughal Empire in India.

Then in the 19th century, it became a protectorate of Britain, which had advanced into Central Asia, and it later became an independent monarchy.

When World War II ended, and British influence disappeared, as the result of a coup d'état, Afghanistan aimed at constructing a socialist nation with Soviet assistance. However, the government was unstable. In particular, because socialism denied religion, the government elicited opposition from the Muslims. For the Soviet Union, which had Muslims in its own territories, it was important to protect the socialist system in Afghanistan at whatever the cost in order to prevent Islamic anti-government movements from spreading within the Soviet Union itself. Further, neighboring Pakistan leaned toward America.

In order to make Afghanistan a stable satellite state, the Soviet Union assassinated its leader and established a puppet administration in Afghanistan.

People who reacted against this engaged in guerrilla warfare in opposition to the Soviet Union. Various Islamic militias from the Middle East supported this war against Soviet forces. America became involved, too, by supporting anti-government forces and supplying them with weapons.

Continuing from the Vietnam War, the Afghan civil war also pitted the two

ケネディ大統領が1963年に暗殺されるという悲劇がおきました。後を継いだリンゼイ・ジョンソン大統領、さらに次のリチャード・ニクソン大統領の時代にベトナム戦争から撤退します。しかしニクソンは、大統領選挙にあたって盗聴を行ったというウォーターゲート事件で、1974年に辞任に追い込まれます。

60年代から70年代は、アメリカの世界でのプレゼンスに微妙な変化が生まれた時期なのです。

ソ連はアフガニスタンの社会主義化に失敗した

ベトナムからアメリカが撤退して6年後、もう一つの軍事大国ソヴィエト連邦がアフガニスタンに侵攻しました。

不安定であったアフガニスタンの社会主義政権を強化することが目的でした。アフガニスタンでは、17世紀以降イランのサファヴィー朝とインドのムガル帝国の間で様々な政権が興亡を繰り返していました。

そして19世紀には、中央アジアに進出してきたイギリスの保護国となったのち、王国として独立します。

第二次世界大戦が終わり、イギリスの影響力がなくなると、アフガニスタンはクーデターによって、ソ連の支援を受けながら社会主義国家の建設を目指します。しかし政権は不安定でした。特に、社会主義が宗教を否定することから、政権はイスラム教徒の反感を買ってしまいます。イスラム教徒を自国にかかえるソ連としては、アフガニスタンの社会主義体制をなんとしても守り、イスラム教徒の反政府運動がソ連国内に飛び火することを防ぎたかったのです。かつ、隣国パキスタンはアメリカよりの国家でした。

そこでソ連はアフガニスタンを安定した衛星国家とするために、指導者を殺害し、傀儡政権を立てたのです。

これに反発した人々がゲリラ戦を展開して、ソ連に抵抗します。実は、この戦闘を中東諸国のイスラム教の民兵が支援していたのです。そして、アメリカもアフガニスタンの反政府活動を支援し、武器を供与します。

ベトナム戦争に続き、アフガニスタンの内戦も、アメリカとソ連と

時代
20世紀1970～80年代
現代

地域
アフガニスタン

分類
戦争【対立】

キーワード
ソ連のアフガニスタン侵攻・イスラム過激派の出現・ソ連の撤退

superpowers—America and the Soviet Union—in a proxy war.

It is quite ironic that Osama bin Laden, the ringleader of the September 11 attacks on America in 2001, participated in this guerrilla activity and received weapons provided by the United States. This resembles to some extent the process by which America, contending against the anti-American administration of Iran, which resulted in the Islamic revolution there, momentarily supported Iraq. It was in the interest of both America and the Soviet Union to give a wide berth to Iran as an Islamic state. However, in Afghanistan, both countries were strongly opposed to one another. This can certainly be seen as an example of how complicated the conflicting interests of international politics really are.

The war in Afghanistan became a quagmire like the one in Vietnam. Ultimately, the Soviet army withdrew in 1989.

Following the Soviets' departure, the Islamic fundamentalist Taliban seized power in of the country.

When America invaded Iraq two years later in the Persian Gulf War, the animosity that the Islamic fundamentalists had directed at the Soviets, who they fought against, was redirected at the Americans. This action was decisive in the discord between America and Islamic societies.

183 In the shadow of the Cold War, wartime chaos on a scale with World War II struck the world

During the period in which Afghnistan was occupied by the Soviet Union, its people suffered enormously from the warfare between the Soviets and those who were opposed to its administration. The scale was so large that there was an insufficient labor pool of males over the age of 16. Village wells were poisoned, rendering them unusable. Mines were planted on roads and in fields. Even children participated in the fighting. Ordinary people's daily lives were devastated.

From the 1960s into the 1970s, the world was deeply impacted by the effects of the Cold War. Following the Second World War, while peace was maintained in the Far East and in the West, strife continued unabated around the world in places like Vietnam, Afghanistan, and countries in Africa. The scale of the damage inflicted on those areas was a match for that caused by World War II. The term Cold War was only a name, and in reality, hot wars unfolded throughout the

いう二つの超大国の代理戦争となったのです。

　皮肉なことに、2001年にアメリカでおきた同時多発テロの首謀者オサマ・ビン・ラディンも、このゲリラ活動に参加し、アメリカから武器の供与を受けていました。それはイスラム革命を経て反米政権ができたイランと敵対したアメリカが、一時的にイラクを支援した経緯と類似しています。イランに対しては、イスラム教国家を敬遠するという意味でアメリカとソ連の利害は一致していました。しかし、アフガニスタンでは両者は強く反発しあったのです。これは、国際政治の利害の複雑さを象徴する事例といえましょう。

　アフガニスタンはベトナム戦争と同様に泥沼化し、最終的にはソ連軍が撤退することになります。1989年のことでした。
　ソ連軍が撤退したあとのアフガニスタンで主導権を握ったのが、イスラム原理主義者タリバンだったのです。
　その2年後におきた湾岸戦争でアメリカがイラクに侵攻すると、アフガニスタンでソ連と戦っていたイスラム原理主義者の敵意がアメリカに向けられるようになります。こうした動きが、アメリカとイスラム社会の確執を決定的なものにしていったのです。

冷戦の陰で、第二次世界大戦に匹敵する 戦禍が世界を見舞った

　ソヴィエト連邦に占領されていた時代、アフガニスタンはソ連とその統治に反発する人々による内戦で、甚大な被害を受けました。その規模は16歳以上の男性の人手が足りなくなるほどで、毒によって村の井戸が使えず、道や田畑に地雷が埋められ、子供まで戦闘に加わるなど、人々の生活そのものが破壊されました。

　1960年代から70年代にかけては、世界中が冷戦の影響を強く被っていました。第二次世界大戦後、極東や欧米では平和が維持された反面、ベトナムやアフガニスタン、アフリカ諸国など、世界中で騒乱が続き、その被害の規模は第二次世界大戦にも匹敵する状況でした。冷戦とは名ばかりで、世界各地で数十万、百万単位で血の流れる熱い戦争が展開されていたのです。

時代
20世紀1960〜80年代
現代

地域
世界

分類
戦争【社会】

キーワード
冷戦の代理戦争・クメール・ルージュの独裁・アフリカの独裁政権・戦乱による貧困と難民問題

world, resulting in bloodshed and casualties in the hundreds of thousands, and even millions.

In Cambodia, which had also been a French protectorate like Vietnam, the monarchy under Norodom Sihanouk was restored, and independence was achieved after the war. When Sihanouk proceeded with socialist policies, the military carried out a coup d'état, and the Khmer Republic came into existence. Following a civil war that broke out in the country, seeking an extremist communist government, the Khmer Rouge, led by Pol Pot, took control of the entire country. During their rule from 1975 to 1979, mandatory relocations were carried out, and those who died from harsh labor and sheer massacres rose into the millions. Following conflict with Vietnam, the Pol Pot regime was deposed, and Cambodia thereafter sought peace under UN supervision.

In numerous cases around the world similar to this, every time a government changed or when a government changed its own policies, it was buffeted by the Cold War policies of the East and West. Moreover, in African cases, there was the added dimension of ethnic conflict, which made the situation even worse.

As one example, in Uganda in Central Africa, the West at first supported Idi Dada Amin, who established a despotic regime. When political instability spread as a result of his dictatorship, Uganda sought support from the East, aligning itself with the socialist nations. In the end, as a result of war with neighboring Tanzania, the Amin government collapsed, and several thousands were slaughtered, lost their homes, and all their possessions. Similar incidents occurred throughout Africa and have still not come to an end.

The poverty, and starvation, and refugee issues that result from the disturbances of war are the severest issues that face today's society.

Following colonization by various Western powers, many countries achieved independence. But in many of those countries, the form of civil society that can support democracy was not cultivated. The government foundation was of little substance, and the system of governance and the legal system were incomplete. When the superpowers reached out to them with military and economic support, they followed the logic of the Cold War, enticed into one of the opposing camps.

As a result, these immature nations were tossed about by the mature powers. A representative example of how this contradiction erupted as a menace to the world at large is the complex circumstances in the Middle East that center around Israel and Iraq.

ベトナムと同様にフランスの保護国になっていたカンボジアでも、ノロドム・シハヌークによる王制が復古し、戦後に独立を達成しました。シハヌークが社会主義的な政策を進めると、軍部がクーデターを起こし、クメール共和国が生まれます。その後の内戦の結果、極端な共産主義政権を目指すポル・ポトに率いられるクメール・ルージュが全国を支配します。彼らが支配した1975年から79年の間、強制移住され、過酷な労働や虐殺で死亡した人々の数は数百万人にのぼるといわれています。ポル・ポト政権は、ベトナムとの対立の後に崩壊し、その後カンボジアは国連の管理のもとに平和を模索します。

　このように、政権が変わるたびに、または政権の方針が転換するたびに西側と東側の冷戦政策に翻弄された例は、世界中に多数あります。しかも、アフリカなどではそれに部族間の対立が加わり、状況が深刻になりました。

　例えばアフリカ中央部にあるウガンダでは、当初独裁政権を樹立したアミンを西欧諸国が支持したものの、その独裁体制による政情不安が拡大すると、ウガンダは東側に援助を求め、社会主義国と連携したのです。結局隣国タンザニアとの戦争などの結果、アミン政権は崩壊しますが、その結果数十万人の人々が虐殺され、家や財産を失っています。こうした事例は、アフリカでは各地におきていて、現在でも終息していないのです。

　戦乱に起因した貧困や飢え、さらに難民の問題は、現在社会が抱える最も深刻な課題なのです。

　欧米列強による植民地化のあと、数々の国が独立しました。しかしそうした地域の多くは民主主義を支える市民社会が育たないまま、政治基盤も貧弱で行政や司法制度も不完全なままでした。そこに軍事、経済での援助を差し伸べる超大国が、冷戦の論理に従って、それぞれの陣営に誘い込もうとしたのです。

　結果として、未成熟な国家を成熟した大国が翻弄することになります。その矛盾が世界の脅威として噴出した代表的な事例が、イスラエルやイラクを軸とした中東地域の複雑な状況だったのです。

184 As a result of the collapse of the Soviet Union, communism has become a mere shell

In the 1980s conditions in the Soviet Union changed.

From the 1950s into the 1960s, the Soviet Union actively meddled in the internal affairs of the socialist orbit, such as the Eastern European bloc, making its presence strongly felt.

When anti-government movements in 1956 rose up to confront the government of Hungary, which had become communist-controlled, the Soviet Union dispatched troops to suppress the uprising. In this Hungarian Revolution there were a number of victims among those who clashed with the Soviets.

Following Joseph Stalin's death, Georgy Maximilianovich Malenkov succeeded to leadership of the Soviet Union. When he in turn was succeeded by Nikita Khrushchev, criticism of the Stalin regime occurred. The reexaminations of Stalin included the purges he carried out under his despotic regime and a fundamental critique of the Stalin personality cult. After Khrushchev was brought down, during the long span of administration maintained by Leonid Brezhnev, the Soviet Union faced chronic economic difficulties. The arms race with America also resulted in heavy expenditures for the country.

Following this, the Soviet Union, while continuing to maintain the Cold War, sought some way of ameliorating tensions with America. This movement also spread into the Eastern European countries, and in Hungary and other countries there were movements seeking democratization. In 1968 when Czechoslovakia aimed at becoming democratic, the Soviet Union led a military intervention in that country.

Following that, in order to maintain the Cold War system, the Soviet Union dispatched troops to Afghanistan and ended up paying a huge price for its long-term bogged-down military adventures there.

After Brezhnev's death, Mikhail Gorbachev succeeded him in 1985 and pursued political and economic reforms known as perestroika, also withdrawing from Afghanistan. However, these reforms gave rise to opposition from the conservatives, and at the same time promoted discord with forces seeking democratization.

The Gorbachev administration, while promoting rapport with the West, sought to disentangle domestic confusion. However, as in the case of the three Baltic states,

ソ連の崩壊によって、共産主義は事実上形骸化した

　1980年代になると、ソヴィエト連邦の状況が変化してきます。

　50年代から60年代にかけて、ソ連は東欧圏をはじめとした社会主義圏の内政にも強く干渉しながら、強い存在感をアピールしていました。

　1956年には、共産化したハンガリーでおきた反政府運動に対して出兵し、それを鎮圧しました。ハンガリー動乱というこの事件ではソ連と衝突した人々が多数犠牲になりました。

　ソ連はスターリンの死後、マレンコフに続いて指導者となったニキータ・フルシチョフのもとで、スターリン批判が行われました。それはスターリンの独裁体制下での粛清やスターリンへの個人崇拝を根本的に見直すものでした。フルシチョフが失脚した後、長期政権を維持したレオニード・ブレジネフの時代、ソ連は慢性的な経済難に見舞われます。アメリカとの軍拡競争もソ連にとって重い支出となりました。

　以後ソ連は、冷戦体制は維持しながら、アメリカとも緊張緩和を模索します。こうした動きは東欧諸国にも伝播し、ハンガリーのみならず、民主化を求める動きが各地に伝播します。1968年には民主化を目指すチェコスロバキアにソ連が主導した軍事介入が実施されました。

　その後ソ連は冷戦体制の維持のために、アフガニスタンにも出兵し、泥沼化した戦闘の長期化という多大の代償を支払うことになったのです。

　ブレジネフが死去したあと、1985年にあとを継いだミカエル・ゴルバチョフは、ペレストロイカと呼ばれる政治経済改革を進め、アフガニスタンからも撤退します。しかし、こうした改革は保守派との対立を生み、同時に民主化を求める勢力との確執も助長してしまいます。

　ゴルバチョフ政権は西欧との融和を進めながら、国内の混乱の収拾にあたります。しかし、バルト三国のように、ソヴィエト連邦内の共

時代
20世紀1980〜90年代
現代

地域
ソビエト連邦

分類
政治【制度】

キーワード
スターリン批判・東欧の民主化運動と弾圧・ゴルバチョフのペレストロイカ・ソ連解体

independence movements in other republics within the U.S.S.R. sought to break away from the Soviet Union. In the end, it was Russia, a member of that union, that withdrew, and with that, the entire U.S.S.R. collapsed. The year was 1991.

With the dismantling of the Soviet Union, to all intents and purposes, the Cold War was over. In China during this period, seeking to recover from the Cultural Revolution, Deng Xiaoping promoted reforms and open-door policies. In 1989 the democratization movement in China led to criticism of the restrictions on freedom of speech and single-party rule by the Communist Party. The government took strong measures to suppress these movements, resulting in the Tiananmen Square Incident. From that point onward, China maintained control through the Communist Party, while it experimented with the introduction of capitalism and promoted economic reforms.

The communism that germinated from Karl Marx and Friedrich Engels in the 19th century therefore became a mere shell. While it still appeared to aim at economic equality through class conflict, it had degenerated into one-party rule, a government by autocracy. Perhaps that is due to the inherent contradiction in a communist state.

185 With the collapse of the Cold War order, a series of tragedies occurred one after another

In the process leading up to the disappearance of the Soviet Union, Eastern Europe underwent major changes.

The Berlin Wall was demolished in November 1989, and as a result West Germany absorbed East Germany, reunifying Germany.

In the process of the crumbling of the Berlin Wall, the Hungarian government acted as a go-between by enabling citizens of East Germany to pass through Hungary on their way to West Germany.

In Eastern Europe, the satellite nations of the Soviet Union began to break away.

Socialist governments in Poland and Romania collapsed in 1989.

As a result of civil war beginning in 1991 in Yugoslavia, the country fell apart, giving rise to present-day Slovenia, Croatia, Serbia, Bosnia, Herzegovina, Montenegro, and Macedonia.

和国からも独立運動がおき、最終的には連邦の共和国の一つであった
ロシアがソ連から脱退する形で、ソ連そのものが崩壊してしまいます。
1991年のことでした。

　ソ連の解体によって、冷戦は事実上終結します。この時期、中国で
も文化大革命からの復興を目指し、鄧小平による改革開放政策が推し
進められていました。1989年、中国では民主化運動が言論の自由と共
産党一党支配への批判へと繋がりかけたとき、政府が強権を発動して
運動を一挙に弾圧した天安門事件がおこりました。その後、中国は共
産党の支配を維持しながら、資本主義の導入を試み、経済改革がさら
に進められたのです。

　19世紀にマルクスやエンゲルスによって発芽した共産主義は、こう
して形骸化してゆきました。それは、階級闘争を通して人々の経済的
平等を目指したものの、一党独裁や独裁者による専制政治へと変質し
ていった、共産主義国家そのものの矛盾が原因だったのかもしれませ
ん。

冷戦の秩序を失った世界で、様々な悲劇が繰り返された

　ソヴィエト連邦が消滅に向かう過程の中で、東ヨーロッパも大きく
変化しました。

　1989年11月には、ベルリンの壁が壊され、その後東ドイツが西ドイ
ツに吸収される形でドイツの統一が実現しました。

　ベルリンの壁が崩壊する過程で、東ドイツの国民がハンガリーを通
して西ドイツへと出国できるよう、ハンガリー政府が仲介したことも
ありました。

　東ヨーロッパでソ連の衛星国家からの離脱が始まっていたのです。

　1989年には、ポーランドでもルーマニアでも社会主義政権が崩壊し
ます。

　また、ユーゴスラヴィアは1991年から始まった内戦によって国が分
裂し、現在のスロベニア、クロアチア、セルビア、ボスニア、ヘルツェ
ゴヴィナ、モンテネグロ、マケドニアといった国家が誕生しました。

時代
20世紀1980～90年代
現代

地域
ヨーロッパ・中国

分類
政治【独立】

キーワード
ベルリンの壁崩壊・東欧
の民主化・ユーゴスラ
ヴィアの解体・ボスニア
紛争・中国の大国化

It remains fresh in our memory that in this process of breaking apart, there were tragic massacres of Croats and Muslim Serbs in Bosnia and elsewhere.

The conflict in Yugoslavia finally came to an end in 2000 when forces from the UN and NATO intervened.

During the Cold War period, due to the discord between America and the Soviet Union, conflicts broke out in numerous areas. Following World War II, with technological innovation and Cold War competition, the quality and effectiveness of weapons advanced far beyond anything that had existed in the past. And in proportion to this, so did the damage in the conflicted areas and the injuries of the people living there.

Ironically enough, however, the framework of the Cold War did provide a kind of world order. That order collapsed, and when it did, the core of one camp—the Soviet Union—broke apart, giving rise to major conflicts throughout the surrounding regions.

Relative to this, the major Western countries, including the United States, benefited from an opportunity to use their influence in Eastern Europe. The Soviet Union collapsed, and Russia, which had been the main power within the alliance, was struggling desperately to recover. Many of the states in the former Eastern European sphere affiliated with the EC and NATO, shifting toward a capitalist economy. Simultaneously, following the collapse of the Soviet Union, various ethnic movements emerged, both within Russia and in the regions surrounding it. Throughout the world, conflicts broke out in the attempt to establish a new order. Later, Vladimir Putin became Russia's president in 2000, and Russia gradually began to recover its national power and to once again project its influence as a powerful state in opposition to the United States.

At the same time, China, which had adopted a capitalist system, developed into the world's second largest economic power and began to compete with America for hegemony. The fact that China developed into a global power also cast a complex shadow over the military balance of power in the Far East. A new, tense relationship, somewhat resembling that of the Cold War arose, pitting America and its allies Japan and Korea against China. Meanwhile, the Chinese government's response to the ethnic movements in Tibet and the Western Regions which it integrated, and its advances into the South China Sea have certainly raised new tensions among countries in the surrounding region. Following the conclusion of the Cold War, the power balance between the world powers is in considerable turmoil.

この過程で、ボスニアなどに居住していたクロアチア人やイスラム教徒がセルビア人民族主義者に虐殺されるなどの悲劇がおきたことはまだ記憶に新しいはずです。

　ユーゴスラヴィアでの紛争は、国連軍やNATO軍の介入によって2000年になってようやく収束したのです。

　冷戦時代には、当事者のアメリカとソ連との確執のために、多くの地域で紛争がおきました。第二次世界大戦後の技術革新と冷戦による競争もあって、武器の質や性能も過去とは比較にならないほど進化しました。そしてそれに比例するように、戦闘地域での被害も人々の受けた傷も深くなりました。

　一方で、皮肉なことに、冷戦という枠組みは世界の秩序でもありました。この秩序が崩壊し、一方の核にあたるソ連が解体されたことは、その周辺に大きな混乱を生むことになりました。

　相対的に、アメリカをはじめとする西側主要国は、旧東欧圏への影響を行使できるチャンスにめぐまれました。ソ連が崩壊し、ソ連の主権を引き継いだロシアが再生へともがく中で、多くの旧東欧圏の国々がECやNATOへ加盟し、資本主義経済へと移行していったのでした。同時に、ソ連が崩壊した後に、ロシア国内やその周辺でおきた民族運動をはじめ、世界各地で新たな秩序を模索した紛争も始まったのです。その後、2000年にウラジミール・プーチンが大統領になって以降、ロシアは次第に国力を回復させ、再び大国としてアメリカに対抗できるプレゼンスを持つようになったのです。

　同時に資本主義の仕組みを取り入れた中国も、世界で2番目の経済大国に成長し、アメリカと覇権を争うようになります。中国が大国へと成長したことは、極東での軍事バランスにも微妙な影を落とします。アメリカと同盟を維持する日本や韓国と、中国との冷戦さながらの緊張関係が生まれたのです。また、中国に統合されたチベットや西域での民族運動への中国政府の対応、中国の南シナ海への進出などが、周辺諸国との新たな緊張へと繋がっているのも事実です。冷戦終結後も、世界は大国のパワーバランスの中で大きく揺れているのです。

186 South Africa became democratized in the 1990s

At roughly the same time that the Cold War order was disintegrating, there were major changes in Africa as well.

During the period when Africa was colonized by the great powers of Europe, large numbers of white settlers arrived in Africa.

Representative of this movement was the Republic of South Africa at the southern tip of the African continent. The republic was already in 1934 a sovereign state independent of Britain, and it maintained policies preferential to whites.

Similarly, Zimbabwe, the state immediately north of South Africa, was at the time of its independence called Rhodesia. As we have seen earlier, this name was taken from that of the British politician Cecil John Rhodes.

In order to improve their state of affairs, people of African ancestry formed an opposition movement. During the Cold War, the supporters of these anti-government movements by black Africans were the Soviet Union and its allied states. Rhodesia collapsed in 1980, and people of African descent established a new state under the new name of Zimbabwe.

However, in South Africa, white supremacy remained unchanged, and a policy known as apartheid was put into practice by which blacks were segregated into specially designated territories and not allowed to live where they chose to. Furthermore, the government dispatched troops into neighboring Namibia and even into that country's neighbor Angola, with the intention of suppressing movements by blacks in all of these areas.

Having established the Civil Rights Act in the 1960s and having reduced discrimination against African Americans, America strengthened economic sanctions against South Africa because of its racial discrimination, and it vigorously sought reforms there. Within the Republic of South Africa, too, there was a movement against apartheid. Many people there began to seek a reconciliation with people of African descent.

After 28 years in prison for opposing South Africa's apartheid laws, Nelson Mandela was set free in 1990. As a result of the democratization movement led by Mandela, a national election in which all of the citizens of the country, black

南アフリカは90年代に民主化された

冷戦が崩壊した頃、アフリカでも大きな変化がありました。

アフリカはヨーロッパ列強の植民地であった頃、数多くの白人系の人々が入植していました。

アフリカ大陸の最南端にある南アフリカ共和国はその代表でした。南アフリカ共和国は、すでに1934年に主権国家としてイギリスから独立していましたが、その後も白人系の人々を優遇する政策を維持していたのです。

南アフリカのすぐ北にあるジンバブエも同様で、戦後に独立した頃の国名は、ローデシアという国家でした。この国名がイギリス人の政治家セシル・ローズの名前にちなんだものであることは、すでに解説した通りです。

この状況を改善しようとアフリカ系の人々は抗議運動を展開します。冷戦時代、こうした黒人系の人々の反政府活動を支援したのがソヴィエト連邦とその同盟国だったのです。ローデシアは1980年に崩壊し、アフリカ系の人々によってジンバブエという国家が成立したのです。

しかし、南アフリカ共和国では、その後も白人至上主義が貫かれ、黒人系の人々を特定の地域に隔離するアパルトヘイト政策を推し進めます。また、隣国のナミビアやさらにその北に位置するアンゴラなどにも派兵し、現地での黒人系の人々の活動を抑えようとしたのです。

60年代に公民権法を制定し、アフリカ系アメリカ人への差別などを軽減したアメリカなどは、南アフリカでの人種差別に対して経済制裁などを強化して、強く改善を求めます。南アフリカ共和国内でもアパルトヘイトに反対する運動がおき、多くの人がアフリカ系の人々との融和を求めるようになりました。

1990年、南アフリカではアパルトヘイトに反対し28年間投獄されていたネルソン・マンデラが釈放されます。彼を軸にした民主化の動きによって、1994年についに全ての国民が参加する総選挙が実施された

and white, were able to participate was held in 1994. As a result of the election, a government was established by the African National Congress (ANC), led by Mandela. He himself became the first president of this reborn South Africa.

South Africa thereafter set as its goal the stabilization of its society by an appeasement policy between black and white citizens. Despite the fact that this gradually took hold, the problems of poverty and crime, resulting from people not receiving sufficient educational opportunities under the apartheid system, continue to cast a dark shadow over the society of South Africa.

In many other African nations, following independence, ethnic conflict has continued to lead to the suppression of human rights and political instability. In Central Africa, in countries including the Democratic Republic of the Congo and Rwanda, horrendous massacres have been carried out due to intertribal hatred.

Following World War II, Japan and Europe recovered, and the countries of Asia continued developing economically. But during that period many African nations' economies were left behind. They have been unable to escape the legacy of poverty, and they have become the global symbol of economic disparity.

187 After the Oslo Accords, the tragedy of "the children of Abraham" continued

Today it is believed that the world's religious populations are made up of 2.4 billion Christians, 1.9 billion Muslims, 1.1 billion Hindus, and 490 million Buddhists. Humanity seems unable to overcome the enmity that comes from the differences between these and other religions.

In September 1993 an agreement called the Oslo Accords was reached between the Palestinian Liberation Organization (PLO), representing the Palestinian refugees, and Israel. Through this agreement, the Palestinian provisional government and Israel acknowledged one another's existence. Amid the collapse of the post-war order during the Cold War, the signing of the accord offered the world one day of hope for a better future.

From the Middle Ages into early-modern times, in contrast with Christianity, Islamic societies were more tolerant of the Jewish people. However, in contemporary society, that concord and tolerance has reversed. The Oslo Accords were supposed to remedy this situation.

のでした。これによって、ネルソン・マンデラの率いる政党、アフリカ民族会議（ANC）による政権が成立したのです。マンデラが新生南アフリカの初代大統領となりました。

南アフリカではその後、黒人系と白人系の人々の融和政策によって社会の安定を目指します。次第にその効果がでてきているとはいえ、アパルトヘイトによって充分な教育を受けられずにいた人々の貧困や犯罪の問題が、社会に暗い影を落としているのも事実です。

そして、アフリカの他の多くの国では、独立後も民族紛争などによる人権の蹂躙や政情不安が続いているのです。中部アフリカにあるコンゴ民主共和国やルワンダなどでは、部族対立による大量虐殺事件もおきています。

戦後、日本やヨーロッパが復興し、アジアでも経済発展が続く中、アフリカの多くの国は経済的にも取り残され、貧困から抜け出せず、世界の格差の象徴となっているのです。

オスロ合意の後もアブラハムの子供達の悲劇は続いた

現在、世界の宗教人口は、キリスト教徒が約24億人、イスラム教徒が約19億人、ヒンドゥー教徒が約11億人、仏教徒は約4億9千万人であるといわれています。そんな宗教の違いからくる憎しみを人類はなかなか克服できません。

1993年9月に、オスロ合意という取り決めが、パレスチナ難民を代表するパレスチナ解放機構（PLO）とイスラエルとの間に締結されました。パレスチナ暫定政権とイスラエルとが、お互いを国家として承認したのです。それは、冷戦という戦後の秩序が崩壊した中で、世界の未来に希望を持てた1日でした。

中世から近世にかけて、キリスト教社会と比べ、イスラム社会はユダヤ人に対して寛大でした。この融和と寛容が現代社会では逆転したのです。オスロ合意はそうした状況を改善するはずでした。

時代
20世紀1990年代
現代

地域
中東

分類
和平【対立】

キーワード
オスロ合意・パレスチナ暫定政権の発足・イスラム社会の混乱・強硬派と穏健派の対立

However, two years later, Israel's former prime minister Yitzhak Rabin, who had supported the agreement, was assassinated by a Jew who opposed the accord. On the opposite side, Palestinian leader Yasser Arafat was denounced by hard-liners who demanded resistance against Israel, and he lost the ability to lead Palestine. Because Arafat was unable to prevent the terrorist actions being carried out on Israel by the hard-liners, he lost the support of the West, and in 2004 he died.

U.S. President Bill Clinton was the negotiator of the Oslo Accords. In a speech he delivered at that time, he referred to both parties using the expression "the children of Abraham." The intention of this reference was to call for rapport between the three Abrahamic traditions: Judaism, Christianity, and Islam.

"Children of Abraham" refers to the Old Testament of the Bible, according to which the prophet Abraham and his two sons, Isaac and Ishmael, play important roles. They are the forefathers of Judaism and Islam, and in addition, Christianity evolved from Judaism. The name Yahweh, who Judaism holds to be the one and only deity, and Allah, who Islam holds to be their one and only deity, refer to the same god. The only difference between the two is the names are different in their respective languages. The ethnic groups and cultures of the region all spring from this common source.

There three religious traditions, which share roots from the mythological past, have over a long period of history, been involved in continuous, bloody antagonistic rivalries. Israel was built out of the desire of the wandering Jewish people for a homeland that began the present Christian era. The Palestinian refugees were driven out of the land of their own ancestors. The clash of these two "wandering peoples" is one source of the problems of today's Middle East.

According to the Oslo Accords, the Gaza Strip in southern Israel and the West Bank of the Jordan River, were to be under autonomous Palestinian authority. However, due to internal conflicts between the moderate and hard-line factions of the Palestinians, and the interventions of the Israelis, hostilities in Palestine have continued unabated. The regional economy has collapsed, and people's daily lives are impoverished and threatened by warfare. They suffer from the deep divisions within Islamic society and an inability to dispel suspicions of Israel and the West as a whole.

しかし2年後、合意を推し進めたイスラエルの
元首相ラビンは、合意に反発するユダヤ教徒の凶
弾に倒れます。また、パレスチナ側の指導者アラ
ファトも、イスラエルへの抗戦を主張する強硬派
から糾弾され、指導力を失ってゆきます。彼はイ
スラエルに対し強硬派が指導するテロ行為を抑え
ることができないことから、最終的には欧米から
の支持も失い失脚し、2004年には死去します。

オスロ合意
調印後に握手をするイスラエルのラビン首相（左）と
PLOのアラファト議長（右）。中央は仲介したビル・ク
リントン米大統領。

Oslo Accords
Israeli Prime Minister Yitzhak Rabin (left) and
PLO Chairman Yasser Arafat (right) shake
hands after the signing. In the center is U.S.
President Bill Clinton, who negotiated the
agreement.

　オスロ合意の仲介役になったのはアメリカの大
統領、ビル・クリントンでした。彼は、その時の
演説で両者を「アブラハムの子供達」と表現しま
した。クリントン大統領はこの表現で、ユダヤ教
とキリスト教、そしてイスラム教といった3つの
宗教の融和を意図していたことになります。

　「アブラハムの子供達」という言葉は、旧約聖書
の預言者アブラハムの二人の子供、イザックとイ
シュマエルが、それぞれユダヤ教徒とイスラム教徒の祖先であるとさ
れていることからきています。しかもユダヤ教を母体にキリスト教が
生まれました。ユダヤ教での唯一神ヤハウェと、イスラム教徒の崇拝
するアラーとは、同じ神がそれぞれの民族で異なった発音で呼ばれて
いるのにすぎないのです。この地域の民族や文化は同じ水源から流れ
出ているのです。

　そんな神話の時代からのルーツを共有する3つの宗教が、その後長年
にわたって血なまぐさい対立を強いられてきたのです。紀元前から流
浪の民であったユダヤの人々の悲願によって建国したイスラエル。そ
してその建国により父祖の地を追われたパレスチナ難民。この二つの
「流浪の民」の対立が、現在の中東問題の原点のひとつとなるわけです。

　オスロ合意で、イスラエル南部のガザ地区と、ヨルダン川西岸にパ
レスチナは自治政府を樹立します。しかし、強硬派と穏健派による内
部分裂とイスラエルの介入で、パレスチナでは戦火が絶えません。地
域の経済は破綻し、人々は貧しさを戦争の脅威に日々さらされている
のです。イスラム社会の深い亀裂と、彼らのイスラエルや欧米への不
信感を拭い去ることはできないのです。

188 Following World War II, humankind experienced a revolution in travel and information

Let us touch on the progress of science and technology since World War II.

The Cold War was a period in which science and technology were applied to military purposes symbolized by competition for nuclear development and the production of nuclear power.

Aeronautical engineering was no exception. By means of the development of jet engines, people were able to travel to different parts of the world in short periods of time.

Meanwhile, through the provision of new infrastructure, such as high-speed trains and expressways, ground transportation also became extremely convenient.

The advancement of transportation methods has resulted in an increase in surplus time for individuals. As a result, people have been able to allocate this additional time toward new forms of productivity and improving their quality of life.

Visual technology, such as television broadcasting, progressed remarkably. People were able to see the affairs of the world around them from their own homes. Accompanying this, entertainment and news broadcasts were created, and large media businesses combining newspapers, books, and magazines began to influence public opinion and consumer behavior.

We should not forget the competition in the development of missile technology during the Cold War. Rivalry led to the Space Race. The Soviet Union placed a man-made satellite in space in 1957 and in 1961 succeeded in a manned space flight. As if to counter these successes, America set forth the Apollo space program and in 1969 succeeded in humankind's first lunar landing.

As the Cold War drew to a close, humankind took hold of a new culture. This was the digital revolution, which brought about one of the biggest transformations since the Industrial Revolution.

Previously, people had only been able to employ steam, electricity, petroleum, or coal as energy to move gears, and thereby change fuel to motive force. With digital technology, however, electric signals could be applied to moving clocks and recording data. Digital technology, furthermore, advanced toward the creation of the Internet, and humankind was able to amass previously unimaginable amounts of information as well as to transmit it with ease.

戦後人類は移動と情報の革命を経験した

　ここで、第二次世界大戦後の科学技術の進歩について触れてみましょう。

　冷戦は、核開発競争などに代表される軍事技術が、原子力発電などのように様々な形で応用された時代でもありました。

　航空技術も例外ではありません。ジェットエンジンの開発によって、人々は短時間で世界各地を移動することができるようになりました。

　一方、高速鉄道や高速道路などの新しいインフラの整備によって、国内での移動も極めて便利になったのです。

　移動手段の発展により、それだけ余剰時間が増えたことで、人々はそうした時間を新たな生産や生活の向上にあてることができるようになりました。

　また、テレビ放送などの映像技術も著しく進化しました。人々は世界でおきた様々な事柄を自宅で見ることができるようになったのです。それに伴って娯楽や報道番組が制作され、新聞や書籍、雑誌などと融合した巨大なメディアビジネスが世論や人々の消費行動に影響を与えるようになったのです。

　冷戦でのミサイル技術の開発競争も忘れてはなりません。それは宇宙開発競争にも繋がりました。1957年に、ソヴィエト連邦が人工衛星を打ち上げ、61年には有人宇宙飛行にも成功します。それに対抗するようにアメリカはアポロ計画を打ち出し、1969年には人類初の有人月面着陸に成功します。

　そして冷戦が終結した頃、人類は新たな文明を手にしました。デジタル革命です。それは、人々の生活に産業革命以来の大きな変化をもたらしました。

　それ以前、人類は蒸気や電気、そして石油や石炭によって発生するエネルギーを歯車などによって動力へ変えることしかできませんでした。それが、電気信号によって時計が動き、物事が記録されるようになったのです。デジタルの技術はさらにインターネットへと進化し、人類は今までにない膨大な情報を集積し発信できるようになったのです。

時代
20世紀後半
現代

地域
共通

分類
技術【社会】

キーワード
科学技術の急速な発展・交通の発展・メディアの発展・デジタル革命

Since the invention of the letterpress printing machine by Johannes Gutenberg, textual information had been printed by machine on paper and distributed. But now, information could be transmitted via the internet. Images and sound, too, could be transmitted directly to people who wanted to receive them. Individuals could also dispatch information with ease. This had a major impact on the behavior of human beings, who since ancient times had been in the habit of writing letters or characters and reading them. At the very beginning of this volume we noted that "the word" was the beginning of "history." With these recent developments, there were new ways of transmitting and receiving "words" in different forms. Gaining access to information became incomparably simplified as a result.

Progress in digital image technology also had a great impact in fields such as medical treatment and scientific research, contributing significantly to the improvement of human life.

At the same time, however, cutting-edge technology was also utilized for military applications. Further, the coming and going of infinite amounts of information has also been easily abused as a tool in inciting people and throwing them into confusion.

189 The world changed with 9-11

Coordinated synchronized terrorist attacks were carried out in America on September 11, 2001.

Multiple aircraft were hijacked and two of them crashed into the twin World Trade Center buildings in New York City, killing over 3,000 people. The crimes were committed by an extremist Islamic organization called al-Qaeda, which opposed American policies in the Middle East. We have earlier seen that the leader of this organization, Osama bin Laden, had at one time received assistance from America in fighting against the Soviet Union in Afghanistan. Since the 9-11 Incident, the world has changed enormously.

The September 11 terror attacks were a tragedy triggered by intricately entangled issues in the Middle East. Upon being attacked, America criticized Afghanistan's Taliban administration for supporting terrorism. By aerial bombing, America caused the Taliban regime, which supported anti-government organizations, to collapse. Because Iraq was also thought to be supporting

グーテンベルクの活版印刷機の発明以来、印刷機によって紙に記され、流通していた文字情報が、インターネットを通して伝達され、映像や音声も同様に情報を求める人の元に送られ、個人も簡単に情報発信できるようになりました。このことは、古代から人類が継承してきた習慣である文字を記し、それを読むという行動にも大きな変化を与えます。本書の冒頭で紹介した、Historyの始まりである「言葉」を伝達し受け取る方法が新しくなってきたのです。情報源へのアクセスも以前とは比較にならないほど簡便になったのです。

　また、デジタルな映像技術の進歩は、医療や科学などの分野にも大きな影響を与え、人類の生活水準の向上にも大きな貢献をしたのです。

　しかし、同時にこうした先端技術は軍事技術としても活用されました。また、インターネットによる無数の情報の行き来は、人々を扇動し、撹乱するノウハウとしても容易に悪用できるようになったのです。

セプテンバーイレブンで世界情勢は大きく変化した

　2001年9月11日、アメリカで同時多発テロがおきました。

　ハイジャックされた複数の航空機がニューヨークの貿易センタービルなどに衝突し、3000人以上の死者を出したのです。犯行は、アメリカの中東政策に抗議するアルカイダというイスラム過激派の組織でした。組織を率いるオサマ・ビン・ラディンが一時アメリカから援助を受けてアフガニスタンでソヴィエト連邦と戦っていたことは、すでに記しました。この事件以来、世界は大きく変化します。

　この同時多発テロは、もつれにもつれた中東問題が引き起こした悲劇でした。テロ攻撃を受け、アメリカはテロを支援していたアフガニスタンのタリバン政権を非難。空爆で反政府組織を支援しタリバン政権を崩壊させます。また、同じくテロを支援しているとして、アメリカは多国籍軍を組織してイラクも攻撃し、サダム・フセイン政権を崩

時代
21世紀
現代

地域
アメリカ合衆国・中東

分類
戦争【国際】

キーワード
アメリカ同時多発テロ・イラク戦争・イスラム国の出現・テロの脅威の高まり

terrorism, America formed a multinational military force to attack it, driving the government of Saddam Hussein to collapse.

However, these actions by this global power aroused further fierce opposition among many Muslims. This became the motive for further acts of terrorism, and in Iraq and Syria, which were exhausted from lengthy fighting, in areas where government authority could not reach, Islamic extremist organizations expanded control, even to the point of establishing the Islamic State (IS). Fundamentalism penetrated the Islamic State, and it imposed strict, almost medieval religious discipline wherever it held power. And it actively supported terrorist activities against any country that was believed to be hostile to Islam.

The fact that the extremist terrorist organization Islamic State held territory under its control was a threat to the world. And the activities of these extremists had repercussions among ethnic groups in African nations, such as Nigeria, in Indonesia, in the southern Philippines, which has a large Muslim population, and among the Uyghurs in China, which the government was eager to suppress.

The anti-government movement which broke out in Tunisia in 2010 and came to be known as the Arab Spring destroyed the Egyptian administration of Hosni Mubarak, who had until them possessed strong influence in North Africa. Moreover, civil conflicts broke out in neighboring Libya and Syria in the Middle East. Islamic State became active in efforts to exert influence in such areas. As a result, people who had lost family members and property flooded toward Europe as refugees.

In the 21st century, Russia continued to recover from the harsh economic disorder that followed the collapse of the Soviet Union. However, the government's interference in domestic ethnic movements caused new terrorist activities. Following the Soviet intervention in Afghanistan, suspicions of Russia became deep-rooted among Muslims. Beginning in the 1990s there also arose an independence movement in Chechen in southern Russia, which led to violent conflict.

Following America's military intervention in Iraq, the administration of George W. Bush gave way to a more moderate administration under Barack Obama. Attempts were made to withdraw troops from Iraq and Afghanistan.

However, societies in the West continue to be menaced by terrorism.

壊に追い込みました。

　しかし、こうした大国の動きは、多くのイスラム教徒の更なる反
発を引き起こします。それが新たなテロ行為の原因となり、戦争で
疲弊したイラクやシリアでは、権力の及ばない地域でイスラム教過
激派組織が膨張し、イスラム国の建国を宣言するに至りました。イ
スラム国は、原理主義を貫き、中世さながらの厳しい戒律を人々に
求めます。そして、イスラム教に敵対すると見なした国へのテロ行
為を積極的に支援したのです。

アメリカのイラク侵攻後に倒
されるサダム・フセインの像
Statue of Saddam Hussein
being toppled after the
US invasion of Iraq.

　イスラム国という過激なテロ組織が支配地域を持ったことは、世界
の脅威となりました。そして、こうした過激派の動きは、ナイジェリ
アなどアフリカ諸国、さらにはイスラム教徒の多いインドネシアやフィ
リピン南部、そしてウイグル族などの民族運動を抑え込もうとする中
国などにも飛び火したのでした。
　2010年にチュニジアでおきた「アラブの春」と呼ばれる北アフリカ
での反政府活動は、それまで強い指導力を持っていたエジプトのムバ
ラク政権を崩壊させます。さらに隣国のリビアや中東のシリアなども
内戦状態に陥ります。イスラム国はこうした地域にも影響力を持とう
と活動します。その結果、家族や財産を失った人々が難民としてヨー
ロッパに押し寄せました。

　一方、21世紀になると、ロシアはソ連崩壊後の厳しい経済混乱から
次第に回復しつつありました。しかし、ロシア国内での民族運動への
政府の介入が、新たなテロ活動を誘発します。ソ連のアフガニスタン
への介入以来、イスラム教徒のロシアへの不信感にも根強いものがあ
るのです。ロシア南部のチェチェンで90年代以降おきた独立運動はそ
のまま激しい紛争となりました。

　アメリカはイラクへの軍事介入の後、ブッシュ政権からより穏健な
オバマ政権へと移行しました。そして、イラクやアフガニスタンから
の撤兵に取り組みます。
　しかし、欧米の社会は未だにテロの脅威にさらされているのです。

190 Humankind is still searching for what a democratic society should be like

If human beings had been like other living organisms and followed the basic principle of the survival of the fittest, their brains might have developed fast, but their fall would have come earlier. Human beings have experienced many wars, yet gradually they have somehow found a way to coexist with people they are hostile to, people with different religious beliefs and ways of thinking. Until now, democracy has been the leading-edge pathway forward.

Democracy is a system which prevents people from settling disputes through the use of force. It is a system recognizing a contractual society in which leaders are chosen by elections. They create laws, and their legislation governs social activities. In this system, when one party in society exerts itself too strongly, people who grow apprehensive seek a compromise through some other force, and a self-correcting function comes into play in balancing society. This self-cultivating function plays a role that is similar to the stabilizing force that keeps a ship on an even keel when it is tossed by waves at sea.

When they became independent, many of the nations of Asia and Africa formally attempted to enter the family of democracies. However, because they did not possess this stabilizing force—which is cultivated through education, social welfare, and the experience of being a civil society—they are still in agony.

In the West and in Japan, which democratized more thoroughly following World War II, people are enduring other trials and ordeals. At present, as a result of the digital revolution, access to and sharing of information has changed greatly. Trends in international society have a major impact on domestic political affairs. As a result of such things as terrorism or the fear of a neighboring country, people tend to develop an inward way of thinking. In such an environment, public opinion is stirred up by populism through the internet and media. One cannot deny that in the background of all of this is the expanding disparity between wealth, poverty, and educational opportunities.

In 2016 in a national referendum, Britain voted to leave the European Union (EU). And in the United States, Donald Trump, who appealed to the public by espousing views on restricting immigration and placing priority on American's national interests above all other considerations, was elected president. Later, in France and the Netherlands, people who were afraid of this wave elected leaders

人類は民主主義社会のあり方を今でも模索している

人類がもし他の生き物のように、弱肉強食の原則だけを追求していたら、他の生物より頭脳が発達していただけに、その滅亡も早かったかもしれません。人類は、無数の戦争を経験しながら、次第に敵対する者、宗教や思想を異にする者との共存の術を見つけだしてきました。民主主義は、現在までのところ、その最先端のノウハウなのです。

民主主義は、人と人とが争いごとを力で解決することを防ぐ制度です。それは選挙で指導者を選び、法を作り、法律が社会活動を規定するという契約社会を認めた制度です。この制度は社会に片方の力が強く働いた場合、それに恐れを抱く人が別の力をもつことで双方が妥協し、社会に天秤のような自己修復作用を作り出そうとしています。この自己修復作用こそが、船が波に翻弄されたときに必要な復元力と同じ効果を社会にもたらしているのです。

アジアやアフリカの国々の多くは、独立したのち、形式的には民主主義国家の仲間入りをしようとしました。しかし、この復元力を生み出すための教育や福祉、そして市民社会の経験の厚さがないために、今なお苦悶しているのです。

また、戦後に民主主義をより徹底させた欧米や日本などでは、別の試練にさらされています。デジタル革命によって、情報へのアクセスや共有方法が大きく変化した現在、国際社会の動向が国内の政治にも大きく影響を与えるようになってきたのです。特にテロリズムや隣国の脅威などにより、人々の考え方が内向きになりがちな環境の中で、ネットやメディアなどを通したポピュリズム（扇動）に世論が左右されるようになったのです。その背景には、そうした国々の中での制度疲労による貧富や教育の格差の拡大があることは否めません。

2016年、国民投票で、イギリスはEUから脱退することになりました。そしてアメリカでは、移民を制限し、アメリカの国益を優先させようと国民に訴えたドナルド・トランプが大統領に選ばれました。その後、フランスやオランダでは、そうした波に脅威を抱いた人々が、移民政策に柔軟でEUを支持する指導者を選挙で選びました。これは民主主義

時代
21世紀
現代

地域
共通

分類
制度【社会】

キーワード
民主主義とは何か•途上国の苦難•ポピュリズムの出現•独裁政権の大国中国

who were more tolerant toward immigration and who supported the EU. This can be seen as a typical agency for restoring democracy.

Meanwhile, under one-party control by the Communist Party, China continues strict control over speech and nationalist movements. After overcoming trials and tribulations following the Opium Wars, China has once again begun to expand as a superpower. In the end, China disregarded the opposition of the citizens of Hong Kong, changing the government system of one-country two-systems, which was agreed upon at the time of reversion from Britain. It imposed strict controls against any activities calling for democratization. Japan and Southeast Asia, conscious of the threat it poses, are trying to find a way to coexist with this powerful nation, which has resurfaced after 200 years.

Today the world is still operating within the framework created following World War II. The rise of Asia, beginning with China, the economic gap within the West and Japan, and issues of immigrants and refugees throughout the world—how did this post-war framework give rise to such realities? This is a problem that the world will have to continue to deal with.

191 The spread of Covid-19 and Russia's invasion of Ukraine have completely changed the world

In 2019 Covid-19 infections were confirmed in China for the first time, and in the blink of an eye, the fear of a pandemic spread around the globe. By 2020 almost every country in the world had closed itself off under quarantines, not only limiting travel across borders but significantly restricting every conceivable activity of people within their own country's borders. In order to somehow maintain business activities, instead of actually communicating in person, businesses have made use of social media and online communications. These events had a major impact on human lifestyles.

In the midst of the anxiety that was stirred up by the pandemic, public opinion in many countries segmented. This divisiveness went so far that following the election of 2020, supporters of the defeated President Trump, in January of the year following the election, broke into the U.S. Capitol. The gaps in the economy and in education expanded, causing serious social divisions to fester, stirring up uneasiness among people around the world.

の修復作用の典型といえましょう。

　一方、中国は、いまだ共産党の一党支配のもと、言論や民族運動を厳しく規制しています。中国はアヘン戦争以来の試練を克服し、再びアジアの超大国として膨張を始めたのです。そしてついに中国は香港市民の抵抗を押し切って、イギリスからの返還時に約束した一国二制度の原則を変更しました。そして香港での民主活動を厳しく統制したのです。日本や東南アジアはその脅威を意識しながら、200年ぶりに強大な国家となった中国とどう共存を図ってゆくか、模索が続いています。

　現在は、第二次世界大戦後に作られた世界の枠組みの延長にあります。中国をはじめとするアジアの台頭や、欧米や日本での格差社会や世界各地での移民や難民の問題を通し、そうした枠組みをどのように現実に即したものに変えてゆくか。それが今後の世界の課題なのです。

ドナルド・トランプ前大統領
2017年1月20日、ワシントンD.C.の米連邦議会議事堂で行われた第58回大統領就任式での大統領就任演説
Former President Donald J. Trump delivered his presidential inaugural address during the 58th Presidential Inauguration at the U.S. Capitol Building, Washington, D.C., Jan. 20, 2017.

新型コロナウイルスの流行とロシアのウクライナ侵攻が世界を一変させた

　2019年、中国で初めて感染が確認された新型コロナウイルスは、瞬く間に世界中をパンデミックの恐怖に陥れました。2020年になるとほとんどの国家が検疫のために国を閉ざし、人々の行き来はもとより、国内でもありとあらゆる人の活動が大きく制限されました。経済活動をなんとか維持するために、人々は実際に出会ってコミュニケーションをする代わりに、ソーシャルメディアやオンライン通信を活用して仕事をします。このことは人類のライフスタイルに大きな影響を与えました。

　また、パンデミックによって煽られる不安の中で、多くの国では民意が分断しています。アメリカでは2020年の大統領選挙の後に、敗北したトランプ前大統領の支持者たちが翌年1月に連邦議会議事堂に乱入する事件まで起こりました。経済や教育の格差が拡大する中で、元々くすぶっていた社会の分断という火種が、実際に世界中で人々の不安を煽るようになったのです。

時代
21世紀
現代

地域
共通

分類
戦争【対立】

キーワード
新型コロナウイルスのパンデミック・社会の分断・新冷戦と権威主義国家・ロシアのウクライナ侵攻

On the global level, the expression "New Cold War" would seem an appropriate way of describing the future in which nations are split into groups. In nations like China and Russia, where authority is centrally concentrated, restrictions on free speech have increased, and other countries have begun to exercise caution toward these authoritarian states. The suppression of the pro-democracy movement in Hong Kong in 2020 affected the guarantee of military security in the Far East region, and it further caused America, Japan, and South Korea to support the independence of Taiwan and to seek to restrain China's advances into the South China Sea, as well as to politically oppose China and North Korea's progress in the development of nuclear weapons. This has led to a new movement in Japan to expand its military strength.

In the Middle East, while the threat of the Islamic State seems to have peaked, the state of affairs in the region remains highly unstable. Added to the issues of nuclear development and the suppression of human rights on the part of Iran, which strongly opposes the U.S., the Middle East continues to experience political instability and the deeply rooted conflict between Israel and the Palestinians. In 2021 the rigid Islamic discipline-supporting Taliban rapidly recovered power, and America's President Biden announced the withdrawal of military forces from Afghanistan. Moreover, in 2023 the once-stable Sudan erupted into civil war, further expanding unease throughout the world.

Such anxieties evolved into a full-scale war when Russian President Putin invaded Ukraine in 2022. As nations that became independent from the former Soviet Union developed stronger relationships with nations of the West, Ukraine attempted to become a member of NATO and that became the trigger for Russia's invasion of Ukraine. Ukrainian President Zelensky appealed to the nations of the world to condemn Russia's outrageous actions, and as his country continued an all-out resistance, Russia was strongly criticized and sanctioned by major nations. This was symbolic of the fact that the New Cold War had in fact for the first time become a truly "hot war." With the continuance of the Covid-19 pandemic and the major chaos caused by Russia's invasion of Ukraine, the world economy was deeply affected. Commodity prices in the Western nations rose steeply, and those countries became deeply concerned about energy shortages.

Before we were able to dispose of nuclear weapons once and for all, we became once again frightened at the prospect of nuclear warfare. Before we were able to halt global warming, we once again have become fearful of the fury of an unrecoverable environmental collapse as a result of warfare.

世界レベルでは「新冷戦」という言葉に表される国家間の分断も未来への不安材料です。中国やロシアのように、権力が中央に集中している国家では、言論統制がますます進み、人々はそうした国家を権威主義国家として警戒するようになりました。2020年の香港での民主化運動の弾圧は、極東地域の安全保障にも影響を与え、台湾の独立を維持させ、同時に南シナ海への中国の進出を牽制しようとするアメリカや日本、韓国と、中国や核開発を進める北朝鮮とが政治的に激しく対立するようになりました。これは日本にとっても新たな軍事力拡張への動きにつながっています。

　そして、中東ではイスラム国の脅威は峠を越したものの、いまだに情勢は極めて不安定です。アメリカと厳しく対立するイランの核開発や人権抑圧の問題に加え、中東各地での政情不安やイスラエルとパレスチナの人々との対立は根深く続いているのです。2021年には、イスラム教の戒律を厳しく実践するタリバンが急激に勢力を挽回し、アメリカのバイデン大統領は米軍のアフガニスタンからの撤退を発表しました。さらに2023年には、一時安定したかに見えたスーダンでも内戦が勃発し、世界中に不安が拡大しています。

　そんな不安が大規模な戦争となっているのが、2022年に始まったロシアのプーチン大統領によるウクライナ侵攻です。旧ソ連から独立した国家が西側諸国との関係強化を続ける中で、ウクライナがNATOに加盟しようとしたことが、ロシアのウクライナ侵攻への導火線となったのです。ウクライナのゼレンスキー大統領は、世界中にロシアの暴挙を訴え、徹底抗戦を続ける中で、ロシアは世界の主要国から強い非難と制裁を受けたのです。これは新冷戦が初めて本格的な熱い戦争になったことの象徴でした。世界経済は新型コロナウイルスのパンデミックに続いて、ロシアのウクライナ侵攻の影響を受けて大きく混乱し、西側諸国も物価の高騰やロシアからの供給が止まったことによるエネルギー不足に悩まされています。

　我々は核が完全に廃棄される前に、再び核戦争の脅威にさらされ、地球の温暖化を食い止める前に、再び戦争による取り返しのつかない環境破壊の猛威に脅かされているのです。

192 In the metamorphosis of power balance around the world, the development of AI casts new challenges

In China, President Xi Jinping, after receiving a long-term extension of his authority in the 2022 National People's Congress, expanded activities in diplomacy, aimed at enhancing his country's influence. Furthermore, Russia's invasion of Ukraine has resulted in a situation where a permanent member of the United Nations Security Council has violated the UN Charter and initiated warfare on another country's territory. While China is a member of the Security Council, it puts great emphasis on maintaining close relationships with Russia. As a result, the very framework of the UN is being shaken. The impact of the United Nations no longer functioning will remain a cause for concern in international politics going forward.

Meanwhile, the world is gradually entering the era of AI. Integrating computers, online functions, and an enormous database accumulated by various mechanisms, AI has begun the process of learning on its own.

The initial phase of this evolution was probably the advance in the development of electric-powered vehicles, which resulted from concerns about protecting the environment. The development of AI to that point all of a sudden became interlinked with commercial needs, such as automated driving and commenced dramatic progress. Through AI services called chatbots, it became possible for students to write essays by simply giving an AI device instructions about what to write.

Whether human beings will accept the convenience of AI or, to the contrary, resist being dominated by AI, there are questions that will need to be dealt with regarding how humans control technological innovations. These issues are already in the process of transforming from science fiction to reality. In the midst of the world and society as a whole splitting apart and humanity confronting varieties of confusion as a result of diversification of values, we are entering an era in which machines learn on their own, accumulate knowledge, and act on their own.

That of course has a major influence on the present state of warfare as exhibited in the Russian invasion of Ukraine. Moreover, the competitive development of technological innovation by AI has—like the competitive development of nuclear weapons during the Cold War era—become a tool that stimulated tensions between nations. Including such issues as cybersecurity, when AI and computer

世界のパワーバランスの変化に、AIの進化が新たな問いを投げかける

中国では習近平国家主席が、2022年の全国人民代表大会で長期政権の強い基盤を維持したことを受け、積極的に外交活動を展開し、自国の影響力の拡大に努めています。そして、ロシアのウクライナ侵攻は、国連安保理の常任理事国が自ら国連憲章を踏みにじって他国の領土で戦争を始めたことになるわけです。中国は同じ常任理事国であるものの、ロシアとの緊密な連携を強調します。このことによって国連の枠組みそのものが揺るごうとしています。国連が機能しなくなったことが、これからの国際政治に与える影響が気になるところです。

時代
21世紀
現代

地域
共通

分類
技術【国際】

キーワード
国連の機能不全・AIによる技術革新・新しい全体主義

一方で、世界はAIの時代へと傾斜しつつあります。コンピューターとオンライン、それに加えて機械が膨大なデータベースを統合し、それを学習する機能が進化を始めました。

端緒となったのが、環境問題への懸念から自動車の電動化が進められたことでしょう。それまでのAIの開発がたちまち自動運転などの商業的ニーズと合致して、飛躍的な進歩を始めたのです。チャットボットと呼ばれるAIによるサービスによって、学生はAIに指示するだけで論文を作成してもらえるようにすらなりました。

人間がAIによる利便性を享受できるのか、あるいは逆にAIに支配されないように、これからの技術革新をどのようにコントロールするべきか。こうした課題がサイエンスフィクションの世界から現実のものとなりつつあるのです。世界や社会が分断され、多様な価値による多様な混乱が人類を見舞う中、我々は機械が自ら学習し知識を蓄積しながら行動する時代を迎えようとしているのです。

もちろん、それはロシアのウクライナ侵攻といった現代の戦争のあり方にも大きな影響を与えてゆくはずです。さらに、AIによる技術革新の競争は、冷戦時代の核兵器の開発競争と同様な新たな国家間の緊張を煽る道具にもなろうとしています。サイバーセキュリティの問題などを含め、AIやコンピューターシステムが攻撃の標的にされたとき、

systems become the target of attacks, it affects even our own lives and economic activities.

The Industrial Revolution occurred as a result of the development of the internal combustion engine, commencing 200 years of major changes in civilization. The AI era is steering us into another such change in human civilization.

However, even as it does this, humankind is continuing to engage in warfare and the same cruel carnage it has carried out in the past. Nations continue to follow their own egos, social conflicts repeatedly occur following events like the Covid-19 pandemic, and people become increasingly inwardly oriented.

One can only hope that public opinion led by AI and social media does not slip in the direction of a new, future form of totalitarianism.

193 Now humankind bears responsibility for all life on the planet

The past two centuries of human history have been a period in which humankind has confronted nature—indeed the planet itself—intensely. During these 200 years, humankind has gone from viewing natural phenomena as awe-inspiring acts of the gods to being capable of understanding them through science. The progress of science and technology has led humanity from an era of production for survival to an era of production for improving quality of life. It heralded the arrival of an era of mass production and consumption.

What this means is that the future of the earth has begun to be entrusted to human hands.

However, the planet and nature possess a power that exceeds human power. These circumstances are unlikely to change. Therefore, as humanity continues wars and environmental destruction, when the Earth begins to feel the pain, much as if it had been stung by a mosquito, it is likely to bring about the destruction of the human beings responsible for it and simultaneously lead to the extinction of many other living organisms on Earth. The trigger will have been the hand of humanity.

From the Industrial Revolution through the digital revolution, the human race has become a presence that has taken ever more responsibility for the earth and all of the life forms that live on it. The vast majority of scientists now agree that human

それは我々の生活や経済活動そのものを脅かすことになるのです。

　内燃機関の開発と進歩によって産業革命が起き、人類の文明が大きく変化を始めて200年。AIの時代は我々をその次の世代へと導こうとしています。

　しかし、それでも人類は戦争を繰り返し、過去と同じように残酷な殺戮を続けています。国家はそれぞれのエゴに従い、人々は新型コロナウイルス流行以後の度重なる社会の混乱で、ますます内向きになりつつあります。

　AIやソーシャルメディアによって誘導される世論が、新たな未来型の全体主義へと傾斜しないことを祈るばかりです。

今、人類は地球の生命全てに責任を持っている

　人類の歴史の直近の200年は、人類が自然、そして地球と激しく向かい合ってきた時代でした。この200年で、人類は自然現象を神のなせる「畏れ多き技」から科学で証明できる現象として認識できるようになったのです。科学技術の進歩は、人類を生きるために生産する時代から、生きる質を上げるために生産する時代へと導きました。大量生産と大量消費の時代の到来です。

　それは、人間の手に地球の運命が委ねられ始めたことを意味しています。

　ただ、地球、そして自然は人間の能力をはるかに超えた力を持っています。その状況はこれからも変わらないはずです。ですから、人間が戦争や環境破壊を続け、地球がちょうど蚊に刺されたような痛みを覚えたとき、地球はその原因となっている人類を破滅させ、同時に地球に住む多くの生命体を絶滅させるはずです。そんな引き金を人類は手にしたといえるのです。

　産業革命から、デジタル革命を経て、人類は、地球と地球に生きる生命体に対して大きな責任を持つ存在へと変化したのです。今や大多数の科学者は、気候危機の原因が人類の活動にあるということを認め

時代
21世紀
現代

地域
共通

分類
人類【社会】

キーワード
大量生産と大量消費・深刻な環境破壊・豊かな社会と幸福な社会・未来に向けて

activity is responsible for the climate crisis. Furthermore, it is undeniable that the weapons and production technology that humankind has taken possession of have tremendous potential to further impact the global environment.

In the 19th century, with the power of the Industrial Revolution, the West colonized Asia and Africa, and maneuvered to gain riches it. With the arrival of the 20th century, the countries of Asia and Africa which opposed these actions learned from Western culture, and using what they learned as levers, they gradually gained strength, and in some places they obtained riches. Japan is a case in point. Today China, Korea, India and Southeast Asian nations are seeking the same affluence.

Unable to overcome the chaos that followed the collapse of the Soviet Union, Russia as well as Brazil in South America, which has faced the same sort of conflict, have gathered people's attention. At one time, countries referred to as BRICs— Brazil, Russia, India and China—may have hoped to become economic powers in the 21st century. Most unfortunately, certain countries in that group have now become the cause of uneasiness around the world.

To be sure, while humankind attains a convenient and abundant society, there remain concerns that humankind is postponing the most important pursuit of a value system that deals with what true happiness and well-being really are. From ancient times in Asia, people cultivated the pursuit of rapport with nature and the universe. Through numerous revolutions and conflicts in the West, people developed the concepts of human rights and individual freedom. What will those values lead to in the future? Will they harmonize with the pursuit of abundance and affluence? These are the questions posed to us after 10,000 years of human history. If we are unable to find an answer to these questions, humans, together with all other life forms on the planet, may become extinct.

When we take a bird's-eye view of world history, we find ourselves at a turning point where we need to calmly reflect on the fact that despite the progress of science and technology, humanity has consistently engaged in conflicts driven by the pursuit of interests, territories, and power. Does it not seem appropriate that we take a calm, composed look back upon where we have come from? Surely we will ask, as the title of Paul Gauguin's painting does, "Where are we going?"

ています。さらに、人類が手にした兵器や生産技術が地球の環境に多大な影響を与える可能性があることも否めない事実です。

　19世紀、産業革命を武器に、欧米はアジアやアフリカを植民地にして、自らを豊かにしようと試みました。20世紀になると、その行為に反抗したアジアやアフリカの国々が、西欧の文明を学ぶことをテコにして、次第に力をつけ、場所によっては富も手にしました。日本はその代表でした。そして、今中国や韓国、インドや東南アジア諸国などが、同様の富を手にしようとしています。

　ソヴィエト連邦の崩壊後の混乱を克服できず迷走するロシア、そして南米ではブラジルなどでも同様の混乱が人々の関心を集めています。一時、BRICsと呼ばれる国々、つまりブラジル、ロシア、インド、中国は21世紀経済を牽引するかもしれないとまで期待されました。しかし、その一部の国が今では世界の不安要因となっていることは残念です。
　確かに、人類が便利で豊かな社会を手に入れながら、真の幸福とは何かという最も大切な価値観の追求を後回しにしつつあることは懸念されます。アジアに古来培われてきた自然や宇宙との融和の追求、欧米で幾多の革命や闘争を経て手にしてきた人権や個人の自由という発想。そうした価値をさらに未来へと繋げることが、豊かさの追求とどう調和するのか。これが人類1万年の歴史の歩みの向こうに問いかけられているのです。その問いかけに答えられないとき、人類は他の生命と共に、地球から抹殺されるかもしれないのです。

　世界史を鳥瞰したとき、人類が科学技術の進歩とは裏腹に、常に利益や領土という縄張り、そして権力を求めた争いを繰り返してきたことを、もう一度冷静に振り返る転換点に、我々は立っているのではないでしょうか。それが、ポール・ゴーギャンが自らの作品で問いかけた、「我々はどこへ行くのか」というテーマを考えることになるはずです。

【ア】

アーリア人 Aryans 9, 12
アイオリス人 Aeolians 16
アイグン条約 Treaty of Aigun 126
アイルランド Ireland 47, 48, 98, 123, 124, 126, 130, 156
アウグストゥス Augustus 23, 24
アウストラロピテクス Australopithecus 2, 3
アクバル Akbar 93
アケメネス朝ペルシア Achaemenid dynasty (of Persian) 13, 15, 16
アショーカ王 Ashoka 18, 19
アステカ Aztecs 83, 84
アダム・スミス Adam Smith 150
アッカド人 Akkadians 7
アッシリア Assyria 13, 15
安土桃山時代 Azuchi Momoyama Period 88, 95
アッティラ Attila 25
アッバース朝 Abbasid Caliphate 36, 38, 39, 41, 42, 43, 49, 62
アテナイ Athens 16, 17, 22
アパルトヘイト apartheid 186
アフガニスタン Afghanistan 9, 19, 28, 49, 80, 114, 182, 183, 184, 189, 191
アブラハム Abraham 13, 35, 39, 187
アフリカ Africa 2, 3, 4, 8, 9, 12, 22, 34, 37, 38, 39, 42, 50, 54, 55, 57, 64, 70, 74, 82, 84, 92, 95, 100, 102, 107, 114, 116, 122, 129, 132, 135, 136, 140, 141, 143, 144, 146, 147, 148, 151, 154, 156, 157, 160, 164, 165, 168, 169, 170, 176, 179, 183, 186, 189, 190, 191
アヘン opium 120, 121, 122, 129, 132, 150
アヘン戦争 Opium War 122, 126, 129, 132, 133, 170, 190
アムル人 Amorites 7
アメリカ America [the United States, the U.S.] 3, 8, 27, 37, 40, 48, 61, 70, 72, 74, 82, 83, 87, 99, 100, 102, 107, 108, 109, 110, 111, 112, 114, 116, 117, 123, 124, 125, 126, 129, 130, 131, 132, 133, 136, 137, 139, 140, 141, 143, 146, 150, 152, 153, 155, 156, 157, 158, 159, 160, 161, 162, 163, 164, 166, 167, 168, 169, 170, 171, 172, 173, 174, 176, 177, 178, 179, 180, 181, 182, 184, 185, 186, 187, 188, 189, 190, 191
アメリカ合衆国 United States of America [the U.S.] 72, 83, 84, 87, 99, 107, 108, 110, 123, 125, 130, 139
アメリカ大陸 American continent 31, 45, 83, 100, 110, 116
アメリカ独立革命 American Revolution 100, 102, 108, 110, 111, 112, 114, 139
アラー Allah 35, 38, 187
アラビア海 Arabian Sea 30, 81
アラビア半島 Arabian Peninsula 35, 36, 37, 54
アラブ Arab 62, 92, 94, 127, 149, 175, 176
アラファト Arafat, Yasser 176, 187
アラブの春 Arab Spring 189
アラブ連合 Arab Union 175
アリウス派 Arianism 26, 37
アリストテレス Aristotle 24, 43, 75
アルカイダ al-Qaeda 189
アルジェリア Algeria 55, 127, 156, 176
アルタミラ Altamira 3
アルファベット alphabet 24
アレクサンドリア Alexandria 23, 27, 30, 75
アレクサンドロス大王 Alexander the Great 17, 18, 19, 20, 23, 24, 25, 43
アングロ・サクソン人 Anglo-Saxons 47, 48
アンコールワット Angkor Wat 63
アンシャン・レジーム Ancien Régime 111
安全保障理事会 Security Council 169, 192
安禄山 An Lushan 40, 41

【イ】

イーリアス Iliad 11
イヴァン雷帝（4世） Ivan the Terrible 94, 104
イエス Jesus 26
イエズス会 Society of Jesus 85, 95, 120
イェニチェリ Janissaries 93
イオニア人 Ionians 16
イギリス (Great) Britain [England] 2, 12, 23, 45, 47, 48, 49, 56, 65, 66, 73, 76, 77, 86, 87, 88, 89, 90, 92, 94, 95, 96, 97, 98, 99, 100, 101, 102, 103, 104, 107, 108, 109, 110, 111, 112, 113, 114, 115, 116, 117, 118, 119, 120, 121, 122, 123, 125, 126, 127, 129, 130, 131, 132, 133, 134, 135, 136, 138, 139, 140, 141, 143, 147, 148, 149, 150, 153, 154, 156, 157, 159, 161, 162, 163, 164, 165, 166, 167, 168, 169, 170, 171, 172, 175, 176, 179, 181, 182, 186, 190
イギリス国教会 Church of England 86, 87, 98
イギリス連邦 Commonwealth of Nations 179
イサベル1世 Isabella I 74
イスタンブール／コンスタンティノープル／ビザンティオン Istanbul; Constantinople; Byzantium 25, 46, 51, 54, 56, 70, 77, 79, 141

イスラエル Israel 13, 174, 175, 176, 183, 187, 191

イスラエル王国 Kingdom of Israel 13

イスラム教 Islam [Islamic beliefs] 8, 14, 16, 26, 35, 36, 37, 38, 39, 41, 42, 43, 46, 49, 50, 51, 54, 55, 56, 62, 63, 64, 67, 69, 70, 71, 74, 79, 80, 81, 82, 92, 93, 94, 107, 127, 154, 182, 187, 189, 191

イスラム教徒 Muslims [followers of Islam] 35, 36, 37, 38, 41, 45, 51, 56, 57, 63, 70, 79, 80, 81, 82, 93, 94, 127, 154, 156, 170, 182, 185, 187, 189

イスラム原理主義 Islamic fundamentalist 36, 182

イスラム国 Islamic State 189, 191

イスラム商人 Muslim merchants 54, 55

イタリア Italy 16, 22, 34, 37, 43, 47, 51, 54, 66, 69, 73, 75, 76, 77, 78, 85, 91, 95, 97, 113, 118, 128, 147, 148, 156, 160, 162, 163, 164, 165, 166, 172

市場 marketplace 57

一神教 monotheistic religion [monotheism] 13, 14, 35, 36, 39, 50

稲作文化 rice culture [rice cultivation] 32, 64

イベリア半島 Iberian Peninsula 34, 36, 37, 38, 42, 71

移民 migrants [immigrants, emigrate] 21, 25, 27, 48, 101, 123, 124, 125, 126, 130, 132, 137, 139, 143, 155, 164, 178, 179, 190

異民族 different [other] ethnic group 28, 34, 40, 50, 59, 80, 134

イラク Iraq 5, 13, 92, 175, 176, 182, 183, 189

イラン（ペルシア）Iran (Persian) 13, 16, 17, 18, 31, 67, 174, 176, 182, 191

イラン・イラク戦争 Iran-Iraq war 176

イラン革命 Iranian Revolution 176

イル・ハン国 Il Khanate 62, 67

殷 Yin 11

インカ帝国 Inca Empire 83, 84, 85

殷墟 Yin Xu 11

イングランド England 48, 87, 88, 98

印刷 printing 73, 75, 136, 188

インターネット Internet 188

インダス Indus 8, 9, 10, 11, 12

インド India 9, 12, 14, 17, 18, 19, 21, 25, 28, 29, 30, 36, 39, 43, 49, 50, 54, 63, 64, 67, 74, 80, 81, 82, 85, 89, 93, 94, 114, 120, 122, 126, 132, 133, 134, 135, 143, 149, 154, 156, 170, 174, 178, 180, 182, 191

インド国民会議 Indian National Congress 154

インドシナ戦争 Indochina Wars 170

インド帝国 the Indian Empire 133, 134

インドネシア Indonesia 63, 64, 94, 97, 114, 120, 126, 135, 170, 189

インド洋 Indian Ocean 30, 54, 63, 64, 80, 81, 82, 91

インドヨーロッパ語族 Indo-European-speaking peoples 9, 22, 47

インノケンティウス3世 Innocent III 56

【ウ】

ヴァスコ・ダ・ガマ Vasco da Gama 74, 80, 81

ヴァロワ朝 Valois dynasty 72

ヴァンダル王国 Vandal Kingdom 34

ウィーン Vienna 45, 79, 80, 81, 92, 94, 117, 118

ウィーン体制 Vienna system 117, 118, 119, 135, 168

ウィーンの包囲 Siege of Vienna 79, 81, 94

ヴィクトリア女王 Queen Victoria 133

ウィクリフ Wycliffe, John 73

ウイグル族 Uyghurs 38, 41, 46, 189

ヴィシー政権 Vichy France 165

ウィルソン Wilson, Woodrow 153

ヴェーダ Vedas 18

ウェストファリア条約 Peace of Westphalia 96, 97

ヴェネチア Venice 54, 56, 63, 66, 69, 75, 79, 82

ヴェネチア商人 Venetian merchant 56, 62

ヴェルサイユ宮殿 Palace of Versailles 112, 128

ヴェルサイユ条約 Treaty of Versailles 153

ヴェルサイユ体制 Versailles system 162, 168

ヴェルダン条約 Treaty of Verdun 43

浮世絵 ukiyo-e 144, 146

ウマイヤ朝 Umayyad Caliphate 36, 37, 38, 42

運河 canal 32, 124

【エ】

英西戦争 Anglo-Spanish War 88

永楽帝 Yongle Emperor 82, 95

英蘭戦争 Anglo-Dutch Wars 99

エーゲ海 Aegean Sea 11, 147

エカチェリーナ2世 Catherine II 119

エジプト Egypt 5, 8, 9, 10, 11, 12, 13, 17, 18, 19, 23, 26, 31, 36, 42, 56, 70, 92, 107, 113, 114, 127, 135, 143, 175, 176

エチオピア Ethiopia 9, 107, 160, 162

エフェソス公会議 Council of Ephesus 27, 53

エリザベス女王（1世）Queen Elizabeth I 77, 87, 88, 98, 104, 111

エルサレム Jerusalem 55, 56, 57, 127, 175

猿人 ape-man 2, 3

袁世凱 Yuan Shikai 142, 149, 152, 161

【オ】

オイラート Oirats 95

オイルショック oil shock 176

王権神授説 divine right of kings 98, 109

黄金（金）gold 54, 55, 74, 101, 124

欧州経済共同体 (EEC) European Economic Community (EEC) 181

欧州石炭鉄鋼共同体 European Coal and Steel Community 173

欧州連合 (EU) European Union (EU) 173, 179, 181, 190

王政復古 restoration 115, 163

王党派 Royalists 98, 99

オーストラリア Australia 179

オーストリア Austria 49, 73, 78, 79, 101, 103, 108, 112, 113, 115, 117, 118, 119, 123, 126, 127, 128, 131, 147, 148, 153, 156, 160, 164

オーストリア継承戦争 War of Austrian Succession 108, 114

オーストリア・ハンガリー帝国 Austro-Hungarian Empire 147, 148, 160

オーストロネシア語族 Austronesian 64

オゴタイ・ハン Ogodei Khan 60, 62

オスマン帝国 the Ottoman Empire 16, 69, 70, 71, 74, 77, 78, 79, 80, 81, 91, 92, 93, 94, 95, 119, 122, 126, 127, 135, 138, 142, 147, 148, 150, 153, 168, 175

オスロ合意 Oslo Accords 187

オットー1世 Otto I 44, 45, 46, 49

オランダ Netherlands [Holland] 77, 88, 89, 90, 95, 96, 97, 98, 99, 100, 103, 107, 110, 114, 120, 126, 135, 153, 165, 166, 170, 190

オレゴントレイル Oregon Trail 124

【カ】

カースト制度 (system of) caste 18

ガーナ王国 Kingdom of Ghana 55

カーバ神殿 Kaaba 35

カール大帝 Charlemagne 43, 44, 49

カール・マルテル Charles Martel 38

階級 (social) class 6, 47, 57, 58, 59, 83, 98, 101, 111, 112, 121, 132

階級闘争 class conflict 131, 160, 184

開拓者 pioneer 124, 132

カエサル Caesar, Gaius Julius 21, 23

夏 Xia 11

科学 science 1, 2, 4, 24, 27, 31, 43, 66, 75, 76, 77, 102, 116, 144, 145, 146, 148, 188, 193

科挙 civil service examination system 58, 80, 121, 142

核拡散防止条約 Treaty on the Non-Proliferation of Nuclear Weapons (NPT) 174

革命 revolution [rebellion, major change] 4, 5, 36, 38, 88, 98, 99, 100, 102, 108, 109, 110, 111, 112, 113, 114, 115, 116, 117, 118, 119, 120, 121, 122, 123, 125, 126, 127, 128, 129, 131, 132, 133, 134, 135,

137, 138, 139, 142, 143, 144, 145, 146, 147, 148, 149, 150, 151, 152, 153, 156, 161, 168, 170, 174, 176, 177, 180, 182, 184, 188, 190, 193

学問 scholarship 21, 76

火刑 burn at the stake 65, 73

カストロ Castro, Fidel 177

課税 taxation 65, 69, 73, 98, 100, 108, 111

合衆国憲法 Constitution of the United States 110, 111

桂タフト協定 Katsura-Taft Agreement 141

カトリック Catholic 26, 27, 37, 43, 44, 45, 46, 49, 51, 56, 57, 66, 68, 69, 72, 75, 76, 78, 82, 84, 85, 86, 87, 88, 89, 90, 96, 98, 100, 102, 103

カニシカ王 Kanishka 29

カノッサの屈辱 Humiliation at Canossa 51, 56

貨幣経済 monetary economy 69, 121

カペー朝 Capetian dynasty 48, 65

鎌倉幕府 Kamakura Shogunate 61, 68, 81

紙 paper 23, 31, 32, 38, 43, 188

カラコルム Karakorum 60, 68

ガリア Gaul 12, 23, 37, 47

カリフ caliph 36, 38, 42, 43, 49

ガリレオ Galileo Galilei 76

カルヴァン Calvin, John 73, 87, 88

カルタゴ Carthage 15, 22, 34

カロリング朝 Carolingian dynasty 37, 38, 43, 48

漢 Han (dynasty) 15, 20, 21, 24, 25, 28, 29, 30, 31, 32, 33, 38

灌漑 irrigating land (Irrigation) 5

漢字 Chinese characters 5, 10, 15, 19, 20, 24, 31, 60

鑑真和上 Jianzhen 50

関税自主権 tariff autonomy 122, 133

ガンダーラ Gandhara 28, 29

ガンディース川 Ganges 12, 29

ガンディー Gandhi, Mahatma 154, 170, 178

カンネーの戦い Battle of Cannae 22

カンボジア Cambodia 63, 64, 126, 135, 170, 177, 183

漢民族 Han Chinese [Han people] 20, 28, 32, 50, 52, 58, 59, 68, 80, 95, 105, 129, 134, 142, 179

【キ】

魏 Wei 28, 29, 31

キエフ公国 Kievan Rus' [Great Duchy of Kiev, Kievan Grand Duchy] 46, 47, 62

議会制民主主義 parliamentary democracy 65, 100, 101, 109, 111, 112

飢饉 famine 47, 123, 126

騎士 knight 44, 51, 56, 57, 65, 66, 69, 77, 93, 111,

128

技術革新 technological innovation 116, 117, 132, 134, 143, 144, 185, 192

魏志倭人伝 Record of Japan in the History of Wei 31

北大西洋条約機構（NATO）North Atlantic Treaty Organization 172

契丹 Khitans 49, 52, 60

騎馬民族 horse-riding (nomadic) people [equestrian people] 32, 52, 53, 60, 80

キプチャク・ハン国 Kipchak Khanate 62, 67, 71, 91

喜望峰 Cape of Good Hope 30, 74, 80, 135

旧人 archaic humans 2, 3

キューバ危機 Cuban Missile Crisis 174, 177, 181

旧約聖書 Old Testament 7, 13, 14, 26, 35, 187

教会大分裂 Great Schism 69

教皇領 Vatican as a domain (Papal States) 37

共産主義 communism 131, 132, 143, 145, 151, 152, 153, 157, 158, 161, 163, 167, 170, 172, 177, 180, 183, 184

共産主義革命 communist revolution 139, 151

仰韶文化（ヤンシャオ文化）Yangshao culture 10

匈奴 Xiongnu 21, 25, 28, 32, 52, 67, 134

恐怖政治 Reign of Terror 113

ギリシア Greece 11, 12, 13, 14, 15, 16, 17, 18, 19, 20, 22, 23, 24, 25, 27, 29, 31, 35, 43, 51, 54, 75, 77, 83, 92, 116, 126, 147, 172

キリスト教 Christianity 14, 16, 25, 26, 27, 28, 29, 35, 37, 38, 39, 43, 45, 46, 48, 49, 50, 51, 52, 53, 55, 56, 57, 62, 63, 70, 71, 72, 75, 76, 78, 79, 82, 84, 85, 87, 90, 93, 94, 95, 97, 101, 127, 129, 131, 134, 137, 140, 145, 164, 175, 187

ギルガメシュ叙事詩 Gilgamesh Epic 7

ギルド guild 57

義和団事件 Boxer Rebellion 140

金（国名）Jin 53, 58, 60, 61

銀 silver 74, 84, 121, 133

金印勅書 Golden Bull 78

キング牧師 Martin Luther King Jr. 178

近代兵器 modern weaponry 152

金融資本 financial capital 143, 144

【ク】

偶像崇拝 idol worship (Idolatry) 43

グーテンベルク Gutenberg, Johannes 73, 75, 136, 188

楔形文字 cuneiform 5, 7

クシャーナ朝 Kushan Empire 29, 30

百済 Baekje 33

クノッソス宮殿 palace of Knossos (Knossos Palace) 11

クフ王 King Khufu 9

グプタ朝 Gupta Empire 30

鳩摩羅什 Kumarajiva 50

クメール・ルージュ Khmer Rouge 183

クリオーリョ criollos 125

クリミア Crimea 94, 101, 104, 119

クリミア戦争 Crimean War 127, 130

クレオパトラ7世 Cleopatra VII 23

グレゴリウス7世 Gregory VII 51

クレタ文明 Cretan civilization 11, 15

クロアチア Croatia 79, 127, 185

クロマニョン人 Cro-Magnon Man 3

クロムウェル Cromwell, Oliver 98, 99

軍国主義 militarism 137, 167, 168

軍事技術 military technology 144, 188

【ケ】

経済制裁 economic sanctions 186

経済封鎖 economic blockade 115, 149, 166, 177

啓蒙専制君主 enlightened despot 105, 108, 119

月氏 Yuezhi 19, 21, 29

ケプラー Kepler, Johannes 76

ケマル・アタテュルク Mustafa Kemal Atatürk 156

ケルト人 Celts 47, 48

ゲルマニア Germania 24, 25

ゲルマン人 Germanic peoples 25, 28, 34, 37, 40, 43, 44, 45, 46, 47, 48, 49, 124, 136, 173

ゲルマン人の大移動 Great migration of the Germanic peoples 25, 47

元 Yuan (dynasty) 61, 63, 68, 75, 95, 105

阮王朝 Nguyen dynasty 134

言語 language 4, 7, 15, 19, 24, 64, 76, 136

元寇 Mongolian Invasions 68

原子爆弾 atomic bomb 167, 173

玄奘三蔵 Xuanzang 39, 50

原人 primitive man [early man] 2, 3, 4

玄宗（Emperor）Xuanzong 39, 40, 41

遣唐使 envoys [emissaries, missions] to the Tang 33, 39, 40, 42, 59

権利の章典 Bill of Rights 99, 100, 111

元老院 Senate 22

言論統制 suppression of [restriction on] freedom of speech 160, 162, 166, 191

【コ】

呉 Wu 28

ゴア Goa 81, 85, 89, 90, 95

小泉八雲 Koizumi Yakumo 2, 4

交易 trade [trading] 4, 5, 8, 11, 12, 15, 16, 18, 29, 30, 38, 46, 54, 55, 56, 61, 62, 63, 66, 67, 68, 70, 74, 80, 81, 82, 89, 91, 95, 99, 104, 114, 121, 132, 173

後ウマイヤ朝 Andalusian Umayyad dynasty 42, 55, 71

黄河 Yellow River 8, 10, 11, 21

康熙帝 Emperor Kangxi 105, 119

工業化 industrialization 139, 157

紅巾の乱 Red Turban Rebellion 68

高句麗 Koguryo 32, 33, 52

鉱山 mine 74, 77, 124

孔子 Confucius 20

黄巣の乱 Huang Chao Rebellion 42

高度経済成長 high economic growth 171, 181

公民権 civil rights 178, 179, 180, 181, 186

公民権運動 civil rights movement 178, 179, 180, 181

高麗 Koryo 61, 68, 80, 106

合理主義 rationality 102, 145

コーカソイド Caucasoid 12

ゴーギャン Gauguin, Paul 2, 4, 7, 12, 193

ゴータマ・シッダルタ Gautama Siddhartha 18

コーラン Quran 35, 36, 38

ゴールドラッシュ Gold Rush 124

後漢書東夷伝 Record of Encounters with the Eastern Barbarians in the History of the Later Han 31

国際軍事裁判所（ニュールンベルク／極東） Nuremberg International Military Tribunal / International Military Tribunal for the Far East 169

国際政治 international politics 49, 92, 100, 119, 129, 143, 149, 152, 182, 192

国際連合 United Nations [UN] 168, 169, 192

国際連盟 League of Nations 153, 159, 161, 168, 169, 175

国粋主義 Nationalism 158

国民議会（フランス革命） National Assembly 111, 112

国民国家 nation-state [national state] 118, 129, 131

国連軍 United Nations forces 169, 185

五胡十六国 Sixteen Kingdoms of the Five Barbarians 28

五・四運動 May Fourth Movement 152, 153, 161

胡椒 pepper 120

コスモポリタン cosmopolitan 19, 40, 59

個性 individuality 144, 146

古代オリンピック Ancient Olympic Games 16

五代十国 Five Dynasties and Ten Kingdoms 42, 49, 52, 58

黒海 Black Sea 12, 25, 45, 91, 92, 94, 127, 172

国家意識 national awareness 4, 137, 157

骨角器 bone tool (bone or horn implement) 4

国家財政 national finance 95, 112, 149

国共合作 United Front 161, 162

コペルニクス Copernicus, Nicolaus 76, 101

コミンテルン Comintern 151

コミンフォルム Cominform 172

コメコン（経済相互援助会議） COMECON 172

コルテス Cortés, Hernán 84

コロンブス Columbus, Christopher 74

コンスタンティヌス帝（1世） Constantine the Great 25, 26

コンスタンティノープル／イスタンブール／ビザンティウム Constantinople; Istanbul; Byzantium 25, 46, 51, 54, 56, 70, 77, 79, 141

【サ】

採集 gathering 3, 5

彩陶 colored earthenware 10

鎖国 close the country to the outside world [national seclusion] 90, 95, 97, 99, 106, 121, 122, 126

ササン朝ペルシア Sassanid Empire (of Persian) 25, 28, 29, 34, 36, 40

サハラ砂漠 Sahara Desert 54, 55, 143

ザビエル Xavier, Francis 84, 85

サファヴィー朝 Safavid dynasty 70, 182

サマルカンド Samarkand 67

サラエボ Sarajevo 148

サラミスの海戦 Battle of Salamis 16

三角貿易 triangular trade 116, 120

産業革命 Industrial Revolution 12, 102, 116, 117, 118, 119, 120, 121, 122, 123, 127, 128, 129, 131, 132, 133, 134, 137, 138, 143, 144, 145, 168, 170, 188, 192, 193

産業技術 industrial technology 144

三権分立 separation of powers 111

三国干渉 Triple Intervention 138

三国協商 Triple Entente 141, 142, 148

三国志 Record of the Three Kingdoms 28

三国同盟（第一次世界大戦） Triple Alliance 142, 148

三国同盟（第二次世界大戦） Tripartite Pact 163, 166

三国防共協定 Anti-Comintern Pact 163

3C政策 3C Strategy 141

30年戦争 Thirty Years' War 96, 98, 99, 104, 126

参政権 right to vote [political right, suffrage] 17, 100, 157

3B政策 3B Strategy 141

サンフランシスコ平和条約 Treaty of San Francisco 171

【シ】

シーア派 Shia Islam 36, 42, 56, 70, 176

シーク教 Sikhism 93, 114

シェイクスピア Shakespeare, William 23, 77

自営農 independent farmer 98

ジェントリ gentry 98, 100, 101

シオニズム Zionism 13

死者の書 The Book of the Dead 9

市場 market 90, 107, 114, 119, 120, 121, 124, 130, 132, 136, 139, 140, 150

士大夫 Shi daifu 58, 59

七月革命 July Revolution 117, 118

七年戦争 Seven Years' War 108, 114

シチリア王国 Kingdom of Sicily 47

ジハード (聖戦) jihad 36, 57

司馬遷 Sima Qian 31

資本家 financier [capitalist] 100, 118, 142

資本主義 capitalism 89, 114, 117, 131, 132, 137, 150, 152, 153, 163, 170, 171, 172, 180, 184, 185

市民階級 middle class [bourgeoisie] 57, 121, 132

シモン・ボリバル Simón Bolívar 125

ジャイナ教 Jainism 18

社会運動 social movement 117, 178, 180

社会主義 socialism 131, 136, 143, 156, 157, 160, 163, 171, 172, 175, 177, 180, 182, 183, 184, 185

社会主義運動 socialist movement 117, 131, 136, 143, 160, 163

ジャコバン派 Jacobins 112, 113

ジャワ原人 Java Man 3

ジャンヌ・ダルク Joan of Arc 65

周 Zhou (dynasty) 11, 13, 15, 20

宗教 religion [teaching] 4, 6, 9, 13, 14, 18, 26, 27, 28, 29, 35, 36, 37, 39, 43, 46, 50, 51, 54, 57, 59, 62, 63, 64, 68, 70, 71, 73, 75, 76, 77, 79, 86, 89, 91, 93, 96, 98, 102, 114, 131, 140, 144, 145, 146, 154, 156, 168, 174, 180, 182, 187, 190

宗教改革 religious reform [Reformation] 26, 37, 69, 72, 73, 74, 75, 76, 78, 84, 85, 87, 88, 96, 102, 116, 126, 136, 156, 168

宗教会議 (公会議) religious conference [council] 27, 37, 39, 51, 53

十字軍 Crusades 38, 51, 52, 53, 54, 55, 56, 57, 69, 70, 75, 103

自由主義経済 liberalist economy 153

重商主義 mercantile system 99, 111

重装歩兵 hoplite [heavily armed infantry] 17, 22

修道院 monastery 73, 85, 86

自由と平等 freedom [liberty] and equality 102, 112, 119

儒教 Confucianism 14, 20, 21, 31, 39, 50, 58, 59, 95, 106, 119, 145, 180

主従関係 lord-vassal relationship (relationship of master and servant) 44

出エジプト Exodus 13

ジュネーヴ Geneva 153, 170

種の起源 On the Origin of Species by Means of Natural Selection 2, 144

シュメール人 Sumerians 5, 6, 7, 8, 15

シュリーヴィジャヤ王国 Srivijaya Empire 63

シュリーマン Schliemann (Heinrich) 11, 12

狩猟 hunting [to hunt] 2, 3, 4, 5, 6, 10, 14, 63, 83, 155

春秋戦国時代 Spring and Autumn and Warring States Periods 15, 20, 31

荘園 manor 40, 44, 47, 51

蒋介石 Chiang Kai-shek 161, 162, 167, 170

蒸気機関 steam engine 116, 117

商業活動 commercial activity 4, 54, 70, 75, 97, 155

象形文字 hieroglyph 5, 9

少数民族 minority ethnic groups [peoples] 40, 41

常設国際司法裁判所 Permanent Court of International Justice 153

浄土宗 Jingtu [Pure Land] school 59

常備軍 standing army 69, 93, 111

縄文時代 Jomon period 5, 10, 64, 83

蜀 Shu 28

植民地 colony [colonial territory] 48, 63, 74, 84, 85, 89, 90, 92, 97, 98, 99, 100, 103, 107, 108, 109, 111, 114, 123, 125, 126, 130, 132, 133, 135, 136, 137, 143, 148, 149, 151, 152, 153, 154, 157, 159, 160, 163, 164, 166, 168, 169, 170, 173, 183, 186, 193

植民地政策 colonial (government) policies 2, 153, 154

贖宥状 indulgences 72

諸国民の春 Spring of Nations 118, 123, 126, 147

諸子百家 Hundred Schools of Thought 20, 31

ジョン王 King John 65

新羅 Silla 33

シリア Syria 9, 13, 36, 92, 175, 176, 189

シリコンバレー Silicon Valley 179

私掠船 privateer 88, 90, 123

シルクロード Silk Road 12, 19, 28, 30, 53, 54, 60, 64, 66, 91

新 Xin 21

晋 Jin dynasty 28

秦 Qin (dynasty) 15, 20, 21, 32, 33, 95

清 Qing (dynasty) 97, 105, 106, 119, 120, 121, 122, 126, 129, 133, 134, 138, 139, 140, 142, 149, 152, 161

辛亥革命 Xinhai Revolution 129, 142, 143, 149, 150, 152, 161

進化論 theory of evolution 2, 4, 144, 145

信教の自由 freedom of religion 14, 26, 72

人権 human rights 17, 112, 117, 132, 157, 169, 173, 178, 186, 191, 193

人権宣言 Declaration of the Rights of Man and of the Citizen 112

人工衛星 man-made satellite 188

人種差別 racial discrimination (Racism) 12, 154, 157, 178, 186

神聖ローマ帝国 the Holy Roman Empire 44, 49, 51, 56, 70, 72, 73, 77, 78, 79, 84, 86, 88, 91, 92, 96, 100, 102, 103, 108, 115, 118, 128, 149, 168

神道 Shinto 35, 50, 54

新バビロニア New Babylonia 13

新約聖書 New Testament 1

侵略 aggression [invasion, make a raid] 8, 32, 45, 49, 89, 90, 95, 157, 160, 163, 164, 173, 178

【ス】

隋 Sui 32, 33, 39, 40, 41

水素爆弾 hydrogen bomb 173

水墨画 ink painting 59, 120

スウェーデン Sweden 46, 96, 101, 102, 104

数学 mathematics 24, 27, 31, 43, 76, 83, 116, 144

スエズ運河 Suez Canal 135, 175, 176

スコットランド Scotland 47, 48, 66, 86, 87, 88, 98

スターリン Stalin, Joseph 156, 157, 167, 173, 180, 184

スターリン批判 criticism of the Stalin regime 184

スパルタ Sparta 16, 17

スペイン Spain 3, 22, 23, 34, 38, 42, 45, 47, 55, 70, 71, 73, 74, 77, 79, 81, 82, 83, 84, 85, 86, 88, 89, 90, 91, 92, 95, 96, 97, 100, 102, 103, 110, 117, 125, 128, 139, 163

スペイン継承戦争 War of the Spanish Succession 103, 104

スペイン内戦 Spanish Civil War 163

スラブ Slav 46, 54, 92, 127, 147

スルタン sultan 49, 93

スレイマン大帝 (1世) Suleyman the Magnificent 79, 91

スンナ派 Sunni Islam 36, 42, 49, 176

【セ】

正教会 Orthodox Church 43, 46, 56, 71, 91, 107

清教徒 Puritan 87, 88, 98

清教徒革命 Puritan [English] Revolution 88, 98, 99, 102, 114

青磁 celadon ware [blue porcelain] 59, 120

聖書 Bible 1, 7, 13, 14, 26, 35, 38, 72, 73, 76, 77, 84, 187

聖職者の叙任権 investiture of the clerics 51

西太后 Empress Dowager Cixi 140

青銅器 bronze [copper] 7, 8, 10, 15, 83

青年トルコ Young Turks 147, 148, 156

西遼 Western Liao 53, 60

セイロン Ceylon 30, 133

世界恐慌 Great Depression 158, 159, 162

責任内閣制 Parliamentary Cabinet system 99

絶対君主制 absolute monarchy 98, 103, 105, 111, 114

セルジューク朝トルコ Seljuq Turks [Empire] 42, 49, 51, 53

セルバンテス Cervantes, Miguel de 77

セルビア Serbia 79, 94, 127, 147, 148, 185

セレウコス帝国 Seleucid Empire 19, 21

宣教師 missionary 56, 62, 84, 90, 95, 119, 120

戦国時代 (中国) Warring States period 15, 20, 32, 39

戦国時代 (日本) Sengoku period 36, 44, 81, 85, 88, 90, 91, 121

禅宗 Zen school 59, 61

専制政治 autocracy 98, 99, 138, 141, 143, 184

戦争犯罪 war crime 169

選帝侯 Elector Prince 78

宣統帝溥儀 Xuantong Emperor / Puyi 142, 161

鮮卑族 Xianbei 28, 32, 52

【ソ】

宋 / 南宋 Song / Southern Song 49, 52, 53, 54, 58, 59, 60, 61, 68, 75, 120

ソヴィエト Soviets 151

ソヴィエト社会主義共和国連邦 (ソ連) Union of Soviet Socialist Republics (Soviet Union) 67, 151, 153, 156, 157, 161, 163, 164, 165, 166, 167, 168, 169, 170, 171, 172, 173, 174, 175, 176, 177, 180, 182, 183, 184, 185, 186, 188, 189, 191, 193

荘子 Zhuangzi 20, 39

ソグド人 Sogdians 40, 41, 67

ゾロアスター教 Zoroastrianism 28, 39

ソロモン王 King Solomon 13

孫文 Sun Yat-sen 142, 149, 152, 161

【タ】

ダーウィン Darwin, Charles 2, 4, 12, 144, 145

タージ・マハル Taj Mahal 93

タイ Thailand 64, 135

第一次世界大戦 World War I [First World War] 79,

118, 127, 141, 142, 147, 148, 149, 150, 151, 152, 153, 154, 155, 158, 159, 160, 165, 168, 175

太陰太陽暦 lunisolar calendar 8

太陰暦 lunar calendar 8

大運河 great canal 32

大韓民国 Republic of Korea 170, 171

大空位時代 Great Interregnum 78

大航海時代 Age of Discovery 54, 74, 75, 80, 88, 90, 95, 107, 120, 156

大乗仏教 Mahayana Buddhism 29

大西洋 Atlantic Ocean [the Atlantic] 45, 70, 74, 90, 109, 115, 123, 155, 169, 172

大西洋憲章 Atlantic Charter 169

第二次産業革命 Second Industrial Revolution 143, 144

第二次世界大戦 World War II [Second World War] 8, 92, 122, 128, 149, 157, 159, 160, 163, 164, 165, 167, 168, 169, 170, 171, 172, 173, 175, 176, 178, 179, 181, 182, 183, 185, 188, 190

対仏大同盟 anti-French Coalition [Coalition against France] 113, 115

太平天国の乱 Taiping Rebellion 129, 134, 142

太平洋 Pacific Ocean [the Pacific] 2, 4, 63, 64, 74, 90, 92, 107, 121, 124, 126, 130, 139, 159, 167, 179

太陽暦 solar calendar 8, 9

大陸横断鉄道 First Transcontinental Railroad 130

大量生産 mass production 117, 143, 155, 193

多神教 polytheistic religion 13, 14, 26, 35, 37

打製石器 chipped stone tool 2, 5

多様性 diversity 18, 179

ダライ・ラマ Dalai Lama 152, 180

タラス河畔の戦い Battle of Talas 38

ダレイオス1世 Darius I 13

ダレイオス3世 Darius III 17

ダンテ Dante, Alighieri 76

【チ】

治外法権 extraterritorial rights 92, 122

地球温暖化 global warming 191

チグリス川 the Tigris 5, 9

治水事業 flood control works (flood control business) 11

地中海 Mediterranean Sea 5, 9, 11, 12, 13, 15, 16, 19, 20, 22, 23, 24, 25, 29, 30, 34, 36, 37, 42, 45, 46, 47, 54, 55, 57, 69, 70, 71, 75, 82, 86, 91, 94, 107, 172

地動説 heliocentric theory 27, 76, 101

血の日曜日事件 Bloody Sunday 141

チベット Tibet 41, 50, 53, 68, 152, 180, 185

ティムール帝国 the Timurid Empire 67, 68, 70, 80

茶 tea 108, 120, 121, 132

チャーチル Churchill, Winston 167, 169, 172

チャガタイ・ハン国 Chagatai Khanate 62, 67

チャンパ王国 Kingdom of Champa 63, 64, 82

中央アジア Central Asia 3, 9, 10, 12, 17, 19, 20, 25, 28, 29, 32, 38, 40, 41, 42, 45, 47, 49, 52, 53, 60, 62, 64, 67, 68, 80, 91, 182

中華思想 China-centered view of the world 20, 59, 134

中華人民共和国 People's Republic of China 131, 170, 171, 180

中華民国 Republic of China 142, 161, 162, 170

中原 Zhongyuan 21

中国共産党 Chinese Communist Party 152, 160, 161, 162, 180

中世 Middle Ages [medieval] 27, 35, 37, 44, 45, 46, 51, 53, 57, 63, 66, 69, 73, 75, 76, 77, 80, 86, 88, 92, 101, 107, 111, 115, 118, 120, 128, 134, 137, 147, 156, 179, 187, 189

沖積世 alluvial epoch 4

中東戦争 Arab-Israeli Wars 175, 176

中東問題 Middle Eastern affairs [discord] 94, 122, 147, 176, 187, 189

長安 Chang'an 21, 39, 40, 41

朝貢 tribute [tributary] 21, 28, 31, 61, 63, 82, 95, 106, 129, 134, 140

チョーサー Chaucer, Geoffrey 76

朝鮮 Korea 17, 21, 29, 32, 33, 46, 50, 52, 54, 61, 64, 68, 80, 81, 82, 95, 106, 120, 129, 134, 138, 140, 164, 170, 171, 172, 174, 181

朝鮮戦争 Korean War 171, 172, 181

朝鮮半島 Korean Peninsula 17, 21, 29, 32, 33, 46, 50, 52, 54, 61, 64, 68, 80, 81, 95, 106, 120, 134, 138, 164, 170, 171

朝鮮民主主義人民共和国 Democratic People's Republic of Korea 170, 171

チンギス・ハン Genghis Khan 60, 62, 67, 68

【ツ】

ツァーリ Tsar 104

ツヴィングリ Zwingli, Huldrych 73

通信技術 communication technology 143

ツングース Tungus 32, 33, 52, 53

【テ】

帝国主義 imperialism 137, 138, 140, 143, 150, 151, 152, 153, 154, 159, 168

鄭和 Zheng He 82

テオドシウス帝 Theodosius 25, 27

手斧 hand ax 3

デカブリストの乱 Decembrist Revolt 119

デカルト Descartes, René 102

デジタル革命 digital revolution 188, 190, 193

鉄器 iron (Ironware) 8, 10, 15, 16, 17, 47

鉄のカーテン iron curtain 172

テニスコートの誓い Tennis Court Oath 112

テムジン Temujin 60

テューダー朝 Tudor dynasty 66

デロス同盟 Delian League 16

天動説 geocentric (theory) 76

デンマーク Denmark 45, 48, 96, 128, 165

天文学 astronomy 31, 116

【ト】

ドイツ Germany 12, 43, 48, 49, 57, 62, 72, 73, 78, 79, 92, 96, 100, 101, 103, 115, 117, 118, 119, 128, 131, 133, 138, 141, 143, 145, 147, 148, 149, 150, 151, 152, 153, 156, 157, 158, 159, 160, 162, 163, 164, 165, 166, 168, 169, 171, 172, 173, 174, 175, 181, 185

ドイツ帝国 German Empire 118, 128, 131, 148, 149, 150

ドイツ農民戦争 German Peasants' War 73

ドイツ民主共和国 German Democratic Republic 172

ドイツ連邦共和国 Federal Republic of Germany 172

唐 Tang (dynasty) [Tang China] 32, 33, 38, 39, 40, 41, 42, 43, 47, 49, 50, 52, 53, 58, 59, 61, 63

統一国家 unified country [unified state] 9, 15, 17, 118, 154

トゥール・ポワティエ間の戦い Battle of Tours-Poitiers 38

トゥキディデス Thucydides 31

道教 Taoism 20, 39, 50

道具 tool [instrument] 1, 2, 3, 4, 15, 144

東西交流 East-West exchange [East-West interchange, trade between East and West] 30, 38, 39, 42, 53, 62, 65, 81, 91, 120

陶磁器 chinaware 59, 120

東南アジア Southeast Asia 12, 28, 30, 38, 50, 54, 61, 63, 64, 81, 82, 91, 94, 95, 114, 135, 166, 190, 193

陶片追放 Ostracism 17

ドーリア人 Dorians 16

土器 earthenware 5, 10

徳川幕府 Tokugawa Shogunate 88, 90, 93, 95, 97, 105, 121, 129, 134

独ソ不可侵条約 Molotov-Ribbentrop Pact 164, 165

独立運動 independence movement [separatist movement, movement for independence] 19, 41, 48, 107, 125, 126, 127, 135, 139, 143, 147, 148, 149, 151, 152, 154, 156, 157, 169, 170, 171, 173, 175, 176, 184, 189

独立宣言 Declaration of Independence 108, 109, 150

ド・ゴール de Gaulle, Charles 165, 181

都市国家 city-state 7, 9, 10, 11, 12, 13, 15, 16, 17, 18, 21, 22, 24, 46, 53, 54, 69, 91, 104

突厥 Tujue 32, 40, 41, 52, 67

ドナウ川 Danube River [the Danube] 45, 79

豊臣秀吉 Toyotomi Hideyoshi 82, 90, 95, 106, 120

トルキスタン Turkestan 41, 49, 53

トルコ Turkey 8, 10, 11, 12, 16, 24, 34, 41, 42, 45, 46, 49, 51, 53, 60, 67, 69, 70, 92, 123, 138, 147, 148, 156, 172

トルデシリャス条約 Treaty of Tordesillas 85

奴隷 slave 9, 13, 17, 26, 49, 56, 74, 84, 102, 107, 109, 116, 117, 125, 130, 132, 135, 157, 178

奴隷解放宣言 Emancipation Proclamation 130

ドレフュス事件 Dreyfus Affair 137, 138

トロイア Troy 11, 12, 16

【ナ】

ナイル川 the Nile (the Nile River) 9

ナショナリズム nationalism 115, 136, 137, 143, 148, 158

ナチス Nazi 12, 158, 162, 163, 164, 175

ナチズム Nazism 137

ナポレオン Napoleon Bonaparte [Napoleon I] 22, 113, 114, 115, 117, 119, 123, 125, 128, 135

ナポレオン3世 Napoleon III 128

ナポレオン戦争 Napoleonic Wars 115, 117, 119, 125, 126, 131, 138, 168

南下政策 policy of southward expansion 94, 119, 127, 138

南京条約 Treaty of Nanjing 122, 129

ナントの勅令 Edict of Nantes 72

南北戦争 Civil War 129, 130, 131, 133, 139, 157, 178

【ニ】

ニーチェ Nietzsche, Friedrich 145

2月革命 February Revolution 118

ニケーア公会議 Council of Nicaea 27

ニコライ2世 Nicholas II 143, 151

西ゴート王国 Visigothic Kingdom 34, 36, 38, 71

西ローマ帝国 Western Roman Empire 25, 34, 37, 40

二足歩行 bipedal 2

日英同盟 Anglo-Japanese Alliance 138, 141, 148

日米安全保障条約 Security Treaty between the United States and Japan 171

日露戦争 Russo-Japanese War 94, 127, 140, 141, 142, 143, 147, 156, 161

日韓併合 Japan officially annexed Korea (Japanese annexation of Korea) 141

日清戦争 Sino-Japanese War 138, 140

日ソ中立条約 Soviet-Japanese Neutrality Pact 165

ニネベ Nineveh 13

日本 Japan 2, 3, 5, 8, 10, 12, 14, 16, 17, 18, 21, 28, 29, 31, 32, 33, 34, 35, 36, 39, 40, 42, 44, 46, 47, 48, 50, 52, 54, 58, 59, 61, 64, 65, 68, 72, 81, 82, 83, 84, 85, 88, 89, 90, 91, 93, 94, 95, 97, 98, 99, 104, 105, 106, 117, 119, 120, 121, 122, 126, 127, 129, 130, 131, 133, 134, 138, 139, 140, 141, 142, 143, 145, 146, 148, 149, 151, 152, 156, 157, 158, 159, 160, 161, 162, 163, 164, 165, 166, 167, 168, 169, 170, 171, 173, 174, 178, 181, 185, 186, 190, 193

ニューイングランド New England 107

ニューディール政策 New Deal 163

ニュートン Newton, Isaac 116

ニューヨーク New York 89, 97, 99, 107, 110, 124, 130, 156, 158, 159, 189

【ネ】

ネアンデルタール人 Neanderthal 3

ネストリウス派 Nestorianism 26, 27, 28, 39, 53, 62

ネルチンスク条約 Treaty of Nerchinsk 105

【ノ】

農業革命 agricultural revolution 116

農耕 agriculture [farming] 5, 6, 7, 8, 10, 14, 15, 17, 44, 52, 53, 63, 83

農耕民族 agricultural people 52, 63

ノヴゴロド Novgorod 46, 57, 91, 104

農奴解放令 Emancipation Reform of 1861 138

農奴制 system of serfdom 104, 138

ノルマンコンクエスト Norman Conquest 48, 49, 50, 98

ノルマン人 Normans 45, 46, 47, 48, 55, 98, 124, 136

バイキング Vikings 45, 46, 47

【ハ】

賠償金 reparations 140, 153, 156, 158

パキスタン Pakistan 9, 14, 19, 93, 170, 174, 182

白磁 white porcelain 59, 120

パクス・ロマーナ Pax Romana 24, 172

バグダード Baghdad 36, 42, 43, 49, 62, 67, 141

バクトリア Bactria 19, 21, 29

バビロン第一王朝 First Babylonian dynasty 7, 8, 15

バビロンの捕囚 Babylonian Captivity 13

ハプスブルク家 House of Habsburg 45, 73, 74, 77, 78, 79, 86, 87, 88, 92, 94, 96, 101, 103, 108, 118, 120, 168

バブル経済 bubble economy 158

ハムラビ王 King Hammurabi 8

ハムラビ法典 Code of Hammurabi 8

破門 excommunication [excommunicate] 43, 51, 56, 65, 86

薔薇戦争 War of the Roses 66, 86, 98

ハラッパ Harappa 9

パリ講和会議 Paris Peace Conference 152, 153

パリ・コミューン Paris Commune 131, 137

パリ条約（アメリカ独立） Treaty of Paris 110

パリ条約（クリミア戦争） Treaty of Paris 127

パリ条約（ECSC） Treaty of Paris 173

パリ不戦条約 Kellogg-Briand Pact 159, 168

バルカン戦争 Balkan Wars 147, 148

バルカン半島 Balkan Peninsula 79, 92, 118, 126, 127, 147, 148, 165

パルティア帝国 Parthian Empire [Parthia] 21, 25

バルト海 Baltic Sea 46, 54, 57, 69, 104, 127

バルト三国 Baltic States 165, 184

バルトロメウ・ディアス Bartolomeu Dias 74, 135

パレスチナ Palestine 13, 56, 149, 175, 176, 187, 191

パレスチナ解放機構 Palestinian Liberation Organization 176, 187

パレスチナ難民 Palestinian refugees 175, 176, 187

パワーバランス power balance [balance of power] 86, 91, 96, 104, 106, 122, 185

ハワイ Hawaii 64, 126, 139, 166

ハンガリー Hungary 45, 46, 62, 79, 118, 126, 147, 148, 160, 184, 185

ハンガリー動乱 Hungarian Revolution 184

漢江の奇跡 miracle on the Han River 181

ハンザ同盟 the Hanseatic League 57, 69

反戦運動 anti-war demonstrations (antiwar movement) 178

ハンニバル Hannibal 22

万里の長城 Great Wall (of China) 21, 28, 32, 53, 95, 105

【ヒ】

東インド会社（イギリス） East India Company 108, 114, 132, 133

東インド会社（オランダ） Dutch East India Company 89, 97, 114

東ゴート王国 Kingdom of the Ostrogoths 34

東シナ海 East China Sea 61, 81, 82

東ローマ帝国 Eastern Roman Empire 34, 35, 36, 37, 43, 46, 49, 51, 54, 56, 69, 70, 77, 91, 92, 93

ヒクソス人 Hyksos 9

飛行機／航空機 airplane / aircraft 144, 152, 155, 189

ピサロ Pizarro, Francisco 84

ビザンティウム／イスタンブール／コンスタンティノープル Byzantium; Istanbul; Constantinople 25, 46, 51, 54, 56, 70, 77, 79, 141

ヒジュラ Hegira 35

ビスマルク Bismarck, Otto von 128, 130, 141

ピタゴラス Pythagoras 24

ヒッタイト人 Hittites 8

ヒトラー Hitler, Adolf 157, 158, 159, 162, 164, 165, 167

百年戦争 Hundred Years' War 65, 66, 69, 86, 92

白蓮教徒 White Lotus Sect 121

氷河期 ice age [glacial period] 3, 4, 5, 31, 83

ピョートル大帝 Peter the Great 104, 105

肥沃な三日月地帯 Fertile Crescent 5, 7, 8, 10, 17

ピラミッド（エジプト）pyramid 9

ピラミッド（マヤ）pyramid 83

ピルグリム・ファーザーズ Pilgrim Fathers 87

ヒンドゥー教 Hinduism (Hindu faith) 14, 18, 30, 35, 50, 63, 81, 82, 93, 114, 154, 170, 187

【フ】

ファシズム fascism 160, 162, 163, 164, 169, 171

ファラオ pharaoh 9

フィリピン Philippines 74, 85, 89, 90, 139, 141, 170, 189

フィリッポス2世 Philippos II 17

フィレンツェ Florence 77

フェニキア人 Phoenicians 15, 22, 34

プエブロ pueblo 83, 84

フス Hus, Jan 73

武断政治 military rule (military government) 58

普通選挙 universal suffrage 118, 157

フッガー家 Fugger family 77

仏教 Buddhism 18, 19, 28, 29, 39, 46, 50, 53, 54, 59, 63, 64, 68, 90, 106, 152, 187

仏像 statue of Buddha [Buddhist image] 29, 146

ブッダ Buddha 18, 29

武帝 Wu Di 21, 25, 31

不凍港 ice-free harbor [port] 104, 106, 126

プトレマイオス朝 Ptolemaic dynasty 19, 23

不平等条約 unequal treaty 122

フビライ Khubilai 61, 62, 68

普仏戦争 Franco-Prussian War 128, 130, 131, 137, 141, 148, 149

プラッシーの戦い Battle of Plassey 132

プラトン Plato 24, 27, 43, 75

フランク王国 Kingdom of the Franks [Frankish Kingdom] 37, 38, 43, 44, 46, 47, 48, 49, 78

フランクフルト国民会議 Frankfurt National Assembly 118

フランス France 2, 3, 12, 16, 23, 34, 38, 43, 47, 48, 49, 51, 56, 57, 65, 66, 68, 69, 70, 72, 77, 79, 86, 87, 88, 92, 94, 96, 97, 100, 102, 103, 105, 107, 108, 110, 111, 112, 113, 114, 115, 117, 118, 119, 123, 125, 126, 127, 128, 129, 131, 132, 133, 134, 135, 137, 138, 141, 143, 145, 148, 149, 150, 153, 156, 158, 159, 160, 163, 164, 165, 166, 168, 169, 170, 172, 173, 174, 175, 176, 177, 181, 183, 190

フランス革命 French Revolution 102, 108, 112, 113, 114, 115, 116, 117, 119, 123, 126, 131, 135

フランス領インドシナ連邦 French Indochina 135

プランタジネット朝 Plantagenet dynasty 65

プランテーション plantation 120, 130

ブルガリア Bulgaria 46, 147, 148

ブルボン朝 the Bourbon dynasty 72, 103, 117

ブレスト・リトフスク条約 Treaty of Brest-Litovsk 151

フレンチ・インディアン戦争 French and Indian War 108

プロイセン Prussia 101, 103, 105, 108, 112, 118, 119, 128, 131

プロイセン-オーストリア戦争 Austro-Prussian War 128

プロテスタント Protestant [Protestantism] 27, 37, 69, 72, 75, 82, 86, 87, 88, 89, 90, 96, 100, 103

プロレタリアート proletariat 151

フロンティア frontier 124, 139

文化大革命 Great Proletarian Cultural Revolution [Cultural Revolution] 180, 184

焚書坑儒 burning books of the Chinese classics and burying Confucian scholars alive (burning books and burying scholars) 20

フン族 Huns 25, 34

文治政治 civilian government 58, 121

文明 civilization 1, 2, 5, 6, 7, 8, 9, 10, 11, 12, 13, 15, 16, 17, 19, 20, 21, 23, 28, 29, 31, 32, 33, 34, 38, 39, 43, 45, 46, 48, 50, 52, 54, 58, 59, 64, 67, 71, 72, 75, 77, 82, 83, 91, 93, 104, 106, 114, 116, 122, 144, 145, 146, 152, 154, 155, 173, 179, 188, 192, 193

【ヘ】

平安時代 Heian period 15, 42, 44, 47, 50, 52, 54, 59

米英戦争 War of 1812 123

米州機構 Organization of American States (OAS) 177

米西戦争 Spanish-American War 139

米墨戦争 Mexican-American War 125, 126

ペイン Paine, Thomas 109

北京 Beijing 3, 61, 68, 95, 105, 129, 140, 152, 161, 162, 170

北京原人 Peking Man 3

北京条約 Convention of Beijing 126, 129

ペスト plague 66, 69, 76

ベトナム Vietnam 61, 63, 64, 82, 126, 134, 135, 157, 160, 166, 170, 172, 177, 178, 180, 181, 182, 183

ベトナム社会主義共和国 Socialist Republic of Vietnam 177

ベトナム戦争 Vietnam war 61, 172, 177, 178, 180, 181, 182

ヘブライ人 Hebrews 13, 26

ペリー Perry, Commodore Matthew Calbraith 122, 126

ペリクレス Pericles 17

ペルシア戦争 Persian War 16, 17, 31

ベルベル人 Berbers 55

ベルリンの壁 Berlin Wall 174, 185

ベルリン封鎖 Berlin Blockade 172

ペレストロイカ perestroika 184

ヘレニズム文化 Hellenistic culture [Hellenism] 17, 19, 21, 23

ヘロドトス Herodotus 16, 31

ペロポネソス戦争 Peloponnesian War 17, 31

ヘンリー8世 Henry VIII 86, 87

【ホ】

封建制度 feudal system (feudalism) 11, 15, 44, 66, 69

亡命政権 government in exile 125, 165

ポエニ戦争 Punic Wars 22

ボーア人 Boer 135

ボーア戦争 Boer War 135

ホー・チ・ミン Ho Chi Minh 170, 177

ポーランド Poland 62, 66, 76, 100, 101, 104, 108, 111, 117, 119, 123, 131, 164, 165, 179, 185

北魏 Northern Wei 28, 32

北爆 bombing campaign in North Vietnam 177

捕鯨 whaling 126

ボストン茶会事件 Boston Tea Party 108

ボスニア Bosnia 70, 79, 94, 127, 148, 185

ボッカチオ Boccaccio, Giovanni 76

ポツダム宣言 Potsdam Declaration 167

ボヘミア Bohemia 73, 78, 96

ホメロス Homer 11

ホモ・エレクトゥス Homo erectus 3

ホモ・サピエンス Homo sapiens 3

ホモ・ハビリス Homo habilis 3

ボリシェヴィキ Bolsheviks 143, 151

ポリス polis 13, 16, 17

ポルトガル Portugal 74, 81, 82, 84, 85, 89, 90, 91, 95, 97, 107, 125

ホロコースト Holocaust 164, 175

ボロブドゥール Borobudur 63

香港 Hong Kong 122, 129, 191

【マ】

マーシャル・プラン Marshall Plan 172, 173

埋葬 buried 3

マウリヤ王朝 Maurya Empire 18, 19, 29

マカオ Macao 81, 85, 89

マグナカルタ Magna Carta 65

マケドニア Macedonia 17, 22, 147, 185

マジャール人 Magyars 45, 46, 147

マスメディア mass media 136, 157

磨製石器 polished stone tool 5

マゼラン Magellan, Ferdinand 74, 75, 85

マテオ・リッチ Matteo Ricci 95

マハラジャ maharaja 154

マムルーク mamluks 49

マムルーク朝 Mamluk dynasty Sultanate 70, 92

マヤ文明 Maya civilization 31, 83

マラッカ Malacca 81, 85, 89, 90, 91, 97

マラトンの戦い Battle of Marathon 16

マリア・テレジア Maria Theresa 108

マリー・アントワネット Marie Antoinette 112, 113

マリ王国 Mali Empire 55

マルクス Marx, Karl 131, 145, 184

マルコ・ポーロ Marco Polo 62

マレーシア Malaysia 64, 81, 85, 89, 94

マレー半島 Malay Peninsula 63, 126

満州 Manchu 95, 105, 106, 129, 134, 142, 161, 167

満州国 Manchukuo 161, 162, 165

満州事変 Mukden Incident 161

マンデラ Mandela, Nelson 186

マンハッタン Manhattan 97

【ミ】

ミケーネ文明 Mycenaean civilization 11, 15, 16

ミケランジェロ Michelangelo Buonarroti 77

南アフリカ South Africa 135, 141, 154, 186

南シナ海 South China Sea 54, 63, 81, 82, 185, 191

南ベトナム解放民族戦線 National Front for the Liberation of the South 177

南満州鉄道 South Manchuria Railway 156, 161

ミャンマー Myanmar 126, 133, 170

明 Ming (dynasty) 21, 68, 80, 81, 82, 89, 95, 97, 105, 106, 119, 120

民主化運動 democratization movement [movement for democratization] 115, 118, 119, 126, 181, 184, 191

民主主義 democracy 100, 101, 115, 157, 173, 179, 183, 190

民族意識 ethnic [racial] awareness 4, 48, 59, 115, 145, 154, 157

民族移動 migration of ethnic groups [ethnic migration] 41, 45, 46, 50, 71, 136

民族主義 nationalism 115, 129, 131, 145, 147, 148, 152, 157, 160, 175, 185

【ム】

ムガル王朝 Mughal Empire 80, 93, 94, 114, 122, 132, 133, 154

ムッソリーニ Mussolini, Benito 160, 162, 166

無敵艦隊 Spanish Armada 89, 90, 91

ムハンマド Muhammad 35, 37

室町幕府 Muromachi Shogunate 68, 81, 82

【メ】

メアリー Mary Stuart 87, 88

明治維新 Meiji Restoration 104, 106, 117, 122, 129, 130, 131, 133, 134, 140

メイフラワー号 Mayflower 87

名誉革命 Glorious Revolution 99, 100, 109, 111, 114

メキシコ Mexico 83, 84, 90, 123, 125, 150, 156

メキシコ共和国 Mexican Republic 125

メソポタミア Mesopotamia 5, 7, 8, 9, 10, 11, 12, 13, 15, 19

メッカ Mecca 35, 36, 92

メッテルニッヒ Metternich, Klemens von 117, 118

メディチ家 Medici 77

メルセン条約 Treaty of Mersen 43

メロヴィング朝 Merovingian dynasty 37

綿花 cotton 107, 116, 130, 132, 133, 154

【モ】

毛沢東 Mao Zedong 152, 162, 170, 180

モーゼ Moses 13, 26, 35

モスク mosque 36, 55, 74

モスクワ Moscow 67, 71, 91, 115, 119, 165

モスクワ大公国 Grand Duchy of Moscow 71, 91, 104

モヘンジョダロ Moenjo-daro 9

モンゴル Mongolia 20, 49, 50, 52, 53, 60, 61, 62, 67, 68, 69, 71, 80, 91, 94, 95, 101, 104, 105, 106, 134, 136, 152

モンゴル帝国 Mongol Empire 60, 61, 62, 67, 68, 69, 70

モンゴロイド Mongoloid 12

モンスーン monsoon 30, 38, 54

【ヤ】

ヤハウェ神 Yahweh 13, 26, 187

弥生時代 Yayoi Period 10, 12, 21, 64

ヤルタ会談 Yalta Conference 167

【ユ】

ユークリッド幾何学 Euclidean geometry 24

ユーゴスラヴィア Yugoslavia 185

ユーフラテス川 the Euphrates 5, 9

遊牧民 nomadic peoples [nomads] 19, 25, 29, 41, 42, 45, 49, 52, 53, 54, 58, 62, 63, 67, 179

宥和政策 appeasement policy 105, 163, 164

ユグノー Huguenot 72, 88, 135

ユスティニアヌス1世 Justinian I 34, 35

ユダヤ人 Jews 13, 26, 66, 137, 162, 164, 168, 175, 187

ユトレヒト条約 Peace of Utrecht 103

ユトレヒト同盟 Union of Utrecht 89

ユンカー Junker 128

【ヨ】

楊貴妃 Yang Guifei 40, 41

煬帝 Emperor Yang of the Sui 32

洋務運動 Self-Strengthening Movement 134

ヨーマン yeoman 98

ヨーロッパ共同体 (EC) European Community 181, 185

ヨーロッパの火薬庫 powder keg of Europe 147

世論 public opinion 109, 130, 136, 137, 139, 162, 166, 177, 188, 190

【ラ】

楽浪郡 Lelang Commandery 21

ラスコー Lascaux 3

ラテン語 Latin 15, 22, 24, 73, 76

ラマ教 Lamaism 68

【リ】

李氏朝鮮 Joseon dynasty 68, 80, 82, 95, 106, 129, 134, 138, 140

立憲王制／立憲君主制 constitutional monarchy 99, 147

リトアニア Lithuania 100, 101, 104

李白 Li Bo 40, 41

リビア Libya 147, 160, 176, 189

琉球王国 Ryukyu Kingdom 81, 82, 106

柳条湖事件 Liutiaohu Incident 161

遼 Liao 52, 53, 58, 60

領主 (feudal) lord 44, 47, 98

リンカーン Lincoln, Abraham 130

【ル】

ルイ 14 世 Louis XIV 103, 105, 107, 111

ルイ 16 世 Louis XVI 111, 112, 113, 115

ルーズベルト Roosevelt, Franklin Delano 163, 167, 169

ルター Luther, Martin 72, 73, 78

ルネサンス Renaissance 75, 76, 77, 114, 116, 146

【レ】

霊長類 primates 2, 4

レーニン Lenin, Vladimir Ilich 143, 151, 156, 160

レオナルド・ダ・ヴィンチ Leonardo da Vinci 77

レコンキスタ Reconquista 55, 71, 80

列強 world [great] powers 63, 70, 81, 91, 92, 94, 96, 100, 101, 104, 105, 108, 111, 112, 113, 115, 117, 119, 121, 122, 125, 126, 127, 129, 130, 131, 133, 134, 135, 136, 137, 138, 139, 140, 141, 142, 143, 145, 148, 149, 150, 152, 154, 157, 159, 163, 168, 169, 173, 177, 183, 186

【ロ】

老子 Laozi 20, 39

労働運動 labor movement 131, 157

労働者 worker [laborer] 9, 116, 117, 123, 131, 136, 143, 151

ローマ Rome 19, 21, 22, 23, 24, 25, 26, 28, 30, 47, 48, 51, 69, 77, 78, 86, 95, 173

ローマ教皇 (Roman Catholic) Pope [papacy] 37, 43, 44, 45, 51, 56, 62, 65, 68, 69, 72, 73, 78, 86, 88, 91, 160

ローマ進軍 March on Rome 160

ローマ帝国 Roman Empire 12, 15, 21, 24, 25, 26, 27, 30, 34, 35, 37, 40, 43, 44, 45, 49, 53, 70, 75, 76, 77, 87, 91, 113, 145, 164, 172, 173

ローマ法 Roman law 24

ローマ法大全 Corpus Iuris Civils 35

ロカルノ条約 Locarno Pact 159

盧溝橋 Marco Polo Bridge 162

ロシア Russia 10, 40, 45, 46, 52, 57, 62, 67, 69, 70, 71, 91, 92, 94, 100, 101, 103, 104, 105, 106, 107, 115, 117, 118, 119, 121, 123, 126, 127, 129, 131, 133, 134, 137, 138, 139, 140, 141, 142, 143, 147, 148, 149, 150, 151, 152, 156, 168, 184, 185, 189, 191, 192, 193

ロシア革命 Russian Revolution 119, 131, 151, 152, 156

ロック Locke, John 109

ロベスピエール Robespierre 113

ロマノフ王朝 the Romanov dynasty 104, 105, 140, 150, 151

ロンドン軍縮条約 London Naval Treaty 159

【ワ】

ワーテルローの戦い Battle of Waterloo 115

ワールシュタットの戦い Battle of Legnica 62

ワイマール憲法 Weimar Constitution 156, 157, 162, 168

倭寇 wako [Japanese pirates] 68, 81, 82, 95, 106

ワシントン Washington, George 108, 110

ワシントン会議 Washington Naval Conference 159

ワルシャワ条約機構 Warsaw Treaty Organization 172

日英対訳 世界の歴史 増補改訂版
A History of the World: From the Ancient Past to the Present

2023年9月7日 第1刷発行

著　者　山久瀬洋二
翻訳者　ジェームス・M・バーダマン

発行者　浦 晋亮
発行所　IBC パブリッシング株式会社
　　　　〒162-0804 東京都新宿区中里町29番3号 菱秀神楽坂ビル
　　　　Tel. 03-3513-4511　Fax. 03-3513-4512
　　　　www.ibcpub.co.jp

印刷所　株式会社シナノパブリッシングプレス

© Yamakuse Yoji 2023
Printed in Japan

ISBN978-4-7946-0781-2